GRATIA PLENA

THE ROUGH GUIDE TO
PORTUGAL

This fifteenth edition updated by
Marc Di Duca, Rebecca Hall and Matthew Hancock

roughguides.com

Contents

Introduction to
Portugal

Portugal is one of Europe's oldest extant nations, an ancient kingdom defended by hilltop castles and dramatic walled towns. First-time visitors are usually struck by the friendliness of the people, the affordable food and wine, and the diversity of a country that is relatively easy to travel round in just a few days. Its cities – notably Lisbon and Porto – amply showcase Portugal's former role as a maritime superpower that ruled the waves from Brazil to East Asia, though it's not all about history: the cities boast some of Europe's best clubs and most adventurous modern architecture. Head inland and there are endless possibilities, from touring wine estates to walking, cycling or kayaking down inland rivers. It is the coast, however, that is the biggest draw. From cliff-backed coves to endless stretches of sandy dunes, you are rarely far from a stunning beach. While its western Atlantic dunes are still relatively unknown to those outside the surfing community, the calmer waters of the Algarve offer the quintessential laidback beach experience.

Portugal's borders have changed little since it became an independent country in the twelfth century. **Mountains** make up the bulk of the frontier with Spain, with the large **rivers** of the Minho in the north and the Guadiana in the south adding to this natural divide. Early Portuguese monarchs fortified the border with a series of **walled towns**, many sited on dramatic hilltops, and these make the border areas some of the most fascinating to visit.

Beaches and high mountains aside, the rest of Portugal is a diverse and verdant country of deep valleys and rolling hills dotted with stone-built villages. For generations, families have eked out a living from the steeply terraced **vineyards** of the mountainous north, and from the **cork oak plantations** roamed by wild boar that dominate the vast agricultural plains of the south.

Portugal's prestige and economy have never regained the heights they attained during the **golden ages** of the fifteenth to eighteenth centuries. The country spent most of the

ABOVE PONTA DA PIEDADE, THE ALGARVE

PORTUGAL

ATLANTIC OCEAN

ATLANTIC OCEAN

SPAIN

Santiago de Compostela

León

Rio Minho
Melgaço
Monção
Valença do Minho
Rio Lima
Caminha
Ponte de Lima
Rio Cávado
Viana do Castelo
Barcelos
Braga
Citânia de Briteiros
Póvoa de Varzim
Guimarães

MINHO

SERRA DE PENEDA-GERÊS

Chaves

Rio Tâmega

SERRA DE MONTESINHO

N103
Bragança

TRÁS-OS-MONTES

SERRA DE MOGADOURO

Mirandela
IP4

Miranda do Douro

DOURO

Vila Real

Mogadouro

SERRA DO MARÃO

Amarante

Porto

Peso da Régua
Lamego

Rio Douro

Vila Nova de Foz Côa

Rio Sabor

Freixo de Espada-à-Cinta

Parque Arqueológico do Vale do Côa

BEIRA LITORAL

Castro Daire

BEIRA ALTA

Francoso

Almeida

Aveiro

Caramulo

Viseu

Celorico da Beira

Vilar Formoso

Tondela
IP3

Guarda
A25

BUÇACO FOREST

R. Mondego

Seia

SERRA DA ESTRELA

Figueira da Foz

Coimbra

Oliveira do Hospital

SERRA DA LOUSÃ

Covilhã

Conímbriga

Lousã

Rio Zêzere

BEIRA BAIXA

Pombal

Leiria

Batalha
Fátima

Tomar

Castelo Branco

Nazaré

Alcobaça

Abrantes

Rio Tejo

A23

Berlenga Islands

Óbidos

Peniche

Entroncamento

Santarém

Castelo de Vide

Marvão

Cáceres

Torres Vedras

Portalegre

SERRA DE SÃO MAMEDE

Madrid

ESTREMADURA

RIBATEJO

Mafra

Vila Franca de Xira

ALTO ALENTEJO

Mérida

Sintra

Cascais

Coruche

Estremoz

Badajoz

LISBON

Setúbal

Montemor-o-Novo

Évora

Elvas

Vila Viçosa

Alcácer do Sal

Os Almendres

Monsaraz

Viana do Alentejo

Reguengos de Monsaraz

Moura

Barragem do Alqueva

Santiago do Cacém

Sines

Mirobriga

Beja

Castro Verde

Serpa

Rio Guadiana

N260

BAIXO ALENTEJO

Vila Nova de Milfontes

Almodôvar

Odemira

Mértola

Rio Mira

Aljezur

SERRA DE MONCHIQUE

N125

Huelva

ALGARVE

Milreu

Lagos

Portimão

Albufeira

Faro

Olhão

Tavira

Vila Real de Santo António

Sagres

N

Metres
1500
1000
500
200
100
0

0   50
kilometres

Valladolid
Salamanca
Córdoba, Cádiz & Granada

FACT FILE

• Including the perimeter of its islands, Portugal boasts 1793 kilometres of **coastline**. Its only neighbour is Spain, and it shares the same **time zone** as the UK.

• There are ten times more Portuguese living overseas than the ten million-strong population that lives in Portugal itself – the bulk of these live in Brazil, though the USA and France both also have over a million **inhabitants of Portuguese descent**.

• Portugal's national dish is **bacalhau**, dried and salted cod, and there are reputed to be 365 different ways of cooking it – one for each day of the year.

• Portugal is the earth's eighth largest **producer of wine** and supplies fifty percent of the world's **cork**.

• There are twelve **UNESCO World Heritage Sites** in mainland Portugal, including towns like Évora and Guimarães, the palaces of Sintra, rock art in the Côa valley, and national monuments at Batalha and Alcobaça.

twentieth century in deep poverty under the dictatorial rule of Prime Minister Dr. Salazar, and while joining the European Union had great initial benefits – funding new roads and communications – Portugal has struggled badly in the recent years of economic crisis. Yet although it remains one of the EU's weakest economies, Portugal is a remarkably unified country – there are no minorities agitating for independence, while rivalry between the north and south consists of little more than gentle mockery. Indeed Portugal is generally a very tolerant nation, and has integrated a substantial population from its **former colonies** in Africa, Asia and Brazil with relative ease. Contemporary Portuguese tastes are influenced by the flavours, sounds and styles of Brazil, Angola and Mozambique in particular.

It's a **Catholic** country – there are ancient churches in every community – and while support for the institutions of the Church may have waned, a belief in **traditional values** remains. The Portuguese have embraced contemporary life without ever quite getting rid of the more appealing aspects of previous centuries. Fully wired town centres have wi-fi hotspots and cell-phone shops by the score, but they also have a butcher, a baker and (quite literally) a candle-stick maker. Children will be both seen and heard at any time of the day or night, as the family remains at the centre of most things.

When times were hard at home, the Portuguese traditionally emigrated to pastures new, but their homeland's blend of tolerance and tradition, its bucolic scenery and year-round sunshine, persuade most emigrants to return at some stage – and it is this same allure that makes the country so appealing to visitors. Prepare to be charmed.

Where to go

The south-facing coast of the **Algarve** is the country's tourist epicentre and justifiably so – it is here that you'll find the archetypal picturesque Portuguese cove beaches, fringed by rock stacks and gentle cliffs, and it doesn't take much to escape the high-rise resorts and golf courses. If it is **beaches** you are after, however, you have almost the entire west coast of the country to choose from. There are expansive stretches of sand not only on the Algarve's western coast, but also in the southern Alentejo, on the coast around Lisbon and north to Figueira da Foz, and along the **Minho coast** north to the Spanish border.

CLOCKWISE FROM TOP LEFT CHIADO BUILDING, LISBON; IGREJA MATRIZ, MÉRTOLA; SURFERS ON GUINCHO BEACH; MARVÃO, ALENTEJO

PORTUGUESE AZULEJOS

Brightly-coloured decorative tiles have been used throughout Portugal since the birth of the nation, making up everything from immense religious scenes covering entire walls of churches to simple geometric patterns on the back of park benches. It was the Moors who introduced the craft in the eighth century – the word derives from the Arabic *al-zulecha*, meaning "small stone". Less studied than stained glass, less famous than frescoes, many *azulejos* are handcrafted works of art, though even mass-produced factory items add flamboyance to otherwise dull buildings. You'll find them all over the country – on churches, houses, cafés and shops, even motorway bridges and metro stations. The **Museu Nacional do Azulejo** in Lisbon (see p.68) is dedicated to them, or you can marvel at the ingenuity and adaptability of the art while catching the train at **Pinhão station** (see p.297), spending the night in the **Palácio do Buçaco** (see p.200) or visiting the church of **São Laurenço** in the Algarve (see p.461).

Many of these beaches extend as far as the eye can see, and are rarely busy even in high summer, but as they face the full power of the Atlantic, they can be dangerous for swimming. It's no big surprise then that many attract serious surfers instead, with **Peniche**, **Figueira da Foz** and **Nazaré** all major surf destinations.

The south of the country is dominated by the enormous **Alentejo** region, whose wide-open spaces, country estates, olive plantations and vineyards invite long drives and leisurely exploration. Here you'll find a Mediterranean-type climate, sun-drenched, whitewashed villages bedecked with flowers and, in early summer, every spire and treetop capped by a stork's nest. Closer to Lisbon is the breeding ground for Portugal's finest horses and for the bulls that still fight in bullrings around the country. Beyond, lies the historic heartland of **Estremadura (now part of the Centro district)**, whose closely grouped towns feature some of Portugal's most famous monuments.

The north of Portugal feels immediately different, and far less Mediterranean in look and temperament – the rolling hills are green and lush, and the coastline cooler, even in

OPPOSITE PORTO'S CATHEDRAL

summer. Terraced vineyards cling to the steep slopes of the **Douro River**, its valley shadowed by one of Europe's most memorable train rides. At the far north of the Porto e Norte district lie the remote towns and villages of **Trás-os-Montes**, while to the west **Peneda-Gerês** is Portugal's only **national park**, a surprisingly verdant landscape of wooded mountains and gushing streams.

Standout city is, of course, **Lisbon**, with its dazzling hilltop and riverside location and alluring mix of old-world charm and modern flair. It's not too much of a stretch to describe it as one of Europe's must-see capitals, though the charms – and wines – of **Porto**, wedged into the Douro river valley, also make an excellent case for a long weekend city break. Other Portuguese towns and cities might not have the same profile, but they are both historical and beautiful – like **Guimarães**, the country's first capital, the religious centre of **Braga**, the handsome university town of **Coimbra**, and **Évora**, another university town with Roman antecedents.

Beyond these attractions, how long have you got? Because in just about every town and village there's a surprise to be discovered. Likeable **Tomar** is home to the impressive headquarters of the Knights Templar, while **Aveiro** is an unexpected treat, set on a series of canals lined with colourful houses. There are sumptuous **monasteries and abbeys** at Batalha, Mafra and Alcobaça and extraordinary **fortified towns** at Almeida, Elvas and Bragança; while in **Fátima**, Portugal boasts one of the world's most revered Catholic shrines.

FOOD FROM AFAR

Portugal's former status as an important trading nation has had a huge influence on world cuisine. The **tempura** method of deep-frying was introduced to the Japanese by sixteenth-century Portuguese traders and missionaries, while the fiery curry-house mainstay **vindaloo** derives from a **vinho** (wine) and **alho** (garlic) sauce popular in Portuguese Goa. Indeed, the use of **chillis** in the East only began when the Portuguese started to import them from Mexico. **Bacalhau** (dried salt cod) started life as a way of preserving fish on board the Portuguese voyages of exploration; another, less exotic, export is marmalade (although the local **marmelada** is actually made from quince). Meanwhile, dishes from Portugal's former colonies crop up time and time again in Portuguese restaurants. Keep an eye out for *mufete* (beans with palm oil and fish) and chicken *piri-piri* (chicken with chilli sauce), which originated in **Angola** and **Mozambique**, *caril de camarão* (shrimp curry) and *chamuças* (samosas) from **Asia**, and **Brazilian** meals such as *feijoada* (pork and bean stew), *picanha* (sliced rump steak) and *rodizio* (barbecue meat buffet).

When to go

A weather map of endless sunshine sums up the situation across the whole of Portugal in **summer**, certainly between June and September, when usually the only daytime variation across the country is a degree or two further up or down the scale from 30ºC. In July and especially August (the Portuguese holiday month), the coastal resorts are at their busiest and prices reach their peak. It's also too hot to do much exploring – if you want to do any serious hiking, or even just walk around the cities, towns and archeological sites, you're better off coming in May or October. Most of the rain falls in **winter**, from November to March, though you can just as easily experience bone-dry winter months and downpours in May and June. The crisp, sharp sunshine makes winter an appealing time to visit central Portugal, while in the south, especially on the coast, it is mild all year round. In the north, on the other hand, it's pretty cold, especially inland where snow is common along the mountainous border areas.

Perhaps the best times of year to visit are in **spring** (ie, from February) – when dazzling flowers carpet hillsides and the almond blossom lights up the countryside – and early **autumn** (October), when the weather is warm but not too hot and the summer crowds have thinned out. The sea, too, is warm in autumn, though the official swimming season only lasts from the beginning of June to mid-September; outside these months – no matter how lovely the weather – outdoor pools and river beach facilities close.

AVERAGE DAILY TEMPERATURES AND MONTHLY RAINFALL

	Jan	Mar	May	Jul	Sep	Nov
LISBON						
Max/min (°C)	14/8	18/10	22/13	27/17	25/16	17/12
Rainfall (mm)	111	109	44	3	33	93
PORTO (COSTA VERDE)						
Max/min (°C)	13/5	15/7	19/10	25/15	24/14	17/8
Rainfall (mm)	159	147	87	20	51	148
FARO (ALGARVE)						
Max/min (°C)	15/9	18/11	22/14	28/20	26/19	19/13
Rainfall (mm)	70	72	21	1	17	65

Author picks

Our authors have visited every corner of Portugal to bring you some unique travel experiences. Here are some of their own personal favourites.

Stay in a castle Be a king or queen for the night at the lovely, tranquil *Forte de São João da Barra*, overlooking the Reserva Natural Ria Formosa, or the *Pousada Dom Afonso II* (p.426) – a historic castle, which has had a stylish, contemporary makeover.

Great walks Fantastic walking trails abound including the epic Rota Vicentina through the unspoilt southwest of the country (p.429) and some terrific mountain paths in the north's Parque Nacional da Peneda-Gerês (p.340).

Classic journeys The train ride along the Douro (p.291) is our favourite – from Porto to Pocinho near the Spanish border.

Party time Stay up all night (and look out for the plastic hammers) at Porto's riotous Festa de São João (p.280).

Coastal beauty spots The tiny Algarve village of Benagil (p.469) marks the start of a clifftop path that leads past an awesome sea cave, while the pretty resort of Vila Nova de Milfontes (p.430) faces a tranquil estuary on the wild Alentejo coast.

Delightful towns Favourites include the ancient hilltop settlements of Marvão (p.407) and Monsaraz (p.413), both with sublime views over the Alto Alentejo, though beautiful Belmonte (p.247) runs a close second.

Magnificent markets Foodies will find the local fish and seafood at Olhão market unbeatable (p.445), while Estremoz market (p.399) sells some of the best Alentejan crafts and local produce, and Barcelos in the Minho (p.320) is the country's most traditional market.

> Our author recommendations don't end here. We've flagged up our favourite places – a perfectly sited hotel, an atmospheric café, a special restaurant – throughout the guide, highlighted with the ★ symbol.

FROM TOP CAVE, BENAGIL; ESTREMOZ MARKET; FESTA DE SÃO JOÃO

24

things not to miss

It's not possible to see everything that Portugal has to offer in one trip – and we don't suggest you try. What follows, in no particular order, is a selection of the country's highlights, including fascinating architecture, outstanding natural wonders, amazing beaches, one stupendous market and a peerless custard tart. All entries have a page reference to take you straight into the Guide, where you can find out more. Coloured numbers refer to chapters in the Guide.

1

ARTESANATO

2

3

7

8

9 MOSTEIRO DA BATALHA
Page 160

The "Battle Abbey" is one of the greatest achievements of Portuguese architecture.

10 KAYAKING ON THE MONDEGO RIVER
Page 198

Even novice kayakers will be enchanted by this gentle float down a verdant valley.

11 ALFAMA, LISBON
Page 65

A village in the heart of the capital, with streets so narrow and precipitous that few cars can enter.

12 SINTRA
Page 112

The hilltop retreat near Lisbon is one of the most scenic in the country, surrounded by opulent palaces and country estates.

13 PARQUE NACIONAL DA PENEDA-GERÊS
Page 340

The country's only national park offers alluring trails past gushing streams and alpine scenery.

14 PASTÉIS DE BELÉM
Page 97

Their version of the delicious flaky custard tartlets have been made and served warm with cinnamon and icing sugar sprinkled over them for more than a century at the *Antiga Confeitaria de Belém*.

15

16

17

18

19

20

21

22

21 SURFING
Page 140

Peniche offers consistently good surfing in a country that is blessed with rolling Atlantic waves.

22 FEIRA DE BARCELOS
Page 320

The country's liveliest and most colourful market shows that rural traditions are alive and well.

23 SERRA DA ESTRELA
Page 237

The highest mountains in Portugal conceal windswept uplands, remote villages and challenging hiking trails.

24 CANAL TRIP, AVEIRO
Page 206

Float through the canals and lagoons of fascinating Aveiro on a brightly coloured boat.

23

24

Itineraries

Whether you've got a few days, a week or longer, here are three itineraries to give you a taste of Portugal's varied attractions. Our Grand Tour takes in the country's unmissable historic towns and natural attractions, while the wine route will guide you around remote rural gems. We also recommend the best beaches in a country famed for its fabulous sands.

GRAND TOUR OF PORTUGAL

Portugal is a small country so you can easily see the best of it quickly. The Grand Tour takes in the must-see destinations.

❶ **Lagos** The Algarve's most historic town, from where the great navigators departed in the Age of Discoveries. See p.479

❷ **Évora** A superbly preserved Alentejan town containing Portugal's finest Roman temple. See p.388

❸ **Elvas** Explore the walls – with their far-reaching views – that encircle this fortified border town. See p.408

❹ **Lisbon** One of Europe's most fascinating capitals is a captivating mix of ancient and contemporary – and beautifully located, overlooking the Tejo river estuary. See p.56

❺ **Coimbra** A former Portuguese capital, the ancient university town also has the superb Roman site of Conímbriga on its doorstep. See p.180

❻ **Serra da Estrela** The country's highest mountains – with its only ski resort – make a great destination for a night in the hills. See p.237

❼ **Porto** A unique city, famed for its wines, football team and amazing riverside cityscape. See p.260

❽ **Parque Nacional da Peneda-Gerês** This wild, rugged mountain region, hugging the border with Spain, is ideal for a walking holiday – or for a panoramic drive. See p.340

WINE ROUTES

Portugal produces terrific wines and its vineyards tend to nestle in bucolic countryside – views and booze, our favourite combination.

❶ **Quinta Miradouro** Cliff Richard's wine estate in the Algarve is a good introduction to Portuguese wines – with the chance of spotting the great man himself. See p.465

❷ **Alentejo wine route** Some of the best Portuguese wines are produced in this beautiful inland region, with top producers located near the historic towns of Beja, Évora and Estremoz. See p.396

❸ **Rota do Vino do Dão** Check out the classic reds produced along the Dão valley. See p.202

❹ **Port wine lodges** No visit to Porto is complete without a tour of the port wine lodges in Vila Nova de Gaia, many overlooking the Douro River. See p.272

❺ **Peso da Régua** The classic port-wine estates can be visited from this town on the Douro, which is also home to the headquarters of the Rota do Vinho do Porto and the Douro Wine Institute's exhibition centre. See p.291

❻ Pinhão The main centre for quality ports with a classic backdrop of Douro wine terraces. **See p.297**

❼ Melgaço Portugal's northernmost outpost is the centre for the country's famed *vinho verde*. The Solar do Alvarinho offers tastings and tours of local estates. **See p.334**

LIFE'S A BEACH

Most people come to Portugal for its beaches and there are hundreds to choose from – here's a tour of the best.

❶ Foz do Minho, Minho Portugal's northernmost beach is a hidden gem, a sandy bank facing Spain across the Rio Minho river estuary. **See p.329**

❷ Nazaré, Estremadura This former fishing village has a great town beach – and is also where the world's largest-ever wave was surfed. **See p.150**

❸ Caparica A favourite for surfers and day-trippers from Lisbon. **See p.128**

❹ Galapos, Parque Natural da Arrábida This beautifully positioned bay has calm waters in one of Portugal's loveliest natural parks. **See p.126**

❺ Comporta, Alentejo Deserted sands stretch as far as the eye can see at this remote part of the northern Alentejo. **See p.426**

❻ Porto Côvo, Alentejo The Portuguese love this unspoilt coast, studded with idyllic sandy coves. **See p.428**

❼ Praia do Amado, Algarve A wild and wonderful stretch of sand with its own surf school in a remote corner of the Algarve. **See p.492**

❽ Praia da Marinha, Algarve A classic cliff-backed cove beach, perfect for families. **See p.469**

BACK TO NATURE

Tour Portugal to see an amazing array of marine life and migrating birds, along with mammals such as badgers, otters and wolves.

❶ Parque Natural da Ria Formosa Protected by five barrier-islands (with great beaches), these wetlands and waterways shelter chameleons, seahorses and aquatic birds. **See p.448**

❷ Cabo de São Vicente Europe's most southwesterly point is part of the little developed Parque Natural do Sudoeste Alentejano e Costa Vicentina. **See p.490**

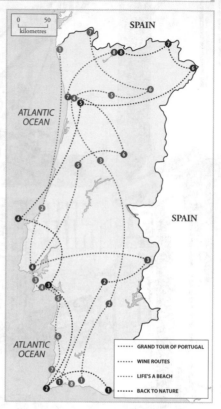

❸ Parque Natural da Arrábida Just an hour south of Lisbon, the coast off this craggy wilderness supports the country's only resident dolphin community. **See p.126**

❹ Ilha da Berlenga It's a 45-minute boat ride to a sea-blasted island packed with millions of puffins, cormorants and seabirds. **See p.142**

❺ Paiva Walkways Take the 8km boardwalk alongside the Paiva River through superb unspoilt terrain, with river beaches on the way. **See p.206**

❻ Parque Natural do Douro Internacional The deep Douro valley demarcates the frontier with Spain, an area of rocks and craggy cliffs that are ideal for birds of prey. **See p.364**

❼ Parque Natural de Montesinho Wolves are said to roam these remote borderlands, a wild, forgotten corner of the country that's ideal for hiking. **See p.372**

❽ Parque Nacional da Peneda-Gerês An almost Swiss mountainscape rich in flora and with its own stumpy garrano ponies. **See p.340**

LISBON TRAM

Basics

Getting there

There are regular direct flights to Lisbon, Faro and Porto from all over Europe and some US cities, though travellers from outside Europe may find it cheaper to fly via London and arrange onward travel from there. If you want to see some of France or Spain en route, or are taking a vehicle, there are overland combinations of ferry, rail and road to consider, though these nearly always work out pricier than flying. Package holidays and tours can be good value, whether it's an Algarve beach holiday or escorted walking tour – and travel agents and specialist tour operators can also provide car rental, hotel bookings and other useful services.

Air, **train** and **ferry fares** are at their highest in school holidays and summer (basically Easter to September), and around Christmas/New Year and Easter week. The cheapest flights from the UK and Ireland are usually with the budget airlines, though watch out for the airport taxes, which can cost more than the flight itself, as well as additional charges for checked luggage and allocated seating. Major scheduled airlines are usually (though not always) more expensive, while specialist flight, discount or online agents can sometimes offer special student and youth fares plus a range of other travel-related services.

Flights from the UK and Ireland

Flying to Faro, Lisbon or Porto takes two to three hours from airports around the UK and Ireland, and usually the cheapest flights are with **budget airlines** such as easyJet, Jet2, Ryanair, Aer Lingus, Monarch Airlines, thomsonfly or flybe. Between them they fly direct from around twenty regional British airports, plus Belfast and Dublin, and although Faro on the Algarve is the most common destination you should be able to find a route that suits you. Not all routes are daily or year-round: some Algarve flights are summer-only, and other

Lisbon or Porto routes have a reduced winter service. **Fares** vary wildly and, depending on promotions, can be as low as £50 or €65 each way, though you'll have to travel off-peak and book a long time ahead to get this sort of deal. Around £120 total for a return flight is more common, but if you're tied to school holidays or book late you're likely to pay nearer £150–200 return.

The main scheduled airlines flying to Portugal are the **national carriers** TAP and British Airways: TAP flies regular services from London to Lisbon and Porto, while BA serves Lisbon and Faro. You'll also be able to arrange add-on sections to London from regional UK airports. They are not necessarily more expensive than the budget airlines, and flight times may be more convenient – that said, you're unlikely to get a rock-bottom deal and the fully flexible fares offered can run into the hundreds.

Flights from the US and Canada

The only direct nonstop services **from the United States** are from New York (Newark) to Lisbon with United Airlines, Lufthansa, or TAP, with fares starting at US$800 return. Flight time is around seven hours. From all other cities you'll need a connecting flight, either via New York or via a European airport with airlines such as British Airways, Delta or Air France – in which case you can add four or five hours to your total travel time, depending on the connection. TAP can also arrange onward flights from Lisbon to Porto or Faro.

From Canada to Portugal, there are direct flights from Toronto with SATA and Air Canada; flight time is 7–8 hours, and fares are around C$1400.

Flights from Australia, New Zealand and South Africa

There are no direct flights to Portugal **from Australia or New Zealand**, but many airlines offer through-tickets with their partners via their European or Asian hubs. Flights via Asia are generally the cheaper option, but fares don't vary as much between airlines as you might think, and in

A BETTER KIND OF TRAVEL

At Rough Guides we are passionately committed to travel. We believe it helps us understand the world we live in and the people we share it with – and of course tourism is vital to many developing economies. But the scale of modern tourism has also damaged some places irreparably, and climate change is accelerated by most forms of transport, especially flying. All Rough Guides' flights are carbon-offset, and every year we donate money to a variety of environmental charities.

the end you'll be basing your choice on things like flight timings, routes and possible stop-offs. If you're seeing Portugal as part of a wider European trip, you might want to aim first for the UK, since there's a wide choice of cheap flights to Portugal once there (see p.25). Or consider a Round-the-World fare, with most basic options able to offer Lisbon as a standard stopover. There are **no direct flights from South Africa**, though you can fly with one of the major European airlines via their home hub.

AIRLINES

Aer Lingus ⓦ aerlingus.com
Air Canada ⓦ aircanada.com
Air France ⓦ airfrance.com
British Airways ⓦ ba.com
Delta Air Lines ⓦ delta.com
easyJet ⓦ easyjet.com
flybe ⓦ flybe.com
Jet2 ⓦ jet2.com
Lufthansa ⓦ lufthansa.com
Monarch Airlines ⓦ flights.monarch.co.uk
SATA ⓦ sata.pt
TAP ⓦ flytap.com
thomsonfly ⓦ flights.thomson.co.uk
United Airlines ⓦ united.com

Trains

Getting from London to Lisbon by train takes around 24 hours and involves taking the **Eurostar** (ⓦ eurostar.com) from London St Pancras to Paris, then Paris to Irun on the Spanish border by high-speed train (TGV) and finally the overnight Sud-Express "train-hotel", which gets you into Lisbon at about 7.30am. It's an enjoyable route, well worth considering, though the cheapest **fares** start at around £200 return (with couchette accommodation on the overnight train). For Porto you change at Coimbra, while there are also direct connections from Lisbon to the Algarve. The alternative route to Portugal is **via Madrid** – this takes two nights (overnight trains from Paris to Madrid and then Madrid to Lisbon), but gives you a day in Madrid en route. The overnight trains have seats (not really recommended) as well as couchettes and cabins complete with showers, plus restaurant, buffet bar and lounge. Our "Overland from Spain" section (see opposite) has more on the various routes.

For **tickets**, the best first stop is the excellent ⓦ seat61.com, which provides full route, ticket, timetable and contact information. You can book the whole journey **online** with Loco2 (ⓦ loco2.com) or Rail Europe (ⓦ raileurope.co.uk).

Information on **rail passes** (principally InterRail and Eurail), which have to be bought before leaving home, is given in our "Getting around" section (see p.27).

Overland from Spain

It's easy to travel by **train** from Spain to Portugal, and there are some rewarding stops en route. Rail passes are valid, though you'll be liable for supplements on many trains.

From Madrid (Chamartin station), the overnight Lusitania Trenhotel takes ten hours and thirty minutes to Lisbon (change at Entroncamento in Portugal for Coimbra and Porto). Prices start at €60 one-way/€96 return for a second-class seat, or €84 one-way/€134 return for the cheapest berth (four-bed cabin); there are also singles, doubles and first-class cabins (*gran classe*) available. **Tickets** can be bought in Madrid at Chamartin, through the Spanish (ⓦ renfe.es) or Portuguese (ⓦ cp.pt) railway companies' websites, or from one of the rail agents mentioned in "Trains" (see above).

From the northeast, the overnight Sud-Express **from the French border at Hendaye/Irun** to Lisbon (around 13hr) passes through San Sebastián (Donostia) and Salamanca, entering Portugal at Vilar Formoso and then calling at Portugal's highest town, Guarda; change at Coimbra for Porto. Tickets start at €40 one-way/€70 return, and again can be bought online or from agents.

From northwestern Spain, two trains a day connect **Vigo** in Galicia to Porto (around 3hr), passing the border at Tuy/Valença on the River Minho, then following the river and coast down via Viana do Castelo.

From **Granada**, **Córdoba** and **Seville** in southern Spain you are well placed to get a bus to the border at Ayamonte/Vila Real de Santo António, for onward transport by bus or train along the Algarve coast.

There are numerous other border **road crossings**, but if you're in a rental car check first whether you're covered to take the vehicle between countries. The major routes from Madrid or Salamanca make for an easy motorway drive to Portugal's biggest cities, but there are some excellent minor routes into the country as well – like those from Zamora to Bragança or Miranda do Douro, or from Cáceres to Castelo Branco.

Driving from the UK

Driving the 2000km or so from the UK to Portugal, using the standard cross-Channel services or

Eurotunnel (Weurotunnel.com) through the Channel Tunnel, takes two full days. It's not a cheap option (factoring in the cross-Channel trip, fuel, tolls, overnight stops and meals), but it is a good way of seeing France and Spain on the way.

The best way of cutting down the driving time is to catch the ferry to northern Spain, though this still leaves a six- to eight-hour drive before you reach Portugal. Brittany Ferries (Wbrittany-ferries.co.uk) sails to **Santander** from Plymouth (1 weekly; 20hr) and Portsmouth (3 weekly; 24hr–32hr) and to **Bilbao** from Portsmouth (2 weekly; 24hr). The one-way **fare** for a car and two passengers starts at £430 from Plymouth to Santander, £424 from Portsmouth to Santander, and £410 to Bilbao, though in summer and school holidays prices can rocket. In winter the Brittany Ferries website often features special deals; note also that fares are cheaper for foot passengers (though everyone has to book some form of seating or cabin accommodation).

Package holidays, tours and city breaks

Standard **package holidays** concentrate on hotels and self-catering apartments and villas in the Algarve's main beach resorts, and bargains can be found online or at any UK high-street travel agent for as little as £125 per person for a seven-night flight-and-accommodation package in the off-season. There are often really good deals for families, though obviously the more bells and whistles you want (beachfront accommodation, pool, kids' clubs etc), the more you pay, while prices are always significantly higher during school holidays.

Other **specialist tour operators** offer a wide range of fly-drive holidays based around accommodation in historic manor houses and *pousadas*, while some feature activities such as birdwatching, horseriding, hiking, biking and wine tours. Prices vary wildly depending on the standard of accommodation, and whether the tours are fully inclusive or not (with guides and meals etc). Most tour operators should also be able to tailor-make a holiday, and arrange flights, accommodation, insurance and car rental.

City breaks are mainly to Lisbon, though you'll also find Porto and even short breaks to the Algarve offered. UK prices start at around £200 for a three-day, two-night break, including return flights and B&B in a modest hotel. Adding extra nights or upgrading your hotel is usually possible too. The bigger US operators, such as American Express and Delta Vacations, can also organize short city breaks to Lisbon on a flight-and-hotel basis.

SPECIALIST TOUR OPERATORS

09°West Portugal ☎ 211 991 086, W 09west.com. Mid-price Lisbon-based company offering a range of birdwatching and walking tours throughout the country.

Arblaster & Clarke UK ☎ 01730 263111, W winetours.co.uk. Sophisticated, upmarket all-inclusive wine-tour specialist offering Douro vineyard walks, port-harvest trips and escorted Portugal tours.

Easy Rider Tours US ☎ 1 800 488 8332, W easyridertours.com. Somewhat pricey guided cycling and sightseeing tours in various Portuguese regions, from a week along the Douro to a nine-day mountain-to-coast trip.

Equitour UK ☎ 0800 043 7942, US ☎ 1 800 656 6163; W equitour .com. Mid-price range horseriding holidays near Lisbon and in the Alentejo and Algarve – price includes accommodation, meals and transfers but not flights.

Formosmar Portugal ☎ 289 817 466, W formosamar.com. Inexpensive tours around the Ria Formosa in the Algarve, based around kayaking, cycling, walking and birdwatching.

Limosa Holidays UK ☎ 01692 580623, W limosaholidays.co.uk. Upmarked operator offering birdwatching in the Alentejo and Algarve. There's some walking involved, and the holidays include flights, meals and transport.

Martin Randall Travel UK ☎ 020 8742 3355, W martinrandall .com. Leading cultural tour specialist, offering small-group, upmarket, expert-led trips either along the Douro by train and boat or to the historic centre of the country. Departures a couple of times a year.

Nature Trails Portugal ☎ 926 543 289, W portugalnaturetrails .com. Inexpensive, guided and self-guided hikes and cycling trips, mostly in the south of the country.

Naturetrek UK ☎ 01962 733051, W naturetrek.co.uk. Mid-price outfit which offers seven- or eight-day spring and autumn botanical and birdwatching trips in the north and south of the country, including gentle walking.

Portugal Walks Portugal ☎ 965 753 033, W portugalwalks.com, W pedalinportugal.com. A nice range of good-value group and individual guided and self-guided walking and cycling holidays throughout the country, ranging from four nights to a week. Flights not included.

Ramblers Worldwide Holidays UK ☎ 01707 331133, W ramblersholidays.co.uk. Long-established walking-holiday operator with inexpensive guided walking trips along the Douro as well as the Algarve, Alentejo and the northern national and natural parks.

Getting around

Portugal is not a large country and you can get almost everywhere easily and efficiently by train or bus. Regional trains are often cheaper and some lines very scenic, but it's almost always quicker to

go by bus – especially on shorter or less obvious routes. You'll obviously have a great deal more flexibility if you drive, and you'll be able to visit more out-of-the-way places in a short trip.

By train

Comboios de Portugal (**CP**; enquiries on ☎707 210 220, ⊛cp.pt) operates all trains. For the most part it's an efficient network with modern rolling stock, while there are some highly picturesque lines in the north that are among the country's best attractions, notably the Douro line from Porto to Pocinho. Be aware that rural train stations can sometimes be a fair way from the town or village they serve – Loulé station and town in the Algarve are 6km apart, for example. **Timetables** (*horários*) for all lines are available from stations and on the CP website, which has a good English-language version.

Most **train services** are designated Regionais (R) or Interregionais (IR), covering the country from Faro in the south to Valença do Minho in the north. Intercidades (IC) are faster and more expensive services, connecting Lisbon to the main regional centres; while the modern, high-speed Alfa Pendulares (AP) trains run from Lisbon to Faro, and from Lisbon to Braga via Santarém, Coimbra, Aveiro and Porto. Urban services (*urbanos*) in Lisbon (to Cascais, Sintra, Setúbal and Vila Franca de Xira) and Porto (to Aveiro, Braga and Guimarães) provide a useful commuter link to local towns, while both cities also have an underground metro system.

Tickets, fares and rail passes

Most visitors simply buy a **ticket** every time they travel; first-class is *primeira classe* or *conforto*, second-class is *segunda classe* or *turística*. Always turn up at the station with time to spare since long queues often form at ticket offices. However, at unstaffed regional stations you can just pay the ticket inspector on board, while major stations have credit-card ticket machines for long-distance IC or AP tickets (on the day of travel or up to thirty days in advance); and you can also buy IC and AP tickets on the CP website.

Fares are extremely good value. A typical regional journey, across the Algarve from Faro to Vila Real de Santo António for example, only costs around €5.20; the Lisbon–Porto route costs around €25 second-class/€36 first-class by Intercidade, or around €32/43 on the fastest Alfa Pendular service.

There are fifty-percent **discounts** for children under 13 (under-5s go free), and for over-65s (ID required; ask for a *bilhete terceira idade*), and 25 percent discounts for those under 25 (ID required).

Seat reservations are obligatory on IC and AP trains, though they are included in the ticket price.

The major pan-European **rail passes** (InterRail and Eurail) are only worth considering if you're visiting Portugal as part of a wider European tour. However, both schemes also have single-country Portugal passes, which might prove better value. The **InterRail Portugal Pass** (⊛raileurope.co.uk) is only available to European residents and allows three, four, six or eight days' train travel within one month, with under-25, adult, family and senior plus second- and first-class versions available. Non-European residents can buy a Portugal rail pass with **Eurail** (⊛eurail.com), typically offering three, four, five or eight days' travel within a month, again in various classes. You can check current prices on the websites, but bear in mind that it often works out cheaper to buy individual tickets as you need them rather than passes, and it's certainly more convenient to be able to choose buses on some routes. All these passes also have to be bought before you leave home, and you might still be liable for supplements and seat reservations on long-distance and high-speed trains.

By bus

Buses connect almost all of the country's towns and villages, with services operated by a wide array of private companies. It can be a little confusing at times: at some bus stations you may find two or more companies running services to the same towns; conversely, buses going to the same destination may leave from different terminals. However, there is a national network of **express buses**, with Rede Expressos (⊛rede-expressos.pt) offering a daily service to destinations across the country. Other key **bus operators** include Rodonorte in the north (⊛rodonorte.pt), Rodotejo in the Ribatejo (⊛rodotejo.pt), Rodoviária do Alentejo in the Alentejo (⊛rodalentejo.pt) and, in the Algarve, EVA (⊛eva-bus.com) and Frota Azul (⊛frotazul-algarve.pt).

You can **book tickets** online or buy them at bus stations and ticket desks (often in cafés by the bus stop/station). Buying tickets in advance is a wise idea, but even in summer in tourist areas the day before is usually fine. **Fares** are good value: the Lisbon–Porto express route and Faro–Lisbon both cost around €20. Under-4s travel free, under-13s

half-price, and there are discounts for under-29s and senior citizens over 65 with relevant identification.

Local and rural bus services go virtually everywhere you're likely to want to go, with the notable exception of remote beaches and some of the natural parks, including much of the Serra da Estrela, Serra de Malcata and Montesinho. Note, however, that services are often restricted to one or two departures a day, or geared towards school dropoffs/pickups and market times – meaning early-morning weekday departures, sometimes only during term times. Many local services are reduced – or nonexistent – at weekends.

The local **bus station** – Rodoviária or Camionagem – is usually the best place to check services and routes. Most companies have **timetables** posted in the ticket-office window and copies to give away, though outside the Algarve it's rare to find anyone who speaks English. Turismos often have bus timetables too.

By car

A massive EU-funded construction programme has improved roads right across the country – particularly in previously remote areas such as Trás-os-Montes and central Portugal – and what appears to be a minor route on a map can turn out to be a beautifully engineered highway. But there are still plenty of winding, poorly maintained rural roads – and you can expect to encounter highway repairs, farm vehicles, roaming animals and locals laden with wood or produce on almost any countryside journey. Other than on city approaches and during rush hour, **traffic** is generally light, though as car ownership has increased dramatically in recent years so too has congestion. It's worth noting, too, that Portugal's accident statistics are some of the worst per capita in the EU, and drink-driving

---

ADDRESSES

Addresses in Portugal are written as: Rua Garrett 32-2º, which means Garrett Street no. 32, 2nd floor; "esq" or "E" (for *esquerda*) after a floor number refers to a flat or office on the left-hand side, "dir" or "D" (for *direita*) is right, *esquina* means corner or junction, and R/C stands for *rés-do-chão* (ground floor). You will often see the following abbreviations used in addresses: Av (for Avenida, avenue) and Trav (Travessa, alley).

---

is not uncommon, despite the strict laws and advertising campaigns.

Most **main roads** are prefixed EN – Estrada Nacional – or just N, with the faster regional highways denoted as IP (Itinerário Principal) or IC (Itinerário Complementar). On the whole, they are two-lane roads, with passing lanes on hills, though stretches near some towns and cities are dual carriageway.

You can pay by credit card at most petrol stations for **fuel** (*gasolina*) – unleaded is *sem chumbo*, diesel *gasóleo*.

Motorways and tolls

The **motorway** (*auto-estrada*) network (prefixed with "A") comprises four- or six-lane toll roads (signposted "Portagem") that link the Algarve with Lisbon, Porto, the main inland towns and the north. Many of the motorways have **toll gates** – take a ticket when you join the motorway, then hand it in at the next toll gate or when you leave, and you'll be told what to pay. Don't drive through the lane marked "Via Verde" (an automatic debit-payment lane), but use any lane with a green light above it – you pay in cash, or with Visa or MasterCard.

Many of the formerly toll-free motorways now use **number plate-recognition** cameras to charge. If you have your own car, there are three somewhat complex ways to pay: full details are on Ⓦ portugaltolls.com. Most car rental companies offer a **transponder** device which records any tolls used; you have to pay extra for these (typically around €20 a week), and the toll fees are settled by way of credit preloaded by the rental company, or by visiting a post office (as you would in a car without a transponder): just tell the post office your car registration number and they will tell you what you owe. However, you can currently only pay two to five days after you have used the road, which is not much good if you're

---

PORTUGAL'S TOP FIVE DRIVES

The **N379-1** through Parque Natural de Arrábida. See p.126
The **N339** from Seia to Covilhã. See p.244
The **N222** from Entre os Rios to Pinhão. See p.290
The **N103** Trans-Trás-os-Montes. See p.378
The **N265** through Parque Natural do Vale do Guardiana. See p.422

using the motorway to the airport for a flight home. In theory, you could be chased for the bill, but it is unlikely.

The tolls are considered expensive by the Portuguese, who tend to use the older routes where possible; driving from Lisbon to Porto or the Algarve costs around €22. However, it's always much quicker by motorway and, with some sections virtually deserted, they are a pleasure to drive.

Rules of the road

Traffic drives on the right: **speed limits** are 50kph in towns and villages (often enforced by tripped "Velocidade Controlade" traffic lights), 90kph on normal roads, and 120kph on motorways and inter-regional highways. Unless there's a sign to the contrary at road junctions (and there rarely is), vehicles coming from the right have **right of way** – it can be horribly confusing, but most drivers use common sense to interpret

PORTUGAL: TRAINS

whose turn it is. Other **road signage** is also poor, particularly at roundabouts, city exits and highway access roads, where signs simply dry up for no reason; often, too, there's little or no warning of turnings at slip-roads and junctions; or destinations may be signposted in one direction and not the other.

Many **car insurance** policies cover taking your car to Portugal; check with your own insurer. However, you're advised to take out extra cover for motoring assistance in case your car breaks down: try motoring organizations like the RAC (W rac .co.uk) or the AA (W theaa.co.uk). Alternatively, you can get 24-hour assistance from the Automóvel Clube de Portugal (W acp.pt), which has reciprocal arrangements with foreign automobile clubs.

Driving licences from most countries are accepted, so there's no need to get an international one before you leave. If you're **stopped by the police** in Portugal, they'll want to see your personal ID or passport, driving licence, and papers for the car (including ownership papers if it's your own car). By law, you should also have a red warning triangle and a fluorescent yellow jacket in the car (provided in rental cars). It pays to be patient and courteous since the police can – and do – levy on-the-spot fines for speeding, parking and other offences. Pleading ignorance won't get you anywhere.

Parking

Many towns and beach resorts are now flooded with traffic, especially in summer, so you may find problems finding a central parking space. Some cities, such as Coimbra, have park-and-ride schemes, while in Porto there are huge car parks at suburban metro stations. When **parking in cities**, do as the locals do and use the empty spaces pointed out to you. A tip of €0.50 to the man doing the pointing will pay them for "looking after" your car. **On-street parking** is usually metered, even in the smallest towns. The price varies, but averages €0.80 an hour, though it's generally free from 8pm until 8am the next morning on weekdays, on Saturday afternoons and all day Sunday. **Garage parking** is always more expensive – up to €10 a day – but where available it's the most secure option.

Car and motorbike rental

Car rental is relatively inexpensive and usually cheapest of all arranged in advance through one of the large multinational chains. Check their websites for special offers. Otherwise, rental agencies (including local firms) are found in all the major towns and at the airports in Lisbon, Porto and Faro. Local rates start at €150 a week with unlimited mileage, theft cover and collision damage waivers; you'll also pay extra for a toll-road transponder (see p.29). Minimum age for rental is 21, though up to and including the age of 25 you'll have to pay a supplement. Note also that when renting a car, UK drivers will need to show a driving licence and provide a **licence code**, which allows the rental company to check if you have any penalty points. The code should be obtained before you travel via W gov.uk /government/news/hiring-a-vehicle.

Collision **insurance** is vital, since without it you'll be liable for costs should the vehicle be damaged – and this includes even minor scratches, easily acquired down unmade tracks or in crowded car parks. Ensure that all visible damage on a car you're picking up is duly marked on the rental sheet. It's definitely worth considering paying the extra charge to reduce the "excess" payment levied for any damage, but these waiver charges (by the day) soon add up. However, you can avoid all **excess charges** in the event of damage by taking out an annual insurance policy with W insurance4carhire.com, which also covers windscreen and tyre damage.

You can also rent mopeds, scooters and low-powered (80cc) **motorbikes** in many resorts, with costs starting at €30–60 a day. You need to be at least 18 (and over 23 for bikes over 125cc) and to have held a full licence for at least a year. Rental should include helmet and locks along with third-party insurance. Helmet use is obligatory.

CAR RENTAL COMPANIES

Auto Jardim W auto-jardim.com
Avis W avis.com
Budget W budget.com
Europcar W europcar.com
Hertz W hertz.com

Taxis

Travelling by **taxi** in Portugal is relatively cheap by European standards, and **meters** are used in towns and cities – an average journey across Lisbon or Porto costs €10–13. **Additional charges** are made for carrying luggage, travelling at weekends or between 10pm and 6am (twenty percent more), and for calling a cab by phone – these charges are all posted inside the cab. You may have to rely on taxis more than you expect, since bus and railway stations are often some way removed from town

centres, while in rural areas there may be no other way to reach your next destination. Outside town limits, the journey is usually charged by the kilometre – the driver should be able to quote you a figure for the trip.

By bike

Cycling is increasingly popular in Portugal, both as a sport and a way to get from A to B, despite the hilly terrain of the interior. In addition, dedicated cycle paths are beginning to appear in major cities, such as Lisbon and Porto, as are long-distance paths along former railways lines, such as the Ecopista do Dão near Coimbra, the Ecopista da Linha do Tâmega near Amarante and the Ecopista near Évora. Specialist outlets, plus hotels, campsites and youth hostels, rent bikes from €10–20 a day; we give details of specific outlets throughout this Guide. A collective of bike-friendly hotels throughout the country, which have repair stations and local cycling routes, is listed at Ⓦ bikotels.com.

Portugal's woeful road-accident statistics mean that **defensive riding** is essential – reflective and fluorescent clothing (or sashes) at night is recommended. In general, it's best to assume that drivers will not obey road signs or regulations – just be prepared. Minor country roads have far less traffic to contend with, but locals know them backwards and so speeding – even around blind corners – is the norm. For more information on cycling abroad, contact the UK's national cycling organization, the **CTC** (Ⓦ ctc.org.uk), though you'll have to join to access their tours and notes on cycling in Portugal.

Collapsible bikes can be taken for free on regional and interregional trains (ie, the slow ones), so long as they're dismantled and stowed in a bag or other cover. Otherwise, bikes can be taken on the Lisbon and Porto urban lines and regional trains from Coimbra – there's usually a small charge during the week, free at weekends. The CP website (Ⓦ cp.pt) has the latest details.

Accommodation

Accommodation in Portugal is pretty good value compared with other western European countries. In almost any town you can find a basic guesthouse or small hotel offering a simple double or twin room for as little as €40, though you'll pay more in Algarve resorts in summer, or year-round in Lisbon or Porto. Moving upmarket, you're often spoilt for choice by some wonderful manor houses and a network of comfortable hotels known as pousadas, many in historic buildings and sited in places of natural beauty. Even in high season you shouldn't have much problem finding a bed in most regions, though the best places in Lisbon, Porto and the Algarve are often booked up days ahead, so advance reservations here are advised.

In hotels, a *quarto duplo* has two single beds, and a *quarto casal* has a large double bed for a couple. A single room – *quarto solteiro* or *individual* – costs around three-quarters of the price of a double. Ask to see the room before you take it, and don't be afraid to ask if there's a cheaper one available (rooms without private bathrooms often cost considerably less). In higher-grade hotels, you'll often get a better rate by booking online or simply by asking, especially out of season or at the end of the day.

Lastly, a word of warning: between November and April, night-time **temperatures** throughout the interior and the north can fall to below freezing. However, few B&Bs or guesthouses have any form of heating other than the odd plug-in radiator, so check out the facilities before taking a room. Similarly, in the height of summer check for a fan or air-conditioning, as nights can be very warm.

Guesthouses and private rooms

A simple **guesthouse** is known as an *alojamento local* – these come with or without en-suite facilities and don't always provide breakfast, but are usually perfectly comfortable and often in characterful old

---

ACCOMMODATION PRICES

All establishments listed in this book have a price quoted. It represents the rate for the **cheapest available double/twin room in high season** (ie, Christmas/New Year, Easter, July and August, and other local holidays), which means that at other times you'll often be able to stay for a lower price than that suggested. Breakfast is included, unless otherwise stated. For youth hostels we give the euro price for a dorm bed, and for campsites we give the price of a pitch plus the price per extra adult, if relevant.

UNUSUAL PLACES TO STAY

A Lagosta Perdida, Montesinho. A haven for hikers at the boutique-style "Lost Lobster". See p.377

Casa do Abrigo, Ilha da Berlenga. Bed down at the old fort on an island nature reserve. See p.143

Convento, Olhão. Stay in style in a beautifully converted Cubist townhouse. See p.448

Há Mar Ao Luar, Setúbal. Enjoy the hilltop views from a converted windmill high above the coast. See p.125

Quinta do Rio Alcaide, Porto de Mós. Relax in the spring-fed pool at this converted paper mill. See p.164

Quinta Nova, Pinhão. Chic rooms and amazing views at a gorgeous Douro wine estate. See p.299

---

townhouses. In seaside resorts and smaller villages, you can also often rent a **room** in a private house, known as a **dormida** or **quarto** – just look around for signs in windows, or check with the local turismo. Room quality and facilities vary greatly: some are little more than a bed in a converted attic, others come with modern bathrooms and air-conditioning. Always ask where the room is before you agree to take it – you could end up far from the town centre or beach. Breakfast is not usually included.

Rates for *alojamentos locais* and *quartos* average €40–50 a night, though in the Algarve in high season expect to pay up to twice as much.

Hotels

Hotels are all classified with one to five stars, and can vary from old buildings with plenty of character, sometimes with owners to match, to top-notch, stylish, luxury resorts. A one-star hotel (which may still be known by its former name as a *pensão* or *residencial*) usually costs €40–60 and may not have en-suite bathrooms or indeed much else other than the bed, a heavy (and almost never used) wardrobe, and perhaps a chair or table. More upmarket places will have modern en-suite rooms, plus TVs, heaters and air-conditioning. Breakfast is usually included: expect coffee, bread and preserves, and possibly some sliced ham and cheese.

At two- and three-star hotels, en-suite doubles cost around €80; many three-star places have air-conditioned rooms with cable/satellite TV, and even swimming pools, so they can be pretty good value. For rooms with all mod cons in four- and five-star hotels, you'll pay anything from €120 to €200, while the very fanciest places – boutique hotels in the Algarve or luxury hotels in Lisbon, for example – attract an international clientele and can pretty much charge what they like. Some cosier places of four- or five-star quality, often in a converted historic building or manor house in a rural location, are known as

estalagems, or inns. All hotels and *estalagems/* inns serve breakfast, usually (though not always) included in the price. In one- and two-star hotels it tends to be continental-style; more substantial buffet breakfasts are provided at three-star places and up.

Pousadas

Pousadas de Portugal (Ⓦpousadas.pt) is a chain of 37 hotels that have mostly been converted from historic properties such as old monasteries or castles, often in dramatic countryside settings. Formerly government-run, they are now efficiently managed by the Portuguese hotel chain Pestana, and can be found all over the country. The larger converted historic buildings are particularly fine, making full use of the old cloisters and chapels, etc, and some have been well modernized by Portugal's top architects. Others are more like small country houses, with an old-fashioned elegance and charm, while facilities and service throughout are equivalent to those in four- and five-star hotels. Most also have a swimming pool, lovely gardens and a good restaurant.

Prices vary considerably depending on the season, day (more expensive on Fri & Sat nights) and location, but start at €100–120 per night, rising to €170–200 for the finest properties. That said, a whole host of promotions (through the website) offer discounted rooms, and there are good deals for anyone over 55.

You can book the *pousadas* through their website, or through the official agents Keytel in the UK (Ⓦkeytel.co.uk) or Petrabax in the US (Ⓦpetrabax.com).

Rural tourism: country and manor houses

An increasingly popular alternative is to stay in a privately owned **country or manor house**. Promoted under the banner of Turismo no Espaço

PICK OF THE POUSADAS

Convento da Graça Tavira, Algarve. Designer-style ancient convent. See p.454
Convento de Évora, Alentejo. Sumptuous comforts in southern Portugal's most charming town. See p.395
Dom Afonso Alcácer do Sal, Alentejo. Dramatic views from a fabulous castle. See p.426
Palácio de Estói Estói, Algarve. A palatial blend of contemporary style and old-fashioned elegance. See p.443
Pestana Palacio do Freixo Porto. A magnificent Baroque riverside palace in Portugal's second city. See p.277
Pousada de São Francisco Beja, Alentejo. A tranquil retreat in a former convent. See p.422
Pousada de Viseu Viseu, Beira Alta. A dramatic conversion of a former hospital. See p.225
Pousada do Castelo, Óbidos. A superb, intimate castle conversion. See p.145
Pousada do Crato, Flor de Rosa, Alentejo. Sumptuous comforts in southern Portugal's most charming town. See p.402

Rural (TER), most are reasonably priced and are subdivided into the following categories: "HR" or Hotéis Rurais (traditional, country hotels); "TH" or Turismo de Habitação (old manor houses and palaces); "CC" or Casas no Campo (simpler country houses); and "AG" or Agro-Turismo (farmhouses, often on working farms or wine estates).

You can book many of these properties via **CENTER** (Central Nacional de Turismo no Espaço Rural ☎258 931 750, ⓦcenter.pt), a non-profitmaking organization which aims to help residents maintain their properties and traditional ways of life – without their support, many houses would either be sold, developed or abandoned. Alternatively, check the websites of the organizations it represents: ⓦsolaresde portugal.pt, ⓦaldeiasdeportugal.pt and ⓦcasas nocampo.net.

Properties range from simple farmhouses offering a couple of rooms on a bed-and-breakfast basis, to country manors complete with period furnishings. Quintas or herdades are farm estate houses, and you can even stay in palaces (palácios), owned by Portuguese aristocrats who have allowed their ancient seats to become part of the scheme.

There are hundreds of properties available, all of which have been inspected and approved by the government tourist office. **Rates** start at around €70 a night, though the grandest places might charge up to €120 for a double/twin room, or a little more for self-contained apartments or cottages within the grounds (sleeping up to six). Large breakfasts are invariably included, while many will provide dinners made from locally sourced ingredients. Others offer activities like fishing, rambling, horseriding and wine tasting.

Villas and apartments

Virtually every area of the country has some sort of self-catering **villa** or **apartment** available for rent, from basic one-room studios to five- or six-bedroom houses complete with grounds and pool. Most UK and European tour operators can find you a suitable place, though in summer the best places are booked up months in advance. The minimum rental period is usually a week, and the best deals are packages, including flights and car rental, with endless tour companies such as First Choice (ⓦfirstchoice.co.uk) and Thomson (ⓦthomson.co.uk), or Western Algarve experts Star Villas (ⓦstarvilla.com).

Youth hostels

There are around forty **youth hostels** (pousadas de juventude) in Portugal, under the umbrella of the youth organization Movijovem and affiliated to the Hostelling International network (ⓦhihostels.com). You'll need a valid membership card, available from your home-based youth-hostel association, or you can join on your first night at any hostel. There are full details of each hostel on the ⓦpousadas juventude.pt website (also in English), and you can book online, directly with the hostels, or call central reservations on ☎707 233 030.

Some hostels are a bit on the basic side, and others are geared towards schools and groups, but they are all in convenient locations for sightseeing or outdoor activities. As well as dorm beds, you can often get larger family rooms or apartments, and even en-suite double rooms. Some of the newer ones – at Parque das Nações (Lisbon) and Guimarães, for example – have been very well designed, while many others have wi-fi, cafés, bars and bike rental as standard.

Prices vary according to season, location and facilities, but dorm beds in most cost between €12 and €18 per person (high season is basically July, August, Easter, Christmas and other public holidays); we have given prices for individual hostels throughout this Guide.

There's also a growing network of **independent** and **boutique hostels**. Prices are similar to those at the *pousadas de juventude*, and most offer double/twin rooms as well as dorms. Some of the new boutique city hostels (such as the *Rivoli Cinema Hostel* in Porto and *Lisbon Lounge* or *Travellers House* in Lisbon) are very classy indeed.

Camping, campervans and motorhomes

There are hundreds of **campsites**, though many are huge, town-sized affairs by or near the beach that also have space for campervans/RVs, caravans and permanent bungalows and apartments. Needless to say, these get very crowded with Portuguese families in summer, though there are also plenty of smaller rural sites offering a quieter experience. The **Roteiro Campista** has details of over 200 campsites on its website (Ⓦroteiro-campista.pt) and booklet, which is widely available in bookshops in Portugal.

Charges are usually per person and per caravan or tent, with showers and parking extra; even so, it's rare that you'll pay more than €8 per person, although those operated by **Orbitur** (Ⓦorbitur.com) – usually with bungalows on site as well – are more expensive. The cheapest place to camp is usually the **municipal campsite** in each town, though these vary in quality and can be very crowded – they are not always recommended.

A few sites require an **international camping card** which gives discounts at member sites and serves as useful identification: many campsites will take it instead of your passport, and it covers you for third-party insurance when camping. The card is available from most home motoring or cycling

organizations and camping and caravan clubs, or check Ⓦcampingcardinternational.com.

Camping outside campsites is legal, though there are restrictions – for example, you can't camp on tourist beaches or in natural parks (other than in designated camping areas). With a little sensitivity you can pitch a tent for a short period almost anywhere else in the countryside, but it's always best to ask locally first – the potential fire risk is taken very seriously in Portugal.

Portugal is a great place to take **campervans** and **motorhomes**. However, it is important not to stop in unauthorized locations to prevent environmental damage; in any case, you may well be moved on by the police. Many campsites have dedicated areas where you can stop for the night. The Algarve tourist board can supply a leaflet (also available on their website, Ⓦvisitalgarve.pt) with details of the Algarve Motorhome Support Network, which aims to support and promote locations for motorhomes, including specific motorhome parks.

Food and drink

Portuguese food doesn't have the same high profile as other European cuisines, with menus usually relying on a traditional repertoire of grilled fish and meat, hearty stews and casseroles, and the ubiquitous salted cod (bacalhau), nearly all served with the same trio of accompaniments – rice, potatoes and salad. There are, of course, blindingly good exceptions to the norm in every town – crispy suckling pig from the local grill house, sardines straight from the boat and slapped on the barbecue, a slow-cooked ragout of wild boar in a country tavern – and these are the kind of simple, earthy dishes that Portugal excels in. Most restaurants are also extremely good value, while Portuguese wine (and not just the famous port) enjoys a growing worldwide reputation – if you're not yet familiar with them, you'll soon come to relish a refreshing glass of vinho verde on a hot day, or a gutsy Alentejo red with your grilled meat.

There's far more choice, style and invention in Lisbon, Porto, the Algarve and in wine regions such as the Douro, where international dishes are widely available and some enterprising chefs are adding a contemporary twist to traditional Portuguese

cuisine. But out in the regions, and particularly in rural areas, simple, traditional menus still dominate. It's surprising, since the Portuguese originally introduced many spices and ingredients to a global market, but other than the odd Chinese or Indian restaurant, pizza place or Brazilian grill house most towns tend to feature resolutely local restaurants. Fast-food joints are widespread, though they are found more often in shopping malls than town centres. We have included a detailed **menu reader** in the Language section (see p.516).

Breakfast, snacks and sandwiches

At **breakfast**, any café, *pastelaria* (pastry shop) or *confeitaria* (confectioners) can provide a croissant or brioche, some toast (*uma torrada*; a doorstep with butter), a simple sandwich (a *tosta mista* is grilled ham and cheese) or some sort of cake or pastry. A *padaria* is a bakery, and any place advertising *pão quente* (hot bread) will also usually have a café attached.

Classic Portuguese **snacks** include *folhadas* (meat- or cheese-stuffed pasties), *croquetes* (deep-fried meat patties), *pastéis* or *bolinhos de bacalhau* (salt-cod fishcakes), *iscas de bacalhau* (battered salt-cod fishcakes with egg), *chamuças* (samosas), *bifanas* (a grilled or fried pork sandwich), and *prego no pão* (steak sandwich).

If you see a sign saying **petiscos**, you can sample Portugal's version of tapas. The range, however, is rarely extensive, and apart from olives, *tremoços* (pickled lupin seeds), a small round of cheese or some small fried fish these dishes tend towards the challenging – stewed snails or octopus salad, for example, or the unspeakable and ubiquitous *orelhas de porco* (crunchy pig's ears).

Restaurants

The quickest way to get trampled to death is to come between the Portuguese and their lunch.
A Small Death in Lisbon, Robert Wilson

Portuguese **restaurants** (*restaurantes*) run the gamut from rustic village eatery to designer hot spot, while meals are also served in a **tasca** (a tavern) and, less commonly these days, a **casa de pasto** (a cheap local dining room). A **cervejaria** is literally a "beer house", usually more informal than a restaurant and typically serving up steaks and seafood. A **marisqueira** is also a seafood place, while a **churrasqueira** specializes in char-grilled meat.

At lunch, most places offer a **prato do dia** (dish of the day), which is often cheaper than choosing from the menu. Many places also offer a more formal **ementa turística** – not a "tourist menu" as such, but a three-course set meal of the day, which may include soup, a drink or dessert; the lot can cost as little as €10–12. Prices, in any case, are rarely off-putting, and for €15–30 a head you could eat well in most restaurants in Portugal, provided you don't choose lobster or quaff the vintage port.

The default size for servings is huge. Indeed, you can usually have a substantial meal by ordering a cheaper **meia dose** (half-portion), or **uma dose** (a portion) between two. Meals are often listed in two sizes on the menu and it's perfectly acceptable to choose a smaller portion. **Lunch** is usually served noon to 3pm, **dinner** from 7.30pm onwards; don't count on being able to eat much after 10pm outside cities and tourist resorts.

Once seated in a Portuguese restaurant, you will be bought a plate of **appetizers**, which may just be bread and portions of butter and sardine spread, but sometimes includes cheese, *chouriço*, prawns or other titbits. None of it is free and you will be charged for everything that you eat – if you don't want it, just say *não quero isto* ("I don't want this"), and make sure you check the bill afterwards. Beware, too, the near-ubiquitous serenade of the traditional Portuguese **television**, even in upmarket or otherwise romantic or fancy restaurants. A request to turn it down or (heaven forbid) off is likely to be met with bemusement.

CLASSIC PORTUGUESE CAFÉS

A Brasileira, Lisbon. A slice of the early 1900s to go with your cake. See p.96
Antiga Confeitaria de Belém, Lisbon. The home-cooked *pastéis de nata* here are second to none. See p.97
Café A Brasileira, Braga. Gilt reliefs and glass-topped tables set the tone for the northern city's finest coffee stop. See p.319
Café Majestic, Porto. A dazzling Belle Époque café. See p.278
Café Santa Cruz, Coimbra. A sumptuous interior inside a former monastery. See p.191
Pastelaria Gomes, Vila Real. Enjoy coffee and cake in this beautifully timeless café. See p.357

OUR FAVOURITE RESTAURANTS

A Choupana, Vila Nova de Milfontes, Alentejo. Grilled fish and meats served right by the crashing Atlantic. See p.432

Adega do Isaias, Estremoz, Alentejo. Country cooking at its best. See p.401

Mini Bar, Lisbon. Portuguese cuisine for the twenty-first century and beyond. See p.98

O Fuso, Arruda dos Vinhos, Ribatejo. Grilled meats don't come fresher than this. See p.177

Rei das Praias, Praia da Caneiros, Algarve. Quality dining on one of the south coast's loveliest coves. See p.471

Robalo, Sabugal. Fresh local produce grilled over a roaring fire. See p.250

Solar Bragançano, Bragança. Excellent regional specialities in a welcoming *casa típica*. See p.372

Vallecula, Valhelhas. Excellent local produce cooked up in an atmospheric old building. See p.244

Portuguese cuisine

Most Portuguese are convinced that theirs is the finest **cuisine** in the world. You may beg to differ – though you're in for a long argument if you voice a contrary opinion – but, at its best, Portuguese food marries locally sourced ingredients (especially fish, seafood, pork and game) with a straightforward preparation that lets the flavours shine through. There is regional variation, though not as much as you'd think – in fact, many ostensibly regional dishes turn up on menus across the country. In most day-to-day restaurants, fancy sauces and fresh vegetables are rare, and the predominant dressing for grills and roasts is olive oil, garlic and lemon, though coriander, cumin and paprika are commonly used in cooking.

Fish and seafood

In any resort or river port you can get fabulous **seafood**, from prawns to barnacles, while **fish** on offer usually includes bream (*dourada*), sea bass (*robalo*), hake (*pescada*), mackerel (*carapau*), salmon (*salmão*, often farmed) and trout (*truta*). The most typical Portuguese fish dish is **bacalhau** (dried, salted cod), which is virtually the national dish, with reputedly 365 different ways of preparing it: served with a boiled egg and black olives, made into a pie, char-grilled or cooked in a traditional copper *cataplana* – the list is endless. The best for first-timers to try are *bacalhau á bras* (fried with egg, onions and potatoes) and *bacalhau com natas* (baked in cream).

Grilled **sardines** provide one of the country's most appetizing smells, and you should definitely try a fish or seafood **cataplana** (stew), named after the wok-like lidded copper vessel in which it's cooked. Also typical of the seaside is **arroz de marisco**, mixed seafood in a soupy rice; *massa de peixe/marisco* is a similar dish but with noodles – *cataplanas*, *arroz* and *massa* dishes are usually served for a minimum of two people. Other specialities include a **caldeirada de peixe**, basically a fish stew, and **açorda** (a bread stew traditionally made from stale bread mixed with herbs, garlic, eggs and whatever farmers found to hand), often served with prawns. *Migas* and *xarém* are regional variations of *açorda*.

Meat and game

Grilled **beef**, **chicken** and **pork** are the mainstays of most menus – pork is especially loved in Portugal, whether it's steaks, chops, ribs, belly or leg. Particularly sought-after is *porco preto*, from the black Alentejan pigs, fed on acorns to give it a sweet flavour. **Presunto** is Portugal's equivalent of Parma ham – a smoked leg of pork preserved in sea salt and cured for months or years. The grill or **barbecue** (*no churrasco*) sees a lot of action, and grilled chicken (almost a second national dish) is usually enlivened by the addition of peppery **piri-piri sauce**. Also ubiquitous are **porco à alentejana** (pork cooked with clams), which originated, as its name suggests, in the Alentejo, and **rojões** (chunks of roast pork, served with black pudding) from the north. **Leitão** (spit-roast suckling pig) is at the centre of many a communal feast, particularly in the interior; **cabrito** (roast kid) is ubiquitous in mountain areas; while another festive inland speciality is **chanfana** (goat stew). Duck (*pato*) is usually served shredded and mixed with rice (**arroz de pato**); rabbit is served in rural areas (a **caçadora**, hunter's style, as a stew), and **game** like wild boar (*javali*), partridge (*perdiz*) or quail (*cordoniz*) is often on menus too.

The Portuguese have long believed that if you eat an animal, you may as well eat all of it, and

VEGETARIAN PORTUGAL

Portuguese cuisine is tough on strict **vegetarians** and you'll be eating a lot of omelettes, chips, salads and pizzas. Nearly everywhere does a basic vegetable soup, though beware of the **caldo verde** – a kale, onion and potato broth – which usually comes with *chouriço* in it. Portuguese fruit is a particular joy, and any market should turn up some excellent local produce. You may even find officially certified *biológico* – **organic** – produce, though it has yet to make much of an impact on mainstream food-buying habits.

In Lisbon, Porto and some parts of the Algarve, there is a reasonable selection of **vegetarian restaurants**, even macrobiotic ones, together with Chinese, Italian and Indian establishments where you should be able to eat well. Also, most towns have **health-food shops** (or supermarkets with health-food sections) where you can find cereal bars, gluten-free biscuits, dried fruit and the like.

offal is common. **Alheiras** are sausages made from bread and chicken, with their roots in the Inquisition, when Jews copied the Catholic passion for sausages while avoiding pork – the best come from Mirandela in the north, and are served grilled or steamed. You might need to steel yourself for a couple of special dishes: Porto's **tripas** (tripe) dishes incorporate beans and spices but the heart of the dish is still recognizably chopped stomach-lining; while **cozido à portuguesa** is a boiled "meat" stew in which you shouldn't be surprised to turn up lumps of fat, cartilage or even a pig's ear. Other traditional dishes use pig's or chicken's blood as a base – the words to look for are *sarrabulho* and *cabidela*.

Cheese

There's a huge range of **regional Portuguese cheese**, a sizeable quantity of which is still handmade (the label D.O.P. guarantees that it was made in its traditional area). A *queijo de cabra* or *cabreiro* is goats' cheese, sheep is *ovelha*, cow is *vaca*, cured is *curado*. *Queijo fresco* and *requeijão* are unpressed curds of sheep's milk, similar to cottage cheese.

Particularly recommended local cheeses to look out for are **Queijo da Serra** (or **Queijo Serrano**) from the Serra da Estrela, which has an almost liquid texture – the traditional method is to cut out a hole on top and scoop up the contents by spoon – and **Azeitão**, a sheep's milk cheese from near Lisbon, which crumbles slightly when you cut it and has a pleasantly astringent taste.

Vegetables and salad

Accompanying nearly every dish will be **potatoes**, either fried or roast in the case of most meat dishes, or boiled if you've ordered fish. The distinction is less marked in tourist resorts on the Algarve and elsewhere, but trying to get chips to come with your grilled trout or salmon in a rural town simply invites incomprehension: fish comes with boiled potatoes and that's that. Most dishes are also served with a helping of rice and salad. Other **vegetables** occasionally make an appearance, like carrots, cabbage or broccoli, usually boiled to within an inch of their lives – a more interesting choice is *grelos* (turnip tops), often turned into a purée, while winter and early spring is the time for chestnuts (*castanhas*), which appear in soups and stuffings. **Salad** is the more common accompaniment to every meal; a *salada mista* is a simple mixed salad of lettuce, tomatoes and onions.

Desserts, cakes, pastries and fruit

In most restaurants, the **dessert** menu rarely goes further than fruit salad, ice cream or things like chocolate mousse and rice pudding. Anything described as a *doce de casa* (house dessert) is invariably a heart-stopping wedge of sugar, cream and egg (our favourite Portuguese recipe begins "Take sixty egg yolks…").

In cake shops, cafés and tea rooms you can seriously indulge yourself in pastries (*pastéis*), buns (*bolinhos*), rolls (*tortas*), tarts (*tartes*) and cakes (*bolos*). There are hundreds of local specialities, starting with the classic Lisbon **pastéis de nata** (custard tarts) and then continuing in glorious profusion by way of **queijadas de Sintra** (Sintra "cheesecakes", not that they contain any cheese), **palha de ovos** (egg pastries) from Abrantes, **bolo de anjo** ("angel cake"), **mil folhas** (millefeuille pastries), **bolinhos** made with beans (*feijão*), carrot (*cenoura*) or pumpkin (*chila*), **bolos de arroz** (rice-flour muffins) and **suspiros** ("sighs" – meringues). From Aveiro, there are incredibly sweet egg-based **ovos moles** wrapped in wafers, while anything labelled **doces conventuais** ("convent desserts") owes its origins to the gastronomic inspiration of nuns past.

Seasonal **fruit** ranges from spring cherries and strawberries to summer melons, peaches and apricots. The grapes arrive in late summer and autumn, as do most pears, apples, plums and figs, while winter is the time for citrus fruits, pomegranates, and immensely sweet *dióspiros* (persimmon or date-plums). Available year-round are bananas from Madeira, and sweet and aromatic pineapples from the Azores.

Wine

Portugal's **wine regions** – notably Alentejo, Bairrada, Dão, the Douro and the historic regions of Estremadura and Ribatejo – have acquired a strong reputation in recent years. Most wines are made in small cooperatives with local grape varieties, many peculiar to Portugal (including some wonderfully named varieties of grape such as Dog strangler and Bastardo).

Portuguese **wine lists** (ask for the *lista de vinhos*) don't just distinguish between *tinto* (red), *branco* (white) and *rosé*, but between *verde* ("green", meaning young, acidic and slightly sparkling) and *maduro* ("mature"), meaning the wines you're probably accustomed to. You'll find a decent selection from around the country in even the most basic of restaurants, and often in half-bottles, too.

Some of the best-known *maduros* are from the **Douro** region: the reds tend to be expensive, though a good, crisp, reasonably priced white is Planalto. Red wines from the **Dão** region (a roughly triangular area between Coimbra, Viseu and Guarda, around the River Dão) taste a little like burgundy, and they're available throughout the country. Quinta de Cabriz from Carregal do Sal (near Viseu) is an excellent mid-range Dão red. The **Alentejo** is another area with a growing reputation – wines from Reguengos de Monsaraz have the strength and full body typical of that region, notably the Monte Velho reds and Esporão Reserva whites from the Herdade de Esporão vineyard. Among other smaller regions offering interesting wines are Colares near Sintra (rich reds), Bucelas in the Estremadura/Lisboa region (crisp, dry whites) and Alenquer from Ribatejo (refreshing whites).

The light, slightly sparkling **vinhos verdes** – "green wines", in age not colour – are produced in quantity in the Minho. They're drunk young as most don't improve with age, but are great with meals, especially shellfish. There are red and rosé *vinhos verdes*, though the whites are the most successful. Casal Garcia and Gato are the two labels you see everywhere; far better are Ponte de Lima and Ponte da Barca. For real quality, try the fuller-strength Alvarinho from Monção and Melgaço, along the River Minho.

Portuguese **rosé wines** are known abroad mainly through the spectacularly successful export of Mateus Rosé. This is too sweet and aerated for most tastes, but other rosés are definitely worth sampling.

Portugal also produces a range of sparkling **wines**, known as *espumantes naturais*. The best of these come from the Bairrada region, north of Coimbra, though Raposeira wines – a little further north from near Lamego – are more commonly available.

Fortified wine, spirits and beer

Port (*vinho do Porto*), the famous fortified wine or *vinho generoso* ("generous wine"), is produced from grapes grown in the vineyards of the Douro valley and mostly stored in huge wine-lodges at Vila Nova de Gaia, facing Porto across the Rio Douro. You can visit these for tours and free tastings; we give full details in the relevant sections of this Guide.

Madeira (*vinho da Madeira*), from the island of the same name, comes in four main varieties: Sercial (a light, dry aperitif), Malvasia (very sweet, heavy dessert wine), Vermelho (a sweeter version of Sercial) and Boal or Malmsey (drier and heavier versions of Malvasia). Also worth trying are the sweet white **moscatel** dessert wines from Setúbal, which – like port and Madeira – also come as yearly vintages.

Domestic **brandy** (the best is *maciera*) and **gin** are fairly unsophisticated and frighteningly cheap. Be warned that the typical Portuguese measure of spirits involves the waiter or bartender pouring from the bottle until you beg them to stop. Order by name if you'd like an international brand that you've heard of.

Local firewaters – generically known as **aguardente** – include *bagaço* (made from distilled grape husks), *aguardente de figo* (from figs), *ginginha* (from cherries) and the very strange *Licor Beirão* (a kind of cognac with herbs). In the Algarve, the best-known firewaters are *brandy mel*, made from honey and the strawberry tree and which tastes a bit like schnapps; and *amêndoa amarga*, made from almonds.

Portugal's main **beer** (*cerveja*) brands, found nationwide, are Sagres and Super Bock, and you'll also see Cristal and Cintra, not that there's much to distinguish any of them. From the tap, order

um imperial (or *um fino* in the north) if you want a regular glass, and *uma caneca* for half a litre. For bottled beer, ask for a mini (20cl) or a *garrafa* (33cl). The standard beer in Portugal is a typical European-style lager (around five percent strength), but the main brands also offer a *preta* (black) beer – a kind of slightly fizzy lager-stout – as well as wheat, fruit-flavoured and non-alcoholic versions, none particularly successful. There's also a growing trend for **craft beers**, such as the Porto-based Sovina and Letra from Braga, which can be interesting; see ⓦcervejaartesanal portuguesa.pt for a full list.

Coffee, tea and soft drinks

The Portuguese take their **coffee** very seriously, and you can order it in a variety of ways. A simple coffee (*uma bica* or *um café*) is small, black and strong, like an espresso; *um carioca* is also small and black, but weaker; *uma chinesa* is large, black and strong. Ordering *um garoto* in Lisbon and the south, or *um pingo* in the north, will get you an espresso-sized coffee with milk; while *um galão* is large and milky but weak, like a latte, and is often served in a glass. If you prefer your coffee reasonably strong and not too milky, ask for *um meia de leite*.

Tea (*chá*) is usually served black; *com leite* is with milk, and to be sure of getting tea with a slice of lemon (as opposed to a lemon-tea drink) ask for *um chá preto com limão*. Herbal teas are known as *infusões*, the most common being camomile (*camomila*), mint (*menta*) and lemon verbena (*lúcia-lima*).

Fresh **orange juice** (*sumo de laranja*) – rather surprisingly for an orange-producing country – can be awkward to find; adding the word *natural* or *fresca* should get you the real thing. If there is a juicer available, ask for it *da maquina* to get it freshly squeezed. **Mineral water** (*água mineral*) – of which the best-known national brands are Vimeiro, Pisões, Pedras Salgadas and Vidago – comes either still (*sem gás*) or carbonated (*com gás*).

The media

Foreign-language newspapers (including the European editions of British papers, plus the International Herald Tribune, Le Monde and the like) can be bought in the major towns, cities and resorts, usually the same day in Lisbon and much of the Algarve or a day late elsewhere.

For an English-language view of what's happening in Portugal, the weekly *Portugal News* (ⓦthe portugalnews.com) is widely available, while *Portugal Resident* (ⓦ portugalresident.com) is aimed principally at expats.

Newspapers and magazines

The most respected Portuguese daily **newspapers** are the Lisbon-based *Diário de Notícias* (ⓦdn.pt) and *Público* (ⓦpublico.pt), and Porto's *Jornal de Notícias* (ⓦjn.pt). While the traditional *Diário de Notícias* is associated by many with the former Salazar regime, *Jornal de Notícias* is more liberal in outlook, and stylish *Público* has the youngest, most sophisticated feel, good for politics and the arts. All have useful daily **listings information** (with good Friday supplements). The best-selling **tabloid** is the right-wing *Correio da Manhã* (ⓦcmjornal.xl.pt), while business daily *Jornal de Negócios* (ⓦnegocios .pt) keeps you up to date with economic issues, and the weekly *Expresso* (ⓦexpresso.sapo.pt) has lots of meaty articles on politics, economics and culture. For fans of Portuguese **sport** (mainly football), *A Bola* (ⓦabola.pt), *O Jogo* (ⓦojogo.pt) and *Record* (ⓦrecord.xl.pt) cover the daily ins and outs of teams and players. Popular current-affairs **magazines** include the long-standing *Visão* (ⓦvisao.sapo.pt), while for coverage of the C-list celeb and reality TV scene you need a copy of *Caras* (ie, Faces, ⓦcaras .sapo.pt), a bit like a Portuguese *Hello!*

Television and radio

There are four domestic **channels**: the state-run RTP1 and 2, and the private channels SIC and TVI. The best is 2, which is a mix of films from all over the world, National Geographic-style documentaries and daily coverage of the arts. The other three channels are heavy on game shows, variety shows, reality TV, and imported or adapted American and British series. Films are nearly always shown in their original language (ie, subtitled rather than dubbed), while you also get a full diet of *telenovelas* (soaps). Some of the most popular soaps are actually Brazilian (saucy historical romps a speciality).

Most Portuguese households and businesses get their TV via **cable** or **satellite** subscription. Even in small two- and three-star hotels you'll often get a couple of foreign-language channels (BBC World, CNN, Eurosport, MTV), while four- and five-star places usually offer an endless range of foreign-language channels plus pay-per-view movie channels.

Portugal has a plethora of national and local **radio stations**. Antena 1 mixes golden oldies and Portuguese music with news on the hour. Antena 2 has classical music, while Antena 3 has the best contemporary sounds and new Portuguese music. Rádio Comercial is the best of the independent stations, playing pop and rock. Radio Renascença is a mainstream station of a religious persuasion; the associated RFM has a younger target audience but its playlist hasn't changed in years. With a short-wave radio you'll be able to tune into the **BBC World Service** (W bbc.co.uk/worldservice).

Festivals

Almost every village in Portugal has its own festival (festa) or traditional pilgrimage (romaria), usually to celebrate the local saint's day or the regional harvest. Some are little more than an excuse for the villagers to hold a low-key procession and picnic or barbecue and dance, while others have become serious celebrations lasting several days and attracting tourists from all over the world.

The great weekly **feiras**, like that at Barcelos in the north, were originally simply markets, but nowadays are a combination of agricultural show, folk festival, amusement park and, admittedly, tourist bazaar. Most towns also put on concerts, dances, processions and events throughout the year (especially between June and September), while an increasing number of **music festivals** are held in Portugal, pulling in giants of the music world: big events include NOS Primavera in Porto (June) and NOS Alive in Lisbon (July). The full lineups are available at W portugalsummerfestivals.com.

Only the major highlights are picked out in the **festival calendar** below. Other local festivals and events are covered in the relevant chapters of this Guide (the Lisbon and Porto chapters both have full listings of festivals in those regions), or check with local turismos and have a look at the websites of the various town halls (Câmara Municipal: usually W cm-nameoftown.pt), which always carry news about forthcoming festivities.

Among major **national events**, Easter week and the Santos Populares festivities – associated with St Anthony (June 12/13), St John (June 23/24) and St Peter (June 28/29) – stand out. All are celebrated throughout the country with religious processions.

Easter is most magnificent in Braga, where it is full of ceremonial pomp, while the saints' festivals tend to be more joyous affairs. In Lisbon, during the saint's day *festa* for Santo António, the Alfama becomes one giant street party. In Porto, where St John's Eve is the highlight of a week of celebration, everyone dances through the streets all night, hitting each other over the head with leeks or plastic hammers.

JANUARY

Epiphany (Dia de Reis) Jan 6. The traditional crown-shaped cake *bolo rei* (king's cake) with a lucky charm and a bean inside is eaten; if you get the bean in your slice you have to buy the cake next year.

FEBRUARY

Carnaval Many areas now have Rio-like carnival parades, with Lisbon and the Algarve towns being good destinations. But Carnaval has much older traditions steeped in springtime fertility rites, and for a glimpse of what it was like before thongs and spangles, check out the masked merry-making of the Entrudo dos Comprades (p.295), near Lamego.

MARCH/APRIL

Easter Holy week (Semana Santa) religious processions in most places, most majestically in Braga, and at São Brás de Alportel in the Algarve (the Festa das Tochas). The Festa da Mãe Soberana in Loulé (Algarve) is one of the country's largest Easter festivals. Another good location is Tomar, where the floral crosses of the procession are ceremoniously destroyed afterwards.

MAY

Sintra Music Festival (W festivaldesintra.pt). Performances throughout May by international orchestras, musicians and dance groups in parks, gardens and palaces in and around Sintra, Estoril and Cascais.

Queima das Fitas Early May. The "burning of the ribbons", celebrating the end of the academic year, reaches its drunken apogee in Coimbra and other university towns.

Festa das Cruzes May 3. The "Festival of the Crosses" is the biggest annual event in Barcelos (Minho).

Fátima (Peregrinação de Fátima) May 13. Portugal's most famous pilgrimage commemorates the Apparitions of the Virgin Mary; also in October (see p.164).

Corpus Christi Vaca das Cordas End of May (or early June). This is a "running of the bull" ceremony in Ponte de Lima with roots in classical mythology.

JUNE

Festa de São Gonçalo First weekend in June. Prominent saint's day celebrations in Amarante.

Rock In Rio Lisboa First week in June (W rockinriolisboa.sapo.pt). Europe's largest rock festival (an offshoot of the enormous Rock in Rio fest) is held in even-numbered years.

Feira Nacional da Agricultura First two weeks in June (W feiranacionalagricultura.pt). Held at Santarém, for ten days from the first Friday, with dancing, bullfighting and an agricultural fair.

Santos Populares Second & fourth weeks in June. Celebrations in honour of Santo António (St Anthony, June 12–13), São João (St John, 23–24) and Pedro (St Peter, 28–29) throughout the country.
Arraial Pride (ⓦ ilga-portugal.pt/lisboapride). Lisbon's increasingly popular gay pride event changes exact date and venue annually but usually takes place towards the end of the month.

JULY

Festa dos Tabuleiros First week in July. Tomar's biggest and most spectacular procession takes place every four years, with the next two being in 2019 and 2023 (see p.170).
Festa do Colete Encarnado First two weeks in July. Held in Vila Franca de Xira, with Pamplona-style running of bulls through the streets.

AUGUST

Festival Sudoeste Second week in Aug (ⓦ sudoeste.meo.pt). Much-heralded four-day rock, indie and electro music festival at Zambujeira do Mar, Alentejo coast (see p.433).
Festas Gualterianas First weekend in Aug. The major festival in Guimarães has been held since the fifteenth century.
Festa do Nossa Senhora da Boa Viagem First weekend in Aug. Seafaring is celebrated at Peniche with religious processions by boat and on land.
Romaria da Nossa Senhora d'Agonia Third weekend in Aug. Viana do Castelo's major annual religious celebration, plus carnival and fair (see p.323).

SEPTEMBER

Romaria de Nossa Senhora dos Remédios First week in Sept. The annual pilgrimage in Lamego comes to a head at the end of the first week, though events start in the last week of August (see p.295).
Festa do Avante! First week in Sept (ⓦ festadoavante.pcp.pt). The Portuguese Communist Party's big annual bash sees three days of live music, events, rallies and speeches in Seixal, a town on the south bank of the Tejo opposite Lisbon.
Feiras Novas Second & third weekends in Sept. The "New Fairs" – a traditional festival and market – held in Ponte de Lima.
Festa de São Mateus Third or fourth week in Sept (ⓦ saomateusemelvas.com). A week's worth of celebrations in Elvas (Alentejo), including a huge religious procession plus the usual fairs and fireworks.

OCTOBER

Feira de Outubro First two weeks in Oct. Bull-running and bullfighting in Vila Franca de Xira.
Fátima Oct 13. The second great pilgrimage of the year at Fátima.

NOVEMBER

Feira Nacional do Cavalo First two weeks in Nov (ⓦ fnc .cm-golega.pt). The National Horse Fair, held in Golegã (see p.173).
São Martinho Nov 11. Celebrations in honour of St Martin, with roots in pre-Christian harvest festivals; coincides with the first tastings of the year's wine, roast chestnuts and Água Pé – a weak wine made from watered-down dregs. At its most traditional in northern Trás-os-Montes, Beira Baixa (particularly Alcains), Golegã, and Penafiel east of Porto.

DECEMBER

Christmas (Natal) Dec 24. The main Christmas celebration is midnight Mass on December 24, followed by a traditional meal of *bacalhau*, turkey or – bizarrely in Trás-os-Montes – octopus.
New Year's Eve (Noite de Ano Novo) Dec 31. Individual towns organize their own events, usually with fireworks at midnight, and the New Year is welcomed by the banging of old pots and pans.

Sports and outdoor activities

Internationally famed for its beaches, golf courses and tennis centres, Portugal also has an ideal climate for a variety of other outdoor pursuits including surfing, windsurfing, walking and adventure sports. Spectators can enjoy top-class football throughout the country, or seek out Portugal's own brand of bullfighting.

Adventure activities

The **outdoor activity** scene is rapidly expanding, with many regions now offering paragliding, abseiling/rap jumping, rafting, canyoning, caving, mountain-biking and 4WD expeditions. There's most scope in the mountain areas – notably the Serra da Estrela and Peneda-Gerês parks – and on the major rivers (Douro, Mondego and Zêzere), but many of the smaller natural parks and reserves also have local adventure outfits. It's always worth contacting operators in advance, since activities are sometimes only for groups and are always heavily subscribed at weekends and during summer holidays. Prices vary considerably, but you can expect to pay from €80 for a day's guided mountain walking, or €90–100 for whitewater rafting or canyoning.

Swimming

Portugal is on the Atlantic, which tends to be cooler than the Mediterranean in summer, but warmer in the winter. The **Algarve** has the country's most popular sandy beaches, many of them sheltered in coves – the sea is warmest on the eastern Algarve, and remains swimmable year-round if you're hardy. The western coast has some stupendous stretches of beach, but they face the

full brunt of the ocean, so you need to beware the heavy undertow and don't swim if you see a red or yellow flag. The EU blue flag indicates that the water is clean enough to swim in – Portugal has an impressive 314 – and that the beach has lifeguards. For a full rundown of the country's **blue flag beaches**, see ⓦblueflag.org.

An unsung glory of central and northern Portugal is its **river beaches** – you'll see signs (*praia fluvial*) everywhere directing you to quiet bends in the local river or to weirs or dramatic gorges. Often, the local municipality erects a summer bar (usually open June to September), and there are often picnic and barbecue areas, and public toilets. Many towns also have a summer outdoor **swimming pool** (*piscina*), also only open from June to September. At indoor municipal pools (open all year) you may have to show your passport, and you'll have to wear a swimming cap.

Bullfighting

Although a traditional Portuguese sport, **bull-fighting** (*tourada*) is nowhere near as popular as it used to be – though you can still watch it, if you really want. Aficionados claim that it is less cruel than in Spain as the bulls are not killed in public, though critics say that it is more cruel as the bull is injured and taunted in the ring, then killed later anyway. Whatever your views, the sport is still legal in Portugal and there are regular fights during the **bullfighting season** (April to October) at bullrings around the country, including Lisbon and Albufeira.

The **Tejo valley**, east of Lisbon, is where many of the country's bulls (and horses) are bred, and local festivals around here involve bullfights and bull-running through the streets, such as at Vila Franca de Xira and Santarém.

Football

Football is Portugal's favourite sport bar none, and it is no surprise to the natives that one of the world's greatest players (**Cristiano Ronaldo**) and top managers (**José Mourinho**) hail from the country. Portugal hosted the 2004 European Championships, which saw the construction of several excellent stadiums, including the Estádio do Dragão in Porto and Benfica's Estádio da Luz. The national team have always punched above their weight and, after being runners-up to Greece in 2004, surprised most people by beating France on their home patch in the final of the **Euro 2016** tournament. Possibly the last international hurrah for Ronaldo, the tournament also saw the emergence of a new wonder-kid, **Renato Sanchez**.

The leading clubs, inevitably, hail from the country's big cities, Porto and Lisbon. Over the last two decades **FC Porto** (see p.276) has swept up every title available, including the national league on many occasions (the win of 1999 made it a unique five times in a row), the European UEFA Cup/Europa League in 2003 and 2011 (when they went the entire league season undefeated under manager Villas-Boas), and – its crowning glory – the European Champions League title in 2004, under José Mourinho. The club is famed for its South American scouting policy, which has brought to Europe previously unknown stars including Deco, Radamel Falcão, Hulk and James Rodrigues.

Lisbon-based **Benfica** (see p.106) experienced a similar golden age in the 1960s, when Mozam-bique-born striker Eusébio was at his masterful height, and have been the more successful team in recent years, being national league winners in 2014, 2015 and 2016. The other big team is **Sporting** (see p.106), also from Lisbon, who are frequently league runners-up. They are known for their excellent youth academy, which has

---

WATCHING THE FOOTBALL

If you're going to a **football game** in Portugal, or watching one on TV, you need to know the basics if you want to join in. Arriving after kick-off, ask *resultado?* (what's the score?) and settle down in time to watch the *guarda-redes* (goalkeeper) make a complete *frango* (cock-up) of a save. The *meio-campo* (midfield) looks decidedly dodgy and your *ponte de lance* (centre forward) keeps getting caught *fora-de-jogo* (offside) – that's when he's not being clattered from behind. That's a *falta!* (foul!) and a *grande penalidade!* (penalty!), surely? If he scores, the TV commentators will invariably celebrate Brazilian-style – *golo!* (try goooooaaaaalllll!) – before referring to the *festa nas bancadas* (party on the terraces) that's now underway. If, on the other hand, you're losing, heaven forbid your team resorts to punting it aimlessly up the field, route-one style – sad to say, the long-ball game is known disparagingly as *o jogo Inglês* (the English game).

nurtured the talents of Cristiano Ronaldo (who they signed from his native Madeira when he was barely a teenager), as well as Luís Nani and England's Eric Dier. Just about every Portuguese citizen supports one of these three teams and, in the provinces, usually one of the lesser, local outfits as well. Of these, Sporting Braga (who reached an all-Portuguese Europa League final in 2011) is the most consistent, though Vitória Guimarães, Estoril Praia and Rio Ave have all played European football in recent years.

Ticket prices for a clash between two big names average €25–50, depending on the seat, though tickets for other games cost a lot less. The **Liga Portuguesa** (Ⓦligaportugal.pt) season runs from the end of August to mid-May, most matches being played on Saturdays and Sundays. Live televised matches are regular fixtures in bars and restaurants, usually on Friday or Sunday evenings, often other days too.

TEAMS AND TOWNS

Some of Portugal's tourist spots are also home to top **league football teams** with regular visits from the likes of Porto, Sporting and Benfica – though if you look at the fixtures list you may be totally unaware where the match is being played. This is because team names don't always match the names of the town they represent. Taking off the ending of *–ense* or *–enses* (which roughly means from the town of) will often help. Here is a list of some top football towns followed by their very different club names:

Barcelos Gil Vicente (Ⓦgilvicentefc.pt)
Belém (Lisbon) Belenenses (Ⓦosbelenenses.com)
Coimbra Académica (Ⓦacademica-oaf.pt)
Funchal (Madeira) Marítimo (Ⓦcsmaritimo.org.pt)
Gimarães Vitória SC (Ⓦvitoriasc.pt)
Olhão Olhanense (Ⓦscolhanense.com)
Setúbal Vitória FC (Ⓦvfc.pt)
Vila do Conde Rio Ave (Ⓦrioave-fc.pt)

Golf

Portugal is a year-round **golf** destination, though exclusivity is often the keyword. Some of the country's finest hotels and villa complexes have golf courses attached, or have connections with a golf club, and the best deals are usually on special golf-holiday packages. Otherwise, **green fees** on 18-hole courses start at around €40, though multi-play packages and discounts are nearly always available; see Ⓦgreenfeesportugal.info. The Greater Lisbon area and the Algarve have the bulk of the courses: for more information consult a specialist tour operator or check online at Ⓦportugalgolf.pt and Ⓦalgarvegolf.net.

Tennis

Many larger Algarve hotels also have year-round **tennis courts**. If you want to improve your game, the best intensive coaching is at the Vale do Lobo Tennis Academy (packages organized by Light Blue Travel; Ⓦlightbluetravel.co.uk); or the Praia da Luz Ocean Club near Lagos (packages via Jonathan Markson Tennis; Ⓦmarksontennis.com).

Horseriding

Horseriding stables around the country offer one-hour or full-day rides, often on Lusitano thoroughbred horses. The main areas for tourist rides are Estoril and Sintra, the Algarve and the Alentejo, while the historic province of Ribatejo lies at the heart of Portugal's equestrian traditions. Prices start from around €30 for an hour's trek, rising to €100–150 for a full day, which usually includes a picnic lunch. For details of *centros hípicos* (riding schools) in a particular area, contact the local tourist office.

Skiing

The only **skiing** is in the Serra da Estrela (usually possible from December to February, sometimes March), though you wouldn't specifically travel to Portugal for it. The slopes lie just below the *serra's* highest point, Torre, with access easiest from Covilhã via Penhas da Saude. The four lifts, ski school, and ski and snowboard rental are operated by Turistrela (see p.245); a day's gear rental starts at €25, one-hour lessons from €30, and you can also book reasonably-priced ski packages. The year-round artificial run at Skiparque, near Manteigas (see p.242), is another option, and this also doubles as an outdoor activity and adventure centre.

Surfing and windsurfing

Surfing in Portugal is renowned throughout Europe, though the currents and the raw power of the swell here require a high level of expertise. Indeed, some of the largest waves ever to have been surfed crash ashore at Nazaré on the central Portuguese coast (see box, p.152). Supertubos on the south side of Peniche is the original surf destination in Portugal – it's one of the few breaks to work in northerly winds – while Nazaré and Ericeira (a World Surfing Reserve) both attract highly talented local surfers and travelling pros. There are international competitions held at all

> **PORTUGAL'S TOP FIVE SURFING BEACHES**
> **Praia do Amado**, Algarve. The best surf of the Algarve's west-coast beaches. See p.492
> **Praia do Coxos**, Ericeira. Challenging surf at Europe's first World Surfing Reserve. See p.135
> **Supertubos**, Peniche. Offers some of the most consistent surfing in the country. See p.141
> **Baleal**, Peniche. Great for surfers of all abilities. See p.141
> **Praia do Norte**, Nazaré. World-record waves for serious surfers. See p.152

these places, as well as at Espinho south of Porto (popular with bodyboarders) and Figueira da Foz near Coimbra, while the more protected west coast of the Algarve, north of Sagres, is excellent for beginners and experienced surfers alike.

The biggest **windsurfing** destinations are Guincho and Praia Grande, north of Lisbon, and round Sines on the Alentejo coast. We've highlighted rental outfits and surf camps in nearly all these places, while good websites include Ⓦwannasurf.com; Ⓦbeachcam.sapo.pt (in Portuguese) for breaks, photos, reports, surf-savvy weather and wave height forecasts; and Ⓦsurfing portugal.com, homepage of the Federação Portuguesa de Surf, which organizes competitions.

Kayaking

Many adventure outfits can organize **river kayaking**, with the Rio Mondego offering an excellent gentle introduction that starts from near Penacova, and is basically a relaxing half-day float downriver towards Coimbra. In addition, **sea kayaking** is increasing in popularity, particularly along the more sheltered southern Algarve coast. Many Algarve resorts now hire out kayaks, if you want to go independently, or offer guided kayak trips that explore the local coves and beaches.

Diving

Scuba diving for beginners is best off Praia do Carvoeiro in the Algarve, where Algarve Dive Experience (Ⓦalgarve-scuba-diving.com) and Divers Cove (Ⓦdiverscove.de) offer standard dives with equipment rental for around €45, plus night and wreck dives for experienced divers, and four-day PADI-accredited Open Water courses from €450. On the west coast, conditions can be more trying, with a strong undertow.

Walking

Portugal only has one **national park** – the Parque Nacional da Peneda-Gerês, in the north – but there are over forty other **protected areas**, designated as

parques naturais (natural parks), *reservas naturais* (natural reserves) or other specifications. You'll find them all listed and profiled on the website of the government's Instituto da Conservação da Natureza (Ⓦicnf.pt – some information in English available). All the main parks, and many of the minor ones, are covered in this Guide and between them account for some of Portugal's most dramatic landscapes – from the high-mountain scenery of the Serra da Estrela to the limestone caves of the Serras de Aire e Candeeiros, or the island hideaway of the Ilha Berlenga to the lagoons, dunes and marshes of the Ria Formosa.

Throughout this Guide we've recommended **walks and hiking trails** wherever possible. All the parks have information centres, and most promote trails and tours within their area. Marked walking routes are becoming more popular, but signage and trail maintenance are extremely patchy. English is rarely spoken, even at main information centres, making it difficult to find out about the status of routes, while there is a real paucity of proper walking maps: we recommend the best ones in our "Maps" section (see p.51).

Shopping

Though most large towns in Portugal have at least one out-of-town shopping centre, in the majority of places people still do much of their purchasing in traditional shops and markets. Old town centres look like they haven't changed much for thirty years or more, with a butcher, a baker and a candlestick-maker on every corner, not to mention a florist, a grocer and a hardware store.

We've pointed out regional handicrafts, specialist shops and markets throughout this Guide, but there's a general rundown below of things you'll see and might want to buy. Some of our town accounts also have their own dedicated shopping sections. Specialist craft and souvenir shops might be able to arrange shipping home for you; otherwise, go to the local post office, where all kinds of insured,

THE CHINESE SHOP

There's scarcely a town in Portugal that doesn't have a **Loja Chinês**, a Chinese-run emporium selling everything under the sun. In many ways, they fulfill the same function as a "pound" or "dollar" shop, selling basic household items really cheaply – if you need two-dozen toilet rolls, a set of tupperware, fifty wine glasses or a washing-up bowl, this is where you come. But they are also good for dirt-cheap toys and electronics – all made in the Far East, guaranteed to break after a couple of hours – and for all those things you never knew you needed, like a Portuguese flag, a *Star Wars* lightsaber or an alarm clock shaped like a man on a toilet.

registered and signed-for services are available; for more information see ⓦctt.pt, which has an English-language version.

Prices are fixed in shops everywhere, though you might be able to negotiate small discounts when buying large souvenirs (or buying in bulk). Open-air markets are a bit more flexible, though don't try haggling for food, drink, clothes or anything that has obviously got a price attached to it – for everything else you can try asking for the best price, and you may get a discount.

Markets

A town's **mercado municipal** (municipal market) is the place to buy meat, fish, fruit, veg and bread. In larger towns they are open daily (not Sunday), usually from 7 or 8am until lunchtime; smaller towns might have a market just once or twice a week. Often, a town's regular market is supplemented by a larger weekly affair, sometimes at a different site in the open air, where you'll also be able to buy clothes, shoes, ceramics, baskets, furniture, flowers, toys, tools and a million-and-one other things you never knew you needed. In the case of the great **weekly markets** at Barcelos (Minho; Thurs), Viana do Castelo (Minho; Fri), Ponte da Barca/Arcos de Valdevez (Minho; Wed), Carcavelos (Lisbon; Thurs), Estremoz (Alentejo; Sat) and Loulé (Algarve; Sat), or the monthly markets at Évora (Alentejo; second Tues) and Santarém (Ribatejo; second/fourth Sun), these constitute a major reason to visit in the first place. The best **flea market** in the country is Lisbon's Feira da Ladra (Tues & Sat), just the place to buy a candelabra or a set of dusty postcards.

Minimarkets, supermarkets and malls

In small villages and towns the **minimercado** (minimarket) is as convenient as convenience-shopping gets, which isn't very if you want a store bigger than someone's front room. **Supermercados** tend to lie on the outskirts of towns – Intermarché, Pingo Doce, Jumbo, Continente and Mini-Preço are the main supermarket names, selling pretty much everything you would expect (though choices can be more limited in out-of-the-way locations), while the pile-'em-high Lidl is increasingly prevalent. In Lisbon, Porto, Coimbra and the Algarve, the **mall** is king. Geared up for whole days out, these giant shopping centres have hundreds of stores, plus cafés, fast-food restaurants, cinemas and kids' entertainment.

Ceramics

Highest-profile souvenirs are probably **ceramics** of all kinds, from traditional *azulejo* tiles to elaborate figurines, cookware to sculpture. The virtual symbol of Portuguese tourism, the ceramic Barcelos cockerel (see p.320), perches on every tat-shop shelf. You can buy rustic, brown kitchen **earthenware** in every market and supermarket for just a few euros, but interesting regional variations include Barcelos' own brown-and-yellow pottery ware, black earthenware (from Tondela) and the almost Aztec-style patterns typical of Santa Comba Dão in the Viseu region. Porches is the centre for the Algarve's pottery and ceramics, while Caldas da Rainha in the historic region of Estremadura is probably the best-known ceramics town – caricatured rustic **figurines** and floral- and animal-inspired plates and bowls have been produced here since the nineteenth century. Estremoz in the Alentejo has an even older heritage, and is also known for its elaborate figurines and its flower- and leaf-festooned pottery.

Carpets, rugs, blankets, tapestries, linen and lace

Hand-stitched **Arraiolos carpets** (from the town of the same name in Alentejo) have a worldwide reputation, and they cost a fortune, but there's

nothing to stop you looking. **Tapestries** from Portalegre (Alentejo) have been known since the seventeenth century, and the *colchas* or **embroidered bedspreads** of Castelo Branco (Beira Baixa) for just as long – again, the high prices and lengthy ordering times mean these are unlikely spur-of-the-moment purchases for most visitors. Hand-woven woollen **rugs** and **blankets** are a more realistic buy, with particularly fine examples from Reguengos de Monsaraz (Alentejo) – you can hang them on a wall. Rustic woolly blankets (and fleece-lined slippers) are also a feature of the mountain villages of the Serra da Estrela – Sabugeiro has hundreds of them displayed in its souvenir shop windows. For embroidered **linen and lace** it's Vila do Conde (north of Porto) that is the best-known centre, though many other fishing towns – such as Peniche and Nazaré (north of Lisbon) – also have a strong bobbin-lace tradition. The biggest and best pieces command high prices, but there's plenty of reasonably priced work available too.

Food and drink

Port wine is the most popular buy, with cheap run-of-the-mill stuff available in supermarkets or gathering dust above the salt cod in old-fashioned grocery stores. For specific names and vintages you'll need to have done your homework since a recent vintage (not yet ready to drink) starts at around €30, with the serious stuff commanding prices of €100 and upwards. Visiting a lodge in Porto or along the Douro is by far the best way to immerse yourself in the subject. Don't miss a drink in the *solares* in Porto or Lisbon either, where you can sample individual glasses from hundreds of different varieties.

Virtually every region in Portugal produces **table wine** (see p.39), often remarkably good. Regional wine routes (past vineyards and estates open to the public) are well signposted, particularly in the Douro, Alentejo, Ribatejo and Dão valley.

Taking food home is more problematic, depending on your country's importation laws, but no one is going to object to a bottle of **olive oil** – the best are now sold like wines, from single estates, particularly in the Douro, where production is an adjunct to the wine business. Other suggestions include a jar of mountain **honey** from the Serra da Estrela, or packs of mountain **herbs** and **teas**, particularly from the Serra do Gerês. Portuguese **cheeses** and **hams** are excellent, though to take them home you may have to get them vacuum-packed (you can buy them like that at Lisbon airport).

Clothes, shoes and accessories

Portugal's textiles industry has traditionally been one of the most important in Europe, and though this has suffered badly from cheap rivals from the Far East, you can still pick up brand-name seconds from many of Portugal's weekly markets. For quality **designer clothes**, however, you have to head to the upmarket malls or larger city centres, particularly Lisbon's Avenida da Liberdade (for international names) or the Bairro Alto (for local cutting-edge styles). Fátima Lopes, Maria Azevedo and Ana Salazar are established names while Alexandra Moura, the duo Alves/Gonçalves and Nuno Gama are also worth looking out for. Some of the larger shopping centres also have designer boutiques; indeed the giant Freeport mall at Alcochete (Wfreeport.pt) is Europe's largest designer discount outlet. Leather goods have a fair reputation in Portugal, particularly **bags** and **shoes** (and belts and briefcases) – most big towns and shopping centres will have a decent selection, though a common complaint is that Portuguese shoe shops don't always stock the larger or wider sizes you might require. Gold and silver **filigree work** is notable – there are some fine shops in Lisbon and Porto – and you'll be able to pick up cheap, hippy-style jewellery at beaches along the Algarve, especially Albufeira.

Travelling with children

As Portuguese society largely revolves around family life, the country is very child-friendly and families will find it one of the easiest European destinations for a holiday. The two main worries for parents in Portugal are cars – which are usually fast moving – and the strong sun. Keep young children covered up between 11am and 3pm, make them wear a hat, and always apply a high-factor sunscreen. Be aware, too, that many castles and monuments are unrailed and may have very steep drops, while sea bathing – especially on the west coast – can be hazardous, with dangerous undertows. Cobbled town centres and stepped alleys are also difficult for anyone with a toddler and a pushchair.

Most **hotels and guesthouses** can provide an extra bed or a cot (*um berço*) if notified in

advance. There is usually no charge for babies and small children who share their parents' room, while discounts of up to fifty percent on accommodation for older children are not uncommon. Babysitting and child supervision are available at most four- and five-star places, though you'll have to pay.

Children are welcome in all **cafés** and **restaurants** at any time of the day. Indeed, waiters often go out of their way to spend a few minutes entertaining restless children; tots may even find themselves being carried off for a quick tour of the kitchens while parents finish their meals in peace. Highchairs (*cadeirinha de bebé*) are normally the clip-on-table variety. Specific child menus are rare, though restaurants will nearly all serve half-portions (*meia dose*) as a matter of course – these are still too much for most children to finish, but the Portuguese often simply order a *dose* or two between the family. Note, however, that restaurants rarely open much before 7.30pm (so British children may need to adjust to eating later than they are used to) and local children are often still up at midnight.

Specific **changing facilities** in restaurants, cafés and public toilets are largely nonexistent, and when you do find them – such as in larger shopping centres – they are usually in women's toilets only.

Fresh milk (*leite pasteurizado*) for **babies** is sold in larger supermarkets; mornings are best as it tends to sell out by mid-afternoon – *gordo* is full-fat, *meio-gordo* half-fat and *magro* skimmed milk. Mini-mercados, smaller shops and cafés generally only stock UHT, which is what most Portuguese kids drink. Nappies/diapers (*fraldas*) are widely available in supermarkets and pharmacies, as are formula milk, babies' bottles and jars of baby food – though don't expect the full range of (or indeed any) organic or salt-free choices you might be used to at home.

Most **museums**, **sights** and **attractions** don't usually charge for small children, while under-12s get in for half-price. On public transport, under-4s go free while 5- to 12-year-olds travel half-price on trains but pay full fare on metros and buses.

Travel essentials

Costs

Portugal remains one of the EU's least expensive destinations, and simple meals and drinks, accommodation and public transport are all still pretty good value. Lisbon, Porto and the Algarve are inevitably the most expensive places to visit, but even here you'll get a better deal on most things than in many other European countries.

As far as a **daily budget** goes, if you always share a room in the cheapest hotels, use public transport and stick to inexpensive restaurants you could have a reasonable time on somewhere between €50 and €80 a day. Stay and eat in fancier places in the main cities and you're looking at more like €120 a day, though if you're holidaying in five-star beach resorts or city boutique hotels this figure won't even cover your room. There's more information about specific prices in the "Accommodation", "Getting around" and "Food and drink" sections.

Most museums, galleries and attractions are fairly inexpensive (and some are free on the first Sunday of the month), but even so it pays to take along any **student/youth discount cards** you may be entitled to, such as the European Youth card (Ⓦeyca.org; also available in Portugal at post offices, youth hostels, and at branches of the Caixa Geral de Depósitos bank – ask for a *Cartão Jovem*). Any **entrance fees** noted in this Guide are for the full adult price; children usually get a discount. **Senior travellers** in Portugal are also entitled to discounts at most museums (it's always worth showing your senior citizen's card or ID), as well as on trains and at the country's *pousadas*.

Value Added Tax (known as **IVA**) varies depending on the goods or services purchased, but can be as high as 23 percent – it's almost always included in the advertised price, though. Non-EU residents can **claim back the sales tax** on purchases that come to over €61.35. You need to ask the shop for a declaration form and then present this to customs at the airport before you fly home: details on Ⓦglobal-blue.com.

Crime and personal safety

By European standards, Portugal is a remarkably crime-free country – people really do still leave their cars and house doors unlocked in the countryside. However, there's the usual **petty theft** in the cities and larger tourist resorts, particularly in the form of pickpockets on public transport and in bus and train stations. Best advice is not to carry too much cash or too many valuables, and leave your passport in the hotel safe where possible. Drivers should never leave anything visible in the car (preferably, don't leave anything in the car at all). In the event of an **emergency**, dial ❶112 for the police or an ambulance.

There are two main police forces: the metropolitan **Polícia de Segurança Pública** (PSP) and the more rural **Guarda Nacional Republicana** (GNR), both of which can handle incidents involving tourists. Most police officers in the Algarve speak some English, but elsewhere it's less usual, so confusion can easily arise. To this end, showing deference is wise: the Portuguese still hold respect dear, and the more respect you show a figure in authority, the quicker you'll be on your way.

Portugal is rarely a dangerous place for **women travellers** and you only need to be particularly wary in parts of Lisbon at night (around Cais do Sodré, at the top end of Avenida da Liberdade, on the metro and on the Cais do Sodré–Cascais train line), in the darker alleys near the river in Porto, and in streets immediately around train stations in the larger towns (traditionally red-light districts).

Electricity

Mains voltage is 220V, which works fine with equipment intended for 240V. Plugs are the European two-round-pin variety; adaptors are sold at airports, supermarkets and hardware stores.

Entry requirements

EU citizens (and most of those from European countries not in the EU) need only a valid passport or identity card to enter Portugal, and can stay indefinitely. Citizens of Canada, the US, Australia and New Zealand do not need a visa for stays of up to ninety days. Most other nationals (including South Africans) will have to apply for a visa from a Portuguese embassy or consulate before departure. Entry conditions can change, however, so it's advisable to check the current situation before leaving home.

If necessary, an **extension to your stay** can be arranged once you're in the country. Extensions are issued by the nearest District Police headquarters or the Foreigners' Registration Service – **Serviço de Estrangeiros e Fronteiras** (W sef.pt) – which has offices in most major tourist centres. You should apply at least a week before your time runs out and be prepared to prove that you can support yourself without working. Extended-stay and work visas are also available from Portuguese embassies or consulates in your own country.

For most EU citizens, a passport or national ID is sufficient to allow indefinite stays as employees, self-employed workers or students. However, you will need to register with various agencies if you are **staying In Portugal**, to access health care etc, and will require a *número de contribuinte* (social security number) to do just about anything else, from opening a bank account to settling an electricity bill.

Health

EU citizens can apply for a **European Health Insurance Card**, which gives access to Portuguese state public-health services under reciprocal agreements. Show the card and your passport at a health centre or hospital for treatment. While the EHIC guarantees free or reduced-cost medical care in the event of minor injuries and emergencies, it won't cover every eventuality – you'll have to pay for X-rays, lab tests and the like, so travel insurance is also essential. If you don't have an EHIC card, you'll be charged for everything and will have to claim it back from your insurance, so get receipts. At the time of writing, British citizens were still covered by the EHIC scheme, but given the 2016 Brexit vote, checking the situation via W ehic.org .uk is advisable before you travel.

Tap water is generally safe to drink, although most Portuguese prefer bottled water (it's very inexpensive in supermarkets). Otherwise, just use common sense: wash and peel fruit and vegetables, and avoid eating snacks that appear to have been sitting in display cabinets for too long. **Mosquitoes** can be a menace in the summer, but mosquito-repellent lotion and coils are widely sold in supermarkets and pharmacies. Use a high-factor **sun block** as the sun is extremely powerful.

For minor complaints go to a **farmácia** (pharmacy); most have a green neon cross outside. There's one in virtually every village and English is often spoken. Pharmacists are highly trained and can dispense drugs that would be prescription-only in Britain or North America. Opening hours are usually Monday to Friday 9am to 1pm and 3 to 7pm, Saturday 9am to 1pm. Local papers carry information about 24-hour or night-time pharmacies (*farmácias de serviço*) and the details are also posted on every pharmacy door.

In an **emergency** dial ☎ 112. Treatment is at the local **Centro da Saúde** (Health Centre) or **hospital**, and somebody usually speaks at least some English. Contact details of other English-speaking doctors can be obtained from British or American consular offices or, with luck, from the local tourist office or a major hotel.

Insurance

You should take out a comprehensive travel **insurance policy** before travelling to Portugal, to cover against loss, theft and illness or injury. A typical policy will provide cover for the loss of baggage, tickets and – up to a certain limit – cash or cheques, as well as cancellation or curtailment of your journey. Most policies exclude so-called dangerous sports unless an extra premium is paid: in Portugal this can mean most watersports and scuba diving are excluded, though probably not things like hiking or bike tours.

If you need to make a claim, you should keep **receipts** for medicines and medical treatment, and in the event you have anything stolen, you must obtain an official **statement from the police** (a *formulário de participação de roubo*).

Internet

The government has invested a lot in communications technology and Portugal is surprisingly switched-on and wireless for a place of its size. You can get online at larger post offices (access by credit card or by buying a prepaid net card), while free **municipal internet** places (called Espaços Internet; locations on 🕾espacosinternet.pt) are widespread, even in very small towns. You can generally also find a PC to use in libraries, youth centres, hostels and many hotels. **Wireless** access is available in many restaurants, bars, shopping malls, town squares and other public "hot spots", usually without charge.

Laundry

Small guesthouses don't really like you doing your laundry in your room – to avoid an incident, it might be better to ask first if there's somewhere you can wash clothes. Hotels generally have a laundry service, but it's usually pretty expensive. It's far better to take your clothes to the local **lavandaria**, where you can get them washed, dried and even ironed at a very reasonable cost – you may have to come back the next day to pick them up.

LGBT travellers

Though traditionally a conservative society, Portugal has become increasingly tolerant of homosexuality, at least in the cities and in the Algarve. In more rural areas, however, old prejudices are ingrained and coming out is still a problem for many. As there is no mention of homosexuality in law, gays have the same rights as heterosexuals by default and the legal age of consent is 16. The best contact is the **Associação ILGA Portugal** (🕾ilga -portugal.pt; English information available), which operates the Centro LGBT, at Rua dos Fanqueiros 40 in Lisbon (Thurs–Sat 6–11pm; ☎218 873 918), an information centre and helpline, which organizes the country's annual Pride festival. The biggest scene is in Lisbon, which has a number of gay bars and clubs.

Mail

Post offices (*correios*; 🕾ctt.pt) are normally open Monday to Friday 8.30 or 9am to 5.30 or 6pm, the smaller ones closing for lunch. Larger branches sometimes open on Saturday mornings, while the main Lisbon and Porto offices have longer hours. However, it's often quicker to buy **stamps** (*selos*) from coin-operated vending machines in streets or inside the offices, or from newsagents. Letters or cards should take three or four days to arrive at destinations in Europe, and seven to ten days elsewhere. *Correio azul* is the equivalent of airmail or first-class, and theoretically (but not always in practice) takes two or three days to Europe, five elsewhere.

ROUGH GUIDES TRAVEL INSURANCE

Rough Guides has teamed up with WorldNomads.com to offer great **travel insurance** deals. Policies are available to residents of over 150 countries, with cover for a wide range of **adventure sports**, 24hr emergency assistance, high levels of medical and evacuation cover and a stream of **travel safety information**. Roughguides.com users can take advantage of their policies online 24/7, from anywhere in the world – even if you're already travelling. And since plans often change when you're on the road, you can extend your policy and even claim online. Roughguides.com users who buy travel insurance with WorldNomads.com can also leave a positive footprint and donate to a community development project. For more information, go to 🕾**roughguides.com/travel-insurance**.

Maps

The best available **country map** is Michelin's *Portugal* (1:400,000) and there are also three regional Michelin maps (north, centre and south) at 1:300,000, while Michelin's *Lisboa Planta Roteiro* is the nearest to an A–Z of the city. A good bookshop or travel store in your own country should be able to provide any of these maps, as will the usual online retailers and specialist stores such as Ⓦ stanfords.co.uk or Ⓦ randmcnally.com. Tourist offices and car rental outlets in Portugal can also usually provide you with a reasonable **road map**, while other maps and more detailed regional plans can be bought at motorway service stations and town and city bookshops.

For **walking and hiking**, the only serious choices are the 1:50,000 topographic sheets produced by the Instituto Geográfico do Exército (Ⓦ igeoe.pt). These cover the entire country, though some haven't been updated for years. Even so, they are the best you'll get; you can buy them online from the Instituto or from Ⓦ stanfords.co.uk, and they're sold at various bookshops in Portugal; outlets are listed on the Instituto website.

Money

Portugal's currency is the **euro** (€), and notes are issued in denominations of 5, 10, 20, 50, 100, 200 and 500 euros, and coins in denominations of 1, 2, 5, 10, 20 and 50 cents and 1 and 2 euros. Up-to-the-minute currency **exchange rates** are displayed at Ⓦ xe.com.

You'll find a **bank** (*banco*) or savings bank/ building society (*caixa*) in all but the smallest towns: standard opening hours are Monday to Friday 8.30am to 3pm. In Lisbon and larger Algarve resorts, some banks also open in the evening, while others have automatic currency exchange machines. **Exchange bureaux** (*câmbios*), which you'll find in Lisbon, Porto and the Algarve, tend to have longer working hours, closing on weekdays at around 6pm, and also opening on Saturdays.

By far the easiest way to get money is to use your bank debit card to withdraw cash from an **ATM** (known as a Multibanco), found in even the smallest towns, as well as at airports. You can usually withdraw up to €400 a day (though only €200 at a time) and instructions are available in English. Make sure you have called your bank to authorise overseas use, and take a note of your bank's emergency contact number in case an ATM

swallows your card. Most European **debit cards** can also be used directly in shops, petrol stations etc, to pay for purchases.

All major **credit cards** are accepted in hotels, restaurants and shops, and for tours, tickets and transport, though don't count on being able to use them in many small hotels, family businesses and rural areas.

Opening hours and public holidays

Opening hours for shops, cafés, restaurants, museums and tourist offices in Portugal tend to be a fluid concept, especially outside the main towns and resorts. Many open late or close early (or don't open at all) if the weather's bad or if not many people are around. We give the official opening hours throughout this Guide, but be aware that these are not always adhered to.

Shops and businesses generally open from 9/9.30am until 12.30/1pm, and then 2.30/3pm until 6/7pm. Most also open all day Saturday from 9am to 7pm, especially in towns and cities, though in smaller towns shops close on Saturday afternoon. Larger **shopping centres** and **malls** stay open seven days a week, often until midnight.

PUBLIC HOLIDAYS

January 1 New Year's Day (Dia Um de Janeiro)

Shrove Tuesday February/March Carnival (Carnaval)

Good Friday March/April (Sexta Feira Santa)

April 25 Liberty Day, commemorating the 1974 Revolution (Vinte Cinco de Abril)

May 1 Labour Day (Dia do Trabalhador)

Late May/Early June Corpus Christi (Corpo de Deus)

June 10 Portugal Day (Dia de Portugal)

August 15 Feast of the Assumption (Festa da Assunção)

Oct 5 Republic Day (Dia da Instauração de República)

Nov 1 All Saints' Day (Dia de Todos os Santos)

Dec 1 Independence Day (Dia da Restauração)

December 8 Immaculate Conception (Imaculada Conceição)

December 25 Christmas Day (Natal)

Restaurants tend to close one day a week, often Sunday or Monday.

Opening hours for **museums**, **churches** and **monuments** vary enormously, but almost all close on Mondays (or Wednesdays for palaces). Some opening hours are **seasonal**, and usually in Portugal "summer" means from Easter until September and "winter" from October until Easter.

On national **public holidays** (see box, p.51) transport services are much reduced. Most museums and galleries also close for the day, though other tourist facilities – restaurants, souvenir shops and the like – tend to stay open. There are also endless **local festivals**, saints' days and holidays when entire villages, towns, cities and regions grind to a halt: for example, June 13 in Lisbon and June 24 in Porto.

Phones

All Portuguese **phone numbers** have nine digits. Landlines start with a 2, mobiles with a 9. Numbers starting with 800 are free; 808 are local-rate calls. To **call Portugal from abroad**, dial your country's international access number + 351 (country code) + nine-digit number. You can search for national phone numbers and addresses for free online at ⓦ pai.pt.

Portugal has one of the highest densities of **mobile phone** (telemóvel) ownership in the world. Most European mobile phones will work in Portugal; note also that in June 2016, **roaming charges** were drastically reduced for mobile phone tariffs that originate in an EU country, and will be abolished completely in 2017. To reduce costs, non-EU citizens could buy a local **SIM card**, though this depends on the model and service provider – Vodafone has shops all over Portugal, for example, including at Lisbon airport.

Smoking

In common with most EU countries, **smoking** is prohibited in all public spaces in Portugal. The ban was introduced in 2008 by the then Prime Minister José Sócrates, who was promptly spotted lighting up on a plane to Venezuela. While not all laws are closely followed by the Portuguese, this one is generally observed – though, of course, smokers can indulge at restaurants and cafés, if they sit at the outside tables.

Time

Portugal is in the same **time zone** as the UK, following GMT in winter. Clocks go forward an hour at the end of March and back an hour at the end of October. If you're coming from Spain, turn your watch back one hour.

Tipping

There is no hard and fast rule for **tipping**, which is not really a Portuguese custom. In a café, restaurant or for taxis, it's customary to round up the bill to the nearest euro or, for big amounts, the nearest note – so leave €25 for a bill of €23.50, for example. You shouldn't feel obliged to leave any tip at all for other services – though needless to say, any you do leave will be gratefully received.

Toilets

Public toilets are neither numerous nor obvious, though a number of cities have installed coin-operated automated toilets. You can generally use the toilets in cafés, though (in theory) you'll have to order something first and sometimes ask for the key. The "facilities" in some places may leave you dazed, though on the whole there's been a significant upgrade in recent years – whoever has the contract for installing automatic light and flush facilities in Portugal is on a roll. A sign reading *Lavábos, Casa de banho* or WC will head you in the right direction, then it's *homens* or *cavalheiros* for men and *senhoras* or *mulheres* for women.

CALLING HOME FROM PORTUGAL

To make an international call, dial the international access code (in Portugal it's ❶ 00), then the destination's country code, before the rest of the number. Note that the initial zero is omitted from the area code when dialling the UK, Ireland, Australia and New Zealand from abroad. Avoid making any calls from hotel phones, which always have very high charges.

Australia international access code + 61
New Zealand international access code + 64
UK international access code + 44

US and Canada international access code + 1
Ireland international access code + 353
South Africa international access code + 27

Tourist information

The Portuguese national tourist board, **Turismo de Portugal**, is a good source of information when planning your trip, while in Portugal itself you'll find a tourist office in most of the larger towns. **Regional offices** offer a broad-brush approach to the region they represent, and some also have useful websites.

On the ground, local or municipal **turismos** can at least supply a town map or accommodation information, though the service available varies wildly from place to place. English is only routinely spoken in offices in the larger towns and resorts and, while some offices are extremely helpful and professional, others treat your visit almost as an intrusion. Often, the best you'll get is a fistful of brochures and directions to the bus station/museum/ferry office, where you'll have to ask all over again.

USEFUL TOURIST WEBSITES

Ⓦ **visitportugal.com** (all Portugal)

Ⓦ **visitlisboa.com** (Lisbon area)

Ⓦ **turismodocentro.pt** (Coimbra and central Portugal)

Ⓦ **uk.visitportoandnorth.travel** (Porto and the north)

Ⓦ **visitalgarve.com** (Algarve)

Ⓦ **visitalentejo.pt** (Alentejo)

Ⓦ **patrimoniocultural.pt** (the Museums Institute website)

Travellers with disabilities

Portugal is slowly coming to terms with the needs of **travellers with disabilities**, though you should not expect much in the way of special facilities. However, people are generally ready to help and will go out of their way to make your visit as straightforward as possible.

Lisbon, Porto and Faro **airports** have ramps, lifts and adapted toilets. You'll also find **ramped access** to some museums and public buildings, while adapted WCs can be found at some train stations and major shopping centres. It's worth bearing in mind that many guesthouses and budget hotels are located on the first floor or higher and don't have lifts. However, most four- and five-star hotels have lifts, ramps and specially adapted bedrooms and bathrooms, while many manor houses and farmhouses have guest rooms on the ground floor.

At **train stations**, wheelchair access is usually possible as far as the platform, but getting from the platform on to the train can be difficult. Parts of Lisbon's **metro** system are also problematic, though Porto's newer system is generally more accessible. **Adapted cars** are available from the larger car-rental companies, and there are reserved disabled parking spaces across the country (though they are not always respected).

Portugal's old **town centres** – specifically their steps and cobblestone alleys – pose their own problems. However, a number of attractive medieval towns and villages have been rehabilitated as part of central Portugal's Aldeias Históricas scheme, which has also meant the construction of some smooth wheelchair-accessible pathways alongside the cobbles.

Some **organizations** at home may be able to advise you further about travel to Portugal, such as Access Travel (Ⓦ access-travel.co.uk), a small **tour operator** offering Algarve accommodation suitable for the disabled. In Portugal, **Accessible Portugal** (Ⓦ accessibleportugal.com) is a specialist in holidays for wheelchair users and people with disabilities, and offers city breaks, tours, accommodation and transfers. The government organization that promotes awareness of disability issues is the **Instituto Nacional Para a Reabilitação** (Ⓦ inr .pt), which has a useful website, though it is only in Portuguese.

Lisbon and around

CASTELO DE SÃO JORGE

1

Lisbon and around

Mainland Europe's westernmost capital, Lisbon is a fascinating and inspiring place to spend a few days, thanks to its wonderful waterfront location, balmy climate and quirky range of attractions that combine a place-that-time-forgot feel with a modern vibrancy that few European cities can match. For much of the twentieth century, Lisbon had little contact with the outside world and, even today, the city retains one foot firmly in the early 1900s. Its hills and cobbled alleys are still served by ancient trams and funiculars that rattle along streets where old-fashioned shops and cafés far outnumber the multinationals. Lisbon's revolution of 1974 and later entry into the EU, however, allowed the city's other foot to stride into the twenty-first century, with a range of excellent modern museums and adventurous architectural projects. Immigrants from Brazil and Portugal's former colonies in Africa add an exotic appeal to the city's culture, and Lisbon is now home to some of Europe's hottest Latin American and African bands and clubs, sitting cheek by jowl with the city's traditional fado bars and restaurants.

A short way inland from Lisbon, the UNESCO heritage site of Sintra enjoys a cool mountainside location, which made it a favoured summer destination for Portugal's royals – their ornate and extravagant palaces make for a fascinating day-trip. It is also just a short hop from Lisbon to some fantastic Atlantic beaches: locals favour the southern coast, with miles of sands along the Costa da Caparica or the small cove beaches between the historic port of Setúbal and the resort of Sesimbra. Easiest to reach, however, are the town beaches of bustling Estoril and the former fishing village of Cascais, both easily accessible by train.

Lisbon

Strung out over a series of hills facing the glistening waters of the broad Tejo estuary, **LISBON** is one of Europe's most handsome cities. Although its modern suburbs are ungainly, the historic centre is relatively compact and easy to explore in just a day or two. The oldest part of the city, the warren of streets that make up the **Alfama**, sits below the spectacularly sited **Moorish Castelo de São Jorge**, its ruined walls facing another hill, the **Bairro Alto** or upper town, famed for its bars, restaurants and vibrant nightlife. The valley between these hills makes up the **Baixa**, or lower town. This neat

ANTIGA CONFEITARIA DE BELÉM

Highlights

❶ Alfama Getting lost in the winding, narrow streets and alleys of Lisbon's oldest quarter is half the fun. **See p.65**

❷ Castelo de São Jorge Despite its bloody past, the castle makes a tranquil haven from the busy city, with its pretty gardens, strutting peacocks and dazzling rooftop views. **See p.68**

❸ Bairro Alto Lisbon's "upper town" is *the* place for a lively night out, with its huge selection of vibrant bars, clubs and restaurants. **See p.72**

❹ Mosteiro dos Jerónimos The magnificent Manueline monastery houses the tomb of Vasco da Gama. **See p.80**

❺ Museu Gulbenkian Lalique's fantastic Art Nouveau jewellery, Flemish masters and Impressionist paintings are all included in this awe-inspiring collection of priceless art and antiquities. **See p.86**

❻ Antiga Confeitaria de Belém Don't miss a melt-in-the-mouth, tasty, flaky, warm custard tart, best eaten in the tiled surroundings of Belém's most traditional café. **See p.97**

❼ Palácio Nacional, Sintra A splendid royal retreat in the beautiful, wooded summer residence of kings. **See p.113**

HIGHLIGHTS ARE MARKED ON THE MAPS ON P.58 & PP.60–61

1

grid of grand eighteenth-century buildings was erected on the rubble of the earthquake which flattened much of the city in 1755, a planned commercial district rebuilt around the historic squares of **Praça do Comércio**, on the riverfront, and the broad **Rossio**. From here, the palm-lined **Avenida da Liberdade** is the main artery inland, rising to the green slopes of the city's central **Parque Eduardo VII**. Key attractions beyond the historic centre include the fantastic art collection of the **Museu Gulbenkian**, just north of the park; the **Museu de Arte Antiga** west of the centre; and the modern art of the **Berardo Collection**, 6km to the west in **Belém**, the suburb from which Portugal's great navigators set sail: the sublime **Mosteiro dos Jerónimos** is one of several monasteries built here to celebrate their achievements. Finally, 5km to the east lies the **Parque das Nações**, the futuristic site of Lisbon's Expo 98, whose main attraction is one of Europe's largest oceanariums.

Brief history

Named Allis Ubbo (calm harbour) by the **Phoenicians**, the administrative capital of Lusitania was renamed Olisipo by the **Romans** when they settled in the western half of Iberia in 210 BC. During the early 700s, **Moors** from North Africa began to exploit trading links from the city they called Lishbuna to their territories to the south, and the

LISBON & AROUND

Torres Vedras

Porto, Santarém & Tomar

Ericeira
Gradil
Sobreiro
Mafra
TAPADA DE MAFRA
Vila Franca de Xira

Azenhas do Mar

Praia das Maçãs
Colares
Praia Grande
Sintra
Cabo da Roca
SERRA DE SINTRA
Convento dos Capuchos
Oriente (Parque das Nações)
Praia de Guincho
Palácio de Queluz
Ponte Vasco Da Gama
Alcochete

LISBON
Rio Tejo
Estoril
Belém
Cascais
Ponte 25 de Abril
Cacilhas
Montijo
Carcavelos
Oeiras
Almada
Seixal
Trafaria
Barreiro

ATLANTIC OCEAN
Caparica
Summer Only
Fonte da Telha

Costa da Caparica

Convento da Arrábida
Palmela
Lagoa de Albufeira
Vila Nogueira de Azeitão
Setúbal
RESERVA NATURAL
Aldeia do Meco
PARQUE NATURAL DA ARRÁBIDA
Tróia
Praia do Meco
Santana
Galapos
Figueirinha
Cetobriga (Roman Ruins)
Sesimbra
Portinho de Arrábida
Rio Sado
Cabo Espichel
Peninsula de Tróia

Sines

HIGHLIGHTS
4 Mosteiro dos Jerónimos
6 Antiga Confeitaria de Belém
7 Palácio Nacional, Sintra

0   10
kilometres

1

city flourished. The Moors set up the Alcáçova – a Muslim palace – on the site of today's castle and settled around some hot springs (*alhama*, today's Alfama). In 1147, Catholics from the north under Afonso Henriques laid siege to Lisbon's castle with a band of ruthless **European crusaders** and, after seventeen weeks of resistance, the Moors finally gave in – they were either killed or forced to live as "New Christians" in the quarter still known as Mouraria. In 1150, with Afonso Henriques now Portugal's first monarch, the Sé (cathedral) was established on the site of the main mosque, and in 1255 Lisbon became the capital of a **Christian** country.

The discoveries

By the fifteenth century, Lisbon was the capital of an expansionist country whose navigational expertise had set up trading routes round half the world. **Vasco da Gama** sailed from Belém to open up a sea route to India in 1498, and within sixty years Lisbon controlled ports from Brazil in the west to Macau in the east. Lisbon became one of the wealthiest cities in Europe, able to fund lavish buildings such as the Torre de Belém, the Mosteiro dos Jerónimos and the palace at Terreiro do Paço. By the early eighteenth century, further funds flooded in from newly discovered gold in Brazil, but this second "golden age" came to a sudden halt with the **Great Earthquake of 1755** (see box, p.73). Under the **Marquês de Pombal**, a new city was rapidly rebuilt in a grid pattern (today's Baixa district), but Lisbon never recovered its economic clout. The city briefly flourished in the mid-nineteenth century, when the Botanical Gardens were considered the best in Europe: a public works programme laid out the Avenida da Liberdade and financed a series of funicular street lifts to serve its hills.

The Salazar era

Political turmoil in the early 1900s saw the end of the Portuguese monarchy and ushered in the reign of **Dr. António de Oliveira Salazar**, who ruled Portugal with an iron fist from 1932 to 1968. An economist, Salazar's policies generated sufficient wealth to fund a wartime Expo in Belém in 1940, the Cristo Rei statue overlooking the Tagus and the impressive Ponte 25 de Abril suspension bridge (originally named the Ponte Salazar). But most of the population failed to prosper under his rule, and by the **1974 revolution** which ushered in democracy, most of Lisbon was stuck in a time warp with little or no economic development.

The modern city

Entry into the EU and a series of events – including **Expo 98**, the hosting of the **European Championships in 2004** and Lisbon's new-found status as a **hub for low-cost airlines** – have seen money and development pour into the city, bequeathing new rail and metro lines and Europe's longest bridge, Ponte Vasco da Gama. The historic *bairros* (districts) and riverfront have also been given makeovers. If some of the renovation has somewhat diminished the city's erstwhile lost-in-time feel, it has also injected a wave of optimism that has made Lisbon one of Europe's most exciting capitals.

The Baixa

The tall, imposing buildings that make up the **BAIXA** (Lower Town; pronounced *bye-sha*) house some of Lisbon's most interesting shops and cafés. Many of the streets are pedestrianized and, by day, they thrum with business folk and street entertainers. Facing the river, these streets felt the full force of the 1755 earthquake that destroyed much of the capital. The king's minister, the Marquês de Pombal, swiftly redesigned the sector with the grid pattern that is evident today, framed by a triangle of broad squares, **Praça do Comércio** to the south, with **Praça da Figueira** and **Rossio** to the north. Within this triangle, three main streets are dissected by nine smaller streets, many of which took their names from the crafts and businesses carried out there, like **Rua da Prata**

GREATER LISBON

HIGHLIGHTS
1 Alfama
2 Castelo de São Jorge
3 Bairro Alto
5 Museu Gulbenkian

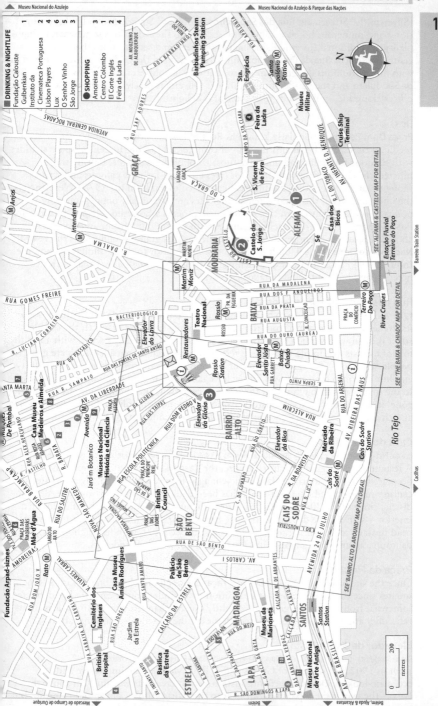

■ DRINKING & NIGHTLIFE	
Fundação Calouste Gulbenkian	1
Instituto da Cinemateca Portuguesa	2
Lisbon Players	4
Lux	6
O Senhor Vinho	5
São Jorge	3

● SHOPPING	
Amoreiras	3
Centro Colombo	1
El Corte Inglés	2
Feira da Ladra	4

N

Rio Tejo

Barbadinhos Steam Pumping Station

Sta. Engrácia

Santa Apolónia Station

Museu Militar

Cruise Ship Terminal

Feira da Ladra

S. Vicente de Fora

ALFAMA

Casa dos Bicos

Sé

Castelo de S. Jorge

MOURARIA

Estação Fluvial
Terreiro do Paço

▶ Barreiro Train Station

Martim Moniz

RUA DA MADALENA

RUA DOS F. ANQUEIROS

BAIXA

RUA DA PRATA

RUA AUGUSTA

RUA DO OURO (AUREA)

Teatro Nacional

Rossio

Baixa-Chiado

Elevador Santa Justa

RUA GARRETT

Terreiro Do Paço

PRAÇA DO COMÉRCIO

River Cruises

SEE 'THE BAIXA & CHIADO' MAP FOR DETAIL

Restauradores

Rossio Station

R. SERPA PINTO

RUA DO ARSENAL

SEE 'ALFAMA & CASTELO' MAP FOR DETAIL

Elevador do Lavra

RUA DAS PORTAS DE SANTO ANTÃO

R. BACTERIOLOGICO

R. LUCIANO CORDEIRO

RUA DO PASSADIÇO

RUA GOMES FREIRE

M Anjos

M Intendente

GRAÇA

C. DO GRAÇA

LARGO DA GRAÇA

AVENIDA GENERAL ROÇADAS

RUA SAP ADORES

CAMPO DA STA. CLARA

DOS BARBADINHOS

AV. MOUZINHO DE ALBUQUERQUE

RUA AFONSO III

M Martim Moniz

DAALMA

RUA DA PALMA

AV. DA LIBERDADE

Elevador do Glória

BAIRRO ALTO

Elevador da Bica

Mercado da Ribeira

Cais do Sodré Station

CAIS DO SODRÉ

M Cais do Sodré

AV. RIBEIRA DAS NAUS

RUA ALECRIM

RUA DO QUEIJO

R. DA BOAVISTA

SEE 'BAIRRO ALTO & AROUND' MAP FOR DETAIL

RUA DOM PEDRO V

PRAÇA ALEGRIA

R. DA GLORIA

RUA DAS TAIPAS

RUA DA ROSA

Museus Nacional História e da Ciência

Jard m Botanico

RUA ESCOLA POLITECNICA

PRAÇA DO PRINCIPE REAL

R. DE SÃO MARÇAL

C. DO COMBRO

RUA DO LORETO

Casa Museu Medeiros e Almeida

M Avenida

PRAÇA DA ALEGRIA

R. ALEX. HERCULANO

RUA CASTILHO

R. ROSA ARAUJO

R. BARATA

RUA DO SALITRE

RUA S. SAMPAIO

RUA DE SÃO MAMEDE

British Council

PRAÇA DAS FLORES

SÃO BENTO

RUA DE SÃO BENTO

Palácio de São Bento

Casa Museu Amália Rodrigues

RUA NOVA SÃO MAMEDE

Cemitério dos Ingleses

British Hospital

Fundação Arpad-sizines

AMOREIRAS

M Rato

R. ALVARES CABRAL

Mãe d'Água

LARGO RATO

PRAÇA DAS AMOREIRAS

RUA SARAIVA DE CARVALHO

RUA DOM JOÃO V

RUA SÃO JORGE

Jardim da Estrela

CALÇADA DA ESTRELA

RUA SANTO AMARO

Basilica da Estrela

ESTRELA

LAPA

AV. DE BRASILIA

Museu Nacional de Arte Antiga

R. DAS JANELAS VERDES

R. SÃO DOMINGOS À LAPA

SANTOS

Santos Station

Museu da Marioneta

MADRAGOA

CALÇADA M. DE ABRANTES

AVENIDA 24 DE JULHO

R.DO 1. INDUSTRIAL

AV. CARLOS I

0	200
	metres

▲ Mercado de Campo de Ourique

▲ Belém

▲ Belém, Ajuda & Alcantara

▶ Cacilhas

1

(Silversmiths' Street) and **Rua dos Sapateiros** (Cobblers' Street). Today, banks, chain stores and numerous hotels and guesthouses disturb these divisions somewhat, though plenty of traditional stores remain, such as the bead and sequin shops that line the central section of **Rua da Conceição**. Pombal also wanted the grid's churches to blend in with his harmonious design, so much so that they are almost invisible – walk along **Rua de São Julião** and the facade of the church of Oliveira is barely distinguishable from the offices alongside it, though its tiled interior is delightful.

Rossio

Praça Dom Pedro IV (popularly known as **Rossio**) has been the city's main square since medieval times, and it remains the hub of commercial Lisbon. Its central space sparkles with Baroque fountains and polished, mosaic-cobbled pavements. During the nineteenth century, Rossio's plethora of cafés attracted Lisbon's painters and writers, though many of the artists' haunts were converted to banks in the 1970s. Nevertheless, the outdoor seats of the square's remaining cafés are perennially popular meeting-points. On the northwestern side of the square, there's a horseshoe-shaped entrance to **Rossio station**, a mock-Manueline complex with the train platforms an escalator ride above the street-level entrances. Opposite, the square's grandest building is the **Teatro Nacional de Dona Maria II**, built in the 1840s. Here, prior to the earthquake, stood the Inquisitional Palace, in front of which public hangings, *autos-da-fé* (ritual burnings of heretics) and bullfights used to take place.

Rua das Portas de Santo Antão

One of Lisbon's first streets to be pedestrianized, **Rua das Portas de Santo Antão** is also its liveliest. Running north from the Teatro Nacional de Dona Maria II, the cobbled street is lined with seafood restaurants and theatres and is usually packed with a healthy mix of tourists and locals. Most of its restaurants have tables outside which are great for people-watching – though this is one of the only streets in town where waiters will try and lure you into their premises if they have tables to fill. The *portas* in the name refer to the town gates through which the street once passed, and though the gates have long gone, it still exudes a sense of history. At no.96, the domed **Coliseu dos Recreios** opened as a circus in 1890 and is now one of the city's main concert venues.

Casa do Alentejo

Rua das Portas de Santo Antão 58 • Daily 10am–10pm • Free • ☎ 213 469 231, ⓦ casadoalentejo.com.pt • Ⓜ Rossio or Restauradores

A restaurant, café-bar and cultural centre, the **Casa do Alentejo** is a sumptuously decorated pseudo-Moorish palace, little-changed for decades. Originally a seventeenth-century mansion and later a casino, it has been dedicated to culture from the Alentejo district since the 1930s. You can just wander in and look around the beautifully tiled interior – some of the decorative tiles are from the original mansion – but most visitors head upstairs to the dining room or the café-bar (see p.97), with its neighbouring ballroom, an amazing, slightly run-down room hung with chandeliers.

Praça da Figueira

Once the site of Lisbon's main market, **Praça da Figueira** has been one of Lisbon's main squares since the 1940s, though the addition of an underground car park has detracted somewhat from its former grandeur. Slightly quieter than the neighbouring Rossio, its cafés offer appealing views of the green slopes of the Castelo de São Jorge above.

Elevador de Santa Justa

Rua de Santa Justa • Daily: June–Sept 7am–11pm; Oct–May 7am–9.45pm • €5 return • Ⓜ Baixa-Chiado

Built in 1902 by a disciple of Gustav Eiffel, Raul Mésnier, the impressive and eccentric-looking **Elevador de Santa Justa** street lift creaks its way up 32m above the Baixa. The exit at the top comes out next to the Bairro Alto's Convento do Carmo, but

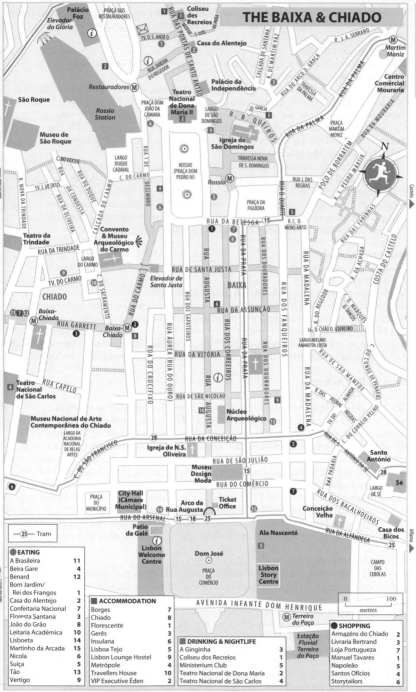

THE BAIXA & CHIADO

— 25 — Tram

Barreiro & River Cruises

1

you can stop first for a drink at the *elevador's* own pricey rooftop café, which has great views over the city and the elaborate metal framework of the lift itself.

Núcleo Arqueológico

Rua dos Correeiros 9 • Book in advance for 45min guided tours Mon–Sat hourly 10am–noon & 3–5pm • Free • ☎ 211 131 004, Ⓦ ind.millenniumbcp.pt • Ⓜ Baixa-Chiado

One of Lisbon's smallest but most fascinating museums, the **Núcleo Arqueológico** lies beneath the Baixa's streets. During the construction of the BCP bank in the 1990s, excavations revealed the remains of Roman fish-preserving tanks, a fifth-century Christian burial place and Moorish ceramics, which can all be seen in this tiny museum. Most of the exhibits are viewed through glass floors or from cramped walkways beneath the modern bank.

If you're interested in discovering more about Lisbon's underground ruins, ask museum staff about early summer visits to the amazing 2000-year-old Roman tunnels that lie beneath the Baixa, whose purpose remains unclear. As the tunnels are usually flooded, they're open to visitors for just three days a year, when they attract enormous queues. Watching people enter the tunnels, accessible only through a manhole cover between tram tracks on Rua da Conceição, is a bizarre sight.

Museu Design Moda

Rua Augusta 24 • Tues–Sun 10am–6pm; but closed for renovation until late 2017 • Free • ☎ 218 886 117, Ⓦ mude.pt • Ⓜ Baixa-Chiado or Terreiro de Paço

Inside a grand former bank, the **Museu Design Moda** houses an impressive collection of design and fashion classics from the 1930s to today, amassed by former stockbroker and media mogul Francisco Capelo. Exhibits include design classics by Charles and Ray Eames and Phillipe Starck, as well as Capelo's collection of haute couture from the 1950s, 1960s street fashion and designer brands of the 1990s, from Paco Rabanne and Pierre Cardin to Alexander McQueen. Check the website for an update on the museum's refurbishment.

Arco da Rua Augusta

Terreiro de Paço • Daily 9am–7pm • €2.50 • Ⓦ visitlisboa.com • Ⓜ Terreiro de Paço

The Baixa's most impressive building is a huge arch, the **Arco da Rua Augusta**, adorned with statues of historical figures, including the Marquês de Pombal and Vasco da Gama. Acting as a gateway to the city, the arch was built to celebrate Lisbon's reconstruction after the earthquake, although it wasn't completed until 1873. You can take a lift up the structure to just below the Clock Room, a small exhibition space centred around the workings of a nineteenth-century clock. From here, you can squeeze up a spiral staircase to the flat roof of the monument, where you'll be greeted by unmissable views across the Baixa and Praça do Comércio. Don't be tempted to stand under the deafening bell here when it strikes – you'll regret it.

Heading north from the arch, the mosaic-paved **Rua Augusta** is the Baixa grid's main pedestrianized thoroughfare, filled with shops, cafés, market stalls and buskers.

Praça do Comércio

Originally built on the site of a royal palace, the arcaded **Praça do Comércio** is Lisbon's main riverfront square, and it was here that Dom Carlos I was assassinated in 1908 during the country's attempts to become a republic. One of Portugal's monarchs is still honoured here, however: the statue at the centre of the square is Dom José, who was king when the city was redeveloped following the 1755 earthquake. The square has been partly pedestrianized in a successful attempt to make it more tourist-friendly, with a panoply of cafés and shops on either side. The secluded Patio da Galé, tucked into the western arcades, hosts frequent events, including the alluring **Peixe em Lisboa** Fish Festival in March/April (see p.105). The north side of the square is the departure point for tram tours of the city, but it's the riverfront side that is perhaps most appealing, especially in the hour

or two before sunset, when people linger in the golden light to watch the orange ferries ply between the Estação Fluvial ferry station and Barreiro on the other side of the Tejo. For a scenic walk, head west along the pedestrianized riverfront to Cais do Sodré (see p.70).

Lisbon Story Centre

Praço do Comércio 78–81 • Daily 10am–8pm • €7, ticket valid for a year • ☎ 211 941 099, ⓦ lisboastorycentre.pt • Ⓜ Terreiro de Paço

The eastern arcades of Praça do Comércio were renovated in 2012 to become **Ala Nascente**, a hub of somewhat touristy cafés and shops, the highlight of which is the **Lisbon Story Centre**. This gives a potted, visual account of the city's history – good for a rainy day, though somewhat pricey for what you get. There are six zones, each dedicated to a phase in Lisbon's history, from ancient myths to the present via the Discoveries. The zones consist of multimedia displays, models, paintings, photos, narrations and filmed re-enactments of key moments – the highlight is a somewhat gory 4D film depicting the 1755 earthquake, and a "virtual" scale model of the modern city.

The Alfama

The Alfama is Lisbon's oldest and most atmospheric quarter, a labyrinthine maze of narrow streets, steps and alleys wrapped round the steep lower slopes of the **Moorish castle**. Walking round the area is a must for any Lisbon visit. It's the street life that's the interest here, much of it continuing in the same way as it has for centuries, with children playing in the squares and alleys, and families cooking fish on tiny grills outside their houses. Appropriately in an area which is home to many **fado clubs**, there is also a museum dedicated to this classic Portuguese genre, while around the Alfama are further distractions in the form of the city's **cathedral**, two historic churches containing national pantheons, a fantastic **market**, and museums dedicated to a Roman theatre, decorative arts and – further east – Portuguese tiles.

The Sé

Largo da Sé • Daily 9am–7pm • Free • **Treasury** Mon–Sat 10am–5pm • €2.50 • **Cloister** Mon–Sat 10am–6.30pm • €2.50 •
☎ 218 876 628 • Tram #28

Lisbon's squat, military-looking cathedral – **the Sé** – is Romanesque in style, with a surprisingly plain and sombre interior. This is because many of its original embellishments were destroyed by the 1755 earthquake, though restoration work in the 1930s saw the reconstruction of the huge and impressive rose window. The cathedral was founded in 1150 on the site of Moorish Lishbuna's main mosque, shortly after the city was taken from the Moors under the direction of the Englishman Gilbert of Hastings, who became Lisbon's first bishop.

Most things of value were placed in the **Treasury**, including the remains of St Vincent, which, according to legend, arrived in Lisbon in a boat guided by ravens – the birds are still a symbol for the city today. Of more interest, however, is the thirteenth-century cloister, which is currently being excavated, to reveal the remains of a Roman house and Moorish public buildings.

ALFAMA WALKS AND VIEWPOINTS

The easiest place to start a wander around the Alfama is along the road below the Sé, which becomes Rua de São João de Praça, and later Rua de São Pedro. Follow this as it twists its way down to the Alfama's lower square, **Largo do Chafariz de Dentro**, home to many of the city's best fado bars and clubs. From here, head uphill and you'll probably get lost in the maze of alleys that wend up past the church of São Miguel to emerge by the **Largo das Portas do Sol**, a viewpoint with a tremendous outlook – a solitary palm rising from the stepped streets against the dome of Santa Engracia and the Tejo beyond. Just round the corner, in front of the Igreja da Santa Luzia, the **Mirádouro da Santa Luzia** has perhaps the city's best views across the Alfama and the river.

1

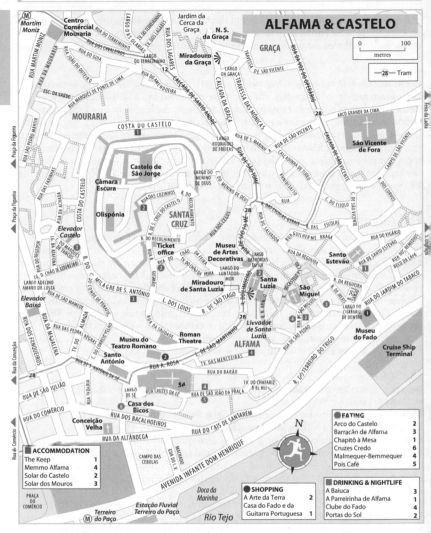

Museu do Teatro Romano

Entrance on Patio de Aljube • Tues–Sun 10am–1pm & 2–6pm • Free • ☎ 218 820 320, ⓦ www. museudelisboa.pt • Tram #28

You can see the sparse ruins of the **Teatro Romano** (57 AD), set behind a grille just off to the left at the junction of ruas São Mamede and Saudade. The finds excavated from the site can be visited at the small adjacent **Museu do Teatro Romano**, which has multimedia explanations of the theatre's history.

Casa dos Bicos

Rua dos Bacalhoeiros 10 • Mon–Sat 10am–6pm • €3, archeological area free • ☎ 218 810 900, ⓦ josesaramago.org • ⓜ Terreiro de Paço

The **Casa dos Bicos** means the "House of Points", which aptly describes its curious walls, studded with pyramid-shaped stones. It was built in 1523 for the son of the Viceroy of India, though only the facade of the original building survived the earthquake. It is now owned by the Saramago organization and hosts regular recitals

and exhibitions dedicated to the Nobel Prize for Literature-winning Portuguese author José Saramago, who died in 2010. The ground floor has been maintained as an **archeological area** where you can view sections of a third-century Roman wall and fish-processing plant, excavated from beneath the building.

Museu do Fado

Largo do Chafariz de Dentro 1 • Tues–Sun 10am–6pm • €5 • ☎ 218 823 470, ⓦ museudofado.pt

Set in the renovated Recinto da Praia, a former water cistern and bathhouse, the **Museo do Fado** is an engaging museum outlining the history of fado and Portuguese guitar by way of wax models, paintings, sounds and descriptions of the leading characters and styles of this very Portuguese music. It's an excellent introduction to fado and worth seeing before you visit a fado house. There's also a small café and a good shop selling fado CDs.

Museu de Artes Decorativas Portugesas

Largo das Portas do Sol 2 • Mon & Wed–Sun 10am–5pm • €4 • ☎ 218 814 600, ⓦ fress.pt • Tram #28

Inside a seventeenth-century mansion, the lovely **Museu de Artes Decorativas Portugesas** displays what was once the private collection of banker Ricardo do Espírito Santo Silva, who offered it to the nation in 1953. Here, you can see some of the best examples of seventeenth- and eighteenth-century applied arts in the country. Highlights include a stunning sixteenth-century tapestry depicting a parade of giraffes, beautiful carpets from Arraiolos in the Alentejo, and oriental quilts that were all the rage in the seventeenth century. The museum also has a courtyard café.

São Vicente de Fora

Largo de São Vicente • Tues–Sun 10am–6pm • Church free, monastery €5 • Tram #28 or bus #34 from Santa Apolónia station and ⓜ Martim Moniz

The church of **São Vicente de Fora** takes its name from its original position *fora* (outside) the city walls. Built on the site where Crusaders perished while fighting the Moors, it remains one of Lisbon's most interesting churches. Begun in 1582 under the Italian architect Felipe Terzi, it was finally inaugurated in 1629 only to be partially destroyed by the earthquake of 1755. It was then restored and in 1855, the former monastic refectory became the official burial site for the kings and queens of the House of Bragança. You can see the tombs of pretty much all the Portuguese monarchs from João IV to Manuel II, the last Portuguese king, who died in exile in England in 1932. Look out too for the tomb of Catherine of Bragança, the widow of England's Charles II. Upstairs rooms trace the history of La Fontaine's fables illustrated on 38 tile panels, but save some energy to climb to the **roof** for spectacular views out over the city. There's also a lovely café by the entrance.

Feira da Ladra

Campo de Santa Clara • Tues & Sat 9am–3pm • Tram #28 or bus #34 from Santa Apolónia station and ⓜ Martim Moniz

Lisbon's twice-weekly **Feira da Ladra** ("thieves' market") sprawls colourfully around the elongated square of Campo de Santa Clara below the impressive dome of the Santa Engrácia church. As well as bric-a-brac and old junk, you'll also find cheap clothes, CDs, crafts, books, prints, antiques of varying quality and the odd novelty (such as night-vision goggles or souvenirs from Portugal's former colonies). Best of all, though, are the people who run the stalls, a motley collection of Lisbon's most interesting characters.

Santa Engrácia

Campo de Santa Clara • Tues–Sun: May–Oct 10am–6pm; Nov–April 10am–5pm • €4 • Tram #28 or bus #34 from Santa Apolónia station and ⓜ Martim Moniz

The white dome of **Santa Engrácia** makes it one of the most recognizable buildings on the city skyline. Begun in 1682, it was not completed until 1966, leading to the expression "a job like Santa Engrácia", one that is never finished. Since 1916, the church has been the

1

Panteão Nacional, housing the tombs of eminent Portuguese figures, including former presidents, the writer Almeida Garrett and Amália Rodrigues, Portugal's most famous fado singer. You can go up to the terrace for dazzling views across the river and city below.

Cruise ship terminal

On most days, an overly large cruise ship docks at the **terminal** below the Alfama. It was built as part of an ambitious riverfront redevelopment plan that has cleared away many of the old warehouses and replaced them with an appealing pedestrianized walkway, which allows you to stroll along the Tagus all the way from Santa Apolónia train station to Praça do Comércio.

Barbadinhos Steam Pumping Station

Rua do Alviela 12 • Tues–Sun 10am–12.30pm & 1.30–5.30pm • €5 • ☎ 218 100 215, ⊕ epal.pt • Ⓜ Santa Apolónia; a 10min walk from the station, off Calçada dos Barbadinhos

The **Barbadinhos Steam Pumping Station** is a small but engaging museum housed in an attractive old pumping station filled with shiny brass, polished wood and Victorian ingenuity. It was built in 1880 to pump water from a nearby river up Lisbon's steep hills, depositing it in a reservoir hollowed out from a former Franciscan convent. It used four steam-powered engines that worked non-stop until 1928, and which you can see demonstrated today. The museum is the main branch of Lisbon's Museus da Água (water museums; see p.73 and p.76), and its exhibits give a fascinating insight into the evolution of the city's water supply.

Museu Nacional do Azulejo

Rua da Madre de Deus 4 • Tues–Sun 10am–6pm • €5; free on the first Sun of the month • ☎ 218 103 340, ⊕ mnazulejo.imc-ip.pt • The museum is 1.5km east of Santa Apolónia station; take bus #794 from Praça do Comércio or Santa Apolónia

One of the most appealing of Lisbon's small museums, the **Museu Nacional do Azulejo** traces the development of tile-making from Moorish days to the present via its hugely impressive collection of *azulejos* (see p.70), covering the main styles of tile from the fifteenth century to the present day. The museum is housed within the church and cloisters of Madre de Deus, a former convent dating from 1509. The church has a Baroque interior, installed after the earthquake of 1755, and retains some striking eighteenth-century tiles depicting scenes from the life of Santo António. Most of the museum is set around the church cloisters, which house many more delights, including Portugal's longest *azulejo* – a 36m tiled panorama of pre-earthquake Lisbon, completed in around 1738 – and some fascinating examples of the large *azulejo* panels known as *tapetes* (carpets). There's also a lovely garden café.

Castelo de São Jorge

Castelo Daily: March–Oct 9am–9pm; Nov–Feb 9am–6pm • €8.50 • Câmara Escura Daily 10am–5pm every 30min, weather permitting • Entry included in castle ticket • ☎ 218 800 620, ⊕ castelodesaojorge.pt • Tram #28 from Rua da Conceição in the Baixa; bus #37 from Praça da Figueira, or tram #12 from Martim Moniz to the Santa Cruz area just east of the castle

Superbly sited on a hilltop with the city and river laid out below, the **Castelo de São Jorge** is rightly Lisbon's most popular attraction. Part of its appeal lies in the fact that much of it is little more than a shell whose restored walls enclose grassy areas where peacocks shelter and cats doze beneath trees. A series of gardens, walkways and viewpoints hidden within the old Moorish walls make this an enjoyable place in which to wander for a couple of hours, with spectacular views over the city from its ramparts and towers.

There was probably a castle here in the Iron Age and by the time the city was under Moorish rule, the building was sufficiently robust to repel the invading Christians for several months until Lisbon finally fell to Afonso Henriques in 1147. Initially, Portugal's monarchs lived in the castle, but they moved out when Manuel I built a new

1

LISBON'S AZULEJOS

Lisbon has some of Portugal's best **azulejos** – brightly coloured, decorative ceramic tiles – and you can see a variety of styles decorating houses, shops, monuments and even metro stations. The craft of decorative tile-making was brought over by the Moors in the eighth century. Originally, the tiles were painted using thin ridges of clay to prevent the lead-based colours from running into each other, and the early Portuguese tiles were produced using the same techniques: the early sixteenth-century **geometric tiles** in the Palácio Nacional in Sintra (see p.113) are a fine example. Portuguese *azulejos* developed their own style around the mid-sixteenth century when a new Italian method – introduced to Iberia by Francisco Niculoso – enabled images to be painted directly onto the clay thanks to a tin oxide coating which prevented running.

At first, **religious imagery** was the favoured form – such as those in the Bairro Alto's Igreja de São Roque (see p.72) – but during the seventeenth century decadent and colourful images became popular. The wealthy Portuguese began to commission large *azulejo* panels displaying battles, hunting scenes and fantastic images influenced by Vasco da Gama's voyages to the East, while huge panels were also commissioned for churches – these often covered an entire wall and became known as *tapetes* (carpets) because of their resemblance to rugs. By the late seventeenth century, blue and white tiles influenced by **Dutch tile-makers** were popular with Portugal's aristocracy, and their favoured images were flowers and fruit. The early eighteenth century saw highly trained artists producing elaborately decorated, multicoloured **ceramic mosaics**, often with Rococo themes.

After the Great Earthquake, more prosaic tiled façades, often with **Neoclassical designs**, were considered good insulation devices, as well as protecting buildings from rain and fire. By the mid-nineteenth century, *azulejos* were being mass-produced to decorate shops and factories, while the end of the century saw the reappearance of figurative designs, typified by the work in the *Cervejaria da Trindade* (see p.99), a vaulted beer-hall in the Bairro Alto. By the 1900s, Portugal had become the world's leading producer of decorative tiles, with **Art Deco** designs taking hold in the 1920s. Lisbon's metro stations boast some of the best of the more modern tiles, with work by artists such as Eduardo Nehry, whose tiles light up Campo Grande, and António da Costa, whose Alice-in-Wonderland-inspired white rabbit can be seen at Cais do Sodré station.

palace down by the river. After that, the castle served as a barracks, prison and children's home until the late twentieth century, when it was substantially renovated to become the tourist attraction you see today. The castle **museum** is in the old Alcáçova (the former palace where the kings lived), with a small multimedia exhibition that details the history of the city together with archeological finds. Inside the Tower of Ulysses, a **Câmara Escura** periscope focuses on sights round the city with English commentary – though the views are almost as good from the neighbouring towers. Better is to explore the **archeological remains**, an excavation site next to the castle that includes the scant remains of an Iron Age house, an eleventh-century Moorish quarter and the ruins of the fifteenth-century Palácio dos Condes de Santiago, built for the Bishops of Lisbon.

Santa Cruz and Mouraria

Take time to explore the areas immediately around the Castelo de São Jorge. Turn left from the castle exit and you are in the tiny **Santa Cruz** quarter, a village in its own right with a school, church and bathhouse. To the north and west of the castle is **Mouraria**, named because this was where the Moors were forced to live when expelled from the castle – today, it's an atmospheric area with some good local cafés.

Cais do Sodré and Bica

Down on the waterfront, **Cais do Sodré** (pronounced *kaiysh doo sodray*) is a colourful but slightly down-at-heel suburb which has become hip thanks to some good restaurants, clubs and bars, many located along Rua Nova Carvalho, aka Rua

Cor-de-Rosa or "pink street", on account of the colour of its tarmac. Many of the area's **waterfront warehouses** have been converted into upmarket cafés and restaurants and by day, in particular, a stroll along its atmospheric riverfront is very enjoyable. Cais do Sodré is also the main departure point for **ferries** over the Tejo – a ride over to the little port of Cacilhas (see p.121) is recommended – while the eponymous station is the terminus for the **rail line** out to Cascais.

Mercado da Ribeira

Av 24 de Julho, Cais do Sodré • Fruit, fish and vegetable market Mon–Sat 6am–2pm; Food stalls Mon–Wed & Sun 10am–midnight, Thurs–Sat 10am–2am • ☎ 212 244 980 • Ⓜ Cais do Sodré

The **Mercado da Ribeira** is Lisbon's main and most historic market. The first market here was built on the site of an old fort at the end of the nineteenth century, though the current structure dates only from 1930. Much of the building is now given over to a vibrant **food hall**, with an impressive range of stalls (most representing top chefs and well-known outlets in Lisbon) and plenty of bench-like tables where you can sit and eat. You pay slightly above the norm for the concept and ambience, but with everything from hams, cheeses and grilled chicken to gourmet burgers, seafood, organic salads and chocolates (not to mention champagne and cocktail bars), you might well find yourself tempted back here again and again.

Elevador da Bica

Entrance on Rua de São Paulo, Bica • Mon–Sat 7am–9pm, Sun 9am–9pm • €3.60 return • Ⓜ Cais do Sodré

With its entrance tucked into an arch on Rua de São Paulo, the **Elevador da Bica** is one of the city's most atmospheric funicular railways. Built in 1892 and originally powered by water counterweights – though now operated electrically – the *elevador* leads up towards the Bairro Alto, via a steep residential street. Take time to explore the surrounding steep side-streets of the Bica neighbourhood, a warren of tightly-knit houses and fine local restaurants.

Miradouro de Santa Catarina

Just off Rua M. Saldanha, Bica • **Kiosk** Daily 10am–dusk, weather permitting • Tram #28

Set on the cusp of a hill, high above the river, the railed **Miradouro de Santa Catarina** has spectacular views over the city and river. Here, in the shadow of the statue of the Adamastor – a mythical beast from Luís de Camões's *Lusiads* – a collection of guitar-strumming New Age hippies often gather around an appealing **drinks kiosk** which has a few outdoor tables.

Chiado

On the west side of the Baixa, the area known as **Chiado** – the *nom de plume* of the poet António Ribeiro and pronounced *she-ah-doo* – was Lisbon's original upmarket shopping area. Many of its former stores were destroyed by a fire in 1988, although the original *belle époque* atmosphere has since been superbly recreated under the direction of eminent Portuguese architect Álvaro Siza Vieira.

Chiado remains a smart shopping district, famed for its cafés especially along Rua Garrett. Of these, **A Brasileira**, Rua Garrett 120 (see p.96), is the most famous, once frequented by Lisbon's literary set and now usually mobbed by tourists.

Museu Nacional de Arte Contemporânea do Chiado

Rua Serpa Pinto 4 • Tues–Sun 10am–6pm • €4.50, free on first Sun of each month • ☎ 213 432 148, Ⓦ museuartecontemporanea.pt • Ⓜ Baixa-Chiado

The stylish **Museu do Chiado** incorporates the former Museum of Contemporary Art, whose original home was damaged during the Chiado fire. The new museum was constructed around a nineteenth-century biscuit factory, hence the presence of the old

1

ovens. Its three floors display the work of some of Portugal's most influential artists since the nineteenth century, including wonderful decorative panels by José de Almada Negreiros, recovered from the San Carlos cinema. Highlights include the beautiful sculpture *A Viúva* (The Widow) by António Teixeira Lopes and some evocative scenes of the Lisbon area by Carlos Botelho and José Malhoa. It also hosts some excellent temporary exhibitions: check the website for details.

Bairro Alto

High above the central city, to the west of the Baixa, the **Bairro Alto** – meaning upper town – has a sleepy, residential feel during the day, its maze of narrow streets enlivened by a few bohemian boutiques. At night, however, it comes to life as many of the city's best bars, restaurants and fado clubs open for business. Many of the Bairro Alto's most interesting thoroughfares lie west of Rua da Misericórdia, a confusing grid of streets, whose buildings are often liberally defaced with graffiti. Traffic is restricted to residents only, and though dodgy characters offering hash still lurk on the corners round the market building on Rua da Atalaia, it's essentially safe at any time if you keep valuables out of sight.

Igreja de São Roque

Largo de Trindade Coelho • **Church** Mon 2–7pm, Tues, Wed & Fri–Sun 9am–7pm, Thurs 9am 8pm; closes 6pm Oct–March • Free • **Museu de São Roque** Same hours • €2.50, free Sun 10am–2pm

Built by Jesuits in the sixteenth century, the **Igreja de São Roque** has a bland Renaissance facade that gives no hint of its interior riches. Inside, impressive *azulejos* and marble decorate the side chapels, while the **Capela de São João Baptista** is thought to be one of the most expensive and lavish chapels of its era. Dom João V commissioned the papal architect to design and build the chapel in Rome, with no expense spared. It was shipped to Lisbon in 1749, but its intricate array of ivory inlays, gold, lapis lazuli and mosaics of John the Baptist took some four years to reassemble and the result is truly remarkable. The most valuable treasures of the church are kept in the adjacent **Museu de São Roque**, which also displays sixteenth- to eighteenth-century paintings and a fairly uninspiring collection of church relics.

Convento and Museu Arqueológico do Carmo

Largo do Carmo • Mon–Sat: June–Sept 10am–7pm; Oct–May 10am–6pm • €3.50 • ☎ 213 478 629, ⓦ museuarqueologicodocarmo.pt

The pretty, enclosed Largo do Carmo holds the entrance to the **Convento do Carmo**, whose beautiful Gothic arches rise majestically above the ruins. Built between 1389 and 1423, and once the city's grandest church, it was badly damaged by the 1755 earthquake. In the nineteenth century its shell was used as a chemical factory but today it houses the splendidly capricious **Museu Arqueológico do Carmo**, home to many of the treasures from Portugal's monasteries, dissolved after the 1834 Liberal revolution. The nave is open to the elements, with columns, tombs and statuary scattered in all corners. Inside, on either side of what was the main altar, are the

---

TRANSPORT TO THE BAIRRO ALTO

To reach the Bairro Alto, you can simply climb the steep Calçada de Glória, but it's more fun to approach via one of the quirky funiculars, which were originally powered by water displacement, and then by steam, until electricity was introduced. Most conveniently, the **Elevador da Glória** (Mon–Thurs 7am–11.55pm, Fri 7am–12.25am, Sat 8.30am–12.25am, Sun 9am–11.55pm; €3.60 return), built in 1885, trundles up from the Praça dos Restauradores, dropping you at the top of the hill on Rua de São Pedro de Alcântara; the adjacent gardens here provide a superb view across the city to the castle. The **Elevador da Bica** (see p.71) drops you on Rua Loreto at the foot of the Bairro Alto, while the **Elevador de Santa Justa** (see p.62), brings you out beside the Convento do Carmo.

THE GREAT EARTHQUAKE

Anyone who witnessed the shocking images of Japan's tsunami in 2011 will have some idea of the disaster which befell Lisbon on November 1, 1755. A quake of around 8.7 on the Richter scale – the largest **earthquake** ever to hit Europe – struck at 9.30am when many people were attending Mass for All Souls' Day. Survivors fled to the open spaces of the riverfront, many to be engulfed by a giant tsunami that followed some forty minutes later. Fires then burned for up to five days and tens of thousands of people lost their lives. The event put a halt to Portuguese colonial expansion, but also led to the development of the study of seismology.

main exhibits, centring on a series of **tombs**. Largest is the beautifully carved, 2m-high stone tomb of Ferdinand I; nearby, that of Gonçalo de Sousa, chancellor to Henry the Navigator, is topped by a statue of Gonçalo himself, holding a book to signify his learning. Other noteworthy pieces include sixteenth-century Hispano-Arabic *azulejos*, an Egyptian sarcophagus (793–619 BC), whose inhabitant's feet are just visible beneath the lid, and, even more alarmingly, two pre-Columbian mummies which lie in glass cases, alongside the preserved heads of a couple of indigenous Peruvians.

Praça do Príncipe Real

North of the tight Bairro Alto grid, the streets open out around the leafy **Praça do Príncipe Real**, one of the city's loveliest squares. Laid out in 1860 and surrounded by the ornate homes of former aristocrats – now largely turned into offices and boutiques – the square is the focal point of Lisbon's gay scene, though by day it is largely populated by children in the play park and locals playing cards under the trees.

Museu da Água Príncipe Real

Praça do Príncipe Real • Tues–Sat 10am–5.30pm • €1 • Tours Wed & Sat at 11am & 3pm, Fri 1pm, €2.50 • Bus #758 or #778 from Chiado

Praça do Príncipe Real's central pond and fountain are built above a covered reservoir that houses the **Museu da Água Príncipe Real**. Steps lead down inside the eerie nineteenth-century reservoir, where you can admire brick and vaulted ceilings, part of a network of underground water supplies that link up with the Aqueduto das Águas Livres (see p.76). Tours – not for claustrophobics – take you along one of these, a humid 410m tunnel that exits at the viewpoint of Miradouro de São Pedro.

Museus Nacional de História e da Ciência

Rua Escola Politécnica 56 • Tues–Fri 10am–5pm, Sat & Sun 11am–6pm; closed Aug • €5, free Thurs 5–8pm; combined ticket with Jardim Botânico €6 • ☎ 213 921 800, ⓦ museus.ulisboa.pt • Bus #758 or #778 from Chiado

Within Lisbon's Polytechnic lies the **Museu de História Natural**, which exhibits a rather sad collection of stuffed specimens tracing the evolution of Iberian animal life. The more appealing **Museu da Ciência** (whose labs featured in the film *The Promise*, starring Christian Bale) includes an imaginative interactive section among its otherwise pedestrian geological displays. Look out for the temporary exhibits, which can be more rewarding.

Jardim Botânico

Rua Escola Politécnica 58 • Daily: April–Oct 9am–8pm; Nov–March 9am–6pm • €2, combined ticket with Museus Nacional de História e da Ciência €6 • Bus #758 or #778 from Chiado

Beyond the Museus Nacional de História e da Ciência, the entrance to the enchanting **Jardim Botânico** is almost completely invisible from the surrounding streets. Portuguese explorers introduced many plant species to Europe, and these gardens, laid out between 1858 and 1878, form an oasis of twenty thousand exotic plants from around the world. There's also a **butterfly house**, called the Lugartagis, which is a greenhouse for breeding butterflies.

1

BAIRRO ALTO & AROUND

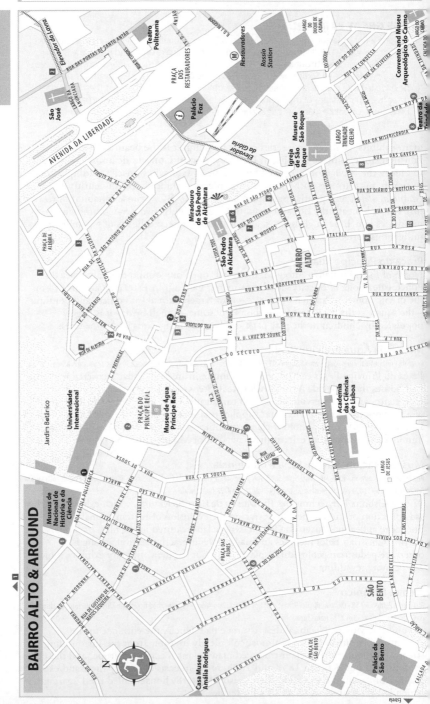

Estrela

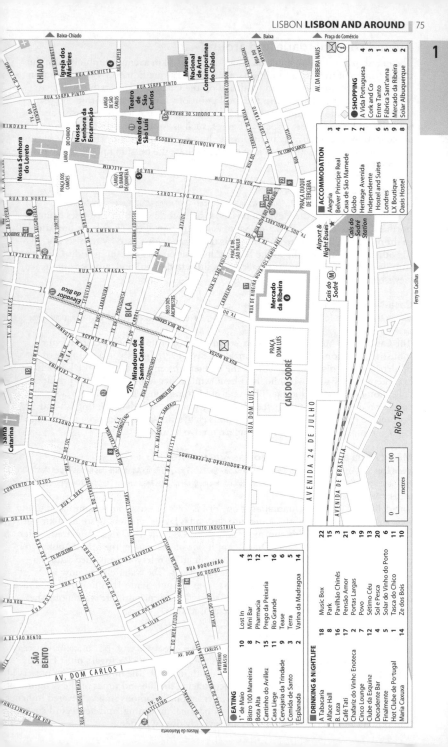

EATING

1° de Maio	10
Bistro 100 Maneiras	8
Bota Alta	7
Cantinho do Avillez	15
Casa Liege	11
Cervejaria da Trindade	9
Comida de Santo	3
Esplanada	2
Lost In	4
Mini Bar	13
Pharmacia	12
Prego da Peixaria	1
Rio Grande	16
Tease	6
Terra	5
Varina da Madragoa	14

DRINKING & NIGHTLIFE

A Tabacaria	18
Alface Hall	8
B. Leza	16
Café Tati	17
Chafariz do Vinho Enoteca	2
Cinco Lounge	7
Clube de Esquina	12
Decadente Bar	4
Finalmente	5
Hot Clube de Portugal	1
Maria Caxuxa	14
Music Box	22
Park	15
Pavilhão Chinês	3
Pensão Amor	21
Portas Largas	9
Povo	19
Sétimo Céu	13
Sol e Pesca	20
Solar do Vinho do Porto	6
Tasca do Chico	11
Ze dos Bois	10

ACCOMMODATION

Alegria	3
Belver Príncipe Real	4
Casa de São Mamede	1
Globo	7
Heritage Avenida	2
Independente, Hostel and Suites	6
Londres	5
LX Boutique	9
Oasis Hostel	8

SHOPPING

A Vida Portuguesa	4
Cork and Co	3
Entre Tanto	1
Fábrica Sant'anna	5
Mercado da Ribeira	9
Solar Albuquerque	2

1

Avenida da Liberdade and around

The grand, palm-lined **Avenida da Liberdade** is a 1.3km avenue climbing from the upper fringes of the Baixa to Lisbon's main park, Parque Eduardo VII. Laid out in the late nineteenth century and modelled on the Champs-Élysées, the broad avenue and its little kiosks form the focal point of various events during the year, including a parade on June 12–13 for St Anthony. It was once the exclusive address for some of Lisbon's most respected figures, such as António Medeiros, whose rich **art collections** are on display in his former home. On the western side of the avenue it's a short walk to the historic **Praça das Amoreiras**, the finishing point of the massive **Aqueduto das Águas**.

Elevador do Lavra

Largo da Anunciada • Mon–Fri 7.50am–7.55pm, Sat & Sun 9am–7.55pm • €3.60 return • Ⓜ Restauradores or Avenida

Dating back to 1882, the **Elevador do Lavra** is a historic street lift that rises from the northern end of Rua das Portas de Santo Antão up one of the city's back-breaking hills, to drop you in a little-visited suburb. It is the *elevador* least used by tourists but, like the other more famous lifts to the Bairro Alto, this one is great fun to ride. Once you've trundled up the hill, it's a short walk to the little **Jardim do Torel**, a park with great views back over the Baixa.

Casa-Museu Medeiros e Almeida

Rua Rosa Araújo 41 • Mon–Fri 1–5.30pm, Sat 10am–5.30pm • €5, free Sat 10am–1pm • ☎ 213 547 892, ⓦ casa-museumedeirose almeida.pt • Ⓜ Avenida

The **Casa-Museu Medeiros e Almeida**, set in the former home of art collector and industrialist António Medeiros e Almeida (1895–1986), gives you a real taste of the opulence of this district of Lisbon in the nineteenth century. Parts of the house have been kept as they were when he lived here, while other rooms display his priceless collection of works, including 2000-year-old Chinese porcelain, an important collection of sixteenth- to nineteenth-century watches, and dazzling English and Portuguese silverware. There are sumptuous eighteenth-century *azulejos* in the Sala de Lago, a room also filled with bubbling decorative fountains.

Mãe d'Água and the Aqueduto das Águas Livres

Mãe d'Água Tues–Sat 10am–12.30pm & 1.30–5.30pm • €2.50 • ☎ 218 135 522 • Ⓜ Rato • **Aqueduto das Águas Livres** March–Oct Tues–Sat 10am–5.30pm • €3 • The aqueduct walk starts around 1km north of Praça das Amoreiras, at Calçada da Quintiha 6 in Campolide; take bus #758 from Amoreiras

The delightful **Praça das Amoreiras** is one of Lisbon's nicest squares, dominated on its west side by the arches of the **Aqueduto das Águas Livres**. Stretching some 60km into the hills above Lisbon, this enormous aqueduct was built in 1748 to pipe fresh water into the city for the first time. On the south side of the square, the **Mãe d'Água** water cistern marks the end of the line for the aqueduct, its reservoir contained within a cathedral-like stone building with Gothic lion heads. The water cistern now hosts occasional exhibitions and has great views from its roof. Some 1km north of the Praça das Amoreiras, you can take an enjoyable fifteen- to twenty-minute walk along the Aqueduto das Águas Livres' 60m-high central section.

Casa Museu Amália Rodrigues

Rua de São Bento 193 • Tues–Sun 10am–1pm & 2–6pm • €5 • ☎ 213 971 896, ⓦ amaliarodrigues.pt • Bus #706 from Praça do Comércio

The **Casa Museu Amália Rodrigues** occupies the house where Portugal's most famous fado singer lived from the 1950s until her death in 1999. The house has been preserved as it was when she lived here, with artefacts tracing the life and times of the daughter of an Alfama orange-seller who became an internationally famous singer. Revered in her lifetime, her death resulted in three days of national mourning, and her record covers, film posters and everyday belongings are lovingly displayed here.

São Bento

São Bento, downhill and west from the Bairro Alto, was home to Lisbon's first black community – originally slaves from Portugal's early maritime explorations. However, the area is best known today for the Neoclassical parliament building, the **Palácio de São Bento** (or Palácio da Assembléia), originally a Benedictine monastery before the abolition of religious orders in 1834. Since the Portuguese government still sits here, it can only be visited by prior arrangement (☎213 919 625), though you get a good view of its steep white steps from tram #28, which rattles right by.

West Lisbon

West of the Bairro Alto sits the leafy district of **Estrela**, best known for its gardens and enormous **basílica**. To the south lies opulent Lapa, Lisbon's diplomatic quarter, where sumptuous mansions and grand embassy buildings peer out majestically towards the Tejo; it's also home to the superb **Museu Nacional de Arte Antiga**, Portugal's national gallery. Down below, on the riverfront, the regenerated district of **Santos** is known as "the design district", with chic shops and bars.

Basílica da Estrela

Calçada da Estrela • **Basílica** Mon–Fri 7.30am–7.45pm, Sat 10am–6.30pm, Sun 3.30–7pm; usually closes for a 2hr lunch from 1pm • Free • **Roof** Mon–Sat 10am–6pm • €4 • Tram #28 from Praça Luís de Camões in Chiado, or #25 from Praça do Comércio

With its landmark white dome visible from much of the city, the impressive **Basílica da Estrela** was commissioned by Queen Maria I (whose tomb lies inside), and completed in 1790. You can visit the flat roof (via 140 steep stone steps) for fine views over the western suburbs, and also walk round the inside of the dome to peer down at the church interior 25m below: not for vertigo sufferers.

Jardim da Estrela

Calçada da Estrela • Unrestricted access • Free • Tram #28 from Praça Luís de Camões in Chiado, or #25 from Praça do Comércio

Opposite the Basílica da Estrela, the **Jardim da Estrela** is a lovely place in which to recover from the climb to the church roof. Small but luxuriantly leafy, the gardens boast an appealing pond-side café and a well-equipped children's playground.

Mercado de Campo de Ourique

Rua Coelho da Rocha • Mon–Wed 10am–11pm, Thurs–Sat 10am–1am • ☎ 211 323 701

Set in a wonderful 1930s building, the **Mercado de Campo de Ourique** has been given a revamp and now not only sells fish, fruit and veg, but also shelters around 20 *tasquinhas* (small food stalls and bars) serving pastries, sushi, *petiscos*, burgers and seafood. There is also occasional live entertainment in the evenings.

Museu Nacional de Arte Antiga

Rua das Janelas Verdes 95 • **Museum** Tues –Sun 10am–6pm • €6, free first Sun of the month • **Gardens** Same hours • Free • ☎ 213 912 800, Ⓦ museudearteantiga.pt • Bus #760 from Praça da Figueira, bus #727 from Belém or a short walk from tram #25

Portugal's national gallery, the **Museu Nacional de Arte Antiga** is home to the largest collection of Portuguese fifteenth- and sixteenth-century paintings in the country, as well as European art from the fourteenth century to the present day, and a rich display of applied art showing the influence of Portugal's colonial explorations. All of this is beautifully displayed in a seventeenth-century palace, once owned by the Marquês de Pombal. The palace was built over the remains of the Saint Albert monastery, most of which was razed in the 1755 earthquake, although its beautiful chapel can still be seen today. The attractive garden and café are worth a visit in their own right.

1

The collection

The museum helpfully highlights its top ten works of art to guide you round the extensive collection. Principal is **Nuno Gonçalves**'s *Altarpiece for Saint Vincent* (1467–70), showing Lisbon's patron saint being admired by people from all walks of life, their faces looking remarkably modern. Equally impressive is **Hieronymus Bosch**'s stunningly gruesome *Temptation of St Anthony* in room 57 – unusually, there's also an image on the back, showing the arrest of Christ. Elsewhere, seek out the altar panel depicting the *Resurrection* by Raphael; Francisco de Zurbarán's *The Twelve Apostles*; a small statue of a nymph by Auguste Rodin and works by Albrecht Dürer, Cranach, Fragonard and **Josefa de Óbidos**, considered one of Portugal's greatest female painters.

The **Oriental art collection** includes inlaid furniture from Goa, Turkish and Syrian *azulejos*, Quing Dynasty porcelain and a series of late sixteenth-century Japanese *namban* screens (room 14), showing the Portuguese landing at Nagasaki. The Japanese saw the Portuguese traders as southern barbarians (*namban*) with large noses – hence their Pinocchio-like features.

Santos

Southeast of the Museu Nacional de Arte Antiga, **Santos** was formerly a run-down riverside area of factories and warehouses, where people only ventured after dark for its well-known nightclubs. Its squares and streets are not particularly alluring, but over the years, artists and designers have moved into the inexpensive and expansive warehouse spaces; it's now become the city's trendy art district, where many of the country's top designers showcase their products, especially around **Largo de Santos**. Hip bars and restaurants have followed in their wake, though much of the district remains fairly run-down – and the area around the Museu da Marioneta retains an earthy, villagey feel to its cobbled backstreets.

Museu da Marioneta

Rua Esperança 146 • Tues–Sun 10am –1pm & 2–6pm • €5, free Sun 10am–1pm • ☎ 213 942 810 • Tram #25, then a short walk

Contemporary and historical puppets from around the world are displayed in the well-organized **Museu da Marioneta**, housed in a former eighteenth-century convent. Highlights include shadow puppets from Turkey and Indonesia, string marionettes, Punch and Judy-style puppets, and faintly disturbing, almost life-sized contemporary figures by Portuguese puppeteer Helena Vaz. There are also video displays and projections, while the final room shows Wallace and Gromit-style plasticine figures and how they are manipulated for films.

Alcântara and the docks

Loomed over by the enormous Ponte 25 de Abril suspension bridge, Lisbon's docks at **Alcântara** have a decidedly industrial hue, with a tangle of railway lines, flyovers and cranes dominating the skyline. Nevertheless, the area is well known for its nightlife, mainly thanks to its dockside warehouse conversions that shelter cafés, restaurants and clubs. It's also home to two good museums tracing Portugal's trading links with the Orient.

Museu do Oriente

Avenida Brasília • Tues–Thurs & Sat–Sun 10am–6pm, Fri 10am–10pm • €6, free Fri 6–10pm • ☎ 213 585 200, ⓦ museudooriente.pt • Tram #15 or #18, or train to Alcântara Mar

Housed in an enormous 1930s *Estado Novo* building, the **Museu do Oriente** traces the cultural links that Portugal has built up with the Orient. Highlights of its extensive collection include valuable nineteenth-century Chinese porcelain, an amazing array of seventeenth-century Chinese snuff boxes and, from the same century, Japanese armour and entire carved pillars from Goa. The top floor is given over to displays on the Gods of Asia, featuring a bright collection of religious costumes and shrines used in Bali and

1

Vietnam, together with Taoist altars, statues of Buddha, some fine Japanese Shinto masks and Indonesian shadow puppets. Vivid images of Hindu gods Shiva, Ganesh the elephant god and Kali the demon are counterbalanced by some lovely Thai amulets. There is also a decent top-floor restaurant.

Doca de Santo Amaro
Tram #15 or train to Alcântara Mar

The intimate **Doca de Santo Amaro** nestles right beneath the humming traffic and rattling trains crossing Ponte 25 de Abril. This small, almost completely enclosed marina is filled with bobbing sailing boats and lined with tastefully converted warehouses. Its international cafés and restaurants are more pricey than usual for Lisbon, but the constant comings and goings on the Tejo provide plenty of free entertainment. Leaving Doca de Santo Amaro at its western side, you can pick up a pleasant riverside path that leads all the way to Belém, twenty minutes' walk away.

Ponte 25 de Abril

Resembling the Golden Gate Bridge in San Francisco, the hugely impressive **Ponte 25 de Abril** was opened in 1966 as a vital link between Lisbon and the southern banks of the Tejo. Around 2.3km in length, the bridge rises to 70m above the river, though its main pillars are nearly 200m tall. It was originally named Ponte de Salazar, after the dictator who ruled Portugal from 1932 to 1968, but took its present name to mark the date of the revolution that overthrew Salazar's regime in 1974. You'll pass over it if you take a bus or train south of the Tejo.

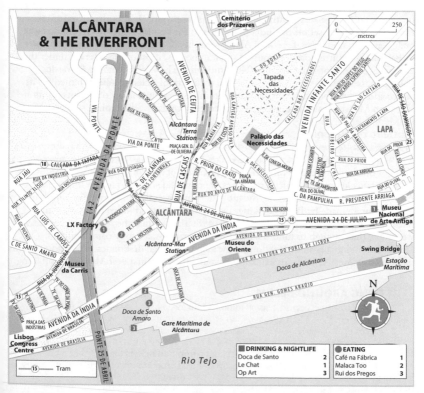

1

Museu da Carris

Rua 1° de Maio 101 • Mon–Fri 10am–6pm, Sat 10am–1pm & 2–6pm • €4 • ☎ 213 613 087, ⓦ museu.carris.pt

The engagingly quirky and ramshackle **Museu da Carris** traces the history of Lisbon's public transport, from the earliest trams and street lifts to the development of the metro. There are three zones, the first with evocative black-and-white photos, uniforms and models. You then hop on a real tram dating from 1901, which takes you to a warehouse filled with historic trams, and then on to another warehouse with ancient buses and models of metro trains. It's great fun for kids especially, who can clamber on board and pretend to drive the vehicles. The south side of the site also has the eye-catching Village Underground, a bizarre medley of old shipping containers and double-decker buses now given over to work spaces for writers and artists.

Museu do Centro Científico e Cultural de Macau

Rua da Junqueira 30 • Tues–Sun 10am–6pm • €3, free Sun 10am–2pm • ☎ 213 617 570, ⓦ cccm.pt • Tram #15

The **Museu do Centro Científico e Cultural de Macau** is dedicated to Portugal's trading links with the Orient and its former colony of Macau, which was handed back to Chinese rule in 1999. There are model boats and audio displays detailing early journeys, and exhibits of Chinese art from the sixteenth to the nineteenth centuries, including an impressive array of opium pipes and ivory boxes.

Belém and Ajuda

Tram #15 (signed Algés) from Praça da Figueira via Praça do Comércio (20min) or Oeiras train from Cais do Sodré

With its maritime history, attractive riverside location and slew of good museums, **Belém** (pronounced *ber-layng*) is rightly one of Lisbon's most popular suburbs. It was from here that Vasco da Gama set off for India in 1497, and the vast **Mosteiro dos Jerónimos** was built here to honour his safe return. Along with the monastery and the landmark **Torre de Belém**, the suburb boasts a group of small museums, most of them set up under the Salazar regime during the Expo in 1940 though the best of the lot, the **Berrardo Collection**, is a more recent addition. Just to the north of Belém is **Ajuda**, famed for its palace and ancient botanical gardens. Bear in mind that quite a few of Belém's sights are closed on Mondays, and many are free on the first Sunday of the month.

Mosteiro dos Jerónimos

Praça do Império • May–Sept Tues–Sun 10am–6.30pm; Oct–May Tues–Sun 10am–5.30pm; restricted access to church on Sat mornings and during Mass • €10, free first Sun of the month; combined ticket with Torre de Belém €12 • ☎ 213 620 034, ⓦ mosteirojeronimos.pt • Tram #15

If there's one building that symbolizes the golden age of the Portuguese discoveries, it's the **Mosteiro dos Jerónimos**, which dominates the north side of the Praça do Império. A UNESCO World Heritage Site, the monastery and its adjacent church were built to fulfil a promise made by Portugal's king, Dom Manuel, should Vasco da Gama return safely from his inaugural voyage to India in 1498. The fact that the spices he returned with were more than enough to fund the building was, perhaps, a happy coincidence. Construction duly began in 1502 under the architect Diogo de Boitaca, who had made his name on the Igreja de Jesus in Setúbal, considered to be the first ever Manueline building.

GETTING AROUND BELÉM

Yellow Bus run a 45min hop-on, hop-off **minibus tour** (departures June–Sept daily every 30min from 10am–1pm & 2–6.30pm; Oct–May Mon–Fri hourly from 10am–noon & 2–5pm, Sat–Sun every 30min from 10am–noon & 2–5pm; €9, valid 24 hours); the circular route starts from in front of the Mosteiro dos Jerónimos, heads up to the palace at Ajuda then returns via the Torre de Belém.

Ask at the ticket offices of the main sites about **combined tickets** that can save money on entry to the main attractions. Note also that you should expect long queues at the attractions in high season: arriving early or late in the day is the best bet.

1

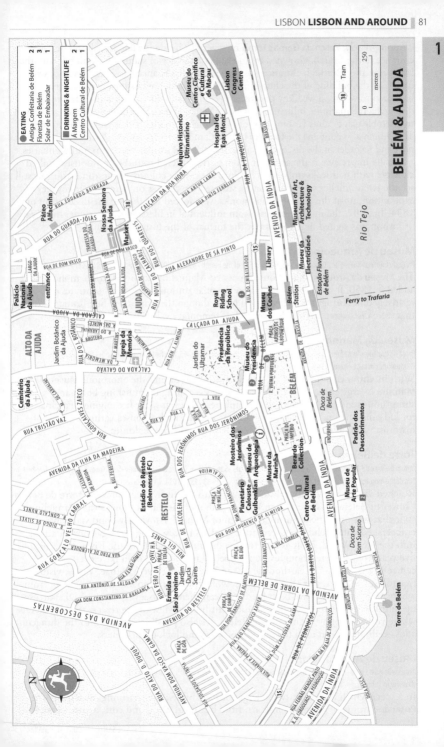

BELÉM & AJUDA

● EATING
Antiga Confeitaria de Belém   2
Floresta de Belém   3
Solar de Embaixadar   1

■ DRINKING & NIGHTLIFE
À Margem   2
Centro Cultural de Belém   1

18 — Train

0   250
metres

Museu do Centro Científico e Cultural de Macau
Lisbon Congress Centre
Hospital de Egas Moniz
Arquivo Histórico Ultramarino
Nossa Senhora da Ajuda
Pátio Alfacinha
Palácio Nacional da Ajuda
entrance
Jardim Botânico da Ajuda
ALTO DA AJUDA
Cemitério da Ajuda
Igreja da Memória
AJUDA
Market
Royal Riding School
Museu dos Coches
Belém Station
Presidência da República
Museu da Presidência
Jardim do Ultramar
Library
Museu da Electricidade
Estação Fluvial de Belém
Ferry to Trafaria
Rio Tejo
Museum of Art, Architecture & Technology
AVENIDA DA ÍNDIA
Estádio do Restelo (Belenenses FC)
RESTELO
Ermida de São Jerónimo
Mosteiro dos Jerónimos
Museu de Arqueologia
Planetário Calouste Gulbenkian
Museu da Marinha
Berardo Collection
Centro Cultural de Belém
Museu de Arte Popular
Padrão dos Descobrimentos
Doca de Belém
Doca de Bom Sucesso
Torre de Belém
BELÉM

N

1

Appropriately, **Vasco da Gama's tomb** now lies just inside the fantastically embellished entrance to the church. Crowned by an elaborate medley of statues, including Henry the Navigator, the 32m-high entrance was designed by the Spaniard João de Castilho, who took over the building of the church in 1517; the portal now forms the obligatory backdrop to weekend wedding photos. The church's interior is even more dazzling, displaying the maritime influences typical of Manueline architecture: the pillars are carved to resemble giant palms fanning out into a ceiling resembling a delicate jungle canopy. The church also contains the **tomb of Luís de Camões** (1527–1570), Portugal's greatest poet and recorder of the discoveries, alongside those of former presidents and dignitaries.

Equally impressive is the adjacent monastery, gathered round sumptuously vaulted **cloisters** with nautical symbols carved into the honey-coloured limestone. You can still see the twelve niches where navigators stopped for confession before their voyages of exploration, until the Hieronymite monks were forced out during the dissolution of 1834. In 2007, the monastery was again influential in blessing future trade: the Treaty of Lisbon was signed here to cement the format of the European Union.

Museu de Arqueologia

Praça do Império • Tues–Sun 10am–6pm • €5, free first Sun of the month • ☎ 213 620 016, ⊕ museuarqueologia.pt • Tram #15

The **Museu de Arqueologia** is housed in a neo-Manueline extension to the monastery, added in 1850. It has a small section on Egyptian antiquities, but concentrates on relatively dull Portuguese archeological finds, though there are a few fine Roman mosaics that were discovered in the Algarve, and its temporary exhibits can be rewarding.

Museu da Marinha

Praça do Império • Tues–Sun: May–Sept 10am–6pm; Oct–April 10am–5pm • €6, free first Sun of the month • ☎ 213 620 019, ⊕ museumarinha.pt • Tram #15

With its entrance opposite the Centro Cultural de Belém, the enormous **Museu da Marinha** is large enough to display real vessels – among them fishing boats and sumptuous state barges, a couple of seaplanes and even some fire engines. Fascinating for kids and anyone interested in maritime history, it also houses various models of historical ships and some artefacts from Portugal's former colonies.

Torre de Belém

Jardim da Torre de Belém, off Avenida Brasília • May–Sept Tues–Sun 10am–6.30pm; Oct–May Tues–Sun 10am–5.30pm • €6, free first Sun of the month; combined ticket with Mosteiro dos Jerónimos €12 • ☎ 213 620 034, ⊕ torrebelem.pt

Reached via a narrow walkway and jutting into the river, the impressive **Torre de Belém** (Tower of Belém) has become an iconic symbol of Lisbon. It typifies the Manueline style that was prominent during the reign of Manuel, its windows and stairways embellished with arches and decorative symbols representing Portugal's explorations into the New World. Built as a fortress to defend the mouth of the River Tejo, it took five years to complete, though when it opened in 1520 it would have been near the centre of the river – the earthquake of 1755 shifted the river's course. Today, visitors are free to explore the tower's various levels, which include a terrace facing the river from where artillery would have been fired. You can then climb a very steep spiral staircase up four levels – each with a slightly different framed view of the river – to a top terrace where you get a blowy panorama of Belém. It's also possible to duck into the dungeon, a low-ceilinged room used to store gunpowder and lock up prisoners.

Museu de Arte Popular

Avenida Brasília • Wed–Fri 10am–6pm, Sat & Sun 10am–1pm & 2–6pm • €2.50, free first Sun of the month • ☎ 213 011 282, ⊕ www.map.imc-ip.pt • Tram #15

In a space which feels slightly too large for its exhibits, the charming **Museu de Arte Popular** chronicles Portugal's folk art, from beautiful wood and cork toys to ceramics,

FESTA DE SANTO ANTÓNIO, ALFAMA (P.65) >

1

rugs and fascinating traditional costumes, including amazing cloaks from the Trás-os-Montes region. Black-and-white photos and old films of folk costumes and dances complete the appeal.

Padrão dos Descobrimentos

Avenida Brasília • Daily: March–Sept 9am–7pm; Oct–Feb 10am–6pm • €4 • ☎ 213 031 950, ⊕ padraodosdescobrimentos.pt • Tram #15

You can't miss the **Padrão dos Descobrimentos** (Monument to the Discoveries), an angular concrete monument in the shape of a caravel. It was built in 1960 to commemorate the 500th anniversary of the death of Henry the Navigator, whose statue stands at the front of the monument, alongside other Portuguese legends. Inside is a temporary exhibition space, though you'll probably just head up in the lift to the top for some fine views of the river, and to look down on the giant marble mosaic map of the world that has been set into the pavement below.

Centro Cultural de Belém

Praça do Império • ☎ 213 612 400, ⊕ ccb.pt • Tram #15

Built to host Lisbon's Presidency of the European Union in 1992, with a stylish pink marble facade, **Centro Cultural de Belém** is one of the city's main cultural centres and is home to the wonderful **Berardo Collection**, as well as putting on regular cultural exhibitions and concerts, plus live entertainment at the weekend.

Berardo Collection

Centro Cultural de Belém, Praça do Império • Daily 10am–7pm • Free • ☎ 213 612 878, ⊕ museuberardo.com • Tram #15

With its entrance via the first floor of the Centro Cultural de Belém, the **Berardo Collection** is a unique assortment of modern art amassed by wealthy Madeiran Joe Berardo. Some of the most celebrated artists of the current and last centuries are displayed, though note that the collection is so large that not all of it can be shown at once, and two floors are given over to temporary exhibits. The best parts of the permanent collection (some of which should be on display) include Eric Fischl's giant panels of sunbathers; Andy Warhol's distinctive *Judy Garland*; and Chris Ofili's *Adoration of Captain Shit*, made with elephant dung. Portugal's Paula Rego is well represented, with works such as *The Past and Present* and *The Barn*, while Francis Bacon, David Hockney, Picasso, Miró, Man Ray, Max Ernst and Mark Rothko usually feature, along with various video artists.

Jardim do Ultramar and the Presidência da República

Jardim Entrance on Calçada do Galvão • Daily: May–Aug 10am–8pm; Sept–April 10am–dusk • €2 • ☎ 213 609 660, ⊕ iict.pt • **President's Palace** Entrance on Praça Afonso de Albuquerque • Tours Sat 10.30am–4.30pm • €5 • ⊕ museu.presidencia.pt • Tram #15

The leafy **Jardim do Ultramar** is a green oasis with hothouses, ponds and towering palms, a lovely place for a shady walk. In the southeastern corner of the garden lies the Portuguese President's official residence, the pink **Presidência da República**, which is open for guided visits at weekends, when the public can look round its lavish state rooms.

Museu dos Coches

Museu dos Coches Avenida das India 136 • Tues–Sun 10am–6pm • €6, free first Sun of the month; combined ticket with Royal Riding School €8 • **Royal Riding School** Praça Afonso de Albuquerque Tues–Sun 10am–6pm • €4, free first Sun of the month; combined ticket with Museu dos Coches €8 • ☎ 210 732 319, ⊕ museudoscoches.pt • Tram #15

Housed in a vast contemporary building, the **Museu dos Coches** (Coach Museum) contains one of the world's largest collections of carriages and saddlery, including a rare sixteenth-century coach designed for King Felipe I. Heavily gilded, ornate and often beautifully painted, the royal carriages, sedan chairs and children's cabriolets, dating from the sixteenth to nineteenth centuries, make a sharp contrast to the stark modern building, which gives great views over Belém and the river.

More coaches from the collection are on display in the former **Royal Riding School** across the road, though they're not really worth the additional entrance fee.

1

Museu da Electricidade

Avenida de Brasília • Tues–Sun 10am–6pm • Free, except for temporary exhibits • ☎ 213 028 130 • Tram #15

Down by the riverside, the extraordinary redbrick **Museu da Electricidade** is an early twentieth-century electricity generating station with cathedral-like windows. The museum's highlights include its enormous original generators, steam turbines and winches – all looking like something out of a science-fiction film. It also makes a fascinating backdrop for regular temporary exhibitions.

Museum of Art, Architecture and Technology

Avenida de Brasília • Ⓦ maat.pt • Tram #15

The impressively futuristic building alongside the Museu da Electricidade is the **Museum of Art, Architecture and Technology**, designed by British architect Amanda Levete in a spaceship-like form that allows you to walk across the top of the curved roof to enjoy some great views over the river. The building had not yet opened to the public at the time of writing, but will host a range of temporary exhibitions presenting the relationship between art, architecture and technology; visit the website for updates and admission information.

Palácio Nacional da Ajuda

Largo da Ajuda • Mon, Tues & Thurs–Sun 10am–6pm • €5, free first Sun of the month • Tram #18 from Praça do Comércio, or bus #729 from central Belém or Calçada da Ajuda • ☎ 213 637 095, Ⓦ palacioajuda.pt

The massive nineteenth-century **Palácio Nacional da Ajuda** sits on a hillside above Belém. The Portuguese royal family ordered its construction in 1802, but it was incomplete when they were forced to flee to Brazil during the invasion of Napoleon's troops in 1807. Despite this, Dom João moved into the palace when he returned to Portugal in 1821. Most of what you see today was commissioned by João's granddaughter Dona Maria II and Dom Ferdinand, and gives an eye-popping insight into the opulent life the royals lived: the queen could warm her feet on a polar-bearskin rug when she got out of bed. There's also an enormous throne and ballroom, while the banqueting hall, full of crystal chandeliers, is highly impressive.

Jardim Botânico da Ajuda

Entrances on Calçada da Ajuda and Calçada do Galvão • Daily: May–Sept 9am–8pm; Oct–April 9am–6pm • €2 • Tram #18 from Praça do Comércio, or bus #729 from central Belém • ☎ 213 622 503, Ⓦ jardimbotanicodajuda.com

Opposite the Palácio Nacional da Ajuda, the attractive **Jardim Botânico da Ajuda** is one of the city's oldest botanical gardens. Commissioned by the Marquês de Pombal and laid out in 1768, it was owned by the royal family until the birth of the Republic in 1910 and substantially replanted in the 1990s. Today, it's a fine example of formal Portuguese gardening, boasting some great views over Belém.

North Lisbon

On a steep slope to the north of the centre, **Parque Eduardo VII** is the city's main park, whose views and tropical greenhouses make for a pleasant escape from the bustle of the city. Northwest, the **Fundação Calouste Gulbenkian** is Portugal's premier cultural centre, combining one of Europe's richest art collections at the Museu Gulbenkian with Portuguese contemporary art at the Centro de Arte Moderna. Beyond are further attractions at Campo Pequeno's **Praça de Touros** (bullring) and the **Jardim Zoológico**, the city's zoo, which lies around 2km northwest of the Gulbenkian.

Parque Eduardo VII

Park Unrestricted access • Free • **Estufas** Daily: April–Sept 9am–7pm; Oct–March 9am–5pm • €3.10, free Sun 9am–1pm • Ⓜ Parque or Marquês de Pombal

The sloping **Parque Eduardo VII**, with its formally laid-out lawns and shrubs, was named in honour of the British King Edward VII when he visited the city in 1903. Its main

1

attraction is the **Estufas** (hothouses), one *quente* (hot) planthouse and one *fria* (cool), filled with tropical plants, pools, palms and cacti. Beyond the hothouses, the top of the park has a viewing platform with commanding views over the city: you can walk over the grassy hillock beyond (with its olive trees, lake and café) to the Gulbenkian museum (see below).

Fundação Calouste Gulbenkian

Avenida de Berna · ☎ 217 823 000, ⓦ gulbenkian.pt · Ⓜ Praça de Espanha or São Sebastião

The **Fundação Calouste Gulbenkian** is Portugal's foremost cultural organization, the legacy of oil magnate Calouste Gulbenkian (see box below). The centrepiece to his foundation is this purpose-built arts complex, constructed in the late 1960s within neatly landscaped grounds. It hosts concerts, performances and temporary exhibitions (check the website for details), though most people come to see the **Museu Gulbenkian**, where the magnate's amazing art collection includes priceless pieces from around the world, dating from ancient Egyptian times to the late twentieth century. Across the gardens, the **Centro de Arte Moderna José Azeredo Perdigão** has more contemporary art, mostly from Portugal but also featuring international names.

Museu Gulbenkian

Fundação Calouste Gulbenkian, Avenida de Berna · Daily 10am–6pm, last entry 5.30pm · €5, free on Sun, combined ticket with Museu de Arte Moderna €8 · ☎ 217 823 000, ⓦ museu.gulbenkian.pt

The biggest pleasure of a visit to the **Museu Gulbenkian** is the chance it offers to compare and contrast pieces of art from so many places in the world and from so many different periods of history. The diverse collection ranges from ancient Egyptian sculptures to twentieth-century Lalique jewellery, via works by heavyweights such as Manet, Monet, Renoir, Turner and Rembrandt.

You start off in the small **Egyptian room** displaying art from the Old Empire (c.2700 BC) up to the Roman era, followed by the **Greco-Roman room** which features beautifully preserved glassware, jewellery and coins. Then move to the **Eastern Islamic arts** section with its Turkish tiles, mosque lamps, sumptuously illustrated manuscripts and fine carpets, while art from the **Far East** includes Chinese porcelain and stunning fourteenth-century lacquerwork from Japan.

The highlight, however, is the **painting collection** – a kind of romp through some of the best art from the European schools, including Flemish masters from the fifteenth century, Rubens' graphic *The Love of the Centaurs* (1635) and eighteenth-century works by Fragonard, Francesco Guardi and Gainsborough – in particular the stunning *Portrait of Mrs Lowndes-Stone*. The big names of nineteenth- to twentieth-century France (Degas, Millet) are all represented, as are Sargent and Turner: don't miss the latter's vivid *Wreck of a Transport Ship* (1810).

CALOUSTE GULBENKIAN

Calouste Sarkis Gulbenkian was the Roman Abramovich of his era, making his millions from oil but investing in the world's best art rather than footballers. Born of wealthy Armenian parents in Istanbul in 1869, he followed his father into the oil industry and became oil consultant to the Ottoman court. In 1911 he set up the Oil Petroleum Company, raking in five percent of the company's vast profits, most of which he invested in England where he chose to live. During World War II, his Turkish background made him unwelcome in Britain, so Gulbenkian moved to Portugal, which offered him tax-free status and a secure home. By his death in 1955, he had accumulated one of the best **private art collections** in the world. His dying wish was that all his collection should be displayed in one place, and this was granted in 1969 – a century after his birth – with the opening of the **Museu Calouste Gulbenkian**. The museum continues to buy works of art with his funds to this day, much of it for the **Centro de Arte Moderna**, which was opened in 1984.

Leave time, too, to explore the **Sèvres porcelain**, Louis XV and Louis XVI furniture and assorted Italian tapestries and textiles. The final room features the wonderful **Art Nouveau jewellery** of René Lalique (1860–1945); the highlight is the fantastical *Peitoral-libélula* (Dragonfly breastpiece) brooch, half-woman, half-dragonfly, decorated with enamel work, gold, diamonds and moonstones.

Centro de Arte Moderna José Azeredo Perdigão

Entrance on Rua Dr. Nicolau de Bettencourt • Daily 10am–5.45pm • €5, free on Sun, combined ticket with Museu de Arte Moderna €8 • ☎ 217 823 000, ⓦ cam.gulbenkian.pt

The **Centro de Arte Moderna José Azeredo Perdigão** can be reached by walking across the gardens from the Museu Calouste Gulbenkian, via an impressive array of sculptures (including a Henry Moore). Inside, the collection embraces Pop Art, installations and sculpture – some witty, some baffling, but all thought-provoking. Twentieth-century Portuguese artists feature strongly: look out for the Lisbon scenes by **Carlos Botelho** (1899–1982), and **Paula Rego**'s portraits: her *Mãe* is outstanding (see box, p.110). Other big names in Portugal are **Almada Negreiros** (1873–1970), whose self-portrait is set in the café *A Brasileira*; and the Futurist colours of **Amadeu de Sousa Cardoso** (1887–1918). Powerful photos by **Fernando Lemos** also feature, as do pieces from major international artists such as David Hockney and Antony Gormley, though these are sometimes lent to other museums.

Praça de Touros do Campo Pequeno

Campo Pequeno • Stadium visits April–Oct 10am–1pm & 2–7pm; Nov–March 10am–1pm & 2–6pm • €3 • ☎ 217 998 450, ⓦ www.campopequeno.com • Ⓜ Campo Pequeno

Built in 1892, the **Praça de Touros do Campo Pequeno** is an impressive Moorish-style bullring seating nine thousand spectators. Portuguese bullfighting takes place here weekly from Easter to September, though you can look around at other times on stadium visits. Surrounded by a ring of lively cafés and restaurants, the bullring also hosts visiting circuses, concerts and occasional events, while beneath it is an underground shopping and cinema complex. Check the website for events and to buy tickets.

Jardim Zoológico

Praça Marechal Humberto Delgado • **Zoo** Daily: March–Sept 10am–8pm; Oct–Feb 10am–6pm • €19.50, under-12s €14 • **Animax** April–Sept Mon–Thurs & Sun 11am–7pm; Oct–March Sat & Sun 11am–7pm • Free • ☎ 217 232 900, ⓦ zoolisboa.pt • Ⓜ Jardim Zoológico

Opened in 1884, the **Jardim Zoológico** has been greatly improved over recent years and now makes for an enjoyable day out, especially if you have children. There's a small cable car, which offers a fine aerial view of many of the enclosures, a reptile house, a boating lake and various animal "shows" – sea lions, macaws and the like – as further diversions. Just by the entrance, the **Animax** amusement park has further rides to rid parents of a few more euros.

Parque das Nações

☎ 218 919 333, ⓦ portaldasnacoes.pt

The former Expo 98 site, **Parque das Nações** – the Park of Nations – lies on the northeastern fringes of the city, and remains a huge attraction for Lisboetas who come here en masse at weekends – it's also a popular riverfront residential area. The main highlight is the **Oceanário** (Oceanarium), though there are plenty of other attractions, from water gardens to a cable car, as well as bars, shops and restaurants, many overlooking Olivais docks and the 17km-long Vasco da Gama bridge. The park is also home to a couple of venues that host major international bands and sporting events: the **Meo Arena** (aka **Pavilhão Atlântico** or Atlantic Pavilion) is Portugal's largest indoor arena; while the elegant **Pavilhão de Portugal** (Portugal Pavilion), with its distinctive, sagging concrete roof, is a multipurpose arena designed by Álvaro Siza Vieira, Portugal's best-known architect.

1

GETTING TO THE PARQUE DAS NAÇÕES

Both the metro and bus #728 from Praça do Comércio leave you in the **Estação do Oriente**, an impressive glass-and-concrete bus and train interchange designed by Spanish architect Santiago Calatrava. From the station, head through the Vasco da Gama shopping centre to the riverfront attractions. The park's website (☎ 218 919 333, ☼ portaldasnacoes.pt) has details of current events.

Oceanário de Lisboa

Esplanada Dom Carlos I • Daily: May–Sept 10am–8pm; Oct–April 10am–6pm • €14, under-12s €9, family ticket €36 • ☎ 218 917 000, ☼ oceanario.pt

Designed by Peter Chermayeff and resembling a set from a James Bond film, the **Oceanário de Lisboa** is one of Europe's biggest and best oceanariums, containing around eight thousand fish and marine animals. Its main feature is the enormous central tank, the size of four Olympic-sized swimming pools, which you can look into from different levels to get close-up views of the sharks and rays. Perhaps even more impressive are the recreations of various ocean ecosystems, such as the Antarctic tank containing frolicking penguins, and the Pacific tank, where otters bob about and play in the rock pools. These areas are separated from the main tank by invisible acrylic sheets, which give the impression that all the marine creatures are swimming together in the same space. On the darkened lower level, smaller tanks contain shoals of brightly coloured tropical fish and other warm-water creatures. Find a window free of the school parties and the whole experience becomes the closest you'll get to deep-sea diving without getting wet.

Pavilhão do Conhecimento Ciência Viva

Alameda dos Oceanos • Tues–Fri 10am–6pm, Sat & Sun 11am–7pm, last entry 1hr before closing • €8, under 17s €5 • ☎ 218 917 104, ☼ pavconhecimento.pt

The **Pavilhão do Conhecimento Ciência Viva** (Knowledge Pavilion for Live Science) hosts excellent temporary exhibitions on subjects such as 3D animation and the latest computer technology, and is usually bustling with school parties. The permanent interactive exhibits – such as creating a vortex in water, a film of detergent the size of a baby's blanket or immobilizing shadows – are particularly good.

The Teleférico

Daily: June to mid-Sept 10.30am–8pm; mid-Sept to Oct & mid-March to May 11am–7pm; Nov to mid-March 11am–6pm • €4 one-way, €6 return

The ski-lift-style **Teleférico** cable car rises up to 20m as it shuttles you across Olivais docks, with commanding views of the Parque das Nações en route. The south end starts near the **Jardins da Água** (Water Gardens), crisscrossed by ponds linked by stepping stones, with enough fountains, water gadgets and pumps to keep kids occupied for hours. The northern end drops you just beyond the **Jardim Garcia de Orta**, a leafy waterside garden displaying plant species from Portugal's former colonies. The garden is overlooked by the **Torre Vasco da Gama**, Lisbon's tallest structure at 145m, which was once part of an oil refinery and now houses the *Myriad Sana* hotel, Lisbon's answer to Dubai's *Burj Al Arab*.

ARRIVAL AND DEPARTURE	LISBON

BY AIR

The airport (☎ 218 413 700, ☼ ana.pt) lies around 9km north of the city centre and has a tourist office (daily 7am–midnight; ☎ 218 450 660), ATMs, 24-hour exchange bureau and car rental agencies.

GETTING TO/FROM THE CENTRE

By taxi The easiest way into the city centre is by taxi and, depending on traffic conditions, a journey to Rossio should take around 20min and cost €12–15, plus €2.50 extra for baggage: note that fares are slightly higher between 10pm and 6am, at weekends and on public holidays. The tourist office at the airport sells taxi vouchers, priced according to the zone or destination you are travelling to. The vouchers allow you to jump the airport taxi queue, but otherwise cost more than a metered ride.

By metro Aeroporto station is at the far end of the red Oriente metro line. To get to the city centre (around 25min;

1

PARQUE DAS NAÇÕES

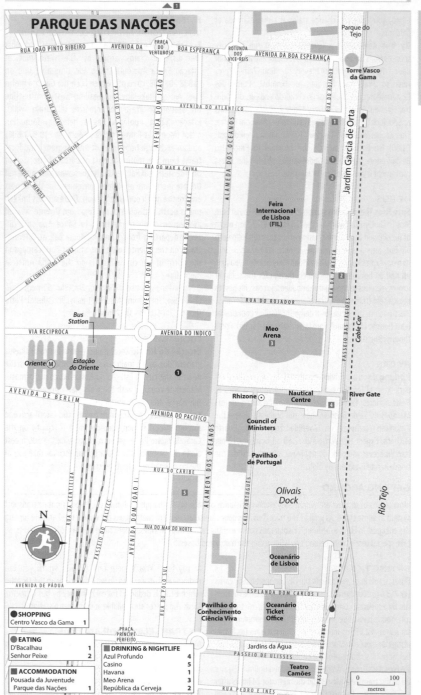

RUA JOÃO PINTO RIBEIRO   AVENIDA DA   PRAÇA DO VENTUROSO   BOA ESPERANÇA   ROTUNDA DOS VICE-REIS   AVENIDA DA BOA ESPERANÇA

Parque do Tejo

Torre Vasco da Gama

ESTRADA DE MOSCAVIDE

PASSEIO DO CANÁRICO

AVENIDA DOM JOÃO II

AVENIDA DO ATLÂNTICO

RUA DO ROJADOR

Jardim Garcia de Orta

R. MANUEL DR. RUI GOMES DE OLIVEIRA

RUA DO MAR A CHINA

ALAMEDA DOS OCEANOS

RUA DO POLO NORTE

Feira Internacional de Lisboa (FIL)

RUA MENDES

RUA CONSELHEIRO LOPO VEZ

RUA DA PIMENTA

RUA DO ROJADOR

Cable Car

PASSEIO DAS TÁGIDES

Bus Station

VIA RECÍPROCA

AVENIDA DO ÍNDICO

Meo Arena

Oriente (M)   Estação do Oriente

1

AVENIDA DE BERLIM

AVENIDA DOM JOÃO II

AVENIDA DO PACÍFICO

Rhizone ⊙

Nautical Centre

River Gate

AVENIDA DE BERLIM

Council of Ministers

Pavilhão de Portugal

RUA DO CARIBE

ALAMEDA DOS OCEANOS

CAIS PORTUGUÊS

Olivais Dock

Rio Tejo

RUA DA CENTIEIRA

5

AVENIDA DOM JOÃO II

RUA DO MAR DO NORTE

N

PASSEIO DO BÁLTICO

Oceanário de Lisboa

AVENIDA DE PÁDUA

RUA DO POLO SUL

ESPLANDA DOM CARLOS I

Pavilhão do Conhecimento Ciência Viva

Oceanário Ticket Office

PRAÇA PRÍNCIPE PERFEITO

Jardins da Água

PASSEIO DE ULISSES

PASSEIO DE NEPTUNO

Teatro Camões

RUA PEDRO E INES

● SHOPPING	
Centro Vasco da Gama	1

● EATING	
D'Bacalhau	1
Senhor Peixe	2

■ ACCOMMODATION	
Pousada da Juventude	
Parque das Nações	1

■ DRINKING & NIGHTLIFE	
Azul Profundo	4
Casino	5
Havana	1
Meo Arena	3
República da Cerveja	2

0   100
metres

1

€1.40) you'll need to change trains at either Alameda or Saldanha.

By bus Aerobus (🔵yellowbustours.com) run two city services from the airport; tickets cost €3.50, and are valid all day on city buses. Aerobus #1 (every 20–30min 7am–11pm) runs to Praça do Marquês de Pombal, Praça dos Restauradores, Rossio, Praça do Comércio and Cais do Sodré train station; Aerobus #2 (every 40min 7.30am 11pm) runs to Sete Rios (for the bus station) and to the financial centre. The cheaper local bus #44 (every 10–15min 6am–midnight; €1.80) leaves from outside the terminal to Praça dos Restauradores and Cais do Sodré station, though this is less convenient if you have a lot of luggage.

BY BUS

Sete Rios The main bus station is opposite the zoo at Sete Rios (🔵Jardim Zoológico on the Gaivota line), 2.5km north of Rossio, and has an information office that can help with all bus arrival and departure details (🔵707 223 344, 🔵rede-expressos.pt). You can usually buy tickets if you turn up half an hour or so in advance, though for the summer express services to the Algarve and Alentejo coast it's best to book a seat (through any travel agent) a day in advance.

Destinations Albufeira (6–8 daily; 3hr 10min); Coimbra (at least hourly; 2hr 20min); Faro (5–6 daily; 3hr 45min); Porto (hourly; 3hr 30min).

BY CAR

Parking If you are driving, head straight for an official car park: central locations include the underground ones at Restauradores; Parque Eduardo VII; Parking Berna on Rua Marquês de Sá da Bandeira near the Gulbenkian; and the Amoreiras complex on Avenida Engenheiro Duarte Pacheco. Expect to pay around €2.50 an hour or €12 per day. Wherever you park, do not leave valuables inside: the break-in rate is extremely high.

BY TRAIN

INTERNATIONAL AND LONG-DISTANCE TRAINS

Estação Santa Apolónia All international and most long-distance trains arrive by the waterfront at Estação Santa Apolónia (fares and timetable info on 🔵808 208 208, 🔵cp.pt), which is on the Gaivota metro line; you can take any bus heading west from outside the station to Praça do Comércio (a 15min walk). Estação Santa Apolónia has a helpful information office (Mon–Sat 8am–1pm & 2–4pm; 🔵218 821 606) and an exchange bureau. Most inter-regional and local trains from the south and east of Portugal also stop at Oriente station at Parque das Nações, which is on the red Oriente metro line and more convenient for the airport and for the north or east of Lisbon. There are bus links to towns north and south of the Tejo from Oriente, as well as frequent train connections to Santa Apolónia (all trains departing from Santa Apolónia call at Oriente). Trains on the Oriente route also stop at Entrecampos in the north of the city, which is on the Linha Amarela metro line.

Destinations Coimbra (hourly; 2hr–2hr 50min); Faro (2–3 daily; 3hr 20min); Madrid (1 daily; 9hr 30min); Porto (hourly; 2hr 50min–3hr 20min).

LOCAL TRAINS

Estação do Rossio Local trains – from Sintra or Queluz via Sete Rios, by the main bus station – emerge right in the heart of the city at Estação do Rossio (🔵cp.pt), a mock-Manueline complex with the train platforms an escalator ride above street-level entrance.

Cais do Sodré Services from Cascais and Estoril arrive at the other local station, Cais do Sodré (🔵cp.pt), on the Caravela metro line – you can either walk the 500m east along the waterfront to Praça do Comércio or take any of the buses heading in that direction.

GETTING AROUND

Most places of interest are within easy walking distance of each other, though it's fun to use Lisbon's public transport system at some stage. As well as the tram, bus, *elevador* (funicular), ferry or metro, taxis are widely used and are among the cheapest in Europe. Although Lisbon ranks as one of the safer European cities, it does have its share of pickpockets, so take special care of your belongings when using the metro and buses.

BUYING TICKETS

Buses, trams and *elevadores* in the city are operated by Carris (🔵213 613 000, 🔵transporteslisboa.pt), while the metro is run by a separate company (🔵213 558 457, 🔵metrolisboa .pt). You can just buy a single ticket (*bilhete simples*, €1.80 for buses, €2.85 for trams, or €1.40 for the metro; €3.60 return for most *elevadores*) each time you ride, but it's much better value to buy one of the available travel passes.

Passes A day-pass (*bilhete 1 dia*; €6) allows unlimited travel on buses, trams, *elevadores* and the metro for 24 hours after you first use it – the first time you buy one, you'll also need

to pay for a Viva Viagem card (€0.50) which you can recharge each day or load up with credits for up to €15, after which €1.25 is deducted for each journey by bus or metro. Cards and passes are available at main metro stations.

BY TRAM, ELEVADOR AND BUS

Most trams, buses and *elevadores* run every 10–15min throughout the day, from around 6.30am to midnight: stops are indicated by a sign marked *paragem*, which carries route details.

Trams (*eléctricos*) These run on five routes, trundling round

the city's oldest and steepest streets, and are worth taking for the sheer fun of it. The most famous route is #28, which runs from Martim Moniz to Prazeres: try and get on at either terminal as the most interesting stretch – from São Vicente to the Estrela gardens via the Alfama and the Baixa – has become so popular that standing-room-only is the norm.

Buses (*autocarros*) These run just about everywhere in the Lisbon area, filling in the gaps to reach the more outlying attractions. Clubbers can take advantage of the *Madrugada* ("Dawn Service") night buses, which operate 12.30–5am. Most night services run to and from Cais do Sodré station, including the useful #201 to the docks via Santos.

Elevadores There are three historic funicular railways and one street lift, along with some newer lifts – each known as an *elevador* – which offer quick access up to Lisbon's highest hills and the Bairro Alto (see box, p.72).

BY CAR

Parking Apart from Saturday afternoons and Sundays, when the city is quiet, driving round Lisbon is best avoided, though it can be useful to hire a car to visit outlying sights, such as Sintra. Parking is very difficult in central Lisbon, so it's best to head for one of the central underground car parks (see p.90). Pay-and-display spots on the street get snapped up quickly and some of the local unemployed get by on tips for guiding drivers into empty spots.

BY TAXI

Fares Lisbon's cream-coloured taxis are inexpensive, as long as your destination is within the city limits; there's a minimum charge of €2 and an average ride across town will cost €8–13. Fares are twenty percent higher from 10pm to 6am, at weekends and on public holidays. All taxis have meters, which should be switched on, and tips are not expected.

Taxi ranks Outside the rush hour taxis can be hailed quite easily in the street, or alternatively head for a taxi rank, found outside the stations, at Rossio and at the southern end of Avenida da Liberdade – you can expect to queue during morning and evening rush hours. At night, your best bet is to ask a restaurant or bar to call a cab for you, or phone yourself (€1 extra): try Rádio Taxis (☎ 218 119 000); Cooptáxis (☎ 217 932 756); or Teletáxi (☎ 218 111 100).

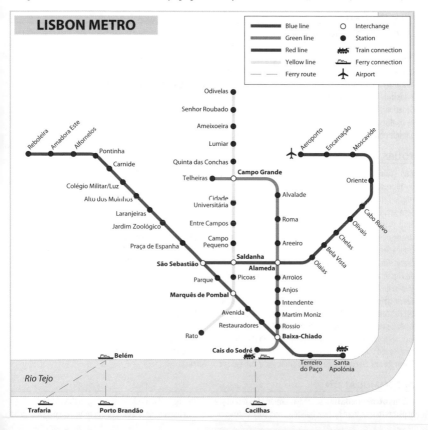

1

TRAM ROUTES

#12 Runs from Praça da Figueira to Largo Martim Moniz via the Alfama.
#15 A modern "supertram" from Praça da Figueira to Algés via Belém; buy tickets in advance or take exact change for automatic ticket machines.
#18 Runs from Cais do Sodré to the Palácio da Ajuda via Santos, Alcântara.
#25 Runs from Praça da Figueira to Campo Ourique via Cais do Sodré, Santos, Lapa and Estrela.
#28 Runs from Largo Martim Moniz to Prazeres, via the Alfama, Baixa, Chiado, São Bento and Estrela.

BY METRO AND LOCAL TRAIN

Metro The most central of Lisbon's metro (Metropolitano) stations are those at Restauradores, Rossio and Baixa-Chiado. The metro is the quickest way to reach outlying sights, including the airport, the Gulbenkian museum, the zoo, bus station and the Oceanarium. Services run daily from 6.30am to 1am.

Local trains The local train line from Cais do Sodré station runs west along the coast to Estoril and Cascais (€2.65 to either). Other local trains depart from the central Rossio station to Queluz (€1.55 one-way) and Sintra (€2.65 one-way).

BY FERRY

Ferries (**w** transtejo.pt) cross the Rio Tejo at various points, offering terrific views of Lisbon. The most useful and picturesque route is from Cais do Sodré to Cacilhas (every 15min; daily 5.20am–1.20am; €1.20). Another attractive route runs from Belém to Porto Brandão and Trafaria (roughly every 1hr; Mon–Fri 6.30am–9.40pm, Sat–Sun 8am–9.10pm; €1.15), from where you can catch buses to Caparica.

INFORMATION

Lisbon Welcome Centre The main Lisbon tourist office, the Lisbon Welcome Centre, is down by the riverfront in Praça do Comércio (daily 9am–8pm; **☎** 210 312 810, **w** visitlisboa.com) and can supply accommodation lists, bus timetables and maps.

Y Lisboa The Y Lisboa tourist office on Rua Jardim do Regedor 50 (daily 10am–7pm; **☎** 213 472 134, **w** visitlisboa.com), to the east of Praça dos Restauradores, has information aimed at young and student travellers.

"Ask Me" In summer, small "Ask Me" kiosks are dotted round town near the main tourist sights, such as on Rua Augusta, Baixa, and opposite Belém's Mosteiro dos Jerónimos (daily 10am–7pm).

Portuguese tourist board On the western side of Praça dos Restauradores in the Palácio da Foz, the main Portuguese tourist board (daily 9am–8pm; **☎** 213 463 314, **w** visitportugal.com) is useful for information on destinations outside Lisbon.

TOURS

Bus tours Yellow Bus (**☎** 213 478 030, **w** yellow bustours.com) operates two hop-on, hop-off open-top bus trips on circular routes: the two-hour Circuito Tejo (June–Sept every 15min from 9am–6pm; Oct–May every 20min from 9am–5.30pm; €16) visits Lisbon's main sites, with clearly marked stops across the city; while the Olisipo tour (June–Sept every 30min from 9.15am–7.15pm; Oct–May every 30min from 9.15am–5.45pm; €16) runs from Praça da Figueira to Parque das Nações via the Alfama and the Museu do Azulejo.

River trips Lisbon by Boat (**☎** 933 924 740, **w** lisbon byboat.com), alongside the Padrão dos Descobrimentos in Belém, offers various rides on rigid inflatable boats (RIBs), including 60min trips to below the Alfama (€35) or 40min high-speed tours (€40).

Tram tours Eléctrico das Colinas (Hills Tour; June–Sept every 25min from 9.30am–7pm; Oct–May every 30min 9.30am–5.30pm; €19; **☎** 213 478 030, **w** yellowbustours .com) takes passengers on a 1hr 20min ride in an antique tram from Praça do Comércio, around Alfama, Chiado and Bairro Alto.

Walks Highly recommended, themed two-hour guided walks are offered by Lisbon Walker (**☎** 218 861 840, **w** lisbonwalker.com; €20). Departing daily from Praça do Comércio at 10am (also March–Oct Fri 2.30pm), they give expert insight into the quirkier aspects of the city's sights including legends, secret histories and spies.

Tuk-tuk tours Departing from outside the Sé cathedral and Sintra train station, various companies offer tours (around €40/hr) in three-wheeled tuk-tuks that can negotiate the steep and narrow streets around the Alfama.

ACCOMMODATION

Lisbon's **accommodation** scene has exploded in recent years, with a host of new places opening, so there is no shortage of places to stay, from historic buildings and palaces to some excellent independent **hostels**. There are real bargains to be

had in the off-season, though between June and September, prices are at their highest and it's advisable to make an **advance reservation** to ensure you get a room. Many of Lisbon's top **hotels** are lined up along and around the Avenida da Liberdade, while the Baixa and the Chiado also have a fair selection of more upmarket places which could not be more central. The most atmospheric part of town is around the Alfama and the castle, while the Bairro Alto is ideal for nightlife, but can be noisy after dark.

BAIXA AND CHIADO

Borges Rua Garrett 108 ☎ 213 461 951, ⓦhotelborges .com; ⓜBaixa-Chiado; map p.63. This is a traditional three-star hotel in a great position for Chiado's shops and cafés. Double or triple rooms are plain and small but good value, though the place often fills with tour groups. **€110**

★**Chiado** Rua Nova do Almada 114 ☎213 256 100, ⓦhoteldochiado.pt; ⓜBaixa-Chiado; map p.63. Stylish hotel designed by Álvaro Siza Vieira – the architect responsible for the Chiado redevelopment – with Eastern-inspired interior decor. The cheapest rooms lack much of a view, but the best have terraces with stunning castle vistas, a view you get from the bar terrace, too. Rooms are not huge but are plush and contemporary. Limited parking available. **€175**

Florescente Rua das Portas de Santo Antão 99 ☎ 213 426 609, ⓦresidencialflorescente.com; ⓜRestauradores; map p.63. One of the best-value options on this pedestrianized street: rooms are spick-and-span and come with TV, a/c and small bathroom. Some rooms are windowless and less appealing, and be prepared for street noise too. **€85**

Gerês Calç. da Garcia 6 ☎ 218 810 497; ⓜRossio; map p.63. The beautifully tiled entrance hall sets the tone in one of the city's more atmospheric central guesthouses, located on a steep side-street just off the Rossio. The variously sized rooms are simply furnished and all have TVs and showers. No breakfast. **€45**

Insulana Rua da Assunção 52 ☎213 427 625, ⓦinsulana.net; ⓜBaixa-Chiado; map p.63. On the top floor of an old Baixa building, above a series of shops, this decent guesthouse has slightly faded en suite rooms with satellite TV. The bar overlooks a pedestrianized street. **€65**

Lisboa Tejo Rua dos Condes de Monsanto 2 ☎ 218 866 182, ⓦlisboatejohotel.com; ⓜRossio; map p.63. This historic Baixa townhouse has been given a sleek makeover, and now combines bare brickwork with cutting-edge design. Wood-floored rooms aren't huge but come with minibars, and downstairs is a boutiquey, Gaudí-inspired bar. Front-facing rooms can be noisy. **€91**

Metrópole Rossio 30 ☎213 219 030, ⓦmetropole -lisbon.com; ⓜRossio; map p.63. Centrally located early twentieth-century hotel, with most of the comfortable rooms (as well as the airy lounge bar) offering superb views over Rossio and the castle. However, the square can be pretty noisy at night. **€135**

VIP Executive Éden Pr dos Restauradores 24 ☎213 216 600, ⓦviphotels.com; ⓜRestauradores; map p.63. Compact studios and apartments sleeping up to four people, in the impressively converted Eden Theatre. Get a ninth-floor apartment with a balcony and you'll have the best views and be just below the rooftop pool and break-fast bar. All studios come with dishwashers, microwaves and satellite TV. Disabled access. Studios **€95**

ALFAMA AND CASTELO

The Keep Costa do Castelo 74 ☎218 854 070; tram #12; map p.66. Beautifully sited, simple guesthouse with a view-laden terrace garden on the street looping around the castle – this is one of the most popular budget options in Lisbon, so book well in advance. Climb up the staircase to the main entrance. Rooms are bright but spartan, though avoid the dingy basement room. Those with a private bath cost €15 more. No breakfast. **€60**

★**Memmo Alfama** Trav das Merceeiras 27 ☎210 495 660, ⓦmemmoalfama.com; tram #28; map p.66. Sleek boutique hotel, hidden behind the facade of a former house, paint factory and bakery. Parts of the ground floor contain the old brick ovens, though the real appeal is the bar and outdoor terraces at the back, complete with small plunge pool, offering sumptuous views over the Alfama and boats plying the Tagus. Rooms are compact and lack much storage space, but have all mod cons; most boast fine views. **€180**

Solar do Castelo Rua das Cozinhas 2 ☎218 806 050, ⓦheritage.pt; bus #737 from Pr da Figueuria; map p.66. Boutique hotel in a historic eighteenth-century mansion, abutting the castle walls on the site of the former palace kitchens. Just fourteen bright, modern rooms cluster round

---

THE CARTÃO LISBOA

If you're planning some serious sightseeing, consider buying a **Cartão Lisboa** (Lisbon Card; €18.50 for one day, €31.50 for two, or €39 for three; ⓦlisboacard.org), which entitles you to unlimited rides on the city's buses, trams, metro and *elevadores*, plus entry to around 25 museums, including the Gulbenkian and Museu de Arte Antigua, as well as discounts of around 25 to 50 percent at other sights and attractions. It's available from all the main tourist offices, including the one in the airport.

1

> **OUR FIVE FAVOURITE PLACES TO STAY**
>
> **Best views**: *Memmo Alfama* (see p.93)   **Retro chic**: *Heritage Avenida* (see p.94)
> **Boutique**: *Chiado* (see p.93)   **Eco-friendly**: *Inspira Santa Marta* (see
> **Budget**: *Travellers House* (see p.95)   p.95)

a tranquil Moorish courtyard, where breakfast is served in summer. **€140**

Solar dos Mouros Rua do Milagre de Santo António 6 ☎ 218 854 940, ⓦ solardosmouros.com; bus #737 from Pr da Figueria; map p.66. A tall, beautifully renovated townhouse done out in a contemporary style, with its own bar. Each of the twelve rooms offers superb views of the river or castle and comes with DVD player and a/c. There's plenty of modern art to enjoy if you tire of the view. Breakfast extra. **€100**

BAIRRO ALTO AND AROUND

Belver Príncipe Real Rua da Alegria 53 ☎ 213 407 350, ⓦ hotelprincipereal.com; bus #758 from Cais do Sodré; map pp.74–75. This small four-star sits on a quiet street just below the Bairro Alto. Just eighteen rooms, each with modern decor and some with balconies – the best ones boast superb city views. If your budget can stretch, go for the top-floor suite with stunning vistas (€180). **€100**

Casa de São Mamede Rua da Escola Politécnica 159 ☎ 213 963 166, ⓦ casadesaomamede.pt; bus #758 from Cais do Sodré; map pp.74–75. On a busy road, this superb seventeenth-century townhouse comes with period fittings, a bright breakfast room and even a grand stained-glass window. The rooms are rather ordinary but all have TV and a/c. Ask about special deals for families. **€90**

Globo Rua do Teixeira 37 ☎ 213 462 279, ⓦ blueangelhotel.com; bus #758 from Cais do Sodré; map pp.74–75. Located in an attractive townhouse with a bar/TV room. The budget rooms are simple but clean and reasonably large (though those at the top are a little cramped and some have no windows). The best rooms have showers and views. No breakfast. **€40**

Independente Hostel and Suites Rua de São Pedro de Alcântara 81 ☎ 213 461 381, ⓦ theindependente .pt; bus #758 from Cais do Sodré; map pp.74–75. Part hostel and part boutique hotel, this fantastic old building was once the Socialist Party HQ and Swiss Embassy and has far-reaching views over Lisbon. The lower floors house dorms (sleeping 6–12), each with towering ceiling, while up the light internal stairwell there are quirky double rooms in the roof spaces, the best with balconies offering river views. There's a downstairs bar and patio and a range of activities, from bar crawls and guided walks to cycle hire. The "Suites" element is in the building next door, offering larger rooms (€125), a library and a hip roof-terrace bar. Dorms **€15**; doubles **€125**

Londres Rua D. Pedro V 53 ☎ 213 462 203, ⓦ pensaolondres.com.pt; bus #758 from Cais do Sodré; map pp.74–75. This wonderful old building has soaring ceilings and a wide range of pleasant rooms with satellite TV, spread across four floors; the best have their own showers (€75), while rooms 402, 409 or 411 have fine city views. Also has rooms sleeping three or four. **€45**

LX Boutique Rua do Alecrim 12 ☎ 213 474 394, ⓦ lxboutiquehotel.pt; ⓜ Cais do Sodré; map pp.74–75. A tasteful makeover of an old townhouse has made *LX Boutique* into a popular small hotel with its own chic restaurant. The floors are named after Portuguese poets and fado singers, and the rooms are stylish and individual, with shutters and tasteful lighting – try and get one with river views rather than looking over the nightlife hub of Rua Nova do Carvalho. **€110**

AVENIDA DA LIBERDADE AND AROUND

Alegria Pr Alegria 12 ☎ 213 220 670, ⓦ alegrianet .com; ⓜ Avenida; map pp.74–75. A friendly, simple place in a great position, on a leafy square (and next to a police station). The spacious, brightly coloured rooms all have TV, but expect some street noise. No breakfast. **€78**

Britania Rua Rodrigues Sampaio 17 ☎ 213 155 016, ⓦ heritage.pt; ⓜ Avenida; map pp.60–61. Designed in the 1940s by influential architect Cassiano Branco, this is an Art Deco gem with huge airy rooms, each with traditional cork flooring and marble-clad bathroom. The hotel interior, with library and bar, has been declared of national architectural importance – and the service is friendly and pleasant too. Breakfast extra. **€175**

Casa Amora Rua João Penha 13 ☎ 919 300 317, ⓦ casaamora.com; ⓜ Rato; map pp.60–61. This lovingly renovated townhouse lies close to the picturesque Praça das Amoreiras. There are five tastefully furnished rooms in the main house and six larger studios (from €145) in a separate building, which are suitable for families. There's also an attractive outdoor patio. **€135**

Dom Carlos Parque Av Duque de Loulé 121 ☎ 213 512 590, ⓦ hoteldomcarlospark.com; ⓜ Marquês de Pombal; map pp.60–61. This is a decent three-star option in a good position near the park, with fair-sized rooms, all with bath, cable TV and minibar. There's also a downstairs bar screening sports events in big TVs. Garage parking. **€96**

★ Heritage Avenida Av da Liberdade 28 ☎ 213 404 040, ⓦ heritage.pt; ⓜ Restauradores; map pp.74–75. In a superb mansion, this hotel blends traditional and contemporary style. Though the dining area/bar is small

(and the gym/plunge pool even smaller), the spruce rooms more than compensate, with tiled bathrooms, retro taps and great cityscapes from those on the top floor. **€148**

★ **Inspira Santa Marta** Rua de Santa Marta 48 ☎ 210 440 900, ⓦ inspirahotels.com; ⓜ Avenida; map pp.60–61. The facade of a traditional townhouse hides a modern boutique hotel which boasts impressive green credentials, including low-energy lighting and recycled or local products. Feng shui-designed rooms are compact but comfy with glass-wall showers and – unusually for Lisbon – coffee-making facilities and free minibars. There are also spa facilities, a games room, stylish restaurant and bar. **€125**

Lisboa Plaza Trav Salitre 7 ☎ 213 218 218, ⓦ heritage .pt; ⓜ Avenida; map pp.60–61. Part of the small, local, highly recommended Heritage chain, whose hotels are all in beautifully renovated historic buildings, this is a tasteful, understated former family home with marble bathrooms, bar and a fashionable rooftop terrace, a short walk from the main Avenida. Friendly staff and good for families. Limited disabled access. **€110**

LAPA

As Janelas Verdes Rua das Janelas Verdes 47 ☎ 213 968 143, ⓦ heritage.pt; bus #727, #760 or tram #25 from Pr do Comércio; map pp.60–61. This discreet eighteenth-century townhouse is just metres from the Museu Nacional de Arte Antiga. It has well-proportioned rooms with marble-clad bathrooms and period furnishings, and a delightful walled garden with a small fountain where breakfast is served in summer. The top-floor library and terrace have stunning river views. **€130**

York House Rua das Janelas Verdes 32 ☎ 213 962 435, ⓦ yorkhouselisboa.com; bus #727, #760 or tram #25 from Pr do Comércio; map pp.60–61. Located in a sixteenth-century Carmelite convent (and hidden from the main street by high walls), the rooms here are chic and minimalist. The best are grouped around a beautiful interior courtyard, where drinks and meals are served in summer, and there's a highly rated restaurant. **€120**

NORTH LISBON

Avenida Park Av Sidónio Pais 6 ☎ 213 532 181, ⓦ avenidapark.com; ⓜ Parque; map pp.60–61. A pleasantly old-fashioned hotel, but with good-sized rooms – beg for one with a view over the park for no extra

price – on a quiet street. There's no bar but price includes a generous breakfast. **€90**

Sheraton Lisboa Rua Latino Coelho 1 ☎ 213 120 000, ⓦ sheratonlisboa.com; ⓜ Picoas; map pp.60–61. The 1970s high-rise is something of an icon in this part of Lisbon and is now a mecca for those seeking five-star spa facilities. Its dated exterior hides some very modern attractions including a heated outdoor pool, swanky rooms and a spectacular top-floor bar and restaurant – dubbed Lisbon's eighth hill, it commands the best views of the city you'll find outside a plane. **€150**

HOSTELS

Lisbon Lounge Hostel Rua de São Nicolau 13–4° ☎ 218 885 312, ⓦ lisbonloungehostel.com; ⓜ Rossio; map p.63. Understandably popular independent hostel in a great old Baixa townhouse full of stripped floorboards and comfy sofas. There's an airy lounge, communal kitchen and laundry service. Dorms sleep four, six or eight, and there are some twin-bed rooms too. Dorms **€22**; twins **€42**

Oasis Hostel Rua Santa Catarina 24 ☎ 213 478 044, ⓦ oasislisboa.com; ⓜ Baixa-Chiado or tram #28; map pp.74–75. In a lovely old townhouse with its own patio garden – complete with palm tree – this welcoming hostel is a stone's throw from the fashionable Miradouro Santa Catarina. Dorms **€24**; doubles **€71**

Pousada da Juventude de Lisboa Rua Andrade Corvo 46 ☎ 213 532 696, ⓦ pousadasjuventude.pt; ⓜ Picoas; map pp.60–61. This is the main city hostel, set in a rambling old building, with a small bar and canteen. There are various dorms sleeping four or six (with shared bathrooms), or doubles with private shower rooms; plus a TV room on the top floor, and breakfast included in the price. Disabled access. Dorms **€17**; doubles **€42**

Pousada da Juventude Parque das Nações Rua de Moscavide 47–101, Parque das Nações ☎ 218 920 890, ⓦ pousadasjuventude.pt; ⓜ Oriente; map p.89. A 5min walk northeast of Parque das Nações, towards the bridge, this well-equipped modern youth hostel has eighteen four-bed dorms and ten double rooms. There's also a pool table and disabled access. Dorms **€17**; doubles **€42**

★ **Travellers House** Rua Augusta 89 ☎ 210 115 922, ⓦ travellershouse.com; ⓜ Baixa-Chiado; map p.63. Right on Lisbon's main pedestrianized street, this award-winning independent hostel has a wonderful

---

SELF-CATERING IN LISBON

There are several fine options for **self-catering accommodation** in Lisbon. As well as ⓦ airbnb .com, good first points of call are ⓦ fadoflats.pt, with places mostly in Chiado and Alfama; ⓦ castleinnlisbon.com, which has apartments right by the castle; or ⓦ travellershouse.com, a hostel which also has four attractive apartments near Elevador da Lavra. The upmarket *Martinhal Chiado* (ⓦ martinhal.com) is an apartment block in the Chiado district geared towards families.

1

high-ceilinged communal lounge, filled with comfy bean bags, and a DVD room. Simple dorms but very comfy doubles. Dorms €26; doubles €80

CAMPSITE
Lisboa Camping Estrada da Circunvalação, Parque Florestal de Monsanto ☎217 628 200,

w lisboacamping.com; bus #714 from Pr da Figueira via Belém; map p.58. The main city campsite – with disabled facilities, restaurants, a swimming pool and shops – is 6km west of the city centre, in the expansive hilltop Parque de Monsanto. The entrance is on the park's west side. Though the campsite is secure, take care in the park after dark. Open all year. Pitch €23

EATING

Lisbon has some of the best-value cafés and restaurants of any European city, serving large portions of good Portuguese food at sensible prices. A **set menu** (*ementa turística*) at lunch or dinner will get you a three-course meal for around €15, though you can eat for even less by sticking to the ample main dishes and choosing the daily specials. **Seafood** is widely available – there's an entire central street, Rua das Portas de Santo Antão, that specializes in it. Options for **vegetarians** are somewhat limited, though *Tão* (see p.98) and *Terra* (see p.99) are worth seeking out. Indian and Chinese restaurants also offer good vegetarian options, as do some of the museum cafés, such as at the Centro de Arte Moderna at the Gulbenkian.

CAFÉS
Lisbon's cafés are its pride and joy, ranging from atmospheric turn-of-the-twentieth-century artists' haunts to Art Deco wonders. The cafés listed below are good for breakfast, coffee and cakes or just a beer during the afternoon; some also serve lunch – expect to eat well for under €12 for a main course and a drink..

BAIXA AND CHIADO
A Brasileira Rua Garrett 120 ☎213 469 547; m Baixa-Chiado; map p.63. Opened in 1905 and marked by a bronze of Fernando Pessoa outside, this is the most famous of Rua Garrett's old-style coffee houses – its outside tables are usually packed. Livens up at night with a more youthful clientele swigging beer outside until 2am, though the attractive interior is its real appeal. Daily 8am–2am.
Benard Rua Garrett 104 ☎211 373 133; m Baixa-Chiado; map p.63. Often overlooked because of its proximity to the better-known *A Brasileira*, this traditional café has an equally ornate interior and an outdoor terrace on Chiado's most fashionable street. It also serves superb cakes, ice cream and coffees. Mon–Sat 8am–11pm.
Confeitaria Nacional Pr da Figueira 18 ☎213 424 470; m Rossio; map p.63. Opened in 1829 and little-changed since, with a stand-up counter selling pastries and sweets below a mirrored ceiling. There's a small side room for sit-down coffees and snacks, and a few outdoor tables. Daily 8am–8pm.
Leitaria Académica Largo do Carmo 1–3 ☎213 469 092; m Baixa-Chiado; map p.63. Take a table in one of the city's nicest, quietest squares, outside the ruined Carmo church. Good for drinks, it also does light lunches. Mon–Sat 7am–11pm.
Martinho da Arcada Pr do Comércio 3 ☎218 879 259; m Terreiro do Paço; map p.63. Beautiful café-restaurant beneath the arches, little-changed from the beginning of the twentieth century when it was frequented by the writer Fernando Pessoa. The restaurant is somewhat

formal, but you can always just call in for a coffee and *pastel de nata* in the attached stand-up café, or have less formal lunches at the outdoor tables. Mon–Sat 7am–11pm.
Nicola Rossio 24–25 ☎213 460 579; m Rossio; map p.63. A former haunt of Lisbon's literary figures, dating back to the seventeenth century, this grand old place is a good stop for breakfast. Outdoor seats are always at a premium and it has occasional live fado. Daily 8am–midnight.
Suíça Rossio 96–104 ☎213 214 090; m Rossio; map p.63. Famous for its cakes and pastries; you'll have a hard job getting an outdoor table here, though there's plenty of room inside – the café stretches across to Praça da Figueira, where the best tables are. Daily 7am–9pm.
Vertigo Trav do Carmo 4 ☎213 433 112; m Baixa-Chiado; map p.63. An arty crowd frequents this brick-walled café with an ornate glass ceiling. Occasional art exhibits and a good range of cakes and snacks. Mon–Thurs 11am–7pm, Fri–Sat 11am–midnight.

ALFAMA, CASTELO AND THE EASTERN RIVERFRONT
Deli Deluxe Av Infante D. Henrique, Armazem B, Loja 8 ☎218 862 070; m Santa Apolónia; map pp.60–61. A modern deli with delectable cheeses, cured meats and preserves, though the riverside café at the back is even more appealing. Grab a seat outdoors and enjoy the range of goodies, from croissants to speciality teas, yoghurts, bagels, salads and cocktails. Mon–Fri noon–midnight, Sat–Sun 10am–midnight; closes 10pm Nov–March.
★ **Pois Café** Rua São João da Pr 93–95 ☎218 862 497; tram #28; map p.66. With its big comfy sofas and laidback ambience, walking into this Austrian-run café feels like eating in someone's large front room. A friendly, young crowd, light meals and home-made snacks, including a great *Apfelstrudel*. Mon noon–11pm, Tues–Sun 10am–11pm.

BAIRRO ALTO AND CAIS DO SODRÉ

Esplanada Pr do Príncipe Real ☎213 470 087; bus #758 from Cais do Sodré; map pp.74–75. Glass pavilion in the square with outdoor seats beneath the shady trees. Great for lunch, as it does a good range of salads, tapas and burgers, and inexpensive mains from €8. Daily 9am–11pm.

Tease Rua Nova da Piedade 15 ☎914 447 383, ⓦtease .pt; bus #758 from Cais do Sodré; map pp.74–75. Specializing in amazing cupcakes and chocolate goodies, this hip, tiled café with jazzy sounds also teases your tastebuds with juices, smoothies and inexpensive light lunches such as quiche and salad. Mon–Thurs 9am–9pm, Fri–Sat 9am–11pm.

BELÉM

Antiga Confeitaria de Belém Rua de Belém 84–92 ☎213 637 423; tram #15; map p.81. No visit to Belém is complete without a coffee and hot *pastel de nata* (custard-cream tart) liberally sprinkled with *canela* (cinnamon) in this cavernous, tiled pastry shop and café, which has been serving them up since 1837. Daily 8am–midnight; closes 11pm Oct–May.

NORTH LISBON

A Linha d'Água Jardim Amália Rodrigues, Parque Eduardo VII ☎213 814 327; ⓜSão Sebastião; map pp.60–61. Facing a small lake, this glass-fronted café at the northern end of the park. It's a tranquil spot to sip a coffee or beer, and serves good-value buffet lunches. Daily 10am–2am, closes earlier in winter.

★**Versailles** Av da República 15A ☎213 546 340; ⓜSaldanha; map pp.60–61. One of Lisbon's most traditional cafés, full of bustling waiters circling the starched tablecloths. It's busiest at around 4pm, when Lisbon's best-dressed elderly dames gather for a chat beneath the chandeliers. Daily 7.30am–10pm.

RESTAURANTS

There are hundreds of restaurants in central Lisbon, many serving no-nonsense local food, inexpensive foreign dishes from the former colonies or modern international fare. Note that on Saturday nights you should reserve a table for the more popular places, such as those in the Bairro Alto and Alfama. Restaurants in the Baixa are good for lunch as most have inexpensive set menus aimed at local workers, while Chiado is the upmarket shopping district with some

good places to eat on its fringes. For more upmarket international food, try the *docas* at Alcântara with its range of fashionable restaurants, most facing the river, or the riverfront Passeio das Tágides out at Parque das Nações, with its long line of moderately priced bars and restaurants specializing in international cuisine.

BAIXA

★**Beira Gare** Pr D. João de Câmara 4 ☎213 420 405; ⓜRestauradores; map p.63. Lisbon's version of a fast-food diner is this stand-up or sit-down café-restaurant serving very good-value snacks and full meals from €7. Constantly busy, which is recommendation enough. Daily 9am–10pm.

Bom Jardim/Rei dos Frangos Trav de Santo Antão 11–18 ☎213 424 389; ⓜRestauradores; map p.63. The "King of Chickens" has branches on two sides of an alleyway connecting Restauradores with Rua das Portas de Santo Antão. There are plenty of tables outdoors, too. A tasty spit-roasted half-chicken with chips is yours for around €8, though it also serves other meat and fish dishes for around €9. April–Oct daily noon–11.30pm; Nov–March Mon–Tues & Fri–Sun noon–11.30pm, Thurs 7–11.30pm.

Casa do Alentejo Rua das Portas de Santo Antão 58 ☎213 405 140; ⓜRestauradores; map p.63. The restaurant of this centre dedicated to Alentejan culture (see p.62) has an ornate interior dining room where you can enjoy sound Alentejan dishes such as *carne de porco à alentejana* (grilled pork and clams) from around €11, as well as a downstairs *taberna* serving inexpensive *petiscos* snacks. Daily noon–3pm & 7–10.30pm.

Floresta Santana Calç. Santana 18 ☎963 945 338; ⓜRossio; map p.63. A short (uphill) walk from the bustle of the Baixa but a world away in terms of atmosphere: this friendly, family-run place is very much a local joint, with excellent-value meals. The fish and meat are fresh and generous and desserts are home-made and huge. Two courses with wine should come to under €12. Mon–Sat 10am–11pm.

João do Grão Rua dos Correeiros 222–228 ☎213 424 757; ⓜRossio; map p.63. One of the best in a row of somewhat touristy restaurants on this pedestrianized street, where appealing outdoor tables tempt you to sit down and sample the reasonably priced Portuguese salads, fish and rice dishes. The marble- and *azulejo*-clad interior is just as attractive. Daily noon–11pm.

OUR FIVE FAVOURITE RESTAURANTS

Best views: *Chapitô à Mesa* (see p.98)
Budget: *Beira Gare* (see p.97)
Modern Portuguese: *Cantinho do Avillez* (see p.98)

Quirky: *Mini Bar* (see p.98)
Traditional: *Varina da Madragoa* (see p.99)

1

Lisboeta Pr do Comércio 31–34 ☎210 407 641, ⓦpousadas.pt; ⓜTerreiro do Paço; map p.63. Inside *Lisbon Pousada* hotel, formerly the Ministry for Internal Affairs, the smart but casual *Lisboeta* serves top-notch contemporary Portuguese cuisine. Expect the likes of scallops with champagne, Alentejo black pork or aged beef. Mains from €25. Daily 1–3pm & 7.30–10pm.

Tão Rua dos Douradores 10 ☎218 850 046; ⓜBaixa-Chiado; map p.63. For a healthy buffet lunch, head to this fashionable, very good-value, Eastern-inspired organic restaurant, with meals from around €7. Tasty vegetarian sushi, risottos, grilled aubergines and salads, along with the occasional fish dish. Mon noon–4pm, Tues–Sat noon–4pm & 6.30–9.30pm.

ALFAMA, CASTELO AND THE EASTERN RIVERFRONT

Arco do Castelo Rua do Chão da Feira 25 ☎218 876 598 ⓦarcodocastelo.wix.com/arcodocastelo; bus #737 from Pr da Figueira; map p.66. This cheerful Goan restaurant specializes in dishes from Portugal's former Indian colony, including a tempting shrimp curry, Indian sausage and spicy bean stew. Despite being right opposite the entrance to the castle, it is good value with mains from around €10. Mon–Sat noon–midnight.

Barracão de Alfama Rua de São Pedro 16 ☎218 866 359; tram #28; map p.66. An unpretentious *tasca* popular with locals, and with non-touristy prices: you can have a full meal here for under €15. Portions are generous, with fine fish and grills. Daily 11am–midnight.

Casanova Loja 7 Armazém B, Cais da Pedra à Bica do Sapato ☎218 877 532; ⓦpizzeriacasanova.pai.pt; ⓜSanta Apolónia; map pp.60–61. The bustling *Casanova* offers pizza, pasta and crostini accompanied by fine views from its outside terrace. It's phenomenally popular and you can't book, so turn up early. Around €18 for a full meal. Daily 12.30pm–1.30am.

★**Chapitô à Mesa** Costa do Castelo 7 ☎218 867 734, ⓦchapito.org; bus #737 from Pr da Figueira; map p.66. Multipurpose venue incorporating a theatre, circus school, restaurant and jazz bar. The restaurant is in an upstairs dining room, reached via a spiral staircase, and serves a range of imaginative mains such as mushroom risotto or black pork with ginger from around €16. The outdoor esplanade commands terrific views over Alfama. Restaurant Mon–Fri noon–midnight, Sat & Sun 7.30pm–midnight; bar open until 2am.

Cruzes Credo Rua Cruzes da Sé 29 ☎218 822 296; tram #28; map p.66. This fashionable little café-restaurant has a jazzy ambience and serves tasty *petiscos* snacks and some less usual (for these parts) dishes such as bruschetta, hummus and burgers (€6–8). It's also a tranquil spot for a drink. Daily 10am–2am.

Malmequer-Bemmequer Rua de São Miguel 23–25

☎218 876 535; tram #28; map p.66. Cheerily decorated and moderately priced place, overseen by a friendly owner. You can have charcoal-grilled meat and fish from around €11 – try the *salmão no carvão* (grilled salmon). Tues 7–10pm, Wed–Sun 12.30–3.30pm & 7–10pm.

CHIADO AND CAIS DO SODRÉ

★**Cantinho do Avillez** Rua dos Duques de Bragança 7 ☎211 992 369, ⓦcantinhodoavillez.pt; ⓜBaixa-Chiado or tram #28; map pp.74–75. In a classy space, with tram #28 rattling by its door, this laidback canteen is the place to sample cuisine from Lisbon's top chef, José Avillez, but at affordable prices. Delectable main courses (€17–21) include the likes of scallops with sweet potatoes, and Alentejan black pork with coriander. Mon–Sat 12.30–3pm & 7pm–midnight.

Casa Liege Rua da Bica Duarte Belo 72–74 ☎213 422 794; ⓜBaixa-Chiado; map pp.74–75. Small, basic and bustling *tasca* at the top of the Elevador da Bica, packed at lunchtimes thanks to its filling and inexpensive dishes such as grilled chicken, sausages and fine *pastéis de bacalhau*. Good house wine, too. Mon–Sat 11am–11pm.

★**Mini Bar** Rua António Maria Cardoso 58 ☎211 305 393, ⓦminibar.pt; ⓜBaixa-Chiado; map pp.74–75. There's certainly a theatrical element to the cuisine in this wacky restaurant-bar inside the Art Deco Teatro de São Luis. Various themed tasting menus feature innovative tapas-style dishes (€3–13) including Algarve prawns, tuna and mackerel ceviche, or beef croquettes. Some of top chef José Avillez's creations are decidedly Blumenthalesque, including amazing edible cocktails and "exploding" olives. Highly recommended. Daily 7pm–1am.

Pharmacia Rua Marechal Saldanha 1 ☎213 462 146; tram #28; map pp.74–75. Part of the Pharmaceutical Society and Museum, this traditional building with a terrace on lawns facing the Tejo is a terrific spot for this quirky café-restaurant decked out with retro pharmacy fittings. The speciality here is tapas (from around €7). It also does daily dinner specials, or just pop in for a drink. Tues–Sun 1pm–1am.

Rio Grande Rua Nova do Carvalho 55 ☎213 423 804; ⓜCais do Sodré; map pp.74–75. It might be on a street full of hip bars, but *Rio Grande* is reassuringly traditional, with *azulejos* on the walls beneath an arched ceiling. The spacious restaurant serves up good-value Portuguese classics such as pork steaks and a good array of fresh fish for under €9. Mon–Tues & Thurs–Sun 12.30–3pm & 6–11pm.

BAIRRO ALTO, PRÍNCIPE REAL AND AROUND

1° de Maio Rua da Atalaia 8 ☎213 426 840; ⓜBaixa-Chiado; map pp.74–75. This *adega* offers simply cooked fish and meat grills with boiled veg and potatoes. You can watch the chef cook through a hatch at the back, adding to

the theatrics. Good daily specials, with mains from around €12. Arrive early to bag a table. Mon–Fri noon–3pm & 7–11pm, Sat noon–3pm.

Bistro 100 Maneiras Largo da Trindade 9 ☎ 210 990 575; Ⓜ Baixa-Chiado; map pp.74–75. In a fine Art Nouveau building, Sarajevo-born chef Ljubmar Stanisic's restaurant and canteen serves a fascinating mixture of interesting mains (game pie or sea urchin with scrambled egg; around €25) and upmarket comfort foods such as salmon sausages and deluxe hamburgers (€18). Mon–Sat 7.30pm–2am.

Bota Alta Trav da Queimada 37 ☎ 213 427 959; bus #758 from Cais do Sodré; map pp.74–75. An attractive old tavern with quirky, boot-themed decor (its name means "high boot") that attracts queues for its large portions of traditional Portuguese food (mains from around €10). It's always packed and the tables sit cheek by jowl; try to get there before 8pm. Mon–Fri noon–2.30pm & 7–10.30pm, Sat 7–10pm.

Cervejaria da Trindade Rua Nova da Trindade 20 ☎ 213 423 506; bus #758 from Cais do Sodré; map pp.74–75. Huge and famous vaulted beer hall and restaurant – the city's oldest, dating from 1836 – with some of Lisbon's loveliest *azulejos* on the walls and a pretty patio garden. It specializes in shellfish, though other dishes are also good (from €12 or so), as is the beer. Mon–Thurs & Sun 10am–midnight, Fri–Sat 10am–1am.

Comida de Santo Calç. Engenheiro Miguel Pais 39 ☎ 213 963 339; bus #758 from Cais do Sodré; map pp.74–75. Popular, pricey but fun Brazilian restaurant serving classic dishes such as *feijoada* (a bean stew), and a fantastic *ensopadinho de peixe* (fish in coconut); also good vegetarian options, with mains €18–20. Mon & Wed–Sun 12.30–3.30pm & 7.30pm–1am; closed for lunch in Aug.

Lost In Rua D. Pedro V 56 ☎ 917 759 282; bus #758 from Cais do Sodré; map pp.74–75. This Indian-inspired little café-restaurant has a great terrace with exhilarating views over town. The menu features prawn curry and veggie burgers (€12–14), and it's a good drinking spot. Mon 4pm–midnight, Tues–Sun 12.30pm–midnight.

Prego da Peixaria Rua Escola Politécnica 40 ☎ 213 471 356; bus #758 from Cais do Sodré; map pp.74–75. Traditional *pregos* are steak sandwiches, but this fashionable restaurant has embraced a whole host of mostly fishy varieties. Choose from the likes of *bacalhau*, tuna, mushroom or salmon with octopus; all are delicious and priced at €9–13. There's a cool interior courtyard and fittings made from recycled materials. Daily 12.30pm–1am.

Terra Rua da Palmeira 15 ☎ 213 421 407; bus #758 from Cais do Sodré; map pp.74–75. Attractive vegetarian and vegan restaurant with a lovely patio garden. There's a good-value all-you-can-eat buffet (around €16) or vegetarian versions of classic Portuguese dishes such as *cozida* stew. Also serves fine Italian ice creams. Tues–Sun 1.20–3.30pm & 7.30pm–midnight.

AVENIDA DA LIBERDADE AND AROUND

Centro de Arte Moderna Rua Dr. Bettencourt, Fundação Calouste Gulbenkian ☎ 217 933 068; Ⓜ S.Sebastião; map pp.60–61. Join the lunchtime queues at the museum canteen restaurant for bargain hot and cold food. Dishes change daily but there's always an excellent choice of salads for vegetarians and a grilled meat and fish dish, plus a selection of tasty desserts. You can eat well for around €8. Daily 10am–5.45pm.

Guilty by Olivier Rua Barata Salgueiro 28 ☎ 211 913 590, Ⓦ guilty.olivier.pt; Ⓜ Avenida; map pp.60–61. Modern diner run by renowned chef Olivier, serving classy comfort foods (hence the name), from pasta and carpaccio to giant pizzas and gourmet burgers (mains €11–17). Just off the Avenida da Liberdade, it's a fashionable spot, too, with night-time DJs. Restaurant daily 12.30–3.30pm & 7.30pm–midnight; bar Mon–Wed & Sun noon–midnight, Thurs–Sat noon–4am.

Marisqueira Santa Marta Trav do Enviado de Inglaterra 1D ☎ 213 525 638; Ⓜ Avenida; map pp.60–61. Slightly touristy but spacious restaurant specializing in seafood: there's a tank with bubbling crabs in one corner. Service is attentive and reasonably priced meals (mains from around €12) end with a complimentary glass of port. Daily noon–midnight.

★ **Ribadouro** Av da Liberdade 155 ☎ 213 549 411; Ⓜ Avenida; map pp.60–61. The Avenida's best *cervejaria*, serving a decent range of grilled meat and fresh shellfish (but no fish) from around €15. If you don't fancy a full meal, order a beer with a plate of prawns at the bar. Very popular, so turn up early or book a table. Daily noon–1am.

SÃO BENTO, LAPA AND SANTOS

Picanha Rua das Janelas Verdes 96, Lapa ☎ 213 975 401; bus #760 from Pr da Figueira; map pp.60–61. Just up from the Museu de Arte Antiga, with an intimate, ornately tiled interior, this specializes in *picanha* (thin slices of beef) accompanied by black-eyed beans, salad and potatoes. Great if this appeals to you (as that's all they do), and for a fixed price of around €20 you can eat as much of the stuff as you want. Mon–Fri 12.30–3pm & 8–11pm, Sat–Sun 8–11pm.

Túnel de Santos Largo de Santos 1 ☎ 912 151 850; tram #15 or #25; map pp.60–61. Lively, modern café-restaurant with outdoor seating facing the square. Inside, a cosy brick-vaulted interior space attracts a young crowd for inexpensive grills, snacks and salads (around €8 and up). Mon–Sat 8am–10pm.

★ **Varina da Madragoa** Rua das Madres 34 ☎ 213 965 533; tram #25; map pp.74–75. Once the haunt of Nobel Prize for Literature winner José Saramago, this lovely, traditional restaurant with grape-embellished *azulejos* on the walls has a superb menu featuring Portuguese dishes such as *bacalhau*, trout and steaks; mains from €10. Tues–Fri 12.30–3.30pm & 7–11.30pm, Sat 7.30–11.30pm.

1

ALCÂNTARA AND THE DOCKS

Café na Fábrica LX Factory, Rua Rodrigues Faria 103 Edf E ☎ 214 010 887; tram #15; map p.79. Set in a small but cosy wooden shed-like warehouse, this arty space is very popular for lunch, with wraps, quiches, baguettes and salads from around €7. There are also a few outdoor tables. Mon–Fri 9.30am–8pm, Sat noon–7pm, Sun 10.30am–7pm.

Malaca Too LX Factory, Rua Rodrigues Faria 103 Edf G ☎ 213 477 082; tram #15; map p.79. This fantastic space has tables wedged between giant old printing presses – a surprising backdrop for fresh Oriental cuisine ranging from wonton soups and green curries to fresh fish, all from around €12. Daily noon–3pm & 7–10pm.

Rui dos Pregos Passeio Doca de Santo Amaro ☎ 967 723 483; tram #15; map p.79. One of the less pricey options hereabouts, set to one side of the docks and with appealing outdoor tables. The speciality here is *pregos* (beef sandwiches), with different varieties from €8. Tues–Sun noon–2am.

BELÉM

Floresta de Belém Pr Afonso de Albuquerque 1A ☎ 213 636 307; tram #15; map p.81. One of the best-value places along this stretch, attracting a largely Portuguese clientele, especially for weekend lunches. Great salads, grills and fresh fish from around €8, eaten inside or on a sunny outdoor terrace. Tues–Sat 9.30am–4pm & 6.30pm–midnight, Sun 9.30am–4pm.

Solar de Embaixador Rua do Embaixador 210–212 ☎ 213 625 111; tram #15; map p.81. Close to the Museu dos Coches, this homely restaurant serves good-value favourites such as *bitoque* (thin steaks), *alheira* sausages and fresh fish at €7–9, with a TV in the corner for company. Mon & Wed–Sun noon–3pm & 7–11pm.

NORTH LISBON

Eleven Rua Marquês da Fronteira ☎ 213 862 211, ⓦ restauranteleven.com; ⓂMarquês de Pombal; map pp.60–61. At the top of Parque Eduardo VII, this Michelin-starred restaurant hits the heights both literally and metaphorically. The interior is both intimate and bright, with wonderful city views. The haute cuisine here is expensive but not outrageous, with a tasting menu at around €76. Mains start at €30: expect the likes of sea bass with chestnuts or suckling pig with passion fruit. Mon–Sat 12.30–3pm & 7.30–11pm.

PARQUE DAS NAÇÕES

D'Bacalhau Rua da Pimenta 43–45 ☎ 218 941 296; ⓂOriente; map p.81. If you want to sample some of the alleged 365 recipes for *bacalhau* – salted cod – this is a good place to come, as it serves quite a range of them, from €9: *bacalhau com natas* (with a creamy sauce) is always tasty. It also offers other dishes, including a selection of fresh fish and meat from €11. Daily noon–4.30pm & 7–11pm.

Senhor Peixe Rua da Pimenta 35–37 ☎ 218 955 892; ⓂOriente; map p.81. "Mr Fish" is widely thought to serve up some of the best fresh seafood in Lisbon – check the counter for the day's catch or choose a lobster from the bubbling tank. Most dishes – from around €15 – are grilled in the open kitchen. Tues–Sat noon–3.30pm & 7–10.30pm, Sun noon–3.30pm.

DRINKING AND NIGHTLIFE

Lisbon's **nightlife** is legendary, though don't expect to see any action much before midnight. There are some great bars where you can get a drink at any time of the day, but clubs – which may not open much before 11pm – generally operate on a "minimum consumption" policy: you buy a ticket at the door which you can get stamped each time you buy a drink at the bar. Designed to stop people dancing all night without buying a drink, which many Portuguese would happily do, the price varies hugely: perhaps €10 if it's a quiet night, more likely around €20–30; keep hold of your ticket to prove you have "consumed" enough (otherwise you pay on exit). The traditional centre of Lisbon's nightlife is the **Bairro Alto**, an intriguing blend of student bars, designer clubs, fado houses and restaurants. The Cais do Sodré district is currently the "in" place, while neighbouring **Santos** also has a trendy reputation. Bars and clubs in **Alcântara and the docks** tend to attract a slightly older, wealthier crowd than those in the centre.

BAIXA

A Ginginha Largo de São Domingos 8; ⓂRossio; map p.63. Everyone should try *ginginha* – Portuguese cherry brandy – once. There's just about room in this microscopic joint to walk in, down a glassful and stagger outside to see the city in a new light. Daily 9am–10pm.

Ministerium Club Ala Nascente 72, Pr do Comércio ☎ 916 931 884, ⓦ ministerium.pt; ⓂTerreiro do Paço; map p.63. The grand, historic buildings of the former Ministry of Finance partly make up the stylish backdrop to this hip club, mostly playing house and techno and attracting top-name DJs. There's a spacious dancefloor, plus quieter zones and a great rooftop café-bar. Sat 11pm–6am.

ALFAMA AND CASTELO

★**Portas do Sol** Largo Portas do Sol ☎ 218 851 299; tram #28; map p.66. With its entrance hidden below street level, this hip spot is an obligatory venue for anyone into sunsets. It's a chic indoor space, though most people head for the comfy sofas and outside seats on the giant terrace, with grandstand views over the Alfama. Pricey drinks, coffees and cocktails, but worth it. Daily 10am–2am.

SANTA APOLÓNIA

Lux Armazéns A, Cais da Pedra a Santa Apolónia ☎218 820 890, ⓦluxfragil.com; ⓜSanta Apolónia; map pp.60–61. This three-storey converted meat warehouse has become one of Europe's most fashionable places to be seen. Part-owned by actor John Malkovich, it was the first place to set up in the docks opposite Santa Apolónia station. There's a rooftop terrace with amazing views, a middle floor with various bars, comfy chairs and sofas, projection screens, and music from pop to jazz and dance, while the downstairs dancefloor descends into frenzy at times. The club is also increasingly on the circuit for touring bands. Thurs–Sun 11pm–6.30am.

BAIRRO ALTO

Alface Hall Rua do Norte 96 ☎213 433 293; bus #758 from Cais do Sodré; map pp.74–75. This quirky café-bar is in a former print works. Now part of a hostel and filled with retro chairs and artefacts, its high ceilings and comfy sofas make it an ideal place to hang out for live music, usually jazz or blues. Daily 1pm–midnight.

★**Chafariz do Vinho Enoteca** Rua da Mãe de Água ☎213 422 079; bus #758 from Cais do Sodré; map pp.74–75. Tucked into steps downhill from Praça do Príncipe Real, this extraordinary wine bar is set in the bowels of a nineteenth-century bathhouse and now serves upmarket wines and other drinks, along with *petiscos* (snacks). Tues–Sun 6pm–2am.

★**Cinco Lounge** Rua Ruben A Leitão 179 ☎213 424 033; bus #758 from Cais do Sodré; map pp.74–75. Run by an affable Brit, this New York-style bar has become legendary for its hundred-plus cocktails: choose from the classics to totally wacky concoctions. A great place to chill out. Daily 9pm–2am.

Clube da Esquina Rua da Barroca 30 ☎929 092 742; bus #758 from Cais do Sodré; map pp.74–75. A buzzy little corner bar with ancient radios on the wall and DJs spinning vinyl on a good, old-fashioned turntable. Great for people-watching and always lively. Mon–Thurs 7pm–2am, Fri–Sat 7pm–3am.

Decadente Bar Rua de São Pedro de Alcântara 81 ☎213 461 281; bus #758 from Cais do Sodré; map pp.74–75. Attached to a boutique hostel, this small, fashionable bar attracts a youthful, laidback crowd. It's best on Thursday and Saturday evenings when there is often live music, usually Latin or jazz. Mon–Wed & Sun

noon–11pm, Thurs noon–1am, Fri–Sat noon–2am.
Maria Caxuxa Rua da Barroca 6–12 ☎965 039 094; ⓦBaixa-Chiado; map pp.74–75. This arty lounge-bar has plenty of space for big sofas and eclectic decor – including record players and aged machinery – though these get lost in the crowds when the DJ pumps up the volume as the evening progresses. Daily 7pm–2am.
Park Calç. do Combro 58 ☎215 914 011; tram #28; map pp.74–75. Reached via a poky entrance inside a car park, this chic rooftop bar comes as quite a surprise. There are potted plants and trees, great cocktails and bar snacks, and a stunning view across the river. Guest DJs and events at weekends. Tues–Sat 1pm–2am, Sun 1–8pm.
★**Pavilhão Chinês** Rua D. Pedro V 89 ☎213 424 729; bus #758 from Cais do Sodré; map pp.74–75. Once a nineteenth-century tea- and coffee-merchant's shop, this is now a bar set in a series of comfortable rooms. Most are completely lined with mirrored cabinets containing some four thousand artefacts from around the world, including a cabinet of model trams. There is waiter service and the usual drinks are supplemented by a long list of exotic cocktails. Daily 6pm–2am.
★**Portas Largas** Rua da Atalaia 105 ☎218 466 379; bus #758 from Cais do Sodré; map pp.74–75. Atmospheric, black-and-white-tiled *adega* with cheapish drinks, background music from fado to pop, and a varied, partly gay crowd, which spills out onto the street on warm evenings. Occasional live music, too. Daily 6pm–2am.
Solar do Vinho do Porto Rua de São Pedro de Alcântara 45 ☎213 475 707, ⓦivdp.pt; bus #758 from Cais do Sodré; map pp.74–75. Opened in 1944, the Port Wine Institute's Lisbon base lures in visitors with over 300 types of port, starting at around €3 a glass and rising to over €25 for a glass of vintage J.W. Burmester. Drinks and snacks such as cheese and hams are served at low tables in the comfortable eighteenth-century former Palácio Ludovice, and it's a good place to kick off an evening. Mon–Fri 11am–midnight, Sat 3pm–midnight.

CAIS DO SODRÉ AND SANTOS

A Tabacaria Rua de São Paulo 75–77 ☎213 420 281; ⓜCais do Sodré; map pp.74–75. In a wonderful old tobacco shop dating back to 1885 – with many of the original fittings – this small, friendly bar specializes in cocktails (from around €7), made with whatever fruits are in season. Mon-Fri noon–1am, Sat 6pm–2am.

OUR FIVE FAVOURITE BARS

Best views: *Portas do Sol* (see p.100)
Best cocktails: *Cinco Lounge* (see p.101)
Best wines: *Chafariz do Vinho Enoteca* (see p.101)

Classic Lisbon: *Portas Largas* (see p.101)
Quirky: *Pavilhão Chinês* (see p.101)

1

Café Tati Rua da Ribeira Nova 36 ☎ 213 461 279, ⓦ cafetati.blogspot.com; Ⓜ Cais do Sodré; map pp.74–75. With stripped walls and upcycled furniture, this has tatty chic decor and a very appealing range of snacks, teas, cakes and wines. Popular for Sunday brunch, it's also lively on Wednesday and Sunday evenings for live jazz. Tues–Sun 11am–1am.

Music Box Rua Nova do Carvalho 24 ☎ 213 430 107, ⓦ musicboxlisboa.com; Ⓜ Cais do Sodré; map pp.74–75. Tucked under the arches of Rua Nova do Carvalho, this cool cultural and music venue hosts club nights, live music, films and performing arts, with an emphasis on promoting independent acts. There's a top sound and light system and a usually hip and happy crowd. Mon–Sat 11pm–6am.

Pensão Amor Rua do Alecrim 19 ☎ 213 143 399; Ⓜ Cais do Sodré; map pp.74–75. The "Pension of Love" is a striking former "house of ill repute" which has retained its eighteenth-century burlesque fixtures and fittings for its current incarnation as a trendy bar/club. Risqué photos, frescoes and mirrors line the walls of a series of ornate rooms, where you can buy cocktails and drinks, browse books in a small erotic bookstore or enjoy occasional live concerts. Mon–Wed & Sun noon–3am, Thurs–Sat noon–4am.

Sol e Pesca Rua Nova do Carvalho 44 ☎ 213 467 203; Ⓜ Cais do Sodré; map pp.74–75. Once a shop selling fishing equipment, this hip bar is located on an up-and-coming street better known for its strip joints. The fishing equipment is now part of the decor, and you can still purchase tinned fish to enjoy with bread and wine. Mon–Sat noon–2am.

ALCÂNTARA AND THE DOCKS

Doca de Santo Armazém CP, Doca de Santo Amaro ☎ 213 963 522; tram #15; map p.79. Though it's slightly set back from the river, this large, palm-fringed club, bar and restaurant has a great cocktail bar on the esplanade. Sun–Thurs 9am–midnight, Fri–Sat 9am–2am.

Le Chat Jardim 9 de Abril ☎ 213 963 668; bus #760 from Pr da Figueira; map p.79. A modern, glass-sided café-bar adjacent to the Museu Nacional de Arte Antiga, *Le Chat* has a terrific terrace which gazes over the docks and Ponte 25 de Abril. Great at any time of the day, it's a particularly fine spot for a cocktail or sundowner. Mon–Sat 12.30pm–2am, Sun 12.30pm–midnight.

Op Art Doca de Santo Amaro ☎ 213 956 787, ⓦ opartcafe.com; tram #15; map p.79. Located in splendid isolation on the fringes of the Tejo, this small glass pavilion morphs from a simple restaurant serving moderately priced grills into an evening bar. In summer, you can sprawl on dockside beanbags and gaze over the

river. After 1am, the mood changes again with vibrant dance sounds. Tues–Fri & Sun 3pm–2am, Sat 3pm–6am.

BELÉM

Á Margem Doca do Bom Sucesso ☎ 916 588 859, ⓦ amargem.com; tram #15; map p.81. Near the stumpy brick-striped lighthouse, this is a chic, sleek and minimalist kiosk/café-bar with stunning views across the river – tables spill out onto the waterfront. There's a good list of cocktails and wines as well as sandwiches, tapas and salads. Mon–Thurs 10am–10pm, Fri & Sat 10am–2am.

PARQUE DAS NAÇÕES

Azul Profundo Rossio dos Olivais, Quiosque 4 ☎ 218 960 004; Ⓜ Oriente; map p.89. Sunny esplanade bar overlooking the glittering docks. Offers a good range of well-priced snacks, fruit juices and wicked *caipirinha* cocktails. Daily 10am–2am; closes 10pm Oct–April.

Havana Rua da Pimenta 115–117; Ⓜ Oriente; map p.89. Lively Cuban bar with an airy interior and outdoor seating. The pulsating Latin sounds ramp up a notch after 11pm when it turns into more of a club. Tues–Thurs & Sun noon–2am; Fri–Sat noon–4am.

República da Cerveja Jardim das Tágides 2.26.01 ☎ 218 922 590; Ⓜ Oriente; map p.89. In a great position close to the water's edge and facing the Vasco da Gama bridge, this modern bar-restaurant specializes in some fine international beers, though sticking to the local Superbock will save a few euros. Steaks and burgers are also on offer, and there's occasional live music. Mon–Sat 12.30pm–1am.

LGBT BARS AND CLUBS

Gay and lesbian nightlife focuses on the Bairro Alto and Praça do Príncipe Real, where a generally laidback group of clubs and bars attracts people of all ages. In "Directory" (see p.107) there's further information on the gay and lesbian scene in Lisbon.

Finalmente Rua da Palmeira 38, Príncipe Real ☎ 213 479 923; bus #758 from Cais do Sodré; map pp.74–75. A first-class disco with lashings of kitsch. Weekend drag shows (at 2am) feature skimpily dressed young *senhoritas* camping it up to high-tech sounds. Daily 11am–6am.

Sétimo Céu Trav de Espera 54, Bairro Alto ☎ 213 466 471; bus #758 from Cais do Sodré; map pp.74–75. Popular with gays and lesbians, this is an obligatory stop for beers and *caipirinhas* served by the Brazilian owner. The great atmosphere spills out onto the street. Mon–Sat 9pm–3am.

LIVE MUSIC AND PERFORMING ARTS

No visit to Lisbon is complete without listening to **fado** – the city's most traditional music – but there's plenty else on offer if this doesn't appeal to you. The many emigrants from Portugal's former colonies have cemented the popularity of **music**

1

from Africa (especially Cabo Verde, Guinea Bissau, Angola and Mozambique) and, of course, Brazil. The Portuguese love their **pop and rock** and big names frequently perform at the venues listed on p.105. The city also has one of Europe's oldest **jazz clubs** and a loyal jazz following. To find out what's on, the best **listings** are in *Agenda Cultural*, a free monthly magazine produced by the town hall, which details current **theatre and opera** shows as well as live music (in Portuguese). An online version is available on ⓦ agendalx.pt. You can usually buy tickets on the night, or, for bigger events, from music store FNAC (Rua Nova do Almada, Chiado) or online at ⓦ ticketline.sapo.pt or ⓦ blueticket.pt.

FADO

Lisbon is the best place in the country to hear fado, a traditional soulful type of music which has its roots in the clubs of the Bairro Alto and Alfama. Most clubs are small and serve pricey food (expect to pay €40–60 a head) , and though you don't have to eat, they usually charge a minimum fee (rarely below €25), which you are expected to spend on food or drink, or you pay on exit. Some of the touristy places can be extremely tacky; we've highlighted below the more authentic experiences.

A Baiuca Rua de São Miguel 20 ⓞ 218 867 284; tram #28; map p.66. Nightly fado *vadio* (using amateur performers) can be heard in this great little tiled *tasca* which serves decent fresh fish and grills. Very atmospheric. Thurs–Mon 8–11pm.

A Parreirinha de Alfama Beco do Espírito Santo 1 ⓞ 218 868 209, ⓦ parreirinhadealfama.com; tram #28; map p.66. Just off Largo do Chafariz de Dentro, this is one of Lisbon's best fado venues, owned by famous fado singer Argentina Santos, and often attracting leading stars and an enthusiastic local clientele. Reservations are advised when the big names appear. Tues–Sun 8pm–1am.

Clube do Fado Rua de São João da Pr 86–94, Alfama ⓞ 218 852 704, ⓦ clube-de-fado.com; tram #28; map p.66. Intimate place with stone pillars and an old well; frequented by a mainly local clientele. Attracts small-time performers, up-and-coming talent and the occasional big names. Daily 8pm–2am.

O Senhor Vinho Rua do Meio à Lapa 18, Lapa ⓞ 213 972 681, ⓦ srvinho.com; tram #25; map pp.60–61. For a truly authentic fado experience, seek out this famous club in upmarket Lapa. It features some of the best singers in Portugal, hence the high prices. Reservations are advised. Mon–Sat 7.30pm–2am.

Povo Rua Nova do Carvalho 32–26 ⓞ 213 473 403; Ⓜ Cais do Sodré; map pp.74–75. This fashionable tavern offers fado from up-and-coming stars (Tues–Thurs and Sun from 9.30pm) along with late-night DJs at weekends in the heart of "pink street". If you just want to eat, there's a great menu of *petiscos* and mains such as mussels with seaweed, *bacalhau* dishes and steaks (€8–21). Daily 6pm–4am.

Tasca do Chico Rua do Diário de Notícias 39, Bairro Alto ⓞ 965 059 670; bus #758 from Cais do Sodré; map pp.74–75. Atmospheric little bar (a fine spot for a drink) which morphs into a very popular fado bar on Mondays and Wednesdays, when crowds pack in to hear the moving songs from 8pm. Daily 7pm–2am.

AFRICAN

B. Leza Cais da Ribeira Nova Armazém B, Santos ⓞ 963 612 816; tram #15; map pp.74–75. Live African music most evenings along with poetry nights and occasional dance lessons. Wed–Sun 10.30pm–4am.

JAZZ

Hot Clube de Portugal Pr de Alegria 48, off Av da Liberdade ⓞ 213 619 740, ⓦ hcp.pt; Ⓜ Avenida; map pp.74–75. Dating from 1948 – making it one of Europe's oldest jazz clubs – the *Hot Clube* hosts top names in the jazz world, along with local performers. Tues–Sat 10pm–2am.

CLASSICAL MUSIC, OPERA AND THEATRE

For details of ballet performances, check the website of the renowned Lisbon-based Companhia Nacional de Bailado (ⓦ cnb.pt).

Casino Alameda dos Oceanos, Parque das Nações ⓞ 218 929 000, ⓦ www.casinolisboa.pt; Ⓜ Oriente; map p.89. This state-of-the-art casino (Sun–Thurs 3pm–3am, Fri & Sat 4pm–4am) offers the usual gambling fodder, but the stunning space – with its glass-cylinder entrance hall – also hosts top shows from Broadway and London as well as major concerts in the performance hall, which has a retractable roof.

Centro Cultural de Belém Pr do Império, Belém ⓞ 213 612 400, ⓦ ccb.pt; tram #15; map p.81. This modern cultural centre has both a large and small auditorium hosting a range of music and dance, from jazz to classical.

Fundação Calouste Gulbenkian Av de Berna ⓞ 217 823 000, ⓦ gulbenkian.pt; Ⓜ São Sebastião; map pp.60–61. There are three concert halls (including an outdoor amphitheatre) at the Gulbenkian, with performances ranging from jazz to chamber to classical, with prestigious guest soloists.

Lisbon Players Rua da Estrela 10, Lapa ⓞ 213 961 946, ⓦ lisbonplayers.com.pt; tram #28; map pp.60–61. Check out performances by this amateur but highly rated English-speaking theatrical group consisting largely of expat actors.

Teatro Nacional de Dona Maria Rossio, Baixa ⓞ 213 250 800, ⓦ teatro-dmaria.pt; Ⓜ Restauradores; map p.63. Puts on regular performances of Portuguese and foreign plays.

Teatro Nacional de São Carlos Rua Serpa Pinto 9,

LISBON EVENTS CALENDAR

Carnival February/March: Brazilian-style carnival parades and costumes, mainly at Parque das Nações.

Lisbon half-marathon March: The half-marathon traces a route across Ponte Vasco da Gama, finishing in Parque das Nações (⊛meiamaratonadelisboa.com).

Peixe em Lisboa March/April: Fish festival held in Pátio da Galé, with masterclasses by top chefs (⊛peixemlisboa.com).

Rock in Rio May: A five-day biannual mega rock festival held in even years, in Parque Bela Vista to the north of the centre (⊛rockinriolisboa.sapo.pt).

Sintra Music Festival May: Performances by international orchestras, musicians and dance groups in parks, gardens and palaces in and around Sintra (⊛festivaldesintra.pt).

Santos Populares June: Street-partying to celebrate the saints' days – António (June 13), João (June 24) and Pedro (June 29). Celebrations for each begin on the evening before the actual day. Santo António is Lisbon's main event.

Arraial Pride June: Gay Pride event, in various venues (⊛arraialpride.ilga-portugal.pt).

Handicrafts Fair June/July: A state-run handicrafts fair, with live folk music, held in Estoril on the Avenida de Portugal, near the Casino. A similar event occurs during the same period at FIL (⊛fil.pt), at the Parque das Nações.

Super Bock Super Rock July: Rock festival featuring local and international bands in various venues (⊛superbock.pt).

Jazz em Augusto August: Jazz festival at the Gulbenkian's open-air amphitheatre (⊛musica.gulbenkian.pt), with a similar event in Cascais.

São Martinho November 11: Saint's day celebrated by the traditional tasting of the year's wine which is drunk with hot chestnuts, in memory of St Martinho, who shared his cape with a poor man.

Natal December: The build-up to Christmas begins in early December with Europe's tallest Christmas tree filling the centre of Praça da Comércio. Distinctive hooped *bolo-rei* (dried-fruit "king cake") appear in shops and *pastelarias*.

New Year's Eve December 31: There are usually fireworks in Praça do Comércio, at Cascais and the Parque das Nações.

Chiado ☎213 253 045, ⊛tnsc.pt; Ⓜ Baixa-Chiado; map p.63. The opera season runs from September to June, and there's also a regular classical music programme inside this lovely building.

Ze dos Bois Rua da Barroca 59, Bairro Alto ☎213 430 205, ⊛zedosbois.org; bus #758 from Chiado; map pp.74–75. Rambling arts venue in a former eighteenth-century palace that hosts various installations, art house films and exhibitions along with occasional concerts. Usually Wed–Sun 6–11pm.

LARGE VENUES

Coliseu dos Recreios Rua das Portas de Santo Antão 96, Baixa ☎213 240 580, ⊛coliseulisboa.com; Ⓜ Restauradores; map p.63. Main indoor city-centre rock, pop and classical venue set in a lovely domed building, originally opened in 1890 as a circus.

Meo Arena Parque das Nações ☎218 918 471, ⊛arena.meo.pt; Ⓜ Oriente; map p.89. Big-name stars play at Portugal's largest indoor venue, which holds up to 20,000 spectators.

CINEMA

Virtually all cinemas show **films with the original soundtrack** (usually American or English) and Portuguese subtitles. Ticket prices are low, usually around €8 (cheaper at matinees and on Monday): you can find listings on ⊛agendalx.pt. There are multi-screen complexes at Amoreiras, Edifício Monumental (Ⓜ Saldanha), El Corte Inglés (Ⓜ São Sebastião), Vasco da Gama in Parque das Nações (Ⓜ Oriente) and Colombo Shopping Centre (Ⓜ Colégio Militar-Luz). As well as the following art-house venues, Lisbon hosts a couple of **film festivals**: the Indie Lisboa film festival in April/May, which showcases independent cinema from around the world (⊛indielisboa.com); and the International Horror Film Festival in September (⊛motelx.org).

Instituto da Cinemateca Portuguesa Rua Barata Salgueiro 39 ☎213 596 200, ⊛cinemateca.pt; Ⓜ Avenida; map pp.60–61. The national film theatre, with twice-daily shows ranging from contemporary Portuguese films to anything from Truffaut to Valentino.

It also has its own small cinema museum.

São Jorge Av da Liberdade 175 ☎213 103 402, ⊛cinema saojorge.pt; Ⓜ Avenida; map pp.60–61. Lisbon's most central cinema shows a mixture of mainstream and art-house movies: it also hosts fairs and temporary exhibitions.

1

SPORTS

Football is the biggest game in Lisbon, and it's usually easy to get match tickets (see below), while summer-season **bullfights** at the Praça de Touros do Campo Pequeno, just off Avenida da República, are the other main spectacle (see p.87). Otherwise, you're going to need to travel out of the capital for sports, either for **golf**, on the upmarket courses around Estoril and Cascais (@portugalgolfe.com), or **watersports**, namely surfing at Caparica (see p.121) and windsurfing at Guincho (see p.110).

FOOTBALL

Daily soccer tabloid *Bola* has fixtures, match reports and news, as does the website @ligaportugal.pt. To buy advance tickets for big games – which cost between €18 and €50 – go to the kiosks (not the turnstiles) at the grounds, or check the club websites.

Benfica Estádio da Luz, Av Gen. Norton Matos ☎707 200 100, @slbenfica.pt; @Colégio Militar-Luz. Lisbon's most famous football team are national and international giants. Their awesome stadium was completely rebuilt in preparation for the 2004 European Championships; it was here that Portugal lost in the final to Greece in front of 65,000 disbelieving spectators.

Sporting Club de Portugal (Sporting Lisbon) Estádio José Alvalade, Rua Professor da Fonseca ☎217 516 000, @sporting.pt; @Campo Grande. Benfica's traditional city rivals play at the nearby stadium, also purpose-built for Euro 2004 and featuring state-of-the-art design, with a capacity of 54,000.

Belenenses Estádio do Restelo, Av do Restelo, Belém ☎211 980 000, @osbelenenses.pt. Lisbon's third team play in a beautifully located stadium in Belém, though they last won the title back in 1946.

SHOPPING

Lisbon has a fantastic array of **independent shops**, many unchanged for centuries, some extremely cutting-edge. There are also some impressive contemporary **shopping malls**, many of which incorporate supermarkets on the ground floor, as well as the more traditional markets, such as the Alfama's Feira da Ladra **flea market**. The Bairro Alto and Chiado are the main centres for alternative **designer clothes** and crafts, while international designer names cluster along Avenida da Liberdade. **Antique shops** tend to be concentrated along Rua do Alecrim in Chiado, Rua Dom Pedro V in the Bairro Alto, and along Rua de São Bento, between Rato and São Bento. Traditional **shopping hours** are Monday to Friday 9.30am to 7 or 8pm (some shops close for an hour at lunch), Saturday 9am to 1pm. However, many of the Bairro Alto shops are open afternoons and evenings only, usually 2 to 9pm or so.

ANTIQUES, ARTS AND CRAFTS

A Arte da Terra Rua de Augusto Rosa 40 ☎212 745 975; tram #28; map p.66. Within historic stables opposite the Sé – some of the handicrafts are displayed in the stone horse troughs – this is a beautiful space selling a range of local arts and crafts, from jewellery and cork products to postcards, preserves and souvenirs. Daily 11am0–8pm.

A Vida Portuguesa Rua Anchieta 11, Chiado ☎213 465 073; @Baixa-Chiado; map pp.74–75. An expensive but evocative collection of retro toys, crafts and ceramics, beautifully displayed and packaged in a former grocer's shop. Mon–Sat 10am–8pm, Sun 11am–8pm.

Cork and Co. Rua das Salgadeiras 10, Bairro Alto ☎216 090 231; @Baixa-Chiado; map pp.74–75. Portugal supplies around fifty percent of the world's cork, and this shop displays the versatility of the product with a range of tasteful cork goods, from bags and bracelets to umbrellas. Mon–Thurs 11am–7pm, Fri–Sat 11am–9pm.

Fábrica Sant'anna Rua do Alecrim 95, Chiado ☎213 222 537; @Baixa-Chiado; map pp.74–75. If you're interested in Portuguese tiles – *azulejos* – check out this factory shop, founded in 1741, which sells copies of traditional designs and a great range of pots and ceramics. Mon–Sat 9.30am–7pm.

Loja Portugueza Rua da Fanqueiros 32, Baixa ☎218 868 211; @Baixa-Chiado; map p.63. A packed treasure-trove of Portuguese crafts and souvenirs, including tasteful mugs, tiles, port and trinkets. Daily 10am–7pm.

Santos Ofícios Rua da Madalena 87 ☎218 872 031; @Terreiro do Paço or tram #28; map p.63. Small shop near the Sé, stuffed with a somewhat touristy collection of regional crafts including some attractive ceramics, rugs, embroidery, baskets and toys. Mon–Sat 10am–8pm.

Solar Albuquerque Rua D. Pedro V 70, Bairro Alto ☎213 465 522; map pp.74–75. A fascinating mix of antique tiles, plates and ceramics dating back to the sixteenth century – great for a browse. Mon–Fri 10am–7pm, Sat 10am–1pm; July & Aug closed Sat.

BOOKS AND MUSIC

Casa do Fado e da Guitarra Portuguesa Largo do Chafariz de Dentro 1, Alfama ☎218 823 470; tram #28 or bus #728 from Pr do Comércio; map p.66. The shop attached to this museum (see p.67) sells an excellent selection of fado CDs, and the staff give expert advice. Tues–Sun 10am–6pm.

Livraria Bertrand Rua Garrett 73, Chiado ☎213 476 122; @Baixa-Chiado; map p.63. Officially the world's oldest general bookshop, having opened in 1773, and once the meeting place of the literary set. Today it sells a good

range of novels in English, plus foreign magazines. Mon–Sat 9am–10pm, Sun 11am–8pm.

CLOTHES AND ACCESSORIES

Entre Tanto Rua Escola Politécnica 42, ☎961 204 571, ⓦentretanto.pt; bus #758 from Chiado; map pp.74–75. Set in a rambling seventeenth-century building, Entre Tanto is an intriguing jumble of stores and fashionable boutiques selling everything from shoes and clothes to perfume and furniture. However, stores do come and go – as does what's on offer. There's a lovely terrace café, too, overlooking the Botanical Gardens. Daily noon–8pm.

Storytailors Calç. do Ferragial 8, Chiado ☎213 432 306; ⓜBaixa-Chiado; map p.63. Set in a suitably stylish bare-brick eighteenth-century former warehouse, the shop interior is as magical as its designer clothes inspired by fairytales. Its haute couture range has been snapped up by the likes of Madonna, Janet Jackson and Lily Allen. Tues–Sat 11am–9pm.

MARKETS

Feira da Ladra Campo de Santa Clara; map pp.60–61. Lisbon's main flea market (see p.67). Tues & Sat 9am–3pm.

Mercado da Ribeira Av 24 de Julho, Cais do Sodré; ⓜCais do Sodré; map pp.74–75. One of Lisbon's most atmospheric covered markets, selling a great selection of fruit, veg and flowers, with an amazing food hall (see p.71). Thurs 7am–2pm.

SHOPPING CENTRES AND SUPERMARKETS

Amoreiras Entrance on Av Engenheiro Duarte Pacheco 2037 ☎213 810 200, ⓦamoreiras.com; ⓜRato; map pp.60–61. This postmodern shopping centre was one of the first in Lisbon, with some 250 shops,

cinemas, restaurants and a hotel. Daily 10am–11pm.

Armazéns do Chiado Rua do Carmo 2, Chiado ☎213 210 600, ⓦarmazensdochiado.com; ⓜBaixa-Chiado; map p.63. A well-designed shopping centre spread over six floors. The top floor has a series of cafés and restaurants, most offering great views over town. Daily 10am–10pm.

Centro Colombo Av Colégio Militar-Luz ☎217 113 600, ⓦcolombo.pt; ⓜColégio Militar-Luz; map pp.60–61. Iberia's largest shopping complex boasts some four hundred national and international stores, restaurants, cinemas and children's play areas. Daily 9am–midnight.

Centro Vasco da Gama Av D. João II 40, Parque das Nações ☎218 930 601, ⓦcentrovascodagama.pt; ⓜOriente; map p.89. Three floors of national and international stores beneath a glass roof permanently washed by running water. Also restaurants, children's areas and disabled access. Daily 9am–midnight.

El Corte Inglês Av António Augusto de Aguiar 31 ☎213 711 700, ⓦelcorteingles.pt; ⓜSão Sebastião; map pp.60–61. Giant Spanish department store spread over nine floors, selling everything from gourmet foods, clothes and sports goods to CDs, books and toys. Mon–Sat 10am–10pm, Sun 10am–8pm.

WINE AND FOOD

Manuel Tavares Rua da Betesga 1A, Baixa ☎213 424 209; ⓜRossio; map p.63. This small, century-old shop sells a great selection of chocolate and national cheeses, plus a basement stuffed with vintage wines and ports. Mon–Sat 9.30am–7.30pm.

Napoleão Rua dos Fanqueiros 68–70, Baixa, junction with Rua da Conceição ☎218 861 108, ⓦnapoleao .co.pt; ⓜTerreiro do Paço; map p.63. Great range of port and wine, with knowledgeable, English-speaking staff. Mon–Sat 9.30am–8pm.

DIRECTORY

Embassies and consulates Australia, Avenida da Liberdade 200–2°, ⓜAvenida (☎213 101 500); Canada, Avenida da Liberdade 198–200, ⓜAvenida (☎213 164 600); Ireland, Avenida da Liberdade 200–4°, ⓜAvenida (☎213 308 200); South Africa, Avenida Luís Bívar 10, ⓜPicoas (☎213 192 200); UK, Rua de São Bernardo 33, ⓜRato (☎213 924 000); US, Avenida das Forças Armadas, ⓜJardim Zoológico (☎217 273 300).

Gay and lesbian The Centro Comunitário Gay e Lésbico de Lisboa at Rua de São Lázaro 88 (Wed–Thurs 6–11pm, Fri 10.30am–midnight, Sat 6pm–midnight; ☎218 873 918; ⓜMartim Moniz) is Lisbon's main gay and lesbian community centre, with its own café. The centre organizes events and is happy to give details of gay-friendly venues. It is run by ILGA whose comprehensive website (ⓦilga -portugal.pt) is in English and Portuguese.

Hospital The main hospital is Hospital de Santa Maria,

Avenida Prof. Egas Moniz (☎217 805 000, ⓦwww.chln .min-saude.pt), close to the zoo (ⓜJardim Zoológico).

Left luggage There are 24hr lockers at the airport (in level 1 of car park 1), the main train stations and bus station (around €8 a day depending on size of bag).

Lost property For anything lost on public transport, call ☎218 535 403.

Police The tourist police station is in the Foz Cultura building in Palácio Foz, Restauradores ☎213 421 634 (daily 24hr). You need a report from here to make a claim on travel insurance.

Post office The main post office is at Praça dos Restauradores 58 (☎213 238 971; Mon–Fri 8am–10pm, Sat 9am–10pm & Sun 9am–6pm), from where you can send airmail and *correio azul* (express mail – the fastest service). There's a 24hr post office at the airport. Stamps (*selos*) are sold at post offices and anywhere that has the sign "Correio de Portugal – Selos" displayed.

1 Around Lisbon

The most popular excursions from the city are to the beach resorts west along the coast from Belém, which can be reached by train from Cais do Sodré (see p.70). There are fine beaches at places such as **Oeiras**, though you only really reach the ocean proper at **Estoril** and **Cascais**. For large, wild stretches of sand, head north to **Guincho**, or cross the Tejo by ferry to reach the **Costa da Caparica**, a 30km stretch of beach to the south of the capital. Further south still, there are good, clean beaches at **Sesimbra** and in the **Parque Natural da Arrábida**, a superb unspoilt craggy reserve, while the large town of **Setúbal** is noted for its Igreja de Jesus, Portugal's oldest Manueline building. Heading inland also pays dividends, with sights such as the elegant **Palácio de Queluz**, while the beautiful town of **Sintra**, a UNESCO World Heritage site in the hills above Lisbon, is a must.

The Estoril coast

Stretching for over 30km west of Lisbon, **the Estoril coast** makes for an easily accessible and enjoyable trip from the city – the train line that hugs this dramatic coast is worth the trip alone. Much of the coast is backed by a seafront promenade, along which you can walk or cycle, and the lively resorts of **Estoril** and **Cascais** in particular make pleasant alternatives to staying in Lisbon.

GETTING AROUND   THE ESTORIL COAST

By train The Linha de Cascais train runs along the Estoril coast stopping at Belém (though fast trains do not stop here), then Oeiras beach and stations beyond to Estoril and Cascais at the end of the line. It leaves Cais do Sodré station roughly every 20min (Mon–Thurs & Sun 5.30am–1.30am, Fri & Sat 5.30am–2.30am; €2.65).

By road The attractive N6 coastal highway (Avenida Marginal) passes through most of the centres along the seafront; the faster A5 motorway (Auto-Estrada da Oeste) is an inexpensive toll road that runs further inland from Lisbon to Estoril – drive west past Amoreiras and follow the signs.

Oeiras and the Palácio do Marquês de Pombal

Palácio do Marquês de Pombal Tues–Sun 10am–6pm • €5, free on Sun • **Palace gardens** Daily: May–Sept 9am–9pm; Oct–April 10am–6pm • Free • ☎ 214 404 8561, ⓦ www.cm-oeiras.pt

The first suburb of any size after Belém is **OEIRAS** (pronounced *oo-air-esh*), where the Rio Tejo officially turns into the sea. The riverside walkways and the beach here have recently been cleaned up, though most people still swim in the ocean pool alongside the sands. The only reason to stop here is to see the grand, turreted **Palácio do Marquês de Pombal**, at Largo Marquês de Pombal, the erstwhile home of the rebuilder of Lisbon; you can also visit the beautifully ornate **gardens**.

Carcavelos

The next town along the train line west of Oeiras, **CARCAVELOS** has the most extensive sandy beach on this part of the coast and is popular with surfers and windsurfers. To reach the **beach**, it's a ten-minute walk from the station along the broad Avenida Jorge V. Try to visit Carcavelos on Thursday morning, when the town hosts a wonderful, rambling **market** on Rua Eduardo Maria Rodrigues, specializing in clothes and ceramics; turn right out of the station and follow the signs.

Estoril

With its fine beach, casino and surviving grandiose villas dotted among the modern apartments, you can see why **ESTORIL** (pronounced *é-stril*) was the favoured haunt of exiled royalty during the earlier half of the last century. These days it's a lively resort, its centre consisting of the palm-lined **Parque do Estoril**, surrounded by bars and restaurants and the enormous **casino**. The **Feira Internacional Artesanato** – handicrafts and folk music festival – is held here in July.

Estoril Casino

Tues–Sat 3pm–3am • Free • Semi-formal attire required • ☎ 214 667 700, ⓦ casino-estoril.pt

During World War II, **Estoril Casino** was a popular hangout for exiled royalty and spies, including James Bond author Ian Fleming who was based here to keep an eye on double agents. He used his experience at the casino as inspiration for his first Bond novel, *Casino Royale*.

Praia de Tamariz

Estoril's fine sandy beach, **Praia de Tamariz**, is backed by cafés, restaurants and a **seafront promenade** that stretches northwest to Cascais, 2km away. A stroll between the two towns is recommended, drifting from beach to bar; the walk takes around twenty minutes. From July to mid-September, a free firework display is held above the beach every Saturday night at midnight.

ARRIVAL ESTORIL

By train The train station is on Estoril's through-road; take the underpass from the station to reach the beach on one side and the town on the other.

ACCOMMODATION AND EATING

Deck Bar Arcadas do Parque 21–22 ☎ 214 680 366. Facing the park, just back from the station, this great little restaurant and café has outdoor tables. A good spot for a drink or snack, it also serves a range of dishes from omelettes and pasta to *bacalhau* and seafood; main courses €8–10. Tues–Sun 8am–2am.

Jonas Bar Passeio Marítimo, Monte Estoril ☎ 214 676 946. On the seafront promenade, around 5min north of Estoril towards Cascais, this is a laidback beach café-bar facing the waves. As well as cocktails and fresh juices, it serves salads, sandwiches and burgers (€5–10) and fresh fish dishes (from €12). Mon–Sat 9am–midnight; closes 8pm Oct–April.

Smart Rua Maestro Laçerda 6, by Rua José Viana 63 ☎ 214 682 164, ⓦ hotel-smart.net. The best budget choice for accommodation, with pleasant rooms and its own pool and bar in a building originally built as an architect's summer house. Free parking. **€85**

Cascais

At the end of the Linha de Cascais train line, **CASCAIS** (*cash-kaysh*) is a handsome resort of grand mansions and former fishermen's houses wrapped round a bay dotted with **sandy beaches**. There's a flash marina and a fort (now a hotel) that guards the harbour, as well as a cluster of appealing museums, including the wonderful **Casa das Histórias**, dedicated to the artist Paula Rego. While the beaches can get pretty mobbed in summer, it has a young vibe and **lively nightlife**.

The mosaic-paved and partly pedestrianized streets of Cascais **old town** have almost as much allure as its beaches. For a wander away from the crowds, stroll up beyond Largo 5° de Outubro into the pretty network of houses on the west side of town, in the streets north of the graceful **Igreja da Assunção**.

Museu do Mar

Rua Júlio Pereiro de Melo • Tues–Fri 10am–5pm, Sat–Sun 10am–1pm & 2–5pm • Free • ☎ 214 815 906

The modern and engaging **Museu do Mar** relates the town's relationship with the sea, via a fascinating collection of model boats, fossils and stuffed fish. There are also stories about and finds from various local shipwrecks, that children, in particular, will enjoy.

Casa das Histórias

Av da República 300 • Tues–Sun 10am–6pm • €3 • ☎ 214 826 970, ⓦ casadashistoriaspaularego.com

You can't miss the distinctive ochre towers of the modernist **Casa das Histórias** – a museum which, unusually, is dedicated to a living artist, Paula Rego, who was made a Dame by Britain's Queen Elizabeth in 2010. The museum, designed by celebrated architect Eduardo Souto de Moura, features around 120 of Rego's disturbing but beautiful collages, pastels and engravings, as well as those by her late husband Victor Willing.

1

Museu Biblioteca Conde Castro Guimarães

Av Rei Humberto II de Itália • Tues–Fri 10am–5pm, Sat & Sun 10am–1pm & 2–5pm • Free • ☎ 214 815 308, ⓦ cm-cascais.pt

On the seafront side of the leafy expanses of the Parque Municipal da Gandarinha, with its mini-zoo and small lake, stands the **Museu Biblioteca Conde Castro Guimarães** within the former grand mansion of the counts of Guimarães. It is now a house museum, and you are free to wander round the opulent rooms filled with period furniture, paintings and the antiques that the family bequeathed to the nation. Its most valuable exhibit is some rare, illuminated sixteenth-century manuscripts.

Palácio da Cidadela

Avenida Dom Carlos I • Wed–Sun 2–8pm • €4 • ☎ 213 614 660, ⓦ cm-cascais.pt

Cascais' **Palácio da Cidadela** was built in the seventeenth century to help defend the mouth of the Tagus, but by 1870, it had become a summer home for the royal family – a role it continued for Portugal's presidents after the birth of the republic in 1910. Today, you are free to wander round the lower-floor exhibition space, though it's worth the entrance fee to visit the top two floors (ask for a non-guided visit unless you understand Portuguese). In the late nineteenth century, parts of the **top floor** were adapted by King Carlos to study oceanography while the ornate **state rooms** of the middle floor have played host to visiting heads of state. There's also a lovely tea room with fine views over the ocean. Just below the fortress is the entrance to the **Marina de Cascais**, an enclave of expensive yachts serviced by restaurants, bars and boutiques.

Santa Marta Lighthouse

Rua do Farol • Tues–Fri 10am–5pm, Sat & Sun 10am–1pm & 2–5pm • Free

The distinctive blue-and-white-striped **Santa Marta Lighthouse** now doubles as a small museum that traces the building's history from a fort in the eighteenth century to the development of optical devices. Don't miss the fine terrace café.

Praia do Guincho

Regular buses from Cascais bus station run the 6km west to **Praia do Guincho**, an enormous sandy beach which curves round a large bay. Often the waves are too big to swim here (take great care of dangerous undertows), though it's a superb place for surfing and windsurfing if you know what you're doing – legs of the World Windsurfing Championships are often held here in August.

PAULA REGO

Paula Rego (born 1935) shot to international prominence in 1990 when she was appointed Artist in Residence at London's National Gallery, and she is now considered one of the world's leading figurative painters. In 2011, she was listed as one of the top 100 most influential living women in the UK's *Guardian* newspaper. Although she has spent most of her life in England – she married English artist Vic Willing – her formative years were spent in Salazar's Lisbon, where she was born. She had a sheltered childhood within the confines of a wealthy family home and she still feels bitter about the way her mother became a "casualty" of a society which encouraged wealthy women to be idle, leaving work to their servants. In Rego's work, women are portrayed as typical of the servants of her childhood: stocky and solid. Other adults are usually viewed with the unsentimental eye of a child, and she paints hairy, bony, yet powerful female figures. Power and dominance are major themes; she revives the military outfits of postwar Portugal for her men and dresses many of her women like dolls in national costume. Several of her pictures convey sexual opposition, the result of a background dominated by the regimes of the Roman Catholic Church and a military dictatorship. Her images are rarely beautiful, but are undoubtedly amusing, disturbing and powerful.

1

Lisbon & Estoril

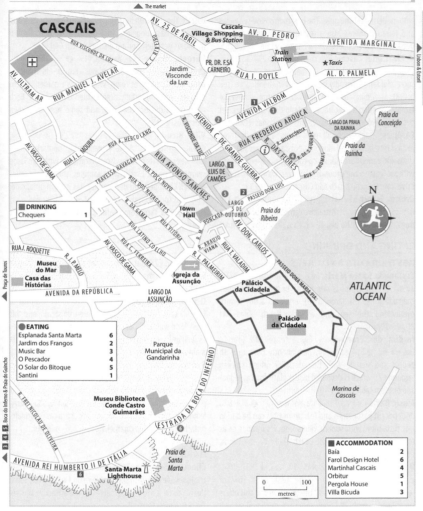

CASCAIS

The market

AV. 25 DE ABRIL

Cascais
Village Shopping
& Bus Station

AV. D. PEDRO

AVENIDA MARGINAL

RUA VISCONDE DA LUZ

R. C. RIBEIRO

Jardim
Visconde
da Luz

PR. DR. F.SÁ
CARNEIRO

Train
Station

★ Taxis

RUA I. DOYLE

AL. D. PALMELA

AV. ULTRAM AR

RUA MANUEL J. AVELAR

AVENIDA VALBOM

Praia da
Conceição

AV. VASCO DE GAMA

RUA J. L. MOURA

RUA A. HERCU LANO

AVENIDA C. DE GRANDE GUERRA

RUA FREDERICO AROUCA

LARGO DA PRAIA
DA RAINHA

R. VISCONDE DA LUZ

R. MISERICÓRDIA

R. DAS FLORES

Praia da
Rainha

TRAVESSA NAVEGANTES

RUA AFONSO SANCHES

LARGO
LUIS DE
CAMÕES

R. DA S.-JORGE

RUA POÇO NOVO

RUA DOS NAVEGANTES

PASSEIO DOM LUIS

R. E. THOMAS

N

R. DA GAMA

RUA VITÓRIA

Town
Hall

LARGO
5 DE
OUTUBRO

Praia da
Ribeira

RUA LATINO COELHO

AV. VASCO DE GAMA

RUA C. FERREIRA

RONCADA

R. M.

AV. DOM. CARLOS I

RUA J. ROQUETTE

R. J. P. MELO

R. L. ARAUJO
VIANA

RUA T. VALADIM

PASSEIO DONA MARIA PIA

DRINKING

Chequers   1

Praia de Touros

Museu
do Mar
Casa das
Histórias

AVENIDA DA REPÚBLICA

Igreja da
Assunção

R. L. PALMEIRIM

LARGO DA
ASSUNÇÃO

Palácio
da Cidadela

ATLANTIC
OCEAN

Palácio
da Cidadela

EATING

Esplanada Santa Marta	6
Jardim dos Frangos	2
Music Bar	3
O Pescador	4
O Solar do Bitoque	5
Santini	1

Parque
Municipal da
Gandarinha

ESTRADA DA BOCA DO INFERNO

Marina de
Cascais

Boca do Inferno & Praia do Guincho

R. FREI NICOLAU DE OLIVEIRA

Museu Biblioteca
Conde Castro
Guimarães

AVENIDA REI HUMBERTO II DE ITÁLIA

Praia de
Santa
Marta

Santa Marta
Lighthouse

0	100
metres	

ACCOMMODATION

Baía	2
Farol Design Hotel	6
Martinhal Cascais	4
Orbitur	5
Pergola House	1
Villa Bicuda	3

ARRIVAL AND INFORMATION

CASCAIS

By train The train station is on Largo da Estação, a couple of minutes' walk from the centre of town.

By bus The bus station is opposite the train station, beneath Cascais Village Shopping, with regular buses to Cabo da Roca (approx hourly; 40min), Guincho (every 1–2 hours; 20 min) and Sintra (approx hourly; 1hr).

Information Cascais' turismo is on Largo Cidade Vitória (daily 9am–6pm; ☎ 912 034 214, ⊛ visitcascais.com); staff will usually phone around on your behalf for private rooms.

ACCOMMODATION

Baía Passeio D. Luis ☎ 214 831 033, ⊛ hotelbaia .com. Modern seafront hotel overlooking the harbour, with a great rooftop pool and bar and a highly regarded restaurant. It has over a hundred rooms, all with a/c and satellite TV, and many with a sea view (book ahead in summer for these). **€125**

★ **Farol Design Hotel** Av Rei Humberto II de Italia 7 ☎ 214 823 490, ⊛ farol.com.pt. Right on the seafront, this is one of the area's most fashionable hideaways, neatly combining traditional and contemporary architecture. A new designer wing has been added onto a sixteenth-century villa, and the decor combines wood and marble

1

with modern steel and glass. The best rooms have sea views and terraces. There's also a restaurant, fantastic fairy-lit outside bar and seapool facing a fine rocky foreshore. **€265**
★**Martinhal Cascais** Rua do Clube 2 ☎ 218 507 788, ⓦ martinhal.com. Taking its name from the hugely successful family-friendly beach resort in the Algarve (see p.488), *Martinhal Cascais* is another sure-fire winner for families wanting top facilities in splendid surroundings. Set between two golf courses, rooms and villas (two-bed €438) are huge with all mod cons, and with three restaurants, indoor and outdoor pools, a fabulous spa, kids clubs and various activities, you could easily spend a week without leaving the grounds. However, it's only a 10min drive from Guincho beach and Cascais centre. **€237**
Orbitur Guincho Lugar da Areia, EN247, Guincho ☎ 214 870 450, ⓦ orbitur.pt. Attractive campsite set among pine trees close to Guincho beach, which is served by bus from

Cascais. The site, with its own tennis courts, minimarket and café, also has bungalows and caravans for rent. Orbitur members get a ten-percent discount. Pitch **€40**
Pergola House Av Valbom 13 ☎ 214 840 040, ⓦ pergolahouse.com. Sumptuous century-old mansion bang in the centre of town, with its own garden, stucco ceilings and wonderfully ornate, tiled dining room. Each room has a distinct character, and some have their own balconies. **€135**
Vila Bicuda Rua dos Faisões ☎ 214 8960 200, ⓦ vilabicuda.com. A very well run, upmarket villa complex set in its own landscaped grounds with two large swimming pools. Excellent for families, the modern villas are well equipped and the complex has its own great café, shop and (pricey) Italian restaurant. But you'll need a car – it's around 3km from central Cascais towards Guincho. **€146**

EATING AND DRINKING

RESTAURANTS AND CAFÉS
Esplanada Santa Marta Av Rei Humberto II de Itália ☎ 961 577 902. This is one of the best places to enjoy charcoal-grilled fish (around €8) served on a tiny terrace overlooking the sea and a little beach. Tues–Sat 10am–10pm.
Jardim dos Frangos Av Combatentes da Grande Guerra 68 ☎ 214 861 717. Permanently buzzing with people and sizzling with the speciality grilled chicken (around €7), which is devoured by the plate-load at indoor and outdoor tables. Daily 10am–midnight.
Music Bar Largo da Praia da Rainha 121 ☎ 214 820 848. Decent pasta, grills and fish (from €14) can be had in this restaurant with superb views from its interior or at tables on the patio above the beach. Daily 10am–10pm; Oct–May closed Mon.
O Pescador Rua das Flores 10 ☎ 214 832 054, ⓦ restaurantepescador.com. The best of a row of restaurants on this street near the tourist office, this offers superior fish meals and good service. A meal will set you

back a good €25, but main courses such as tuna cooked in garlic are sublime. Mon 6.30–11pm, Tues–Sat noon–3pm & 6.30–11pm.
O Solar do Bitoque Rua Regimento 19 de Infantaria, Loja 11 ☎ 918 580 343. *Bitoques* are thin steaks, and this lively local with outdoor seating specializes in various types as well as inexpensive burgers, salads and fresh fish; most mains under €10. Mon–Sat 10am–midnight.
Santini Av Valbom 28F ☎ 214 833 709. Opened by an Italian immigrant just after the World War II, *Santini's* ice creams arc legendary in these parts. Fresh, natural ingredients produce delicious fruity flavours such as mango, strawberry, lemon and passion fruit or "classics" such as chocolate, pistachio, almond and caramel. Daily 11am–midnight.

BARS
Chequers Largo Luís de Camões 7 ☎ 214 830 926. Lively English-style pub with sports shown on TV and so-so food; the big draw is the outdoor tables on the attractive square. Daily 9.30am–2am.

Sintra

The attractive, verdant town of **SINTRA** warrants at least a day of anyone's itinerary, though two or three days would allow you to make the most of its fabulous surroundings. The cooler air of the hilltop town made it the preferred summer retreat for Portugal's royalty; over the years it has also attracted the rich and famous, and inspired countless writers, including Lord Byron (who begins his epic poem *Childe Harold* in "Cintra's glorious Eden") and Gothic-novel writer William Beckford. It was awarded UNESCO World Heritage status in 1995 because "the cultural landscape of the Serra and the town of Sintra represents a pioneering approach to Romantic landscaping that had an outstanding influence on developments elsewhere in Europe".

The town's historic centre spreads across the slopes of several steep hills. Dominating the centre of **Sintra-Vila** are the tapering chimneys of the **Palácio Nacional**, surrounded by an array of tall houses painted in pale pink, ochre or mellow yellow, many with

STRANGE HAPPENINGS IN SINTRA

Sintra has been a centre for **cult worship** for centuries: the early Celts named it Mountain of the Moon after one of their gods and the hills are scattered with ley lines and mysterious tombs. Locals say batteries drain in the area faster than elsewhere and light bulbs seem to pop with monotonous regularity. Some claim this is because of the angle of iron in the rocks, others that it is all part of the **mystical powers** that lurk in Sintra's hills and valleys. There are certainly plenty of **geographical and meteorological quirks**. In the woods around Capuchos, house-sized boulders litter the landscape as if thrown by giants, while a white cloud – affectionately known as the queen's fart – regularly hovers over Sintra's palaces even on the clearest summer day. Exterior walls seem to merge with the landscape as they are quickly smothered in a thick layer of ferns, lichens and moss. And its castles, palaces, mansions and follies shelter tales of Masonic rites, insanity and eccentricity that are as fantastical as the buildings themselves.

ornate turrets and decorative balconies peering out to the plains of Lisbon far below. All this is highly scenic – though summer crowds can swamp its narrow central streets, and once you've seen the sights, you're best off heading to the surrounding attractions up in the hills. Easiest to reach are the **Castelo dos Mouros** and the extraordinary **Palácio da Pena** – both visible on the wooded heights above town – or the lush gardens of **Monserrate**, though you'll need a car to see the **Convento dos Capuchos**.

Sintra's annual **festa** in honour of St Peter is held on June 28 and 29, while in May the **Sintra Music Festival** puts on classical performances in a number of the town's buildings, including the Palácio Nacional. The end of July sees the **Feira Grande** in São Pedro, with crafts, antiques and cheeses on sale.

Palácio Nacional

Largo da Rainha Dona Amélia • Daily: March–Oct 9.30am–7pm; Nov–Feb 9.30am–5.30pm • €10 • ☎ 219 237 300, ⓦ parquesdesintra.pt

Best seen early or late in the day to avoid the crowds, the sumptuous and wonderfully atmospheric **Palácio Nacional** largely dates from the reign of Dom João I (1385–1433), making it the oldest surviving palace in Portugal, though sadly, after the fall of the monarchy in 1910, most of the surrounding walls and medieval houses were destroyed. Embellished by a series of monarchs – notably Manuel I (1495–1521) – the palace displays a range of architectural styles from Moorish tiles to Manueline decorations and Gothic battlements.

On the lower floor of the palace, you'll pass through the beautiful **Sala dos Cisnes** (Hall of Swans), a reception room named after the painted swans on its ceiling, and the **Sala das Pegas** (Hall of Magpies). The story goes that Dom João I had the room decorated with as many magpies as there were women at court, implying that they were all magpie-like gossips after he was allegedly caught canoodling with one of the servants.

The highlight of the upper floor is the gallery above the palace chapel. Beyond here, a succession of state rooms leads to the **Sala das Brasões**, a dazzling domed hall embellished with 72 coats of arms representing Portuguese nobility. Finally, back down on the ground floor don't miss the **kitchens**, whose roofs taper into the 33m-high chimneys which are the palace's distinguishing features.

Quinta da Regaleira

Daily: April–Sept 10am–8pm; Oct & Feb–March 10am–6.30pm; Nov–Jan 10am–5.30pm • 90min tours every 30min–1hr; reservations essential • €10; unguided visits €6 • ☎ 219 106 650, ⓦ regaleira.pt

Just a five-minute walk southwest of town on the Seteais–Monserrate road, **Quinta da Regaleira** is one of Sintra's most elaborate estates, laid out at the start of the twentieth century, and declared a UNESCO World Heritage Site in 1995. The estate was designed by Italian architect and theatrical set designer Luigi Manini for wealthy landowner António Augusto Carvalho Monteiro. The Italian's sense of the dramatic is

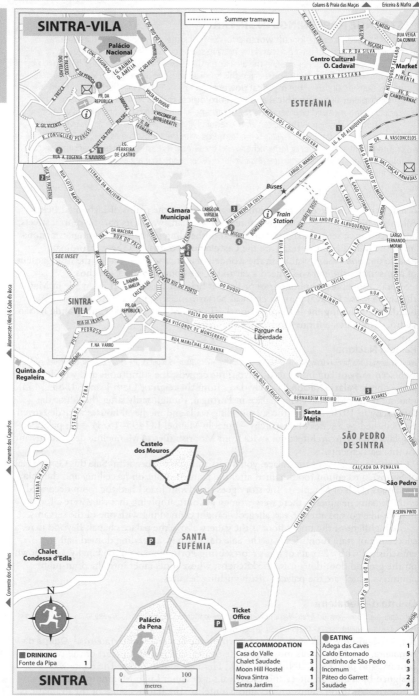

Colares & Praia das Maças   Ericeira & Mafra

········· Summer tramway

SINTRA-VILA

Palácio Nacional

PR. DA REPÚBLICA

LG. FERREIRA DE CASTRO

RUA A. EUGENIA F. NAVARRO

Centro Cultural O. Cadaval

Market

ESTEFÂNIA

RUA CÂMARA PESTANA

Câmara Municipal

LARGO DR. VIRGILIA HORTA

Buses

Train Station

LARGO D. MANUEL I

SEE INSET

SINTRA-VILA

PR. DA REPÚBLICA

RUA GIL VICENTE

PEDROSO

F. NA VARRO

Parque da Liberdade

Quinta da Regaleira

VOLTA DO DUQUE

SÃO PEDRO DE SINTRA

Santa Maria

CALÇADA DA PENALVA

São Pedro

R SERPA PINTO

Castelo dos Mouros

SANTA EUFÉMIA

Chalet Condessa d'Edla

N

Palácio da Pena

Ticket Office

Cruz Alta

■ **DRINKING**
Fonte da Pipa   1

SINTRA

0   100
metres

■ **ACCOMMODATION**
Casa do Valle   2
Chalet Saudade   3
Moon Hill Hostel   4
Nova Sintra   1
Sintra Jardim   5

● **EATING**
Adega das Caves   1
Caldo Entornado   5
Cantinho de São Pedro 6
Incomum   3
Páteo do Garrett   2
Saudade   4

Monserrate (4km) & Cabo ¢s Roca

Convento dos Capuchos

Convento dos Capuchos

obvious: the principal building, the mock-Manueline **Palaço dos Milhões**, sprouts turrets and towers, though the interior is sparse apart from some elaborate Rococo wooden ceilings and impressive Art Nouveau tiles. The surrounding **gardens** are more impressive and shelter fountains, terraces, lakes and grottoes. The most memorable feature is the **Initiation Well**, inspired by the initiation practices of the Knights Templar and Freemasons. Entering via a Harry Potter-style revolving stone door, you can walk down a moss-covered spiral stairway to the foot of the well and through a tunnel, which eventually resurfaces at the edge of a lake.

Monserrate

Estrada da Monserrate • Daily: March–Oct 9.30am–7pm; Nov–Feb 10am–5pm • €8 • ☎ 219 237 300, ⓦ parquesdesintra.pt • Bus #435 from Sintra station, via Sintra-Vila, departs every 30min or so

About an hour's walk west of the Quinta da Regaleira, the fabulous gardens and palace of **Monserrate** are most associated with William Beckford, a wealthy MP and author of the Gothic novel *Vathek*. He rented the estate from 1793 to 1799, after he was forced to leave Britain when caught in a compromising position with a 16-year-old boy. He set about improving the place, by landscaping a waterfall and recreating elements of his estate at Fonthill in Wiltshire.

Half a century later, a second immensely rich Englishman, Sir Francis Cook, bought the estate, with scarcely less ambitious plans. Cook imported the head gardener from Kew to lay out succulents and water plants, tropical ferns and palms, and just about every known conifer. For a time Monserrate boasted the only lawn in Iberia and it remains one of Europe's most richly stocked **gardens**, with over a thousand different species of subtropical trees and plants.

From the entrance, paths lead steeply down through tree ferns and lush undergrowth to a ruined chapel, half-engulfed by a giant banyan tree. From here, lawns take you up to Cook's main legacy, the construction of a great **palace** inspired by Brighton Pavilion, with its mix of Moorish and Italian decoration – the dome is modelled on the Duomo in Florence. The interior has largely been restored after years of neglect and you can now admire the amazingly intricate plasterwork which covers almost every wall and ceiling. Don't miss the billiard room, with superb views over the coast. The park also has a decent café.

Castelo dos Mouros

Daily: March–Oct 9.30am–8pm; Nov–Feb 10am–6pm • €8 • ☎ 219 237 300, ⓦ parquesdesintra.pt • Bus #434 from Sintra station or Sintra-Vila

From Sintra, it's a pleasant, if steep, walk up to the spectacular ruined ramparts of the **Castelo dos Mouros**, the "Castle of the Moors" (30–40min): start at the Calçada dos Clérigos, near the church of Santa Maria, from where a stone pathway leads all the way up to the lower slopes, where you can see a Moorish grain silo and a ruined twelfth-century church. To enter the castle itself, you'll need to buy a ticket at the main entrance on the road up from Sintra. Built in the ninth century, the castle was taken from the Moors in 1147 by Afonso Henriques, Portugal's first monarch: the ruins of a Moorish mosque remain. The castle walls were allowed to fall into disrepair over subsequent centuries, though they were restored in the mid-nineteenth century under the orders of Ferdinand II. The castle is partly built into two craggy pinnacles, and views from up here are dazzling both inland and across to the Atlantic. Excavations have revealed the ruins of Muslim houses, thirty Medieval Christian graves and ceramic vases dating back to the fifth century BC.

Palácio da Pena

Estrada da Pena • Daily: March–Oct 9.45am–7pm; Nov–Feb 10am–6pm • Palace, gardens & Chalet Condessa d'Edla €14; Chalet Condessa d'Edla & gardens €9.50; gardens only €7.50 • ☎ 219 237 300, ⓦ parquesdesintra.pt • Bus #434 from Sintra station or Sintra-Vila to the ticket office, every 20min; the shuttle bus between the ticket office and palace is €3 return

From the ticket office (which lies at the bottom of the park below the palace), it's a

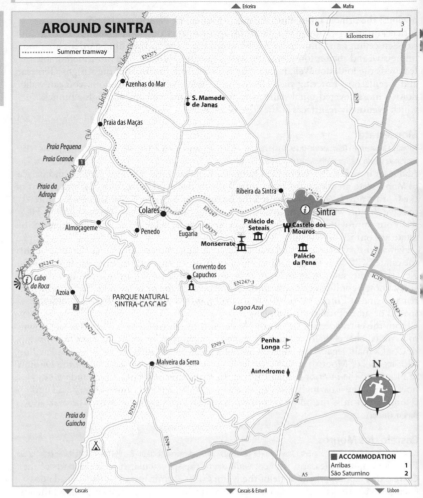

AROUND SINTRA

··········· Summer tramway

0   3
kilometres

▲ Ericeira   ▲ Mafra

Azenhas do Mar

S. Mamede
de Janas

Praia das Maças

Praia Pequena
Praia Grande

Praia da
Adraga

Ribeira da Sintra

Colares

Sintra

Almoçageme   Penedo

Eugaria

Palácio de
Seteais

Castelo dos
Mouros

Monserrate

Palácio
da Pena

Cabo
da Roca

Azoia

PARQUE NATURAL
SINTRA-CASCAIS

Convento dos
Capuchos

Lagoa Azul

Penha
Longa

Malveira da Serra

Autodrome

N

Praia do
Guincho

■ ACCOMMODATION
Arribas   1
São Saturnino   2

▼ Cascais   ▼ Cascais & Estoril   ▼ Lisbon

short ride on a shuttle bus or a twenty-minute walk up through the **gardens** – a stretch of rambling woodland with a scattering of lakes and follies – to the fantastical **Palácio da Pena** itself. Resembling something out of a Shrek film, with its ornate medley of domes, statues and towers, the palace was built in the late 1840s by the German Baron von Eschwege on the site of a former monastery – whose chapel remains inside the palace today. Queen Maria II's husband, Ferdinand of Saxe-Coburg-Gotha, requested some of the embellishments, which embrace various architectural styles from Moorish to Manueline. The palace was subsequently used as a summer retreat for the royals, and Queen Amélie, mother of the last king of Portugal, stayed the night here before the royals were driven into exile at the birth of the Republic in 1910. The **interior** of the palace is also highly impressive, packed with furniture, paintings and imposing statues – the ballroom and royal dining room are particularly lavish. You can also look round the mock-alpine **Chalet Condessa d'Edla** in the grounds, built by Ferdinand in the 1860s as a retreat for his second wife.

Convento dos Capuchos

9km southwest of Sintra on the EN247-3 • Daily: March to Oct 9.30am–8pm; Nov–Feb 10am–6pm • €7 • ☎ 219 237 381, Ⓦ parquedesintra.pt

Built in 1560, the **Convento dos Capuchos** is known as the "cork convent" because of its cork doors and cell-like rooms, cut from rock and also lined with cork. This natural insulation gave the resident monks a modicum of comfort in otherwise incredibly basic conditions. It's hard not to be moved by the simplicity of the place, which was occupied for almost three hundred years before finally being abandoned in 1834 by its seven remaining monks. You can enter some of the **penitents' cells** by crawling through 70cm-high doors; here, and on every other ceiling, doorframe and lintel, panels of cork are attached, which were taken from the surrounding woods. Elsewhere, you'll come across a washroom, kitchen, refectory, tiny chapels, even a bread oven set apart from the main complex.

ARRIVAL AND DEPARTURE   SINTRA

By train Sintra station is on Avenida Dr. Miguel Bombarda, a 10–15min walk from Sintra-Vila, the historic centre of the town, with trains from Lisbon's Rossio and Sete Rios stations roughly every 20min (45min; €2.65 one-way).

By bus Buses from Cascais (approx hourly; 1hr), stop outside Sintra train station.

GETTING AROUND

Local buses Local buses depart across the street from the train station, with bus #403 to and from Cabo da Roca (every 1–2 hr; 40min) and #441 to the Sintra beaches (see p.118). Bus #434 takes a circular route from Sintra station and Sintra-Vila to the Pena Palace and the Castelo dos Mouros via São Pedro (every 20min; €5 return), while bus #435 goes from Sintra station and Sintra-Vila to Quinta da Regaleira and Monserrate gardens (approx every 45min; €2.50 return).

Bus pass If you want to visit several sights in the area, including the coast, consider a Day-rover ticket, which allows travel on all the local buses run by Scotturb (Ⓦ scotturb.com; €12 for seven journeys within a year).

Tram A summer-only tram runs from Sintra to the coast via Colares (April–June and Sept Fri–Sun 3 daily; July–Aug 3–6 daily; 50min; €3).

Tuk-tuk tours Various tuk-tuk tours depart from outside the station, with prices starting at around €40/hr for two people.

INFORMATION

Information Sintra turismo (daily 9.30am–6pm, until 7pm in Aug; ☎ 219 231 157, Ⓦ cm-sintra.pt) lies just off the central Praça da República. There's also a small turismo desk at Sintra station (same hours). Ask at the tourist offices about combined tickets that can save money on entry to the main sites.

ACCOMMODATION

Casa do Valle Rua da Paderna 2 ☎ 219 244 699, Ⓦ casadovalle.com. Though steeply downhill from the historic centre, this charming guesthouse still commands unbeatable views across the wooded slopes of Sintra. There are various rooms, from top-floor doubles with the best views, to ground-floor rooms with their own terraces. All the rooms access a beautiful garden with its own pool. Good for families, with interconnecting rooms. **€90**

Chalet Saudade Rua Dr. Alfredo Costa 21 ☎ 210 150 055, Ⓦ saudade.pt. This tall eighteenth-century chalet has been superbly renovated, retaining many of its quirky original fittings. The interior is all parquet flooring, swirling stairways, stained glass and beautiful *azulejos*. Stairs take you down three floors to rooms of varying sizes: €10 extra gets you the one opening onto the garden. Breakfast is extra. **€70**

Moon Hill Hostel Rua Guilherme Gomes Fernandes 17 ☎ 969 831 095, Ⓦ moonhillhostel.com. Near Sintra station, this fantastic hostel has friendly staff, stylish decor

and a range of contemporary rooms from en-suite doubles with a view of the castle to tidy dorms with smart bunk beds. There's a communal kitchen and lounge with a wood burner for the winter and a terrace and patio for chilling out in summer. Dorms **€20**; doubles **€60**

Nova Sintra Largo Afonso d'Albuquerque 25 ☎ 219 230 220, Ⓦ novasintra.com. This hotel is in a big mansion above a decent restaurant, which has a raised café-terrace overlooking the busy street. Modern rooms, all with cable TV, bath and shiny marble floors. **€95**

★ **Sintra Jardim** Trav dos Álvares ☎ 219 230 738, Ⓦ hotelsintrajardim.pt. The best mid-range option in the area, this rambling old building has soaring ceilings, wooden floors and oodles of character. There's a substantial garden with a swimming pool and the giant rooms can easily accommodate extra beds – so it's great for families. You'll need to book ahead in summer; in winter there's a log fire in the communal lounge. **€80**

1

EATING AND DRINKING

There's a great **market** – with antiques and crafts, as well as food – held in São Pedro's main square, 2km southeast of Sintra-Vila, on the second and last Sunday of every month. Good restaurants are thin on the ground around Sintra; the best are close to the station. Local specialities include *queijadas da Sintra* – sweet cheese pastry-cakes.

CAFÉS AND RESTAURANTS

Adega das Caves Rua de Pendoa 2–10 ☎ 219 239 848, ⓦ adegadascaves.com. Bustling café-bar beneath *Café Paris*, attracting a predominantly youthful local clientele; good-value salads and baguettes as well as inexpensive grills from around €9. Daily 9am–2am.

Caldo Entornado Rua Dr. Alfredo Costa 22 ☎ 219 243 719 ⓦ incomumbyluissantos.pt. Close to the station, this upmarket restaurant and wine bar is run by chef Luis Santos. His stints in some of Switzerland's top restaurants are reflected in a menu featuring the likes of scallops with mushroom risotto, black linguini with seafood or steak with sweet potatoes, though the ingredients are local and top quality. Mains from €15. Mon, Wed–Fri & Sun noon–midnight, Sat 4.30pm–midnight.

Cantinho de São Pedro Pr D. Fernando II 18 ☎ 219 230 267 ⓦ cantinhosaopedro.com. Large, stone-walled restaurant overlooking an attractive courtyard just off São Pedro's main square. Slightly formal service but excellent food at reasonable prices. Try the daily specials (around €9), which are usually good value. On cool evenings, a log fire keeps things cosy. Daily noon–3pm & 7.30–10pm.

★ **Páteo do Garrett** Rua Maria Eugénia Reis F. Navarro 7 ☎ 219 243 380. Bar-restaurant with a dark interior, though the lovely, sunny patio has great views over the village. It serves standard Portuguese meals, such as monkfish rice, from around €12 – or just pop in for a drink. May–Dec Thurs–Tues 11am–11pm; closes 2pm Jan–April.

Saudade Av Dr. Miguel Bombarda 6 ☎ 212 428 804, ⓦ saudade.pt. This buzzy café used to be a factory selling *queijadas* and has a warren of rooms and its own art gallery, with occasional live music. As well as cakes, scones and sandwiches, it serves some interesting *petiscos* snacks such as Madeiran garlic bread and regional cheeses. A wide range of drinks and teas includes Gorreana tea from the Azores. Daily 8.30am–8pm.

BARS

Fonte da Pipa Rua Fonte da Pipa 11–13 ☎ 219 234 437. This laidback bar with low lighting is one of the few bars in this part of town, and sits next to the lovely fountain (*fonte*) the street is named after. Daily 9pm–3am.

The Sintra coast

West of Sintra the road winds around through the hills to **PRAIA GRANDE**, the best beach on this section of coast, certainly for surfers. In August the World Bodyboarding Championships are held here, along with games such as volleyball and beach rugby. Plenty of inexpensive cafés and restaurants spread along the beachside road. Just north of Praia Grande is the larger resort of **PRAIA DAS MAÇÃS**, a lively little holiday village with plenty of bars and restaurants sprawled round a broad expanse of sand – a good place to spend a day or two. Sintra's **historic tramway** offers the most picturesque, if rather slow, route to the coast: opened in 1904, the tram trundles along from the northeast part of Sintra to the coast at Praia das Maçãs via Colares.

The most visited part of this coast, however, is **CABO DA ROCA**, 14km southwest of Praia Grande and officially the most westerly point in mainland Europe – the tourist office in the souvenir shop and café here sells a certificate to prove it. It's an enjoyable trip to get here, though the cape itself offers little more than a lighthouse below which Atlantic breakers slam the cliffs.

ARRIVAL AND INFORMATION

THE SINTRA COAST

By bus Bus #441 runs from Sintra train station to Praia Grande and Praia das Maçãs (every 1–2hr; around 30–40min). Bus #403 runs approx hourly to Cabo da Roca from both Sintra (40min) and Cascais train stations (40min).

By tram The tram runs from the start of the N247, just north of Avenida Heliodora Salgado in Sintra-Estefânia to

Praia das Maçãs (April–Sept Fri–Sun 3 daily, 6 daily Sat & Sun in July and Aug; 50min; €3). Check the local timings with the Sintra tourist board as service interruptions seem to be the norm.

Information The Cabo da Roca turismo is in the souvenir shop on the headland (daily 9am–8pm; closes 7pm Oct–May; ☎ 219 280 891, ⓦ cm-sintra.pt).

1

ACCOMODATION

Arribas Av A. Coelho 28, Praia Grande ☎ 219 289 050, ⓦ hotelarribas.pt. This slightly dated three-star dominates the seafront at the north end of the sands. The rooms, however, are enormous and the hotel boasts sea pools, a restaurant and café-terrace with great sea views. **€120**

São Saturnino Azóia ☎ 219 289 686, ⓦ saosat.com.

Reached down a steep track – look for the sign on the left on the way to Azóia/Cabo da Roca – this former convent dates from the twelfth century and sits in a valley where time seems to stand still. The six rooms, three suites and self-catering apartment all come with wooden beams and low ceilings. There's a small outdoor pool and lots of terraces with stunning views. **€140**

Palácio de Queluz

Largo do Palácio, Queluz Belas • Daily 9am–5pm; gardens open till 6pm May–Sept • €10, or €8 after 3.30pm; gardens only €5 • ☎ 219 237 300, ⓦ parquesdesintra.pt • Take the Sintra line train from Rossio to Queluz-Belas station (every 20min; 20min, €1.85): turn left out of the station and walk down the main road for 15min, following signs through the town until you reach a vast cobbled square, Largo do Palácio

Around 13km northwest of Lisbon city centre and 16km southeast of Sintra, the **Palácio de Queluz** is one of Portugal's most sumptuous palaces. Commissioned in 1747 by Dom Pedro, brother of King José I, its striking Rococo exterior and formal gardens were clearly influenced by the Palace of Versailles. It was built as a summer residence for the royals, but ended up being the permanent home of Dona Maria I, aka Maria the Mad. She married her uncle Dom Pedro, and became queen after José I's death in 1777, but after the death of her husband in 1786, Maria suffered severe psychiatric problems and is said to have alarmed visitors who could hear her screaming from her palace bedroom. The palace was occupied and pillaged by French forces during the Napoleonic wars, when the Portuguese royal family fled to Brazil, though plenty of priceless works of art survived. Palácio de Queluz is now preserved as a museum, with its original artwork displayed alongside pieces installed on the royal family's return to the palace in 1821, and is still pressed into service now and again to accommodate state guests and dignitaries, as well as hosting events for the Sintra music festival.

The palace and gardens

Visitors first enter the **Throne Room**, lined with mirrors surmounted by paintings and golden flourishes. Beyond is the more restrained **Music Chamber** with its portrait of Queen Maria above the French grand piano. Smaller quarters include bed and sitting rooms, a tiny oratory swathed with red velvet, and a **Sculpture Room**, whose only exhibit is an earthenware bust of Maria. Another wing comprises an elegant suite of public rooms – smoking, coffee and dining rooms – all intimate in scale and tastefully decorated. The **Ambassador's Chamber**, where diplomats and foreign ministers were received during the nineteenth century, echoes the Throne Room in style, with one side lined with porcelain chinoiserie. In the end, though, perhaps the most pleasing room is the simple **Dressing Room** with its geometric inlaid wooden floor and spider's-web ceiling of radial gilt bands.

Outside, the formal **gardens** consist of low box hedges and weatherworn statues spreading out from the protection of the palace wings, while small pools and fountains, steps and terracing form a harmonious background to the building.

South of the Rio Tejo

The south bank of the river Tejo was linked to Lisbon only by ferry until 1966, when the "Salazar Bridge" was built. Renamed the **Ponte 25 de Abril** after the 1974 Revolution, this huge suspension bridge opened up the south bank to the encroaching city. **Cacilhas** is the port you'll arrive at if you come by ferry, while **Caparica** is the main resort along the superb Costa da Caparica, which stretches for some 20km to the south.

Cacilhas

Daily ferries from Lisbon's Cais do Sodré (5.20am–1.20am; every 15min; €1.20; ⓦ transtejo.pt)

The most enjoyable way to approach the southern bank of the Rio Tejo is to take the ferry from Lisbon's Cais do Sodré to the little port of **CACILHAS**. The blustery ride grants wonderful views of the city, as well as of the Ponte 25 de Abril, though it's the line of **seafood restaurants** along the riverfront that attracts most Lisboetas to make the crossing. The moderately priced riverside *Cervejaria Farol* is a good bet, though if you head towards the bridge along the Cais do Ginjal you'll find plenty of others with great Lisbon outlooks.

Dom Fernando II e Gloria

Tues–Sun 10am–5pm • €4 • ☎ 917 841 149, ⓦ dfernando.marinha.pt

Just past Cacilhas's main bus station, the moored nineteenth-century frigate, **Dom Fernando II e Gloria**, is now home to an interesting museum. Dating from 1843, it was the last military frigate built by the Portuguese, and assisted in preserving Portugal's colonies in India. It was decommissioned in 1878 and was left to rot in the Tagus until 1990, when it was artfully restored; today, displays recount what life was like for its crew during the nineteenth century.

Elevador Panorâmico da Boca do Vento

Daily 8am–midnight • €2 return

Just along the waterfront from the Cacilhas ferry terminal is the foot of the **Elevador Panorâmico da Boca do Vento**, a sleek, modern elevator which whisks you up the cliff face to the old part of the neighbouring town of **Almada**. From the top there are fantastic views over the river and city, while the surrounding streets are highly atmospheric.

Cristo Rei

Av Cristo Rei 61 • Daily 9.30am–6.30pm • €4 • ☎ 212 751 000, ⓦ cristorei.pt • Bus #101 from Cacilhas

On a steep cliff above Almada, facing Lisbon across the Tejo, stands the Rio-like **Cristo Rei** (Christ the King) statue, built in 1959 as part of a church. A lift shuttles you up the interior of the statue to a viewing platform, 80m above the ground, with dramatic vistas over the Ponte 25 de Abril, the river and the city.

Caparica

Allegedly named after the discovery of a cloak (*capa*) full of golden coins, **CAPARICA**, at the northern end of the Costa da Caparica, is Lisbon's main beach resort. It's high-rise, tacky and packed at weekends in summer, but don't let that put you off – the family atmosphere, restaurants and seaside cafés full of tanned surfers make it a thoroughly enjoyable day out. From the main **Praça da Liberdade** (home to the market, supermarkets and banks), the pedestrianized **Rua dos Pescadores** – lined with cafés, restaurants and inexpensive guesthouses – heads down to the seafront. The **beach** itself stretches north towards Lisbon and south away into the distance. The water is of good quality, though beware the dangerous undertow.

Transpraia railway

June–Sept daily every 30min from 9am–7pm • €7.50 return, or €4.50 for first nine stops • ☎ 212 900 706, ⓦ transpraia.pt

A mini-railway, **Transpraia**, runs along Caparica's 8km or so of dunes to **Fonte da Telha** – if you're after solitude, just take the train to the last stop and walk. There are nineteen mini-train stops, most with a beach-café or two, and each with its own particular atmosphere: the earlier stops tend to be family-oriented, later ones are on the whole more fashionable, while stop 18–19 is something of a gay hangout.

By bus From Cacilhas take the Via Rapida bus (approx every 30min, daily 7am–9pm; 30min). Alternatively, bus 161 leaves from Areeiro in Lisbon (every 30–60min, daily 7am–12.45am; 40min–1hr).

Information The turismo is near the beach at Frente Urbana de Praias (Mon–Sat 9.30am–1pm & 2–5.30pm, closed Sat Oct–March; ☎212 900 071, ⓦ m-almada.pt).

ACCOMMODATION AND EATING

O Barbas Catedral Apoio de Praia 13 ☎212 900 163. This is the best of the dozens of fish and seafood restaurants in a row of modern wood-framed buildings on the promenade. It serves up affordable paella, *cataplana* and fresh fish (around €9). Daily noon–midnight; closed Wed Oct–April.

Orbitur Av Afonso de Albuquerque ☎212 901 366, ⓦorbitur.pt. Caparica's most central campsite is well-equipped, complete with a café and minimarket, though it gets pretty packed in August. Pitch €40

Real Caparica Hotel Rua Mestre Manuel 18 ☎212 918 870, ⓦrealcaparicahotel.com. Close to the beach and the centre, this small hotel is one of the best-value central options, with some of the en-suite rooms having sea-facing balconies. €50

Setúbal and Palmela

Some 50km south of Lisbon, **SETÚBAL** is a bustling and fairly industrial port, though its historic, pedestrianized centre is both lively and highly attractive, set round a series of squares and narrow alleys filled with decent shops and restaurants. It's a pleasant place to spend some time – take a dolphin trip or look round the remarkable Igreja de Jesus – while its ferry link over the wide Sado estuary gives easy access to miles of long sandy beaches.

Igreja de Jesus and Museu de Setúbal

Largo de Jesus • **Church** Tues–Sun 9am–noon & 2–5pm, closed public hols • Free • **Museum** Tues–Fri 11am–2pm & 3–6pm, Sat 11am–2pm & 2–6pm, Sun 2–6pm • Free • ☎ 265 537 890

Stranded in a somewhat bleak stretch of town, the **Igreja de Jesus** is one of the most important churches in Portugal. It was founded in 1490, and was a pioneer of the Manueline style that was developed by its architect Diogo de Boitaca (see box, p.169). Its most striking feature is its twisted columns, resembling ropes and made using the local stone from Arrábida. The beautiful *azulejo* tiles were seventeenth-century additions. To find out more about the church and its treasures, visit the somewhat dry **Museu de Setúbal**, housed in a former monastery adjacent to the church.

Casa da Baía

Av Luísa Todi 468 • Daily 9am–10pm; closes 8pm mid-Sept to May • Free • ☎ 265 545 010, ⓦvisitsetubal.com.pt

Housed in an eighteenth-century former convent, which later became an orphanage, **Casa da Baía** is still partly run by former orphans. It now houses the city's tourist office as well as a cultural centre and exhibition space, with its own wine shop (good for regional wines), restaurant and café in the internal courtyard.

Castelo São Felipe

ⓦ visitsetubal.co.pt

The **Castelo São Felipe**, signposted off the western end of Avenida Luísa Todi, was built on the orders of Spanish king Felipe II in 1590. It's a grand structure, harbouring an *azulejo*-lined chapel and protected by sheer walls of overpowering height. Legend has it that a series of secret tunnels connects the castle with the coast, but any proof was lost in the Great Earthquake of 1755. The castle was closed for essential repairs at the time of writing (check the website for updates and admission information), but when it reopens you can enjoy superb views over the mouth of the Sado estuary from its walls.

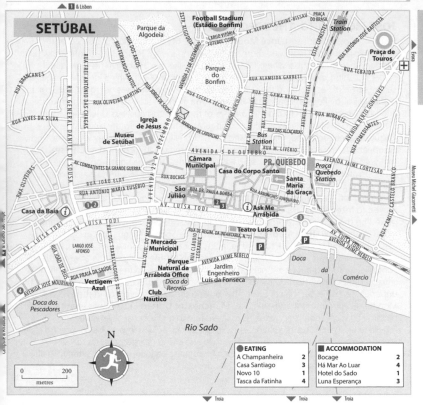

SETÚBAL

Parque da Algodeia
Football Stadium (Estádio Bonfim)
Train Station
Praça de Touros
Parque do Bonfim
Igreja de Jesus
Museu de Setúbal
Bus Station
Câmara Municipal
Casa do Corpo Santo
PR. QUEBEDO
Praça Quebedo Station
São Julião
Santa Maria da Graça
Casa da Baía
Ask Me Arrábida
Teatro Luísa Todi
Mercado Municipal
Parque Natural da Arrábida Office
Jardim Engenheiro Luís da Fonseca
Doca do Recreio
Vertigem Azul
Club Náutico
Doca da Comércio
Doca dos Pescadores
Rio Sado

N

0   200
metres

● EATING		■ ACCOMMODATION	
A Champanheira	2	Bocage	2
Casa Santiago	3	Há Mar Ao Luar	4
Novo 10	1	Hotel do Sado	1
Tasca da Fatinha	4	Luna Esperança	3

Tróia   Tróia   Tróia

Casa do Corpo Santo

Rua Corpo Santo 7 • June to mid-Sept Tues–Fri 9am–12.30pm & 2–5.30pm, Sat 3–7pm; mid-Sept to May Tues–Fri 9am–12.30pm & 2–5.30pm, Sat 2–6pm • €1.50 • ☎ 265 534 222

Take a peek inside the small but beautiful **Casa do Corpo Santo**, built in 1714 as a nobleman's palace and later used as a fishermen's fraternity. It's now a small museum celebrating the fisherman's craft. The upper floor has a painted ceiling, Baroque chapel and walls decked in superb *azulejos* showing scenes of São Pedro, patron saint of fishermen.

The riverfront

Most of Setúbal's **riverfront** is functional and unattractive, but it's worth strolling out past the **Doca de Pescadores** fishing harbour, where colourful boats moor up at the end of the day and fishermen still tend their nets. Continue southwest – parallel to Avenida José Mourinho – and you pick up a pedestrianized riverfont path to the slightly scruffy town **beach**, where the *Rockalot* kiosk café is a good spot for a seaside drink; if you want to swim, you're better off heading to Arrábida (see p.126).

Tróia

Across the Sado estuary, and reachable by ferry from Setúbal (see p.125), loom the high-rise apartments of **Tróia**, a surprisingly glitzy resort complete with marina and golf course, which looks like it's been beamed in from the Algarve. It sits at the tip of a large sand-spit which is fringed on the Atlantic side by a superb, sandy **beach** – if you have your own transport, however, you're best off heading further south to the quieter sands at Comporta (see p.426).

1

JOSÉ MOURINHO: THE SPECIAL ONE

Setúbal's most famous son, **José Mourinho**, is one of Europe's most successful and controversial football managers. Born in Setúbal on January 26, 1963, Mourinho grew up supporting Vitória Setúbal where his father was goalkeeper. He began his managerial career coaching their junior team after a modest playing career, which included a spell at Sesimbrense of Sesimbra, up the coast. His big break, however, was being former England manager Bobby Robson's translator at **Barcelona**. He exploited what he learnt from the English manager to turn round the fortunes of the previously useless União Leiria, which alerted Porto to his managerial talents. Under Mourinho, Porto swiftly landed the Portuguese league, Portuguese Cup and UEFA Cup (all in 2003), and they were crowned European Champions in 2004. His fame was cemented when he moved to **Chelsea** later that year and promptly won back-to-back league titles (they had not won a league title previously for half a century). Calling himself "the special one", Mourinho was booted out by the London club in 2007 when it was felt he was getting bigger than the club itself, but after a year off – mostly spent back in Setúbal – his career blossomed further, when he moved to **Inter Milan**. Here, he not only won back-to-back Italian league titles, but also picked up the European Champions League in 2010. His phenomenal success continued when he moved to **Real Madrid**, where he won the Spanish league title in 2011, and he was subsequently lured back to London in 2013 for a second stint with Chelsea, winning them the league yet again in 2015. Nevertheless, his off-the-field persona always attracts controversy. Booted out from Chelsea after a disastrous start to the 2015–16 season, he stirred up the Italian media with the same aplomb as he did in the UK and made himself unpopular in some quarters of Spain after poking the Barcelona coach in the eye. Mourinho's appointment as manager of **Manchester United** in 2016 was seen as a mixed blessing by many: controversy seems as inevitable to his career as silverware.

Despite his wealth and international profile, Mourinho remains loyal to his Portuguese roots. He married his childhood sweetheart (they have two children) and continues to visit his family in Setúbal. Not surprisingly, he has become a Portuguese national hero, and Setúbal's seafront road was recently renamed Avenida José Mourinho.

Tróia Ruínas Romanas

1km northeast of the Tróia passenger ferry terminal, and just northwest of the car ferry terminal • June–Aug Tues–Sat 10am–1pm & 3–6.30pm; Sept–Oct & March–May Sat 10am–1pm & 3–5.30pm • €5 • ☎ 265 499 400, ⓦ troiaresort.pt

The **Ruínas Romanas** are an impressive site that was once the Roman town of Cetobriga. It grew up from the first century AD as a fish-salting centre, before being abandoned in the sixth century, probably after an earthquake and tsunami. You can still see the stone tanks where the fish were preserved before being exported to Rome.

Palmela

The small town of **PALMELA**, 10km north of Setúbal, has an impressive medieval **castle**, now a hotel (see p.125), from which stunning views give out over the coast and the Parque Natural da Arrábida. It is also the centre of a wine-producing area, hence the town's major annual event, the **Festa das Vindimas**. Held in September, it celebrates the first of the year's wine harvest, with processions, fireworks, grape-treading and running of the bulls.

ARRIVAL AND GETTING AROUND
SETÚBAL AND PALMELA

By bus Setúbal and the surrounding area are served by TST buses (ⓦ tsuldotejo.pt), which arrive at and depart from the bus station on Avenida 5 de Outubro, a 5min walk from the pedestrianized centre.

Destinations Cacilhas (hourly; 50min–1hr); Lisbon's Praça de Espanha (every 30–60min; 1hr); Palmela (approx hourly; 20min), Sesimbra (approx hourly; 30min).

By car The fast A2 from Ponte 25 de Abril whisks you to Setúbal from Lisbon in around 40min; it's about the same from Lisbon airport via Ponte Vasco da Gama. There is metered parking on the main Avenida Luísa Todi, and free car parks down by the ferry terminal.

By light railway Setúbal and Palmela are both on the Fertagus light railway line (ⓦ fertagus.pt) from Lisbon's

Entrecampos and Sete-Rios stations (hourly; 50min to Palmela; 1hr to Setúbal).

By train Conventional trains run from Lisbon's Entrecampos station to Setúbal (approx every 30min; 1hr 10min; timetable on ☎ 707 127 127, ⓦ cp.pt), which drop you at Praça do Brasil, north of the town centre; local trains use the more central Praça Quebedo station at the eastern end of Avenida 5 de Outubro.

By ferry Car ferries ply the Sado estuary between Setúbal and Tróia (daily every 30–60min: from Setúbal 7.30am–10pm; from Tróia 8am–10.40pm; €3.95 per person single, cars from €15; ☎ 265 235 101, ⓦ www .atlanticferries.pt); expect long queues in summer. There's also an hourly passenger catamaran (daily, approx hourly: from Setúbal 6.20am–1am; from Tróia 6.45am–1.30am; €3.50 per person single).

INFORMATION AND ACTIVITIES

Information Setúbal's turismo is in the Casa da Baía (see p.122), Avenida Luísa Todi 468 (daily 9am–10pm; closes 8pm mid-Sept to May; ☎ 265 545 010, ⓦ mun-setubal.pt), and can give information about local jeep safaris, wine tours, birdwatching and canoeing/kayak hire.

Dolphin-watching tour Vertigem Azul, Rua Praia da Saúde 11D, near the harbour (☎ 265 238 000, ⓦ vertigemazul.com), runs wonderful 3hr dolphin-watching trips to see a resident pod of bottle-nosed dolphins, either in the Sado estuary or along the coast (daily, weather permitting, at 9.30am & 2.30pm, minimum eight people; €35 per person).

ACCOMMODATION

Bocage Rua de São Cristovão 14, Setúbal ☎ 265 543 080, ⓦ hoteisbocage.com. This is Setúbal's best budget option, right in the heart of the pedestrianized old town. The rooms are attractive and well-maintained with private bathrooms, a/c and TV. **€60**

Há Mar Ao Luar Estrada do Forte de São Filipe, Setúbal ☎ 265 220 901, ⓦ wonderfulland.com/maraoluar. Close to the Castelo, with dazzling views across the Sado estuary, this has various rooms and apartments dotted around grounds whose centrepiece is an old windmill, which you can stay in (€125). There's also a lovely outdoor pool. **€75**

Hotel do Sado Rua Irene Lisboa 1–3, Setúbal ☎ 265 542 800, ⓦ hoteldosado.com. Perched on a hilltop above a residential part of town, this renovated mansion has a modern extension with plush rooms, the best sharing the great views from the terrace and restaurant. **€70**

Luna Esperança Av Luísa Todi 220, Setúbal ☎ 265 521 780, ⓦ lunahoteis.com. Overlooking the main avenue, this high-rise has functional but pleasantly minimalist rooms, the best on the fourth and fifth floors, which stay clear of the street noise and offer views of the bay. There's also a decent restaurant and attractive top-floor breakfast room. Good value. **€75**

Pousada de Palmela Castelo de Palmela, Palmela ☎ 212 351 226, ⓦ pousadas.pt. Once the headquarters for the Order of Santiago, the convent in Palmela's castle has been restored and extended into a fabulous *pousada*, incorporating the original cloisters within the design and boasting panoramic views from all points. There's also a quality in-house restaurant. **€130**

EATING AND DRINKING

Good-value fish and seafood **restaurants** abound at Setúbal's waterside Doca dos Pescadores. There are also plenty of places to eat around the atmospheric **Mercado Municipal** (Tues–Sun 7.30am–2pm); in summer, the market area is considerably expanded with clothes and touristy bric-a-brac. **Nightlife** in Setúbal revolves around the outdoor café-bars along Avenida Luísa Todi and the grid of streets north of the Doca dos Pescadores.

A Champanheria Av Luísa Todi 414, Setúbal ☎ 265 220 996, ⓦ champanheria.com.pt. Classy oyster and champagne bar-restaurant whose owner is a champion of the Slow Food Movement. Tapas and oysters are the speciality (up to €10), though it also serves interesting mains such as prawn stew with coconut rice, from €15. Tues–Sat 12.30–3pm & 7–11pm, Sun 12.30–4pm.

Casa Santiago Av Luísa Todi 92, Setúbal ☎ 265 221 688. This friendly locals' place close to the ferry port is famed for serving one of Setúbal's specialities, *chocos* (fried cuttlefish), a bit like squid. If you don't fancy it, there are also various *bacalhau* and rice dishes from around €9. Mon–Sat noon–3pm & 6–10pm.

Novo 10 Av Luísa Todi 422–426, Setúbal ☎ 265 525 212. Local hero José Mourinho (see box, p.124) is said to favour this *marisqueira* with a big terrace facing the avenue, and it is easy to see why: great fish, seafood and the likes of barbecued goat. Prices are moderate, with mains around €12. Mon, Tues & Thurs–Sun noon–midnight.

Tasca da Fatinha Rua da Saúde 56, Setúbal ☎ 265 232 800. Good waterside restaurant right on the fisherman's dock, dishing up piles of fresh fish (around €10) straight from the outside grill. Daily noon–midnight.

1

Parque Natural da Arrábida

Just 7km southwest of Setúbal, the craggy, scrub- and wood-covered slopes of the Serra da Arrábida rise to around 500m above a dramatic coastline dotted with cove beaches. It's stunningly beautiful, though surprisingly little known to tourists: home to wildcats, badgers, polecats, buzzards and Bonelli's eagles, the region has had protected status since 1976 and makes up the **Parque Natural da Arrábida**. Walking guides are available from the park's main office in Setúbal (see p.127), though to get the most from the park you'll need a car – indeed, the spectacular N379-1 ranks as one of the most dramatic drives in Portugal. Note, however, that from July to August, a one-way system is in place on the narrow coastal road through the park, which operates westwards-only from 8am to 7pm (though the inland N10 and N379-1 roads operate both ways).

Convento da Arrábida

Tours Wed–Sun only, reservations essential • €5 • ☎ 212 197 620, ⓦ foriente.pt

Accessible on the N379-1, the highly picturesque, stacked white buildings of the **Convento da Arrábida** were built by Franciscan monks in 1542. Abandoned in the late nineteenth century, the buildings were restored in the 1950s and are now owned by the Fundação Orient, who use the spaces for seminars and conferences. Tours take in the original monastery building, gardens, shrines and the lodgings for pilgrims – with stunning ocean views from most of the site.

Portinho da Arrábida and Galapos

The most attractive destination on the coast, around 4km south of the convent down the winding N10, is the tiny harbour village of **PORTINHO DA ARRÁBIDA**, where a cluster of waterside restaurants and former fisherman's houses face the clear waters of the Bay of Setúbal – walk round the bay to the east to reach the coast's best beach, **Galapos**, which you can also reach from the coast road to Setúbal. Portinho's harbour is guarded by a tiny seventeenth-century fort, now housing the **Museu Oceanográfico** (Tues–Fri 10am–4pm, Sat 3–6pm, closed Sat in August; €3.50; ☎ 265 009 982), which displays marine animals from the region both live – in a small aquarium – and stuffed.

Praia da Figueirinha and the coast road

The six to seven kilometres of snaking coast road from Portinho da Arrábida towards Setúbal are dotted with various superb cove beaches – look for parking signs or the huddle of cars above them. **Praia da Figueirinha** is the largest and most accessible beach, a lovely stretch of sand, though the waters here – as elsewhere on this coast – tend to be colder than on the western beaches facing the main Atlantic.

José Maria da Fonseca manor house and wine vaults

Rua José Augusto Coelho 11–13, Vila Nogueira de Azeitão • Daily: April–Oct 10am–noon & 2–5.30pm; Nov–March 10am–noon & 2.30–4.30pm • 45min tour €3 • ☎ 212 198 940, ⓦ jmf.pt • Bus #768 from Setúbal, roughly hourly Mon–Sat

The highlight of the otherwise unexceptional village of Vila Nogueira de Azeitão (just outside the park boundary) is the **José Maria da Fonseca manor house and wine vaults**. The company has been producing quality wines in this region since the nineteenth century, including the local Setúbal Moscatel. The tour of the house, gardens and three wine cellars (including the impressive Teares Novo cellar, rammed with giant barrels) includes a free tasting.

GETTING AROUND   **PARQUE NATURAL DA ARRÁBIDA**

By bus Getting around by public transport is tricky. In July and August buses from Setúbal run along the coast as far as Praia da Figueirinha roughly every 30min (daily 9am–7pm).

The rest of the year, you can only skirt round the park on buses from Setúbal to Sesimbra via Vila Nogueira de Azeitão (Mon–Fri 11 daily,) that take the main road, well back from the coast.

INFORMATION AND ACTIVITIES

Information The Ask Me Arrábida information office is in Setúbal at Travessa Frei Gaspar 10 (daily: 10am–1pm & 2–6pm, until 7pm April–Sept; ☎916 442 247, ⓦmun -setubal.pt), and can provide information on walking in Arrábida as well as information on the Setúbal region as a whole. It doubles as a shop selling local handicrafts, with the remains of Roman fish-preserving tanks visible under its glass floor.

Diving and boat trips Certified divers can rent equipment from the Centro de Mergulho diving school, Casa 5, Pontinha da Arrábida (☎919 807 289, ⓦportinhodivers.com), or you can take diving lessons; the waters here are some of the clearest on the entire Portuguese coast. In summer, the company also offers boat trips along the coast.

ACCOMMODATION

Casa d'Adôa Casa 3, Pontinho da Arrábida ☎212 180 689, ⓦcasadaadoa.com. This lovely house right on the seafront has a sunny patio garden and a variety of fresh-feeling rooms, all with minibar, a/c and satellite TV; two have kitchenettes, as does a larger family room (€150). Breakfast extra. **€60**

Picheleiros Vale de Picheleiros S. Caetano ☎212 181 322, ⓦclubecampismobarreiro.pt. This well-equipped campsite, just outside Azeitão (a short drive from the park and the coast), comes complete with minimarket, café and children's playground. Pitch **€12.40**

EATING

★**O Galeão** Portinho da Arrábida ☎212 180 533. The best of the restaurants facing the water, with a terrace resting on stilts so you can guiltily peer down at the relatives of what's probably on your plate: sea-fresh fish and seafood, from €10–14. Mon & Wed–Sun 8am–midnight.

Sesimbra and around

The main resort on the Bay of Setúbal, **SESIMBRA** is largely a day-trip destination for Lisbon residents who come here for the long sandy strip of beach, **Praia da California**, facing relatively still waters. Apartment buildings mushroom across the low, bare hills beyond the narrow streets of the attractive old centre, whose endless rows of café-restaurants are all filled to the gills in summer. The crowds, however, are largely Portuguese and out of season it's an atmospheric place, with elderly fishermen gathering in groups on the seafront promenade to chat. It also makes a good base to explore the coast to the west, including the wild **Cabo Espichel** and the southern stretches of the **Costa da Caparica**.

Fortaleza de Santiago

Fort Daily 9.30am–8pm • Free • **Museum** Tues–Sun: May–Sept 3–7pm & 8.30–11pm; Oct–April 10am–1pm & 2.30–5.30pm • €3 • ⓦ museusesimbra.pt

Sesimbra was an important port during the Portuguese Discoveries, when Dom Manuel lived here for a while. The **Fortaleza de Santiago** was built in the seventeenth century as part of the country's coastal defences, but in the eighteenth century it became a seaside retreat for the Portuguese monarchs. Today, it is the hub of the town's social calendar and hosts frequent craft fairs, concerts and is the start point of the bizarre **Clown Parade** (officially the world's largest), when people in clown costumes gather during the Feb/March carnival. At other times, you are also free to wander rounds its low walls and visit its café, with fine views across the beach. Parts of the castle are given over to a modest **Museum of the Sea**, tracing the town's links with the Atlantic through multimedia displays, photos and old navigational aids.

Porto de Abrigo

It's a pleasant walk from the centre of Sesimbra along the seafront Avenida dos Náufragos to the town's fishing port, **Porto de Abrigo**, with its brightly coloured boats. Various **boat trips** operate out of the port in summer; get the latest timetables from the tourist office (see p.128).

1

Castelo de Sesimbra
Daily 7am–8pm; closes 7pm Oct–May • Free

High above Sesimbra, the imposing Moorish **Castelo** is a short drive or a stiff half-hour climb from the centre. Dating from the tenth century, it was substantially renovated in the 1930s: within the walls are a pretty eighteenth-century church, **Nossa Senhora do Castelo**, a small **archeological museum**, a cemetery and a café. Climb round the battlements, which give amazing panoramas over the surrounding countryside and coastline.

Cabo Espichel and Nossa Senhora do Cabo
Eleven kilometres west from Sesimbra lies **Cabo Espichel**, a dramatic cape facing the full force of the Atlantic. Here you'll find the eighteenth-century church of **Nossa Senhora do Cabo**, lined on two sides by arcaded lodgings for pilgrims, with a weatherworn chapel perched above the rocks beyond. The whole place has an end-of-the-world air – and it seems appropriate that dinosaur footprints have been discovered on the nearby Praia dos Lagosteiros.

Costa da Caparica
It's an easy drive from Sesimbra to the southern beaches of the **Costa da Caparica**, a surprisingly verdant and undeveloped stretch of coast. A few kilometres to the north of Cabo Espichel is the little village of **Aldeia do Meco**, from where a path cuts down to the superb (partly naturist) beach of **Praia do Meco**, though beware of the huge breakers here. The calmest strip of beach is by the **Lagoa de Albufeira**, a little further south, where you'll find a sheltered lagoon, popular with sea birds (including flamingoes) and fine to swim in.

ARRIVAL AND INFORMATION   SESIMBRA AND AROUND

By bus Sesimbra's bus station is halfway up Avenida da Liberdade, a 5min walk from the seafront.
Destinations Aldeia do Meco (Mon–Sat 5 daily; 30min); Cabo Espichel (2 daily at 1.30 and 2.50pm, return at 2.05 and 3.30pm; 20min); Lagoa de Albufeira (1–2 daily; 40min); Lisbon's Praça de Espanha (hourly; 1hr); Setúbal (roughly hourly; 30min).
By ferry and bus Coming from Lisbon in summer, it's usually much quicker to take the ferry across to Cacilhas and pick up the hourly bus there

(around 45min), as the main bridge road is often jammed with traffic.
By car In season and at weekends, parking in central Sesimbra is a nightmare – head for the signed free car park near the football stadium.
Information Sesimbra's helpful turismo is inside the Fortaleza de Santiago (Mon–Fri 9.30am–8pm, Sat & Sun 9.30am–6pm; ☎937 405 904, ⓦvisitsesimbra.pt), and can give details of jeep tours, tuk-tuk tours and boat trips in the area.

ACCOMMODATION

Hotel do Mar Rua Gen. Humberto Delgado 10, Sesimbra ☎212 288 300, ⓦhoteldomar.pt. Enormous, slightly impersonal three-star spreading uphill above Sesimbra's western beach. The older parts are showing their age, but most rooms command superb sea views, as does the top-floor restaurant. There's also a garden with pool. Parking. **€175**
Náutico Av dos Combatantes 19, Sesimbra ☎212 233 233, ⓦresidencialnautico.com. Steeply uphill above the western end of the beach (and the *Hotel do Mar*), this is Sesimbra's best affordable option: a comfortable modern place with spacious rooms, some with great sea views (balcony rooms are €15 extra). **€80**
Sana Park Av 25 de Abril 11, Sesimbra ☎212 289 000, ⓦsesimbra.sanahotels.com. An excellent upmarket choice, this boutiquey hotel has glass lifts, sauna and pool,

restaurant and groovy rooftop bar (open to non-guests). The plush rooms are all en suite, though you'll pay €30 more for a sea view. **€170**

CAMPSITES
Campimeco Praia das Bicas, Aldeia do Meco ☎212 683 393, ⓦcampigir.com. About 2km northwest of Aldeia do Meco, just off Praia das Bicas, a fabulous stretch of sand, this large campsite comes complete with tennis courts, restaurant, pool and minimarket. Pitch **€12**
Forte do Cavalo Porto de Abrigo, Sesimbra ☎212 288 508, ⓦroteiro-campista.pt. This is a well-located campsite just past the fishing port, a short walk from central Sesimbra and the beach; there's a fine café as well as a minimarket and games room. Pitch **€11**

EATING AND DRINKING

Sesimbra's local delicacy is *salmonete* (red mullet), which in these parts feeds off a certain seaweed that makes it extra flavoursome. At night, families crowd the line of restaurants east of the fort, along Avenida 25 de Abril, and round the little Largo dos Bombaldes, with its warren of cobbled alleyways and inexpensive restaurants spreading uphill. West of the fort along the seafront is where most of the music **bars and cafés** are found.

SESIMBRA

A Sesimbrense Rua Jorge Nunes 19 ☎ 212 230 148. Friendly family-run local joint just back from Largo dos Bombaldes, serving no-nonsense soups, sardines, salads and grills from €10, with a few outdoor seats in summer. Mon & Wed–Sun 12.30–3.30pm & 6.30–10.30pm.

O Modesto Largo de Balbaldes 4 ☎ 919 197 323. This traditional restaurant has been going since 1934 – so you can expect reliably tasty dishes. Its speciality is *chocos* (cuttlefish; from €7.50), served in various ways, though it also does other fish and seafood dishes for not much more. Daily noon–3pm & 7–10pm.

Por do Sol Av dos Náufragos 23–1° ☎ 212 232 251. For a change from the usual Portuguese fare, the "Sunset" serves a range of good-value pizza, pasta and salad (from around €8) in an upstairs dining room with superb views across the beach. Tues–Sun 12.30–3pm & 7.30–11pm.

Ribarmar Av dos Náufragos 29 ☎ 212 234 853. For an upmarket option, it's hard to beat this location, with tables right on the seafront. Prices aren't outrageous, with fresh fish from €9, though plump for seafood and it's €20 upwards. *Arroz* dishes (€40 for two) are always good and filling. Daily noon–4pm & 7–11pm.

X-up Av dos Náufragos 13 ☎ 962 331 528. This sophisticated cocktail bar is right on the seafront: it's a great place for a drink, with regular party nights and guest DJs. Daily 10am–4am.

LAGOA DE ALBUFEIRA

O Lagoeiro Estrada Lagoa de Albufeira ☎ 212 681 929. Just back from the beach overlooking the lagoon, *O Lagoeiro* is the perfect spot for grills, drinks or snacks – the speciality is *caldeirada* (a tasty fish stew). Around €15 a head. Daily 8.30am–11pm.

Estremadura and Ribatejo

ILHA DA BERLENGA

Estremadura and Ribatejo

Now rebranded as south Centro de Portugal and northwest Alentejo, the historic districts of Estremadura and Ribatejo have some of the most famous buildings in Portugal. The monastery at Alcobaça, the extraordinary abbey at Batalha and the headquarters of the Knights Templar in Tomar are all easily accessible, even by public transport, and offer a fascinating glimpse into the country's tangled past. Other attractions are equally high profile, from the walled medieval town of Óbidos to the tremendous castle at Leiria, while the obscenely ornate palace-monastery of Mafra always intrigues. Heads are also turned by the shrine at Fátima, the country's (and, indeed, one of the world's) most important pilgrimage sites.

Along the Costa da Prata (the Silver Coast) the main resorts are the holiday fleshpots of **Ericeira** and **Nazaré**, though there are several smaller, perhaps more charming resorts – notably **São Martinho do Porto** – and plenty of less crowded beaches too. Ferries sail from **Peniche** to the remote offshore bird sanctuary of the **Ilha da Berlenga**, while inland, getting off the beaten track means delving into the spectacular underground caverns around **Porto de Mós** and viewing the amazing nearby sauropod tracks, all of which lie within the **Parque Natural das Serras de Aire e Candeeiros**.

Contrasting with the fertile agricultural land and market gardens of Estremadura is the flatter plain Northwest Alentejo (formerly Ribatejo) – the traditional bull-breeding territory that runs alongside the banks of the **Rio Tejo**. The river valley itself boasts some of Portugal's richest **vineyards**, while **Santarém** has the province's longest history.

Ericeira

Perched on a rocky ledge 30m above a series of fine sandy beaches, **ERICEIRA** offers one of the few natural harbours between Cascais and Peniche. During the nineteenth century boats left from here to trade with countries as far away as Scotland and Brazil. Later, it provided a welcome escape route for Portugal's last monarch, Dom Manuel II – "The Unfortunate" – who hightailed it to the harbour at Ericeira on October 5, 1910, fleeing into exile as Portugal finally jettisoned its monarchy.

Popular with surfers year round – it's just south of Europe's first World Surfing Reserve (see p.135) – and certainly a busy resort in peak season when people flock here from Lisbon, Ericeira remains a laidback and highly attractive place of narrow lanes and whitewashed houses picked out in cobalt blue. It's also renowned for excellent seafood – the town's name is said to derive from the words *ouriços do mar* (sea urchin).

Highlights

① Ericeira coast Try out the surf at the beaches round this little resort, proclaimed a World Surfing Reserve in 2011. **See p.132**

② Tapada Nacional de Mafra Walk, cycle or picnic in this impressive walled park, once the hunting ground for the palace at Mafra. **See p.137**

③ Ilha da Berlenga Take the boat from Peniche to a rocky, windswept island bird-sanctuary. **See p.142**

④ Medieval streets of Óbidos After the coach tours have left, explore the atmospheric streets of this walled medieval town. **See p.143**

⑤ Nazaré For seaside frolics, you can't beat the biggest, brashest resort on the Costa da Prata. **See p.150**

⑥ Alcobaça The twelfth-century monastery at Alcobaça is one of Europe's most impressive Cistercian monuments. **See p.153**

⑦ Grutas de Mira de Aire Visit the most spectacular underground caves in the country, with a water park right next door. **See p.162**

⑧ Tomar The stunning Convento de Cristo is the undisputed highlight, but Tomar itself is a gem of a town. **See p.167**

HIGHLIGHTS ARE MARKED ON THE MAP ON P.134

Around Praça da República

Much of the town centre is pedestrianized, with the pretty **Praça da República** at its hub, ringed with cafés and *pastelarias*; there's a daily market nearby. Below town, the working fishermen's port of **Porto de Pesca** is overlooked by the whitewashed chapel of Santo António (patron saint of Portuguese fishermen), and there's a beach by the port, though it's a bit scrappy and often crowded.

The beaches

The main street, Rua Dr. Eduardo Burnay, leads from Praça da República towards the town's principal beach, **Praia do Sul**, while north of the port, Praia dos Pescadores, is **Praia do Norte**, with **Praia do São Sebastião** a fifteen-minute walk ahead, past the next headland.

ESTREMADURA & RIBATEJO

HIGHLIGHTS

1 Ericeira coast
2 Tapada Nacional de Mafra
3 Ilha da Berlenga
4 Medieval streets of Óbidos
5 Nazaré
6 Alcobaça
7 Grutas de Mira de Aire
8 Tomar

WORLD SURFING RESERVE

The Ericeira coast is famous as the heartland of Portuguese surfing, and was named a World Surfing Reserve in 2011, which aims to preserve the globe's coasts and surfing culture. The first in Europe, it was awarded reserve status because of its high density of surf breaks and its established surfing culture. The reserve actually starts four kilometres north of Ericeira at Praia da Empa and continues north to São Lourenço. Surfers rate the biggest challenge to be the so-called Cave off Praia dos Coxos, while the World Surfing Championships have been held at **Praia da Ribeira d'Ilhas** (5km north), which also hosts the annual Quicksilver Pro Portugal professional surf event. To get an idea of the cliffs, bays and waves along the coast, visit the small surf museum space above the Ericeira tourist office (see below), which has interactive displays.

2

You can also take a bus from Praça dos Navegantes to reach less-developed beaches further out: the best is at **Foz do Lizandro** (2km south), where the river guarantees safe bathing whatever the state of the sea.

ARRIVAL AND DEPARTURE   ERICEIRA

By bus The bus station is up on the main N247 highway, but passengers are dropped at the top of Rua Prudêncio Franco da Trindade, which leads down in a couple of minutes to the main square. Full timetables on ⓦ www.mafrense.pt. Destinations Lisbon's Campo Grande (roughly hourly; 1hr 40min), Mafra (hourly; 20min) and Sintra Portela (hourly; 50min).

By car Ericeira is a quick (45min) drive from Lisbon on the A21 motorway via Mafra. There's limited access to the old town by car, and parking is easiest near the market (free) or in the underground Parque Navegantes at Praça dos Navegantes (expensive).

INFORMATION AND ACTIVITIES

Information The turismo, Rua Dr. Eduardo Burnay 46 (daily 10am–7; ☎261 861 095 ⓦcm-mafra.pt) has details of local accommodation while upstairs there's a small surf museum.

Surfing There are various surf schools and camps in the area; recommended for beginners is Na Onda (ⓦ ericeirasurf.com, no phone) at Foz do Lizandro. Lessons start at around €30 a session.

ACCOMMODATION

Hotels and guesthouses are generally good value, though anywhere in the main part of town can be guaranteed to be noisy in high season. The ones listed below are open all year round (not all are), and prices are generally a good bit lower outside July and August.

Ericeira Hostel Largo Santa Marta 4a ☎261 869 841, ⓦ ericeirahostelspa.com. This is part upmarket hostel and part classy guesthouse. The big draws are the breakfast room/lounge with fab views over the Praia dos Pescadores, and the little jacuzzi in the internal courtyard. Rooms are bright and jazzy, though you pay €35 extra for sea views. You can also use their bikes and they can arrange surf lessons. Three-bed dorms €50, doubles €120

Fortunato Rua Dr. Eduardo Burnay 45 ☎261 862 829, ⓦpensaofortunato.com. A range of simple en-suite rooms, some with a terrace (for which you'll pay €10 extra): the best are the west-facing ones at the top with good views of Praia do Sul. Breakfast is included but only June–Sept. Garage parking available. €70

★**Vila Galé** Largo dos Navegantes 1 ☎261 869 900, ⓦwww.vilagale.pt. Ericeira's top hotel – a large green-tiled 1950s edifice – exudes an old-fashioned elegance. Superbly sited on a rocky promontory overlooking Praia do Sul, you'll have your sleep gently stirred by the sound of crashing waves. You pay a little more for sea views or terraces, but all rooms are plush. The landscaped grounds feature three gorgeous sea pools, and there's also a bar, restaurant and health club. Parking available. €180

★**Vinnus** Rua Prudêncio Franco da Trindade 19 ☎261 866 933, ⓦresidencialvinnus.com. Close to the market and main square (with parking opposite), this is the best budget option. En-suite rooms are bright and individually decorated, the best with small balconies, and others have a kitchenette (€15 extra). No credit cards. Breakfast extra. €55

EATING

Ericeira has a glut of good restaurants, thanks to holiday-makers from Lisbon who demand a decent dinner. Local seafood specialities are the coastal shellfish or *arroz* (rice), *massada* (pasta) and *feijoada* (beans) *de mariscos* – rich,

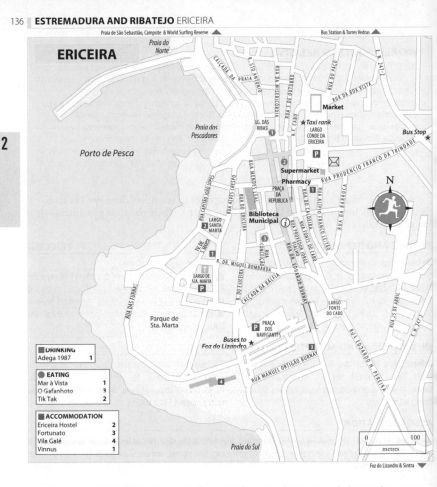

Foz do Lizandro & Sintra ▼

soupy servings of seafood made for sharing. You'll pay more if you eat with a sea view – the better-value restaurants tend to be in the town centre.

Mar à Vista Rua de Santo António at Largo das Ribas ☎ 261 862 928. A wonderful place above the Praia dos Pescadores, with three basic nooks to dine in and the freshest shellfish in Ericeira. It's a great place for *cataplanas*, *arroz* dishes, or crab and lobster, though expect to pay at least €30 a head. Mon, Tues & Thurs–Sun noon–10pm.

O Gafanhoto Rua da Conceição 8 ☎ 261 861 514. There are few frills in this friendly backstreet joint, but you get a decent choice of char-grilled meat and freshly caught fish

at budget prices (from around €10–11). Wed–Mon noon–4pm & 7–11pm.

★Tik Tak Rua 5 de Outubro 7 ☎ 261 863 246 ⊛ restaurantetiktak.wordpress.com. A fashionable place with outdoor tables on a cobbled street, serving great grills and fish (dishes mostly €9–16). Order the fantastic *arroz de tamboril* or *arroz de polvo* (monkfish or octopus rice, around €15) and it's easily enough for two people. Tues–Fri 7–11pm, Sat & Sun 11.30am–3.30pm & 7–11.30pm.

DRINKING

The bars around the modern Praça dos Navegantes, near Praia do Sul, attract a young crowd, especially at weekends, but most of the "in" places (for which, read surfer-friendly) are out of town.

Adega 1987 Rua Alves Crespo 3 ☎ 261 861 220. This great little tiled bar is full of bikes and surf boards. There's a

long list of tasty tapas (€4–8) and various inexpensive drinks. Mon 6pm–3am, Tues–Sun 3pm–3am.

Mafra and around

The small town of **MAFRA** is synonymous with the vast monastery-palace, the **Mosteiro Palácio Nacional de Mafra**, built by the recklessly extravagant king Dom João V. It's only 12km from Ericeira, so makes an easy half-day trip from the coast, or you can see it en route from Lisbon or Sintra. Drivers will also be able to call in at the nearby **Tapada de Mafra** park and at the craft village at **Sobreiro**, on the road between Mafra and Ericeira.

2

Mosteiro Palácio Nacional de Mafra

Terreiro Dom João V • Mon & Wed–Sun 9am–6pm, last entry 5pm; guided tours take 1hr 30min • €6, under-12s free, and free on first Sun of the month • ☎ 261 817 550, ⓦ palaciomafra.pt

Construction of the **Mosteiro Palácio Nacional de Mafra** started in 1717, and it was originally planned to be a modest Franciscan monastery, built to honour the birth of the king's first child. But Dom João V's reign coincided with Portuguese holdings in Brazil producing vast mineral wealth, and this bonanza changed everything. The simple monastery became a lavish palace, with hundreds of monks in residence to care for the royal souls. The resulting building was a magnificent, over-the-top Baroque statement of intent, completed in just thirteen years by the gruelling labour of thousands (of whom hundreds died). The oft-quoted figures tell a tale of grandiose excess – a 200-metre-long facade, 1200 rooms, over five thousand doorways and windows, 156 staircases, and two soaring bell towers over the basilica containing 98 bells, the largest carillons in the world.

There's little humanity or empathy at work in the seemingly endless royal apartments, and it's hard to imagine a life lived in these cavernous chambers. All the rooms are recreations from when João VI fled to Brazil in 1808 in the face of the French advance and took all the furniture and valuables with him. However, there is at least one original piece – the bed in which the last Portuguese monarch, Manuel II, slept the night before he went into exile in England. Some of the rooms are simply shocking, like the **Sala dos Troféus**, where the furniture, including the chandeliers, is made from antlers and upholstered in deerskin. The undoubted highlight is the stupendously decorated **library**, with its 90-metre-long tiled floor. Forty thousand books are still in place here, kept free of insect infestation by a colony of tiny bats that lives in the eaves.

Tapada Nacional de Mafra

Portão de Codeçal, Mafra • Daily 9.30am–5pm • Walking trails €6.50; train €15; bike rides from €10; horse rides €20/hr (reservations advised ☎ 261 817 050) • Mon–Fri Sat & Sun and hols • ☎ 261 814 240, ⓦ tapadademafra.pt

Six kilometres north of Mafra on the Gradil road is the **Tapada de Mafra**, once the palace's extensive hunting grounds. The park is still entirely walled, and there are wild boar and deer within, though it's now set up for public visits for walks, bike rides and other activities. Access to the trails is limited to certain hours in the morning and afternoon, and it'll take two or three hours to get round. There are also falconry displays and children's and family activities, while at weekends and public holidays, you can tour the park on a road train. There's even a nine-room house if you fancy staying (€450 a night).

Aldeia Típica Museu José Franco

Sobreiro, 5km northwest of Mafra on N116 • Daily 10am–6pm • ☎ 261 815 420

En route to Ericeira, at the small village of **Sobreiro**, you'll find the **Aldeia Típica** craft village and museum, which was established by artist José Franco. It's particularly geared up for families, who enjoy looking round the traditional workshops, water mills and craft outlets, all displaying tools, furniture and artefacts collected over many years. The *adega* here is a good place to stop for lunch, serving local wine, bread and moderately priced meals.

2

WATCH OUT, WOLVES ABOUT

In a hidden forest valley just 20km north of Lisbon, the **Iberian Wolf Recovery Centre** houses a dozen or so wolves in natural enclosures. There are only around three hundred wolves left in the wild in Portugal, mostly in the northern mountains, with another two thousand in Spain. Those living at the centre were brought here after being rescued from illegal captivity or were transferred from other zoos – they won't be released again into the wild.

The centre is run by the not-for-profit organization **Grupo Lobo** (ⓦ lobo.fc.ul.pt), which campaigns for wolf preservation and public education, and offers **guided 1hr 30min visits** to see the wolves (Sat, Sun and public holidays: May–Sept at 4pm & 8pm, Oct–April at 3pm & 4.30pm; €5, under-18s €3; ☎261 785 037 or ☎917 532 312; English spoken); you have to book in advance, but the day before is usually fine. You'll get to walk around the enclosures and see (hopefully) some of the wolves up close, and you can then buy as many postcards, T-shirts, key-rings and wolf-adoption packs as you can manage to boost the centre's funds. They also have a volunteer programme.

To get here, follow the brown signs for the "Centro de Recuperação do Lobo Ibérico", which is 7km from Malveira, off the N8 Torres Vedras road; look for the turn at the Picão/Carapiteira junction and then it's 2km up a minor road, eventually a track (but fine for cars), which leads to the reception centre.

ARRIVAL AND INFORMATION   MAFRA

By bus Mafrense buses run roughly hourly from Lisbon Campo Grande (35 min–1hr 30min) or from Sintra Portela (45min), stopping near Mafra's monastery/palace. There are also hourly buses from Ericeira (20min).

By car A vast car park outside the palace soaks up the day-trip trade.

Information The turismo is in the palace, to the right of the basilica (Mon & Wed–Fri 10am–5pm, Sat & Sun 10am–1pm & 2–5pm; ☎261 817 170, ⓦcm-mafra.pt).

Torres Vedras and around

TORRES VEDRAS is a pleasant if fairly nondescript town, though for a short period during the Peninsular War against the French it was at the forefront of a desperate European struggle. With Lisbon judged to be under threat, the Duke of Wellington ordered the secret construction of the Linhas de Torres, the so-called "Lines of Torres Vedras". Within a year in 1810, Wellington's troops, plus gangs of militias and conscripted locals, built an extraordinary network of almost 150 forts and impregnable defensive positions. The British–Portuguese forces then carried out a scorched-earth policy in front of the Lines and sheltered behind them, thwarting the under-supplied French army, which was subsequently forced to retreat to Spain. Wellington's seemingly desperate tactic was a military triumph – though the cost to the local population was severe.

There's little evidence of this drama on display in the modern town, bar some surviving fortress ruins nearby. Still, there's a pleasant kernel of cobbled lanes in the centre, at its best around the central Praça 25 de Abril, where an obelisk commemorates the battles. Otherwise, the **castelo** is the only notable sight and, after a drink at one of the cafés on the square it's probably time to move on – Lourinhã or the local beaches to the northwest make a better overnight stop, while Alenquer and the Ribatejo wine country are just a thirty-kilometre drive to the east.

Castelo

Entrance off Rua de São Miguel • Tues–Sun 10am–7pm, closes 6pm from Sept–May • Free

Above the old town of Torres Vedras sits the **Castelo**, which was once a popular royal residence. It was here, in 1414, that Dom João I confirmed the decision to take the Moroccan outpost of Ceuta – the first overseas venture leading towards the

future Portuguese maritime empire. The castle was reduced to rubble by the earthquake of 1755, but the battlements have been restored and in spring the slopes are carpeted with red poppies.

Praia de Santa Cruz and around

Thirteen kilometres northwest of Torres Vedras, the resort of **Praia de Santa Cruz** marks the start of a string of local beaches that runs all the way north to Peniche. Santa Cruz itself is eminently missable, its wide beaches backed by a contagious rash of apartments and villas, and boasting a campsite the size of an independent country. Far better to push on the 5km north to the duned sands of **Porto Novo** (follow signs initially for Lourinhã), which has restricted its development to a strip of four simple guesthouses with restaurants, just above the sandy bay at the mouth of the Rio Maceira.

Areia Branca

If you're looking for an overnight beach stop somewhere near Torres Vedras, **Areia Branca** ("White Sand"), 21km north, is the most enticing option. Little more than a fishing village thirty years ago, it's now been fully developed but it remains a congenial place of low-rise apartments filling a shallow bowl above a sandy beach, with a promenade of café-bars where surfers hang out. To stretch your legs and soak up the views, follow the walk signposted 3km up the coastal road to the seventeenth-century Forte de Paimogo.

ARRIVAL AND INFORMATION

AREIA BRANCA

By bus Regular daily buses run to Areia Branca from Lisbon (8 daily; 1hr 13min); Peniche (8 daily; 20min) and from Torres Vedras, via Lourinhã (8 daily; 30min).

Turismo Largo do Turismo (daily June–Aug 9.30am–12.30pm & 2–6pm; ☎261 422 167, ⦿ cm-lourinha.pt).

ACCOMMODATION AND EATING

Casal dos Patos Alameda Ver o Mar 1 ☎261 413 768, ⦿ casaldospatos.com.pt. This German-owned property is a hilltop villa with great views, sited on the road directly above the beach. There are four double rooms (closed Nov–Feb) – though not all have the views – and various cottages, bungalows that sleep 4–8, and chalet-like "surf houses" with dorms and doubles. Surf house dorms €25, main house doubles €64, bungalow for 4 €80

Pousada da Juventude Praia de Areia Branca ☎261 422 127, ⦿ microsites.juventude.gov.pt/portal/en. For once, budget travellers have the edge in town, as there's a good youth hostel right on the sands, where you can wake to the sound of crashing waves. Dorms €14, doubles €45

Residencial Dom Lourenço Av António José do Vale 4–6 ☎261 422 809, ⦿ domlourenco.com. On the road out of town, this straightforward seaside hotel has fine if functional rooms and apartments, and a decent restaurant below (mains €9–12). Doubles €50, apartments €60

Lourinhã

Just inland, 3km from the beach at Areia Branca, the small market town of **LOURINHÃ** touts itself as "Capital dos Dinossáuros", on account of the many Jurassic-era fossils retrieved from the local coastline, now on display at the local museum. After a visit here, you might to climb up to the church viewpoint or eat at one of the fairly basic restaurants that line up around the central square and along the pedestrianized street beyond the museum. The town is known for its *aguardente Lourinhã*, Portugal's only demarcated brandy, so expect to be offered a nip at the end of a meal. There's also a fruit and vegetable **market** (mornings only, closed Sun & Mon) and an outdoor flea market on the first Monday of every month.

Museu da Lourinhã

Rua João Luís de Moura 95 • Daily 10am–1pm & 2.30–6.30pm, closed Mon Sept–June • €4 • ☎261 414 003, ⦿ museulourinha.org

The excellent **Museu da Lourinhã**, right in the centre of town, is definitely worth a visit.

It has a separate dinosaur pavilion containing, among other things, dinosaur egg nests and the oldest dinosaur embryos in the world. These are pretty amazing, and tend to overshadow the rest of the museum, but the rooms devoted to local trades and crafts are fascinating too.

INFORMATION LOURINHÃ

Turismo Largo António Granjo, by the main square (Mon–Fri 10am–12.30pm & 2–5.30pm; ☎261 410 127, ⓦcm-lourinha.pt). Pick up leaflets for a couple of local waymarked walks, including the 7km trail out to the beach at Areia Branca, or for local *turismo rural* options.

Peniche and around

In the fishing town of **PENICHE**, determined touts hawk rooms and a glut of harbourside seafood restaurants vie for tourists. But although the balance of life is changing here, Peniche has yet to be seduced entirely from its roots. Gangs of fishermen still repair nets at the harbourside, while the first weekend in August sees the boisterous festival of **Nossa Senhora da Boa Viagem**, during which there's a blessing of the fleet, plus fireworks, bands and dancing in the street.

The town was an island up until the fifteenth century, when the surrounding area silted up and now a narrow isthmus, with gently sloping beaches either side, connects it to the mainland. Unsightly development stretches along the coast, and though it's not the most handsome of towns, inside the walled town there is a small grid of attractive narrow streets dominated by a fortress, near the busy harbour and marina. Boats from here run out to the Ilha da Berlenga (see p.142), while many visitors use Peniche as a base to explore the fabulous beaches either side of town – rated some of the best surf beaches in the country – or to visit the church at Atouguia da Baleia.

Fortaleza de Peniche

Campo da República • Tues–Fri 9am–12.30pm & 2–5.30pm, Sat & Sun 10am–12.30pm & 2–5.30pm • €2 • ☎262 780 116

The sixteenth-century **Fortaleza** was a much-feared jail during the years of Portugal's

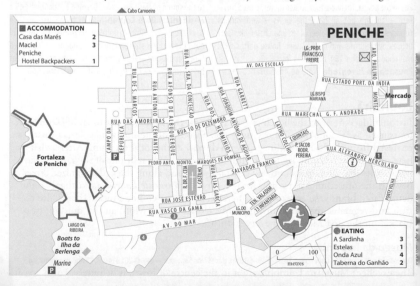

ACCOMMODATION
Casa das Marés	2
Maciel	3
Peniche Hostel Backpackers	1

PENICHE

EATING
A Sardinha	3
Estelas	1
Onda Azul	4
Taberna do Ganhão	2

dictatorship, and later housed refugees from the former colonies. Despite a fresh coat of paint here and there, it's still a formidable place of bare yards and high walls; the bleak *parlatório* (prisoners' receiving room) houses a small exhibition commemorating those imprisoned here. Further within the fort is the municipal museum, while on the top floor you can see the old cells and solitary-confinement pens.

Cabo Carvoeiro and Baleal

Beyond the fortress, to the west, it's 2.5km to the tip of **Cabo Carvoeiro**, a rugged peninsula topped by a lighthouse, where the waves smash against the weathered rock pillars. South of town (along the Caldas da Rainha–Lisbon road) and east towards Baleal/Ferrel, you'll find the duned **surf beaches**, with periodic beach bars, boardwalks and surf-camps. Most appealing of these is **Baleal** itself, 5km northeast of Peniche, an islet-village joined to the mainland by a narrow causeway. This is perfect for both surfers and swimmers, as there are beaches either side of the causeway so one side usually catches the waves and the other is more sheltered. There are miles of sands either side of the attractive village, which has an array of bars, cafés and restaurants overlooking the sands at both ends.

Atouguia da Baleia

The other local excursion is the five-kilometre drive east along the N114 (Caldas da Rainha–Lisbon road) to the village of **Atouguia da Baleia** – *baleia* means "whale". These magnificent creatures were hunted off the shores here when Atouguia was a thriving port. The parish church of São Leonardo is said to have been built from the bones of whales washed up on the shore, and is full of small treasures, such as a curious fourteenth-century stone relief of the Nativity and a calcified whalebone propped up in the corner.

ARRIVAL AND DEPARTURE

PENICHE AND AROUND

By bus The bus station lies outside the town walls – it's a 10min walk into the centre, across the Ponte Velha to the main Rua Alexandre Herculano.

Destinations Areia Branca (8 daily; 20min); Baleal (Mon–Fri roughly hourly; Sat & Sun 8 daily; 10min); Caldas da Rainha (3 daily; 30min); Lisbon (9 daily; 1hr 35min); Óbidos (4–7 daily; 35min); São Martinho do Porto (3 daily; 50min); Torres Vedras (8 daily; 30min).

By car There's pay parking all over town, including by the gardens outside the turismo and on the harbour front, and there's free parking up by the fortress. At Baleal, there's a large car park on the mainland side of the causeway.

By boat The harbour, for boat trips and the ferry to Berlenga (see p.142), is close to the fortress.

INFORMATION AND ACTIVITIES

Information Turismo, Rua Alexandre Herculano (daily 9am–1pm & 2–7pm; closes 5pm from Oct–May; 📞 262 789 571, 🌐 cm-peniche.pt). They hand out a free surf-guide to the local beaches, including Supertubos and the other local breaks.

Boat trips In addition to Viamar ferry (see p.142), which runs to Ilha de Berlenga in the summer months, sea-charter companies based at the harbour offer year-round (except Dec) fishing trips and cruises, either around the local coastline (from €9 for an hour) or out to Berlenga. Operators include Turpesca (📞 963 073 818) and Julius (📞 262 782 698 or 📞 917 601 114, 🌐 julius-berlenga.com .pt), and although departures depend on the weather and season, in summer there are several daily excursions, usually departing in the morning and including a stop on Berlenga and a visit to the caves along the coastline. Ticket prices are pegged to those of the ferry, so you shouldn't pay more than €20 for the trip.

Diving Peniche is a big watersports centre, particularly for surfing, but also for diving. Dive operators include Haliotis (🌐 haliotis.pt) – one-day dive trips in the gin-clear waters off Ilha Berlenga cost around €110, though cheaper coastal dives are also available.

Surfing You can rent gear from any of the local surf-camps, including Baleal Surfcamp (🌐 balealsurfcamp .com), PH Surf School (🌐 penichehostel.com) and Peniche Surf Camp in Baleal (🌐 penichesurfcamp.com). Group lessons cost from €35 (individual sessions from €80), while each camp also has accommodation (hostel-style or apartments and private rooms). One-week inclusive courses for beginners cost around €550 in July and August, cheaper outside high season.

2

ACCOMMODATION

Casa das Marés Praia do Baleal, 5km northeast of Peniche ☎262 769 200/255/371, ⓦcasadasmares1 .com, ⓦcasadasmares2.wix.com and ⓦcasadasmares .com. At the far end of Baleal village (over the causeway), by the chapel, this is actually three conjoined houses run separately by members of the same family, each offering B&B, with views either of the sweeping sands or back across to Peniche. Breakfast is served on the terrace overlooking the small fishermen's beach where the boats are winched ashore. There's parking at the front. **€90**

Maciel Rua José Estêvão 38 ☎262 784 685. A good budget option, with pleasant rooms and a highly polished interior of wooden floors, rugs, plants and coordinated decor. **€60**

★**Peniche Hostel Backpackers** Rua Arquitecto Paulino Montêz 6, 1st floor ☎969 008 689, ⓦpenichehostel.com. A friendly surfers' and backpackers' place in a renovated house just inside the town walls, across from the turismo. It's kind of boutiquey, with two small, four-bed mixed dorms and three double rooms available, plus a kitchen and lounge. They can arrange lessons at their own surf school, and you can also rent boards and bikes. Dorms **€20**, doubles **€50**

EATING

A dozen or so **restaurants** along Avenida do Mar all offer grilled fish at reasonable prices (mains from around €10), plus pricier *arroz* and shellfish dishes. To check out the daily catch, visit the **Mercado Municipal** (off Rua Arquitecto Paulino Montêz; closed Mon), full of voluble fishwives sipping a *bica* as they exchange news. Your best bet for a drink and a view of the world going by is one of the handful of harbourside **bars** on Avenida do Mar, while Baleal beach has a few bars popular with the surf crowd.

A Sardinha Rua Vasco da Gama 81–93 ☎262 781 820, ⓦrestauranteasardinha.com. The best of the backstreet options is a good-value, family-run place serving the full range of fish and seafood, from sardines to clams, with dishes starting from around €9. Best bet is the grilled mixed fish for €12.50, which is enough for two. You can sit outside on the narrow street in summer. Daily 11.30am–4pm & 6.30–10.30pm.

Estelas Rua Arquitecto Paulino Montêz ☎262 782 435 ⓦrestaurantestelas.pt. Acclaimed as the best restaurant in town, serving super-fresh fish and seafood in a breezy contemporary dining room. Most mains are from €15–20, and it's the place to try classics like *cataplana de marisco*, John Dory and big steaks. Daily noon–4pm & 7pm–midnight.

Onda Azul Av do Mar 38 ☎262 787 224 ⓦrestauranteestelas.pt. The "Blue Wave" has harbour views from its outdoor terrace, so it's a popular lunch choice. There's the usual grilled-fish menu in three languages, though daily specials are always worth a look, such as roast octopus with potatoes in olive oil. Mains from around €12. Daily noon–3pm & 7–midnight.

Taberna do Ganhão Largo das Amigas do Baleal 1, Baleal ☎911 878 095. Opposite the causeway on the islet side, this has a cosy interior and a fine terrace facing the beaches. There's a good range of *petiscos* and main courses, from mussels, spicy shrimps and sautéed clams (€8.50–13.50) to tuna and beef steaks (€14–15). Mon, Tues & Thurs–Sun 10am–10.30pm.

Ilha da Berlenga

The craggy, ocean-ravaged **Ilha da Berlenga** lies 10km offshore from Peniche – it's usually visible from Cabo Carvoeiro. Taking up just two-and-a-half square kilometres, the island is uninhabited except for a few fishermen, because the island has been declared a **natural reserve**, home to thousands upon thousands of sea birds, including gulls, puffins and cormorants. The birds are entirely dominant – visitors, you get the feeling, are just about tolerated as long as they don't venture into the ubiquitous perching and roosting areas.

At the main landing dock, with its small fleet of fishing boats, there's a tiny sandy beach that's a mere golden notch in the cliffs. This gets ridiculously busy in summer, though you're unlikely to come to Berlenga just for the beach. The water is lovely however, and fantastic for snorkelling. The only buildings on the island are a few huts and concrete houses above the harbour, a lighthouse on the heights and – across one shoulder of the island, reached by the only track – the highly romantic seventeenth-century **Forte de São João Baptista**, on a rocky islet the other side of a stone bridge and one of the few options for accommodation. Striding out across the island seems like an attractive idea, but be warned – there's no shade, and the ever-present screeching, swooping birds make a restful picnic unlikely.

ARRIVAL AND DEPARTURE   ILHA DA BERLENGA

By ferry The ferry from Peniche is operated by Viamar (€20 return, under-12s €10; ☎ 262 785 646, ⓦ viamar -berlenga.com) and takes around 45min – longer if the sea is rough (it can be a very bouncy ride). Departures are from Peniche marina below the fort and run mid-May to mid-September, with up to three ferries a day in July and August

(9.30am, 11.30am & 5.30pm; return at 10.30am, 4.30pm & 6.30pm), and one daily at other times (10am; return at 4.30pm). There's a limit of 300 tickets sold each day (ticket office open 8.30am–noon & 3–5.30pm). In July and August, get there in good time for a ticket; outside these months it's not usually a problem.

ACCOMMODATION AND EATING

Facilities on the island are limited, though it's remote and interesting enough a destination to attract a fair number of tourists. There's a campsite, a hostel, one hotel and a small minimarket (only open in summer when everything else is). There's also a bar and restaurant at the hotel, but as everything is shipped in, prices are high. Advance reservations are essential everywhere – don't turn up expecting to stay without one.

Área de Campismo de Berlenga ☎ 262 789 571, ⓔ campismo.berlenga@cm-peniche.pt. Reservations for the small island campsite need to be made through Peniche turismo. It's not exactly a luxury spot, more a rocky ledge in a fantastic location, and you'll need to be pretty self-sufficient unless you plan on eating in the hotel. Open 1 July–15 Sept. Pitch <u>€10.30</u>
★**Casa do Abrigo** Forte de São João Baptista ☎ 912 631 426 (Mon–Fri after 7pm), ⓔ berlengareservasforte @gmail.com. This rudimentary refuge housed in the fort can't be beaten for location, if not sybaritic comfort. There are simple private bed spaces for 1 or 2 people (*cubatas*)

and dorms (sleeping up to six). It's a cold-water shower, generator-off-at-midnight kind of place – bring your own cooking utensils (there is a kitchen), sleeping stuff and towels. Open 15 May–15 Sept; it's a bit cheaper outside July and August and if you stay more than two nights. Dorms <u>€20</u>; *cubata* bed spaces <u>€22</u>
Residencial Mar e Sol ☎ 262 750 331, ⓦ restaurante maresol.com. There are just six rooms at the only hotel, above the harbour. Meals in the restaurant are based around the fish landed at the harbour below, which is pretty good for food miles (dishes start at around €14). Open May–Oct. Restaurant 9am–midnight. <u>€100</u>

Óbidos and around

ÓBIDOS is thoroughly charming – a very small town, completely enclosed by medieval walls – and although much was rebuilt after the 1755 earthquake, it retains a captivating feel with its cobbled alleys and whitewashed houses. To the Portuguese it's known as the "Wedding City", after a custom whereby the ancient kings gave the village to their queens as a wedding present. Perhaps more curiously still, five hundred years ago the sea reached the foot of the ridge on which Óbidos stands and boats were once moored below its walls. As the sea later retreated, it left a fertile green plain and the distant Lagoa de Óbidos, with the town now marooned inland. In 2015, it was designated a UNESCO City of Literature because of its literary heritage and contemporary creative scene. Not surprisingly, Óbidos hosts some good **festivals:** a March Chocolate Festival; a summer festival (July to September), which includes a ten-day medieval fair, opera at the castle and other concerts and events; a Classical Music Festival (October) and a big Christmas Fair (details for each at the turismo).

Naturally enough, such an attractive, history-laden place attracts visitors by the coach-load, while the land below the walls shows ever-increasing development. However, it's really just the main street that gets overly congested, and you only need to climb the side alleys or the perimeter walls to escape the throngs.

While here, don't miss the chance to visit the Bacalhôa Buddha Eden gardens, a short drive to the south (see p.144).

Rua Direita

The main entrance to town is through the **Porta da Vila**, housing a tiled oratory, beneath which someone is usually displaying handmade lace. Beyond stretches the

main street, **Rua Direita**, a run of restored houses, gift and craft shops, galleries and cafés. Ginjinha d'Óbidos, the local cherry liqueur, is much in evidence, along with the ubiquitous ceramics and embroidery.

Rua Direita climbs eventually to Dom Dinis's massively towered **castle**, whose keep now houses a rather splendid *pousada*. There's also access at various points to the **town walls** – at times, a hair-raising walkway with no handrail – from where you can enjoy the views over the surrounding plain.

Museu Municipal

Praça de Santa Maria, off Rua Direita • Daily 10am–1pm & 2–6pm • Free • ☎ 262 955 557

The handsome central square, overlooked by pillory and portico, is flanked on one side by the former town hall, now the **Museu Municipal**, notable principally for its work by **Josefa de Óbidos** (1630–1684), one of the most renowned of all Portuguese painters. Although she was born in Seville, Josefa lived here in Óbidos in a convent for most of her life. First known for her etchings and miniature paintings, she later moved on to wonderfully detailed, full-scale religious works of art. Her portrait of powerful priest Faustino das Neves is the museum's highlight (though it's not always on display).

Igreja de Santa Maria

Praça de Santa Maria • Daily: April–Sept 9.30am–12.30pm & 2.30–7pm; Oct–March 9.30am–12.30pm & 2.30–5pm • Free

At the back of the main square, the **Igreja de Santa Maria** has a homely interior lined with blue seventeenth-century *azulejos* and an altarpiece attributed to Josefa de Óbidos. The church was the venue of the wedding of the 10-year-old king, Afonso V, who married his 8-year-old cousin, Isabel, in 1444.

Bacalhôa Buddha Eden

13km south of Óbidos at Quinta dos Loridos, Carvalhal Bombarral • Daily 9am–6pm, last entry 5.30pm • €3, plus €3 for land train • ☎ 262 605 210 ⓦ buddhaeden.com • It's a short drive off junction 12 of the A8 motorway (follow signs initially for Carvalhal)

The extraordinary **BACALHÔA BUDDHA EDEN** gardens are set in 35 hectares of highly imaginatively landscaped grounds; cobbled paths head off past palm-lined lakes, lawns and a dazzling array of statues and sculptures – you can take a land train if you don't fancy the walk. The gardens were originally laid out in 2007 after the Taliban's destruction of the Bamiyan Buddha statues in Afghanistan by wealthy philanthropist José Berardo, hence the garden's name and the predominance of Buddha statues, including a giant reclining Buddha and the 21-metre high Buda Gigante. The gardens have subsequently been expanded to include both contemporary and African sculpture sections. One section of garden is filled with life-size statues of buffalos, lions and other creatures, many made from recycled materials in a bamboo wood. A blue smurf-like army of replicas of the Xian Terracotta Warriors also lines one of the immaculately kept lawns. The combination of exotic art against the Portuguese backdrop of vineyards, olive and cork groves is highly appealing, and there is a café and restaurant as well as a shop selling the neighbouring Quinta's wines at very good-value prices.

ARRIVAL AND INFORMATION
ÓBIDOS

By bus Buses stop outside the Porta da Vila, by the turismo.

Destinations Caldas da Rainha (every 30min–1hr; 15min), Nazaré (Mon–Fri roughly hourly; Sat & Sun 5 daily; 45min) and Peniche (6–12 daily; 35min).

By car It's an easy drive to Óbidos from Caldas da Rainha (6km to the north) or Peniche (24km west), while from Lisbon it's around an hour's drive up the A8 motorway. There's a large car park by the turismo, immediately outside the Porta da Vila; or there's free parking over the road in wasteground lot by the aqueduct.

By train There's a minor train station at Óbidos (8 daily services from Caldas da Rainha, 6min), but it's a fair walk from the walls, below the town.

Information Turismo, outside the Porta da Vila (May– Sept daily 9.30am–7.30pm; Oct–April Mon–Fri 9.30am–6pm, Sat & Sun 9.30am–12.30pm & 1.30– 5.30pm; ☎ 262 959 231, ⓦ cm-obidos.pt).

ACCOMMODATION

Accommodation generally scores high on charm, especially in the old townhouses or country manors that play on Óbidos' genteel image. Most is mid-range or above – budget travellers should hunt out private rooms advertised in the windows of houses along Rua Direita, where you should be able to get something for €50 or €60.

★**Casa das Senhoras Rainhas** Rua do Padre Nunes Tavares 6 ☎ 262 955 360, ⓦ hotelsenhorasrainhas .com. The only serious rival to the *pousada do Castelo* is this exceptional boutique-style hotel at the bottom of the old town, by the walls. Rooms are charming rather than cutting-edge, with smart marble bathrooms and a soothing colour scheme – some have a private terrace – and there's a lovely courtyard. The restaurant (closed Tues, & Wed lunch) meanwhile offers a fine-dining experience – say seafood gazpacho and pork loin with a *moscatel* glaze – for around €50 a head. **€110**

★**Casa de São Tiago** Largo de São Tiago 1 ☎ 262 959 587, ⓦ casas-sthiago.com. Beautifully restored family house, dripping with vines and climbing flowers, just below the castle on Rua Direita. It's peaceful and friendly, and the rooms have wrought-iron bedsteads, tiles and rugs, and views either over the lemon trees or to the castle walls. Breakfast is served in the walled courtyard. **€80**

Casa d'Óbidos Quinta de São José, 1km south of town, near Senhor da Pedra church ☎ 262 950 924, ⓦ casadobidos.com. Classy nineteenth-century manor house in lovely gardens, with a swimming pool and tennis court. There are nine rooms in the house, and a cottage in the grounds. **€90**

Louro Rua da Antiga Estrada Real, Casal da Canastra ☎ 262 955 100, ⓦ hotelouro.com. A modern, refurbished inn, around 500m from the walls – walk away from Porta da Vila, past the car parks. The en-suite rooms offer a comfortable night at a good price (and outside July–Oct rates drop to €50–60). The rear rooms have valley and town-wall views, parking is easy, and there's a manicured garden and outdoor pool. **€68**

Pousada do Castelo ☎ 210 407 630, ⓦ pousadas.pt. One of the country's finest *pousadas*, sited within the castle and approached through an intimate courtyard over-looked by carved windows. There are only 17 rooms, 8 of them in a new wing, all done in a lavish Portuguese country style, and making good use of the original stone walls and other features. The top room is the duplex suite in one of the castle towers, complete with canopied bed fit for a king. Guests tend to eat in the restaurant (mains around €25), where there's a classy take on traditional country food. For parking, follow the *pousada* signs. **€200**

Rainha Santa Isabel Rua Direita ☎ 262 959 323, ⓦ obidoshotel.com. The carefully preserved facade hides an up-to-date twenty-room hotel with lounge and bar. There's a period feel inside – wooden floors and beams, blue-tiled bathrooms, dried flowers and leather armchairs – while the rooms vary in size and outlook, though the best have rooftop views. **€60**

EATING

Restaurants are geared towards day-trippers, so prices are high and multi-language menus ubiquitous. To eat with the locals you need to head 1km out of town (on the N8 Caldas da Rainha road, 15min walk) to the cobbled square by the unfinished rotunda church of Senhor da Pedra, where there's a handful of moderately priced restaurants serving grills, fish and rice dishes.

Adega do Ramada Trav Josefa d'Óbidos, off Rua Direita ☎ 262 959 462. Simple grill house with summer esplanade seating in the alley. Steaks, lamb chops, pork, sea bass and salmon (€12–14) are all prepared on the outdoor charcoal grill. Daily noon–10.30pm.

★**Esplanada Miradouro** Largo de Jogo da Bola, off Rua Talhada ☎ 913 657 192. Wedged against the walls at the upper end of town, and with superb views back over the rooftops, this small kiosk café-bar has tables set out under spreading beech trees. There are slightly pricey sandwiches, toasts and salads (€4–7) but it's a perfect stop for a drink: try the fresh fruit juice or the *ginjinha* liqueur. Mon & Wed–Sun 11am–2am.

O Pretensioso Largo do Postigo 2 ☎ 262 950 021. The dishes are a little different at this old house set inside the lower walls, such as a *bacalhau papillote* with an almond-and-*broa* crust or duck with a honey and port-wine sauce (mains €14–18). If the weather's kind you can also eat in the charming garden, shaded by an orange tree. Tues–Sun noon–3pm & 7–11pm.

★**Vila Infanta** Largo do Santuário do Senhor da Pedra, 1km south, Caldas da Rainha road ☎ 262 959 757. The best-value meals are just out of town at this friendly, family-run grill restaurant, where you can eat a full meal for around €15, which is the price of a main course at many places in Óbidos. Mon, Tues & Thurs–Sun noon–3pm & 6.30–10pm.

DRINKING

Ibn Errik Rex Rua Direita 100 ☎262 959 193. This townhouse bar on the main through road has been in business for half a century. Bottles hang from every available space, and there's a carafe of the local *ginjinha* on every table. April–Sept only: Mon & Wed–Sun 10am–2am, closes earlier in bad weather.

Lagar da Mouraria Trav da Mouraria, near Santa Maria church ☎919 937 601. Idiosyncratic bar fashioned from an old wine press – there are seats in a small courtyard and inside where an enormous, gnarled wooden beam bisects the room. They do tapas-style snacks and pizzas, too, though these are nothing special. Daily 11am–2am.

Caldas da Rainha

CALDAS DA RAINHA means "Queen's Spa", and was named for Dona Leonor, wife of Dom João II. She was sufficiently taken by the therapeutic powers of the bubbling waters here that she founded a hospital in 1484, around which the town gradually grew up to service the growing popularity of the **spa**. Its heyday was probably in the nineteenth century, although Caldas today shows little of its regal past: once through the drab modern outskirts, however, there's a pleasant centre focused on the modern spa buildings. Pretty much everything of interest lies in, or just outside, the tranquil **Parque Dom Carlos I**, a lovely, extensive landscaped park with two diverting museums, a small lake and a garden café.

Caldas is also not a bad place for souvenir hunting: its **embroidery** has a national reputation, though it's best known as a **ceramics** centre. There's a lively outdoor fruit, vegetable and flower **market** every morning in the central Praça da República – Monday sees the addition of clothes, shoes and household goods. The lanes running downhill from the central Praça da República lead to Largo da Rainha Dona Leonor and the impressive buildings of the royal spa complex, notably the **Hospital Termal** (founded the year after the queen's first visit, in 1485) and the **Balneário Novo** (New Baths) built in 1855, though neither is now open to the public.

Nossa Senhora do Pópulo

Largo da Capa • Mon–Fri 9.30–11am & 2–5pm • Free • ☎ 262 832 029

Around the back of the spa, the hospital church of **Nossa Senhora do Pópulo** (built in 1500) is covered in blue-and-yellow *azulejo* tiles and has an impressive Manueline belfry. Inside the sacristy, there's a *Virgin and Child* by Josefa de Óbidos.

Museu de José Malhoa

Parque Dom Carlos I • Tues–Sun 10am–1pm & 2–7pm, closes 6pm from Oct–Easter • €3, free on the first Sun of the month, and under-12s free • ☎ 262 831 984, ⓦ mjm.imc-ip.pt

The main attraction in the municipal park is **Museu de José Malhoa**, largely dedicated to the works of the Caldas-born painter **José Malhoa** (1855–1933), Portugal's leading nineteenth-century exponent of naturalism, a master of costume, genre scenes and country life. There are also works by many of Malhoa's contemporaries on display, particularly those of the so-called "Grupo do Leão", a collection of artists, writers and intellectuals (named after a Lisbon beer-hall), of which Malhoa was a prominent member.

In the basement, don't miss the ceramics by **Rafael Bordallo Pinheiro** (1846–1905), notably his masterpiece, the life-sized models representing the Passion. It's Pinheiro who is most closely associated with the famous Caldas da Rainha pottery. His naturalist tableware (cabbage-leaf bowls, butterfly plates and the like) is still hugely popular, while in the enduring caricature of "Zé Povinho" – a bearded peasant in black hat, with no respect for authority – Pinheiro created a true Portuguese archetype.

CLOCKWISE FROM TOP FÁTIMA (P.164); CONVENTO DE CRISTO, TOMAR (P.168); IBERIAN WOLF SANCTUARY (P.138) >

Faianças Artisticas Fabrica Bordallo Pinheiro

Rua Rafael Bordallo Pinheiro 53 • **Factory shop** Mon–Sat 10am–7pm, Sun 2–7pm • Free • **Casa-Museu San Rafael** by appointment only • €2 • ☎ 262 880 568, ⓦ bordallopinheiro.com

The ceramics factory founded by Pinheiro in 1884, the **Faianças Artisticas Fabrica Bordallo Pinheiro**, lies on the street that bears his name, which runs around the back of the municipal park. The factory shop ("Loja") is filled with colourful glazed earthenware, from typical figurines to contemporary dinner services; the adjacent **Casa-Museu San Rafael** displays a selection of remarkable historical pieces by Pinheiro and his craftsmen, though you'll need to book a visit in advance.

Museu da Cerâmica

Rua Ilídio Amado 97, just up the road from the Pinheiro factory • Tues–Sun 10am–7pm (closes 5.30pm from Oct–April) • €2, free on Sun 10am–2pm • ☎ 262 840 280 ⓦ museudaceramica-en.blogspot.co.uk

The other place to pursue the subject of Caldas' ceramics is the **Museu da Cerâmica**. It's set in a delightful rustic stone villa, and contains more of Pinheiro's original work as well as providing an overview of the whole history of Caldas pottery. There are some extraordinary naturalistic pieces here – lobster-garlanded dishes, griffins entwined with snakes, fish-head jars, cabbage-leaf bowls – all protected from harm by staff who follow you around the creaking floors at a not-so-discreet distance.

ARRIVAL AND INFORMATION

CALDAS DA RAINHA

By bus The bus station (Terminal Rodoviário) is at Rua Coronel Sueiro Brito 35, around a 5min walk from Praça da República.
Destinations Foz do Arelho (3–8 daily, though hourly on Sat & Sun in July & Aug; 25min); Leiria (6 daily; 1hr 20min); Lisbon (hourly; express service 1hr 10min, otherwise 1hr 30min); Nazaré (10 daily; 40min); Óbidos (every 30min–1hr; 15min); Peniche (3 daily; 30min).

By car Caldas is 6km north of Óbidos. There's pay parking in Praça 25 de Abril and along Rua de Camões in front of the park, though if you continue around the park heading out of town, the street parking becomes free.

By train The train station is on the west side of the town; it's a 5min walk from there to the turismo, down Avenida 1 de Maio. Heading north from Caldas da Rainha, the trains stay inland until São Martinho do Porto, 13km south of Nazaré – for Foz do Arelho, you need to take the bus instead.
Destinations Leiria (6 daily; 45min–1hr); Lisbon (up to 7 daily; 2hr 10min); and São Martinho do Porto (6 daily; 10min).

Turismo Praça 25 de Abril (daily 10am–6pm; ☎ 262 240 000, ⓦ www.cm-caldas-rainha.pt), at the side of the modern town hall. From here, Praça da República is a 5min walk away: walk down Rua Engheneiro Duarte Pacheo from the turismo, turn right on Rua Heróis da Grande Guerre, then left down pedestrianized Rua Almirante Cândido dos Reis.

ACCOMMODATION

Casa dos Plátanos Rua Rafael Bordallo Pinheiro 24 ☎ 262 841 810. The in-town manor-house option is this restored eighteenth-century property set in a quiet corner behind the spa and park. No credit cards. Closed Nov–Jan. **€70**

Dom Carlos Rua de Camões 39A ☎ 262 832 551, ⓦ domcarlosportugal.com. Traditional old hotel, opposite the park. It's a bit musty, and furnishings and decor have seen better days, but it's a useful standby if you just want a bed for the night. No credit cards. **€40**

EATING AND DRINKING

Pastelaria Baía Rua da Liberdade 33 ☎ 262 832 349. Overlooking the quaint Largo Dom Leonor and the Hospital Termal, lovely *azulejos* on the outside show the bakers preparing the tempting array of regional sweets, pastries and cakes which sit in the counter inside, though the phallic meringues are somewhat x-rated. Mon–Sat noon–3pm & 7–10pm.

Sabores d'Italia Pr 5 de Outubro 40 ☎ 262 845 600, ⓦ saboresditalia.com. It's rare to get proper Italian food in Portugal and, though not cheap, it's worth it for this buzzy place on an attractive square five minutes' walk from the park. They serve home-made pasta and daily fish and meat specials (€16–25), plus pizzas too (€10–15). Tues–Sun 12.30–2.30pm & 7–10pm.

Tijuca Rua de Camões 89 ☎ 262 824 255. The best budget choice, a simple basement restaurant opposite the park, with a traditional menu (rabbit stew, octopus rice) and most dishes costing €8–9. The chicken casserole (*frango na púcara*) is good, served in an earthenware pot. Mon–Sat noon–3pm & 7–10pm.

Foz do Arelho

The small village of **FOZ DO ARELHO**, 8km west of Caldas da Rainha, sits 1km back from a beautiful, sheltered lagoon beach, which is overlooked by a couple of cafés. The road continues a further 500m or so to another tremendous beach where river meets ocean, and here there's a promenade of fancier bars and restaurants. It's not really overdeveloped – this is more a holiday-home place than a resort – and outside July and August you'll have the wide, white sands to yourself. On the lagoon itself, the **Lagoa de Óbidos**, fishermen stand in the shallow waters next to their boats, attending to their nets.

ARRIVAL AND DEPARTURE
FOZ DO ARELHO

By bus There are direct Rodotejo buses out to Foz from Caldas da Rainha (Mon–Fri roughly hourly, fewer at weekends), a 20min ride.

By car With a car you can drive northwest from Caldas along the N360, which takes you past the tranquil Lagoa de Óbidos, and then out along the coast via Foz do Arelho on a breezy clifftop route – a much better option than taking the busy N8 or the motorway.

ACCOMMODATION

Penedo Furado Rua dos Camarções 3 ☏ 262 979 610, ⓦ hotel-penedofurado.com. This is the best of two small hotels, signposted to the right up a side street as you pass through the village. It's a homely place with spacious rooms and distant lagoon views – prices shoot up in August, but are better value the rest of the year. **€80**

Quinta da Foz Largo do Arraial ☏ 262 979 369, ⓦ quintadafoz.co. The other good option is *Quinta da Foz*, right in the village (off the square), a sixteenth-century manor house with a bar, and five pretty rooms. Expect echoing quarters, vintage tiles and antique beds. No credit cards. **€90**.

EATING AND DRINKING

The presence of some rather fashionable bars in Foz village and dotted around the lagoon tells you what kind of place this is in summer, when the city crowds descend from Lisbon. Much of the action is out at the ocean beach where a line of bars and seafood restaurants vies for your attention. They're all a bit showy, a bit pricey and often a bit disappointing.

O Central Rua Francisco Almeida Grandela 81 ☏ 262 978 523. Best place to eat in the village is this bar and restaurant on the main through-road. A welcoming family dishes up bumper-sized platters of grilled meat and fish, *cozido*, pizza and *bacalhau*, and you'll spend €8–10 at lunch, perhaps twice that at dinner. Daily 11am–midnight.

São Martinho do Porto

Lying 10km north of Foz, **SÃO MARTINHO DO PORTO** is the main and most appealing resort between Peniche and Nazaré. Low-key and largely low-rise, it's an easy-going place favoured by families. The reason for São Martinho's popularity is its beach, a glorious sweep of sand that curls around an almost enclosed bay and shelves gently into the sea, making its waters wonderfully warm and calm. You could easily spend days tramping the boardwalks and dune paths around the bay, hiring a kayak or pedalo (around €8 an hour) or climbing the ochre cliffs above the quayside to the lighthouse. There's also an older part of São Martinho to explore, up the steep hill behind the more modern bay-side streets – the easiest way up is to take the **ascensor** (daily: June–Sept 10am–midnight; Oct–May 10am–9pm; free), a lift departing from inside the turismo building, which whisks you to an upper square with sweeping town and bay views.

ARRIVAL AND INFORMATION
SÃO MARTINHO DO PORTO

By bus Buses stop on Rua Conde de Avelar, a short walk from the seafront.
Destinations Caldas da Rainha (Mon–Fri roughly hourly; Sat & Sun 7 daily; 25min); Nazaré (Mon–Fri roughly hourly; Sat & Sun 4 daily; 15min).

By train The train station (services from Caldas da Rainha and Leiria) is on Largo 28 de Maio, which is an easy walk from the sea front.
Destinations Caldas da Rainha (6 daily; 10min); Leiria (6 daily; 35–50min).

Information The turismo is in the heart of the town, two blocks from the bay promenade, at Rua Vasco da Gama 8 (Tues–Sun 9.30am–1pm & 2–6.30pm; ☏ 262 989 110, ⓦ cm-alcobaca.pt).

ACCOMMODATION AND EATING

Atlântica Rua Miguel Bombarda 6 ☏ 262 980 151, ⓦ hotelatlantica.pt. The best budget option, with pleasant rooms in a jaunty blue-and-white guesthouse that's just two blocks from the seafront. €85

★ **Cais 24** Rua Cândido dos Reis 24 ☏ 262 999 213. This modern restaurant is in a great position on the harbourfront on the northern Cais (quay) side of the bay. The friendly and helpful staff will talk you though the day's catch in the cooler cabinet which usually includes turbot, John Dory and bass (around €15–20 a head), though you pay less for the likes of chicken *piri-piri* and *bitoques* (€9–12). Daily 10am–2am.

Carvalho Rua Vasco da Gama 23 ☏ 262 980 151. The *Atlântica* guesthouse restaurant is as good as any of the eating places in the centre, with a summer terrace and a good range of Portuguese and international dishes including pizzas and giant helpings of paella. Mains from €8. Tues–Sun 11am–11pm.

★ **Palace do Capitão** Rua Capitão Jaime Pinto 6 ☏ 262 985 150, ⓦ hotelpalacecapitao.com. The finest accommodation in town is a beautifully restored mansion overlooking the central promenade. The inlaid parquet floors and hand-painted wallpaper set the tone for what is an elegant house with comfortable rooms – though not all have sea views. They have an elegant bar and *Casa de Chá* too (daily 11am–11pm), which makes a rather nice place for afternoon tea and cakes. €100

Nazaré

Some websites and holiday brochures claim **NAZARÉ** as one of Portugal's most picturesque seaside resorts, and if you come out of season you might just about agree. But in summer, the crowds are far too heavy for the place to cope with and the enduring characteristics are lines of souvenir stalls and identikit fish restaurants with a touch of hard-edged hustle. While elderly local women still don traditional headscarves and embroidered aprons, their trays of fish have been replaced by cheap souvenirs and signs advertising rooms – and the colourful sardine boats that used to be hauled up along the beach at night now dock at an out of town harbour. However, as long as you don't expect a cosy village, and are steeled for peak-season crowds, Nazaré is highly enjoyable, with all the restaurants, facilities and knockabout cheer of a busy resort. It's not just summer either that rocks: New Year's Eve on Nazaré beach is one of the biggest parties in Portugal, while the annual Carnaval parades are rumbustious all-night affairs.

The beach

The long sweep of the seafront promenade is backed by a tight warren of narrow alleys and streets filled with houses advertising rooms and simple restaurants, with the occasional small square letting in the light. The main **beach** is a large expanse of clean sand, packed with bathers and multicoloured sunshades in summer, while further beaches stretch north beyond the headland. The water might look inviting on calm, hot days, but it's worth bearing in mind that swimming off these exposed Atlantic beaches can be dangerous. Nazaré has a worldwide reputation among **surfers** seeking serious waves (see box, p.152) – always heed warning signs and swim only where directed to do so.

Sítio

Ascensor da Nazaré (funicular), lower station at Largo do Elevador • Daily roughly every 15 mins: Oct–May 7.30am–8.30pm; June, July & Sept 7.30am–midnight; Aug 7.30am–2am • €2.40 return

The original settlement here was built at the attractive village of **Sítio**, 110m up a dramatically slumped rock face above the north end of the town, to avoid pirate raids. Legend tells of a twelfth-century knight, Dom Fuas Roupinho, who, while out hunting, was led up the cliff by a deer. The deer dived into the void and Dom Fuas was

saved from following by the timely vision of Nossa Senhora da Nazaré, in whose name a church was subsequently built. You can reach Sítio, and the church, by taking the funicular from town, which rumbles up to a *miradouro* at the top.

The picturesque main church square is ringed by souvenir shops and patrolled by formidable *varinhas* (fishwives) touting knitwear, dried fruit and nuts. The views down to the town and beach are sensational, while following the road downhill from the square takes you out to the *farol* (lighthouse) from where you get a fine view over Praia do Norte.

ARRIVAL AND DEPARTURE

NAZARÉ 2

By bus The bus station is on Avenida do Município, five minutes west from the seafront.

Destinations Alcobaça (hourly; 20min); Caldas da Rainha (10 daily; 40min); Leiria (5–7 daily; 40min);

NAZARÉ

Funicular to Sítio

Largo do Elevador

RUA DO ELEVADOR
TRAV. DE ELEVADOR
R. FIGUEIRAS
RUA DE SÃO GIÃO
RUA DO LEIRIA
RUA GUILHIM
LARGO DAS CALDEIRAS
RUA DO AMPARO
PRAÇA SOUSA OLIVEIRA

RUA DR. RUI ROSA
AVENIDA DA INDEPENDÊNCIA NACIONAL
AVENIDA DE OLIVENÇA

RUA MOUZINHO DE ALBUQUERQUE

RUA DOS FORNOS
R. GOMES FREIRE
RUA DA ROSA
RUA ADRIÃO BATALHA
RUA FRANÇA BROGES

PRAÇA DR. MANUEL DE ARRIAGA
RUA DA SAUDADE
RUA DAS FLORES
RUA J. B. SOUSA LOBO
RUA GIL VICENTE
RUA GIL VICENTE
RUA DA BONANÇA
RUA TRÊS DE SETEMBO

RUA DA BONANÇA
RUA TRÊS DE SETEMBRO
RUA DA PÁTRIA
RUA DO ALECRIM
RUA DA PAZ
RUA REGENERAÇÃO
RUA DA LIBERDADE

RUA SUB VILA
RUA MOUZINHO DE ALBUQUERQUE

AVENIDA DA REPÚBLICA

RUA DA GRAÇA
RUA DAS ABEGORIAS
RUA DOS LAVRADORES
RUA ANTÓNIO C. J. ARANJO
RUA DOS CALAFETES
RUA J. MANUEL
RUA DOS PESCADORES
R. DAS BERLENGAS
RUA DOS MARINEIROS
RUA DAS CABANAS

RUA OCCIDENTAL
RUA DOS BARRANCOS

Police Station

AVENIDA VIEIRA GUIMARÃES
RUA ALVES REDOL
(i) Market
RUA SUB VILA

RUA DA CARIDADE
RUA DAS TRAINEIRAS
RUA BANCO MARTINS
RUA DAS TRAINEIRAS

Bus Station

AVENIDA DO MUNICÍPIO
Centro Cultural de Nazaré

N

0   100
metres

DRINKING
Casa O Santo   1

EATING
A Tasquinha   2
O Casalinho   1
Rosa dos Ventos   3

ACCOMMODATION
À Hotel Maré   2
Mar Bravo   3
Praia   6
Quinta do Campo   5
Ribamar   4
Vila Conde Fidalgo   1

S (6km), Train Station (6km); Orbitur Campsite, Leiria & Alcobaça

Vale Paraíso Campsite & Lisbon

Port & Marina

São Martinho do Porto

2

RIDING GIANTS

Facing the full brunt of the Atlantic, Nazaré's Praia do Norte has an underwater gully that tapers towards the land, further amplifying waves that are already enormous. As a result, in certain weather conditions, the coast here can produce some of the **world's biggest swells**. These monsters attract the big names in surf and over recent years, several claims have been made for riding the biggest ever waves. English plumber Andrew Cotton rode a 24-metre wave in February 2014, though the previous year Hawaiian Garrett McNamara broke his own record when he surfed a 30-metre giant at the same place. The lighthouse at Sítio is the place to watch when the surfers try their luck, though it is an extremely dangerous game. Brazilian Maya Babeira might have been riding a similar 30-metre giant when she fell off her board. She was knocked unconscious and had to be rescued by the support jet ski. Inexperienced surfers should stay well clear, though Nazaré's main beach offers a more modest, safer surfing experience for much of the year.

Lisbon (2–4 daily; 2hr); Óbidos (Mon–Fri roughly hourly; Sat & Sun 5 daily; 45min); and São Martinho do Porto (4–8 daily; 20min).

By car A one-way system filters traffic away from narrow streets and up and down the flanking thoroughfares. There's pay parking in a large car park behind the market, or free spaces along the seafront starting after the cultural centre and library (heading towards port and marina).

By train The nearest train station is 6km inland, at Valado, on the Alcobaça road, though connecting buses do run regularly into town. It's easiest, however, to come by bus.

INFORMATION

Turismo Nazaré's turismo is by the market building on Avenida Vieira Guimarães (Daily: Aug 9am–9pm; April–July & Sept 9.30am–12.30pm & 2.30–6pm; Oct–March 9.30am–1pm & 2.30–6pm; ☎ 262 561 194, ⊛ cm-nazare.pt).

ACCOMMODATION

Nazaré is awash with **private rooms** and you'll be approached by touts throughout town – expect to pay up to €60–80 in high season, though much less for most of the year. In August a local bus runs on a circuit from town out to the two nearby **campsites** and back (*Orbitur* ⊛ orbitur.pt, and *Vale Paraíso* ⊛ valeparaiso.com), but there's no transport there the rest of the year.

À Hotel Maré Rua Mouzinho de Albuquerque 10 ☎ 262 550 180, ⊛ hotelmare.pt. Modern mid-range comforts are on offer at this modern hotel just back from the seafront. All rooms come with little balconies, some of which share the fine view enjoyed by the top-floor breakfast room. **€110**

★Mar Bravo Pr Sousa Oliveira 71 ☎ 262 569 160, ⊛ marbravo.com. The most upmarket seafront choice has smallish rooms but all have an ocean view (balcony €17 extra) and are handsomely styled with good marble bathrooms. There's an equally refined fish and seafood restaurant downstairs (closed Tues from Nov–March), where you can eat really well for €30 or so. **€122**

★Praia Av Vieira Guimarães 39 ☎ 262 569 200, ⊛ hotelpraia.com. Designer four-star hotel that's actually a couple of hundred metres from the beach (despite the name) but otherwise fully lives up to expectations. The rooms have blond-wood furniture, smart bathrooms and big balconies with sea or hill views; there's a year-round rooftop pool (covered in winter) and a terrific terrace with sweeping views. **€160**

Quinta do Campo Rua Carlos O'Neil 20, Valado dos Frades, 6km east of Nazaré ☎ 262 577 135, ⊛ aquintadocampo.com. A rather grand estate whose eight double rooms and apartments are traditional but elegant, with heavy wood furniture and immaculate white linen. There are also extensive grounds that contain a pool and tennis courts. **€100**, apartments **€130**

Ribamar Rua Gomes Freire 9 ☎ 262 551 58 ⊛ hotel ribamarnazare.com. Rooms (above a restaurant) are small, with frilly fabrics and tiny bathrooms tiled with *azulejos*. Some have the original wooden flooring and plaster cornicing, while others overlook the beach, though you'll pay a bit more for a sea view. **€90**

★Vila Conde Fidalgo Av da Independência Nacional 21 ☎ 262 552 361, ⊛ condefidalgo .planetaclix.pt. The best budget choice is set back up the hill from the sea (10min walk), with parking outside. It's a secluded complex of simple rooms and apartments, separated by plant-filled patios and ceramic-tiled walkways. Furnishings are basic but adequate, with a fridge and TV in each room, and kitchenettes in the apartments (which can sleep four). No breakfast and no credit cards. Doubles **€50**; apartments **€70**

EATING

The main concentrations of **restaurants**, **cafés** and **bars** are along the seafront Avenida da República, in the squares and alleys behind, and near the lower funicular station. Menus are broadly similar – plenty of grilled fish – and prices at most don't vary by more than a euro or two.

★ **A Tasquinha** Rua Adrião Batalha 54 ☎ 262 551 945. Just far enough off the seafront to be a locals' choice, this is the hands-down winner for very reasonably priced tavern-style food. It's a wooden bench and check-tablecloth joint, and you may have to queue, but it's worth it for the tasty meat and fish grills or special dishes like *atum cebolada* (tuna with onions), with most options costing €9–11. Tues–Sun noon–3pm & 7–10pm.

O Casalinho Pr Sousa Oliveira 7 ☎ 262 551 328 ⓦ restaurantemarisqueiraocasalinho.pt. Alfresco dining in the square, or in the contemporary dining room. You can expect good sea bass, squid kebabs, sardines, grilled bream and the like for around €10, or a fine *cataplana* at €25 for two – it's not really the place to go if you don't want fish. Daily 11am–11pm, closes Thurs from Oct–May.

Rosa dos Ventos Rua Gil Vicente 88 ☎ 918 267 127. A small, attractively tiled dining room with a couple of tables on an outside terrace. Grilled meats are tasty, but this is the place to come for seafood: the clams, shrimps and lobster are superb. Mains mostly €9–13. Daily 11am–11pm, closes Thurs from Oct–May.

DRINKING

Casa O Santo Trav do Elevador 11 ☎ 262 085 128. This cosiest of *adegas* is the nearest thing to a pub in town, good for a thimbleful of local wine or a beer with *petiscos* such as fresh clams or prawns. Tables spill onto an attractive pedestrianised street. Daily noon–midnight, closes Tues from Nov–March.

Alcobaça

The vast Cistercian monastery at **ALCOBAÇA** was founded in 1153 by the first king of Portugal, Dom Afonso Henrique, to celebrate his decisive victory over the Moors at Santarém six years earlier. Building started soon after and – with royal patronage assured – by the end of the thirteenth century it was the wealthiest and most powerful monastery in the country. Nearly a thousand monks and lay-brothers lived here running a veritable business empire based on market-gardening, farming, fishing, forestry and trading. Notorious tales of the lavish lifestyle at Alcobaça were a staple of the writings of early travellers, who found the monastic excesses shocking and titillating in equal measure. The dissolution of the Portuguese monasteries in 1834 put an end to all this, but the buildings still stand as an extraordinary monument to another age.

A visit to the monastery can comfortably occupy a couple of hours. Alcobaça itself is a small and fairly unremarkable town, though the Rio Baça winds attractively through the few remaining old-town streets. The ruined hilltop castle provides the best overall view of the monastery, while down below in town there's a large market building (the market is held on Monday) and attractive public gardens.

Mosteiro de Alcobaça

Daily: April–Sept 9am–7pm; Oct–March 9am–6pm; last entry 30min before closing • Monastery €6, under-14s free & free first Sunday of the month; entry to church free; joint ticket with Batalha and Tomar's Convento do Cristo €15 • ☎ 262 505 120, ⓦ mosteiroalcobaca.pt

For centuries a centre of study, contemplation and religious doctrine, the **Mosteiro de Alcobaça** still possesses an overwhelming power that's also at least partly related

---

ALCOBAÇA FESTIVALS

The middle of November every year sees the **Mostra de Doces Conventuais**, a weekend of feasting on conventual sweets and pastries and fruit liqueurs from convents, monasteries and cake shops in Portugal, Spain and France. During the **Cister Música** (ⓦ cistermusica.com) festival in May or June you can catch concerts in the abbey and elsewhere.

to its historic and architectural significance. Founded in the very early years of the Portuguese kingdom, its overall construction took centuries, with major expansions and additions mirroring each notable era of Portuguese imperial might. In particular, Alcobaça stands as the first great early-Gothic building in Portugal – both abbey church and medieval cloister are the largest of their types in the country, while the church is also the burial place of Dom Pedro and Dona Inês de Castro, whose story echoes down through the ages as one of enduring love (see box below). The monastery has had multiple uses since Portugal's religious orders were dissolved in 1834 – from prison and barracks to school and nursing home. A UNESCO World Heritage Site since 1989, today it's effectively a museum, owned and run by the state.

Sala dos Reis

The ticket desk for the monastery is immediately inside the church, on the left, by the entrance to the **Sala dos Reis** (Hall of Kings). The monarchs in question are those who ruled Portugal for its first six hundred years, from founder Afonso Henrique to Dom José I, who died in 1777 and under whom the final additions and alterations were made to the monastery. Their statues are all on display, along with vivid eighteenth-century *azulejos* that tell the story of the founding of the monastery.

Claustro do Silencio

From the Sala dos Reis you enter the heart of the monastery, the **Claustro do Silencio** (Cloister of Silence), off which are located the wider monastic quarters. It was built in the reign of Dom Dinis (probably finished around 1311) and is a beautiful space – indeed, it's one of the largest cloisters in Europe. In the sixteenth century a Manueline upper storey was added by notable architect João de Castilho, giving the medieval Gothic cloister a renewed grace and elegance. There's also a beautiful hexagonal *lavabo* with Renaissance fountain, which was where the monks washed before entering the refectory.

Refectory and kitchen

The monks took their meals in the **refectory**, but the celebrated feasting at Alcobaça came with an attached duty – as they ate, the Scriptures were read to the assembled brothers from the elegant stone pulpit. The medieval **kitchen** was lost to renovations in the seventeenth century. By the time awed travellers were

---

DOM PEDRO AND DONA INÊS DE CASTRO

The two extraordinary, carved, fourteenth-century tombs in the abbey church at **Alcobaça** shine a light on a doomed medieval romance. **Prince Pedro** (1320–1367), son of Afonso IV and heir to the Portuguese throne, was married to Constance of Castile, but fell in love with her maid, **Inês de Castro** (1320–1355), who was from a noble Galician (ie Spanish) family. The two continued an affair, despite the disapproval of the king, who feared a creeping Spanish influence in the Portuguese court. Following Constance's death in 1345, Afonso IV banished Inês and forbade her marriage to Pedro, but the pair wed in secret in Bragança in the far north of the country. With Inês's brothers and other Spanish nobles favoured by Pedro, and Afonso in danger of losing control of his court, the king moved to more radical measures, and ordered his daughter-in-law's murder. She was killed in **Coimbra** in 1355, sparking a revolt by Pedro against his own father. Afonso died two years later, and when Pedro succeeded to the throne in 1357 he assuaged his grief with the commissioning of two elaborate tombs, which he placed foot to foot in the abbey church – allegedly, so that they could see each other when they rose again. Inês' corpse was transferred here from Coimbra and ceremonially reinterred – not before, according to gory legend, Pedro placed her rotting body on the throne and insisted the court honour his lost queen by kissing her hand.

enjoying monastic hospitality a century later, the food was prepared in the vast, arcaded "new" eighteenth-century kitchen, whose scale still retains the power to impress. An enormous central chimney rests on wrought-iron legs, with water brought into the building via a hydraulic canal system – the size of the water-basin set into the floor gives you an idea of just how much pot-boiling and pan-scrubbing went on here.

ARRIVAL AND INFORMATION ALCOBAÇA

By bus From the market and the nearby bus station it's a 5min signposted walk to the monastery, crossing the river en route.

Destinations Batalha (8 daily; 40min); Leiria (1–2 daily; 30min); Lisbon (4 daily; 2hr); and Nazaré (roughly hourly; 20min).

By car There's free parking in the large car park off the avenue above the monastery, and plenty more near the market and gardens. The town centre has improved immeasurably since through-traffic was diverted away from the monastery, opening up the facing square, Praça 25 de Abril.

Information The turismo, Rua 16 Outubro 17 (daily 9am–1pm & 2–6pm; ☎ 262 582 377, ⓦ cm-alcobaca.pt), is on the square, opposite the monastery, and can supply wholly unnecessary maps of the town.

ACCOMMODATION AND EATING

Alcobaça has a limited but relatively inexpensive choice of **accommodation**, mostly near Praça 25 de Abril, where a ring of cafés and restaurants has grandstand views. **Restaurants** are predictably touristy, with little to choose between them – for cheap meals, locals favour the restaurant at the *Coraões Unides*.

António Padeiro Rua D. Maur Cocheril 27 ☎ 262 582 295. Just up the alley from the main square, this long-standing restaurant is a refined spot for a meal. The food's traditional, like everywhere in town, but it's the best place for something like *cabrito*, *cozido* or grilled fish, with lunch dishes from around €8, otherwise mains at €12–15. Daily noon–3.30pm & 7–10pm.

Challet Fonte Nova Rua da Fonte Nova 8 ☎ 262 598 300, ⓦ challetfontenova.pt. A boutique hotel in an aristocratic nineteenth-century villa, furnished with antiques but tempered with an interior-designer's eye. They have an associated spa as well, with the house secreted on a backstreet off Rua Frei Estevão Martins, to the side of the turismo. Parking. **€120**

Coraões Unides Rua Frei António Brandão 39 ☎ 262 582 142, ⓦ coracoesunidos.pt. Large rooms in a dated guesthouse, just off the square, some with side views to the monastery. The old-fashioned restaurant downstairs is a reliable place for an inexpensive meal (the *ementa turística* is around €14) – *frango na púcara*, a tasty chicken casserole, is the house speciality, with *cozido* served on a Sunday. Restaurant open daily noon–3pm & 7–11pm. **€40**

Pastelaria Alcôa Pr 25 de Abril 44 ☎ 262 597 474. This little café bills itself as the "masters" of traditional sweets and pastries and it has awards to prove it, notably the best *pastéis de nata* in Portugal award. That's no mean feat, and the flaky custard tarts truly are unmissable. Daily 8am–7.30pm.

Leiria and around

The old royal castle at **LEIRIA** peers out over a charming town that comes as something of a surprise for many visitors. Surrounded by modern suburbs and a swirling one-way system, it holds no great sights save the castle itself, but the pretty old streets and squares in the centre are worth a wander. As a student town Leiria has enough good restaurants and bars to make the evenings go with a swing.

The old town spreads out around the arcaded **Praça Rodrigues Lobo**, lined with attractive cafés and named for the statue of the local poet (1580–1622) who became one of Portugal's most famous early writers. In fact, Leiria's literary connections go back even further than this – in 1480, the town had one of Portugal's first printing presses, which was run by Jews who printed in Hebrew. An antiques and crafts fair is held in the square on the second Saturday of each month. Leiria is also handily poised for the fine beaches of the **Pinhal de Leiria** to the west, which spread either side of the pretty resort of São Pedro de Moel.

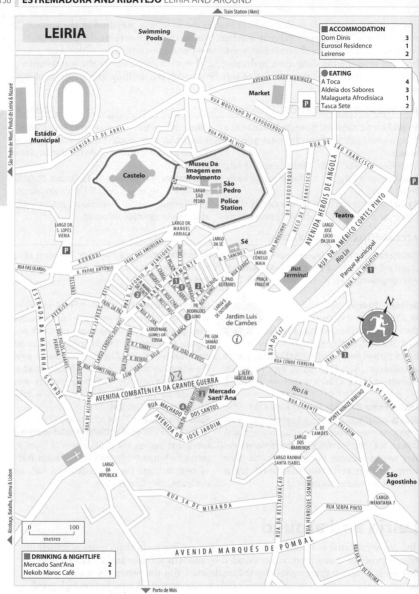

Castelo de Leiria

Rua do Castelo • Tues–Sun 9.30am–6.30pm, closes 5.30pm from Oct–March • €4 • ☎ 244 813 982

Leiria's **Castelo** was an early site in the battle for control of what was to become the kingdom of Portugal. Taken from the Moors by Afonso Henriques in the twelfth century, it became a royal favourite and in the fourteenth century was the main residence of Dom Dinis. It's been much altered since (the battlements are modern reconstructions), though it's still an impressive sight, crowning the crags above town. You can see the former royal palace within the castle walls, while inside the keep is a

small museum containing displays of armour and archeological finds. There's also the shell of the old church of **Santa Maria de Penha**, which dates from around 1400.

The entry fee also allows entry to a couple of missable museums, the Museu da Imagem em Movimento, a cinema museum just outside the castle entry; and the Moinho do Papel, a modest paper mill museum, to the southwest of the centre.

Largo da Sé

Outside the walls, on the edge of the old town, stands the sixteenth-century cathedral, or **Sé**, which was built during the reign of Dom João III. Look across the square here to the impressively tiled pharmacy opposite – once the meeting place of a literary circle surrounding novelist **Eça de Queirós**, who lived in Leiria for a year in 1870–71. His novel, *The Sin of Father Amaro* (1876), draws heavily on his experiences in this provincial cathedral city.

ARRIVAL AND DEPARTURE

LEIRIA

By bus It's easiest to arrive by bus, as the bus terminal is right in town on Avenida Heróis de Angola.

Destinations Alcobaça (1–2 daily; 30min); Batalha (5 daily; 15min); Coimbra (roughly hourly; 50min); Fátima (5–9 daily, 25min); Lisbon (roughly hourly; 1hr 50min); Nazaré (5–7 daily; 40min); Porto de Mós (7 daily; 35min); São Pedro de Moel (Mon–Sat 3–7 daily; Sun 1 daily; more in July–Aug; 45min); and Tomar (1 daily; 1hr).

By car Leiria is about 35km northeast of both Alcobaça and Nazaré, and 70km (under an hour's drive) south of Coimbra. Driving into Leiria, if you follow the signs for "centro", you end up in a one-way system of some

devilment. Although metered street parking and pay car parks are widely advertised, parking in the centre can be pricey. Far better to avoid the one-way system and park in the free car parks on the outskirts (near the market and river), which isn't too long a walk into town.

By train The train station is 4km north of town – either wait for a connecting bus into the centre, or take a taxi (around €6).

Destinations Caldas da Rainha (6 daily; 45min–1hr); Figueira da Foz (3 daily; 1hr 20min); Lisbon (4–6 daily; 1hr 15min–3hr 20min); and São Martinho do Porto (6 daily; 35–50min).

INFORMATION

Information The turismo is on Jardim Luís de Camões (Mon–Fri 9am–6pm, Sat–Sun 9am–1pm & 2–6pm;

☎ 244 814 770, ⓦ cm-leira.pt), a 5min walk across from the bus station.

ACCOMMODATION

The very cheapest accommodation is found in the narrow old-town streets off Praça Rodrigues Lobo – though note that none of these places has parking, and you won't be able to drive to them to unload.

Dom Dinis Trav de Tomar 2 ☎ 244 815 342, ⓦ hotelddinis.pt. Across the bridge from the turismo, and up a steep side-street – it's signposted and there's adjacent parking. It doesn't look much from the outside, but the rooms are bright and double-glazed against street noise. **€45**

Eurosol Residence Rua Comissão da Iniciativa 13 ☎ 244 860 460, ⓦ eurosol.pt. Leiria's stark but central four-star choice provides stylish, modern apartments

(studios, or one- and two-bedroom), plus gym, sauna, pool and underground parking – it's signposted from the ring road. **€66**

★ **Leiriense** Rua Afonso de Albuquerque 6 ☎ 244 823 054, ⓦ hotelleiriense.com. A firm favourite for some years, offering cool, quiet rooms with parquet floors and handsome wooden furniture. There are a fair few single and twin rooms, so it's useful for solo travellers. The location is ideal, and it's good value for money. **€45**

EATING

Pretty Praça Rodrigues Lobo has the most popular **cafés** in town as well as some somewhat pricy restaurants, each with tables spilling onto the square.

★ **A Toca** Rua Dr. Correia Mateus 40–44 ☎ 244 832 221. Come here for large portions of traditional, well-cooked food – the *bife a vaca* arrives sizzling in an earthenware

dish and the *espetada de tamboril* is excellent. It's the best restaurant on the street, with mains from around €13. Mon, Tues & Thurs–Sun noon–3pm & 7–10.30pm.

2

Aldeia dos Sabores Pr Rodrigues Lobo 23 ☎ 244 837 130. The most appealing of the cafés on this attractive square, with marble table-tops and a sumptuous array of croissants, cakes and pastries. Mon–Sat 7.30am–8pm, Sun 8.30am–8pm; open until midnight in July and August.

Malagueta Afrodisíaca Rua Gago Coutinho 17 ☎ 244 831 607. Contemporary style that comes as something of a shock in old-town Leiria, and a fun menu to boot – Adam in the Adam-and-Eve fountain outside the tourist office certainly seems to have benefited from its aphrodisiacal

qualities. Expect plenty of fragrant curries – fish and prawn – but also a good chicken *fajita*, Brazilian *vatapá* (fish in palm oil), and a rare vegetarian selection. Dishes mostly €9–14. Mon–Thurs & Sun 12.30–2.30pm & 7–11pm, Fri 12.30–2.30pm & 7pm–midnight, Sat 7pm–midnight.

Tasca Sete Rua Maria da Fonte 6 ☎ 962 238 621. A small and cheery backstreet diner with bargain set menus only: expect a daily changing fish or meat dish with a dessert and drink for around €8. Mon–Sat noon–2pm & 7–9pm.

DRINKING AND ENTERTAINMENT

The **bar scene** is concentrated on Largo Cândido dos Reis and Rua Barão de Viamonte – you'll find all kinds of places tucked away in the alleys off here, from student dives to quite sophisticated lounge bars.

Nekob Maroc Café Rua Gago Coutinho 23 ☎ 244 892 082. Right in the heart of the old town, this fashionable Moroccan bar is a popular choice for a night out. Daily 8.30pm–2am.

Mercado Sant'Ana Largo de Santana 3 ☎ 244 839

528. This attractive former market building is now a cultural space which hosts frequent festivals and live music events. Opening times vary depending on the event; details on ⓦ viralagenda.com/pt/p /mercadosantanaleiria.

Pinhal de Leiria

One of the finest stretches of coastline in the country flanks the **PINHAL DE LEIRIA**, a sprawling pine forest west of Leiria and stretching north of São Pedro de Moel. It's what passes for an ancient forest in Portugal – the pines were first planted by farmers in the fourteenth century as a protective measure against encroaching sand dunes. Later, the trees were an essential resource when it came to fitting our ships during the Portuguese "Discoveries". There are **bike lanes** and tracks throughout the forest, while beyond the dunes lie vast white-sand beaches soaking up the thundering breakers from the Atlantic. By public transport, the only realistic target is the small resort of São Pedro de Moel (see below), though cyclists and drivers will be able to find better, more isolated spots. Expect any of the **beaches** near São Pedro to be packed in July and August – the straight, fast, coastal road north and south has been upgraded to cope with heavy summer traffic. Come any other time and you'll have the sands to yourself.

São Pedro de Moel

SÃO PEDRO DE MOEL, 22km west of Leiria, is a largely laidback resort where old buildings have been renovated and new ones erected with an eye for tradition. Although it's now firmly a holiday place, it still resembles in part the fishing village it once was, with many houses boasting wooden balconies, louvred windows and climbing roses. A restored cobbled square sits back from a small central beach, while just to the north, 1km past the lighthouse, **Praia Velha** provides a fantastic sweep of sand. You can walk here – follow signs for "praias" from the roundabout – though the equally fine southern beaches of **Paredes** and **Pedra do Ouro** are a short drive away.

A bike lane runs through the trees all the way from São Pedro to the more developed resort of **Praia da Vieira**, 15km north (or a 15min drive), with a long line of beachfront cafés and deckchairs staked out under bamboo parasols.

ARRIVAL AND DEPARTURE   SÃO PEDRO DE MOEL

By bus Buses from Leiria to São Pedro sometimes involve a change at Marinha Grande, the congested small town

halfway between Leiria and the coast (Mon–Sat 3–7 daily; Sun 1 daily; more in July–Aug; 45min).

ACCOMMODATION

Even in high season you should be able to find accommodation, since most local visitors come for the day or stay in holiday homes here. Still, making an advance reservation in August isn't a bad idea. Several places advertise "*quartos*" on the road down from the roundabout towards the clifftop; bear left near the church and you'll soon find the square and beach at the bottom of town.

★**Água de Madeiros** Rua da Ribeira 13, Água de Madeiros, 3km south of São Pedro de Moel ☎244 599 324, ☻aguademadeiros.com. Sitting in a valley cleft, near often deserted sands (out of season, at least), there are twelve simple but cosy rooms, some of which have sea views, plus a bar, pool and terrace. The beach is just 100m away. **€85**

Mar & Sol Av da Liberdade 1 ☎244 590 000, ☻hotelmaresol.com. São Pedro's main hotel sits on the cliffs above the sea. It's a three-star that's had a face-lift, so the rooms are in cool, contemporary colours (a balcony and sea views cost €20–45 more), and the swish restaurant has big picture windows overlooking the beach. **€90**

Miramar Rua dos Serviços Florestais 2 ☎244 599 141 ☻miramarhotel.pt. The largest of several guesthouses, just down from the roundabout. It's a family-friendly place – some rooms have bunk-beds, there's a restaurant downstairs and it offers bike hire. Rooms vary in size, the best with balconies (€18 extra). You might want to ask to see a couple of rooms first. **€65**

Parque Orbitur Rua Volta do Sete ☎244 599 168, ☻orbitur.pt. The closest campsite to town is also the best, in the trees and just 600m from the beach. The site has a pool with slides, plus bar and restaurant, as well as rooms, chalets and bungalows for rent. Pitch **€23**, doubles **€50**

EATING AND DRINKING

Brisamar Rua Dr. Nicolau Bettencourt 23 ☎244 599 520. Regarded as the best in town, and augmenting its Portuguese menu with things such as Greek salad, pasta or tuna steak (mains from around €13). But you have to sit inside and there's no sense of being at the seaside. It's a block over from the *Miramar*. Daily 12.30–3pm & 7.30–10pm; closed Mon in winter.

Estrela do Mar Av Marginal ☎244 599 245. Hard to beat for location, tucked into the cliffs above the main beach and with a lot of outdoor seating. You should just be able to get a drink outside meal times and soak up the

views. Otherwise, the fish choice depends on what's been caught that day, and mains cost from around €11. Daily noon–11pm; closed Thurs in winter.

★**O Pai dos Frangos** Praia Velha ☎244 599 158. Unmissable beach restaurant which prepares sensational mixed kebabs (pork and bacon-wrapped prawns), plus grilled chicken, seafood rice and fresh fish (most dishes €9–12). There's no better place for lunch – on the small outdoor terrace, or at tables by the huge picture windows. Tues–Sun 11am–11.45pm; shorter hours in winter.

Batalha

Eleven kilometres south of Leiria stands the Mosteiro de Santa Maria da Vitória, widely known as the **Mosteiro da Batalha** (Battle Abbey). Built to commemorate a great national victory – the defeat of Castilian forces at the decisive Battle of Aljubarrota in 1385 – the abbey in turn became a great national monument and has been a UNESCO World Heritage site since 1983. Successive monarchs lavished funds upon its construction, and over two centuries Batalha became one of Portugal's most celebrated buildings – a hybrid Gothic and Manueline masterpiece that's both royal pantheon and an expression of national pride.

Most visitors see the abbey and leave – to be honest, there isn't anything attractive about the village itself, though it's peaceful once the tour buses have left. To complete the trip – and learn more about the history behind the founding of the abbey – it's also worth driving out to **São Jorge**, 4km south of present-day Batalha and site of the actual battle in question, where there's a useful interpretation centre.

Brief history

The dynasty of Burgundian kings lasted over 250 years, until 1383 and the death of Fernando I. Even during the good times, in the early years of the Portuguese kingdom, Castilian Spanish nobles and kings had an eye for making trouble – the death of a Portuguese king seemed like too good an opportunity to miss, especially since

Fernando's widow Leonor, now ruling as regent, subsequently married her only daughter Beatriz to Juan I of Castile. With an illegitimate heir of Fernando's also contesting the throne – one João, Grand Master of the noble Portuguese house of Aviz – the stage was set for a showdown, which duly came at the **Battle of Aljubarrota** (August 14, 1385). Although the sheer force of numbers and power all seemed to be on the side of Castile, they had not bargained on a canny promise that João made to the Virgin Mary – he vowed that if the Portuguese won, she would get a brand-new abbey and eternal gratitude. João's army prevailed in a battle that sealed the independence of Portugal, the first stones of the "Battle Abbey" were laid the following year in 1386, and Grand Master João became Dom João I (initial king of the Aviz dynasty which subsequently ruled until 1581).

2

Mosteiro da Batalha

Largo Infante Dom Henriques, Batalha • Daily: April–Sept 9am–6.30pm; Oct–March 9am–6pm; last admission 30min before closing • Main church free; Cloisters and Capelas Imperfeitas €6, free on the first Sunday of the month; joint ticket with Alcobaça and Tomar's Convento do Cristo €15 • ☎ 244 765 497, ⓦ mosteirobatalha.pt

The abbey at Batalha took more than a century to build, though the overall ornate French-Gothic structure owes its style and substance to the work of the first two long-serving architects, Afonso Domingues and the Catalan architect known as Master Huguet. English influences are explained by the Portuguese Crown's alliance with England since 1373 – Dom João I later married Philippa of Lancaster, the daughter of John of Gaunt – and it's possible to see the hand of medieval English architects in the abbey's nave and chapterhouse. With a wealthier, more confident age came a richer design, and in the late fifteenth and early sixteenth centuries Batalha's architects worked in a masterful Manueline style, transforming the abbey into a dazzling statement of Portuguese pride. Batalha has been in the hands of the state since the dissolution of the monasteries in 1834 and is, in essence, a museum.

Capela do Fundador

It's the **Capela do Fundador** (Founder's Chapel) that lies at the heart of Batalha's raison d'être. The abbey might have had its origins in thanks for divine help in battle, but Dom João I put it to work to bolster his authority and that of the House of Aviz by ordering the construction of a royal pantheon (completed by the architect Huguet around 1433). João and his English wife Philippa were its first occupants – their joint tomb is a suitably regal affair, and their statues, rather cutely, hold hands, to symbolize the enduring relationship between Portugal and England. Four royal princes also have tombs in the chapel, all of them sons of João and Philippa and three of them very definitely eclipsed by the fourth and most famous – **Prince Henry the Navigator**, the man who drove the first wave of Portuguese explorations south to Africa.

Claustro Real and Sala do Capítulo

The first departure from the overall Gothic tenor of the abbey can be seen in the **Claustro Real**, or Royal Cloister. Diogo de Boitaca – royal architect to Dom Manuel I – arrived at the abbey in 1509 with a commission to spend some of the kingdom's increasing wealth, and added intricate carved decorations to the cloister, typical of the daring Manueline style. The columns supporting the arches and stone screens are an ornate, entwined tangle of spirals, branches, leaves, flowers and shells.

Opening off one side of the cloister is the abbey's chapterhouse, the **Sala do Capítulo**, the nerve-centre of the early abbey, where the monks congregated to discuss important matters. It's the undoubted masterpiece of the architect Huguet, with a daring star-vaulted ceiling, nineteen metres across, that has no visible support. Legend has it

that only condemned prisoners were allowed to work on its construction because the vault was considered so unsafe, and that Huguet had to sleep beneath his completed ceiling on the first night to prove his doubters wrong. However, it did stay up – and has done for centuries – and the chapterhouse now commemorates Portugal's "unknown soldiers", with ceremonial sentries watching over a tomb containing the remains of two unidentified combatants from World War I.

Capelas Imperfeitas

Behind the apse of the main church are the so-called **Capelas Imperfeitas** (Unfinished Chapels) – you have to leave the main complex to see them and walk around the back. They were commissioned by Dom Duarte, crowned king in 1433 on the death of his father João I, and were intended as Gothic funereal chapels, but work stopped with the early death of the king in 1437 and that of his architect Huguet a year later. There matters may have rested, but for the later intervention of Dom Manuel and his millions, and more importantly his masterful architects, notably Mateus Fernandes who worked here from 1490 onwards. The towering, fifteen-metre-high portal was transformed into an extraordinary Manueline latticework, while inside the octagonal space virtually every inch bristles and froths – tree branches, ropes, angels, molluscs, linked chains, vegetation, keyhole arches and many other conceits in delicate stone. The seven interior funereal chapels were eventually completed – two contain the tombs of Dom Duarte and his wife Leonor, placed here much later – but the upper storey is still unfinished, giving the chapels their name.

São Jorge: the battle site

The Battle of Aljubarrota was fought on a plain 10km northeast of Aljubarrota itself, at the small hamlet of **São Jorge**, 4km south of Batalha. When the fighting was over a small chapel was built and remains at the entrance to the village today. The battle lasted only one hour, but it was a hot day and the commander of the victorious Portuguese forces, Nuno Álvares Pereira, complained loudly of thirst; a jug of fresh water is still placed daily in the porch of the chapel in his memory. Legend has it that Aljubarrota itself was defended by its baker, Brites de Almeida, who fended off the Castilian army with her baking spoon. This fearsome weapon dispensed with seven soldiers, whom Brites promptly baked in her oven.

Centro de Interpretaçao da Batalha de Aljubarrota

Av Dom Nuno Álvares Pereira 120, São Jorge • Tues–Sun 10am–5.30pm • €7, under-17s €5.50 • ☎ 244 480 060, ⓦ fundacao-aljubarrota. pt • The centre and battle site are signposted on the IC2/N1, a short drive from Batalha.

A short path leads from the chapel to the impressive **Centro de Interpretaçao da Batalha de Aljubarrota**, which tackles the battle itself, the contemporary political intrigue and much more besides. It takes a hands-on multimedia approach, so not only do you visit the battlefield but then see a video re-enactment of the day's combat; there's also plenty for children to do, and a café on site.

ARRIVAL AND INFORMATION   BATALHA

By car The large abbey car park is the most convenient place to leave your car, though there's plenty of overspill parking in the village beyond.

By bus Buses stop on the cobbled square-cum-car park, Largo 14 de Agosto de 1385, at the top end of which the abbey is visible, on the right, standing alone surrounded by a bare plaza.

Destinations Alcobaça (8 daily; 40min); Fátima (Mon–Fri 3 daily; 40min), Leiria (roughly hourly; 15–30min) and Lisbon (5 daily; 2hr).

Information Turismo, Praça Mouzinho de Albuquerque, next to the monastery (daily 10am–1pm & 2–6pm; ☎ 244 765 180).

ACCOMMODATION AND EATING

There are some budget rooms in town, and a decent hotel or two in the vicinity, though Batalha doesn't really warrant an overnight stop (Alcobaça or Leiria are nicer places to stay). The **cafés** that flank the abbey plaza are the best places to soak up the views, though none of the **restaurants** stands out – all offer standard menus at moderate prices.

Casa do Outeiro Estrada de Fátima 15 ☎ 244 765 806, ⓦ casadoouteiro.com. Signposted 100m up a side road, this small boutique hotel with swimming pool has fifteen bright rooms, all with terrace (€10 extra for abbey view). It's very contemporary – white walls, wooden floors, stylish furniture and plenty of light – there's a gym and billiard room, and home-made preserves and cakes served at breakfast. Also offers bike hire at €15 a day. **€65**

Restaurante Vitória Largo da Misericórdia ☎ 244 765 678. The *churrasqueira* here, beneath the guesthouse of the same name, is where the locals come for grilled chicken and pork, straight from the grill at bargain prices. There's a shaded terrace for diners. It's just up from the bus stop (or, from the main road, behind Totta bank) – if it's busy then *Casa das Febras*, across the way, offers more good-value dining. Daily noon–3pm & 7–10pm.

Porto de Mós and around

Eight kilometres south of Batalha lies the small riverside town of **Porto de Mós**, with its distinctive castle. Further south and east extends the **Parque Natural das Serras de Aire e Candeeiros**. There are walking trails in both the Aire and Candeeiros ranges, but the park is best known for its fabulous **underground caves**, which all lie in a rough triangle between Porto de Mós and Fátima, on the west side of the A1 motorway. Meanwhile, across the motorway on the east side of the Serra de Aire, Portugal has its own Jurassic Park where you can walk with dinosaurs at the **Pegadas dos Dinossáurios**.

Castelo de Porto de Mós

Porto de Mós • May–Sept Tues–Sun 10am–12.30pm & 2–6pm; Oct–April Tues–Sun 10am–12.30pm & 2–5.30pm • €1.55 • ☎ 244 499 637, ⓦ municipio-portodemos.pt

High above town, nestled in the folds of the hills, the grandiose **Castelo de Porto de Mós** was built in the thirteenth century. It was given to Nuno Álvares Pereira in 1385 by the grateful Dom João I, in recognition of the general's victory at the Battle of Aljubarrota – significantly, the Portuguese army had rested here on the eve of the battle – and was later turned into a fortified palace. Severely damaged in the earthquake of 1755, the castle has been renovated piecemeal since, and now boasts rather too pristine electric-green tiled towers.

Parque Natural das Serras de Aire

The **Parque Natural das Serras de Aire** is a mix of rugged limestone hills, crags and upland farmland divided by ancient stone walls. There are three sets of caves open to the public in the natural park (and a fourth, Moeda, off the N356 road between Batalha and Fátima), but unless you are a real fan, a visit to one will probably suffice. As it happens, the largest and most spectacular, at Mira de Aira, is the only one directly accessible by bus.

Grutas de Mira de Aire

Mira de Aire, 13km southeast of Porto de Mós • Daily: April & May 9.30am–6pm; June & Sept 9.30am–7pm; July & Aug 9.30am–8pm; Oct–March 9.30am–5.30pm • €6.60, under-11s €3.90, under-5s free; combined entry with Parque Aquático €13.20, under-11s €9.70 • ☎ 244 440 322, ⓦ grutasmiradaire.com

It's a fabulous drive out into the hills along the N243 from Porto de Mós to the **Grutas de Mira de Aire**, Portugal's largest show caves. There's parking right outside, or it's a signposted one-kilometre walk from the town bus stop. The 45-minute guided tour ends up at a natural lake filled with fountains 110m below the surface, taking in a galaxy of stalactites, stalagmites and oddly shaped rock formations with curious names – "Octopus Gallery",

the "Organ", the "Conch" – en route. To exit, you take the lift up and emerge beside the **Parque Aquático** water park (summer only), which is a great place to cool off – there are half-day (€6.40) and full-day tickets (€8) available for this, and you can visit independently of the caves. Outside on the road, several cafés and restaurants cater for the crowds.

Grutas de Alvados and Santo António

July & Aug daily 10am–6.30pm; Sept–June Tues–Sun 10am– 5pm • Each site €5.80, under-11s €3.60, or combined ticket (Visita Conjunta) €9, under-11s €6 • Ⓦ grutasalvados.com, Ⓦ grutassantoantonio.com

The **Grutas de Alvados**, 12 kilometres southeast of Porto de Mós, contain a variety of natural halls and underground lakes, though it's the **Grutas Santo António** that are the bigger draw – the latter has the most impressive stalagmites and stalactites of any of the local caves. The turn-off for these caves is signposted from the N243 before you reach Mira de Aire – you could jump off the Mira de Aire bus, but it's then a three-kilometre walk to Alvados and then another 1km to Santo António.

Pegadas dos Dinossáurios

Estrada de Fátima, Bairro • Tues–Sun 10am–12.30pm & 2–6pm; mid-March to mid-Sept Sat & Sun open until 8pm • €3 • ☎ 249 530 160, Ⓦ www.pegadasdedinossaurios.org • The site is just outside the village of Bairro, off the N360 – you'll pick up the signs at Boleiros if you head towards Fátima (via Minde) after seeing the caves

In a quarry around 10km south of Fátima, paleontologists made an extraordinary discovery in 1994 – namely the oldest and longest set of preserved sauropod tracks found anywhere in the world. The tracks date back 175 million years, and were made as the large herbivores plodded through a shallow lagoon, later preserved as limestone. They are now on display *in situ* at the excellent **Monumental Natural das Pegadas dos Dinossáurios**, where a gravel walkway circles the site on high before dropping down to the quarry floor. You can clearly see the footprints (*pegadas*) – hundreds of them, exceptionally well preserved – and follow their route across the stone. By the spacing, paleontologists reckon that some of the sauropods were up to 30m long. There's an explanatory film (in Portuguese) shown at the ticket office, though it's hard to resist the temptation to make straight for the tracks.

ARRIVAL AND INFORMATION   PORTO DE MÓS

By bus The bus station is a short walk from the riverside gardens.

Destinations Leiria via Batalha (7 daily, 35 mins), Mira de Aire (Mon–Fri 4–5 daily, 25 mins). Timetable Ⓦ rodotejo.pt.

Information Turismo, Jardim Municipal (Mon–Sat 10am–1pm & 2–6pm; ☎ 244 491 312, Ⓦ www.municipio -portodemos.pt).

PASS THE SALT

Of all the things uncovered in the Aire e Candeeiros natural park over the years (stalactites, Roman cobblestones, dinosaur footprints), the oddest is surely salt – mined here since ancient times. It's still produced near the town of Rio Maior, at the foot of the Serra dos Candeeiros, where a wide bed of concrete-lined **salt pans** (*marinhas do sal*) exploits the bed of rock salt under the local mountains. Workers at the cooperatively owned **Salinas Naturais de Rio Maior** pump salty water from a well and then subject it to various concentration and evaporation techniques in the tanks and pans on view. It's a process that has been going on, in some shape or form, since the twelfth century. There's most activity between June and September, but you can see something at most times of the year since many of the old wooden salt sheds have been turned into craft stores, salt shops and rustic taverns, and there are even a couple of restaurants where you'll get a good grill-lunch with the salt workers. The sheds themselves are curious works, with weathered boards, gnarled olive-wood posts and ancient wooden locks. The salt pans lie 3km north of Rio Maior (off the IC2/N1), but signposting is patchy. Coming into the town centre, follow scant signs for "Marinhas do Sal" and "Salinas" (on the Alcobertas road); you're there when you see the Wild West-style wooden buildings overlooking the salt-beds.

2

Casa dos Matos Rua D. Fuas Rupinho, Alvados ☎ 244 440 393, ⓦ casadosmatos.com. An attractive, contemporary country home on the way to the Alvados caves, with plenty of exposed stone and coordinated fabrics, plus an outdoor pool and pretty terrace. The breakfasts are good, using locally sourced produce. **€85**

Quinta do Rio Alcaide Rua do Catadouro 528, Rio Alcaide ☎ 966 164 342, ⓦ rioalcaide.com. Nearest to town, 1km out of Porto de Mós, the serene *quinta* is a converted paper mill with guest rooms (including in the windmill), as well as self-catering studios and larger apartments. There's also an attractive swimming pool in the grounds. **€60**

Fátima and around

The simple farming village of **FÁTIMA** changed forever on May 13, 1917, when – according to the witnesses themselves – the Virgin Mary announced herself to three young children. It was the first of six apparitions that transfixed first Portugal and then the Catholic world, which now regards Fátima as a fixture on its pilgrimage calendar, second only to Lourdes in France. As Fátima's celebrity has increased exponentially, so has its size and importance. Farming village no more, Fátima has a basilica that attracts millions – not to mention hotels, pilgrims' hostels, cafés and restaurants, as well as souvenir shops that each year explore new levels of tackiness.

Quite what you make of it all depends largely on your beliefs – it is, after all, a place built entirely on faith. To see it through the eyes of believers you really need to come during the major **annual pilgrimages** (May 12–13 and October 12–13), when hundreds of thousands of people gather here from throughout the country. Most walk and for a few weeks before the dates each year, it's common to see pilgrims in reflective jackets, marching along Portugal's highways in the blazing heat, with some completing the final part of their journey shuffling penitently down the esplanade on their knees. The death of the last surviving child witness, Lúcia, in 2005, was marked as a national event – amid blanket media coverage she was buried in the basilica in February 2006, and it's no exaggeration to say that the entire country came to a halt to watch.

Fátima also makes a good base to visit the attractive hilltop town of **Ourém**, 12km to the east.

Santuário de Fátima

Information office, next to Capelinha das Aparições, daily 9am–1pm & 2.30–6pm • ☎ 249 539 600, ⓦ santuario-fatima.pt

At the heart of the entire sanctuary is the simple **Capelinha das Aparições** (Chapel of the Apparitions), built on the spot where the Virgin supposedly appeared. This was the first building constructed here, and still marks the end of pilgrimage for millions of visitors each year, though it's now entirely overwhelmed by the other buildings that have sprung up over the intervening years. The mighty **Basílica de Nossa Senhora do Rosário de Fátima** was begun in 1928 and consecrated in 1953 – inside are the tombs of Lúcia, Jacinta and Francisco. In front is the gargantuan esplanade – capable of holding a million worshippers – over which Gregorian chanting wafts from flanking speakers. At the top of the esplanade stands another epic church, the circular **Basílica de Santíssima Trindade** (Holy Trinity Basilica), a dramatic contemporary space that can hold nine thousand pilgrims.

There are regular daily Masses held in both the chapel and main basilica – times are posted (some are in English) – and a torchlit procession at dusk, the largest of which is on the twelfth day of each month.

For all but the most devout, a tour around the rest of the widely advertised "attractions" in town is largely an exploration of the grotesque and the kitsch, from the Wax Museum ("29 scenes!, 112 figures!") to the Museum of Apparitions 1917 ("Be present during the Vision of Hell!"). Every shop window, meanwhile, displays an endlessly inventive array of

FROM TOP NAZARÉ (P.150); MOSTEIRO DE ALCOBAÇA (P.153) >

2

MIRACLES, SECRETS AND PILGRIMAGES

The three Fátima children – Lúcia, Jacinta and Francisco – were looking after sheep when the **Virgin Mary** descended from Heaven. Celestial lights flashed as she introduced herself and then requested that the children return five more times – each time on the thirteenth of the month – until October, at which time all would be revealed. The children reported their vision and, slowly, over the months, enthusiastic crowds grew at the appointed times – not put off in the slightest by the fact that the Virgin remained stubbornly invisible to anyone other than the three children.

The October gathering was the largest by far, with thousands in collective thrall to an event that became known as the **Miracle of the Sun** – a technicolour burst of light and fire, accompanied by wondrous healings. Of the three children, it was Lúcia only who was chosen to receive – and keep – the famed three **Secrets of Fátima**, directly from the Virgin. She revealed two in the 1940s – unsurprisingly apocalyptic visions and vague prophecies about world war – and wrote the third down in a sealed envelope entrusted to the Pope. After decades of speculation, the third secret was revealed in May 2000, another typically vague prediction that apparently predicted the attempt on Pope John Paul II's life in 1981.

Lúcia's fellow witnesses both died in the European flu epidemic of 1919–20, while **Lúcia** herself later retreated to the Convent of Santa Teresa near Coimbra. Cocooned from the outside world as a Carmelite nun, she was known by all in Portugal as Irmã (Sister) Lúcia. The elderly bespectacled nun made an unlikely pin-up, but her image is as ubiquitous in Fátima as that of the Virgin herself, set poignantly against the fading, black-and-white childhood photographs of Jacinta and Francisco, cast forever in a supporting role by their early deaths.

artigos religiosos. You can get an awful lot of tacky souvenirs for just a few euros – Apparition snowflakes, Virgin Mary keyrings, bottled Fátima water, Sister Lúcia desk ornaments – or spend hundreds on a gilded statue of a martyred saint.

Ourém

With its cosy nest of medieval lanes, a clutch of old stone houses and a church or two, the pretty town of **OURÉM** lies 12km to the east of Fátima. From the lower new town, Vila Nova de Ourém, a winding road climbs for 2km up to Ourém castle, crowning a hill above the town. Ourém's heyday was in the fifteenth century, when the fourth count of Ourém, Dom Afonso, built several grand monuments and converted the castle into a palace. The castle was virtually destroyed by Napoleon's forces, but is now largely restored. You can walk around its parapet, walls and towers for a marvellous, sweeping panorama, with the basilica of Fátima visible away to the west.

ARRIVAL AND INFORMATION

FÁTIMA AND AROUND

By bus Fátima's bus station is on Avenida Dom José Alves Correia da Silva, which is the main through-avenue between the rotundas – turn right along the avenue and walk for 500m to reach the turismo.

Destinations Batalha (Mon–Fri 3 daily; 40min), Leiria (5–9 daily, 25min); Lisbon (roughly every 30min; 1hr 30min) and Tomar (1 daily; 45min).

By car With Batalha 18km northwest, Leiria 25km northwest and Tomar 35km east, Fátima and the basilica lie just off the A1 motorway, flanked by two large traffic circles

(*rotundas*) – Rotunda Norte, nearest the bus station, is the one with the statues of the three shepherd children. Vast car parks ring the basilica, and provided you don't coincide with a pilgrimage you'll find street parking in the town as well.

By train Fátima is also on the main Lisbon–Porto train line, but the Estação de Fátima is 25km east of town and there's not always an immediate bus connection.

Information Turismo, Avenida Dom José Alves Correia da Silva (Tues–Sat 9am–1pm & 2–6pm, longer hours during pilgrimage times; ☎ 249 531 139, ⓦ turismodocentro.pt).

ACCOMMODATION AND EATING

FÁTIMA

Outside the major pilgrimages and weekends there's plenty of **accommodation** to go round. The turismo's map of town (also viewable online) lists thirty options alone.

During the pilgrimages (when most accommodation is booked up months in advance and prices double) people camp around the Basílica. All this said, it's hard to recommend spending the night in Fátima basilica – nearby

Ourém is a better option (see below). It really is a very small place, with nothing to do, and while there is also a glut of **cafés and restaurants**, they are all geared towards tourists and pilgrims and none is particularly inspiring.

OURÉM

Pousada de Ourém Largo João Manso ☎ 249 540 930, ⓦ pousadas.pt. The *pousada* has been fashioned from several fifteenth-century buildings to create a stylish hotel, most of whose rooms have far-reaching views (though only three have balconies). There's a nice terrace-bar and courtyard, while across the street from the reception is a fabulous terrace and outdoor pool with more extensive views. The restaurant offers a contemporary twist on traditional regional dishes. **€130**

Tomar

TOMAR is a charming, small town on the banks of the Rio Nabão – close enough to Lisbon for a day-trip, handsome enough and certainly interesting enough to warrant an overnight stay. Its old quarter is typically attractive, laid out as a grid of cobbled streets centred on a fine square, and there are riverside strolls to enjoy and green woods for picnicking. But standing sentry over town, high on the hill above, is the real reason for a visit – the mighty **Convento do Cristo**, founded (along with the town) in 1160 as the headquarters of the Order of the Knights Templar, scourge of the Moors and defenders of the faith. Castle and town both survived Moorish siege and attack in 1190, after which Tomar prospered in line with the gradual establishment of Portugal as a regional and, later, imperial force.

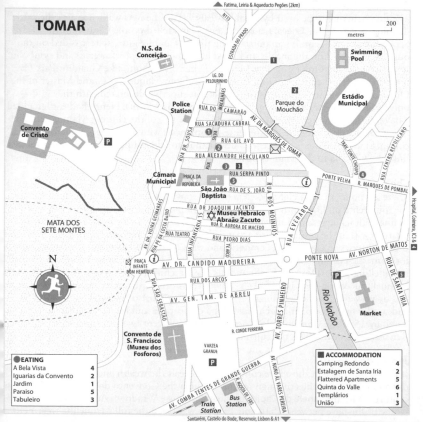

EATING	
A Bela Vista	4
Iguarias da Convento	2
Jardim	1
Paraíso	5
Tabuleiro	3

ACCOMMODATION	
Camping Redondo	4
Estalagem de Santa Iria	2
Flattered Apartments	5
Quinta do Valle	6
Templários	1
União	3

2

Convento de Cristo

Estrada do Convento • Daily: June–Sept 9am–6.30pm; Oct–May 9am–5.30pm; last entrance 30min before closing; closed public holidays • €6, under-12s free, free the first Sunday of the month; combined ticket with Alcobaça and Batalha €15 • ☎ 249 315 089, ⓦ conventocristo.pt • It's a 15min walk uphill from the town centre; free parking outside

The dramatic **Convento de Cristo** is one of Portugal's most important historical buildings – serving, unusually, as both military nerve-centre and religious foundation. Now a UNESCO World Heritage site, it was built by Gualdim Pais, a knight who had served under Afonso Henriques in battles against the Moors in Portugal. In 1157 he was appointed Grand Master of the **Order of the Knights Templar**, and moved their base from Soure in central Portugal, south to strategically important land overlooking the Rio Nabão at what became Tomar. When the powerful Templar order was later suppressed – it was seen as a challenge both to European rulers and the Papacy – it was simply re-established in Portugal in 1319 as the **Order of Christ**, with the castle at Tomar again its headquarters. The Order was later at the centre of Portugal's emerging maritime empire, and under Prince Henry the Navigator – an illustrious Grand Master indeed – the castle also became both lavish palace and monastic centre.

It's an enormous complex, and though you could whip around the main highlights in an hour, a longer tour could easily take two or three hours. You're given a comprehensive English-language guide and floorplan on entry, and there's a café inside with terrace seating.

Charola, nave and portal

The first structure to be built by Gualdim Pais within the new walls was also the castle's defining structure, the **Charola**, a round temple modelled on the Church of the Holy Sepulchre in Jerusalem. It's an outstanding piece of architecture, sixteen-sided on the outside, octagonal on the inside, and must have made a deeply powerful and symbolic impression on the Order's medieval knights – many of whom, like Gualdim Pais himself, had travelled to the Holy Land. Under Dom Manuel I – Grand Master of the Order of Christ as well as king – the chapel was superbly decorated with the polychromatic statues and rich paintings you see today. Prince Henry had earlier added a **nave** to the round temple, greatly expanding the size of the church; Manuel rebuilt this in the flamboyant style that became synonymous with his name, in particular commissioning master architect João de Castilho to add a superb decorative **portal** that links the Charola to the Manueline church.

The cloisters

There are no fewer than eight cloisters in the Convento do Cristo, most added during the fourteenth and fifteenth centuries as the complex underwent massive expansion, in line with its increasing influence. Not only did Prince Henry build himself palatial quarters within the castle, he also expanded the monastic quarters, adding two lovely tiled cloisters, the **Claustro do Cemitério** and the **Claustro da Lavagem**, the latter used for domestic tasks like the washing of monks' robes. The main cloister received its first remodelling under Dom Manuel I and his court architect João de Castilho, but it was Manuel's successor, João III (1521–57), who transformed this central feature of what was by now a full working monastery. Work on the **Claustro Príncipal** began in 1557 and, under first the Spanish architect Diogo de Torralva and then the Italian Filippo Terzi, by 1591 the Convento do Cristo had a magnificent two-storey arcaded Renaissance cloister that's the equal of anything in the country.

Janela do Capítulo

If there's one place in the entire complex that reveals the wealth and care lavished on the buildings – and thus the high regard in which the Convento do Cristo was held for centuries – it's the **Janela do Capítulo** (Chapter House Window). Added to the west facade of the nave between 1510 and 1513, it was given the full Manueline treatment

MANUELINE ARCHITECTURE

With the new-found wealth and confidence engendered by the "Discoveries" came a distinctly Portuguese version of Late Gothic architecture. Named after King Manuel I (1495–1521), the **Manueline style** is characterized by a rich and often fantastical use of ornamentation. Doors, windows and arcades are encrusted with elaborately carved stonework, in which the imagery of the sea is freely combined with both symbols of Christianity and of the newly discovered lands.

The style first appeared at the Igreja de Jesus (1494–98), in **Setúbal**. This relatively restrained building is the work of Diogo Boitaca, who later supervised the initial construction of the great Jéronimos monastery at **Belém** a few kilometres downstream from Lisbon. Commissioned by the king, this is a far more exuberant structure with an elaborately carved south portal opening onto a nave where the vaulting ribs seem to sprout out of the thin, trunk-like columns like leaves from a palm tree. Belém was the point from which many of the Portuguese navigators set forth, and the new building was largely subsidized by the new, lucrative spice trade.

The Jéronimos monastery is the most unified expression of the new style, but Manuel I also commissioned lavish extensions to existing buildings, such as the Convento de Cristo at **Tomar**, which is arguably the most brilliant and original expression of Manueline decoration. The armillary sphere – a navigational instrument – became the personal emblem of King Manuel, and frequently appears in Manueline decoration. It can be seen at the great abbey at **Batalha**, whose Capelas Imperfeitas (Unfinished Chapels) are also smothered in ornamentation (including snails and artichokes) that seems to defy the material from which it's carved. Not all Manueline architecture was ecclesiastical: there were also palaces, like that of the Dukes of Bragança at **Vila Viçosa**, and castles, like the one at **Évora Monte** where the whole of the exterior is bound by a single stone rope. Most famous of all secular constructions is Lisbon's **Torre de Belém**, a fortress built on an island in the River Tejo which incorporates Moorish-style balconies, battlements in the form of shields, and even a carving of a rhinoceros.

Manueline architecture did not continue much beyond the fourth decade of the sixteenth century. Indeed, so meteoric was the rise and fall of Manueline art within the reign of Dom Manuel that, to some extent, it must have reflected his personal tastes. In the reign of Manuel's successor, King João III, a more austere religious atmosphere prevailed in which the decorative excesses of the Manueline style were replaced by the ordered sobriety of Italian classicism.

by sculptor Diogo de Arruda, who rolled out every maritime and imperial motif he could muster in one masterful decorative sweep around what is – let's not forget – a mere window (albeit a very large window into a very important church). There are twisted ropes, knots and swirls, coral and vegetation, and crosses and globes in glorious profusion. Access to see the window and the west facade is from the **Claustro de Santa Bárbara**, next to the Claustro Príncipal.

Mata Nacional dos Sete Montes

Praça Infante Dom Henriques • Daily: May–Sept 8.30am–7.30pm; Oct–April 8.30am–5.30pm • Free

Originally the convent gardens, this is now a large park where local residents flock at the weekend for picnics or a stroll in the woods. There is an area of formal topiary by the entrance, with a series of marked trails. Note there is no access to the convent from here.

Praça da República

The gridded streets of the old town converge on the central **Praça da República**, where you'll find a statue of Tomar's founding father, Gualdim Pais, and a ring of handsome seventeenth-century buildings including the old town hall. Here, the **Igreja de São João Baptista** (Tues–Sun 10am–noon & 2–6pm; free) dates from at least a century earlier and presents an interesting melange – octagonal bell-tower, sculpted Manueline doorway and paintings inside by Gregório Lopes (1490–1550), one of the most significant artists to emerge from the so-called "Portuguese School" of the sixteenth century.

Museu Hebraico Abraão Zacuto

Rua Dr. Joaquim Jacinto 73 • May–Sept Wed–Sun 10am–1pm & 3–7pm; Oct–April Wed–Sun 10am–1pm & 2–6pm • Free • ☎ 249 329 823

Tomar's excellently preserved fifteenth-century synagogue, now the **Museu Hebraico Abraão Zacuto**, is named after the Spanish astronomer Abraham Zacuto, who prepared navigational aids for Vasco da Gama. There's little to see inside save some surviving Hebraic inscriptions, as well as gifts donated by visitors, but the fact that it stands at all is reason enough to visit. Following the expulsion of the Portuguese Jews in 1496, the temple was abandoned and later served as a prison and then private house, before being adopted as a national monument.

Museu dos Fósforos

Convento de São Francisco, Avenida General Bernado Faria • Visits by appointment only at the tourist office ☎ 249 329 823, May–Sept Wed–Sun 10am–noon & 3–7pm; Oct–April Wed–Sun 10am–noon & 2–6pm • Free

The old convent of São Francisco, facing Varzea Grande, might tempt you with its **Museu dos Fósforos**, which claims Europe's largest collection of matchboxes. Indeed, it does hold forty thousand or so – although its boast of it being "a singular description of universal history and culture" is pushing it a bit. Visits need to be booked first at the tourist office.

Aqueduto Pegões

Out of town, you can get great views of the stunning seventeenth-century **Aqueduto Pegões**, built to supply the convent with water. The best place to see it is 2km from Tomar, signposted (Pegões) off the N113 Leiria road, where a double-storey L-shaped sweep strides across a fertile valley.

ARRIVAL AND INFORMATION   **TOMAR**

The adjacent train and bus stations are on Avenida Combatentes da Grande Guerra, within easy walking distance of the centre. Head directly north across the open space of Varzea Grande and you'll soon hit Avenida Dr. Cândido Madureira – the turismo is at its western end.

By bus There are services to and from Fátima (1 daily; 45min), Leiria (1 daily; 1hr) and Lisbon (3 daily; 1hr 45min–2hr 30min).

By car Tomar is 130km northeast of Lisbon. Free parking is available on the vast Varzea Grande, in front of the bus station. Anywhere else near the old town, or across the

---

THE FESTA DOS TABULEIROS

Tomar is renowned throughout the country for its **Festa dos Tabuleiros** (literally, the Festival of the Trays). It can be traced back to Queen Isabel who founded the Brotherhood of the Holy Spirit in the fourteenth century, though some believe it to derive from an ancient fertility rite. Whatever its origins, it's now a largely secular event, held at four-yearly intervals during the first week of July; the next event is in 2019.

The festival starts on the first Sunday with the **Cortejo dos Rapazes** or "Boys' Procession" (for schoolchildren), with the **Cortejo do Mordomo** on the following Friday, when the costumed festival coordinators parade their carriages, carts and cattle (symbols of the sacrificial oxen that were once presented).

The main procession is on the final Sunday. The **Cortejo dos Tabuleiros** consists of several hundred young women wearing white, each escorted by a young man in a white shirt, red tie and black trousers. Each woman carries on her head a tray with thirty loaves threaded on vertical canes, intertwined with leaves and paper flowers, and crowned with a cross or a white dove – the symbol of the Holy Spirit. The resulting headdress weighs 15kg, and is roughly person-height – hence the need for an escort to lift and help balance it. There's music and dancing in the flower-filled streets, traditional games, fireworks at dawn and dusk, and a bullfight the night before the procession.

bridge in the more modern part, is either zealously metered or restricted.

By train There are direct trains to Tomar from Lisbon (approx hourly; 1hr 50min–2hr 30min) and Santarém

(approx hourly; 45min–1hr).

Information Turismo Municipal, Avenida Dr. Cândido Madureira (Daily 10am–12.30pm & 2–6pm; ☎ 249 329 823, ⊚ cm-tomar.pt).

ACCOMMODATION

Camping Redondo Rua do Casal Rei 6, Poço Redondo, 10km northeast of Tomar ☎ 249 376 421, ⊚ campingredondo.com. This pretty, rural campsite, under English–Dutch ownership, also has two stone cottages and four wooden chalets to rent – prices run from €60 to €85 a night. There's also budget accommodation in a two-person caravan (€40 per night) or pre-erected six-person tents (€45). Pool, café-bar (camp dinners in summer) and breakfast are available, and you're only a few kilometres from the local lake. From Tomar, follow signs for IC3 (Coimbra) and then Junceira, Fonte de Dom João and Poço Redondo. Pitch €12, plus €2.50 per car

Estalagem de Santa Iria Parque do Mouchão ☎ 249 313 326, ⊚ estalagemsantairia.com. This secluded island retreat has spacious balconies onto the park, whose mature trees screen off the traffic. Rooms are on the tired side, but it's old-fashioned in the nicest possible way, and the restaurant is pretty good value too (mains from €12) in quietly elegant surroundings. Car access is from the riverside avenue across the narrow bridge. €50

★ **Flattered Apartments** Rua Santa Iria 11 & 21 ☎ 939 146 262, ⊚ flatteredapartments.com. Perfect for families, these compact but very tastefully furnished apartments are

inside a lovely traditional townhouse of polished wood floors, big wooden shutters and high ceilings. There's a kitchenette, coffee machine and dishwasher and some come with lovely views towards the castle. A superb breakfast (around €14 extra) is delivered on request. One bed apartments €75, two-bed apartments €115

Quinta do Valle Guerreira, Santa Cita, 7km south of Tomar ☎ 249 381 165 or ☎ 966 814 941, ⊚ quintadovalle.com. Lovely old *quinta*, now divided into self-catering apartments sleeping two to four people. Breakfast is included (served in the apartments) and there's an outdoor pool and rambling gardens. Doubles €92; four people €128

Templários Largo Cândido dos Reis 1 ☎ 249 310 100, ⊚ hoteldostemplarios.com. The smartest hotel in the town centre is a large, modern four-star overlooking the river, with a health spa and rather fine indoor pool, plus easy parking. Balconies overlook the riverside lawns. €88

União Rua Serpa Pinto 94 ☎ 249 323 161. This deservedly popular place (book in advance in summer) has an air of grandeur, especially in the lovely breakfast room and period-piece of a bar. Bathrooms might be on the elderly side, but most rooms are generously sized. No credit cards. €45

EATING

A Bela Vista Rua Marquês Pombal 68 ☎ 249 312 870, ⊚ restaurantebelavista.pai.pt. A rustic place by the river with a delightful covered terrace underneath an old house. It serves traditional Portuguese dishes – roast *cabrito* and *leitão* are house specials – but there are also fish and rice dishes, all around €10–13, though half portions at €7–8 will suffice. Mon 12.30–2.30pm, Wed–Sun 12.30–2.30pm & 7–11pm.

Iguarias da Convento Rua Silva Megalhães 77–79 ☎ 249 316 154. A modern deli-cum-tapas bar with seats out on a pedestrianised street. There's a fine array of tapas to choose from: local hams, cheeses, sausages and snails (all around €4–6), or you can just pop in for a glass of local wine or beer. Tues–Sun 10.30am–9.30pm.

Jardim Rua Silva Magalhães 54 ☎ 249 312 034 ⊚ restaurantejarimtomar.com. With a separate entrance on Rua Sacadura Cabral, this is a warren of a place with different

dining areas, including a little back garden. The speciality is giant toasted-sandwich *francesinhas* (from €7), though it also does large portions of well-prepared salmon, pork and whole grilled squids, all around €8–9. Mon, Wed–Fri & Sun 9am–3pm & 6pm–midnight, Sat 6pm–midnight.

Paraíso Rua Serpa Pinto 127 ☎ 249 312 997. A Tomar institution with marble pillars and tables on the main pedestrianized street, ideal for a coffee or drink at any time of day. Mon 9am–2pm, Tues–Sat 8am–2am, Sun 8am–8pm.

★ **Tabuleiro** Rua Serpa Pinto 140 ☎ 249 312 771 ⊚ restaurantetabuleiro.wordpress.com. Semi-smart, family-friendly restaurant serving traditional food (roast pork, *bacalhau*, veal, *arroz de peixe*, steak) in coronary-inducing portions – a *dose* (€15) will easily feed two, or choose half portions for €8–9. Desserts are all home-made, and the owner summons up menu guidance in half a dozen languages. Mon–Sat noon–3pm & 7–10pm.

ENTERTAINMENT

Tomar has a wide cultural programme, detailed in the monthly *Agenda Cultural*, available from the turismo. Look out for performances by the Fatias de Cá **theatre company** (⊚ fatiasdeca.net), who stage spectacular events – Shakespeare productions, *The Name of the Rose*, sound-and-light shows – occasionally in the Convento do Cristo or the Mata dos Sete Montes park as well as the Castelo de Almourol (see p.172).

East along the Rio Tejo

Following the Tejo valley to the east, you will pass the remarkable castle at **Almourol** and, at the confluence of the Rio Tejo and Rio Zêzere, the pretty town of **Constância**. There's another historic castle at **Abrantes**, 12km further east, and an even more extraordinary one at Belver, east of Abrantes, on the north bank of the Tejo. The whole route is an enjoyable approach to the towns of the northern Alentejo or the Beira Baixa, and it's covered by train (the Lisbon–Covilhã service), but drivers are going to have the best of it since you're unlikely to want to stop anywhere for long.

Castelo de Almourol

Vila Nova da Barquinha, 27km south of Tomar • Ferry departures from Cais Junto ao Castelo, opposite the castle • March–Oct Tues–Sun 10am–1pm & 2.30–7.30pm; Nov–Feb Tues–Sun 10am–1pm & 2.30–5pm; castle open same hours • Ferry €2.50 return; castle €2.50 • ☎ 249 720 358

Castles rarely come cuter than the **Castelo de Almourol**, which clings to a craggy islet in the Rio Tejo. You arrive via a little ferry that departs from a car park opposite the castle itself. Once ashore, you can climb through the trees to the castle, where there's a beautiful rural panorama from the tall central keep. Back above the quayside car park, a bar with a shady terrace serves snacks and sandwiches. Boats (Tues–Sun roughly hourly from 10am–7pm, fewer in winter, €4 single) also run to the castle from the river esplanade in the village of Tancos, 2km to the west, which is home to the nearest train station.

Constância

3km east of Almourol • By train, get off at Praia do Ribatejo-Constância, the stop after Almourol

Sited on a hillside spilling down to riverfronts on both the Tejo and Zêzere, the small town of **CONSTÂNCIA** is worth a quick stop. It's typically attractive in that old-town Portuguese way, with a historic centre of cobbled streets and whitewashed buildings. It's best known, however, for its association with **Luís de Camões**, author of Portugal's great national epic poem, *Os Lusíadas* – the riverside Camões gardens are based on those described in the poem. Constância is at its liveliest during the **Festa dos Barqueiros**, on Easter Monday, with parades and traditional boats on the Tejo.

Abrantes

Overlooking the Rio Tejo, 15km east of Constância, **ABRANTES** has a historic kernel of pretty narrow alleys and squares lined with crumbling houses that lies hidden at the centre of a dreary modern town. It looks its best in spring and summer when flowers on Rua da Barca and in the Jardim da República are in bloom; the views are also impressive. The high point – in all respects – is the town's much-restored early fourteenth century **castelo** (Tues–Sun 10am–1pm & 2–5.30pm; free), from where there are more sweeping vistas. Recent excavations here have revealed fifteenth-century frescoes and a ninth-century Islamic tower.

Castelo de Belver

Belver, 35km east of Abrantes • Tues–Fri 10am–1pm & 2–6pm; Sat–Sun 2–6pm; closed last weekend of each month • €2 • ☎ 926 386 094, ⊕ cultura-alentejo.pt

The **Castelo de Belver** is one of the most famous in the country, with a place in dozens of Portuguese legends. The name comes from *belo ver* (beautiful to see), the supposed exclamation of a medieval princess, waking up to look out from its keep at the river valley below. It dates from the twelfth century, when the Portuguese frontier stood at the Tejo, the Moors having reclaimed most of the territories to the south. Stunningly sited

– and virtually impregnable, as failed Moorish attack after failed Moorish attack revealed – the beautifully restored battlemented walls and keep are a dramatic reminder of how hard the early Portuguese nation had to work at keeping its independence. An exhibition space inside details the castle's history through maps and multimedia displays.

ARRIVAL AND DEPARTURE   **CASTELO DE BELVER**

Although technically in the Alentejo, Belver is best approached from Abrantes, by train at least.

By train The train station is directly below the village beside the river (4 daily trains from Abrantes, 25min). If you take the train further towards Castelo Branco, look out for the striking rock gorge at Vila Velha de Ródão, known as the Portas do Ródão (see p.255).

Golegã

GOLEGÃ, on the west bank of the Rio Tejo, midway between Tomar and Santarém, is a pleasant riverside town which calls itself "Capital of the Horse", a claim it backs up with black-horse silhouettes hanging outside virtually every business. It is best known for its **Feira Nacional do Cavalo** (National Horse Fair), held during the first two weeks of November. The fair incorporates celebrations for St Martin's Day on November 11, when there's a running of the bulls and a grand parade of red-waistcoated grooms. Other than during the *feira*, Golegã makes for a brief visit: the sixteenth-century **Igreja Matriz** flanks its main square, a couple of cafés put out tables under the trees, while the old market has been turned into a small shopping complex.

Casa-Estúdio Carlos Relvas

Largo Dom Manuel I · Tues–Sun 10am–1pm & 2–6pm · Free · ☎ 249 979 120, ⓦ casarelvas.com

Golegã's **Casa-Estúdio Carlos Relvas** was the home of Carlos Relvas – father of José Relvas, who proclaimed the Portuguese Republic in Lisbon in 1910. Relvas Senior had an interest in the newly discovered art of photography, early examples of which are displayed, while the house itself is a whimsical pavilion of wrought iron and glass set in landscaped gardens.

Santarém

Strategically sited **SANTARÉM**, set on a plateau on the banks of the Rio Tejo, already had a long history before Portugal was ever an independent nation. An important Roman trading city was sited here, and from the eighth to the twelfth centuries Shantarin was one of the most cultured Moorish cities on the Iberian peninsula. Accordingly, its conquest in 1147 by Afonso Henriques was hugely significant and in later medieval times Santarém became a royal favourite, decorated with grand Gothic buildings and hosting regular meetings of the Cortes (Parliament). There's little if nothing left of Roman or Moorish times but, with its two exquisite churches and surviving old-town alleys and squares, modern Santarém remains a pleasant place to visit – not least for the unrivalled view across the plains from the Portas do Sol, the former site of the Moorish citadel and Reconquista castle.

Praça Sá da Bandeira

The market and municipal gardens mark the northern edge of the town, with the spacious **Praça Sá da Bandeira** just beyond. This is named for the Marquês de Sá da Bandeira (1795–1876), Portuguese prime minister in the 1830s and the town's most famous son, whose statue is overlooked by the fussy Baroque facade of the Jesuit **Igreja**

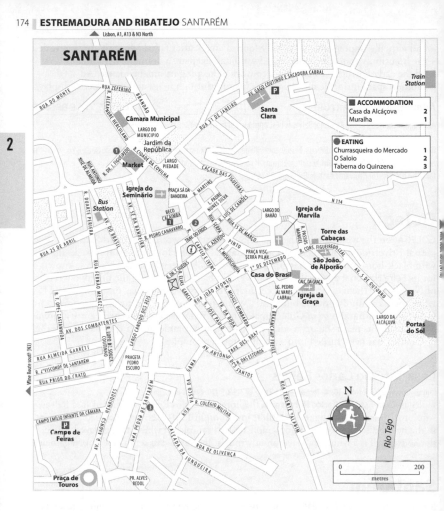

do Seminário (1676). The largely pedestrianized old town lies beyond, with Rua Serpa Pinto and Rua Capelo e Ivens threading towards the signposted Portas do Sol, about fifteen minutes' walk away, with the best of the churches conveniently en route.

Igreja de Marvila

Praça Visconde Serra do Pilar • Tues–Sat 9am–12.30pm & 2–6pm, Sun 9.30am–12.30pm & 2–5.30pm • Free

Although one of the oldest churches in town, the **Igreja de Marvila** – at the end of Rua Serpa Pinto – had a Manueline makeover, which is especially noticeable in the sculpted doorway. Inside are brilliant seventeenth-century *azulejos* covering every centimetre of the nave.

Igreja da Graça and the Casa do Brasil

Largo Pedro Álvares Cabral • Tues, Wed & Sat–Sun 9.30am–12.30pm & 2–5.30pm, Thurs–Fri 10am–12.30pm & 2–5.30pm • Free

The fifteenth-century **Igreja da Graça**, with its impressive rose window, is Santarém's most architecturally interesting church. Inside, it's the elaborately carved sarcophagus of Pedro

de Meneses, the first Governor of Ceuta (died 1347), which draws the eye, though Portuguese people know the church as the burial place of **Pedro Álvares Cabral**, discoverer of Brazil in 1500. A simple tombstone set in the floor near the Meneses sarcophagus marks the spot, with Cabral "the discoverer" honoured more prominently outside the church by a heroic statue – cross in one hand, sword in the other. The Cabral family lived in Santarém, and a house by the church thought to be theirs (though with no real evidence) is now the **Casa do Brasil** (entrance on Rua Vila de Belmonte 13–15, ☎243 304 652), a cultural centre with art and other exhibitions (closed Sundays).

2

Igreja de São João de Alporão

Largo Zeferino Sarmento • Currently closed for refurbishment, but normally Wed–Sun 9.30am–12.30pm & 2–5.30pm • ☎ 243 377 290, ⓦmuseu-santarem.org

Opposite the fifteenth-century clock tower of the Torre das Cabaças is the city's modest Núcleo Museológico de Arte e Arqueologia (archeological and medieval art museum), housed in the twelfth-century church of **São João de Alporão**. Its Romanesque portal gives way to a later Gothic interior, containing the remarkable Gothic tomb of one Duarte de Meneses, governor of Portuguese India from 1522–1524.

Portas do Sol

End of Avenida 5 de Outubro • Daily: May–Sept 9am–10pm; Oct–April 9am–6.30pm • Free

The Moors, naturally enough, picked the best vantage point for their fortified town, atop the plateau overlooking the Rio Tejo and beyond. Afonso Henriques too, and all subsequent overlords of Santarém, kept the walls secure, though today's stone battlements have been much restored over the centuries. The castle site is now a municipal garden known as the **Portas do Sol**, the "Gates of the Sun" – a pleasant spot to stroll and sip a coffee at the modern kiosk café in the shade of the trees. A swashbuckling statue of Afonso Henriques commemorates his pivotal capture of the town.

ARRIVAL AND INFORMATION   SANTARÉM

By bus The bus station is close to the old centre, on Avenida do Brasil.

Destinations Abrantes (3–7 daily; 1hr 25min); Évora (2 daily; 2 hr); Fátima (3 daily; 45min); Lisbon (4–7 daily; 1hr 20min).

By car It's 80km, and under an hour's drive, from Lisbon to Santarém. Parking in the old town is impossible, though there are pay-parking spaces (free at weekends) around the market and down Avenida Sá da Bandeira, near the bus station. There's also free parking a little way out by Santa Clara church.

By train The train station is 2km north, below the town, with buses into the centre leaving every 30min; a taxi will cost €6.

Destinations Castelo Branco (6–10 daily; 2hr–3hr); Covilhã (5 daily; 3hr–4hr 5min); Lisbon (every 30min–1hr; 1hr–1hr 20min); Tomar (roughly hourly; 45min–1hr); and Vila Franca de Xira (every 30min–1hr; 30–40min).

Information Turismo, Rua Capelo e Ivens 63 (Mon–Fri 10am–6pm, Sat & Sun 9.30am–1pm & 2–5.30pm; ☎243 304 437, ⓦcm-santarem.pt).

ACCOMMODATION

★**Casa da Alcáçova** Largo da Alcáçova 3 ☎243 304 030, ⓦalcacova.com. The premier choice in town, this aristocratic seventeenth-century manor house at the

shoulder of the Portas do Sol has jaw-dropping river views. Antiques, original fireplaces and magnificent beds (including some four-posters) furnish the eight

SANTARÉM'S FESTIVALS AND MARKETS

For two weeks in June (starting the first Friday of the month) Santarém's **Feira Nacional da Agricultura** celebrates all things rural and agricultural, with displays of bullfighting, folk dancing, local arts and crafts, and country traditions. The town also hosts an annual **Festival de Gastronomia** (third and fourth week of October, ⓦfestivalnacionaldegastronomia.pt), where you can taste all sorts of regional specialities. In addition, a large **market** sprawls around the bullring on the second and fourth Sunday of every month.

2

rooms – dressing gowns and slippers are supplied. Drinks are served in the elegant lounge, and there's a lovely pool and outdoor eating area. Parking available. **€145**
Muralha Rua Pedro Canavarro 12 ☎243 322 399.

Simple budget rooms in a family-run place adjacent to a surviving chunk of the city walls. A couple have balconies over the street, but otherwise it's fairly unremarkable. No credit cards. **€45**

EATING

Santarém's choice of restaurants is good, though hardly any are open on Sundays. Rua Dr. Jaime Figueiredo, the street behind the market, is the place to look for an inexpensive meal. Among local specialities there's *fataça na telha* (mullet cooked on a hot tile), which has its origins in the fishing village of Caneiras, 5km south of town.

Churrasqueira do Mercado Rua Dr. Jaime Figueiredo 24 ☎243 326 839. A basic grill house behind the market, one of the few places open on a Sunday night – when you'll be watching football with the locals (you should be supporting Sporting). The grilled chicken is really good – the thermonuclear *piri-piri* sauce is optional, and you can eat well for under €10. Daily 11am–3pm & 7–11pm.
O Saloio Trav do Montalvo 11, off Rua Capelo e Ivens ☎243 327 656. Popular with local families, and boasting a

little outdoor patio, this traditional, tiled *casa de pasto* is good value for money – most dishes around €7. Mon–Fri 11am–9.30pm, Sat 11am–4.30pm.
Taberna do Quinzena Rua Pedro de Santarém 93–95 ☎243 322 804, ⓦquinzena.com. One of the oldest eating places in the region, in business for well over a century. Traditional steaks, meat grills and daily specials are served in a no-nonsense *tasca* with a serious bullfighting obsession – a full meal costs around €25–30. Daily 11am–11pm.

The Ribatejo wine routes

Wine has been produced on the banks of the Tejo for around two thousand years and, while it's long had a reputation for quantity rather than quality, the offerings of some new producers have recently begun to acquire an international profile. Many **vineyards** offer tours and tastings. The **N118** marks the most attractive route north of Santarém, taking in several small towns and *quintas* en route to Chamusca, 28km away. There's nothing much to stop for in Almeirim (once the site of a royal summer palace), Alpiarça or Chamusca, but local **wine producers** line the road at intervals, open for sales to the public; look for signs saying "*vinho do produtor*".

South of Santarém, the **N3** towards Vila Franca and Lisbon is a great road if you're not in a hurry. The drive can occupy half a day, with stops at the interesting Museu Rural e do Vinho in **Cartaxo** and the historical sites around **Azambuja**, plus a detour for lunch in one of the pretty towns of **Alenquer** or **Arruda dos Vinhos**.

Cartaxo

Fourteen kilometres south of Santarém, the small town of Cartaxo is the self-declared "Capital do Vinho". The **Museu Rural e do Vinho** (Avenida 25 de Abril; Tues–Sun 9.30am–12.30pm & 2.30–5.30pm; €1.40; ☎243 701 257) is the single best place to investigate the subject – as well as the exhibits, you can taste (for a tiny fee) and buy the local wines here.

The museum is housed in the signposted Quinta das Pratas, a municipal park and sports complex on the outskirts of town.

Azambuja

AZAMBUJA, 13km to the southwest of Cartaxo, is known for its red wines made from the Periquita grape, though the town itself isn't worth a stop. However, for a true off-the-beaten-track sight, follow the signs from town to the **Vala de Azambuja**, a 26-kilometre-long canal built parallel to the river by the Marquês de Pombal, designed to drain the land when the Rio Tejo was in flood. Three kilometres up a dirt road (fine for cars; signposted "Palácio") stand the forlorn ruins of the **Palácio das Obras Novas**,

once used as a staging post for the steamers plying the route from Lisbon to Constância in the nineteenth century. It's beautifully sited by the river, though red signs warn you to keep out of the rickety structure.

Alenquer

At Carregado, the N3 meets the N1, and offers a choice of routes further into the rolling hills. Five kilometres north, and perched on a hill above the Alenquer river, **ALENQUER** mainly produces lemony-flavoured white wines and has some decent local restaurants in which to sample them. Traffic chokes the main road alongside the river, but it's an enjoyable climb up to the attractive upper town, where you can visit the Manueline cloisters of the church and convent of São Francisco, the oldest Franciscan house in Portugal, built during the lifetime of St Francis of Assisi.

Arruda dos Vinhos

It is in the valleys around **ARRUDA DOS VINHOS**, 13km west of Carregado, that the region's vineyards are at their most attractive. It's a pretty town, too, with an enormous eighteenth-century public fountain and handsome Manueline church, but is top-heavy with restaurants and estate agents, both the consequence of the weekend influx of Lisboans.

EATING AND DRINKING · ARRUDA DOS VINHOS

★**O Fuso** Rua Cândido do Reis 94, Arruda dos Vinhos ☎ 263 975 121. A rustic barn of a restaurant where vast slabs of meat and *bacalhau* are grilled over open fires. It's not particularly cheap (meals from around €25–30) but it is excellent, and you can drink the fresh, Beaujolais-style Arruda (also known as Arruta) red wines. Daily noon–11pm.

Vila Franca de Xira

The bustling west-bank city of **VILA FRANCA DE XIRA**, 45km downriver from Santarém, makes a rival claim to be the capital of the Ribatejo, but it's a poor second to Santarém and only worth the effort of a visit for aficionados of the Portuguese bullfight. The rearing of bulls and horses dominates the local economy: there's a School of Bullfighting here, and posters everywhere announcing forthcoming fights, while Vila Franca celebrates its obsession in café names and statues.

The two big annual events are the **Festa do Colete Encarnado** ("Red Waistcoat Festival", which refers to the costumes of the mounted horsemen of the plains), held over several days in the first two weeks of July; and the **Feira de Outubro** (October Fair), in the first two weeks of the month (details for both on ⓦwww.cm-vfxira.pt). On both occasions there are bullfights, with the animals running through the streets chased by the bold (and drunk) – inevitably, injuries are sustained.

Without a bullfight to detain you, it's hard to linger long in the few restored streets around the town hall; it's nicest down at the riverside gardens by the train station, where there's an old fisherman's *bairro* with a couple of restaurants – in March and April local restaurants in town all celebrate the shad, a Tejo river fish.

ARRIVAL AND DEPARTURE · VILA FRANCA DE XIRA

By train Vila Franca is on a fast commuter line to Lisbon with 2–3 hourly services to Lisbon's Oriente station (30 mins) and 1–2 hourly services to Santarém (30–40min).

By car It's just a 40min drive from Lisbon to Vila Franca up the fast A1. However parking is tricky in the central area: you'll need to look for metered spots or signed central car parks.

Coimbra and the Beira Litoral

BIBLIOTECA JOANINA, COIMBRA

Coimbra and the Beira Litoral

The province of Beira Litoral is dominated by the city of Coimbra, which, with Guimarães, Lisbon and Porto, forms the quartet of Portugal's historic capitals. Situated on a steep hill above the Rio Mondego, it's a wonderfully moody place of ancient alleys and lanes, twisting and climbing around the country's oldest university. As a base for exploring the region, the city can't be beaten, with Portugal's most extensive Roman site, Conímbriga, 16km to the southwest, the castle at Montemor-o-Velho, 32km west, and the delightful spa town of Luso and ancient forest of Buçaco under an hour's journey to the north.

Beira's coastline, from Figueira da Foz north as far as Porto, remains one of the least spoiled in Portugal, backed by rolling dunes and pine forests. There's some development around the pretty lagoon town of **Praia de Mira**, but the only major resort is **Figueira da Foz** and even this remains mostly local in character. To the north of the region, **Aveiro** is one of Portugal's most attractive provincial towns and sits on an elaborate network of canals.

Following the delightful **Rio Mondego** upstream from Coimbra, you'll come to see why it has been celebrated so often in Portuguese poetry as the "Rio das Musas" – River of the Muses. A tributary of the Mondego, the **Dão**, is the source of some of the country's finest wines, while there's an equally beautiful route along the **Rio Vouga** up to the pretty little town of **Vouzela**. To the north is the impressive convent at **Arouca**, and the *serras* of Freita and Arada, both peppered with remote hamlets and offering more scenic routes for drivers. To the south lies the **Serra do Caramulo**, where the village of **Caramulo** makes a good base for mountain pursuits. East of Coimbra, as the land slowly rises towards the mountainous Beiras region and the Serra da Estrela, the first foothills are encountered in the **Serra da Lousã** and the **Serra do Açor**, rustic regions containing a range of pretty settlements such as riverside **Góis** and the incredibly sited schist village of **Píodão**.

Coimbra

Hugging the banks of a broad stretch of the sluggish Rio Mondego, handsome **COIMBRA** (pronounced *queem-bra*) is famed for its historic hilltop university, dating from 1290, with its awe-inspiring Baroque library. Coimbra was capital of a fledgling Portugal from 1143 to 1255 and, for a relatively small town, retains an impressive number of historical monuments, including ancient convents and two cathedrals. Its old town, curving round the hilltop where the university is located, oozes both history and a vibrancy resulting from the presence of around twenty thousand students who ensure the city is well-stocked with good-value cafés, bars and restaurants, some playing Coimbra's jaunty version of fado. It's a worthwhile destination at any time of the year

TRADITIONAL BOATS, AVEIRO

Highlights

❶ Velha Universidade, Coimbra Wind your way up to the splendidly sited university, with its striking Baroque library. **See p.186**

❷ Roman ruins at Conímbriga Mosaics, baths, forum, aqueduct and a mighty defensive wall survive at Portugal's finest Roman site. **See p.192**

❸ Serra do Açor Explore this little-visited mountain range full of unexpected delights – schist villages, river beaches, mountain walks and elegant old bridges. **See p.195**

❹ Kayaking down the Mondego Take a gentle paddle down the meandering and

picturesque Rio Mondego between Penacova and Coimbra. **See p.198**

❺ Mata Nacional do Buçaco Spend the day in the shaded Buçaco forest, and then drop down into the neighbouring spa town of Luso for afternoon tea. **See p.199**

❻ Aveiro Cruise on one of the traditional brightly-painted boats, known as *barcos moliceiros*, through the atmospheric canals of Aveiro. **See p.206**

❼ Figueira da Foz Central Portugal's finest resort, boasting one of Europe's widest beaches, and some great local walks. **See p.212**

HIGHLIGHTS ARE MARKED ON THE MAP ON P.182

(the depths of winter perhaps excepted), though the best time to visit is May, when students celebrate the end of their studies with a series of festivities – come in August when the students have gone and locals are on holiday, and you'll find the town strangely quiet.

Brief history

There was a settlement here in **Roman** times and the remains of the Roman Crypto-porticus are on display in the town's excellent Museu Machado de Castro. The **Moors** occupied the city from 711, using it as a trading centre for almost three hundred years

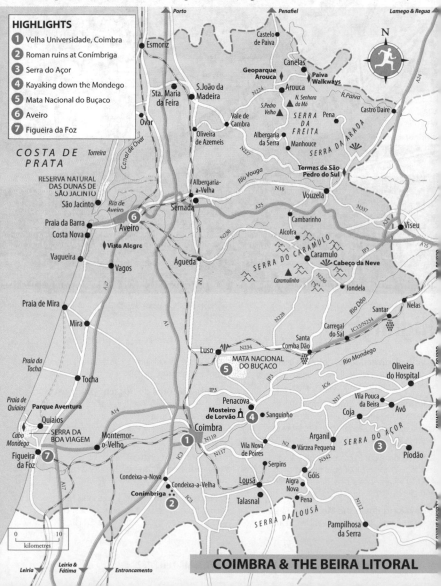

HIGHLIGHTS

1. Velha Universidade, Coimbra
2. Roman ruins at Conímbriga
3. Serra do Açor
4. Kayaking down the Mondego
5. Mata Nacional do Buçaco
6. Aveiro
7. Figueira da Foz

COIMBRA & THE BEIRA LITORAL

– today's Arco de Almedina gateway marks the entrance to a former Moorish medina. In 1143, shortly after the **Christian** Reconquista of 1064, Coimbra became the country's **capital** thanks to its position between the Christian north and Moorish south. During this time, the Sé Velha was built, along with the Convento de Santa Cruz. With Portugal expanding south, Lisbon became the capital in 1255, though Coimbra took on the role of cultural capital with the founding of its **university** in 1290, one of the world's first. For a time the university, too, moved to Lisbon before returning to be permanently housed in Coimbra's former royal palace in 1537. The Biblioteca Joanina was added in the eighteenth century and the university was further expanded by the New State in the mid-twentieth century. During term time its students now make up around a sixth of the population.

Baixa

Curling from the riverfront round the slopes of the upper town, the **Baixa**, or lower town, is an atmospheric warren of narrow streets and alleys housing traditional grocers' shops, tiny restaurants, cafés and the odd fashionable boutique. The main shopping streets, both of which are pedestrianized, are **Rua Ferreira Borges** and its continuation, **Rua Visconde da Luz**. Just off the former, the aptly named **Rua Quebra Costas** (Backbreaker Street) ascends very steeply to the upper town through the old city gate, **Arco de Almedina**, and is lined with some of the city's most fashionable bars and cafés.

Igreja de Santa Cruz

Praça 8 de Maio • Mon–Fri 9am–5pm, Sat 9am-12.30pm & 2–5pm, Sun 4–5.30pm • Church and sacristy free; chapterhouse and cloister €2.50 • ☎ 239 822 841

Facing the pretty little Praça 8 de Maio, the **Igreja de Santa Cruz** is one of the oldest monastery churches in Coimbra and is the resting place of some of the country's earliest monarchs. Dating from 1131, the *azulejo*-lined interior of the church contains the tombs of **Afonso Henrique**, proclaimed Portugal's first king in 1143, and **Sancho I** (1185–1211); it was also where St Anthony of Padua studied in the early thirteenth century. In the sixteenth century, at the height of Portugal's maritime expansions, the church was remodelled by Diogo de Boitaca, the architect behind Lisbon's famous Jerónimos monastery. It was Boitaca who added the ornate **Sala do Capítulo** (chapterhouse) and the beautiful **Cloister of Silence**, with its scenes from the Passion of Christ by French artist Nicolas de Chanterene. The over-the-top and rather incongruous neo-Gothic triumphal arch outside the church was added in the nineteenth century.

Sé Velha

Largo da Sé Velha • Mon–Sat 10am–5.30pm • €2.50 • ☎ 239 825 273

Coimbra's first cathedral, the **Sé Velha**, was consecrated in 1184 when Portugal was still battling with the Moors to the south, hence its narrow slit windows and imposing fortress-like battlements. The only external embellishment is the faded Renaissance **Porta Especiosa** ("beautiful door") in the north wall. Inside, the sixteenth-century additions are marginally more ornate, with a gilded wooden **altarpiece** and attractive **azulejos**, while the Gothic **cloisters** date from 1218. By 1772, the cathedral was supplanted by the slightly bland Sé Nova ("new" cathedral), further up the hill.

Museu Nacional de Machado de Castro

Largo Dr. José Rodrigues • Tues 2–6pm, Wed–Sun 10am-6pm • €4 • ☎ 239 853 070, ⓦ museumachadocastro.pt

Coimbra's most interesting museum, the **Museu Nacional de Machado de Castro** is

3

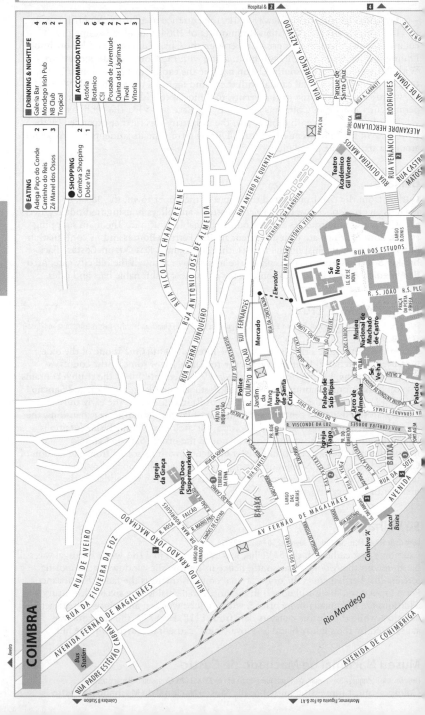

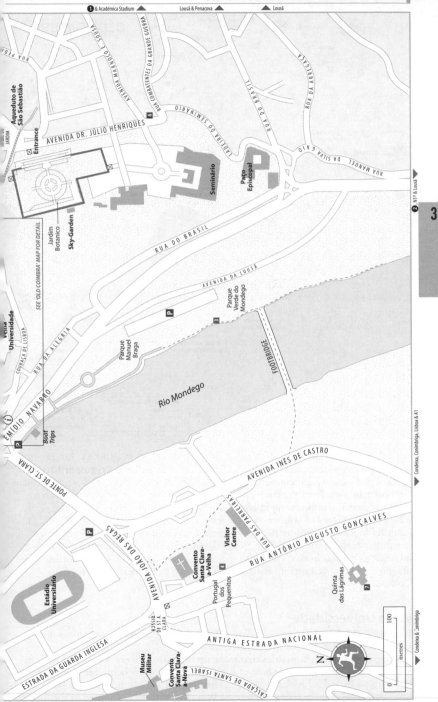

① & Académica Stadium ▲   Lousã & Penacova ▲   ▲ Lousã

② , N17 & Lousã ▶

3

Aqueduto de São Sebastião

Entrance

AVENIDA DR. JÚLIO HENRIQUES

Seminário

Paço Episcopal

RUA PEDR...

RUA PEDRO

AVENIDA MARNOCO E SOUSA

RUA COMBATENTES DA GRANDE GUERRA

LADEIRA DO SEMINÁRIO

RUA DO BRASIL

RUA DA ARREGAÇA

RUA MANUEL DA SILVA GAIO

Jardim Botânico

Sky-Garden

RUA DO BRASIL

SEE 'OLD COIMBRA' MAP FOR DETAIL

Velha Universidade

COURAÇA DE LISBOA

RUA DA ALEGRIA

AVENIDA DA LOUSÃ

Parque Verde do Mondego

P

Parque Manuel Braga

3

FOOTBRIDGE

Rio Mondego

EMÍDIO NAVARRO

P

Boat Trips

PONTE DE ST. CLARA

i

AVENIDA INÊS DE CASTRO

◀ Condeixa, Conímbriga, Lisboa & A1

AVENIDA DE JOÃO DAS REGAS

P

PASSEIO DE ST. CLARA

Estádio Universitário

ESTRADA DA GUARDA INGLESA

Museu Militar

Convento Santa Clara-a-Nova

Convento Santa Clara-a-Velha

Portugal dos Pequenitos

Visitor Centre

RUA DAS PARREIRAS

RUA ANTÓNIO AUGUSTO GONÇALVES

Quinta das Lágrimas

7

4

ANTIGA ESTRADA NACIONAL

CALÇADA DE SANTA ISABEL

N

0   100   metres

◀ Condeixa & Conímbriga

3

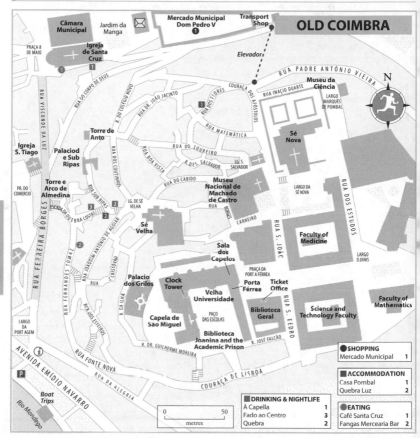

housed in an impressive twelfth-century former bishop's palace. This was built on top of Portugal's most important Roman building, the extraordinary **Cryptoporticus**, a series of first-century underground galleries which you can visit in the basement today (and partially view from the streets outside). Named after a local eighteenth-century royal sculptor, the museum highlights Coimbra's cultural importance over the years, with a dazzling array of artefacts such as religious sculptures, jewellery – including a beautiful fourteenth-century necklace – ceramics, furniture, textiles and paintings mostly dating from the fourteenth to the eighteenth centuries. There are also some interesting artefacts from the Orient including eighteenth-century snuff bottles, while the museum's café-restaurant boasts what might just be the best views from any Coimbra eatery.

Velha Universidade

Paço das Escolas; ticket office on Praça da Porta Férrea • Daily: Mid-March to Oct 9am–7.30pm; Nov to mid-March 9.30am–1pm & 2–5.30pm • €9, €2 extra for the clock tower • ☎ 239 859 884, ⊛ uc.pt

The imposing modern structures that make up the main university – mostly built in the 1940s and 50s – give little hint of the riches hidden away behind the white facades of the broad Paço das Escolas square. Accessed via the seventeenth-century Porta Férrea (the "iron gate" that once stood here), the **Velha Universidade** is housed in the former

royal palaces. You'll need to buy a ticket to look round it, though you're free to enjoy the city views from the terrace to one side of the square.

Biblioteca Joanina and the Academic Prison

Highlight of the Velha Universidade – and indeed all Coimbra – is the **Biblioteca Joanina**, a Baroque confection of cleverly-marbled wood, gold leaf, imposing frescoed ceilings and elaborate trompe-l'oeil decorations. The ancient library was installed in 1717 by Dom João V, whose portrait surveys his legacy from the library walls, which are lined with some 250,000 books dating back to the twelfth century – though these do fade into the background a bit against the backdrop of all the Baroque elaboration. The library only opens every twenty minutes – your time will be written on your ticket. With luck you won't be hemmed in by a big group, but at busy periods, you'll be ushered on from the library after a few minutes to the so-called **Academic Prison** in the basement below. This proved that studying was once no laughing matter: until 1832, the windowless cells were used to punish students found guilty of the heinous crimes of disrespect, book damage and contestation (arguing with teachers). The prison's upper levels were used as a book store.

3

Capela de São Miguel and Sala dos Capelos

After leaving the library, glance into the adjacent **Capela de São Miguel** (knock for entry), a sixteenth-century chapel with a splendid eighteenth-century trumpet-adorned Baroque organ clamped to the wall and floor-to-ceiling *azulejos*. Leave the chapel and from the square outside head up the grand double stairway to the **Sala dos Capelos**. This grand hall was once part of the royal palace and then became an ornate venue for students to sit their exams, beneath the portraits of former monarchs and university rectors and an impressive ceiling of over a hundred wooden panels. The rooms are still used to award degree certificates and for students to defend their PhD theses. Previous graduates include epic poet Luís de Camões, writer Eça de Queiros and twentieth-century dictator Salazar. Don't miss the narrow, vertigo-inducing balcony outside that affords breezy city views.

The clock tower

€2; not covered by Universidade ticket

Those with a head for heights can climb the somewhat claustrophobic 184 steps that spiral to the top of the eighteenth-century **clock tower** for spectacular views over the entire area. The tower is nicknamed *cabra* (the goat), an unaffectionate term lamenting its role in summoning students to lessons.

Museu da Ciência

Largo Marquês de Pombal • Tues–Sun 10am–6pm • €5 • ☎ 239 854 350, ⓦ museudaciencia.com

Partly housed in one of the university's original chemistry laboratories, the excellent **Museu da Ciência** (Science Museum) gathers together a substantial collection of scientific paraphernalia that has been in use at the university since the eighteenth

---

REPÚBLICAS

The grid of streets that spread around the university buildings is made up of the so-called **Repúblicas**, co-operative buildings first set up in the fourteenth century under Dom Dinis to provide subsidized accommodation for students. Generally rambling houses with tiny rooms, they are ideal for a communal student lifestyle – though have the added bonus of coming with their own cooks – and are little-changed from the 1960s and 1970s, when they were breeding grounds for dissenters to the Salazar regime. You might be able to sneak in for a peek round a República – students are usually quite welcoming to foreign visitors.

century. The **collection** includes around 24,000 objects ranging from maps and books to botanical collections from Portugal's former colonies, medical equipment, stuffed animals, preserved insects, fossils and rare gemstones. The museum also has more cutting-edge interactive displays and exhibits dedicated to modern science, including a section on light and matter, looking at how light works and how it affects our universe.

Jardim Botânico

Calçada Martim de Freita, entrance on Bairro Sousa Pinto • **Gardens** Daily: April–Sept 9am–8pm; Oct–March 9am–5.30pm • Free • ☎ 239 855 216, ⊛ uc.pt/jardimbotanico • **Sky-Garden** Daily: March & Oct 10am–5.30pm; April–Sept 10am–8pm; Nov & Feb Sat & Sun 10am–5.30pm, weather permitting • €24 • ☎ 916 665 449, ⊛ skygardenadventure.com

Partly hidden beneath the impressive sixteenth-century **Aqueduto de São Sebastião**, Coimbra's **Jardim Botânico** is Portugal's oldest botanical garden, founded in the eighteenth century – its main greenhouse, built in 1856, was one of the country's first structures to use iron. Today the garden is a tranquil retreat from the town's bustle, its paths and steps meandering down into sunken lawns past fountains, lakes, shady palms and enormous banyan trees. Other attractions include dazzling azaleas and an impressive collection of medicinal plants. For the more active, the **Sky-Garden** tree-top adventure course gives you the chance to clamber through the trees along a series of ladders, zip-lines and even a suspended bike.

Convento de Santa Clara-a-Velha

Rua das Parreiros • Visitor centre Tues–Sun: May–Sept 10am–7pm; Oct–April 10am–5pm • €4; English-language audioguide €1.50

Built by the river on flat grassland, the fourteenth-century Gothic convent of **Santa Clara-a-Velha** was founded in 1330 by Queen Isabel, Coimbra's patron saint and wife of Dom Dinis. Isabel was buried here, along with Inês de Castro (see p.154), though when the convent was abandoned in the seventeenth century because of persistent flooding, Isabel's tomb was moved to the higher Santa Clara-a-Nova in 1677 (see below). Neglected and immersed in silt for over three hundred years, the old convent was then carefully excavated and now forms the centrepiece of a visitor centre in a modern building across the lawns. Here you can find out about religious life in medieval times before looking round the convent itself. The well-preserved interior includes the remains of the tiny cells, tiled floors and a surprisingly neat communal loo.

Convento de Santa Clara-a-Nova

Alto de Santa Clara • Daily: May–Sept 8.30am–7pm; Oct–April 8.30am–6pm • €1, cloister €2 • ☎ 239 441 674

With the original Convent of Santa Clara prone to annual flooding, it was decided to build a new convent on higher ground, and construction of the **Convento de Santa Clara-a-Nova** ("the new") began in 1649. Its exterior has a military appearance – indeed it was used as a hospital during the Peninsular Wars – but once inside you'll find beautiful **cloisters** (added in 1733) and an attractive Baroque **church**, housing the ornate stone tomb of Queen Isabel. The Queen's remains, however, were placed in a silver and crystal urn in 1696, which now sits behind the main altar.

Portugal dos Pequenitos

Rossio de Santa Clara • Daily: Jan, Feb & mid-Oct to Dec 10am–5pm; March–May & mid-Sept to mid-Oct 10am–7pm; June to mid-Sept 9am–8pm • €9.50, under-13s €5.95, under-3s free • ☎ 239 801 170, ⊛ portugaldospequenitos.pt

No time to visit Portugal's most famous monuments? Then head to this enclosed area of parkland, where **Portugal dos Pequenitos** displays a beguiling collection of (rather large) scale models of the country's major architectural attractions – though since it was built

in the 1940s by local collector Bissaya Barreto, there are no contemporary buildings here. There are also three small but moderately interesting museums featuring miniature copies of costumes, boats and furniture from the sixteenth century to today. It's not as much fun for the kids as you might expect, with little in the way of hands-on fun.

Quinta das Lágrimas

Rua António Augusto Gonçalves • Gardens mid-March to mid-Nov Tues–Sun 10am–7pm; mid-Nov to mid-March Thurs–Sun 10am–5pm • €2 • ☎ 239 802 380

The **Quinta das Lágrimas** (Estate of Tears), now a luxury hotel (see p.190), was once an estate hideaway for medieval Portugal's star-crossed lovers Dom Pedro and Inês de Castro. In the **gardens**, so legend has it, Inês was brutally murdered on the orders of King Afonso IV – her tears (*lágrimas*) as she died lent the estate its name. Her lover, meanwhile, the crown prince Pedro, rose in open revolt against his own father and later extracted a gory revenge upon the murderers (see box, p.154). As well as being home to some ancient plant species, the gardens also host the **July Art Festival**, with plays, music and exhibitions (☷festivaldasartes.com).

ARRIVAL AND DEPARTURE COIMBRA

By bus The main bus station is on Avenida Fernão de Magalhães (a 15min walk northwest of the centre), for Transdev services (☎239 855 270, ☷transdev.pt) to Figueira da Foz, Aveiro, Condeixa-a-Nova and Conímbriga; intercity Rede Expressos buses (☎707 223 344, ☷rede-expressos.pt); Rodoviária Beira Litoral (☎239 855 270, ☷rede-expressos.pt) regional services; and Rodonorte (☎239 825 190, ☷rodonorte.pt) services to the mountain Beiras and the north. Moisés Correia de Oliveira buses (☎239 828 263, ☷moises-transportes.pt) to Montemor-o-Velho and Figueira da Foz stop on Avenida Fernão de Magalhães, just up from Largo do Arnado.

Destinations Arganil (2–3 daily; 1hr 40min); Condeixa, for Conímbriga (2 daily; 30min); Covilhã (2–4 daily; 3hr 15min); Figueira da Foz (hourly; 1hr–1hr 15min); Góis (2–3 daily; 1hr 15min); Gouveia (3–4 daily; 2hr); Guarda (?–4 daily; 2hr 5min); Leiria (10–14 daily; 50min); Lisbon (at least hourly; 2hr 20min); Luso via Buçaco (Mon–Sat 2–5 daily; 40min); Montemor-o-Velho (approx hourly; 40min–1hr); Penacova (up to 16 daily Mon–Fri; 45min–1hr); Porto (approx hourly; 1hr 30min); Praia de Mira (1–2 daily; 1hr 15min); Santa Comba Dão (hourly; 1hr 20min); Viseu (approx hourly; 1hr 15min–1hr 25min); Vouzela (1–3 daily; 1hr 50min).

By train There are two train stations – Coimbra A and Coimbra B. All long-distance and express trains call only at Coimbra B, 2km northwest of the centre, from where local trains connect to Coimbra A – you don't need another ticket but allow 20mins connection time.). Riverside Coimbra A (often just "Coimbra" on timetables) is right at the heart of the city, on the edge of the Baixa. You can check train timetables online at ☷cp.pt.

Destinations Alfarelos, for Montemor-o-Velho (every 30min; 35min); Aveiro (hourly; 1hr); Braga (hourly; 2hr–3hr 50min); Figueira da Foz (hourly; 1hr–1hr 10min); Guarda (7 daily; 2hr 30min–3hr); Lisbon (hourly; 2hr–2hr 50min); Luso-Buçaco (3 daily; 30min); Porto (hourly; 1hr 30min–2hr 30min); Santa Comba Dão (3 daily; 1hr).

GETTING AROUND

You can walk across central Coimbra in around 20min, though the university is right at the highest part of town – and the stepped streets and alleys take it out of you in the summer heat – so you may want to take one of the local buses or the *elevador* street lift.

By bus The local bus network is run by SMTUC (☷smtuc .pt) – bus #103 runs from Coimbra A station via the market up to the university, while the #3 (daily) runs along the same route to Praça da República. In addition, the little electric Linha Azul buses (Mon–Fri, plus Sat mornings in summer) run on a circular route through the otherwise pedestrianized Baixa.

By elevador The useful *elevador* (Mon–Sat 7.30am–10pm, Sun & hols 10am–10pm; €1.60), rises from next to the market on Avenida Sá da Bandeira to Rua Padre António Vieira, a short walk from the Sé Nova in the upper town.

By taxi There are taxi ranks outside Coimbra A and B train stations, by the police headquarters near Praça 8 de Maio, and in Praça da República. To call a cab, ring Politaxis (☎239 499 090).

Tickets Integrated tickets for buses and the *elevador* are sold on board Coimbra's buses (€1.60 per journey), though it's cheaper to pre-buy tickets (3 journeys €2.20; 11 journeys €6.40; one-day pass €3.50) from kiosks or from SMTUC transport shops (Mon–Fri 7am–7pm) – there's one in Praça da República and another by the *elevador* next to the market (also open Sat 8am–1pm).

3

SCHOOL'S OUT

Coimbra's biggest bash of the year is the **Queima das Fitas** in May, when the ritual academic "burning of the ribbons" is accompanied by the mother of all parties in a week-long, alcohol-fuelled series of gigs, dances and parties. The coloured ribbons worn by students represent the various faculties, and the week's main parade sees decorated faculty floats followed by black-caped students winding down the hill from the university; every night the focus shifts to the riverside arena where big names in music rock the city until the small hours.

INFORMATION

Turismo Centro de Portugal The regional tourist office, at Avenida Emídio Navarro by Largo da Portagem, facing the Ponte Santa Clara (Oct–Easter Mon–Fri 9am–6pm; Easter–Sept Mon–Fri 9am–8pm, Sat, Sun & hols 9.30am–1pm & 2.30–6pm; ☎239 488 120, ⓦturismodocentro.pt), is useful for city enquiries and staffed with English speakers. It hands out the free street map and the useful *Coimbra Viva* guide and cultural agenda.

TOURS AND ACTIVITIES

City tours Hop-on-hop-off, 1hr open-top bus tours are run by Fun(tastic) Coimbra (mid-May to Oct Tues–Sun, departures on the hour 10am–noon & 3–5pm; €10.80; ⓦyellowbustours.com) and leave from Largo da Portagem: the bus ticket includes free access to some of the city's museums and discounts at others. Odebarca runs one-hour city tours by tuk-tuk for €7.

Boat cruises One-hour cruises on the Rio Mondego are run by Odabarca (May–Sept Tues–Sun departures on the hour from 3–7pm; Oct–April departures at 3, 4 & 5pm; €6.50; ☎969 830 664, ⓦodabarca.com), departing from beside Parque Dr. Manuel Braga.

Watersports O Pioneiro do Mondego (☎239 478 385, ⓦopioneirodomondego.com) runs downriver kayak trips between the nearby town of Penacova and Coimbra (see p.198), as does Caminhos d'Água (2hr lesson from €50, equipment rental from €10; ☎969 049 470, ⓦcaminhos dagua.com), who can also arrange windsurfing on the river in Coimbra.

ACCOMMODATION

Astória Av Emídio Navarro 21 ☎239 853 020, ⓦalmeidahotels.com; map pp.184–185. You can't miss the historic dome of this historic three-star hotel with grand Art Deco communal areas. Unfortunately its best days have gone, and though all the rooms are a/c and double-glazed, most are in need of a revamp. Nevertheless front-facing rooms have wonderful river views and there's secure parking 200m away. €73

★**Botânico** Bairro de São José 15 ☎239 714 824, ⓦhotelbotanicocoimbra.pt; map pp.184–185. One of Coimbra's best for the price, this modern business hotel is up near the botanical gardens and, although right on the main road, the rooms are double-glazed and quiet, with polished wooden floors and rugs. €49

★**Casa Pombal** Rua dos Flores 18 ☎239 835 175, ⓦcasapombal.com; map p.186. Coimbra's most charming choice – and the only place to stay in the old town – is this very friendly Dutch-run townhouse near the university. Rooms are small but pretty, with wooden floors, rugs and throws, some peering down over the rooftops to the river – room eight has a great view from the bath. A splendid breakfast is served in the tiled dining room and there's a small patio-garden,– it's a real home-from-home. En-suite rooms cost more (€65). €54

CSI Rua Bernardim Ribeiro 76 ☎964 826 060; map pp.184–185. In Portugal's most famous university town, why not experience life in a student dorm? The rooms at this sensitively renovated block to the east of the old town feature antique sinks, heaters and strong wi-fi signal. There's access to a kitchen but all bathrooms are shared. No check-in – your key is left in a cloth envelope at the entrance. €25

Pousada de Juventude Rua Dr. Henriques Seco 14 ☎239 829 228, ⓦpousadasjuventude.pt; map pp.184–185. Above Parque Santa Cruz, and ideally sited for the bars and clubs around Praça da República, this fairly modern hostel has standard four- to six-bed dorms as well as private en-suite twin rooms, plus a patio and kitchen. Reception is open 8am–midnight. Dorms €12, doubles €30

Quebra Luz Escada da Quebra-Costas 18 ☎912 278 779, ⓦquebra-luz.com; map p.186. On Coimbra's famously steep approach to the old town, this great little guesthouse has four simple but spacious rooms, the best with balconies looking over the street (others face a courtyard garden). The cheapest rooms share a bathroom, but there are also two en-suite rooms (€65). No breakfast. €45

Quinta das Lágrimas Rua António Augusto Gonçalves ☎239 802 380, ⓦquintaslagrimas.pt; map pp.184–185. The city's swankiest address lies on the other side of the river from the old town. A historic stately house set in acres of beautiful gardens and grounds, it's a classy affair with some regally decorated

palace and garden rooms, as well as more contemporary options. Staff lurk in each corner to attend to every whim. The Garden Spa has various treatments, plus pool, sauna and Turkish bath, and there are two restaurants – the more formal *Arcadas* is an expensive gourmet affair. Website deals offer the best rates. **€170**

Tivoli Rua João Machado 4 ☎ 239 858 300, ⓦ tivolihotels .com; map pp.184–185. The city's most central four-star hotel doesn't have much of a location (out near the bus station), though it's less than 10mins walk to the historic centre. Rooms are unexciting but modern and comfortable, and there's an indoor pool, gym and garage parking. **€61**

★**Vitoria** Rua da Sota 9–11 ☎ 239 824 049, ⓦ hotelvitoria.pt; map pp.184–185. The best of the budget options near the station has smart en-suite rooms, most decked out with wooden flooring and furniture. You can also get a good breakfast in the family restaurant downstairs (€3.50 extra). **€59**

EATING

★**Adega Paço do Conde** Rua Paço do Conde 1 ☎ 239 825 605; map pp.184–185. Choose your meat, add chips, salad and wine and you have a filling meal at this locally renowned *churrasqueira*, with a dining room either side of a shady covered terrace. The smoky grill is in the entrance where locals queue for takeaway. Main courses cost between €5 and €12. Mon–Sat noon–midnight.

★**Café Santa Cruz** Pr 8 de Maio ☎ 239 833 617; map p.186. Set in part of the sixteenth-century monastery buildings next to the Igreja de Santa Cruz, Coimbra's most appealing café is a great coffee and cake halt with dickie-bowed waiters and marble tabletops. There are tables in the vaulted stone interior, but on a sunny day it's nicer on the terrace above the square. Slightly more expensive than you're average Portuguese café, but the setting is special. Daily 8am–11pm.

Cantinho do Reis Terreiro da Erva 16 ☎ 239 824 116; map pp.184–185. The sun-trap terrace is the big attraction here, on the edge of a brutally renovated square.

The food attracts a steady stream of hungry locals – it's best for simple fish and grills, with reliable *bacalhau* dishes and a tasty house steak. Mains around €10. Mon–Sat noon–1am.

Fangas Mercearia Bar Rua Fernandes Tomás ☎ 934 093 636; map p.186. This cool, vaguely retro dining room is a laidback place to enjoy some tasty tapas (€6 a plate) and drinks at any time of the day or night. The menu changes according to the season and there's lilting fado on CD. Daily noon–3.30pm & 7pm–1am.

★**Zé Manel dos Ossos** Beco do Forno 12 ☎ 239 823 790; map pp.184–185. Easy to miss, this atmospheric little joint is behind an inconspicuous door, tucked behind *Hotel Astória*. Little more than a few tables, and walls adorned with messages of praise, the service is brisk and friendly, and the regional food excellent – around €15 for a decent meal, from soup to coffee. If you don't want to queue, arrive at opening time. Mon–Fri noon–3pm & 7.30–10pm, Sat noon–3pm.

DRINKING AND NIGHTLIFE

BARS, CAFE-BARS AND CLUBS

★**Galeria Bar Santa Clara** Rua António Augusto Gonçalves 67 ☎ 239 441 657, ⓦ galeriasantaclara.com; map pp.184–185. Relaxed gallery-café-bar with a large terrace overlooking Santa Clara-a-Velha and the river beyond. It's a great place for a coffee or a late drink, with exhibitions, music nights and other events. Mon–Fri noon–2am, Fri & Sat noon–3am.

Mondego Irish Pub Parque Verde do Mondego ☎ 239 837 092; map pp.184–185. Right by the river, so ideal for an afternoon beer or sundowner drinks, this relaxed bar hosts live music Thurs & Fri nights. *Mondego* was closed for repairs

at the time of writing following flood damage in early 2016, but is expected to reopen swiftly. Daily noon–4am.

NB Club Rua Venâncio Rodrigues 11–17 ☎ 968 771 904; map pp.184–185. Glitzy club attracting a mixture of students and older locals, with top DJs, themed nights and lots of house (though Fridays are often revival nights). Opening times can vary according to events. Tues & Thurs–Sat 11.45pm–6am.

★**Quebra** Rua de Quebra Costas 45–49 ☎ 239 841 174; map p.186. Coimbra's top student music bar hangout, tucked away on the steps leading down from the Sé Velha. There's a tiny terrace for drinks, and live music and DJ sets

3

COIMBRA FADO

Coimbra fado is distinguished from the Lisbon variety by the fact that it uses a slightly different guitar and is sung exclusively by males, usually in the traditional dark cape of the university. Themes are often translations of famous poems, and in general it is slightly more upbeat than the Lisbon variation. It's performed year-round in the city's **fado clubs**, but you'll find it far more atmospheric if you catch an **open-air performance** in the old town in summer. The student celebrations in May are a good bet for impromptu fado sessions, and this is also the best time for big-name gigs. *Fado ao Centro* (see p.192) is a good place to get a taster of the music.

3

later in the evening – check the website for details. Mon–Fri noon–4am, Sat 2pm–4am.

Tropical Pr da República 35, corner of Rua Alexandre Herculano ☏ 239 824 857; map pp.184–185. The pick of the República café-bars, this studenty joint on two levels heaves at the weekends. The pavement tables get swamped, while the barman roves around with trays of ice-cold Super Bocks. Daily 10am–5am.

FADO CLUBS

★**À Capella** Rua do Corpo de Deus, Largo da Vitória ☏ 239 833 985, ⓦ acapella.com.pt; map p.186. If you're going to catch just one fado performance, make it here, in the atmospheric surroundings of this converted medieval chapel with its own bar. There's usually one show a night (€10–15), beginning at 9.30pm. Daily 8.30pm–2.30am.

Fado ao Centro Rua Quebra Costas 7 ☏ 239 837 060, ⓦ fadoaocentro.com; map p.186. This small venue is a superb place to sample fado from Coimbra and Lisbon. Things kick off with a short film about fado, then performers explain the meaning of the songs and give sample performances. The ticket price (€10) includes a free glass of port. It's popular, so try to get your ticket in advance. Performances daily at 6pm.

SPORTS AND THEATRE

Football Established by some sporty students in 1876, Académica claims to be Portugal's oldest football club. It generally struggles to stay in the top division but its modern stadium, Estádio Cidade de Coimbra (Rua Dom Manuel I; ⓦ academica-oaf.pt), which seats 30,000, is highly impressive and also hosts summer concerts.

Theatre The Teatro Académico de Gil Vicente, on Praça da República (☏ 239 855 630, ⓦ tagv.info), is Coimbra's cultural hub with a full calendar of theatre, art-house movies and music.

SHOPPING

Coimbra Shopping Av Dr. Mendes Silva 211–251 ☏ 239 708 758, ⓦ coimbrashopping.pt; map pp.184–185. This large shopping mall has a hypermarket and a vast array of stores including clothes shops (Mango, Sportzone), toyshops, jewellers and just about everything else. Mon–Thurs & Sun 8.30am–11pm, Fri & Sat 8.30am–midnight.

Dolce Vita Rua General Humberto Delgado 207–211 ☏ 239 798 090, ⓦ dolcevita.pt; map pp.184–185. Near the city stadium, the Coimbra branch of this giant shopping-centre chain has a range of local and international stores as well as a huge supermarket, cinemas, cafés and restaurants. Mon–Thurs & Sun 8.30am–1am, Fri & Sat 10am–midnight.

Mercado Municipal Dom Pedro V Rua Olímpio Nicolau Rui Fernandes ☏ 239 833 385; map p.186. Close to the post office, this is the biggest market in the region, selling a medley of fresh fruit, veg, fish, flowers, clothes and souvenirs. Mon–Sat 7am–7pm.

DIRECTORY

Hospital Hospital da Universidade de Coimbra, Praceta Prof Mota Pinto (☏ 239 400 400, ⓦ www.chuc.min-saude.pt).

Police Main PSP HQ is at Rua Olímpio Nicolau Rui Fernandes (☏ 239 797 640), across from the post office.

Post office The main post office is on Avenida Fernão de Magalhães 223, near Largo do Arnado; other central offices are on Rua Olímpio Nicolau Rui Fernandes, just below the market, and on Praça da República (all Mon–Fri 8.30am–6.30pm).

Conímbriga

Portugal's most important Roman site, **Conímbriga** is just 16km southwest of Coimbra – an easy day-trip – and around a kilometre south of the pleasant market town of **Condeixa-a-Nova** (signed off the IC3 road to Tomar), where you could easily spend the night. The excavations and remains you can see today are just a fraction of the Roman town that flourished from the last year BC until around 4 AD, and which once spread beneath land now occupied by the little village of **Condeixa-a-Velha**, where the remains of a huge amphitheatre remain hidden.

The site

Daily 10am–7pm • Site and museum €4.50 • ☏ 239 941 177, ⓦ conimbriga.pt

As you enter the site you'll find a large car park with ticket office, separate museum and two cafés – handy, as you'll need to allow a good two to three hours to see everything.

Once through the gates you'll be faced by the remains of a paved **Roman road** which once ran from Olisipo (Lisbon) to Braccara Augusta (Braga). To the right of this is the impressive first-century **House of the Fountains** – covered to protect it from the elements – whose floors still display beautiful polychrome mosaics. To the left of here are the remains of other wealthy family homes – some with mosaic panels – as well as shops.

Up until the fourth century, the inhabitants lived well and peacefully, but their lives changed dramatically when Swabian attacks became increasingly common. Those who could afford to leave quickly departed for the safety of Rome, while those who remained decided to build the site's most prominent feature, a **vast defensive wall** 4m thick, which could only be entered via giant double gates. The wall virtually cut Conímbriga in two: the part of town between the wall and today's ticket office was abandoned, with the rest of the settlement being protected between the wall and the natural defences of a ravine on the other side.

Today, you can see further **houses** beyond the wall: the biggest boasts around forty rooms and was once owned by a first-century aristocrat, Cantaber – reconstructed pillars show how impressive it was. Little remains of the other main structures, which include shops, an early **Christian basilica**, and a **water cistern** that formed part of a 3km-long aqueduct. You can also visit the partially reconstructed **Forum**, a broad space built around a temple dedicated to Roman gods, that was once the hub of the town.

Museu Monográfico de Conímbriga

The small but excellent **Museu Monográfico de Conímbriga** displays fascinating finds from the excavations, presented thematically. Cabinets detail the minutiae of various trades (glass-making, ironmongery, weaving, even house building) and aspects of daily life including coins hoarded because of fear of attack and an array of implements that show the Romans were a vain lot: there are sumptuous carved hairpins and jewellery you'd admire today. The section on health and hygiene contains scalpels, needles and some quite alarming "probing spoons". On the other side of the museum are displayed the larger spoils – statues of torsos, carved lintels, gargoyles from temples, monochromatic mosaics, remarkably bright mural fragments, and inscribed slabs, pillars and tombstones from the necropolis.

ARRIVAL AND DEPARTURE   CONÍMBRIGA

By bus Buses run from Coimbra to Conímbriga (around 25min) but there are only two or three a day during the week, making a visit tricky. Another option is to take the regular bus to Condeixa-a-Nova and walk the remaining 2.5km. Weekend services are greatly reduced.

By taxi A taxi from Coimbra to Conímbriga will cost around €9.

ACCOMMODATION AND EATING

Other than the two cafés, there are no facilities at the site of Conímbriga and the closest **restaurants** and **accommodation** can be found in the nearby town of Condeixa-a-Nova, 1km away, which is a pleasant provincial place to spend the night.

O Cabritino Rua Francisco de Lemos 9, Condeixa-a-Nova ☎ 239 944 111. Just down the road from the *pousada* (towards the centre of town), this is a handsome fine-dining restaurant with a summer terrace and garden. Goat is the speciality, though you can also find good steaks and fresh fish dishes for €12–16. Mon–Sat noon–11.30pm, Sun noon–4pm.

O Regional do Cabrito Pr da República 14 ☎ 239 944 933. Right on Condeixa-a-Nova's main square, with a few outdoor tables, this simple, friendly place is very good value, with main courses from €6: try dishes such as *bacalhau*, salmon or the local speciality – as perhaps you may gather from the restaurant names – *cabrito* (roast kid goat), usually slow-roasted and served with roast potatoes and greens. Tues–Sun 11am–11pm.

Pousada de Santa Cristina Rua Francisco Lemos, Condeixa-a-Nova ☎ 239 944 025, ⓦ pousadas.pt. In a relatively modern building – built in 1993 on the site of a fourteenth-century palace – this lacks the wow factor of some of Portugal's *pousadas* but still makes a very pleasant base, with comfy rooms (the bottom ones with a terrace) looking over the hills beyond town and the extensive lawns, which feature a pool. There's also a good in-house restaurant and bar. **€128**

THE SERRA DA LOUSÃ'S ALDEIAS DO XISTO

Hard lives in the mountains led to the desertion of many typical upland **aldeias do xisto** (schist villages), some of which are beginning to develop fledgling rural-tourism businesses. Five villages above Lousã (Casal Novo, Talasnal, Cerdeira, Chiqueiro and Candal) form part of central Portugal's **Schist Village Scheme** (ⓦaldeiasdoxisto.pt), which promotes sustainable tourism and other projects, such as establishing waymarked walks and craft shops, and reviving village festivals and customs. The website includes details of local adventure-tour outfits as well as the limited accommodation that is available in the villages. You can drive up yourself – even though not all the roads are surfaced, they are usually fine for normal cars – or follow our circular walk from Lousã castle (see box, p.195) which leads to both **Casal Novo** and **Talasnal**, the latter with the bonus of the restaurant *Ti'Lena* in a restored schist house.

Serra da Lousã

The rugged hills of the **Serra da Lousã**, only 25km southeast of Coimbra, make a fine day-trip from the city, though you'll probably need to stay the night if you're planning any serious exploration. The handsome town of **Lousã** is the main base (easily accessible by bus from Coimbra), providing access to a series of **aldeias do xisto**, or mountain schist villages, that were largely depopulated in the 1960s but are now gradually being revived and regenerated in response to the increasing interest in rural tourism.

Lousã

LOUSÃ retains an attractive old core within a wider modern town, with the forested green slopes of the *serra* rising behind. A few *casas brasonadas* (heraldic mansions) survive in the older streets, while the grand town hall speaks loudly of more prosperous times. The best days to visit are Tuesdays and especially Saturdays, when the covered **market** is in full swing and stallholders come into town from the outlying villages to hawk their produce, including the local speciality, Licor Beirão. It was a pharmacist from Lousã who originally came up with the secret recipe and this sickly sweet, herb-flavoured cognac-like drink is now consumed all over Portugal. Otherwise, Lousã's only real attraction is its miniature **castle**, though if you're not driving it's a stiff uphill walk to reach it. At the castle, there's a river beach and pool, as well as the good but pricey *Burgo* restaurant (see below), beyond which stepped paths climb up the hillside beyond past a succession of caves, terraces and viewpoints.

ARRIVAL AND DEPARTURE   LOUSÃ

By bus From Coimbra, southbound buses (see p.189) run sporadically throughout the day, often stopping in Lousã en route. There are also 2–4 daily services (Mon–Fri) between Lousã and Góis (45min) and one daily service (Mon–Fri) to Arganil in the Serra do Açor (1hr 10min).

ACCOMMODATION, EATING AND DRINKING

Burgo Nossa Senhora da Piedade, Lousã ☎239 991 162. Near the castle, this old watermill has been converted into a cosy restaurant specializing in dishes from the Serra da Lousã, including chestnut soup, *javali* (wild boar), grilled goat and rabbit with chestnuts. Mains €10–14. Mon–Sat 12.30–3.30pm & 7.30–10pm.

Casa Velha Pr Sá Carneiro 14, Lousã ☎239 991 555. There's a long menu of Portuguese standards and regional cuisine at this rustic-style restaurant, and portions are vast, so a *dose* (portion; €7–12) easily feeds two. Dishes include *pataniscas de bacalhau* (cod cakes) and *feijoada de lebre* (hare stew with beans). Mon–Tues & Thurs–Sun 11am–11pm.

Martinho Rua Carlos Reis 3, Lousã ☎239 991 397. Lousã's cheapest accommodation is at the *Martinho* – to get there, head up the hill from the town hall square and turn left. Set inside a low white building, the rooms are simple but pleasant, and some have balconies. **€50**

Meliá Palácio da Lousã Rua Viscondessa do Espinhal, Lousã ☎239 990 800, ⓦpalaciodalousa.com. In the old

town, beyond the town hall, this boutique hotel is housed in a seventeenth-century former ducal mansion. The chic rooms come in contemporary style, with the best in the original building, though some are in a modern wing. There's also a bar, a restaurant and a swimming pool. **€60**

Ti'Lena Talasnal ☎ 933 832 624. In an ancient stone building, this village restaurant is only open at lunch from Friday to Sunday and it's best to call ahead to let them know you're coming. Although the menu is fairly limited (*cabrito, chanfana, bacalhau*), the food is great: expect to pay around €20 for two courses and drinks. Fri–Sun noon–3pm.

Serra do Açor

East of Lousã stretches the **Serra do Açor**, a mountain range that borders the Serra da Estrela further to the northeast. It's a very attractive region, a mix of bucolic river valleys, pine and eucalyptus forest and the higher traditional schist villages of the mountains proper. **Góis**, 20km northeast of Lousã, is the gateway, prettily set in a river valley, with the small market town of **Arganil** another 13km to the north. Less accessible but worth the effort is the marvellous schist village of **Piódão**, high in the peaks.

3

Góis and around

GÓIS is beautifully set on the Rio Ceira, crossed by an arched sixteenth-century bridge which leads up to a sloping cobbled square backed by a couple of old-town streets. There's not a lot to occupy you here, but Góis comes into its own in summer (June to early Sept) when boardwalks are erected and white sand imported to construct a fantastic river beach, with a waterside bar and kayaks to rent. Other favourite local **river beaches** include that at **Várzea Pequena**, 5km west, or you can head into the hills for walks around the Góis schist villages – brown signposts off the Lousã road (N342) lead up to the tiny village of **Aigra Nova**, where there's a **craft shop/café** run by a local not-for-profit agency, Lousitânea, at Rua dos Bois (daily 10am–6pm; ☎ 235 778 644, ⊕ lousitanea.org), and a good circular waymarked **mountain hike** (10km; 4hr) through three other ancient schist villages in varying stages of restoration.

A HIKE INTO THE SERRA DA LOUSÃ

This three-hour, 6km circular hike in the **Serra da Lousã** provides marvellous views and a fascinating glimpse of mountain village life.

From the *Burgo* restaurant near Lousã's castle, walk up the stone steps to the end of the picnic areas, and follow the sign to Casal Novo and Talasnal. The steep rocky path climbs for 1km until it reaches a junction; follow the right-hand fork and after 700m or so you will emerge onto a wider track, which you should follow uphill until it joins a second similar track – turn left and continue the ascent. As the path comes clear of the trees your toil is rewarded by stunning views of the valley below. At the top of this path turn left and continue upwards to where you meet an unsurfaced road; Talasnal is visible to your left, or you can head right to sleepy **Casal Novo**, which spills down the hillside.

Retrace your steps, ignoring the track you came up, and continue in the direction of **Talasnal**, probably the most beautiful of the Serra da Lousã's villages with a harmonious mix of ruined and restored cottages amid stunning mountain views. Once you've wound round the side of the mountain you descend to the entrance of the village, whose narrow, higgledy-piggledy passageways are worth a wander.

To exit Talasnal, follow the stream downhill, passing numerous small dwellings in various states of repair to your left and right. Continue downwards on a path mostly marked by dry-stone walls on both sides. When the trail meets a T-junction turn left downhill and cross the river via an old stone bridge. Follow the good, easily navigable path all the way back to the river pools, keeping an eye out for occasional fallen logs blocking the path and the dizzy drop to your right. A well-earned dip in the pools below the castle makes a refreshing end to the walk.

GÓIS MOTORBIKE FESTIVAL

Góis is pretty quiet for most of the year, though it perks up in August, no more so than for the huge **motorbike rally** (Concentração de Góis) organized by the Góis Moto Clube (ⓦgoismotoclube.pt). This attracts up to forty thousand bikers for a good-natured four-day festival of bike shows, radical sports, live bands and DJs – a tent city lines the river just outside town in the middle of the month.

Arganil

The N342 winds through the trees for 13km from Góis, finally descending to the small town of **ARGANIL**, which has a pedestrianized main street full of traditional shops and a couple of cafés by the square. By far the best day to visit is a Thursday when Arganil's regional weekly **market** takes place on the open-air space above town, from early morning onwards. Part market, part bazaar, it sells everything from a garden spade to a dining-room suite, and it's particularly good for cheap clothes, shoes, local basketware and agricultural hardware and supplies. Inside the market building, there's a simple first-floor *churrasqueira* where everyone goes to eat grilled chicken or *leitão* (suckling pig) for lunch – you'll get the works for just a few euros.

Piódão

From Arganil, it's around an hour's beautiful drive via Coja to **PIÓDÃO** (pronounced *pee*-oh-*dow*), a traditional schist village set on a steeply terraced mountainside. Despite the slight theme-park atmosphere, its narrow streets are great to explore and the whole village affords superb valley views. There's a small **museum** on Largo Cónego Manuel Fernandes Nogueira (daily: June–Sept 10am–1pm & 2–6pm; Oct–May 9am–1pm & 2–5pm; free), which provides an insight into traditional village life with displays on subjects such as emigration, local industries and agriculture. You can follow a couple of short **walks** from Piódão into the countryside – these are well signposted from the village, or pick up walk leaflets from the information office in the museum.

ARRIVAL AND DEPARTURE   SERRA DO AÇOR

By bus Rodoviária da Beira Litoral buses run 2–3 times daily from Coimbra to Arganil (1hr 40min) via Góis (1hr 15min). There are also 2–4 daily services (Mon–Fri) from Lousã to Góis (45min) and one daily service (Mon–Fri) to Arganil via Góis (1hr 10min).

By car You'll obviously have far more flexibility with your own transport – and a car is essential to visit Piódão or any of the secluded picnic spots and river beaches that make this area so beguiling.

INFORMATION

Góis turismo Largo Francisco Inácio Dias Nogueira (Mon–Fri 10am–1pm & 2–5pm, Sat & Sun 10am–1pm & 3–5pm; ☎ 235 770 113, ⓦcm-gois.pt).

Piódão turismo Inside the museum on Largo Cónego Manuel Fernandes Nogueira (daily: June–Sept 10am–1pm & 2–6pm; Oct–May 9am–1pm & 2–5pm; ☎ 235 732 787).

ACCOMMODATION AND EATING

Casa das Videiras Carapinhal ☎ 235 778 073, ⓦbedandbreakfastcentralportugal.com. For a lovely rural retreat, head to this English-owned B&B, 7km west of Góis on the N2, Vila Nova de Poiares road. There's a summer pool, a pretty patio affording the grounds and meals are available. **€50**

Casa Santo António Rua de Santo António, Góis 18

☎ 235 770 120. Just off the central square in a traditional building, the simple, unmarked *Casa Santo António* has the only official accommodation in Góis. It can be chilly in winter (ask for a heater and extra blankets), but at other times it's cosy and welcoming, with its own snooker table in the bar and a generous breakfast. **€40**

CLOCKWISE FROM TOP FIGUEIRA DA FOZ (P.212); CONÍMBRIGA (P.192); COIMBRA OLD TOWN (P.180) >

Penacova and around

PENACOVA, 22km northeast of Coimbra, is spectacularly sited on a crag high above the **Rio Mondego**. There is little to the place itself – a pint-sized square overlooked by a town hall, and a modest cobbled historic quarter laid out along the ridge – but for stunning views of river and valley make a beeline for the terrace of the *Café Turismo*, by the side of the town hall. You can walk the 2km from the café down to a great little river beach, **Reconquinho**, where you can swim alongside a seasonal café. Penacova's **market** is on the second Thursday of the month – look out for the highly elaborate toothpicks that are a local speciality, hand-carved from willow.

Mosteiro de Lorvão

Lorvão, 7km southwest of Penacova • Tues–Sat 9am–12.30pm & 2–6.30pm • Free • ☎ 918 216 726

Set in a a beautiful valley in the wooded hills above Penacova, the **Mosteiro de Lorvão** is an ancient monastic foundation that is able to trace its its history back to the sixth century AD, making it one of the oldest monasteries in Europe. What you see now dates from the sweeping alterations made in the seventeenth and eighteenth centuries. Today the building houses a psychiatric hospital and a small **museum** that contains paintings and what was left of the monastic wealth after the place was looted in the nineteenth century. If you visit on the last Sunday of the month, you'll coincide with the village of Lorvão's open-air **market** – or visit one of the village cafés for a *pastel de Lorvão*, an almond-based sweet traditionally made in the monastery.

ARRIVAL AND INFORMATION   PENACOVA

By bus The bus from Coimbra (Mon–Fri 3 daily; 25min) stops in the main square.

Information Penacova's turismo is opposite the town hall on Largo Alberto Leitão (daily: mid-March to mid-Oct 10am–1pm & 2–6pm; mid-Oct to mid-March 10am–1pm & 2–5pm; ☎ 239 470 300, ⓦ cm-penacova.pt).

ACCOMMODATION AND EATING

A Cota Azenha do Rio ☎ 239 474 841. The best place in town for traditional Penacova specialities, including lamprey rice, eel fritters and steaks, all from around €10. The restaurant has lovely river views, although it's way below town by the bridge on the EN110. Daily noon–10pm.

Avenida Av Abel Rodrigues da Costa ☎ 239 477 142, ⓦ pensaoavenida.com. Penacova's best budget choice is the traditional *Avenida*, centrally located just down the hill from the main square. It is more than a bit on the elderly side and you pay an extra €10 for your own bathroom, but it does have a good, inexpensive restaurant attached. **€25**

O Panorâmico Largo Alberto Leitão 7 ☎ 239 477 333. Next to the town hall, *O Panorâmico* (as the name suggests) enjoys a spectacular view down the valley and slightly upmarket fare such as lamprey and duck rice at €11–16. Daily 11am–11pm.

KAYAKING THE MONDEGO

The Mondego is one of the only rivers in Portugal in which it's possible to kayak comfortably all year round, and the 18km, 3–4 hour **kayaking trips** (€22.50 a head) are a real highlight of any visit to the region. Penacova-based O Pioneiro do Mondego (☎ 239 478 385, ⓦ opioneirodomondego.com) was the first company to offer kayaking tours and can arrange pick-ups or meeting points at various spots along the river between Penacova and Coimbra. Once on the river you'll be guided downstream with a gentle current – and the odd set of gentle rapids – taking you down pine- and eucalyptus-lined valleys, where black kites fish in summer and grape vines dangle over the river in autumn. You end up on a river beach where you can swim before being taken back to your starting point.

The Mata Nacional do Buçaco and Luso

Around 30km northeast of Coimbra, the **Mata Nacional do Buçaco** (National Forest of Buçaco) is a walled, former monastic hilltop retreat, with its own royal palace, the Palácio do Buçaco (now a five-star hotel). These days the forest – partly wild and partly landscaped – is a hugely popular place for an outing with Portuguese day-trippers, who descend in droves at weekends for picnics, but it's large enough to escape the crowds and makes a great

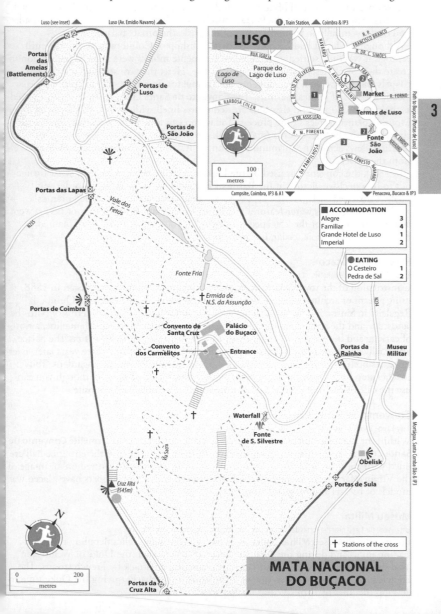

LUSO

Parque do Lago de Luso

Lago de Luso

Market

Termas de Luso

Fonte São João

Portas das Ameias (Battlements)

Portas de Luso

Portas de São João

Portas das Lapas

Vale dos Fetos

Fonte Fria

Ermida de N.S. da Assunção

Portas de Coimbra

Convento de Santa Cruz

Palácio do Buçaco

Convento dos Carmelitos

Entrance

Portas da Rainha

Museu Militar

Waterfall

Fonte de S. Silvestre

Obelisk

Via Sacra

Cruz Alta (545m)

Portas de Sula

Portas da Cruz Alta

ACCOMMODATION	
Alegre	3
Familiar	4
Grande Hotel de Luso	1
Imperial	2

EATING	
O Cesteiro	1
Pedra de Sal	2

✝ Stations of the cross

MATA NACIONAL DO BUÇACO

day out. It's easily accessible by car or bus, or you could walk the 2km (steeply uphill) from **Luso**, a little spa town famed for its mineral waters, which bubble out on the main square.

Buçaco forest

Cars €5; pedestrians and cyclists free • ☎ 231 937, ⊛ fmb.pt

The real joy of Buçaco is the chance to wander freely around 105 hectares of forest, below towering trees, stumbling across hidden water features, lakes and the occasional dazzling view, such as from the **Portas de Coimbra**. There are few signs, but most paths lead back eventually to the focal point of the park, the ornate palace.

Although the forest had been owned by the Bishop of Coimbra since the eleventh century, it was only settled in 1628 when Carmelite monks were granted permission to create their own "desert" on the wooded hilltop. Here, they constructed a series of chapels and hermitages, the **Convento dos Carmelitos**, in an attempt to recreate the ascetic lifestyle of biblical hermits. The **Convento de Santa Cruz** (see below) was erected as their main church, and they also created routes lined with chapels to the "Sacred Mount", planting trees in the process. Today you can follow the **Via Sacra**, lined with chapels, to the heights of **Cruz Alta**, a "high cross" at the top of a hill, which gives dazzling views across the surrounding country: it's around a forty-minute walk here from the palace.

In 1810, the convent was used by the Duke of Wellington as a base for what turned out to be a decisive victory in the Battle of Buçaco, before the religious order was finally disbanded in 1834. The area was then developed into a romantic botanical garden, when today's water-features and beautiful **Vale dos Fetos** (Valley of Ferns) were laid out, and many of the 250 species of tree that you can see today were planted, including giant sequoia, cedar, firs and pines.

Palácio do Buçaco

☎ 231 937 970, ⊛ almeidahotels.com

Construction of the royal **Palácio do Buçaco** in the middle of the forest began in 1888, using a team of architects including Luigi Manini, who built the dramatic Quinta da Regaleira in Sintra; indeed, Buçaco has a lot in common with Sintra in terms of both the landscape and the style of architecture. The impressive palace is mock-Manueline, a riot of carving and beautiful *azulejo* tiles, topped by a dramatic pinnacled turret. The palace was finally completed in 1907, only for the Republic to be declared three years later. Ever since, it's been a five-star hotel, surrounded by sumptuously landscaped gardens. Tour coaches stop by in droves and as a result casual visitors are discouraged, though you can use the café or bar after 3pm. At other times, there is a public café opposite.

Convento de Santa Cruz

Daily 10am–1pm & 2–6pm • €2

Within the palace grounds you can visit the small but attractive Carmelite **Convento de Santa Cruz**. As you enter, you'll notice that the door and ceiling of the entrance hall are lined with cork. Look out, too, for the curious little **side-chapel** centred on an image of the Virgin Mary breastfeeding a baby Jesus, around which worshippers have placed wax models of breasts and pregnant women.

Museu Militar

Just outside the forest near the Portas da Rainha • Tues–Sun 10am–12.30pm & 2–5pm • €2

Buçaco's small **Museu Militar** contains charts, uniforms and relics detailing the events leading up to and during the Battle of Buçaco (1810), when the Duke of Wellington used the heights of the area to successfully withstand an attack by French troops. The French sustained heavy losses, one of Napoleon's first setbacks, giving the Duke time to develop the lines of Torres Vedras further south.

Luso

A spa town for well over a hundred years, **LUSO** – 3km downhill by road from Buçaco – still draws crowds of Portuguese to take its waters, and visitors are welcome to try the various treatments at the **Termas de Luso** (May–Oct; ⊛maloclinictermasluso.com), which is run by the Malo Spa company. Locals fill bottles and plastic containers with free spa water from the **Fonte São João** spring – Luso water is sold all over the country – next to which is an old-fashioned Art Deco *casa do chá* (tea room), with a terrace overlooking the central gardens and spa buildings. There's also a great little daily fruit-and-veg **market** just down from the tourist office, while a souvenir market (lace, basketware, football shirts and regional cakes) sets its stalls out between the town's roundabouts. After a turn around the small town centre and municipal park with its little lake, head up past the souvenir market stalls to pick up the stepped path to Buçaco.

ARRIVAL AND INFORMATION

LUSO AND BUÇACO

By bus All non-express buses from Viseu take a short detour through the forest, stopping at the Palácio do Buçaco, and again by the Portas da Rainha (for the Museu Militar) en route to Luso (Mon–Fri 5 daily, Sat 2 daily; 1hr 45min). Services from Coimbra to Luso run 4 daily (Mon–Fri), and 2 daily on Sat (40min).

By train Three afternoon services leave Coimbra A, and take 30mins to reach Luso–Buçaco station; it's a 15min walk into town from the station – take the road on the left.

Information Luso turismo is opposite the *Grande Hotel*, near the post office on the main Rua Emídio Navarro (June to mid-Sept Mon–Fri 9am–12.30pm & 2–7pm, Sat & Sun 9.30am–1pm & 2.30–6pm; mid-Sept to May daily 9.30am–12.30pm & 2–5.30pm; ☏231 939 133, ⊛turismo-centro.pt). They give out free fold-out maps of the town and forest.

ACCOMMODATION

★**Alegre** Rua Emídio Navarro 2, Luso ☏231 930 256, ⊛alegrehotels.com. Just 100m up the road to Buçaco, this impressive building with a grand entrance, once home to a count, is full of nineteenth-century style and polished wood. The best of the high-ceilinged rooms have balconies (€15 extra) and great views, and there's also a small bar and a swimming pool in the pretty garden. The owner is a real expert on local history. Parking. **€50**

Familiar Rua Ernesto Navarro 34, Luso ☏231 939 612. Just up the Buçaco road from town, this is a charming old house with a variety of rooms: a few have small balconies and some sleep up to four people. No credit cards. Parking available. **€35**

Grande Hotel de Luso Rua Dr. Cid de Oliveira 86, Luso ☏231 937 937, ⊛hoteluso.com. The region's top address, the yellow, turreted *Grande Hotel* is a four-star Art Deco beauty with tastefully designed rooms, most with balconies. There's an Olympic-sized outdoor pool, as well as an indoor pool and hot tub, kids' club and parking. **€80**

★**Imperial** Rua Emídio Navarro 25, Luso ☏231 937 570, ⊛residencialimperial.com. Great value, and a good location by the *casa do chá* and *fonte*. These are modern digs with comfortable en-suite rooms complete with sturdy furniture – some rooms sleep four, and there's a good, inexpensive restaurant downstairs (which is often closed at quiet times). **€42**

EATING

O Cesteiro Rua Monsenhor Raul Mira, Luso ☏231 939 360. A 5min walk from the town centre (keep going past the turismo), this local favourite serves a typical regional menu, including duck rice, roast goat and a good steak, with mains at €8–13.50. Mon, Tues and Thurs–Sun noon–3pm & 7–10pm.

Pedra de Sal Rua Dr. Francisco Diniz 33, Luso ☏231 939 405, ☏restaurantepedradesal.com. One of Luso's smarter options, with crisp service and a menu featuring the likes of *porco preto*, steak, or squid-and-prawn kebab for €12–13. Daily 12.30–3pm & 7–10pm.

The Dão valley wine route

The route northeast from Coimbra along the IP3 sweeps through the **valley of the Rio Dão**, a name synonymous in Portugal and beyond with high quality **wine**. The Dão is a tributary of the Mondego and flows through the heart of the demarcated region where some of the country's finest red wines are produced. Most of the wine estates lie either side of the river valley to the northeast of **Santa Comba Dão**, and you can spend a

happy day pottering through the region's small country towns, following winery signs on the **Rota do Vinho do Dão** to pretty villages like **Santar**. It's a hilly, granite area, cold and rainy in winter, but hot and dry in the sweltering summers, when the wooded slopes are particularly susceptible to ravaging forest fires.

Santa Comba Dão and the Dão valley

The small market town of **SANTA COMBA DÃO**, a little over 50km from Coimbra, marks the start of the Dão wine region. Its only claim to fame is as the home town of António de Oliveira Salazar (1889–1970), the Portuguese dictator and leader of an authoritarian regime that lasted forty years, who was born (and is buried) in the nearby village of Vimeiro. There's not much to the town itself, save a very small historic centre and some grandstand views of the tumbling river and the Aguieira *barragem* (reservoir). However, you can explore the surroundings on the disused Dão valley rail line from Santa Comba Dão to Viseu, which is now the **Ecopista do Dão**, a 48km cycleway and footpath, the longest in the country (ⓦecopista-portugal.com).

Santar

Around 30km northeast of Santa Comba Dão, near Nelas, **SANTAR** is a very attractive village in the heart of Dão vineyards. Cobbled backstreets lined with handsome stone mansions lead up to the main square, where you'll find the **Paço dos Cunhas de Santar** (Tues–Sun 10am–10pm; free; ☎232 960 140), a restored seventeenth-century mansion which now runs wine tastings, wine workshops and cookery courses.

ARRIVAL AND DEPARTURE   SANTA COMBA DÃO AND THE DÃO VALLEY

By bus Buses leave Coimbra approx hourly for Santa Comba Dão (1hr 20min).

By train Around three daily trains leave Coimbra B station, and four daily from Coimbra A, for Santa Comba Dão (1hr).

By car In order to reach most of the wine estates, which are well signed on the roads, you will need your own car.

ACTIVITIES

Wine tours and tastings For details of wineries open to the public for tours and tastings, look online at ⓦglobalwines.pt. Some of the estates in the area are small family concerns and require appointments, while others are very much set up for public visits, like the Paço dos Cunhas de Santar (see above) and Quinta de Cabriz (daily 9am–10pm; free; ☎232 960 140), 3km from Carregal do Sal (off the IC12), which makes some terrific reds and interesting sparkling wines, and has its own restaurant.

ACCOMMODATION AND EATING

Quinta do Rio Dão Escolha Verde ☎963 444 663, ⓦquintadoriodao.com. The charming Dutch-owned *Quinta do Rio Dão* is an organic estate by the river, 2km from Santa Comba Dão. Accommodation is in B&B rooms in the main house or rustic self-catering cottages in the grounds, and organic orange juice and home-made estate preserves are served at breakfast. You can splash about on the water in the *quinta*'s kayaks or rowing boat, and it's also near the start of the *ecopista*, with bikes available for guests to rent. Minimum stay conditions in high season. **€65**

Serra do Caramulo

Beyond Santa Comba Dão, the IP3 bears away from the Dão valley and the views are soon of the **Serra do Caramulo**, breaking to the northwest. The eastern turn-off point for the mountains is the small, unassuming town of **Tondela**, 20km from Santa Comba Dão, from where the minor N230 winds through a succession of tiny villages at the heart of the mountain range, including **Caramulo** itself, a twisting 19km from Tondela. This is the only worthwhile overnight stop, with a fantastic museum, and makes a good hiking base; most of the other *serra* villages are little more than hamlets, surrounded by rhododendrons, brightly coloured azaleas and thick green shrubs growing wild on the

hillside. After Caramulo, the N230 descends to **Águeda**, western access point to the mountains, 37km from Caramulo, which is close to the main north–south routes between Coimbra and Aveiro/Porto.

Caramulo

Tucked beneath the granite outcrops and wind turbines of the high Beiras *serra*, the straggling village of **CARAMULO** glories in some staggering views. It's a somnolent place, with a belvedere garden and vast, shady chestnut trees at its heart, while several waymarked footpaths radiate from the village through neighbouring hamlets and up to the local peaks. The summit of the highest, **Caramulinho** (1075m), is a 5km drive from the village, while at **Cabeço da Neve** (a 4km drive) there's another sweeping viewpoint. The best walk is the circular **Rota dos Caleiros** (8.2km; 3–4hr), which is detailed in a leaflet available from the turismo (see below): it picks its way past the old stone aqueducts (*caleiros*) and granite boulders around Caramulinho, with magnificent views east to the Serra da Estrela and west to the Atlantic Ocean.

Museu do Caramulo

Rua Jean Lurçat 42 • Daily 10am–1pm & 2–6pm; closes at 5pm in winter • €7 • ☎ 232 861 270, ⓦ museu-caramulo.net

The extraordinary **Museu do Caramulo** was founded by two brothers with a love of "art and automobiles" and displays everything from primitive religious sculpture to souped-up Harley-Davidsons. Once you've browsed through the Picasso sketches and sixteenth-century tapestries, it's on to the superb collection of vintage and 21st-century cars and motorcycles, most of which are in working order and given a run-out every September for the **Caramulo Motorfestival** (ⓦ caramulo-motorfestival.com).

ARRIVAL AND INFORMATION   CARAMULO

By car There is no public transport to Caramulo, so you'll need a car to explore.

Information Caramulo turismo, Avenida Jerónimo de Lacerda 750 (Mon–Fri 9am–1pm & 1.30–5pm,

Sat & Sun 10am–12.30pm & 2.30–5.30pm; ☎ 232 861 437 ⓦ visitcaramulo.org). You can pick up walking brochures here as well as lots of other information on the area.

ACCOMMODATION

Hotel do Caramulo Av Dr. Abel Lacerda ☎ 232 860 100, ⓦ hoteldocaramulo.pt. The town's flagship sleep is the four-star *Hotel do Caramulo*, with spa and leisure

facilities, including indoor and outdoor pools, a decent restaurant and bar, and unbeatable views towards the Serra da Estrela. **€115**

Vouzela and the Rio Vouga

North of Caramulo, and just beyond the fast Aveiro–Viseu road (A25), **Vouzela** is an attractive Beira town set on the beautiful **Rio Vouga** and makes a fine destination if you feel like taking in a little of backwater Portugal. Bus services run from Coimbra and Aveiro and, on reaching the Vouga, follow the route of the old train line along the river on the N16. For drivers there are equally bucolic approaches, from Caramulo to the south (N228) or from Viseu and the IP5 to the east, from where the minor N337 makes a particularly memorable approach. Beyond the town lies the spa resort of **São Pedro do Sul**, on the Rio Sul, which flows down from the lovely Serra da Arada that flanks Vouzela to the north.

Vouzela

VOUZELA's old centre is built around a shallow river, crossed by a low **Romanesque bridge**, overhung by willow and bordered by attractive manor houses. Beyond are the

---

FOREST FIRES AND THE BOMBEIROS VOLUNTÁRIOS

Portugal's famed green countryside is ravaged each year by **forest fires**, and the problem has worsened markedly in the last decade – it's estimated that ninety percent are caused by some sort of human activity, whether that be arson or carelessness with cigarettes, bonfires and barbecues. Matters aren't helped by the country's timber industry, which has replaced native tree species with the highly lucrative and highly flammable eucalyptus and pine. Peak fire season is midsummer, but in drought years forest fires break out as early as January and as late as November. You don't need to drive through central and northern Portugal for long before seeing the evidence of past fires – hillsides burned black and torched trees – or the telltale plumes of thick smoke from the latest conflagration. On the worst days, ash falls to the streets in distant towns and cities, and major train lines and motorways are closed.

Extraordinarily, the firefighting service that has the unenviable task of dealing with the problem is almost entirely voluntary. The country's twenty thousand or so **Bombeiros Voluntários** make up over ninety percent of Portugal's firefighting forces, with the few (and far better equipped) professional corps (Bombeiros Sapadores) based in the cities or working privately for the country's timber and paper-pulp concerns. You'll see Bombeiros Voluntários vehicles in every region – helping out with ambulance duties too as part of their remit – and the volunteers are usually the first and only firefighters on the scene when a blaze breaks out. Equipment and vehicles are old and often wholly inadequate; in the past, urgent appeals to the EU have led to specialist aircraft and foreign crews arriving to help.

It is, of course, horribly dangerous work and firefighters lose their lives every year. For this reason – and for their astonishing success rate in saving local homes and properties – the Bombeiros Voluntários have an almost heroic status in Portugal. Rare is the town without a street or avenue named after them, while proud **municipal statues and memorials** to their deeds proliferate.

---

riverside gardens, manicured lawns and municipal pool, all towered over by the **viaduct** of the former railway which stretches across a narrow terraced gorge. You can cross both bridge and viaduct on an 8km circular walk – a board at the top of the gardens by the viaduct shows the route. Within Portugal, the town is best known for its *pasteis de Vouzela* (a very sweet egg-based pastry) and the local *vinho Lafões* (a wine similar to *vinho verde*).

Museu Municipal

Praça Morais de Carvalho • Tues–Fri 9.30am–1pm & 2–5.30pm, Sat & Sun 2–5pm • Free

From the Rio Vouga, narrow Rua São Frei Gil climbs up past manor houses to a small square where you'll find the **Museu Municipal**, housed in the attractive building of the eighteenth-century law courts. The museum has a fairly uninspiring collection of archeological remains and sacred art, though the room of old toys is more diverting. A third room hosts temporary exhibits.

Termas de São Pedro do Sul

☎ 232 720 300, ⊛ termas-spsul.com

Four kilometres northeast of Vouzela is the thermal resort area of **TERMAS DE SÃO PEDRO DO SUL**, possibly the oldest spa in Portugal, though now offering modern treatments. It was used by the Romans and Portuguese royalty – Dom Afonso Henriques is said to have bathed his wounded leg here after the battle at Badajoz – and remains among the most attractive in the country. Its position beside the Vouga, with pine trees all around, certainly lends it charm and the resort makes for a pleasant side-trip from Vouzela.

ARRIVAL AND INFORMATION   VOUZELA AND THE RIO VOUGA

By bus Vouzela bus station is at Avenida Sidónio Pais.
Destinations Aveiro (2–3 daily; 1hr 10min); Coimbra (5 daily; 1hr 50min); Lisbon, via Coimbra (3 daily; 4hr 10min); Porto (1–2 daily; 2hr 30min); São Pedro do Sul (1–2 daily; 15min).

Information Vouzela turismo, Avenida João de Melo 23 (Mon–Sat 10am–6pm, Sun 2–6pm; reduced hours in winter; ☎ 232 740 070, ⊛ cm-vouzela.pt), is in an old market building, which also sells local handicrafts.

ACCOMMODATION AND EATING

Casa de Fataunços Fataunços ☎ 232 772 697. In the village of Fataunços, roughly halfway between Vouzela and São Pedro do Sul, this beautifully restored eighteenth-century manor house is a fantastic country retreat with its own grounds, swimming pool and tennis court. Painting, theatre and dance courses are available, and there's a games room. **€60**

Casa Museu Rua Ribeiro Cardoso 6, Vouzela ☎ 232 771 514, ⓦ casamuseu.com. Opposite Vouzela's museum, and with similarly historic touches, the eighteenth-century *Casa Museu* is an elegantly decorated townhouse with grandly medieval bare stone walls, chunky antique furnishings and pristinely stylish rooms. **€60**

Ferreira Rua Barão da Costeiro 3, Vouzela ☎ 232 771 650, ⓦ residencialferreira.com.pt. Around 50m down the hill from the Praça da República, *Ferreira* is Vouzela's best budget option, a pleasantly old-fashioned place with twelve simple en-suite rooms in an old townhouse. **€30**

O Meu Menino Av Sidónio Pais 6, Vouzela ☎ 232 771 335. Just down from the bus station, this large restaurant serves up reasonably-priced local dishes such as *feijoada*, home-made sausages and rabbit: you can eat well here for around €10. Daily 9am–10pm.

O Regalinho Rua Teles Loureiro 18, Vouzela ☎ 232 771 220. Vouzela's swankiest option, just off Praça da República, where you can expect to pay around €13 a plate for very well executed regional food (roast goat, veal, *bacalhau*). Mon & Wed–Sun noon–2.30pm & 7–9.30pm.

3

Arouca and the Serra da Freita

A winding, undulating 43km route from Vouzela heads over the 1000m peaks of the **SERRA DA FREITA** to Arouca, via a beautiful, terraced landscape littered with dolmens, crumbling villages and waterfalls. Vines grow on precipitous slopes, while the roads snake through pine forest and then high across the heather-dotted moorland. A regional map available from Arouca turismo (see p.206) details all the local sights and attractions, as well as several breathtaking hikes, and you could easily spend a day or two touring and walking in the hills.

Arouca

AROUCA is a handsome little town which – though largely unbothered by tourists – is a real gem. It was probably established by the Romans, though nothing of the period remains; today, the town is famous for its **monastery**, the main reason to visit. The central square holds a couple of pavement cafés, and the medieval backstreets are great for a bit of aimless wandering, with some beautiful old houses bedecked with wisteria.

Mosteiro de Santa Maria de Arouca

Largo de Santa Mafalda, Avenida 25 de Abril • Accompanied visits, sometimes in English, Tues–Sun 9.30am–noon & 2–5pm • €3.50 •
☎ 256 943 321, ⓦ museudeartesacradearouca.weebly.com

Arouca has always been associated with the vast, medieval **Mosteiro de Santa Maria de Arouca**, whose imposing walls loom over the main road that cuts through town. In the kitchen there are huge fireplaces that give an idea of the number of its former inhabitants, while the Baroque **church** (which you can see without buying a ticket; enter from the main road) holds richly carved choir stalls and a great organ with 1352 notes, played on rare occasions by one of the country's few experts. The convent peaked in importance when Dona Mafalda, of whose dowry it had formed a part, found her marriage to Dom Henriques I of Castile annulled and retired here to a life of religious contemplation. In the **museum** upstairs, you can see some of Queen Mafalda's most prized treasures, including an exquisite thirteenth-century silver diptych.

Geoparque Arouca

Canelas, 10km northeast of Arouca (N326) • **Visitor centre** Sat 10am–noon & 2.30–5pm, Sun 2.30–5pm; private visits also available
Tues–Fri with advance reservations • Admission to centre €2, guided walking tour €8 • ☎ 916 352 917, ⓦ aroucageopark.pt

Local heart-rates increased slightly following the discovery of an extraordinary **fossil site** at Canelas, containing an amazing series of 400-million-year-old trilobites and

gastropods. This sits within the wider **Geoparque Arouca** and to see the fossils you need first to go to the park visitor centre, which is on the left-hand side of the N326 before you turn off for Canelas.

Paiva Walkways

Daily: Nov–March 9am–5pm; April–Oct 7.30am–8pm • €1 • ⓦ passadicosdopaiva.pt

A major new attraction in the region, the **Paiva Walkways** comprise 8km of timber trails on the left bank of the Paiva River, which provide a zigzagging, often toe-curlingly steep route through some of the most attractive landscapes of the Geoparque Arouca. You can start at the southern end at Areinho or the northern terminus at Espiunca; allow at least three hours to complete the route.

ARRIVAL AND INFORMATION

AROUCA

By bus There are regional buses from Porto to Arouca (via São João de Madeira), though to make the magnificent journey over the Serra da Freita, you'll need your own car.

Information The modern, interactive Arouca turismo is at Rua Abel Botelho 4 (Mon–Fri 9am–12.30pm & 2–5.30pm, Sat & Sun 9.30am–1pm & 2–5.30pm; ☎ 256 940 258, ⓦ cm-arouca.pt).

ACCOMMODATION AND EATING

NaturVeredas Merujal ☎ 256 947 723, ⓦ naturveredas .com. A nice pine-forest campsite, 1km south of Arouca, with little wooden cabins (sleeping 2–4; from €27) and a bunkhouse available, as well as a bar-restaurant on site. Tent pitch **€2.50** plus **€3.50** per adult; bunk-house **€10**
São Pedro Av Reinaldo de Noronha ☎ 256 944 580, ⓦ hotelspedro.com. Arouca's best hotel is a three-star affair, 5min on foot up the main road from the square (take

the left fork, to Castro Daire, at the top). Rooms just about deserve their price tag and the best afford wonderful views from small balconies. **€70**
Tasquinha da Quinta Rua 1 de Maio ☎ 256 944 080. Around the corner from the turismo, the *Tasquinha da Quinta* offers excellent regional dishes for around €10, including the local speciality, *arouquêsa* beef. Daily noon–3pm & 7–10pm.

Aveiro and around

The substantial inland town of **AVEIRO** lies south of Porto on the edge of a system of coastal lagoons which stretch for around 40km both north and south. Until the mid-1500s, it was a vibrant coastal port but the local economy was devastated when the river mouth silted up and the hinterland turned to swamp. At the beginning of the nineteenth century, however, canals were dug to open up the town and drain the marshes, creating saltpans and facilitating the harvesting of seaweed, and the town began to flourish once more. Today, Aveiro's economy depends increasingly on tourists, with visitors attracted to the "Venice of Portugal" by boat rides on the canals, Art Nouveau buildings and the nearby **Vista Alegre** factory, famed for its ceramics. The town's closest beaches – at **Barra** and **Costa Nova** – are built up and packed in summer, but still good fun, while the **São Jacinto nature reserve** provides coastal attractions of a more peaceful kind.

Aveiro

Aveiro has a compact centre of handsome buildings and open squares, though what strikes most are its **canals**, looped over by footbridges and plied by colourfully painted cruise boats. Stand on the bridge (actually a busy roundabout) over the **Canal Central** and most of central Aveiro is within a couple of minutes' walk. The town's traditional industries are recalled by imposing statues of local workers on the bridge, notably the *salineira* with her salt tray. Pastel-coloured houses line Rua João Mendonça on the north side, with the old town streets and **Mercado do Peixe** (fish market; Tues–Sat 7am–1pm) just behind. Other arms of the canal branch off at intervals, with tiled houses facing each other across the water.

Aveiro has a preponderance of **Art Nouveau buildings**, the legacy of returning wealthy emigrants in the early years of the twentieth century. At the top of the pedestrianized Rua Coimbra, Praça da República is flanked by the blue snowflake-design tiled facade of the seventeenth-century **Igreja da Misericórdia** and the **Câmara Municipal**, a century older.

Museu de Aveiro

Avenida Santa Joana Princesa • Tues–Sun 10am–6pm • €4 • ☎ 234 423 297

Apart from a boat trip, the town's must-see attraction is the wonderful **Museu de Aveiro**, housed inside the fifteenth-century **Convento de Jesus**. Its finest exhibits all relate to Santa Joana, a daughter of Afonso V who lived in the convent from 1472 until her death in 1489. Barred from becoming a nun because of her royal station and her father's opposition, she was later beatified for her determination to escape from the material world (or perhaps simply from an unwelcome arranged marriage). Her tomb and chapel are strikingly beautiful, as is the convent itself, and there's a fine collection of art and sculpture – notably a series of naïve seventeenth-century paintings depicting the saint's life.

Vista Alegre

Ílhavo • **Museum, chapel and palace** May–Sept Tues–Fri 9am–6pm, Sat & Sun 9am–12.30pm & 2–5pm; Oct–April Tues–Fri 9am–6pm, Sat & Sun 10am–12.30pm & 2–5pm • €2.50 • **Vista Alegre shop and factory shop** Mon–Sat 9.30am–7.30pm • ☎ 234 320 600, ⓦ vistaalegre.com • Buses (signed Ílhavo) leave approx hourly from outside Aveiro station and take 20min

Portugal's celebrated **Vista Alegre** porcelain works was established in 1824 at Ílhavo,

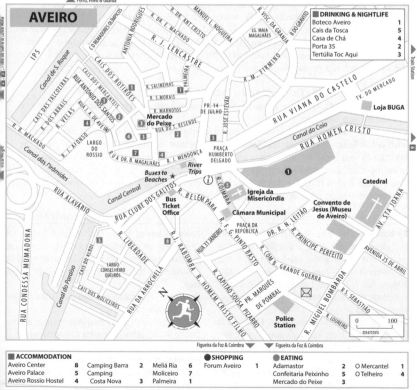

around 5km southwest of Aveiro. It soon acquired royal patronage and expanded from a simple porcelain and glass factory to an estate with its own workers' village, along the lines of the model villages built by enlightened British entrepreneurs of the period. Today, there's a **museum**, the founder's **palace**, and a tiled and frescoed seventeenth-century **chapel** to visit, as well as a Vista Alegre **shop** (porcelain, crystal, silverware) and factory shop for seconds.

Praia da Barra and Costa Nova

Buses to Praia de Barra and Costa Nova depart from outside Aveiro train station, or from Rua Clube dos Galitos (approx hourly; Praia de Barra 15min; Costa Nova 25min)

Aveiro's nearest beach lies 9km west, at **Praia da Barra**, a large, developed stretch of sand overlooked by the Iberian peninsula's tallest lighthouse. There's more of the same at **Costa Nova**, 3km south of Barra, though the development here is ameliorated by an attractive line of candy-striped wooden buildings facing inland over the lagoon.

São Jacinto

From Aveiro, catch the bus from the Rua Clube dos Galitos stop to the end of the line at Forte da Barra – not be confused with Praia de Barra (approx hourly; 15min); a connecting boat runs from here across the water to São Jacinto (approx hourly; 5min; €1 single)

On the north side of the lagoon from Aveiro, and accessible by boat from Forte da Barra, is the beach and nature reserve of **SÃO JACINTO**, a thriving little port with a handful of dockside cafés and restaurants. With a military base at one end and a forest of cranes cluttering the skyline, it's not beautiful, but there is an enormous dune-fringed **beach** twenty minutes' walk away.

North of São Jacinto the minor N327 (and summer bus service) runs all the way up the lagoon to the beach at **Torreira**. There's another small resort at **Furadouro**, 26km from São Jacinto, where a long stretch of pine-fringed dunes marks the point at which the distinctive Ria countryside finally comes to an end.

Reserva Natural das Dunas de São Jacinto

No set hours • Free • ☎ 234 831 063, ⓦ sig.riadeaveiro.pt • The reserve entrance is a 10min walk from the São Jacinto boat jetty, out of town along the road to Torreira

Parts of São Jacinto's beach, plus the encroaching pine forest, have been preserved within the **Reserva Natural das Dunas de São Jacinto**, where boardwalks and paths are laid out through the marram grass and past willow-shrouded ponds. More than a hundred bird species have been spotted here, including goshawk, teal and widgeon. You can pick up a free map from the visitor centre for a self-guided 7km walk through the reserve, which takes around two and a half hours.

ARRIVAL AND INFORMATION

AVEIRO AND AROUND

By bus Tickets for Rede Expressos (express) services to Lisbon, Coimbra, Porto and other destinations are available from a special ticket point (Tues–Thurs 7am–noon & 12.30–7pm, Fri 7am–noon & 12.30–9.30pm, Sat 7–11am & 1–6.30pm, Sun 7–11am & 1–9.30pm) on Rua Clube dos Galitos. Buses leave from across the road.

Destinations Coimbra (4–5 daily; 45min); Figueira da Foz (3–4 daily; 1hr 10min); Lisbon (7 daily; 3–4hr); Porto (roughly hourly; 2hr 45min); Praia de Mira (1 daily; 1hr); and Vouzela (3 daily; 1hr).

By car Parking can be difficult, as metered on-street

parking is limited to two hours (though free on Sat afternoon & Sun) – try Largo do Rossio by the canal or the streets around the train station. The covered car park beneath Praça Marquês de Pombal is best for longer stays.

By train The train station is on Largo da Estação, a 15min walk east of the centre.

Destinations Coimbra (at least hourly; 1hr); Espinho (hourly; 30min); Lisbon (hourly; 2hr 30min); Porto (at least hourly; 30min–1hr).

Information Aveiro turismo is at Rua Clube dos Galitos 2 (daily 9am–6pm; ☎ 234 377 761, ⓦ turismo-centro.pt).

FROM TOP PIÓDÃO (P.196); MATA NACIONAL DO BUÇACO (P.199) >

3

AVEIRO CANAL TRIPS

On Aveiro's main Canal Central, the traffic consists largely of **barcos moliceiros**, the traditional flat-bottomed lagoon boats with raised prows, colourfully adorned with paintings of flowers and scantily-dressed women. Once used to transport kelp, they now almost exclusively serve as cruise boats, and a trip on them is something of a must. Numerous companies offer 45-minute **boat tours** departing from either side of the Canal Central (departures every 30min or so, daily 10am–6pm, longer hours in July & Aug; 45min; €7.50). The trips usually pass down the main canal to local saltpans and back into town with surprisingly knowledgeable rowers giving an interesting commentary on local history; if you're (un)lucky, this may be accompanied by a song or two.

GETTING AROUND

By bike Bicycles are available free from the green-trimmed "Loja BUGA" kiosk (daily 10am–7pm), at the back of the Forum Aveiro shopping mall, just across the footbridge (in front of the old market). You will need to to show ID to get a bike, but you get use of it for a whole morning or a whole afternoon.

By taxi Taxis are available from in front of the train station; they also wait at the bottom of Rua Viana do Castelo, near the bridge. To book a taxi, call Central de Táxis (☎ 234 343 266).

ACCOMMODATION

AVEIRO

★ **Aveiro Center** Rua da Arrochela 6 ☎ 234 380 390, ⓦ hotelaveirocenter.com. This good-value family hotel offers air-conditioned doubles, triples (€100) and family rooms (€115) with shower or bath, overlooking a quiet street or a pretty patio at the back. The staff are courteous, there's on-street parking nearby and a generous buffet breakfast included. **€75**

Aveiro Palace Rua de Viana do Castelo 4 ☎ 234 421 885, ⓦ hotelaveiropalace.com. Aveiro's top address is this grand old building in a prime location, by the bridge and canal. Comfort levels are high, with four-star standards, plush rooms with spotless modern bathrooms, and an attractive first-floor bar. The rates here are not as high as you might expect. **€90**

★ **Aveiro Rossio Hostel** Largo do Rossio, corner Rua João Afonso de Aveiro 1 ☎ 234 041 538, ⓦ aveirorossiohostel.com. Not just a hostel – though it does have very attractive dorms – but also a very appealing guesthouse, with bright, spacious rooms in a high-ceilinged townhouse. There's also a pleasant communal lounge. Dorms **€20**; doubles **€70**

Meliá Ria Cais da Fonte Nova ☎ 0808 234 1953, ⓦ melia.com. A short walk from the old centre, Aveiro's smartest four-star hotel is a striking glass-and-steel box belonging to the Meliá chain, overlooking the canal and artificial lake. Rooms (some with balconies) are pretty stylish too, and there's a spa and pool, restaurant and garage parking (fee charged). **€100**

Moliceiro Rua Barbosa de Magalhães 15–17, Largo do Rossio ☎ 234 377 400, ⓦ hotelmoliceiro.com. Arguably the best upmarket choice in town, this is a contemporary four-star affair. Rooms come in earthy tones with dark-wood furniture and marble bathrooms; some overlook the canal, others the rear street, and there's a good buffet breakfast. Limited parking out the front. **€127**

Palmeira Rua da Palmeira 7–11 ☎ 234 422 521, ⓦ residencialpalmeira.com. A bright and cheerful budget choice in the old quarter, between the fish market and the Canal de São Roque. The rooms vary in standard and decor, but most have a shower or bath, cable TV, and the owner is a helpful, friendly type. **€45**

THE BEACH

Camping Costa Nova Costa Nova ☎ 234 722 441, ⓦ campingcostanova.com. Beachside campsite in the same style as its sister site at Praia da Barra, though potentially a little quieter. Pitch **€4.10**, plus **€3.95** per adult

Camping Praia da Barra Praia da Barra ☎ 234 965 111, ⓦ campingbarra.com. Summer beachside campsite outside of town with plenty of facilities; rooms, bungalows and apartments for rent, but not really suitable if you're looking for a quiet few days by the beach. Pitch **€4.10**, plus **€3.95** per adult

EATING

Aveiro has some excellent **restaurants** that serve local specialities such as eels and shellfish from the lagoons, usually served fried, with rice (*arroz*), or as a stew (*ensopado*), and accompanied by powerful Bairrada wine. You should also try the

celebrated Aveiros *ovos moles*, a confection of heavily sweetened egg yolk cream in a wafer shell, normally in the shape of seashells and fish.

Adamastor Trav do Lavadouro 1 ☎ 234 347 777. Facing the fish market, this bare-brick *cervejaria* doesn't look much from the outside, but the wooden benches in its two huge dining rooms fill up fast at mealtimes thanks to the enormous portions of fantastic fresh fish, as well as dishes such as *caril de gambas* (prawn curry), *arroz de marisco* (€30 for two) and a few meat dishes. Mains are €9.50–13. Daily 10am–3pm & 6pm–2am.

Confeitaria Peixinho Rua de Coimbra 9 ☎ 234 423 574. Many places in Aveiro sell the signature local tooth-rotter, *ovos moles*, but to taste the town's best head to this tiny bakery near the river. A kilo costs €22. Daily 9am–8pm.

★ **Mercado do Peixe** Largo da Pr do Peixe ☎ 234 241 928. In the rafters of the fish market, with crisp decor, attentive service and exceedingly fresh fish and seafood, as well as a range of steaks with various sauces. There's also a good-value weekday lunch deal, and great views out to the Ria or to the square below from the tiny terrace. Mains €12–22. Mon–Sat noon–3pm & 7.30–11pm, Sun noon–3pm.

O Mercantel Rua António dos Santos 16 ☎ 234 428 057. Established by a former fishmarket worker, as you'd expect this place excels in fresh fish such as *dourada*, squid and lobster, with mains at €8.50–20. The *arroz de marisco* (€45 for two) is said to be the best in town. Tues–Sun noon–midnight.

★ **O Telheiro** Largo da Pr do Peixe 20–21 ☎ 234 429 473. At this traditional but buzzy *adega*, you can sit at the bar, or at rustic wooden benches and tiled tables. It serves a good range of tapas-style starters (all €4–6), tender beef (try the *bife á caçarola*), *enguias fritas* (fried eels) and a terrific *lulas grelhados* (grilled squid); main courses cost €9–16. Tues–Sat 8am–midnight, Sun 9am–5pm.

DRINKING AND NIGHTLIFE

The liveliest **bar area** is immediately around the fish market, where tables are scattered across the cobbles. A 10min walk from here, there's another line of late-opening canal-side bars along **Cais de São Roque**, some set in renovated salt storage barns. The town's big annual festival is the **Festa da Ria** (last two weeks of Aug), celebrated with boat races, folk dances, and competitions for the best decorated *barcos moliceiros*. The other major event is the **Festa de São Gonçalinho** (second week of Jan).

Boteco Aveiro Cais dos Botirões. Whether you're after a laidback coffee and sandwich at lunchtime or a sundowner when the day is done, this simple, cool canalside bar is a sound option. Pull up a bean bag by the water and watch the world go by. Daily 10am–2am.

Cais da Tosca Rua Cais Do Alboi 12 ☎ 234 421 579. In a modernized canalside warehouse, this funky pub offers superb *petiscos*, served both indoors and out next to the water. Staff are super-friendly and there's a great atmosphere on summer evenings. Mon–Thurs & Sun 11am–midnight, Fri & Sat 11am–2am.

Casa de Chá Rua Dr. Barbosa Magalhães 9–11. Behind the modest Art Nouveau Museum, this is a great little tea room and bar (also accessed from Travessa do Rossio), serving tea, cakes and coffee by day and a mean range of cocktails by night. Best on a summer's evening. Mon–Sat 10am–late.

Porta 35 Rua do Tenente Resende 35 ☎ 911 532 016. This fashionable bar has a dark-red exterior and a funky interior where you can enjoy *petiscos* and great burgers. There's often a DJ on hand playing jazzy, relaxed tunes. Mon–Thurs noon–3pm & 7–11.30pm, Fri & Sat noon–3pm & 7pm–2am, Sun noon–4.30pm & 7–10.30pm.

Tertúlia Toc Aqui Pr do Peixe ☎ 913 006 553. Fashionable fish-market bar, whose name (which isn't signed – it's the one with the blue facade) means "play here", and on more raucous nights, that's exactly what you can do with the instruments that hang on the back wall. Daily 10pm–2am.

SHOPPING

Forum Aveiro Rua Batalhão de Caçadores 10 ☎ 234 379 500, ⊕ forumaveiro.com. On the south side of the bridge, by the canal, this huge mall should cater to your every shopping need, with a whole panoply of local and international stores as well as a several restaurants, cinema screens and even a roof garden. Most shops daily 10am–11pm.

DIRECTORY

Football The local club, Beira Mar (⊕ beiramar.pt), usually do pretty well in Portugal's top league, though rarely get near to filling their state-of-the-art stadium (capacity 32,800), which was built for the 2004 European championships.

Hospital Hospital Distrital, Avenida Dr. Artur Ravara (☎ 234 378 300).

Police Praça Marquês de Pombal (☎ 234 302 510, ⊕ psp.pt).

Post office Praça Marquês de Pombal 23 (Mon–Fri 9am–6pm).

Praia de Mira

South of Aveiro, **PRAIA DE MIRA** is the only resort of any size until you reach the full-scale development of Figueira. Though very quiet and a bit dreary out of season, from June to September it's a lively place set on a small lagoon known as **Barrinha**, its cobbled quayside planted with palms. The one long main street barrels past the lagoon towards the sea, where a seemingly endless dune-backed **beach** stretches to either side. It's ideal for beach-lounging, though the resort also makes an good base for low-key walking and cycling (see box below).

The coastline immediately south of Praia de Mira consists of a virtually deserted 30km stretch of stupendous beaches, mostly backed by pine trees, planted to stabilize the low-lying dunes. The sands are only easily accessible at a couple of points – **Praia de Tocha**, with its unusual wooden fisherman's houses, around 12km south of Praia de Mira; and the even quieter **Praia de Quiaios** (pronounced *key-aysh*), another 11km south (avoid the extremely rutted forest road to get here, sticking to the N109–8 instead). Both are popular summer resorts but dead out of season, and you'll need a car to get to them.

ARRIVAL AND INFORMATION

By bus There are infrequent direct buses to Praia de Mira from Aveiro (1 daily; 1hr), Figueira da Foz (2 daily; 45min) and Coimbra (1–2 daily; 1hr 15min), but you'll usually have to change in Mira, the inland town 7km to the east.

Information The turismo (daily 9am–1pm & 2–5pm; ☎231 480 550, ⓦcm-mira.pt), on Avenida da Barra, is a restored *palheiro* (hayloft), built on stilts by the water and once typical of the region – it now doubles as the municipal museum dedicated to Mira's traditions and trades.

Surfing Surf lessons (around €25) and equipment hire are offered by Secret Surf School (☎915 480 890, ⓦsecretsurfschool.com).

ACCOMMODATION AND EATING

A Cozinha Av da Barrinha ☎231 471 190. The most appealing of the line of places facing the lagoon is the modern *A Cozinha*, where you can sit outside and eat fresh fish or the likes of octopus rice and *feijoada*; mains from around €8. Daily noon–3pm & 7.30–10.30pm.

Mira Villas Aldeamento Mira Villas ☎231 470 100, ⓦmiravillas.com. The upmarket *Mira Villas* is around 2km from the village, close to the lagoon. Set in an exclusive tourist development, it's a modern four-star with its own pool, bar and restaurant. The rooms have small kitchenettes and some have balconies, but you'll need a car to get here. €115

Pousada de Juventude Parque Campismo de Jovens ☎231 472 288, ⓦpousadasjuventude.pt. The seasonal youth hostel is signposted from the road by the *Orbitur* campsite – advance bookings are essential, as it's usually busy with groups. Closed Oct–May. Dorms €12; doubles €27

Senhora da Conceição Av Cidade de Coimbra 217 ☎231 471 645, ⓦhotelsradaconceicao.com. On the main avenue by the lagoon and GALP station, this two-star hotel is a good budget option – ask for one of the rooms at the back, which have lagoon views over the rooftops. €64

Figueira da Foz

Facing what the town claims to be Europe's widest beach, **FIGUEIRA DA FOZ** is the largest and busiest seaside resort on this coast, its fabulous beach attracting a vibrant holiday crowd throughout the summer. It's not an immediately attractive place

---

HIKING AND CYCLING AROUND PRAIA DE MIRA

Praia de Mira is very well set up in terms of local walks and cycle routes. The tourist office has leaflets detailing two great walks: the **Route of the Lakes** is a four-hour jaunt round the Barrinha lagoon inland to the Lagoa de Mira and back, while the **Route of the Mills** is a slightly longer walk via a series of watermills. Alternatively, you can follow the **Pista Ciclo-pedonal**, a 25km cycle route that heads inland along canals towards Mira then north towards Aveiro.

– ugly high-rise blocks line up along the seafront – though the tight grid of **central old town** streets around the ultra-modern casino brim with shops and pavement cafés that give this seaside settlement and working port its own distinct and rather pleasant identity.

The town has a diverting **municipal museum**, but most visitors are here for the enormous sandy **beach**, which is 2km long and very wide – it takes a good ten minutes to reach the sea across the sands. Waves here can be pretty huge, making it a popular spot for **surfers**, who also frequent the nearby **Praia do Cabadelo**, on the other side of the Rio Mondego. The seafront suburb of **Buarcos**, around twenty minutes' walk northwest of the centre of town, has some interesting restaurants as well as a diminutive **maritime museum**.

Museu Municipal Dr. Santos Rocha

Rua Calouste Gulbenkian • Jul & Aug Tues–Sun 9.30am–7pm; Sept–June Tues–Fri 9.30am–5pm, Sat & Sun 2–7pm • Free

On the edge of the town park, Parque das Abadias, the **Museu Municipal Dr. Santos Rocha** displays an impressive collection of items partly amassed by the avid local collector and archeologist Dr. Santos Rocha. It includes a number of fascinating items from Portugal's former colonies, such as Indo-Portuguese furniture and African instruments, as well as some religious sculptures, ancient coins and an impressive archeological section.

AN ESTUARY WALK NEAR FIGUEIRA DA FOZ

Figueira da Foz turismo has details of several **waymarked walks** in the area, including the 4km **Rota das Salinas**, an interesting estuary route around the saltpans that you glimpse from the bridge on the way into town. The walk begins 7km out of Figueira, at Armazens de Lavas, where you can leave your car by the small **Núcleo Museológico do Sal** (May to mid-Sept Wed–Sun 10.30am–12.30pm & 2–6.30pm; mid-Sept to April Thurs–Sun 10.30am–12.30pm & 2–4pm; €1), which details the history of salt production in these parts. Salt has been produced in the Mondego estuary for almost a thousand years, and around fifty *salinas* still operate between May and September each year. A boardwalk leads out across the saltpans, past weatherbeaten plank huts with salt bags piled outside. The well-signposted circular route takes about an hour (at a brisk stroll), through a pretty estuarine habitat of hedgerow flowers, rustling stands of bamboo and salt-tolerant shrubs. Black-winged stilts and other estuarine birds are a common sight, while the return leg of the path runs along the muddy banks of the Mondego, where a few fishermen still eke out a living from their painted wooden boats.

Buarcos

Buses to Buarcos run from outside the bus and train stations (Mon–Fri 17 daily, Sat & Sun approx hourly), also stopping in town at Rua da Liberdade

Figueira's seafront road and promenade are lined with apartment buildings and cafés as far as the suburb of **Buarcos** at the northern end. This is arguably the most pleasant part of Figueira, with a row of candy-striped fish restaurants right on the beach and a huddle of pastel-coloured fishermen's houses lurking behind what remains of the old defensive sea wall.

Núcleo Museológico do Mar

Rua Governador Soares Nogueira 32 • Mon–Fri 9am–1pm & 2–5pm • Free • ☎ 233 402 840 •

Buarcos is also home to the tiny **Núcleo Museológico do Mar**, a mildly diverting museum which records the area's former seafaring life, and explores how fishing and fishermen have shaped the town with models, photos, pictures and diagrams.

Serra da Boa Viagem and Parque Aventura

Parque Aventura Serra da Boa Viagem • May–Sept daily 10am–9pm • €10–17, depending upon your route • ☎ 916 536 555, ⓦ lusoaventura.com

North of Buarcos and the Cabo Mondego headland, the **Serra da Boa Viagem** is a hilly, wooded reserve with shaded picnic areas and woodland walks, including one detailed on a turismo pamphlet (*Rota da Boa Viagem*). You can test your climbing skills here at the **Parque Aventura**, an aerial forest adventure course with zip-wires, rope bridges, clamber nets and treetop obstacles – there's a height and age restriction on some of the routes. From central Figueira, the Serra is a ten-minute drive or an energetic thirty-minute cycle; follow the signpost from the coastal road at the northern end of Buarcos.

ARRIVAL AND DEPARTURE

FIGUEIRA DA FOZ

By bus The bus station is on Avenida Saraiva de Carvalho, a 20min walk east of the town centre and beach.

Destinations Aveiro (3–4 daily; 2hr); Caldas da Rainha (3–4 daily; 2hr); Coimbra (hourly; 1hr–1hr 15min); Leiria (7 daily; 1hr 30min); Lisbon (4 daily; 2hr 45min–3hr).

By car Parking is a bit tricky in August but there's plenty of space during the rest of the year, either in the huge free car park near the clock tower (good for campervans) or anywhere along the long promenade, heading northwards.

By train The train station is next to the bus station on Largo da Estação.

Destinations Caldas da Rainha (3 daily; 3hr); Coimbra (hourly; 1hr 15min); Leiria (3 daily; 2hr).

By taxi There's a rank outside the train station, or call Radio Taxis (☎ 233 420 880).

INFORMATION

Information Figueira da Foz turismo (daily 9.30am–1pm & 2–5.30pm; ☎233 422 610, ⓦcm-figfoz.pt) is on Avenida 25 de Abril, in the parade of cafés near the clock tower. There's another in Buarcos at the Núcleo Museológico do Mar, just back from the seafront at Rua Governador Soares Nogueira 32 (Mon–Fri 9am–1pm & 2–5pm; ☎233 402 840).

ACTIVITIES

Football The local club, Naval, Avenida 1 de Maio, plays at the small Estádio Municipal, and has spent a few seasons bobbing between the top and second divisions.

Surfing Escola de Surf da Figueira at Praia do Cabadelo (☎918 703 363, ⓦsurfingfigueira.com) offers lessons and also rents out surf gear.

Swimming pool Piscina de Mar, Avenida 25 de Abril (June–Sept 10am–8pm; €7; ☎961 791 921), is a popular outdoor saltwater swimming pool, with a terrace and bar.

Waterpark Aquapark, Avenida Dom João II 70, Cabo Mondego, Buarcos (mid-June to mid-Sept daily 10.30am–7pm; €8.50; ☎233 402 720, ⓦteimoso.com), is a fun waterpark with slides, chutes, a kids' play area and restaurant.

ACCOMMODATION

Aliança Rua Miguel Bombarda 12 ☎233 422 197, ⓦhotelalianca.net. One block from the seafront, this has light, well-presented rooms with double-glazed windows and cable TV; some have balconies where you can sneak a view of the sea. There's a pleasant bar and restauant downstairs. **€80**

Aviz Rua Dr. Lopes Guimarães 16 ☎233 422 635. This well-cared-for place with a friendly owner is on a quiet side-street, not far from the seafront, and you can park outside. Rooms are on the small and chintzy side, but are good quality with polished wooden floors, carved furniture, double-glazing and cable TV. **€60**

Costa de Prata Largo Coronel Galhardo 1 ☎233 426 620, ⓦcostadeprata.com. Recently renovated, this hotel is right on the seafront with some neat Art Nouveau touches: director's lamps and muted decor in the communal areas, a top-floor breakfast room and front rooms which boast fab sea views – avoid the back rooms: they lack a view and only some had been modernized at the time of writing. **€70**

Eurostars Oasis Plaza Av do Brasil ☎233 200 010, ⓦeurostarsoasisplaza.com. Big, bold and rising confidently from the seafront, this new hotel has quickly become the town's premier place to stay. Like a ship setting out to sea, the shape of the building means everyone gets a sea view. Rooms are immaculate studies in hotel comfort and staff are superbly regimented. Breakfast is a whopping €18 extra. **€105**

★Paintshop Hostel & Bar Rua Clemencia 9 ☎233 436 633, ⓦpaintshophostel.com. In the old part of town, this is a great English-run hostel with high-ceilinged dorms sleeping up to six, and three comfortable double rooms with shared bathroom on the top floor, all in a deceptively large townhouse. There's a communal kitchen/lounge with pool table, patio area and a bar for sports TV and film nights. The very friendly owners can arrange surf lessons, bike hire and theme nights (bar crawls, pizza and barbecues). Free parking and breakfast. Closed end-Oct to March. Dorms **€20**; doubles **€50**

Wellington Rua Dr. Calado 23–27 ☎233 426 767, ⓦhotelwellington.pt. A reasonable, modern and central hotel, the three-star *Wellington*, three blocks from the beach, has tasteful rooms with en-suite bathrooms and cable TV, as well as its own bar. **€65**

EATING

Caçarola I Rua Cândido dos Reis 65 ☎233 424 861. Late-opening shellfish bar and restaurant with daily specials of crab, lobster, clams and the like. Mains start at €10–15, but there's also a lot of dishes whose price is calculated per kilo (€18.50–85). There's a streetside deck for alfresco dining. Daily noon–3pm & 6.30pm–1am.

Gelataria San Remo Largo D.M. Barraca 26, Praia de Buarcos ☎233 425 309. Something of a Buarcos institution, this is renowned for its fabulous crêpes, waffles and Italian ice cream, which come in an array of exotic flavours from around €1.50 a scoop; or you can just call in for a drink. It's in a lovely high-ceilinged former townhouse with a fine outdoor terrace facing the beach. Daily: April–Sept 8am–2am; Oct–March 8am–midnight.

Marégrafo Petisqueira Av Infante D. Pedro, Praia de Buarcos ☎ 233 433 150. Just steps from the beach, choose between tables on the cobbles or the beautifully tiled townhouse dining room to enjoy flavoursome tapas (€3–8) and the best Portuguese wines in town. Gets very busy at mealtimes so booking is a good idea. Daily noon–2am.

Núcleo Sportinguista Rua Praia da Fonte 14–17 ☎233 434 882. You pay a little more if you're not a member of the Sporting Lisboa supporters club, but it's still a real bargain for the set meals (€8) in this buzzy glass building where the green-and-white of Sporting dominate. The menu features fish (salmon, octopus rice and the like) or meat (grilled chicken, pork etc) as well as a soup starter.

The mixed fish (around €8.50) is a safe bet. Daily 11.30am–3pm & 7–10pm.

Plataforma Av Infante D. Pedro, Praia de Buarcos ☎ 233 422 055. Right on the beach at the Buarcos end, by the car park, this is great for fish and shellfish with a sea view. It's not cheap – around €25 a head – but the fish is straight from the boat, and the daily specials are chalked on a board, from barnacles to lobster. Daily 11am–midnight.

Volta & Meia Rua Dr. Francisco António Dinis 64 ☎ 233 418 381, ⓦ voltaemeia.com. This trendy new restaurant in the heart of town serves up wholesome international dishes and imaginatively crafted Portuguese favourites in an informal dining room. The focus is on using the best ingredients possible in nutritious filling mains (€5–9). Great home-style cakes and other desserts. Mon & Wed–Fri noon–3pm & 6.30pm–midnight, Sat & Sun noon–midnight.

DRINKING AND NIGHTLIFE

BARS AND CLUBS

Areias de Sabores Av do Brasil, Praia da Claridade ☎ 233 415 336. You can't miss this bar-restaurant right on the beach: just look for the area of palm trees that gives it its name. Food is pricey, but a sunset drink on the terrace is a treat. Mon & Wed–Sat 10.30am–midnight, Sun 10am–6pm.

Cristal Rua Académico Zagalo 28. This smart little bar is popular after dark for its lively streetside terrace – inside, DJs play music late into the night. Tues–Thurs 8pm–2am, Fri & Sat 8pm–4am.

NB Club Rua Cândido dos Reis ☎ 916 455 943. Inside the original casino building and opposite the new one, this is Figueira's top club venue, with two dancefloors usually playing house or disco, though it doesn't warm up until well after midnight. Opens for special events in addition to the Saturday party night. Sat 11pm–6am.

Perfumaria Pub Rua Dr. Calado 37 ☎ 233 426 442. On the scene for some 35 years, this is a laidback,

wood-panelled, arty bar on two levels connected by a spiral staircase, with a pool table and a good (if pricey) cocktail list. Daily 5pm–4am.

★**Zeitgeist Café** Rua Francisco António Dinis 82–84 ☎ 233 429 759. This modern café-bar serves a decent selection of cocktails, and there's a DJ set and live music most Wednesdays (from midnight). Daily 10am–4am.

ART AND ENTERTAINMENT

Casino Figueira Rua Dr. Calado 1 ☎ 233 408 400, ⓦ casinofigueira.com. One of the north's glamorous nights out, though not that exclusive. There's a fancy bar, all the usual games and slot machines, as well as frequent concerts and shows. Mon–Thurs & Sun 3pm–3am, Fri & Sat 4pm–4am.

Centro de Artes e Espectáculos Rua Abade Pedro ☎ 233 407 200, ⓦ cae.pt. This modern cultural centre near the municipal museum hosts some surprisingly big acts (from Stomp to the Moscow State Ballet) as well as arthouse movies, various events and exhibitions.

SHOPPING

Mercado Municipal Passeio Infante D. Henrique 42. At the southern end of the beach near the remains of an old sea fort, Forte de Santa Catarina, the Mercado Municipal is good for fresh produce as well as beachwear, lace, embroidery and other crafts. Daily: April–Sept 7am–7pm, Oct–March 7am–4pm.

DIRECTORY

Hospital Across the river from the town centre: Hospital Distrital da Figueira da Foz, Gala, São Pedro (☎ 233 402 000, ⓦ www.hdfigueira.min-saude.pt).

Police PSP, Rua de Mortágua ☎ 233 407 560.
Post office Passeio Infante Dom Henrique 41–42 (Mon–Fri 9am–6pm).

Montemor-o-Velho

Thirty-two kilometres west of Coimbra, the keep and crenellated silhouette of the castle at **MONTEMOR-O-VELHO** brood over the flood plain of the Mondego. After it was taken back from the Moors at the end of the eleventh century, Montemor became a favoured royal residence – it was here in 1355 that Dom Afonso IV met with his council to decide on the fate of Inês de Castro, and here, thirty years later, that João of Avis received the homage of the townspeople on his way to Coimbra to be acclaimed Dom João I. Despite this royal attention, the town never really prospered, and there's not a lot to modern-day Montemor-o-Velho, though come on the second and fourth Wednesday of the month and you can experience the sprawling morning **market** which spills across the plain in the lee of the castle.

Castelo de Montemor-o-Velho

Rua Condessa de Valenças • Tues–Sun: June–Sept 10am–7pm; Oct–May 9.30am–5.30pm • Free • ☎ 239 687 316

Originally built in the thirteenth century, but with sixteenth-century additions, the **Castelo de Montemor-o-Velho** has little to see inside, save a Manueline church with a beautiful wooden ceiling, said to have been designed by Diogo de Boitaca of Belém fame. However, the views of the surrounding countryside from the walkways are stunning, the lawns are a good place to let children run free and there's a nice terrace-café.

ARRIVAL AND DEPARTURE   MONTEMOR-O-VELHO

By bus Running roughly hourly on weekdays (less frequently at weekends), Moisés buses (☎ 239 629 114, ⓦ moises-transportes.pt) stop at Montemor-o-Velho en route between Figueira da Foz (30min) and Coimbra (1hr).

By train The nearest train station is 5km southwest of town at Alfarelos, with regular services from Coimbra (every 30min; 35min) and Figueira da Foz line (hourly; 30min). A taxi between Alfarelos station and Montemor-o-Velho costs around €6.

EATING

A Grelha Av Fernão Mendes Pinto 3148 ☎ 239 689 372. Below the castle on the main street, this is the best place for lunch or an evening meal. The speciality is *charruscão da quinta*, a giant mixed grill, although the fresh fish is also good – try the sardines. Mains around €9. Sun–Fri 11am–11pm.

3

Beira Alta and Beira Baixa

SORTELHA

Beira Alta and Beira Baixa

The two historic mountain provinces of Beira Alta (Upper) and Beira Baixa (Lower) feature some of the most spectacular landscapes in the country, from upland plains of enormous boulders to towering mountain peaks. This harsh but beautiful landscape was home to the mighty warrior Viriatus, who used its remote wildness to his advantage when repelling the Romans. Later, as Portugal strived for nationhood, many of the towns along and near the disputed border with Spain acquired mighty castles, still in existence today.

The ancient town of **Viseu** is the pleasant capital of **Beira Alta** province and the only place of any real size in the region. The fast east–west A25 links Viseu to the mountain-top town of **Guarda** – with Spain another 40km to the east – while to the north, between the highway and the Douro River, are the high-sited castle-towns of the **planalto** (or tableland). Some, like medieval, walled **Trancoso**, or the star-shaped fortress town of **Almeida**, are worth a day of anyone's time.

South of the main highway rises the **Serra da Estrela** mountain range, whose landscape is protected under the auspices of the **Parque Natural da Serra da Estrela**. Mountain villages, tumbling rivers and glacial valleys are linked by an extensive series of hiking trails, though there's also road access to the major settlements, notably the enjoyable small town of **Manteigas**. The park's southeastern boundary is flanked by the university town of **Covilhã**, handy for the winter ski fields and the ascent of mainland Portugal's highest mountain, Torre.

South and east of Covilhã lies the sombre plain of the lower province, **Beira Baixa**, whose parched landscape has its own mysterious beauty, dotted with cork, carob and olive trees. **Castelo Branco** in the south is the provincial capital, but most tourist attention is centred on the ancient hilltop villages rising dramatically from the surrounding plains, notably **Sortelha** and **Monsanto**. There's historic interest, too, in pretty **Belmonte**, halfway between Covilhã and Guarda, and in the extensive Roman remains at isolated **Idanha-a-Velha**. Meanwhile, in the border hills and reservoirs of the **Serra da Malcata**, there are hiking, biking and wildlife-spotting opportunities.

Viseu

On a plateau between the coast and the mountains, **VISEU** is one of Portugal's best-kept secrets. It was named "Viso" by the Romans because of its great views, and it was from an embankment just outside town that Viriatus, the head of a local independence movement, waged war against its Roman occupiers. According to most polls, modern Viseu has the best quality of city life in Portugal, and it doesn't take long to find out why. Its **old town**, clustered round a sturdy cathedral, is wonderfully unspoilt, while a burgeoning modern town is made up of wide avenues, leafy parks, a university and

NATURAL SWIMMING POOL, SERRA DA ESTRELA

Highlights

❶ Museu de Grão Vasco, Viseu Explore the works of one of Portugal's greatest artists in Viseu's fine museum. **See p.223**

❷ Trancoso This beautifully preserved walled town is the best overnight stop in the Beira Alta tableland. **See p.232**

❸ Fortified walls of Almeida The extraordinary fortifications here are built in the form of a twelve-pointed star. **See p.234**

❹ Hiking in the Parque Natural da Serra da Estrela The mountain town of Manteigas is the best base for *serra* walks, including the half-day circuit to the Poço do Inferno waterfall. **See p.242**

❺ Belmonte An unsung treasure of a town, from the picturesque castle to its restored Jewish quarter. **See p.247**

❻ Village stay, Sortelha Stay the night in one of the restored houses in this walled village. **See p.249**

❼ Monsanto Houses hewn out of granite cling to a boulder-strewn hillside below a formidable castle. **See p.251**

❽ Idanha-a-Velha A mysterious ancient village set amid the burned plains of Beira Baixa. **See p.253**

HIGHLIGHTS ARE MARKED ON THE MAP ON P.222

diverse array of shops, including the eye-popping **Palácio do Gelo** shopping centre. The town is also close to some of Portugal's best vineyards: fruity local Dão wines can be found in all of the restaurants. The main annual event is the agricultural fair-cum-festival of the **Feira de São Mateus**, which runs from mid-August until its climax on September 21 (Dia do São Mateus).

The old town

The lower town centres on the large square outside the town hall, known as the **Rossio**, from where you can climb up to the granite **Porta do Soar**, the fortified gateway to the jumble of alleys of the old town immediately behind the cathedral. **Rua Direita** offers a

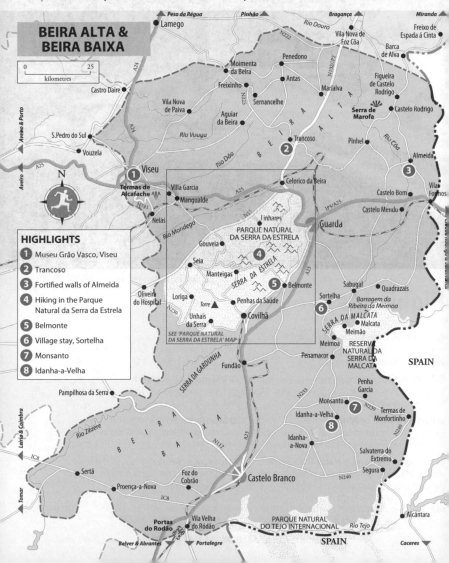

BEIRA ALTA & BEIRA BAIXA

0   25
kilometres

Peso da Régua   Pinhão   Bragança   Miranda
Lamego   Rio Douro   Freixo de Espada á Cinta
Vila Nova de Foz Côa   Barca de Alva
Moimenta da Beira   Penedono   Figueira de Castelo Rodrigo
Castro Daire   Freixinho   Antas   Castelo Rodrigo
Vila Nova de Paiva   Sernancelhe   Marialva   Serra de Marofa
Aguiar da Beira   Rio Vouga   Pinhel   Rio Côa   Almeida
S.Pedro do Sul   Trancoso   Vila Formoso
Vouzela   Pisão Dão   Castelo Bom
Viseu   Celorico da Beira   Castelo Mendo
Termas de Alcafache   Villa Garcia
Nelas   Mangualde   Linhares   Guarda
Rio Mondego   PARQUE NATURAL DA SERRA DA ESTRELA
Gouveia   Sabugal   Quadrazais
Seia   Barragem da Ribeira da Meimoa
Manteigas   Belmonte   SERRA DA MALCATA
Oliveira do Hospital   Loriga   Sortelha   Malcata
Torre   Penhas da Saúde   Meimão
Unhais da Serra   Covilhã   RESERVA NATURAL DA SERRA DA MALCATA
SEE 'PARQUE NATURAL DA SERRA DA ESTRELA' MAP   Meimoa   SPAIN
Penamacor
Pampilhosa da Serra   Fundão   Penha Garcia
SERRA DA GARDUNHA   Monsanto   Termas de Monfortinho
Idanha-a-Velha
Rio Zêzere   Idanha-a-Nova   Salvaterra do Extremo
Sertã   Foz do Cobrão   Segura
Proença-a-Nova   Castelo Branco
Portas do Ródão   Vila Velha do Ródão   PARQUE NATURAL DO TEJO INTERNACIONAL   Rio Tejo   Alcántara
Belver & Abrantes   Portalegre   SPAIN   Caceres

Aveiro & Porto
Aveiro
Leiria & Coimbra
Tomar

HIGHLIGHTS

1. Museu Grão Vasco, Viseu
2. Trancoso
3. Fortified walls of Almeida
4. Hiking in the Parque Natural da Serra da Estrela
5. Belmonte
6. Village stay, Sortelha
7. Monsanto
8. Idanha-a-Velha

GRÃO VASCO AND GASPAR VAZ

Little is known about Vasco Fernandes, universally known as **Grão Vasco**; it can only be said that he was born in or near the city of Viseu, probably in 1475, and that he died in 1542 or 1543. There was no major artist living in Viseu at the time to mentor the young Vasco Fernandes, so it's assumed that he trained in Lisbon or even abroad. Even more problematic for art historians is that virtually all the works associated with him – up to one hundred by some counts – have had to be identified by comparisons with the only two that he definitely signed, and with his known work on the surviving altar panels for Lamego and Viseu cathedrals. In many cases, his attributed works are collaborations, particularly with his Viseu contemporary **Gaspar Vaz** (1490–1569).

second approach to the old town, along a winding medieval street that mixes boutiques and gift shops with key-cutters, florists, grocers and undertakers, many of the buildings displaying sixteenth-century Manueline windows and coats of arms. At the northern end of Rua Direita – just beyond the theatre, on the main avenue – stands the other surviving town gate, the **Porta dos Cavaleiros**. Beyond here, on the outskirts of town, lies the **Parque do Fontelo**, a municipal park laid out across the woods and gardens of the old bishop's palace.

Museu Almeida Moreira

Rua Almeida Moreira • Tues 2–6pm, Wed–Sun 10am–1pm & 2–6pm • Free • ☎ 232 427 471, ⓦ cm-viseu.pt

Near the Rossio, up a tiled staircase on Rua Almeida Moreira, the attractive **Museu Almeida Moreira** has an eclectic display of Impressionist art, furniture and porcelain, displayed in the former home of Francisco Almeida Moreira, local collector and first director of the Museu de Grão Vasco (see below).

The Sé

Praça da Sé • Mon–Sat 9am–noon & 2–6pm, Sun 9am–noon & 2–7pm • Free

The wide cathedral square, Praça da Sé, is lined with noble stone buildings, including the striking twin-towered **Sé**, a Romanesque-Gothic cathedral built in the thirteenth century, but substantially added to over the years. The **interior** is truly striking, with a ribbed stone ceiling typical of Manueline architecture – look for the chunky knots in the ribs. After viewing the interior, head out to the neighbouring set of **cloisters**, where you can't fail to notice some very attractive *azulejo* panels.

Museu de Grão Vasco

Adro da Sé • Tues 2–6pm, Wed–Sun 10am–6pm • €4, free first Sun of the month • ☎ 232 422 049

Housed in the former Bishop's palace next to the cathedral, the **Museu de Grão Vasco** is Viseu's star attraction. It displays religious paintings and artefacts, including some beautiful Oriental porcelain and textiles, but the main draw here are the paintings by local boy Vasco Fernandes, better known as "The Great Vasco" (Grão Vasco), widely regarded as one of Portugal's best painters (see box above). His earliest work on display here is the fourteen panels tracing the *Life of Christ* (1501–06), which were commissioned for the altarpiece of Viseu cathedral – note the vivid *Adoration of the Magi* which topically presents Balthasar as a Brazilian-inspired Indian with feathered headdress (Brazil had been "discovered" by the Portuguese in 1500). His most famous work is *St Peter on His Throne* (1530–35) – the painting has a freestanding mounting that allows you to see how the original frame was dovetailed together. There are also many works created by Grão Vasco with collaborators, and several by **Gaspar Vaz**, mostly depicting the apostles.

ARRIVAL AND INFORMATION	VISEU
By bus The bus station is down Avenida Dr. António José de Almeida, a 5min walk north of the Rossio.	**Destinations** Castelo Branco (4 daily; 2hr 30min–3hr); Coimbra (approx hourly; 1hr 15min–1hr 25min); Covilhã

4

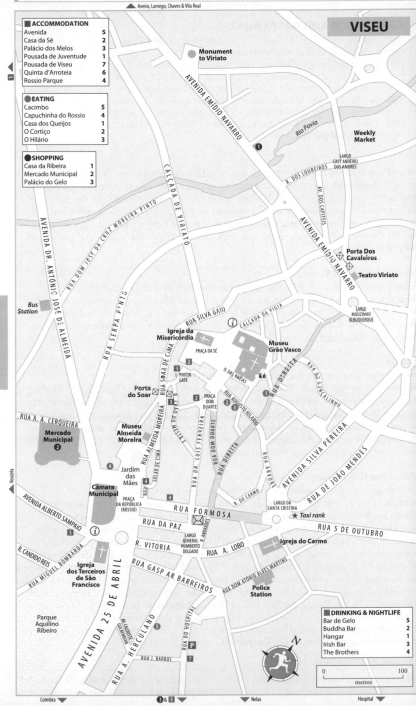

VISEU

▲ Aveiro, Lamego, Chaves & Vila Real

■ ACCOMMODATION
Avenida	5
Casa da Sé	2
Palácio dos Melos	3
Pousada de Juventude	1
Pousada de Viseu	7
Quinta d'Arroteia	6
Rossio Parque	4

● EATING
Cacimbo	5
Capuchinha do Rossio	4
Casa dos Queijos	1
O Cortiço	2
O Hilário	3

● SHOPPING
Casa da Ribeira	1
Mercado Municipal	2
Palácio do Gelo	3

■ DRINKING & NIGHTLIFE
Bar de Gelo	5
Buddha Bar	2
Hangar	1
Irish Bar	3
The Brothers	4

Monument to Viriato

Weekly Market

Porta Dos Cavaleiros

Teatro Viriato

Bus Station

Igreja da Misericórdia

Museu Grão Vasco

Porta do Soar

Sé

Museu Almeida Moreira

Jardim das Mães

Mercado Municipal

Câmara Municipal

Igreja do Carmo

Taxi rank

Igreja dos Terceiros de São Francisco

Parque Aquilino Ribeiro

Police Station

0   100
metres

Coimbra ▼   ❸ & ❺ ▼   Nelas ▼   Hospital ▼

(6 daily; 1hr 30min–2hr); Guarda (6 daily; 1hr 10min); Lisbon (hourly; 3hr 30min); Luso-Buçaco (5–7 daily; 1hr 45min); Mangualde (2–3 daily; 20min); Porto (approx hourly; 1hr 45min).

By car There's metered parking all over the centre, though there's a 4hr limit – it's better to use the open-air car park on Rua do Hospital, by the *pousada*, where there's no time limit and you pay when you leave.

Information The big modern regional turismo in Casa do Adro on Adro da Sé (mid-June to mid-Sept Mon–Fri 9am–6pm, Sat & Sun 9am–1pm & 2–6pm; mid-Sept to mid-June Mon–Fri 9am–6pm, Sat & Sun 9.30am–12.30pm & 1.30–5.30pm; ☎ 232 420 950, ⓦ turismodocentro.pt) has information about the whole region as well as free internet and wi-fi. The municipality also runs a small information booth on the Rossio (daily: April–Sept 10am–6pm; Oct–March 10am–5pm; ☎ 232 427 427), where the staff are a bit more knowledgeable about the city itself.

ACCOMMODATION

Avenida Av Alberto Sampaio 1 ☎ 232 423 432, ⓦ hotelavenida.com.pt. The location is excellent, and it exudes a stately air, with antiques and attractive photos in the communal areas. The smallish rooms and cramped bathrooms don't quite match up though, and there's street noise at the front. **€55**

★ **Casa da Sé** Rua Augusta Cruz 12 ☎ 232 468 032, ⓦ casadase.net. This small luxury hotel doubles as an antiques shop: the period furniture and fittings that decorate the communal areas and rooms are all for sale (from €30 to over €300). The rooms are varied, but all are plush with eighteenth-century flourishes – *azulejo*-lined bathrooms, period lamps, antique chairs and paintings. The superior Grão Vasco room is the one everyone wants. Small bar downstairs. **€80**

Palácio dos Melos Rua Chão do Mestre 4 ☎ 232 439 290, ⓦ hotelpalaciodosmelos.pt. Right by the Porta do Soar gate, this hotel offers boutique, city-centre accommodation with style. Superior rooms in the main building retain a period feel, some with balconies; there's a more contemporary style in the annexe and in the classy restaurant. There's also parking – follow signs for Centro Histórico and then Porta do Soar. **€67**

Pousada de Juventude Rua Aristides Sousa Mendes, Portal do Fontelo ☎ 232 413 001, ⓦ pousadasjuventude .pt. Viseu's backpacker choice is a plain, modern hostel by the main city park, a 10min walk northeast of Rossio, with five en-suite double rooms and mini-dorms with either four or five beds. Dorms **€12**; doubles **€27**

★ **Pousada de Viseu** Rua do Hospital ☎ 232 457 320, ⓦ pousadasofportugal.com. The country's largest *pousada* is a super-stylish conversion of a historic hospital, which opened in 1842 – photographs throughout the building show the work in progress. Spacious cherrywood rooms with granite bays – top-floor ones have terraces – overlook Viseu, while lounge seats occupy the soaring glass-topped cloister-courtyard. It's a very calm space, with an outdoor pool, titchy indoor pool plus gym, spa (in the former hospital chapel), restaurant and parking. **€105**

Quinta d'Arroteia Póvoa de Sobrinhos ☎ 232 478 450, ⓦ quintadarroteia.com. Exposed granite walls, a full-sized snooker table, an open fire in winter and a large pool in summer – perfect for a relaxing few days away from it all. It's located 3km east of town on the N16 (Mangualde road). Cash only. **€70**

★ **Rossio Parque** Rua Solar de Cima 55 ☎ 232 422 085, ⓦ pensaorossioparque.com. A real treat if you can land one of the better rooms since they're large and airy, some with a view of the Rossio (though the cheaper rooms are smaller and more cell-like). Breakfast is good, served in the popular restaurant downstairs. **€35**

EATING, DRINKING AND NIGHTLIFE

For the cheapest **eating**, look along Rua Direita where several old-fashioned *tascas* and *casas de pasto* turn out full meals at lunch for around €7. The presence of students means there's a fairly lively nightlife scene, with most of Viseu's late-night **bars** found in the old town near the Sé and Misericórdia churches.

RESTAURANTS

★ **Cacimbo** Rua Alexandre Herculano 95 ☎ 232 422 894, ⓦ cacimbo.pt. Run by a cackle of dinner ladies, this tiny contemporary takeaway with local food is tops for an utterly reliable meal. Choose from local sausages, octopus, chicken and custardy desserts, ideal for self-caterers. Mains are mostly €5–10. Daily 9am–10pm.

Capuchinha do Rossio Pr República (Rossio) 16 ☎ 232 435 710. Ask anyone in town to recommend the best place for a coffee and cake halt and they're more than likely to direct you to this long-established café opposite the town hall. The fried steak or omelette sandwiches (€2) make a filling lunch and the sweet fare is superb. Tues–Sat 8am–10pm.

Casa dos Queijos Trav Escadinha da Sé 9 ☎ 232 422 643. In the heart of the old town, the "House of Cheese" is a quirky tavern full of smelly mountain cheeses and – up a narrow, creaky staircase – a traditional restaurant serving grilled meat and fish. Mains €6–9. No credit cards. Mon–Sat 8am–8pm.

★ **O Cortiço** Rua Augusto Hilário 45 ☎ 232 423 853. This snug little restaurant boasts walls filled with messages

4

of praise from heartily satisfied customers. The food is strictly traditional and a cut above most in town, and though dishes (feijoada, local black pudding, roast goat and octopus) range from €11.50 to €20, many of them will feed two. The menu has a couple of interesting translations, such as "rotten codfish" for bacalhau. Tues–Sat 11am–11pm.

O Hilário Rua Augusto Hilário 35 ☎232 436 587. Named after a famous late-nineteenth-century fado singer from Viseu, this friendly place just down from the Sé serves tasty pataniscos (cod cakes) and steak in Madeira wine for €6.50–10. No credit cards. Mon–Sat 9.30am–11pm.

BARS AND CLUBS

★Bar de Gelo Palácio do Gelo, Quinta da Alagoa ☎232 483 931, ⓦbardegeloviseu.com. Viseu's coolest bar, despite being on the ground floor of a shopping centre. Why? Because the bar itself, the chairs and the sculptures are entirely made from permanently cooled ice imported from Canada: it costs €10 to enter, which gives you 30min inside and includes the hire of coat and gloves to keep you

warm at −9°C while you down one of their excellent cocktails from an ice glass. Daily 2pm–midnight.

Buddha Bar Largo da Misericórdia ☎232 469 531. Buddha-themed lounge bar where young professionals go to soak up the mellow atmosphere, with the occasional guest DJ playing the latest sounds – there's a great outdoor terrace. Daily noon–2am.

Hangar Estrada do Aeródromo ☎936 014 763. For the determined clubber, there's a cool converted aircraft hangar outside the city near the aerodrome (on the Lamego road) where house is played well into the morning. Fri–Sun 10pm–late.

Irish Bar Largo Pintor Gata 7–8 ☎232 436 135. This Irish-themed bar draws a mixed crowd and sits on a charming square that catches the afternoon sun, so it's ideal for an early evening drink. Also has occasional live music. Mon–Fri 9am–2am, Sat & Sun 1pm–2am.

The Brothers Rua Formosa 22 ☎232 440 391. Viseu's top coffee bar and after-dark venue is this permanently busy place with an old-fashioned vibe, decorated in the banknotes and tennis rackets of yesteryear. Coffee, tapas, wine, cocktails and live music are all on the menu. Daily 8.30am–2am.

SHOPPING

Casa da Ribeira Largo Nossa Sra Conçeição ☎232 429 761. The Casa da Ribeira is home to a foundation that aims to maintain traditional arts and crafts, and there's usually someone on hand to show you the working loom and potters' wheel. There's plenty of traditional work to purchase, from the typical black Tondela earthenware to Viseu stained-glass and decorative ironwork. There's also studio space where contemporary sculptors, basket-weavers and wood restorers work. Tues–Sat 9am–12.30pm & 2–5.30pm.

Mercado Municipal Av Dr. António José de Almeida. The two floors of the modern, domed Mercado Municipal, just west of Rossio, are interesting to visit though the range

of goods is limited. Mon–Fri 6.30am–7pm, Sat 6.30am–3pm.

Palácio do Gelo Quinta da Alagoa ☎232 483 900, ⓦpalaciodogelo.pt. Most Portuguese cities boast giant shopping centres these days, but this one is truly impressive, with a basement water feature that blasts a jet of water the full height of its seven floors. As well as the usual panoply of local and international shops, there are also six cinema screens, an ice rink, bowling alley, restaurants and the famous Bar de Gelo ice bar (see above). It's around 2km from the centre: walk past the pousada and keep going. Most shops daily 10am–11pm.

DIRECTORY

Hospital Hospital Distrital de Viseu, Avenida Rei Dom Duarte (☎232 420 500, ⓦwww.hstviseu.min-saude.pt).
Pharmacy Farmácia Confiança, Rua Formosa 10 (☎232 480 340).
Police Rua Dom António Alves Martins (☎232 480 380).

Post office Largo General Humberto Delgado (Mon–Fri 9am–7pm).
Taxis There's a rank at the end of Rua Direita at Largo Monzinho Albuquerque (☎232 429 453).

Mangualde and around

MANGUALDE, 15km east of Viseu along the A25, is a well-to-do town which traditionally flourished thanks to its position on the trading routes between the mountains and the coast. As a result, a tree-lined avenue leads into a centre of noble mansions, pick of which is the tiled baronial eighteenth-century **Palácio dos Condes de Anadia** on Largo Condes de Anadia (Mon–Fri 2–6pm; €5; ☎232 622 366), packed with period furniture and beautiful azulejos. Try and visit the town on a Thursday, when the weekly **market** enlivens the central streets.

Live Beach

Av Nossa Senhora do Castelo • Mid-June to mid-Sept daily 9am–7pm • €4.50, or €2.50 after 4.30pm • ☎ 932 543 488, ⓦ livebeach.pt

A side road just outside Mangualde is the unlikely setting for **Live Beach**, which locals proudly proclaim is Europe's first artificial beach, complete with 22,000 square metres of sand, salt water and all the paraphernalia associated with a real beach. In reality, it's just a large swimming pool faced by a flat bank of sand, but on a hot summer's day you'll certainly appreciate the space and chance to soak up the rays, while the bars and restaurant are good value. After 7pm the venue is also used for frequent party nights and concerts that go on until the early hours; check the website for details.

Termas de Alcafache

Spa Mid-April to mid-Nov • ☎ 232 479 797, ⓦ termasdealcafache.pt

A couple of kilometres northwest of Mangualde, the **Termas de Alcafache** sit by a Roman-era bridge which crosses the Rio Dão over a rock cleft. It's a charming little spot, with bathing in the gentle river, grassy picnic areas, a signposted riverside walk, and a couple of cafés that put out seats near the bridge. You can also take various treatments in the sulphurous waters at the **spa building** (see website for prices).

ARRIVAL AND INFORMATION

By bus There are 2–3 daily buses to Mangualde from Viseu (20min) and Guarda (50min).

By train The train station is 2km south of the town centre, on Rua da Estacão, with 6 daily services to Guarda (1hr) and two to Coimbra (1hr 35min).

MANGUALDE AND AROUND

Information Mangualde turismo, Largo Dr. Couto (Mon–Fri 9am–6pm, Sat 10am–noon & 2–4pm, Sun 10.30am–noon & 2–3.30pm; ☎ 232 613 980, ⓦ turismode mangualde.pt), is adjacent to the Câmara Municipal, and has printed local driving and hiking routes.

ACCOMODATION AND EATING

Casa de Darei Darei ☎ 232 613 200, ⓦ casadedarei.pt. A few kilometres out of Mangualde on the Penalva do Castelo road (north of the A25), in the midst of Dão valley vineyards, *Casa de Darei* is a working winery with B&B rooms, a private river beach and hiking and biking trails. **€100**

Moinhos do Dão c/o Café Pinheiro, Rua Principal 27, Tibaldinho ☎ 232 610 586, ⓦ moinhosdodao.nl. Around 10km west of Mangualde (it's signed from the Fagilde exit on the A25) down a 1.5km track (fine for cars, take it slowly), you'll find this supremely relaxed ecofriendly holiday retreat on the Rio Dão. The owners have fashioned cheerily rustic accommodation, mostly self-catering: as well as double rooms, there are studios in the old mill buildings (from €50) and log cabins (from €50). You might have to share a bathroom or fetch your own drinking water, and lighting is almost all by candle, but it's great fun for kids; while veggie-friendly meals are served communally most nights under the spreading fig tree. Six-night stays are preferred. Doubles **€50**

O Valério Rua dos Combatentes da Guerra 48, Mangualde ☎ 232 611 955. This rustic restaurant (meals from €15) serves portions that are legendary: never mind a *meia dose* (half-portion), it's the only place in Portugal we've found offering a quarter-portion of most dishes. Fab for pork, duck rice, eels and much more. Mon–Fri 11am–4pm & 8–10pm, Sat 11am–4pm.

Guarda

GUARDA, 70km east of Viseu, is Portugal's highest city, at an altitude of over 1000m. With a somewhat dour old town made of solid granite, its name is apt, as the original fortifications helped to guard the residents – and the mountain hinterland – from Spanish invaders. There's not much left of the fortifications, but the historical core retains an air of dignified grandeur, especially in the streets around the cathedral. Locals will tell you their city is *forte, farta, fiel e formosa* (strong, wealthy, loyal and beautiful), though come on an overcast winter's day and you may prefer to use *fria e feia* (cold and ugly). Either way, it makes a laidback base from which to explore the surrounding area.

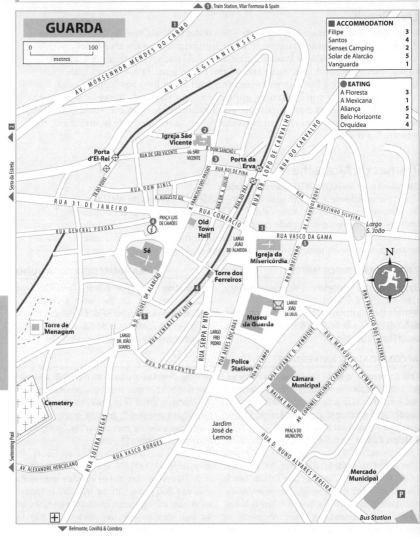

, Train Station, Vilar Formosa & Spain

GUARDA

0 — 100 metres

Serra da Estrela

AV. MONSENHOR MENDES DO CARMO

AV. B. V. EGITANIENSES

Igreja São Vicente

Porta d'El-Rei

RUA DE SÃO VICENTE

IG. SÃO VICENTE

R. DOM SANCHO I

Porta da Erva

RUA DR. LOPO DE CARVALHO

RUA DO CARVALHO

RUA DOM DINIS

R. FRANCISCO DOS PASSOS

RUA RUI DE PINA

RUA DR. A. JÚLIO

RUA DO PAZ

RUA

RUA MOUZINHO SILVEIRA

RUA DE ALBUQUERQUE

Largo S. João

RUA 31 DE JANEIRO

R. AUGUSTO GIL

RUA COMÉRCIO

RUA GENERAL POVOAS

PRAÇA LUÍS DE CAMÕES

Old Town Hall

LARGO JOÃO DE ALMEIDA

Igreja da Misericórdia

RUA VASCO DA GAMA

RUA MUZINHO

Sé

Torre dos Ferreiros

R. D. MIGUEL DE ALARCÃO

RUA TENENTE VALADIM

LARGO JOÃO DE DEUS

Museu da Guarda

RM FRANCISCO DOS PRAZERES

N

Torre de Menagem

LARGO DR. JOÃO SOARES

RUA SERPA PINTO

LARGO FREI PEDRO

RUA ALVES ROÇADAS

Police Station

RUA DO CAMPO

RUA MARQUÊS DE POMBAL

RUA DO ENCONTRO

Cemetery

RUA SOEIRA VIEGAS

RUA VASCO BORGES

Jardim José de Lemos

RUA IGARTE D. HENRIQUE

Câmara Municipal

R. BALHA E MELO

AV. CORONEL ORLINDO CARVALHO

PRAÇA DO MUNICÍPIO

Swimming Pool

AV. ALEXANDRE HERCULANO

RUA D. NUNO ALVARES PEREIRA

Mercado Municipal

P

Bus Station

Belmonte, Covilhã & Coimbra

The Sé

Praça Luís de Camões • Tues–Sun 9.30am–1pm & 2–5pm • €1

The heart of the historic centre is dominated by the granite hulk of the **Sé**, a cathedral whose construction took around 150 years to complete (1390–1540). Not surprisingly it embraces various architectural styles, from its fortress-like Gothic exterior – including grotesque gargoyles – to later Manueline flourishes inside, including enormous twisted pillars and an intricate network of stone vaulting supporting the ceiling.

The fortifications

Around the Sé you can see what's left of Guarda's original medieval fortifications. To the southeast lies the tall **Torre dos Ferreiros** (Blacksmiths' Tower; closed to the public),

while the medieval jumble of streets between the old city gates – the **Porta da Erva** and **Porta d'El-Rei** – make up the old Jewish quarter and are the city's most ancient and interesting. You can climb the steps of the Porta d'El-Rei for some distant *serra* views.

Torre de Menagem

Daily: April–Sept 10am–1pm & 2–6pm; Oct–March 9am–1pm & 2–5pm • Free • ☎ 217 224 372

In a lonely spot to the southwest of the Sé, the former keep, the **Torre de Menagem** is, at 1056m, the highest point in the city: there are fantastic views from the top, though it's a scramble up through a hatch in the roof to get there. Inside the keep you can watch a moderately engaging twenty-minute 3D film tracing the history of the fortifications and town. The views of the surrounding hills, with their communications antennae and wind turbines, and down onto the Sé, are equally spectacular from below the tower or from its roof.

Museu da Guarda

Rua Alves Roçadas 30 • Tues–Sun 10am–12.30pm & 2–6pm • €3 • ☎ 271 213 460

The city's history, art and culture is explored in the **Museu da Guarda**, housed in the seventeenth-century former seminary and bishop's palace. There are some interesting Roman and prehistoric objects, sculptures, paintings and historic furniture, though you'd probably only want to visit on a wet day.

ARRIVAL AND INFORMATION   GUARDA | **4**

By bus The bus terminal is on Rua Dom Nuno Álvares Pereira, below the market – it's a 15min (uphill) walk to the cathedral square.

Destinations Almeida (Mon–Fri 1 daily; 1hr 10min); Belmonte (3 daily; 25min); Braga (4 daily; 2–4hr); Castelo Branco (7 daily; 1hr 40min); Coimbra (1 daily; 2hr 45min); Covilhã (9 daily; 45min); Figueira de Castelo Rodrigo (Mon–Sat 1 daily; 1hr); Lisbon (8 daily; 4hr); Manteigas (Mon–Fri 2 daily; 1hr 20min); Sabugal (Mon–Fri every 2hr, Sat 1 daily; 45min); Seia (Fri & Sun 1 daily; 1hr 10min); Trancoso (1 daily; 1hr 35min); Vila Nova de Foz Côa (Mon–Fri 1 daily; 1hr 30min–2hr 15 min); Viseu (6 daily; 1hr).

By train Guarda's train station is 5km northeast and downhill from the town centre, out towards the A25

– there's a regular bus service up to the bus station, and taxis outside.

Destinations Coimbra (6 daily; 2hr 30min–3hr); Lisbon (6 daily; 4hr–5hr); Mangualde (6 daily; 1hr); Porto (7 daily; 3hr 35 min–4hr 25min).

By car There's metered parking (two-hour maximum) all over the town centre, though these spaces are free after 1pm on Saturday and all day Sunday. Alternatively, there's free parking at any time in the square outside the market or along Avenida dos Bombeiros Voluntários Egitanienses, to the north of the centre.

Information The turismo is on Praça Luís de Camões 21 (April–Sept daily 9am–1pm & 2–6pm; Oct–March Mon–Fri 9am–5.30pm, Sat & Sun 9am–12.30pm & 2–5.30pm; ☎ 271 205 530, ⊕ www.mun-guarda.pt).

ACCOMMODATION

Filipe Rua Vasco da Gama 9 ☎ 271 223 658. Van Gogh prints and marble in the public areas give way to more traditional rooms with parquet floors and heavy wood furniture, not to mention some rather garishly tiled bathrooms. Rooms 103, 104 and 108 have the best views of the Misericórdia church. €40

★**Santos** Rua Tenente Valadim 14 ☎ 271 205 400, ⊕ hotelsantos.pt. Stylishly built around – and through – part of the original medieval city walls, this hotel has a glass lift that rises past suspended internal terraces and exposed stonework to rooms that frame views of the cathedral or countryside within granite sills. Beds are comfortable, and a decent buffet breakfast is included.

Street parking almost outside (provided you can find your way there). €46

Senses Camping Quinta do Rio, Faia ☎ 910 488 800, ⊕ sensescamping.com. A 15min drive (or €15 taxi ride), 8km northwest of Guarda, this stylish "glamping" site is run by a former DJ and sculptor. The rural riverside site has ready-erected bell tents (for 2–4 people, from €35 a night) and luxury "safari" tents (perfect for families, from €45), as well as wooden cabins sleeping two (from €40) and plenty of tranquil pitches. There's an on-site pool, bar and restaurant serving home-grown organic veg, while activities on offer include yoga, massage, arts workshops and horseriding. Pitch from €3, plus €3 per adult

★**Solar de Alarcão** Rua D. Miguel de Alarcão 25–27 ☎271 214 392. Almost next to the Sé, this magnificent granite manor house dating back to the seventeenth century boasts atmospheric rooms with huge antique mirrors, chandeliers, carved wooden ceilings and vintage shutters, while secure parking is available in the courtyard. Advance reservations essential. No credit cards. €55

Vanguarda Av Monsenhor Mendes do Carmo ☎271 208 390, ✆naturaimbhotels.com. The rooms in Guarda's most contemporary hotel feature gleaming bathrooms and sweeping views. It's on the edge of town (a 15min walk), though drivers will pass it on the way up from the A25 – you can't miss the steel wave-style roof. €53

EATING

Most of the town's **restaurants** are to be found between the Sé and the Igreja de São Vicente, with half a dozen alone squeezed into narrow Rua Francisco dos Passos. There really isn't too much variety on offer, although regional specialities – *chouriçada* (spiced sausage), *morcela* (black pudding), *cabrito* (kid), *javali* (wild boar) and trout from Manteigas – are all widely available.

★**A Floresta** Rua Francisco dos Passos 40 ☎271 212 314. Warm and welcoming with tiled arches and colourfully laid tables, this is arguably Guarda's best place to eat. Admire the old photos of the town on the walls as you enjoy *chouriçada*, *morcela* and *cabrito*, all between €10 and €18 a plate. The tourist menu is great value at €7.50, and portions serve two. Daily noon–4pm & 7–11pm; Oct–April closed Mon.

A Mexicana Av Monsenhor Mendes do Carmo 7 ☎271 211 512. No Tex-Mex here, just creatively prepared and presented Portuguese food with a modern twist: fish with shrimp sauce, clam soup and the like for around €20. Mon, Tues & Thurs–Sun noon–3pm & 7–10pm.

Aliança Rua Vasco da Gama 8 ☎271 222 235. Packed through the week, serving local dishes for local people – so, lots of pork and not much finesse. A good stop for lunch though, with mains around €8.50. Daily noon–2.30pm & 7.30–9.30pm.

Belo Horizonte Largo de São Vicente 2 ☎271 211 454. A Guarda institution for over sixty years. A kindly old chef and matronly waitresses dish up meals from a menu strong on regional specialities (*chouriçada*, grilled goat, hare stew) that cost between €8.50 and €14. Tues–Sat 10am–midnight, Sun 10am–4pm.

Orquídea Pr Luis de Camões 19 ☎271 211 431. Possibly Guarda's best café, with a full range of tooth-rotting treats and inexpensive sandwiches. Daily 7.30am–midnight.

DIRECTORY

Hospital Hospital Distrital, Avenida Rainha Dona Amélia (☎271 200 200).
Pharmacy Farmácia Central, Largo Dr. João Almeida (☎271 211 972).

Police Largo Frei Pedro da Guarda (☎271 222 022).
Post office Largo João de Deus 22–24 (Mon–Fri 8.30am–6pm).
Taxis There's a rank on Rua Alves Roçadas (☎271 221 863).

The Beira Alta planalto

Beyond Guarda and the mountains lies the **Beira Alta** tableland, or *planalto*, with its ancient, scattered villages separated by mile after mile of boulder-strewn scrub. It's a land of harsh winters, where even potatoes were hard to grow – in bygone days, roast or dried chestnuts were used as a substitute, plucked from the large trees that signal the entrance to many of the villages. Still, there's a history here that's central to Portugal's identity, starting with the border castles that typify the eastern *planalto*, in particular the stunning star-shaped fortress of **Almeida**. Other castles and fortified settlements of particular interest are those at **Castelo Rodrigo**, to the north of Almeida, **Castelo Bom** and **Castelo Mendo** to the south, and **Penedono** and **Marialva** to the northwest. There's a bygone wealth in the region, too, that sprang from the merchant trade of medieval Jewish settlements like **Trancoso**, which is easily the most attractive small town in the *planalto*. With a car, you could see the whole region in a couple of days, with the best overnight stops at Trancoso, Almeida or Marialva, with its upmarket holiday village.

TRANCOSO (P.232) >

Trancoso

TRANCOSO is still largely contained within an attractive circuit of medieval walls. It's an uncommonly atmospheric little town, full of cobbled alleyways, well-kept gardens, shady squares and restored churches, all of which represent a tangible civic pride. It was here that Dom Dinis married the 12-year-old Isabel of Aragon in 1282, and later gave her the entire town as a gift; the wedding was solemnized in the small **Capela de São Bartolomeu**, not far from the town's surviving main gate, the **Portas d'el Rei**, which is surmounted by the Trancoso coat of arms.

Castelo

June–Sept daily 9.30am–12.30pm & 2–6pm; Oct–May Tues–Fri 9am–12.30pm & 2–5.30pm, Sat 9.30am–12.30pm & 2–5pm, Sun 9.30am–12.30pm & 2–4.30pm • Free

Like most *planalto* settlements, Trancoso grew up around its **castelo** – and like any town with a castle, trouble was generally to be expected from one quarter or another. Even once the Moors had been finally vanquished, there were still centuries during which armies came and went across the tablelands, using Trancoso as a base or a defensive position. It's surprising that the walls have survived at all – never mind that they remain in such good condition – while its well-restored towers can be seen from afar as you drive towards town.

Casa do Gato Preto

Largo Luís Albuquerque • No public access

Medieval Trancoso had a large Jewish community, which enjoyed a relatively harmonious existence here (as in the rest of Portugal) until the late fifteenth century when Dom Manuel I ordered Jews to be expelled from the country. The former rabbi's house in Trancoso is known as the **Casa do Gato Preto** (House of the Black Cat), its facade featuring a prominent Lion of Judah. Other buildings in the old town also display features that hark back to a prosperous Jewish community quietly going about its business until religion and politics stepped in. The oldest

TRANCOSO

0   100
metres

BANDARRA, THE COBBLER-PROPHET

The statue in Trancoso's Praça do Municipio might at first seem puzzling – a gentleman with a cobbler's last and shoe, and a rolled parchment in hand. It is the supposed likeness of the town's most famous son, **Gonçalo Bandarra**, a humble sixteenth-century shoemaker given to versifying – and, more to the point, coming up with **prophecies** that predicted the end of the world and the return of a hero-like king to save Portugal. The Inquisition took a dim view of this sort of thing and Bandarra was punished, and his verses banned, but the prophecies took on a life of their own with the later destruction of the cream of Portuguese nobility at the battle of Alcácer-Quibir in Morocco (1578). The young crusader-king Dom Sebastião – killed in battle – was held by many to be the hero-king who would one day return to free Portugal from the Spanish yoke, and Bandarra was posthumously elevated to the status of a Nostradamus figure. He was eventually honoured with a tomb in the town's Igreja de São Pedro.

houses, for example, have separate doorways, one for business and one used by the family, while others are marked with carved crosses, ordered by the Inquisition (active in Portugal from the 1530s onwards) to show that the inhabitants were "New Christian" converts.

ARRIVAL AND INFORMATION
TRANCOSO

By bus Buses stop near the Portas d'el Rei and the turismo. The easiest way to get to Trancoso by bus is the hourly service from Guarda to Celorico da Beira, from where there are two daily buses on to Trancoso. There are also services from Lamego (1 daily Mon–Fri; 1hr 30min), and Viseu (1 daily Mon–Fri; 1hr 10min), and express services to and from Bragança (1 daily Mon–Fri; 3hr) and Lisbon (1 daily Mon–Fri; up to 5hr).

By car Trancoso is 44km north of Guarda, just off the N102: parking isn't usually a problem, though things are much busier on market day, Friday.

Information The turismo is at Portas d'el Rei (June–Sept daily 9am–12.30pm & 2–5.30pm; Oct–May Tues–Fri 9am–12.30pm & 2–5.30pm, Sat 10am–12.30pm & 2–5pm, Sun 10am–12.30pm & 2–4.30pm; ☎271 811 147, ⓦ cm-trancoso.pt).

ACCOMMODATION

Convento Nossa Senhora do Carmo Freixinho ☎254 594 080, ⓦhoteldocarmo.com. For charming rural accommodation, drive 31km northwest of Trancoso on the N226 to the village of Freixinho, just beyond Sernancelhe. The hotel here is a splendidly restored sixteenth-century convent with simple, rustic rooms and a dining room situated in the former chapel. **€60**

★**Dom Dinis** Av da República 10 ☎271 811 525, ⓦdomdinis.net. Unpromisingly sited above the post office (follow signs for "Correios" to find it), this place picks up markedly inside where rooms have laminate floors, good bathrooms, central heating and wall-mounted fans. Not much of a view, it's true, but it puts on a great spread for breakfast (an extra €4.50 per person) – fresh orange juice, *presunto*, cake and home-made jam. Private parking. **€32**

Turismo de Trancoso Rua Prof Irene Avillez ☎271 829 200, ⓦhotel-trancoso.com. This swish four-star affair on the southeast edge of town (a 10min walk) seems out of place in homely Trancoso, and when guests are thin on the ground you'll rattle around the building. The 49 rooms are modern, there's a gym and sauna, and rates hit rock bottom in winter. **€65**

EATING

★**Àrea Benta** Rua dos Cavaleiros 30A ☎966 310 789. The town's best place to eat, offering handsomely prepared meals – say, grilled squid with coriander vinaigrette, *cabrito* (kid) with chestnuts, or black-pepper steak – in an arty setting. Most main courses cost €8–12. Tues–Sat 12.30–3pm & 7.30–10pm, Sun 12.30–3pm.

O Brasão Rua Adriano Moutinho 3 ☎271 811 767. A simple, traditionally tiled place, where you know what to expect the minute you walk through the door: steaks, grills, chops and sausages, with nothing costing much more than €9. Mon–Fri noon–2.30pm & 7–10pm, Sun noon–2.30pm.

O Museu Largo de Santa Maria de Guimarães ☎271 811 810. The dishes of the day in this homely place are good value at around €7; otherwise it's €9–12 for grilled meat and fresh fish, with advance orders required for the speciality fondues and raclettes. Tues–Sun noon–3pm & 7–10pm.

4

Penedono and around

Isolated **PENEDONO** has a simply wonderful castle, the lichen-encrusted **Castelo Roqueiro**, visible from afar as you drive closer. The castle emerges from its granite base, and from the top there are far-reaching views, although the Rapunzel-style turrets and sparsely railed walkways are not for the faint-hearted.

Antas

Six kilometres south of Penedono, on the Trancoso road, lies the small village of **ANTAS** – an *anta* is a megalithic tomb, and a modern recreation of one sits in the traffic roundabout on the main road. Follow the sign from here, through the village, east for 3.5km up a country road, and then park by the roadside sign for "Necrópole Megalítica da Lameia da Cima". It's a 1.5km walk from here up a dusty track to two megalithic **burial chambers**, 5000 years old, formed by overlapping stones. The capstones are missing, but it's a scene of some mystery, with sweeping views down across the distant plain. If you're not travelling to the Alentejo, where more dramatic examples await, it's worth the hour's walk there and back.

Marialva

The tiny village of **MARIALVA** is dominated by its castle: here, within a complete circuit of walls dating from 1200, lies a deserted village where town hall, prison, watchtowers and houses stand in ruins, overgrown with olive trees and overrun by geckos. Depopulated for obscure reasons, the only buildings restored in modern times are the sixteenth-century **Igreja Matriz**, the stone keep and a lone bell-tower, with a geometrically cobbled square and *pelourinho* below. A timetable of hourly visits is posted (daily 10am–6pm; €1.50), but in practice you can ask at the turismo, and they'll let you in to wander through the roofless buildings, haphazard streets and doorways leading nowhere – it's an eerie experience.

ARRIVAL AND INFORMATION   MARIALVA

By car There's no public transport to Marialva; it's 23km north of Trancoso, just off the N102, a quick drive on a good road; there's also a winding, 28km back-road route from Penedono via Mêda.

Information The concrete-box turismo (daily: June–Sept 10am–1.30pm & 3.30–7.30pm; Oct–May 9.30am–12.30pm & 2–6pm; ☎ 279 859 288, ⓦ cm-meda.pt) is below the castle gates.

ACCOMMODATION AND EATING

Casas do Côro Largo do Côro ☎ 917 552 020, ⓦ casasdocoro.pt. A mini-village-within-the-village of restored granite houses, terraces and gardens offering relaxed overnight accommodation. Minimalist chic vies successfully with four-poster beds and stone walls, while the outdoor pool is set amid manicured lawns and olive trees. Double rooms and independent houses with kitchenette (sleeping from four; €230) are available; breakfast is included, and there's a restaurant serving dinner. Doubles **€145**

Almeida and around

The most impressive of all Portugal's fortified border settlements is surely **ALMEIDA**, within a mere cannon-shot of Spain. It's a handsomely preserved eighteenth-century stronghold, laid out in the shape of a twelve-pointed star and well worth the effort of a visit – particularly during the twice-monthly **feiras** (on the eighth day and last Saturday), and the annual bash on September 1. The village within is charming, while a 3km walk around the **walls** – now overgrown with grass, and grazed by horses – shows you the true extent of the fortifications, though you can only really appreciate their shape by looking at the aerial-shot postcards sold in the gift shops. If your interest is piqued, two more frontier fortresses – **Castelo Bom** and **Castelo Mendo**, around 20km south of Almeida – are both also easily seen in a quick trip from town by car or en route to the A25, which they straddle.

Almeida played a key role in the **Peninsular War**. Besieged here in 1810 by the Napoleonic army, the garrison held out for seventeen days until, on July 26, a barrel of gunpowder ignited and began a devastating fire. That should have been it for the town, and the remaining survivors gave themselves up, but they were reprieved when the Duke of Wellington later arrived with full army in tow – the French army disappeared into the night and Almeida was saved.

The town defences

Almeida's walls enclose a warren of cobbled lanes and whitewashed houses, punctuated by airy squares – inside the walled town, you'll also find the village post office, a bank with ATM, a grocery shop and a few cafés. The main entrance is still through the original two consecutive defensive tunnel-gates of the **Portas de São Francisco**, complete with a wide, dry moat between inner and outer walls. Immediately inside the gates, to the left, are the long infantry barracks, while a right turn, past the gardens and along the walls, leads to the **Casamatas** (opposite the fire station), an underground storage area with a capacity for five thousand men and their supplies.

You'll easily find your way up to what's left of the **castle**, blown up in 1810, the foundations now exposed under a modern walkway. Behind here, in one of the star-points, is the **picadeiro**, the restored cavalry barracks and horse-training area, whose stables offer short riding lessons and horse-and-buggy rides around town.

Castelo Bom

Tiny **Castelo Bom** preserves walled fortifications above an ancient village just 7km west of the Spanish border at Vilar Formoso, and 20km south of Almeida. The Duke of Wellington's forces secured the whole area during 1812 and 1813 while advancing into Spain, with Wellington himself headquartered at a house in a nearby village – hence the brown tourist sign with the incongruous English place-name "Wellington".

Castelo Mendo

Four kilometres west of Castelo Bom, and 20km south of Almeida, the preserved medieval village of **Castelo Mendo** is a gem. Two headless Celtic granite pigs guard the main gateway, through which cobbled streets twist up to a grassy knoll topped by a roofless church and the sketchy remains of the castle keep. It's a glorious spot, sitting on the lip of a sheltered bowl of land, with views across the undulating countryside.

ARRIVAL AND INFORMATION

By bus Buses stop in the square outside Almeida's main gate, with services from Guarda (Mon–Fri 1 daily ; 1hr 10min), and Sabugal/Castelo Branco (Mon–Fri 3 daily; 1hr 30min–2hr).

By car Almeida is 45km northeast of Guarda; drivers can

ALMEIDA AND AROUND

park in the square outside the main gate.

Information The turismo is at Portas de São Francisco, just inside the inner gate (Mon–Fri 9am–12.30pm & 2–5.30pm, Sat, Sun & hols 10am–12.30pm & 2–5.30pm; ☎ 271 570 020, ⓦ cm-almeida.pt).

ACCOMMODATION AND EATING

Accommodation within Almeida's walls is not too badly priced, given the location and atmosphere. There are cheaper rooms outside the walls, by the petrol station, just down from the main gate, though the main road can be noisy; ask for a room at the back. If you don't eat in the *Fortaleza*, you'll probably end up down here anyway as both cheaper hotels have good-value **restaurants**.

A Muralha Bairro de São Pedro ☎ 271 571 744, ⓦ amuralha.pt. Opposite the petrol station, with decent en-suite rooms that have French windows opening on to balconies. The restaurant downstairs serves a reputable steak. **€40**

★**Casa Pátio da Figueira** Rua Direita 48 ☎ 963 367 237.

Four refined rooms nestled in a charming townhouse around the corner from the *Fortaleza*. It's very pretty inside, with exposed stone walls and tiled floors, and there are lovely gardens and a secluded swimming pool. Cash only. **€80**

Fortaleza de Almeida Rua das Muralhas ☎ 271 574 283, ⓦ hotelparadordealmeida.com. Formerly the *pousada*, this

was built strictly for the views, across the rooftops to Spain. Inside it's a comfortable 1980s' rustic pastiche – agricultural equipment on the walls and 21 rooms with four-posters and enclosed latticework balconies. A decent restaurant (mains around €18) serves regional cuisine, and shares the views with a shaded terrace. There's parking outside – follow the signs. Restaurant daily noon–10pm. **€85**

Granitus Largo 25 de Abril ☎ 271 574 834. A down-to-earth place, just outside the main gate, with a stand-up local bar where the bus drivers and policemen often congregate. Inexpensive meals are served in the dining room, and there are a few café tables outside. You'll eat a good dinner for €16, lunch for less. Daily 11am–11pm.

Morgado Bairro de São Pedro ☎ 271 574 412. At this slightly frayed guesthouse adjacent to the petrol station, the prevailing colours are brown (bathroom tiles and furniture) and yellow (bedspreads). That said, it has a welcoming restaurant with fresh fish on the menu most days. **€40**

Castelo Rodrigo and around

The obvious route north of Almeida is up the N332 towards the Douro. After 20km – and 3km before the town of Figueira de Castelo Rodrigo – look for the signs to **CASTELO RODRIGO**, a fortified medieval settlement cresting an isolated hill. In recent years, its huddled houses and cobbled alleys have been fully restored. Inevitably, there are tour buses, a couple of gift shops and cafés, and a slightly unreal, slightly sterile air, but it's a great place to spend a couple of hours, with the terrific views on all sides being the main distraction.

The village is surrounded by a new road, punctuated by three surviving thirteenth-century gates – it's best to park outside if you have a car. Near the southeastern **Porta do Nascente** – facing the town of Figueira below – an inscription above the cemetery warns: "Consider with attention this place of terror, the end of this duplicitous world's vanities", a possible allusion to the castle's long and often violent history. Suitably chastened, enter the village, where the gatehouse now contains the *Sabores do Castelo* shop and bar, selling cheese, honey, smoked meats, local wines and liqueurs.

The castle

Daily: Oct–May 9am–6pm; June–Sept 9am–8pm • €1; pay the at the adjacent turismo

Castelo Rodrigo's **castle** is built on a rocky outcrop, and remains impressive despite having been torched and sacked in the seventeenth century. The admission fee allows you to scramble round the hollow ruins, but there isn't really a lot to see; the view of the surrounding hills is quite impressive, however.

Figueira de Castelo Rodrigo

Below Castelo Rodrigo, you'll inevitably pass through the bigger town of **Figueira de Castelo Rodrigo**, and it's an attractive enough place with a broad central square with fountains and a large church topped by a stork's nest. It provides a minor route to Barca d'Alva (the last settlement on the Douro River), a wonderfully scenic 20km to the north, or it's 35km from Figueira to Vila Nova de Foz Côa and its rock carvings.

Serra de Marofa

To or from Castelo Rodrigo, you might as well divert up to the **Serra de Marofa** viewpoint – signposted at the Pinhel junction on the Almeida road – an antennae-festooned summit, with a Rio-like Christ in Benediction looking out over Castelo Rodrigo, with Spain beyond.

ARRIVAL AND INFORMATION

CASTELO RODRIGO AND AROUND

By car Without your own car, Castelo Rodrigo is an unlikely visit. There is a bus from Guarda (1 daily Mon–Sat; 1hr 15min), but this runs only to Figueira de Castelo Rodrigo (ie not the restored village) and then on to Foz Côa.

Information Castelo Rodrigo turismo is next door to the castle (daily: Oct–May 9am–6pm; June–Sept 9am–8pm; ☎ 271 311 277, ⏥ cm-fcr.pt). Figueira de Castelo Rodrigo turismo is on Largo Mateus de Castro (Mon–Fri 9am–12.30pm & 2–6pm; ☎ 271 311 365).

ACCOMMODATION

★**Casa da Cisterna** Rua da Cadeia 7, Castelo Rodrigo ☎ 917 618 122, ⓦ casadacisterna.com. Up at the castle you'll find this stylish, designer conversion of a village house, next to the old water cistern. Accommodation is split between the main house, garden and annexe, and prices vary according to room, but all are lovely, whether stone-walled mezzanine suite or rustic-chic romantic bolthole. **€65**

Falcão de Mendonça Rua Álvaro Castelões 20, Figueira de Castelo Rodrigo ☎ 271 319 200 ⓦ falcaodemendonca.com. Just off the town square near

the turismo stands a refurbished 1820 mansion offering the best lodgings in town. There's a small covered swimming pool, courtyard bar and a silver-service atmosphere at the hotel's moderately priced restaurant, a formality ruined slightly by the "Greatest Hits" radio piped in the background. **€75**

Transmontano Av 25 de Abril 66, Figueira de Castelo Rodrigo ☎ 271 313 263. The budget choice in town, at the top end of Figueira's square, with scuffed en-suite rooms on three floors, lackadaisical service and an inexpensive restaurant. **€40**

The Serra da Estrela

The peaks of the **Serra da Estrela** are the highest mountains in Portugal, rising dramatically to the southwest of Guarda. The range is basically a high alpine plateau cut by valleys, from within which emanate two of the country's greatest rivers, the Mondego and Zêzere – the only rivers to begin and end in Portugal rather than crossing the border from Spain. The mountains – snowcapped into late spring – soon impose themselves upon any approach, while the lower flanks on either side of the range reveal a patchwork of small villages that retain much charm. The odd Portuguese visitor comes to the *serra* to **ski** in winter; many more clog the narrow roads in summer looking for picnic space. A network of **hiking trails** covers the peaks and valleys, though relatively few people take to the paths to explore the region.

Around 1000 square kilometres of the mountain range is protected as the **Parque Natural da Serra da Estrela**, which stretches for around 55km from north to south and around 25km east to west at its widest point. From the west, access is from the N17, through the small service towns of **Seia** or **Gouveia** and then on over the high mountain roads, deep into the park; the smaller western-flank villages of **Linhares**, **Folgosinho** and **Loriga** offer a prettier introduction to the mountain landscape. The valley town and spa of **Manteigas**, pretty much in the centre of the park, is the single best base for hiking and touring, while the tiny ski industry – such as it is – centres on the road between 1993m **Torre**, the country's highest peak, and **Covilhã**, south of Manteigas. Covilhã lies just outside the park proper, and is the only town of any size in the region.

GETTING AROUND

THE SERRA DA ESTRELA

By public transport Covilhã and Guarda can be reached by train or bus, and there are bus services to Seia and Gouveia, but none across the park itself or to any of the more interesting villages, except Manteigas.

By car Drivers could see all the sights in a couple of days

– a good route starts from Seia, climbs to the heights of Torre, cuts down the glacial valley road to Manteigas, then switchbacks west again to Gouveia and north to the pretty villages of Folgosinho and Linhares.

MOUNTAIN LIFE

In the last decades of the twentieth century, and to a lesser extent more recently, life in the mountains changed almost beyond recognition. Farmers have moved from **stone mountain houses** to more modern dwellings on the valley floor while many of the former intensively cultivated Zêzere valley terraces have been abandoned in favour of spreading **pine plantations**. Meanwhile local village production is often now directed towards tourists – delights such as the local *queijo da serra*, an unctuous **mountain cheese**, as well as rye bread, fruit preserves, **honey** from the fertile valleys and blankets made from the wool of grazing upland sheep are all widely available.

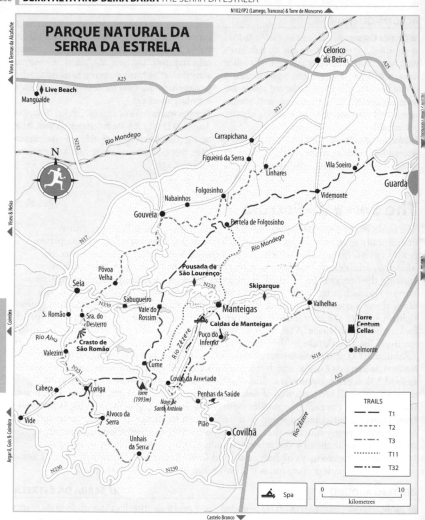

PARQUE NATURAL DA SERRA DA ESTRELA

Linhares

The most historic village on the western flank of the Serra da Estrela is **LINHARES**, 6km off the N17 (20km southwest of Celorico da Beira and the A25) and 810m up, high on a slope overlooking the Mondego valley. It's a highly picturesque jumble of old stone houses linked by steps and cobbled alleys, offering fabulous views across the plains below. Near the parish church a path branches off towards Figueiró da Serra to the west (part of the T2 hiking trail), following a section of an old, paved **Roman road** – it's a lovely route, though the next stop, Folgosinho (see opposite), is around three hours away.

Castelo

Mon–Fri 10am–1pm & 2–6pm • Free

Built on an enormous outcrop of granite at the top of the village, the twin towers of the **castelo** date from 1169 when Linhares was a strategic military outpost. One of the towers

had a clock added in the seventeenth century – you can go inside the tower and see its granite weights, while there are tremendous views to enjoy from high on the castle walls.

ACCOMMODATION AND EATING   LINHARES

Cova da Loba Largo da Igreja, Linhares ☎ 271 776 119, ⓦ covadaloba.com. Opposite the church, this is a surprisingly modern and trendy-looking restaurant with a range of well-presented meat and fish dishes at €13–15; the trout is always good and there's usually a vegetarian option. Mon, Tues & Fri–Sun 11.30am–midnight.

Quinta do Adamastor Rua do Hospital 215, Figueiró da Serra ☎ 271 770 010, ⓦ quintadoadamastor.com. With lovely gardens, an impressive outdoor pool and restaurant, this is a wonderful rural escape 7km

southwest of Linhares on the road to Folgosinho, set in a nineteenth-century stone mansion with ornate fittings. Cosy rooms with scrubbed wood floors come with a/c and minibars. **€90**

Taberna do Alcaide Linhares ☎ 271 776 578, ⓦ tabernadoalcaide.serradaestrela.com. This country tavern serves local cheese, *serra* lamb and the like at around €9 for a main course, though it only opens at weekends. It also has three pretty if simple rooms, two en suite. Restaurant Sat & Sun 9am–midnight. **€40**

Folgosinho

FOLGOSINHO, 14km southwest of Linhares along a bumpy country lane (head back towards Carrapichana and turn left before the N17), is 100m higher than Linhares, with a mountain tang to the air, and is topped by not so much a castle as a perky, turreted clock tower clinging to the crags. There's a tree-shaded village square and a central kernel of granite houses, a few of which tout local produce and woolly jumpers (though it's shepherds' cloaks that are the more traditional habit). It's 11km by road to Gouveia from Folgosinho, or around three hours' walking on the T2 trail, whose paint-marks you can pick up in the village.

EATING   FOLGOSINHO

O Albertino Largo do Adro de Viriato 8 ☎ 238 745 266, ⓦ oalbertino-folgosinho.com. An earthy restaurant with a very meaty menu (suckling pig, wild boar, goat and veal dominate), with most dishes accompanied by *arroz de cabidela* (rice cooked with blood). Mains €11–17.50. Tues–Sat noon–4pm & 7.30–10.30pm.

O Mocas Rua do Outão 8 ☎ 927 974 263. Cheery *Mocas* has a downstairs café and upstairs restaurant, with an

inexpensive menu of half a dozen daily dishes (around €8) including the speciality sausage, *morcela*. The unusual name of the restaurant, which means "stubs", is explained (in English) on the plaque outside, but it might have been better if they had kept it to themselves, since it's a reference to a particularly nasty kitchen accident that befell the present owner's grandfather. Mon & Wed–Sun 11am–11pm.

Gouveia

GOUVEIA is a small provincial town of well-kept gardens and terrace-cafés, with a striking blue-tiled Baroque **Igreja de São Pedro** – everything of interest is within five

---

HIKING IN THE PARQUE NATURAL DA SERRA DA ESTRELA

In theory, various **hiking trails** cut across the Parque Natural da Serra da Estrela, though it's much harder to walk in the *serras* than it should be. The **park information offices** tend not to have English-speaking staff, and it's rare for the personnel to have any first-hand experience of the trails – often, you'll simply be pointed to dated or unreliable hiking guides and maps. Moreover, the **waymarking** (red-and-yellow paintmarks) in the park is unreliable: maintenance doesn't appear to be a priority and signposting at village trailheads is woeful or nonexistent. Well-prepared walkers will need to be self-sufficient in order to complete the longer trails. The best time to walk is from May to October. For the **day-hiker**, who just wants a taste of the mountains, try the easy circular route from Manteigas to the Poço do Inferno waterfall (see box, p.242). Alternatively, you could tackle a short stretch of the lower-level T2 – Linhares to Gouveia, via Folgosinho, is a good full day's walk, with facilities in each place – though you'll need to take a taxi back to your starting point.

minutes' walk of the church. Although there are few onward buses into the mountains, it makes a good and lively base from which to explore the Serra da Estrela villages if you have a car. There's also a bustling Thursday **market**.

Museu de Abel Manta

Ria Direita 45 • Tues–Sat 9.30am–12.30pm & 2–6pm, Sun 10am–noon & 2–5pm • Free • ☎ 238 493 648, ⓦ cm-gouveia.pt

Set inside seven small rooms of an interesting seventeenth-century former winery, the **Museu de Abel Manta** houses a wide selection of contemporary Portuguese art donated by Gouveia-born artist and architect Abel Manta (1888–1982). Not many of the works are particularly memorable, one exception being the pieces by the man himself. Abel Manta lived and worked in Lisbon, Paris and Funchal, and his evocative paintings beautifully capture some of the towns and characters he encountered.

ARRIVAL AND INFORMATION   GOUVEIA

By bus Buses pull up in the centre of town, with regular services to Coimbra (3–4 daily; 2hr), Lisbon (3–4 daily; 4hr 30min) and Seia (Mon–Fri 3 daily; 30min).

Information The modern turismo is in the Jardim da Ribeira (daily 9.30am–12.30pm & 2–6pm; ☎ 238 083 930, ⓦ cm-gouveia.pt), a small park below the market building.

ACCOMMODATION AND EATING

Monteneve Av Bombeiros Voluntários 12 ☎ 238 490 370, ⓦ montenevehotel.com. In operation for just over a decade, this hotel within two restored houses is the best deal in town, with well-dressed en-suite rooms above a café. The entrance is a little tricky to find even though it's on the main through-road. **€55**

O Júlio Rua do Loureiro 11A ☎ 238 498 016. This strictly traditional place offers dishes like wild boar with onions, rabbit stew, or local kid and game from around €10 – prices are a little steep for what you get. Mon &

Wed–Sun noon–3pm & 7–9.30pm.

★ **Quinta das Cegonhas** Nabainhos ☎ 238 745 886, ⓦ cegonhas.nl. There are two double rooms and two apartments (€65) to rent at this Dutch-owned seventeenth-century manor house, which revels in its country location (6km east of Gouveia on the Folgosinho road) and sweeping views. There's also a shady campsite (open all year), swimming pool, bar and restaurant. Tent pitch **€3**, plus **€4** per adult, doubles **€60**

Seia and around

The largest town on the western side of the Serra da Estrela, **SEIA**, 16km southwest of Gouveia, is well located as a base for mountain trips – though only if you have your car, as there's no onward public transport. The town centre is small indeed, and not particularly historic, but where Seia scores is its proximity to smaller, higher villages, such as **Sabugueiro**, and for the direct road route up to Torre peak, 30km to the southeast (see p.244).

Museu do Pão

Tues–Fri & Sun 10am–6pm, Sat 10am–10pm • €5 • ☎ 238 310 760, ⓦ museudopao.pt • The museum is a steep 1km above the town centre, on the Sabugueiro road

The quaint **Museu do Pão** features rustic reconstructions of bread-making equipment and a traditional mill – if nothing else, you could emerge knowing the word for bread in 125 languages. The terrace café has excellent views and there's also a decent restaurant and traditional *mercearia* (grocers) where you can buy home-made bread.

Sabugueiro

At a lofty 1050m, **SABUGUEIRO**, 10km east of Seia, is said to be Portugal's highest village, a cachet that has led to some rampant overdevelopment, certainly along the main road, which is now nothing more than a drive-through shopping experience. Mountain cheese, ham, rye bread, honey, leather coats, woolly slippers and fluffy mountain-dog toys are piled high in the rash of souvenir shops – real mountain-dog pups (*cães*) are sold as a sideline, yelping piteously in tiny roadside cages. The surviving **old village** is at the

bottom of the hill, near the Rio Alva. The slate-roofed stone cottages are in varying states of repair, although many have been restored and can be rented for a night's stay, but you'd do far better to visit on a day-trip from Seia or press on to Manteigas, 25km to the east.

ARRIVAL AND INFORMATION

SEIA AND AROUND

By bus Seia's bus station is on the ring-road at the bottom of town, a few hundred metres from the centre.

Destinations Coimbra (3–6 daily; 1hr 45min); Covilhã (Mon & Sun 1 daily; 1hr 40 min); Gouveia (Mon–Fri 3 daily; 30min); Guarda (Fri & Sun 1 daily; 1hr 10min); Lisbon (3 daily; 3 hr 30min–4hr).

Information Seia's turismo is opposite the market on Rua Pintor Lucas Marrão (Mon–Sat 9am–12.30pm & 2–5.30pm, Sun 9am–1pm; ☎ 238 315 336).

ACCOMMODATION AND EATING

Camelo Av 1 de Maio 16, Seia ☎ 238 310 100, ⊛ eurosol.pt. Agreeable, central three-star hotel with brightly coloured rooms, manicured grounds with a swimming pool, and a bar and restaurant. Follow the road through town (São Romão direction) to find it. €53

★ **Casas da Ribeira** Pôvoa Velha ☎ 238 311 221, ⊛ casasdaribeira.com. Ten delightful stone-built houses in an ancient village, 5km east of Seia and signposted off the Sabugueiro road, ranging from studios to three-bed cottages, all equipped with kitchens, central heating, wood-burning stoves and fireplaces. A breakfast of fresh bread, ham, cheese and preserves is delivered to your door in the morning.

Minimum two-night stay; no credit cards. Studios €60

Estalagem de Seia Av Dr. Afonso Costa, Seia ☎ 238 315 866. Eighteenth-century townhouse with a granite staircase and a pleasant garden pool. Features and furnishings are a bit long in the tooth, but the relatively low price reflects this. It's just off the roundabout by the post office. No credit cards. €60

Restaurante Regional da Serra Av dos Combatentes da Grande Guerra 12–14, Seia ☎ 238 312 717. Just off the bottom of Praça da República, this place serves river trout, *cabrito* (kid), sausages and other tasty regional fare, with mains at €7–10. Things get busy around lunchtime. Daily noon–11pm.

Loriga

The minor N231 road south of Seia (signposted initially to São Romão) winds for 18km to **LORIGA**, sitting at 770m above agricultural terraces that slope steeply down to the Loriga River. The fast-flowing water once powered woollen mills, and still irrigates the fields, while the settlement itself dates back at least to Roman times – there are traces of the Roman road signposted near Loriga and at **Valezim** just to the north.

INFORMATION

LORIGA

Information Loriga turismo is on the N231 into the village (Tues–Sat 9am–12.30pm & 2–5.30pm, Sun 9am–1pm; ☎ 238 951 175, ⊛ cm-seia.pt).

ACCOMMODATION

Casa do Meio da Vila Trav do Figueiredo 6 ☎ 238 953 401, ⊛ casadomeiodavila.net. Double rooms in a restored rustic stone village house; there's a two-night minimum stay (three in high season); the website also features other larger houses that sleep up to ten. €55

O Vicente Rua Gago Coutinho 2 ☎ 238 953 127, ⊛ ovicente.com. Out on the N231, this welcoming place doubles as a crafts shop and restaurant, with decent rooms upstairs (three-night minimum stay in high season). €55

Manteigas

If there's one town in the Serra da Estrela with a true mountain air it's **MANTEIGAS**, 700m up, whose whitewashed houses run along the contour above the Rio Zêzere. The approach from any direction is dramatic: from Sabugueiro and the west the road winds down in convoluted switchbacks; from Belmonte and the east the river scenery is at its most bucolic; while from the south there is the breathtaking descent down the glacial valley of the Rio Zêzere. The latter route brings you into town past the therapeutic spa of **Caldas de Manteigas** and to the fertile valley bottom of the Zêzere, with Manteigas itself spreading across the steep slope opposite.

4

There's no public transport further into the park from town, but with a car you can use Manteigas as a base to visit Torre, the glacial valley and ski fields, and the nearby villages. The town is on two of the official **walking trails**, but local routes are on the tough side since – south and west at least – you have to climb steep and far to get anywhere. There's one easy circular walk to the Poço do Inferno (see box below); most other routes are point-to-point, requiring a taxi ride out or back, which can be easily arranged.

Skiparque

Largo Relva da Reboleira Sameiro • Daily 10am–5pm • Half-day activities and ski lessons start at €25; 4hr guided walks cost €10 a person (min four people) • ☎ 275 980 090, ⓦ skiparque.pt

The **Skiparque** is an artificial winter-sports slope and adventure park 8km east of Manteigas down the N232 Belmonte road. It's open all year round for dry-slope skiing and snowboarding, plus everything else from mountain-biking to hang-gliding and guided walks, as well as swimming at a river beach; there's also a campsite (see p.244), restaurant and bar. It pays to call ahead to book activities since it's either heaving (at winter and weekends) or otherwise deserted.

ARRIVAL AND INFORMATION   MANTEIGAS

By bus Bus services to Manteigas are limited to weekdays (though not public holidays) and are liable to change. Manteigas turismo can confirm times, but currently there are buses to/from Guarda (Mon–Fri 1 daily; 1hr 20min), Covilhã (Mon–Fri 1 daily; 1hr 30min) and Belmonte (Mon–Fri 1 daily; 45min).

Information The English-speaking turismo (Aug Wed–Sun 9am–1pm & 2–6pm; rest of the year Tues–Sat 9am–1pm & 2–6pm; ☎ 275 981 129, ⓦ cm-manteigas.pt) is below GALP petrol station, opposite a small park and café.

ACCOMMODATION

★**Albergaria Berne** Quinta de Santo António, Manteigas ☎ 275 981 351, ⓦ albergaria-berne .planetaclix.pt. A friendly family takes good care of you in this simple, pine-furnished inn where the seventeen rooms have their own baths. There's a large swimming pool and a moderately priced restaurant where you can tuck into local

---

A CIRCULAR WALK FROM MANTEIGAS TO THE POÇO DE INFERNO

The best circular walk **from Manteigas** is to the **Poço de Inferno waterfall** and back, which takes around four hours. Most of the paint-mark trail signs are missing or faded, but it's a straightforward route with some gorgeous views. The walk starts in the Zêzere valley bottom, from the small bridge and picnic area reached down the steep road behind the turismo in Manteigas.

Cross the bridge, turn left (signposted "Leandres") and walk for 500m along the road, past the recycling plant, before turning right onto a clear forestry track. Keep straight on, ever upwards through the woods – the first yellow paint-sign is on a tree on the right-hand side (6min) and there isn't another until you reach a ruined white house in a clearing (45min) marked with the words "Matas Nacionais".

Five minutes' walk after the house is the only turn off the main path – to the left (with paint-marks before and after the turn). In another fifteen minutes the path ends at a bend in a tarmac road. Walk uphill (there's a yellow paint-mark almost immediately) and it's twenty minutes further up the road to the **Poço do Inferno**, "Hell's Well", where the Leandres River pours down the narrow gorge into clear pools overlooked by viewing platforms.

To return, follow the minor road around past the falls, heading back towards Manteigas. This road actually runs steadily down to Caldas de Manteigas, though this would be a long (8km) and unnecessary return to Manteigas itself. Instead, after an hour, at a large water tank by the right-hand side of the road (there's also a white house, just before a small bridge), turn right down an ancient track – walled in parts – which drops in zigzags through the trees. Ultimately, there are several divergent paths, but as long as you keep going downhill you'll end up in the group of houses by the *Albergaria Berne* (another 30min) – from where it's a steep fifteen-minute climb into Manteigas proper.

specialities including Beira sausages and grilled kid. It's down at the bottom of the town, by the river – a very steep 15min on foot, or by car follow the signs coming in on the Caldas–Torre road. Restaurant Tues–Sat noon–2.30pm & 7–9.30pm, Sun 7–9.30pm. €60

Casa das Obras Rua Teles de Vasconcelos, Manteigas ☎ 275 981 155, ⓦ casadasobras.pt. Follow the blue signs in town to find this restored early nineteenth-century mansion, enlarged from an even older eighteenth-century dwelling. Some rooms are a little on the dim side, but the faded dining room murals, games room, uneven floorboards and cellar-like bar are a joy, and there's an enchanting garden with fruit trees and a wonderfully secluded swimming pool. €68

Pensão Serradalto Rua 1 de Maio, Manteigas ☎ 275 981 151. The fifteen spotless rooms here have wooden ceilings and wonderful views. The communal terrace is one of the best spots in Manteigas for a sunset beer, while full-length windows in the restaurant look out to the valley below – steak cooked on a hot stone at your table is the speciality. No credit cards. €45

Pousada de São Lourenço Pehas Douradas ☎ 275 980 050, ⓦ pousadas.pt. Reached by a series of switchbacks (follow signs from town) this marvellous *pousada*, 12km west of Manteigas, is best enjoyed in winter when log fires are roaring in the wood-panelled bar and the tartan curtains are drawn against howling mountain winds. That said, there are superlative views at any time of the year, and more great views from the restaurant. €110

Relva da Reboleira Largo Relva da Reboleira, Sameiro ☎ 275 980 090, ⓦ skiparque.net. Set in the Skiparque, this year-round place is the area's most convenient campsite, near its own river beach and with a café and good facilities. Pitch €5

Soadro do Zêzere Estrada Nacional 232, Valhelhas ☎ 275 487 114, ⓦ soadro.com. Some 17km east of Manteigas, this inn is a sympathetic restoration of an old village house, with plenty of exposed stone and burnished wood, and half a dozen unflashy but good-value rooms. There's a decent restaurant on the premises, too. €55

EATING

★**Dom Pastor** Rua Sá da Bandeira, Manteigas ☎ 275 982 920. Tucked away in an idyllic little lane by the river, *Dom Pastor* offers a creative take on traditional cuisine. It's a calm, contemporary space, constructed using local materials, and you can expect dishes such as fillet of perch with shrimp sauce, or *bacalhau* with a corn-bread crust (mains €10–12). Daily 9am–midnight.

Luso Pizza Rua Teles de Vasconcelos 15–17, Manteigas ☎ 275 982 628. The wheels of pizza at this miniscule restaurant/takeaway just behind the park office are the genuine article, and with prices at €7–10 it's a great deal

for the truly hungry. Some outdoor tables. Daily 11am–3pm & 7pm–midnight.

★**Vallecula** Pr Dr. José de Castro, Valhelhas ☎ 275 487 123. One of the best places to eat in the region, it's worth a special trip out to Valhelhas (17km east of Manteigas) for the superior dining on offer. The restaurant occupies an old stone house on the village square and the menu showcases the best of local produce, with lamb, pork, rabbit, beef or game preceded by a starter of soft cheese with herbs, for example. Prices are fair (mains around €14), the owner affable and the regional wine list impressive. Tues–Sun noon–11pm.

Torre and around

The trans-mountain N339 between Seia and Covilhã climbs right across the bleak, scoured landscape of Portugal's highest mountains. The peak is known as **Torre** (1993m) after the stone *torre* (tower) added on the orders of Dom João VI in 1817 to raise the height to a more impressive 2000m. There's something typically Portuguese about that gesture, as there is about the summit shopping centre, with outlets all selling smelly cheese and woolly slippers. Impressive in winter, when the ski lifts and surrounding slopes are bustling with skiers, at other times the natural beauty and grandeur at the top of Portugal's highest mountain is disfigured somewhat by the coach parking, radar domes and concrete buildings that house a café and restaurant.

It goes without saying that the route there is the best thing about Torre, and there's no better approach than the 15km from Manteigas up the dramatic glacial **Zêzere valley**. The valley road joins the N339 at the **Nave de Santo António** plateau, where you turn right for Torre (7km). En route to the peak you pass the vast statue of **Nossa Senhora da Boa Estrela**, carved into a niche in the rock, to which there's a massive procession from Covilhã on the second Sunday in August.

Penhas da Saúde
Ski passes €25 per day, equipment hire €25 per day • ☎ 275 314 727, ⑩ skiserradaestrela.com

Around 10 km below Torre (towards Covilhã) lies the ski resort of **Penhas da Saúde** (1900m). The ski season runs from November to April, but outside this time, it's a rather desolate-looking place with few facilities save a sprinkling of accommodation and some cafés. You can stretch your legs at the reservoir above, or stop on the way further down to Covilhã at a couple of signposted strolls, like that to **Pedra do Urso** (Bear Rock).

ACCOMMODATION   **PENHAS DA SAÚDE**

Pousada de Juventude ☎ 275 335 375, ⑩ pousadasjuventude.pt. The huge 163-bed youth hostel is at 1500m, so the superb views are a given, and it also has a self-catering kitchen and bar, and some private en-suite rooms. Dorms €12, doubles €40

Covilhã

Just outside the eastern park boundary, and 44km south of Guarda, the prosperous town of **COVILHÃ** lies immediately below the highest peaks. It's busiest on winter weekends, when it's used as a base for trips to the ski slopes, but it has a life independent of the mountains, which makes it an agreeable place to visit at any time. Virtually every thoroughfare looks out across the plain below or up to the mountain crags – the café in the pretty town gardens has the best view, serenaded by practice sessions in the music conservatory opposite.

Praça do Município
Covilhã's favourite son is **Pêro de Covilhã**, who set out in 1487 to search for Prester John (legendary Christian priest and king) in what is now Ethiopia. He never found Prester John and never returned to Portugal, though Vasco da Gama found his report about India useful when he made his own celebrated voyage there in 1498. In front of the town hall on **Praça do Município** there's a huge, polished granite slab depicting Pêro de Covilhã's voyages and a decidedly queasy-looking statue of the man himself.

Museo de Lanifícios
Rua Marquês d'Ávila e Bolama • Tues–Sun 9.30am–noon & 2.30–6pm • €2, under-16s free • ☎ 275 319 724, ⑩ museu.ubi.pt

A market town since the Middle Ages, Covilhã developed a textile industry in the seventeenth century using wool from the local sheep, which also provide the milk for the renowned *queijo da serra* (mountain cheese). Later, the woollen industry harnessed water-power from the mountain streams; factories today, down on the plain below town, are powered by hydroelectricity. You can view the enormous vats used in the traditional wool-dyeing processes in the **Museo de Lanifícios**, located in the former Real Fábrica de Panos (Royal Textile Factory), a short walk downhill from the centre.

ARRIVAL AND DEPARTURE   **COVILHÃ**

By car Parking in the town centre is metered (4hr maximum; free after 8pm and on Sun). For longer stays, use the large, free parking area below the fire station (*Bombeiros*) – from the public gardens, head up past the *Covilhã Parque* hotel and *Telepizza*, turn sharp left at the garage (Pneus) and there's a blue parking sign immediately on the left.

By bus and train The train and bus stations straddle a small park 2km below the town, but a bus runs up the hill from here every 10min and drops you at the local bus terminal outside the PSP (police station), where there's a bus information kiosk.

Bus Destinations Belmonte (3 daily; 30min); Castelo Branco (5 daily; 1hr); Guarda (6 daily; 45min); Lisbon (4–9 daily; 3hr 35min–6hr); Manteigas (Mon–Fri 1 daily; 1hr 30min); Penhas da Saúde (Aug 2 daily, July & Sept 1 daily; 35min); Seia (Mon–Fri & Sun 1 daily; 2hr); Viseu (2–6 daily; 2hr).

Train Destinations Castelo Branco (7 daily; 50min); Lisbon (5 daily; 3hr 40min–5hr 15min).

4

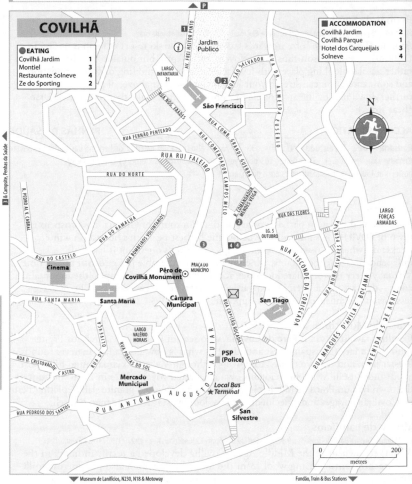

ACCOMMODATION

There's a limited choice of **accommodation** in the old centre, while several business-oriented three- and four-star places are found below town (not really walking distance), down the road out to the main highway. Note that prices fall everywhere in summer.

★**Covilhã Jardim** Rua São Salvador 40 ☏ 275 322 140, ⊚ hotelcovilhajardim.com. Located by the public gardens, this superb guesthouse has fifteen smart en-suite rooms, some with French windows and little balconies. The central location and friendly family who run the place make the prices something of a steal; there's also pay parking right outside, and a café-bar (see opposite) on the ground floor. **€65**

Covilhã Parque Av Frei Heitor Pinto ☏ 275 329 320, ⊚ covilhaparquehotel.com.pt. This two-star, 134-room hotel is ten floors high and affords the best views in town,

at least from the front rooms. Things are not quite as swish as the reception area suggests, with slightly worn decor and bathrooms on the basic side. But discounted summer rates are excellent, and there's direct access from the fire-station parking area. **€35**

Hotel dos Carqueijais Penhas road, N339 ☏ 275 319 120, ⊚ turistrela.pt. For serious views, head towards the mountains, 5km northwest of Covilhã, to this four-star ski-oriented inn, with panoramic bar and restaurant, plus summer outdoor pool. Expect prices to be a lot higher at weekends in winter. **€68**

Solneve Rua Visconde da Coriscada 126 ☎ 275 323 001, ⓦ solneve.pt. This traditional three-star hotel overlooking the main traffic circle and square has smart, business-like rooms, either "standard" or "superior" (the latter come with a hot tub-bath and cost €10 or so more), and there's also a pool, spa and parking. **€41**

EATING

Covilhã Jardim Rua São Salvador 40 ☎ 275 322 140. On the ground floor of the *Covilhã Jardim* guesthouse, Covilhã's nicest café-bar has stone walls, odd boxy furniture and a lovely terrace, and makes a pleasant place to while away a couple of hours. Daily noon–10pm.

Montiel Pr do Município 33–37 ☎ 275 322 086. Typical café and *pastelaria* downstairs, restaurant upstairs, filled to bursting with families for Sunday lunch. The menu concentrates on regional specialities, from trout to *cabrito* (kid), and although some dishes are pricey the *pratos do dia* cost around €7 for a *meia dose* or €12 for a portion big enough for two. Daily 9am–10.30pm.

Restaurante Solneve Rua Visconde da Coriscada 126 ☎ 275 323 001, ⓦ solneve.pt. This restaurant within the *Solneve* hotel is a cavernous downstairs affair, and offers pretty unbeatable value, serving up traditional local fare; main dishes around €9. Daily noon–10.30pm.

Ze do Sporting Rua Comendador Mendes Veiga 19 ☎ 275 334 127. Locals plump for the steaks and grills (including fish and seafood) at this popular *churrasqueira* – prices start at €8, though it's more like €15 for a decent steak. It's down a backstreet behind the *Solneve*. Tues–Sat noon–3pm & 7–10pm, Sun noon–3pm.

Beira Baixa

The area east of Covilhã and the A23 motorway forms the upper boundary of the **Beira Baixa**, a landscape of undulating, heather-clad hills that extends to the Spanish border. The sun-bleached fields, grazing livestock and extensive olive groves provide a distinct contrast to the *serra* scenery, with visits concentrating on a series of fortified towns and fascinating villages. With a car you can see the whole region in a couple of days, and the best overnight stops are either at the underrated town of **Belmonte** or in one of the atmospheric houses of medieval **Sortelha**. On the other hand, travel by public transport is particularly difficult and slow. Only Belmonte and **Sabugal** can be reached easily by bus, though if you're determined you'll also get to Sortelha, while the provincial capital of **Castelo Branco** (on the Lisbon–Covilhã train route) has services to **Monsanto** and **Idanha-a-Nova**. But isolated destinations, such as **Idanha-a-Velha** and the **Serra da Malcata** nature reserve, are impossible to see by public transport.

4

Belmonte

The delightful small town of **BELMONTE** springs one of the best surprises in the Beiras, a charming place of sun-dappled squares, stone houses dripping with flower-filled windowboxes and lazy dogs basking on the cobbles. There are curiosities at every turn, such as the unusual pillory in the shape of an olive press, or the fire-blackened tree stumps outside the castle, which are the site of Christmas Eve carols and gambols. Meanwhile, in the Zêzere river valley, which Belmonte overlooks, vast peach and cherry orchards splash a blaze of colour each spring.

Castelo and Igreja de Santiago

Largo de Santiago • April to mid-Sept Tues–Sun 9am–12.30pm & 2–6pm; mid-Sept to March Tues–Sun 9.30am–1pm & 2–5.30pm • Castelo free; Igreja €1

For the Portuguese Belmonte is best known as the birthplace of **Pedro Álvares Cabral** (1467–1520), the "discoverer" of Brazil, who was born in the tidily restored **Castelo** overlooking town. Cabral's father received the castle from Dom Afonso V, and adapted it as the family residence, though it later fell into disrepair. The **Igreja de Santiago**, just outside the castle walls, contains the Cabral family pantheon (though not the tomb of Pedro Álvares, which is in Santarém), while one of two tiny stone chapels on a hillock

PARKS, PATHS AND PROJECTS IN BEIRA BAIXA

The lower (*baixa*) Beira region is a surprisingly good place for **hiking** and **outdoor activities**; better, in many ways, than the higher Serra da Estrela. It's the result of a diverse set of interconnecting development projects, the main result of which is a growing series of reliable, waymarked **footpaths** and readily available information. Castelo Branco sits at the centre of the so-called **Naturtejo Geopark** (📞 272 320 176, 🌐 naturtejo.com), part of a wider pan-European project, while a large section of Tejo River hinterland is contained within the **Parque Natural do Tejo Internacional** (🌐 icnf.pt); "internacional" because it's mirrored on the Spanish side of the river too. There are good local walk circuits in many towns and villages, particularly between Monsanto, the Spanish border and Idanha-a-Nova, and also around the so-called **aldeias do xisto** (schist villages; 🌐 aldeiasdoxisto.pt), west of Castelo Branco; we've highlighted the best in the Beira Baixa section of this chapter, and you can pick up route leaflets and information in any local turismo. There's even a long-distance hiking trail, the **GR12-E7** (total 80km), that connects Termas de Monfortinho on the Spanish border with Idanha-a-Nova (some of the shorter walks connect with this; details on the local council website 🌐 cm-idanhanova.pt).

opposite is inscribed with the Cabral family coat of arms – two goats within a shield. The Cabral trail also extends to the main through-road named in his honour, where there's a statue of the explorer clutching a large cross.

Judaria

Belmonte's restored **Judaria (Jewish quarter)** is tucked below the southern wall of the castle. Belmonte once maintained one of Portugal's largest Jewish communities and records show that there was a synagogue here as early as 1297, but this fell into ruins after the Inquisition, when many Jews fled the country or were forced to convert to being "New Christians". You should be able to look into the Jewish quarter's modern **Sinagoga** (synagogue), while behind Largo do Pelourinho, in the old town, the **Museu Judaico**, at Rua da Portela 4 (mid-April to mid-Sept Tues–Sun 9am–12.30pm & 2.30–6pm; mid-Sept to mid-April Tues–Sun 9.30am–1pm & 2–5.30pm; €2.50) explores the history of Portuguese Judaism.

The town museums

All museums Rua Pedro Álvares Cabral • Mid-April to mid-Sept Tues–Sun 9am–12.30pm & 2.30–6pm; mid-Sept to mid-April Tues–Sun 9.30am–1pm & 2–5.30pm • Combined admission to all museums (plus Museu Judaico and Igreja de Santiago) €7.50 • 📞 275 088 698

All the town **museums** apart from the Museu Judaico are located along the main Rua Pedro Álvares Cabral – start with the interpretation centre, **À Descoberta do Novo Mundo**, installed in the former Cabral palace, across from the town hall, which covers the New World discoveries of Cabral and others. Opposite lies the **Ecomuseu do Zêzere**, housed in a barn-like granite building, formerly a granary owned by the Cabral family, and which provides the natural and geological background on the Zêzere River. For an investigation of the local olive oil industry, follow the signs around the corner to the **Museu do Azeite**, housed in the former municipal olive-oil press.

Torre de Centum Cellas

No access • The tower is just off the N18: drive 600m along the road from the Belmonte junction towards Guarda and then 400m up a side road to the right

A couple of kilometres north of Belmonte, the extraordinary **Torre de Centum Cellas** presents a very odd picture – rather like a child's brick building – with the further curiosity that no one quite knows what it was – though it's thought that it may have formed part of a Roman villa, and survived due to later use as a watchtower. The stone

tower measures around 10m by 8m and stands three storeys high, and there are no fewer than forty intact window and door frames.

ARRIVAL AND INFORMATION

By bus Buses drop you at the end of Rua Pedro Álvares Cabral, a 500m walk from the centre; long-distance express buses stop at Gingal junction on the N18, 2km below town. Destinations Covilhã (3 daily; 30min); Guarda (3 daily; 25–45min); Lisbon (4 daily; 4hr); Manteigas (1 daily; 45min); Sabugal (1 daily; 1hr 30min).

By car Belmonte is just 26km south of Guarda and 20km northeast of Covilhã, and it's also a handy stop en route to the Serra da Estrela, with Manteigas just 27km to the west. It's easy to park for free on the road into town, or up by the castle.

Information The turismo is in the Castelo (Tues–Sun 9.30am–12.30pm & 2.30–5.30pm; ☎275 911 488, ⓦcm-belmonte.pt).

ACCOMMODATION AND EATING

Casa do Castelo Largo de Santiago ☎275 181 675, ⓦcasadocastelo.net. Located right outside the castle, offering good rooms at a decent price, a terrace café with sweeping views and a granite-walled restaurant serving upmarket regional food; mains are €11–14, though the *prato do dia* for lunch is better value at €8. Restaurant Tues–Sun 11.30am–10.30pm. **€60**

Pousada Convento de Belmonte Serra da Esperança ☎275 910 300, ⓦpousadas.pt. The rather elegant rooms in this restored convent combine natural textures, light and space. There's a plunge-pool and terrace, and an excellent restaurant, where you'll eat smarter versions of traditional dishes for around €40 a head. It's 1km south of town – follow the signs. Restaurant daily 12.30–3pm & 7.30–10pm. **€130**

Sortelha

Twenty kilometres east of Belmonte, **SORTELHA** rises dramatically amid an unearthly, undulating highland plateau strewn with giant glacial boulders. It's an ancient place that, for most of its existence, has gone about its business quietly, though the wonderful rock-built fortress suggests some frontier excitement in times past. Today it presents itself as a museum piece – with some beautifully restored lodgings available – since the number of permanent residents in the old town barely struggles into double figures. From the modern quarters on the Sabugal road it's a five-minute walk uphill (follow "Castelo" signposts) to the fascinating walled **old town** – or you can drive up and park outside the main gate. A tight web of cobbled lanes wends between squat stone houses with red-tiled roofs, while rough carved steps in the castle keep offer a grandstand view over the valley below and the rock-speckled hillsides beyond.

ARRIVAL AND DEPARTURE

By car Reaching Sortelha by public transport is practically impossible, given buses are scheduled around school dropoffs and pickups, and run in term-time only – you'll need your own wheels to get here.

ACCOMMODATION AND EATING

Sortelha has some enticing rustic **accommodation**, but advance reservations are recommended (and note that there are no credit card or banking facilities in Sortelha). As well as the **café** and **restaurant** in the old town there are a couple of places to eat on the main road below.

Bar do Forno Esplanada ☎271 388 034. Friendly café with a stone-flagged terrace, right beneath the castle walls. There are sausage and cheese *petiscos* and other snacks, or they will rustle you up a steak and chips for under €10. Daily 10am–9pm.

★**Casa da Lagariça** Calç. de Santo Antão 11 ☎271 388 116, ⓦcasalagarica.com. This delightful old stone village house, fashioned from a former grape store, is a wonderfully atmospheric place to stay. Accommodation is in two doubles or a twin room, which share two bathrooms, a fully equipped kitchen and a lounge. Prices go up to €80 in peak summer and winter season, but it's more reasonable at other times. **€55**

Dom Sancho I ☎271 388 267. The only proper restaurant in the old town, just inside the main gate, with a rustic stone-walled interior. Sample meat grills and game from a strictly traditional menu (mains €12–18), or you can just have a drink in the downstairs bar. Tues–Sat noon–2.30pm & 7–10pm, Sun noon–3pm.

4

Sabugal

SABUGAL is a pleasant place, rising uphill from the Côa riverside, and with a small old-town area of winding streets and noble mansions. The hill is topped by the neatly restored **Castelo do Sabugal** (April–Sept Tues–Fri 9.30am–1pm & 2–6.30pm, Sat & Sun 10am–1pm & 2–7pm; Oct–March Tues–Fri 9.30am–1pm & 2–5.30pm, Sat & Sun 10am–1pm & 2.30–5.30pm; €1); you can look around inside the castle walls, and enjoy pretty views over the river, but the setting isn't a patch on that at Sortelha. Most visitors will just drive on by, though Sabugal does make a good base for visiting the Serra da Malcata reserve (see below), as accommodation and restaurants are far better here than at the other town near the reserve, Penamacor, which is 35km to the south.

ARRIVAL AND INFORMATION
SABUGAL

By bus The bus station is at the bottom of town, by the market. Destinations Belmonte (1 daily; 1hr 30min); Castelo Branco (Sun–Fri 1 daily; 2hr); Guarda (Mon–Fri every 2hr, Sat 1 daily; 45min); Penamacor (Sun–Fri 1–2 daily; 1hr); Sortelha (Sept–June Mon–Fri 1 daily; 30min).

Information The turismo is in Castelo do Sabugal (April–Sept Tues–Fri 9.30am–1pm & 2–6.30pm, Sat & Sun 10am–1pm & 2–7pm; Oct–March Tues–Fri 9.30am–1pm & 2–5.30pm, Sat & Sun 10am–1pm & 2.30–5.30pm; ☎ 271 751 046, ⓦ cm-sabugal.pt).

ACCOMMODATION AND EATING

★ **Robalo** Largo do Cinema 4 ☎ 271 753 566. By far the best place to eat in town, and frankly worth a major detour in its own right. It serves trout from the Rio Côa, its own smoked sausage and fantastic lamb, steaks or *bacalhau*, all grilled over huge fireplaces burning holm oak; everything is served with organic salad and a garlic-and-pepper sauce that should have UN weapons' inspectors on alert; you can eat amazingly well for around €25. Restaurant Mon–Sat noon–3pm & 7.30–10pm; Sun noon–3pm. Doubles **€45**

Sol Rio Av Infante D. Henrique 58 ☎ 271 753 197. Down by the river bridge on the way into town, with eleven decent budget rooms with castle or river views, and a modest restaurant serving regional food (mains at €10–15). Restaurant Mon–Thurs, Sat & Sun noon–3pm & 7–10pm. Doubles **€35**

Reserva Natural da Serra da Malcata

ⓦ icnf.pt

Between Sabugal and Penamacor, and reaching east from two local reservoirs to the Spanish border, spreads the **Reserva Natural da Serra da Malcata**. It's one of the least-visited Portuguese nature reserves – access isn't easy, and you really need to bike or hike to get much out of it – but it rewards the effort. If you're very lucky, you might get a glimpse of a wild boar among the trees, or catch sight of the magnificent golden eagle or black vulture. What you won't see – despite the emblem on all the promotional material – is the **Iberian lynx**, which is under serious threat of extinction. The last lynx was caught in the park in 1992, and there's been no sign of one now for many years – fewer than two hundred are believed to exist in the wild, all now in Spain.

The reserve covers 16,000 hectares of heather-clad hills and oak woodland, with the reserve headquarters in Penamacor (see p.251). They can usually rustle up an English-speaking member of staff, and the office also sells a map and separate walking booklet in English. Note that not all the **hiking trails** are currently signposted, as neglect, forest fires and vandalism have taken their toll – but you can always follow our directions instead.

Barragem da Ribeira da Meimoa

To combine a scenic drive and walk, take the Penamacor road south of Sabugal and turn off after around 4km for the village of **Malcata**, near the Barragem do Sabugal. Just before you reach the village, turn off on a new minor road (not shown on most maps, signposted to Meimão) to wind right through a dramatic line of wind turbines before dropping into the rustic village of **Meimão**. From here, follow signs for "Barragem", which lead you above the edge of the reservoir and right to the dam wall of the **Barragem da Ribeira da Meimoa** (in total, a 20km drive from Sabugal).

A HIKE IN THE RESERVA NATURAL DA SERRA DA MALCATA

An easy hike, the **Espírito Santo** trail (4.6km; 1hr 30min), through typical Malcata heather and oak-wood scenery, starts near the village of Quadrazais. We hesitate to say you can't get lost, but it would be difficult.

Drive 15km down the minor but good 538 road from Sabugal. At Quadrazais, take the Vale de Espinho road and 500m down this road take the right turn down a good dirt track (signposted "Reserva Natural, Rio Côa") for 300m to the River Côa. Drive over the bridge to the parking and picnic area and then walk up to the trail information board. Don't turn left for the chapel, but head straight up the track by the side of the wire fence, and turn right when you reach a T-junction after 750m. The track skirts the flank of a hill, through pine nurseries, and after 1.25km meets another T-junction at a ruined building, where you turn left (a wooden "PR1" marker shows the turn). Continue for another 1km, through shady groves of oak, reaching a left turn on a rise with wind turbine views (again, there's a wooden "PR1" marker). Turn left here and it's then 1.6km around the other flank of the hill, dropping down to the chapel and river, where you started.

It's nice to combine this walk with lunch at the appealing *Trutal Côa* restaurant (Mon, Tues & Thurs–Sun lunch and dinner; ☎ 271 606 227), located at the trout farm, just a few kilometres away – it's 2km before the village of Vale de Espinho.

You can cross the wall and park and then try to follow the 8km (2hr) trail, which is shown on the information board here, but suffers from a lack of signs. At the very least, you can walk out along the waterside track for a couple of kilometres and enjoy the views. The nearest facilities are further down the Penamacor road, at **Meimoa** (not to be confused with Meimão), 13km from Penamacor, which has a couple of simple restaurants.

4

Penamacor

Just outside the Reserva Natural da Serra da Malcata, **PENAMACOR** has another medieval **castle**, not as impressive as those in Sabugal and Sortelha but still offering great views over the Serra da Malcata towards Spain. It's reached by a short but punishing climb up from the newer part of town, and the restored walls enclose a dilapidated village that's been getting a face-lift in recent years. Back down the hill, the **public gardens** have more sweeping views over the southern plains of the Beira Baixa – there's an outdoor café here.

ARRIVAL AND INFORMATION

RESERVA NATURAL DA SERRA DA MALCATA

By car Penamacor is 34km southwest of Sabugal; it's just a 35min drive between the two. You'll need a car to get to the reserve, as there is no public transport. Once there, you're best off walking or cycling round the reserve itself.

Information The Reserva Natural da Serra da Malcata HQ is in Penamacor, at Rua António Ribeiro Sanches 60 (Mon–Fri 9am–12.30pm & 2–5.30pm; ☎ 277 394 467, ⊛ icnf.pt); to find it, follow the main street uphill from the gardens and around to the left towards the church.

Monsanto and around

Ancient **MONSANTO** jealously guards its title of the "most Portuguese" village in the country, an award originally bestowed in 1948. Sited high on a hill above the plain, its houses huddle between giant granite outcrops, their walls moulded around enormous grey boulders – in the case of the **Casa de Uma Só Telha** ("the house with only one tile"), the entire roof is formed from a single rock. A few houses lie abandoned, but on the whole Monsanto seems to be doing well from Spanish day-trippers and from tourists still searching for the "real" Portugal. Gift shops aside, facilities are limited to a couple of cafés and a small *mercearia* (grocer's), but there's enough to do if you decided to stay the night and it certainly is an experience.

A fine driving **circuit east and south of Monsanto** leads to some fascinating border outposts, each with a well-marked walking trail. You can do it easily in a day, with time for a walk or two, before returning to Monsanto via Idanha-a-Velha (90km total trip).

A walk around Monsanto

A leaflet available from Monsanto turismo dutifully details every church, chapel, cross, decayed mansion and restored fountain in the village. The main cobbled path heads up to the **castelo** (always open; free), 700m up and offering remarkable views across the parched plains to the distant mountains. An enjoyable walk leads you around the castle and rock outcrops in a couple of hours, also dropping down to **São Pedro de Vir-à-Corça** chapel, in a grotto of cork trees below the crags. You'll pick up the walk-posts all over town, and there's an information board outside the turismo.

Penha Garcia

Heading down the N239, it's a 10km drive east from Monsanto to the similarly crag-bound village of **Penha Garcia**. A splendid trail (3km; 1hr) climbs up to the skeletal castle and then down into a rather magical **gorge** below a dam wall, where fossils of the furrows of giant trilobites have been found (some are on display in the village antiquary). There's a swimming area cut into the gorge terraces, with the trail leading back to the village via a fascinating series of old mills and watercourses. You can have a drink in a bar built into the former forge, while at weekends some of the local women fire up the village's communal oven and make bread to sell to visitors.

Salvaterra do Extremo

From Penha Garcia, the road sweeps on another 12km towards the Spanish border and the eminently missable collection of spa hotels and pensions that make up Termas de Monfortinho. However, turn south here at the roundabout (for Zebreira and Castelo Branco) and it's 15km down the N240 for the turn-off to sleepy **Salvaterra do Extremo**, which sits a little way inland from the Rio Erges (Erjas in Spanish), a tributary of the Tejo, which delineates the border. A signposted **trail** (10km; 3–4hr) takes in the old village, river and surrounding olive groves, but even if you're not up for this, at least walk the first 1km section down an ancient stone pathway to the river viewpoint and bird hide, where eagles and vultures soar on the thermals.

Segura

A back road from Salvaterra do Extremo leads directly to **Segura** to the south (signposted as 6km, but more like 9km), a small church-topped village also right on the Rio Erges and border. A waymarked 10km **trail** (3–4hr) takes you through more fine scenery, and includes the remains of the area's old lead mines.

Alcântara and the Spanish border

From Segura, it's around 35km to Idanha-a-Velha, via Zebreira, or 60km to Castelo Branco, but you might find a dash across the border irresistible. Just 20km southwest, across the Roman bridge at the border and down a fast road, is the small Spanish town of **Alcântara**. This sits high above the Rio Tajo (the Tejo in Portuguese) and is crossed by a magnificent bridge, also Roman. In the part-abandoned old town, crumbling mansions and churches have been colonized by storks, whose unearthly machine-gun chatter accompanies any stroll through the quiet streets.

ARRIVAL AND INFORMATION   MONSANTO AND AROUND

By bus Buses to Monsanto from Castelo Branco (1–2 daily) stop at the parking area immediately outside the old village; the return service is at the early hour of 7.15am (though at 2.30pm on Sunday).

By car Monsanto is 48km northeast of Castelo Branco, and 25km south of Penamacor. There's a newer settlement right at the bottom of the hill and, further up, a small parking area outside the old village – don't be tempted to drive any further in.

Information Monsanto's turismo is on Rua Marquês da Graciosa (June–Sept daily 10am–1pm & 2–6pm; Oct–May daily 9.30am–1pm & 2–5.30pm; ☎ 277 314 642). Walk up from the parking area to the church and turn right along the main street for the turismo and – eventually – the castle.

ACCOMMODATION AND EATING

Casa do Chafariz Rua Marquês da Graciosa ☎ 916 931 120, ⓦ casadochafariz.com. A short (signposted) walk along the main street from the turismo, this is a refurbishment of an old Monsanto house, with rooms built into the rock outcrops. Breakfast is available for a small extra charge. €42

Estalagem de Monsanto Rua de Capela 3 ☎ 277 314 481, ⓦ monsanto.homestead.com. The fully renovated small village inn offers ten en-suite rooms – nothing fancy, but perfectly good for the night. There's a reasonably priced restaurant and bar on the premises, too, offering a set menu for €10; otherwise mains are €5–15. Restaurant daily 8–10pm. €70

Petiscos & Granitos ☎ 277 096 050. Eating out is fairly restricted in Monsanto – there are more gift shops than restaurants – but this restaurant-tavern on the way up to the castle is good for an atmospheric meal of *bacalhau*, roast kid or fish stew among the boulders. It's a bit on the pricey side (mains around €20), but the views are great. Daily 10am–midnight; closed Wed in winter.

Idanha-a-Velha

The isolated village of **IDANHA-A-VELHA** is 15km south of Monsanto by road, though closer by footpath. It might seem a forgotten backwater now, but it was a large Roman city in the first century BC and was later an important Visigothic settlement – one legend proudly records that the famous Visigothic king Wamba (reigned 672–680 AD) was born here, though at least two places in Spain claim him as well. Local folklore also has it that the inhabitants were driven from the village by a plague of rats during the fifteenth century, after which time the village fell into terminal decline. People do still live in Idanha-a-Velha today – grazing sheep on the plains and tending allotments down by the river – but it often seems almost deserted. Indeed, the village looks much as it must have done when the rats moved in, and perhaps not very different from when the Romans left, either.

4

The old town

Set amid burned plains and olive groves, the old village is still partly girded by a massive **Roman wall**. Down by the languid river, the **Roman bridge** is still in use, while roses and vines are trained up the weathered walls of the houses, many built from plundered Roman stone. A stork's nest tops the ancient **basilica** – signposted as the Sé – while outside here stand the ruins of the **bishop's palace** and an even earlier Roman house. Perhaps the most fascinating restoration is of the old oil press or **Lagar de Varas**, with an ingenious pressing system utilizing two huge tree trunks, with roots intact. The basilica and the olive-oil-press building should be open during turismo office hours (April–Sept daily 10am–1pm & 2–6pm; Oct–March daily 9.30am–1pm & 2–5.30pm; see below), but if not, just ask.

ARRIVAL, INFORMATION AND EATING

IDANHA-A-VELHA

On foot There's no public transport to the village, although there is a great footpath from Monsanto (7km; 2hr). Walk down to the São Pedro de Vir-à-Corça chapel from Monsanto (red-and-yellow marks) and, behind the chapel, pick up the red-and-white markers that run down ancient tracks, through cork and olive groves, to Idanha-a-Velha. You wouldn't want to walk back uphill, though, so arrange a taxi in Monsanto first.

Information The turismo is on Rua da Sé, behind the Lagar (April–Sept daily 10am–1pm & 2–6pm; Oct–March daily 9.30am–1pm & 2–5.30pm; ☎ 277 914 280, ⓦ cm-idanhanova.pt.

Eating and drinking There is a café in the village by the *pelourinho*, but the nearest restaurants and accommodation are in Idanha-a-Nova, 20km to the southwest (see below).

Idanha-a-Nova

The local municipal centre of **IDANHA-A-NOVA** is "nova" only in comparison with ancient Idanha-a-Velha. High above the nearby dam and Rio Ponsul, it presents a likeable, little-visited *zona antiga* of noble mansions and imposing churches. Not all has been tidily restored, and it's much the better for it, though the local council is making strenuous efforts to promote the town and its surroundings.

With history repeating itself in a rather neat way, there's a new town (*zona nova*) set even higher above the old – Idanha-a-Nova-Nova, if you like – where the planners have put the bus station, cultural centre, library and residential suburbs.

ARRIVAL AND DEPARTURE   IDANHA-A-NOVA

By car Idanha-a-Nova is 40km northeast of Castelo Branco and a 20km drive from the old village of Idanha-a-Velha, to the northeast. There are buses from Castelo Branco (1 daily Mon–Fri; 1hr), though it's extremely unlikely that

Idanha-a-Nova falls into any must-see itinerary – it does, however, make a handy base (or coffee stop en-route) for seeing Idanha-a-Velha.

ACCOMMODATION AND EATING

Estrela da Idanha Av Joaquim Morão ☏ 277 200 500, ⓦ estreladaidanha.pt. Up in the new town, this very agreeable three-star hotel sits right on top of the hill. There's a covered outdoor pool, and smart, spacious rooms with balconies and big views, and if you'd rather not eat in the restaurant it's just a 20min walk down into town. **€68**

★ **Helana** Rua José Silvestre Ribeiro 35 ☏ 277 201 095, ⓦ helana.com. There are one or two defiantly elderly cafés in town as well as this ubiquitously signposted stalwart,

which serves a mix of pizzas, pasta and regional Portuguese dishes, including river-fish soup and sautéed wild mushrooms. You can eat for €15–20. Mon & Thurs–Sun noon–2.30pm & 7.30–10.30pm.

Pousada de Juventude Pr da República 32, ☏ 277 208 051, ⓦ pousadasjuventude.pt. There's not a lot of budget accommodation around in these parts, so it might pay to detour to Idanha-a-Nova for hostel dorms and rooms in a grand, restored mansion in the centre of town. Dorms **€12**; doubles **€30**

4

Castelo Branco and around

As capital of the Beira Baixa, **CASTELO BRANCO** has an air of prosperity compared to many of the nearby villages. Various frontier wars have robbed the town of much of its age-old history, save the sixteenth-century former town hall, a few handsome mansions, and some castle ruins at the top of town, where a garden *miradouro* offers sweeping views. Otherwise, it's a pleasant enough, predominantly modern place of sweeping boulevards, squares and parks, with a broad, leafy central avenue that's been opened up for pedestrians – there's also a daily **market** at the **Mercado Municipal**, down Avenida 1º de Maio, near the turismo. That said, you don't have to head very far out of town for some peace, quiet and natural beauty, with a string of stunning viewpoints and ancient villages within easy reach.

Jardim do Paço Episcopal

Rua Bartolomeu da Costa • Daily: Oct–April 9am–5pm; May–Sept 9am–7pm • €2

Flanking one side of Castelo Branco's remaining old town is the **Jardim do Paço Episcopal**, the eighteenth-century garden of the old bishop's palace, whose twin showpiece staircases sport elaborate historic statues – on one, figures of the Apostles; on the other, the successive kings of Portugal, including three that, curiously, are much smaller than the others. The latter are the figures of the Spanish Habsburg rulers, Felipe I, II and III, whose sixty-year reign in Portugal is still cause for resentment (hence their diminutive size).

Museu Tavares Proença Júnior

Largo Dr. José Dias Lopes • Oct–April Tues–Sun 10am–6pm; May–Sept Tues–Sun 10am–7pm • €2, free Sun mornings • ☏ 272 347 880

The former bishop's palace now houses the **Museu Tavares Proença Júnior**, whose pride and joy is its large display of embroidered bedspreads, known as *colchas*. These lavish status symbols were originally produced in India and China where wealthy Portuguese commissioned them from local artisans. The craftspeople duly incorporated motifs from their own myths and culture – typically animals, flowers and mythical figures – which subsequently influenced Portuguese manufacturers in Castelo Branco.

Vila Velha de Rodão
27km southwest of Castelo Branco, down the A23 motorway

A quick drive out of town takes you to **Vila Velha de Rodão** on the Rio Tejo. Don't go into the village. but keep on the Portalegre road until you reach the bridge and a brown sign pointing across the railway tracks for "Portas do Rodão"; at the top of the hill, turn at the "Ermida" sign. From the balcony in front of the restored Castelo de Rodão keep there are stupendous views of the serpentine Tejo River and the sheer walls of the **Portas do Rodão** (Rodão Gates) – the jaw-droppingly beautiful gorge that confronts rail passengers on the Lisbon–Castelo Branco line.

Foz do Cobrão
Follow the sign outside Vila Velha de Rodão for Alvaiade (7km) and, once there, follow a brown tourist sign to Foz do Cobrão for another few kilometres

Foz do Cobrão is one of the region's typical schist villages, spectacularly sited in arid hills close to the **Portas de Vale Mourão** gorge – there's a viewpoint on the road in, just before the village. The schist villages hereabouts (known as *aldeias do xisto*) are all seeing sustainable tourist investment of one kind or another, and the fruits in Foz do Cobrão are a **river beach** (*praia fluvial*) and a circular 11km (4hr) **hiking trail** that takes in the gorge and, depending on your luck, the storks, eagles, vultures and otters that inhabit the valley. Park outside the *Restaurante Vale Mourão* at the top of the village, where there's a walk information board.

ARRIVAL AND INFORMATION

By bus From Castelo Branco's bus station, turn right and t's a short walk up to the main Alameda da Liberdade. Destinations Covilhã (5 daily; 1hr); Guarda (5 daily; 1hr 40min); Lisbon (7 daily; 2hr 30min); Monsanto (Mon–Fri 2 daily, Sun 1; 1hr 30min); Penamacor (Sun–Fri 1–2 daily; 1hr 20min); Viseu (2–5 daily; 2hr 30min–3 hr).
By car Grab a parking space where you can along the two avenues (Av 1° de Maio and Avenida de Nuno Álvares) approaching the Alameda da Liberdade, which is the main

CASTELO BRANCO AND AROUND

thoroughfare through Castelo Branco. Or try Largo de São João near the Paço Episcopal gardens.
By train Castelo Branco train station is 500m from the main Alameda da Liberdade, down Avenida de Nuno Álvares, with regular services to Covilhã (7 daily; 50min) and Lisbon (6 daily; 2hr 50min–4hr).
Information The Castelo Branco turismo is on Avenida de Nuno Álvares 30 (daily 10am–1pm & 2–6pm; ☎272 330 339, ⓦcm-castelobranco.pt).

ACCOMMODATION AND EATING

CASTELO BRANCO
Churrasqueira da Quinta Rua Dr. Henrique Carvalhão 4A ☎272 326 406. A short walk from the railway station, this neighbourhood *churrasqueira* is the real deal, with steaks coming straight off a smoky grill. The same company operates four takeaways around town. Mains €6–11. Mon–Sat noon–3pm & 7–10pm.
Império Rua dos Prazeres 20 ☎272 341 720, ⓦimperiodorei.pt. Behind the post office, in a quiet street close to the cathedral – follow Alameda da Liberdade around towards the gardens and museum. A friendly place with air-conditioned rooms and gleaming bathrooms; downstairs rooms are gloomier but cool in summer. No credit cards. **€50**
★**O Jardim** Rua da Figueira 29–31 ☎272 342 850, ⓦrestauranteojardim.com. Cosy restaurant with a big local reputation. Lunch is a bargain, but the *à la carte* prices are hardly off-putting, with grills from around €8 and

house specials for €8–13, including great steaks – and many come specially for the prawn curry. It's signposted up an alley between Alameda da Liberdade and Largo da Sé, opposite Farmácia Ferrer, just before the post office. Mon, Tues & Thurs–Sun noon–3pm & 7–10pm.
Rainha Dona Amélia Rua Santiago 15 ☎272 348 800, ⓦhotelrainhadamelia.pt. Smart, spacious rooms in warm tones make this the town's best mid-range choice. The three-star hotel itself is a bit traditional (a restaurant no one uses, souvenirs no one buys), but there's a buffet breakfast and garage parking. It's off the bottom of Avenida 1° de Maio. **€46**
Tryp Colina do Castelo Rua da Piscina ☎272 349 280, ⓦsolmelia.com. The fanciest place in town has a lofty location by the castle, rooms with soft-focus interiors and breathtaking views from the balconies and bar. There's also parking, a health club with sauna, Turkish baths and squash courts. Website room-only deals start at around €45. **€55**

Porto and the Rio Douro

PORTO RIVERFRONT

5

Porto and the Rio Douro

Lisbon might be the country's capital, but Portugal's second city, Porto, is very definitely not second best. Dramatically situated at the mouth of the Rio Douro, it's a massively atmospheric place that's well worth a couple of days of your time – more if you plan to make a serious assault on the famous port wine lodges of Vila Nova de Gaia, located just across the river. For a convenient trip to the seaside, the pretty town of Vila do Conde, 45 minutes to the north, offers a taste of what's to come as you head up the coast towards the Minho. East of Porto, meanwhile, the N15 or much faster A4 motorway runs inland to the *vinho verde*-producing towns of Penafiel and Amarante, the latter perhaps the single most attractive town in the region, set on the lazy Rio Tâmega.

Inevitably, however, it's the **Rio Douro** ("River of Gold") that defines the region, winding for over 200km from the Spanish border to the sea, with port wine lodges and tiny villages dotted above intricately terraced hillsides. It was once a wild and unpredictable river, though after the port-producing area was first demarcated in the eighteenth century, engineering works soon tamed the worst of the rapids and opened up the Douro for trade. The railway reached the Spanish border by the end of the nineteenth century, while the building of hydroelectric dams and locks along the river's length in the 1970s and 1980s turned the Douro into a series of navigable ribbon lakes.

In recent years, **Porto** itself has been undergoing a massive tourism boom and this is reflected in the many hotels now on offer, many of which are of the boutique variety. For eating and going out you'll be spoilt for choice, as areas have been gentrified with new restaurants and bars opening up.

It's possible to cruise all the way from Porto to Barca d'Alva on the Spanish border, while the drive along the Douro also makes for an unforgettable journey. But take the train at least part of the way if you can, since the main **Douro train line** captures some of the area's best scenery – particularly once you've reached the rough halfway point, marked by the port wine town and cruise centre of **Peso da Régua**. Just to the south of Régua, a slight detour takes in the delightful Baroque pilgrimage town of **Lamego** and the fascinating churches and historic buildings of its little-explored surroundings. Beyond Régua, the main stop is the idyllically set wine-town of **Pinhão**, and the train line continues to cling to the river as far as its terminus at **Pocinho**, though the Douro itself still has a way to go, winding on to the border at **Barca d'Alva**. However, following the uppermost reaches of the Douro is impossible by road beyond Pinhão, with the N222 finally veering south of the river to reach the extraordinary collection of paleolithic rock engravings near **Vila Nova de Foz Côa**.

PORT WINE CELLAR, VILA NOVA DE GAIA

Highlights

❶ Fundação Serralves, Porto Don't miss this designer-style contemporary art gallery, which is surrounded by the city's most enjoyable park. See p.271

❷ Touring the port wine lodges, Vila Nova de Gaia Wine tastings and tours galore are offered by the country's leading port wine producers. See p.272

❸ Rio Douro river cruise Pass under the city bridges, or let the vineyards drift by, on a trip along the "River of Gold". See p.275

❹ Amarante A dreamy riverside town that's an upmarket weekend getaway. See p.286

❺ Lunch on the Douro Enjoy an alfresco

riverside lunch at the stylish *DOC* restaurant near Peso da Régua. See p.292

❻ Manor house stay, Lamego This pretty town is known for its *quintas* and *solares* – manor houses located in the surrounding area – that offer restful nights in beautiful surroundings. See p.293

❼ Pinhão Road, rail and river hug the Rio Douro as far as this beautifully sited port-producing town with stunning local accommodation choices. See p.297

❽ Rock art at Foz Côa These rock engravings are some of the world's oldest works of art, dating back over 20,000 years. See p.299

HIGHLIGHTS ARE MARKED ON THE MAP ON PP.260–261

5 Porto

While *Portus Cale* (the Romans' "sheltered port") has a long history, modern **PORTO** largely eschews its distant past and presents itself to visitors as a busy commercial city rather than a prettified tourist destination. If that puts you off, it shouldn't, because commerce is written into Porto's DNA, from the great trading river at the heart of the city to the Baroque churches and Neoclassical buildings funded by merchants who made good. If it's never quite what you'd call gentrificd – especially in the old riverside back-alleys – modern Porto does at least look better now than it has done for decades. Since 2001, when it was declared European City of Culture, many of the streets and squares have been reconstructed and historic buildings restored, particularly in the riverside *bairro* of **Ribeira** – now a UNESCO World Heritage Site – where the waterfront cafés and restaurants are an obvious attraction.

Once you've scooted around the commercial centre and seen the cathedral, the only two essential cultural attractions are the applied-art collections of the **Museu Nacional Soares dos Reis** and the world-class **Fundação Serralves** museum of contemporary art. Otherwise, tourism in Porto generally consists of lounging at a dockside café, enjoying a cruise on the Douro, swigging port across the river in **Vila Nova de Gaia** or taking the antique tram out to the local beach at **Foz do Douro**, at the mouth of the Rio Douro.

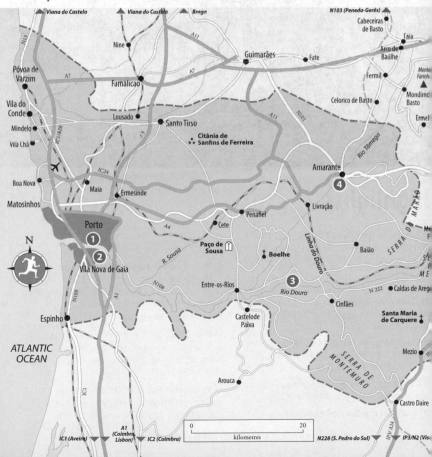

Avenida dos Aliados

5

Not quite all roads lead to the **Avenida dos Aliados** (just "Aliados" to locals), but most do. At the foot of the broad avenue – in the area known as Praça da Liberdade – are a couple of pavement cafés and an equestrian statue of Dom Pedro IV; at the head stands the statue of celebrated local boy Almeida Garrett (1799–1854), poet, novelist, dramatist and Liberal politician. Behind the statue at the top of the avenue is Porto's city hall, the **Câmara Municipal**, while off the bottom the **Estação de São Bento** doubles as a train station and one of the city's grandest buildings – the entrance hall contains twenty thousand magnificent *azulejos* depicting two great themes, namely the history of transport and the history of Portugal.

Mercado do Bolhão

Rua Formosa • Mon–Fri 7am–5pm, Sat 7am–1pm

The heartbeat of the busy commercial area centred on Rua Formosa is the two-storey, wrought-iron **Mercado do Bolhão**. Time may have taken its toll on the structure, but it's still the principal place in the city centre to buy meat, fish, fruit, vegetables and handicrafts. It's particularly good for bread (sold from little cabins in the middle), flowers and dried mountain herbs and teas, while one stall sells nothing but enormous mounds of garlic.

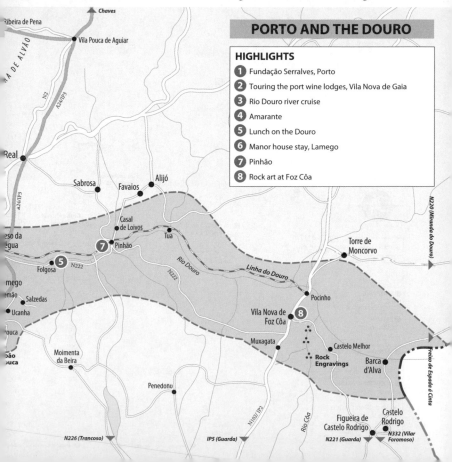

PORTO AND THE DOURO

HIGHLIGHTS

1. Fundação Serralves, Porto
2. Touring the port wine lodges, Vila Nova de Gaia
3. Rio Douro river cruise
4. Amarante
5. Lunch on the Douro
6. Manor house stay, Lamego
7. Pinhão
8. Rock art at Foz Côa

5

Torre dos Clérigos

Rua São Filipe Nery • **Tower** April–Oct daily 9.30am–1pm & 2.30–7pm; Nov–March daily 10am–noon & 2–5pm • €2, binoculars €3 • **Church** Daily 8.45am–12.30pm & 3.30–7pm • Free • ⓦ torredosclerigos.pt

The best vantage point in the city centre is from the top of the Baroque **Torre dos Clérigos**, which towers 75m above the streets. The slender finger was the tallest building in Portugal when completed in 1763 and, having puffed up the two hundred-odd stairs, you can enjoy the sweeping views (you can rent binoculars at the ticket desk). Before you leave, step through the door into the associated church, the **Igreja dos**

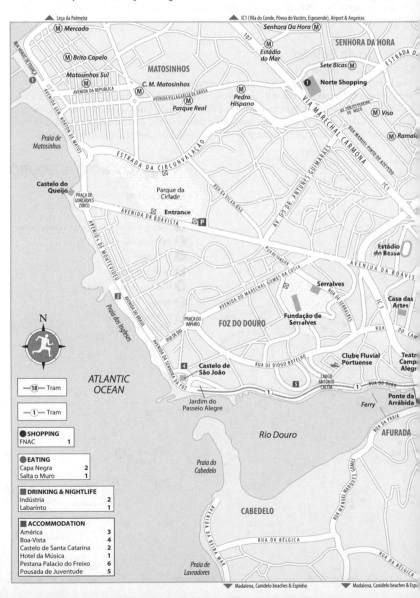

N

ATLANTIC
OCEAN

—18— Tram

—1— Tram

● **SHOPPING**
FNAC   1

● **EATING**
Capa Negra   2
Salta o Muro   1

■ **DRINKING & NIGHTLIFE**
Indústria   2
Labarínto   1

■ **ACCOMMODATION**
América   3
Boa-Vista   4
Castelo de Santa Catarina   2
Hotel da Música   1
Pestana Palacio do Freixo   6
Pousada de Juventude   5

Clérigos – designed, like the tower, by busy Porto architect Nicolau Nasoni, who, after half a lifetime spent in his adopted city, was buried in the church at his own request. Be sure to also check out the bookstore.

Around the Jardim da Cordoaria

The main university building in Porto flanks one side of the **Jardim da Cordoaria**, whose gigantic plane trees shelter impromptu card and chess games. There are more

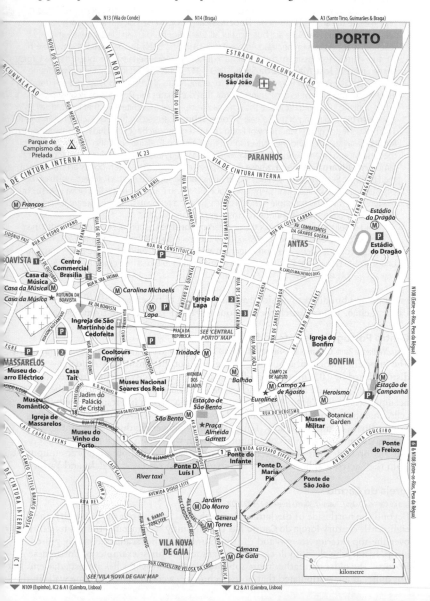

PORTO'S ARCHITECTURE

Porto's churches provide one of the country's richest concentrations of **Baroque** architecture. The style was brought to Portugal by Italian painter and architect **Nicolau Nasoni** (1691–1773), who arrived in Porto at the age of 34, and remained here for the rest of his life. The church and tower of Clérigos is his greatest work, though his masterful touch can also be seen in the cathedral and adjacent bishop's palace, and at the churches of Misericórdia, Carmo, Santo Ildefonso and São Francisco. All are remarkable for their decorative exuberance, reflecting the wealth derived from Portugal's colonies.

In the second half of the eighteenth century, out went the luxuriant complexity of Baroque and in came the studied lines of the **Neoclassical** period. Neoclassicism also incorporated hints of Gothic and Baroque art, but most of all, was influenced by an Islamic style, which reached its apotheosis in the Salão Árabe of the Palácio da Bolsa. By the turn of the twentieth century Porto's Neoclassicism had acquired a distinctly French Renaissance touch, thanks largely to the architect **José Marquês da Silva** (1869–1947), who studied in Paris. His most notable works were São Bento railway station, the exuberant Teatro Nacional São João, and the distinctly less elegant monument to the Peninsular War that dominates the Rotunda da Boavista.

Not until the 1950s did Porto see the emergence of a style of architecture that it could call its own, with the beginning of the so-called **Porto School**, centred on the city's School of Fine Arts. This proved fertile ground for many of Porto's contemporary architects, including Eduardo Souto Moura (Casa das Artes, and the conversion of the Alfândega), Alcino Soutinho (the conversion of the Casa-Museu Guerra Junqueiro, and Amarante's Museu Amadeo Sousa Cardoso), and – most famously – **Álvaro Siza Vieira**, whose masterpiece in Porto is the contemporary art museum at the Fundação Serralves (1999). Earlier works of his can be seen in Leça da Palmeira, north of the city, such as the Piscina de Mar swimming pool (1966) and Casa de Chá da Boa Nova (1963), both hidden in the rocks by the shore – the Casa de Chá was a renowned café-restaurant for years but has currently been sadly abandoned to the elements and vandals.

A word should also be said about the city's famous **bridges** – there are five more besides the landmark Ponte Dom Luís I (see p.268), notably the Ponte do Infante, whose central 280m reinforced-concrete arch is the world's longest, and further east upriver, Gustave Eiffel's iron railway bridge, Ponte Dona Maria Pia. The best way to see them is to take a river cruise (see p.275).

monumental buildings to all sides, and a grouping of pavement cafés flanking Praça de Parada Leitão. You can catch the tram out towards Foz do Douro from here too.

Centro Português de Fotografia
Campo Mártires da Pátria, Cordoaria • Tues–Fri 10am–12.30pm & 3–6pm, Sat, Sun & hols 3–7pm • Free • ☎ 220 046 300, ⓦ www.cpf.pt

The imposing Neoclassical building to the south of the Jardim da Cordoaria – distinguished by 103, mostly barred, windows – was the city's eighteenth-century prison, the Cadeia da Relação, which remained in use until 1974. It's now the headquarters of the **Centro Português de Fotografia**, which has restored the building's cells, chambers, workshops and internal courtyards and converted them into rather extraordinary exhibition spaces. Temporary shows cover anything from vintage Portuguese photography to contemporary urban work from Brazil and elsewhere. On the top floor there is a collection of antique cameras and photographic equipment, from the "stereo-graphoscope" of 1885 to all manner of classic Kodaks and Yashicas.

Igreja do Carmo
Rua do Carmo • Daily: 7.30am–7.30pm • Free • ☎ 223 322 928

Beyond the north side of the Jardim da Cordoaria, across from the university, the eighteenth-century **Igreja do Carmo** has two instantly recognizable traits – its deliriously over-the-top exterior *azulejos* and the four saints atop the facade, seemingly poised to jump. Inside, the elegant gilt carvings are among the finest examples of Portuguese Rococo. The older and rather more sober **Igreja das Carmelitas** lies almost adjacent, but not quite, as a law stipulated that no two churches were to share the same wall (in this

case perhaps to hinder amorous liaisons between the nuns of Carmelitas and the monks of Carmo). As a result, what is probably the **narrowest house in Portugal** – barely 1m wide, and with its own letterbox – was built between them and, though now empty, remained inhabited until the 1980s.

Museu Nacional Soares dos Reis

Rua Dom Manuel II 44 • Tues 2–6pm, Wed–Sun 10am–6pm • €5, free on Sun & hols 10am–2pm • ☎ 223 393 770, ⓦ museusoaresdosreis.pt

A five-minute walk from the Jardim da Cordoaria, behind the hospital, stands the **Museu Nacional Soares dos Reis**. Serralves aside, it's the best museum in Porto and in fact was Portugal's first designated art museum, founded in 1833 to preserve works confiscated from dissolved monasteries and convents. The present building, into which the collection moved in the 1940s, was once a royal residence that served as the French headquarters in the Peninsular War.

The museum takes its name from sculptor António Soares dos Reis (1847–89), whose best-known work, *O Desterrado* (The Exile), is here, along with an extensive display of Portuguese art from the sixteenth to twentieth centuries. But it's the **applied and decorative art** that's perhaps most engaging – the museum contains excellent collections of gold jewellery, religious silverwork, Portuguese glassware, earthenware and textiles, Chinese ceramics, French furniture, and painted screens and lacquered cabinets from the Far East. Special exhibitions concentrate on particular periods, artists or themes, and you could spend hours here browsing; there's also a garden and a good café.

Jardim do Palácio de Cristal

Rua Dom Manuel II • Daily: April–Sept 8am–9pm; Oct–March 8am–7pm • Free • ☎ 225 320 080

The **Jardim do Palácio de Cristal**, whose centrepiece pavilion – a kind of concrete tea-cosy – replaced a far more elegant 1860s iron-and-glass "Crystal Palace", hosts various concerts and events, and there's a popular open-air self-service café by the lake. It's the surrounding **gardens** that are the real draw, however, with an avenue of lime trees and lovely river views from high vantage points on the south side. The municipal library is sited near the main entrance, while other buildings and galleries put on exhibitions, workshops, summer concerts and children's activities.

Sé and around

Terreiro da Sé • **Cathedral** Daily: April–Sept 9.30am 12.30pm & 2.30–7pm; Oct–March 9.30am–12.30pm & 2.30–6pm • Free • ☎ 222 059 028 • **Cloisters** Daily: April–Sept 9.00am–12.15pm & 2.30–6.30pm; Oct–March daily 9am–12.15pm & 2.30–5.30pm • Cloisters, Sala Capitular and Tesouro €3

Porto's cathedral, the **Sé**, commands the eastern heights above the river, and there's a case for making this your first stop in the city, because the view from the terrace – of the old-town streets tumbling down towards the Douro – puts everything into perspective. On the north tower (the one with the bell), look for the very worn bas-relief depicting a fourteenth-century ship – a reminder of Portugal's (and Porto's) maritime past. Despite its great age – construction began in the twelfth century – there's no real sense of majesty inside the cathedral, with altar and chapels making little impact in the darkness. The **cloisters**, however, are a different matter, their arched walls filled with magnificent Baroque *azulejos*. Architect Nasoni added a grand, granite staircase, which climbs from the cloisters to the restored **Sala Capitular** (Chapter Room), with more *azulejos*, painted ceiling panels and views from the shuttered windows. In the **Tesouro** (Treasury), meanwhile, is the usual boggling array of silver and gold – beautifully lit for once.

On the south side of the Sé stretches the grandiose frontage of the **Paço Episcopal** (not open to the public), the medieval archbishop's palace that was also rebuilt by the designer of much of eighteenth-century Porto, Nicolau Nasoni.

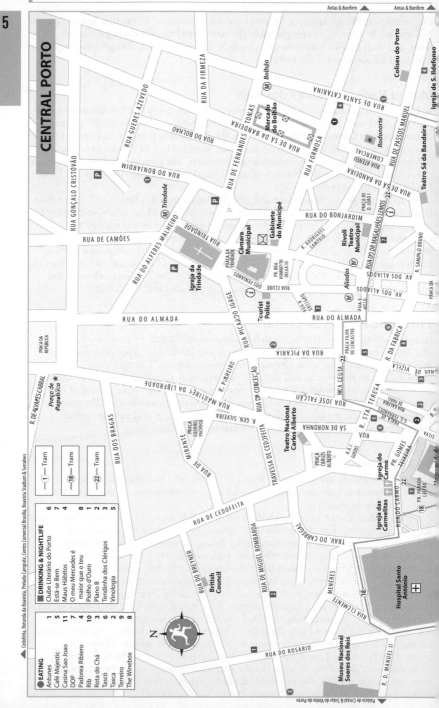

CENTRAL PORTO

Antas & Bonfim ▲   Antas & Bonfim ▲

Coliseu do Porto

Igreja de S. Ildefonso

RUA DA FIRMEZA

M Bolhão

RUA DE SANTA CATARINA

Mercado
do Bolhão

RUA DE SÁ DA BANDEIRA

RUA GUEDES AZEVEDO

RUA DO BOLHÃO

RUA TOMÁS

RUA DE FERNANDES TOMÁS

RUA FORMOSA

RUA DE PASSOS MANUEL

Rodonorte

CENTRO
COMERCIAL
ATENEU

Teatro Sá da Bandeira

RUA DE SÁ DA BANDEIRA

RUA GONÇALO CRISTÓVÃO

RUA DO BONJARDIM

P

M Trindade

PRAÇA DE
D. JOÃO I

RUA DO BONJARDIM

Camara
Municipal

Gabinete
do Municipé

R. RODRIGUES
SAMPAIO

RUA DR DR MAGALHÃES LEMOS

Rivoli
Teatro
Municipal

M Aliados

R. SAMPAIO BRUNO

RUA DE CAMÕES

P

RUA DO ALFERES MALHEIRO

RUA DA TRINDADE

PRAÇA DA
TRINDADE

Igreja da
Trindade

PRAÇA DE
GOMES
TEIXEIRA

PR. BBA.
HUMBERTO
DELGADO

RUA CLUBE
DOS FENIANOS

Tourist
Police

AV. DOS ALIADOS

AV. DOS ALIADOS

PRAÇA DA

RUA DO ALMADA

RUA PICARDO IGARE

RUA DO ALMADA

PRAÇA DA
REPÚBLICA

RUA DA PICARIA

PRAÇA FILIPA
DE LENCASTRE

R. DA FÁBRICA

RUA DE VIZELA

RUA DOS BRAGAS

R. DE CAMPOS CABRAL

Praça de
República ★

RUA DE S. MARTIRES DA LIBERDADE

R. PIMHEIRO

R. DA CONCEIÇÃO

R. JOSÉ FALCÃO

RUA CEITA

R. STA TERESA

R. GÁLERIA
DE PARIS

PRAÇA DE
PARIS

G.G. FERNANDES

RUA DE
MIRANTE

PRAÇA
CORONEL
PACHECO

R. GEN. SILVEIRA

TRANESSA DE CEDOFEITA

Teatro Nacional
Carlos Alberto

SÁ DE NORONHA

R.A.T.
GUEDES

PRAÇA
CARLOS
ALBERTO

Igreja do
Carmo

PR. GOMES
FERREIRA

RUA DE CEDOFEITA

RUA DO BREYNER

British
Council

RUA DE MIGUEL BOMBARDA

Igreja das
Carmelitas

RUA DO CARMO

PR. PARADA
LEITÃO

TRAV. DO CARREGAL

RUA DO ROSARIO

RUA CLEMENTE

MENERES

Museu Nacional
Soares dos Reis

R. D. MANUEL II

Hospital Santo
António

N

— 1 —Tram

—18—Tram

—22—Tram

● EATING
Antunes   5
Café Majestic   5
Casina Sao Joao   11
DOP   7
Padorea Ribiero   4
Rib   10
Rota do Chá   3
Tascó   6
Taxca   2
Terreiro   9
The Winebox   8

■ DRINKING & NIGHTLIFE
Clube Literário do Porto   6
Está-se Bem   7
Maus Hábitos   4
O meu Mercedes é
maior que o teu   8
Piolho d'Ouro   1
Plano B   2
Tendinha dos Clérigos   3
Vinologia   5

◀ Cedofeita, Rotunda da Boavista, Preiada Campoite, Centro Comercial Brasília, Boavista Stadium & Serralves

Palácio de Cristal & Solar do Vinho do Porto ▼

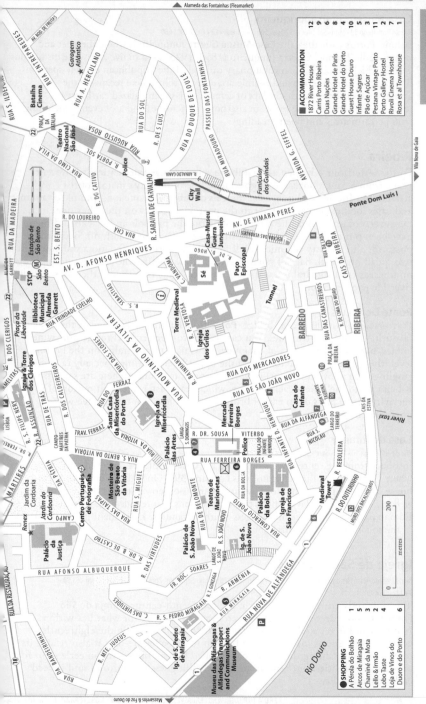

Alameda das Fontainhas (Fleamarket)

5

	ACCOMMODATION
12	1872 River House
9	Carris Porto Ribeira
6	Duas Nações
8	Grande Hotel de Paris
4	Grande Hotel do Porto
10	Guest House Douro
5	Infante Sagres
3	Pão de Açúcar
11	Pestana Vintage Porto
2	Porto Gallery Hostel
7	Rivoli Cinema Hostel
1	Rosa et al Townhouse

SHOPPING	
A Pérola do Bolhão	1
Arcos de Miragaia	5
Chaminé da Mota	3
Lello & Irmão	2
Lobo Taste	4
Loja de Vinos do Duoro do Porto	6

Vila Nova de Gaia

Massarelos & Foz do Douro

Rio Douro

Ponte Dom Luís I

5

Casa-Museu Guerra Junqueiro

Rua de Dom Hugo 32 • Mon–Sat 10am–5.30pm, Sun 2–5.30pm • €2 • ☎ 222 003 689

Behind Porto's cathedral, the **Casa-Museu Guerra Junqueiro** is where the poet and writer Abílio Manuel Guerra Junqueiro (1850–1923) used to live and write his famous works, which reflected the revolutionary turmoil of the Republican era. He spent his lifetime collecting Iberian and Islamic art, and the rooms here recapture the atmosphere of the era with displays of ceramics, glassware, glazed earthenware, jewellery and textiles. The museum also hosts an active calendar of events, including fado performances and poetry readings.

Ribeira

Porto's waterfront – known as the **Ribeira** – has changed dramatically in recent years, from a rough dockside cargo zone to one of the city's major tourist attractions. The arcaded quayside, the **Cais da Ribeira**, is one long run of restaurants and cafés looking across the river to the port wine lodges on the other side. However, come down in the morning – before the parasols and blackboard menus have been put out – and the Ribeira still ticks along in local fashion. Between the postcards and touristy ceramics you'll find dusty grocery stores and a warehouse or two, piled high with bags of potatoes. Meanwhile, behind the arcades and heading up towards the cathedral is a warren of stepped alleys that thumb their noses at the riverside gentrification.

Ponte Dom Luís I

Porto's iconic double-decker bridge, **Ponte Dom Luís I**, provides one of the city's favourite photo opportunities. You can walk across either level to the port wine lodges, bars and restaurants of Vila Nova de Gaia – there's traffic on the bottom level, the metro across the top – and the upper level crossing especially (a nerve-jangling 60m above the water) is worth doing at least once. There are steps from the Ribeira up to the lower-level walkway, which lead past a café built on top of the surviving stone piers of an earlier bridge – a great location for a coffee with an unrivalled bridge and river view.

Casa do Infante

Rua da Alfândega 10 • Tues–Sun 9.30am–1pm & 2–5.30pm • Museum €2, exhibitions often free • ☎ 222 060 400

Just back from the central riverside stands the **Casa do Infante**, believed to be the house where Prince Henry the Navigator was born in 1394. Once the Crown's customs house, and later part of the Royal Mint, the mansion now contains the city archives as well as a museum displaying finds from excavations that revealed the remains of a large Roman palace. The prince himself gets a rather grandiose monument just up the road in the square also bearing his name.

Igreja de São Francisco

Rua do Infante Dom Henrique • Daily: March–June & Oct 9am–7pm; July–Sept 9am–8pm; Nov–Feb 9am–6pm • €3.50 •
☎ 222 006 493

The city's only truly Gothic church, the fourteenth-century **Igreja de São Francisco** (now deconsecrated), is even more remarkable for what lies within. Not only did it get a fabulously opulent Rococo makeover in the eighteenth century – the gilded interior has to be seen to be believed – but it also retains its catacombs, containing thousands of scrubbed human bones. It's an eerie sight for modern sensibilities, but reflects an earlier willingness to confront, and indeed embrace, mortality.

FROM TOP FUNDAÇÃO SERRALVES, PORTO (P.271); TORRE DOS CLÉRIGOS, PORTO (P.262) >

5

Palácio da Bolsa

Rua Ferreira Borges, at Praça do Infante Dom Henrique • Guided tours daily: April–Oct 9am–6.30pm; Nov–March 9am–12.30pm & 2–5.30pm • €8 • ☎ 223 399 090, ⓦ palaciodabolsa.com

For an indication of the wealth pouring into Porto from the nineteenth century, join a tour of the stock exchange, the **Palácio da Bolsa**, whose interior halls display an almost obscene level of richness. You don't need to buy a ticket to see the dramatic iron, glass-and-tile **Patio das Nações** courtyard, a veritable cloister of commerce, whose side rooms contain a craft-and-jewellery store, wine bar and shop. But to delve any deeper into the building, to encounter over-the-top salons like the extraordinary **Salão Árabe** – inspired by the Alhambra in Granada – you'll have to bear with the rather pricey and fact-heavy guided visits.

Santa Casa da Misericórdia do Porto

Rua das Flores 15 • Daily: April–Sept 10am–6.30pm; Oct–March 10am–5.30pm • €5 • ☎ 220 906 960, ⓦ mmipo.pt/en-gb

The collections of paintings, sculptures and jewellery on display in the **Santa Casa da Misericórdia do Porto**, are organised and displayed in themed rooms ranging from the fifteenth to eighteenth centuries. The sixteenth-century church, which was modified in the eighteenth century, is part of the museum and was also an official stamp for pilgrims who were on their way to Santiago de Compostela.

Along the river

It's around 2km from the Ribeira along the riverfront pavement and quayside to the Ponte da Arrábida (heading west towards Foz do Douro). This is a good half-hour's walk, enough for most people to get a flavour of the Douro and you can then jump on the tram or bus #500 back to the city centre or on to Foz and the beach.

Museu das Alfândegas and Alfândegas Transport and Communications Museum

Rua Nova de Alfândega • Tues–Fri 10am–1pm & 2–6pm Sat, Sun & hols 3–7pm • €7.50 • ☎ 223 403 000, ⓦ www.amtc.pt

The Neoclassical Alfândega, or Customs House, was constructed on the riverbank between 1860 and 1880. It's a vast building that was originally designed to store the cargo of up to forty ships, but now is in service as the **Museu das Alfândegas**, which recounts the history of Porto, its trades and industries.

The Customs House also contains the **Alfândegas Transport and Communications Museum** – the "car through time and space" exhibition entertainingly relating to the development of the motor car. It also houses the first-ever car brought to Portugal in 1895 from Paris.

Museu do Vinho do Porto

Rua de Monchique 45–52 • Tues–Sat 10am–5.30pm, Sun 10am–12.30pm & 2–5.30pm • €2, free on Sat & Sun • ☎ 222 076 300

Housed in a handsome eighteenth-century former wine warehouse, the **Museu do Vinho do Porto** details the city's take on the history of the port wine trade. In many ways, this is the history of Porto itself and the museum passionately tackles the subject – displays and exhibits chart the development of the port wine business, linking the trade with the fortunes of the major port-wine families and showing how the city grew to become synonymous with wine in just a matter of decades.

Museu do Carro Eléctrico

Alameda Basílio Teles 51 • Mon 2–6pm, Tues–Sun 10am–6pm • €4 • ☎ 226 158 185, ⓦ museudocarroelectrico.pt

All Porto's trams make a fitting halt on the riverside outside the **Museu do Carro Eléctrico**. In the echoing spaces of a former power station, you can admire Iberia's oldest streetcar (1872) alongside many other gleaming vintage specimens.

Rotunda da Boavista

The northwestern edge of the city centre – 2km from downtown Aliados – is marked by the large park-cum-roundabout, which is called the Praça Mouzinho de Albuquerque but is more commonly known as the **Rotunda da Boavista**. The mighty obelisk in the centre commemorates the defeat of the French in the Peninsular War (1808–14), with a Portuguese lion squatting on top of a vanquished French eagle.

Casa da Música

Av da Boavista 604 • Guided tours daily at 11am and 4pm in English and Portuguese • €7.50 • ☎ 220 120 210, ⓦ www.casadamusica .com • **Building and shop** Mon–Sat 9.30am–7pm, Sun & hols 9.30am–6pm • **Restaurant** Mon–Thurs 12.30–3pm & 7.30–11pm, Fri–Sat 12.30–3pm & 7.30–midnight • Ⓜ Casa da Música

Rem Koolhaas' **Casa da Música** – a vast white wedge on a bare esplanade – looks as if the Mother Ship has landed, an impression reinforced by the steel staircase leading up into the black mouth of the entrance. It was a coup for Porto, a flagship part of its urban regeneration programme, and opened to great fanfare in 2005. Attending a concert or event is clearly the best way to see the building, but there are daily, hour-long guided visits if you want to know more about its dramatic design and construction.

Igreja de São Martinho de Cedofeita

Largo do Priorado, off Rua Aníbal Cunha • Mon–Sat 8–10am & 5–7pm

Located a few blocks off the Rotunda is the very simple **Igreja de São Martinho de Cedofeita**, which some claim has its origins as far back as the sixth century AD – making it the oldest church in Iberia. However, the existing Romanesque building is a thirteenth-century remodelling of a church whose existence can only be dated with certainty to 1118. Whatever its origins, Cedofeita is unique in being Portugal's only Romanesque church to have kept its original dome, supported by bulky exterior buttresses.

Fundação Serralves

Rua Dom João de Castro 210 • **Museum** April–Sept Tues–Fri 10am–7pm, Sat, Sun & hols 10am–6pm; Oct–March Tues–Fri 10am–5pm, Sat, Sun & hols 10am–7pm • **Park** April–Sept Tues–Fri 10am–7pm, Sat, Sun & hols 10am–8pm; Oct–March Tues–Sun 10am–7pm • Museum & park €8.50; park only €4; both free Sun 10am–1pm • ☎ 226 156 500, ⓦ serralves.pt • Ⓜ Casa da Música, or bus #502 from Bolhão or bus #203 from Rotunda da Boavista

If there's a must-see cultural attraction in Porto it's the contemporary art museum and park run by the **Fundação Serralves**, 4km west of the centre. The **Museu de Arte Contemporânea** is the work of Porto architect Álvaro Siza Vieira, and is a minimalist triumph of white facades and terraces strikingly set in an overwhelmingly green park. There's no permanent collection, instead several changing exhibitions a year draw on the works of Portuguese and international artists, mainly from the 1960s to the present day. Other exhibitions are held in the separate, pink Art Deco **Casa de Serralves** in the grounds.

You can get an idea of the main building from the outside, and from the terrace café, more formal restaurant and museum shop (all free to enter), which means if the exhibitions aren't to your taste, you miss nothing by just visiting the **park**. Indeed, many people prefer this to the museum itself and it's easy to spend a lazy afternoon here, winding along swept gravel paths and clipped lawns before descending wooded tracks to the herb gardens and farmland beyond, grazed by goats and cattle. There are art installations dotted around and a tea house (open weekends only in winter) in a glade with a vine colonnade. July and August see a sequence of "Jazz no Parque" (Jazz in the Park) **concerts** held in the gardens.

Foz do Douro

5km west of the city centre • Bus #500 from São Bento, bus #203 from the Serralves museum and park, to central Foz, or #502 from Bolhão to Castelo do Queijo • Tram #1 (from Ribeira), or #18 (Igreja do Carmo) down to the terminus at Massarelos and change there to tram #1

Foz do Douro, formerly a fishermen's quarter but a distinctly more upmarket beach

5

A DAY BY THE SEA

The easiest beach escape from Porto is to **Foz do Douro** (tram, or bus #500) – really, if all you want is a paddle in the rock pools, a lie on the sand and a beachside beer, there's no need to go anywhere else. **Matosinhos** (metro Line A), further north, is where the locals go to eat seafood and for a night's clubbing, and there are beaches and more restaurants across the Rio Leça at **Leça da Palmeira** (an easy walk from Matosinhos or bus #507 from Senhora da Hora or Matosinhos metros). The **Vila Nova de Gaia** beaches (buses #902/#906), across the Douro to the south, have extensive sands and big campsites. Further south still, is the resort of **Espinho**, which is 18km from Porto (frequent local trains from São Bento; 35min). Once the darling of northern Portugal's monied classes, the resort is now largely ruined by unchecked construction that has taken place since the 1970s. A better day-trip option is by metro (Line B) to the north of the city: the old seafaring town of **Vila do Conde** (see p.283) is easily the best target, though the brash resort of **Póvoa de Varzim** just beyond (at the end of Line B; 1hr from Porto) might tempt you with its 8km of sands.

suburb these days, is on several bus routes, but it's a nice idea to take the tram at least one way – these drop you by the riverside gardens in Foz. The confluence of river and ocean is dominated by the squat **Castelo de São João**, beyond which stretch several kilometres of coves and beaches, backed by the cafés and bars of Avenida do Brasil, which becomes the hub of Porto's summer nightlife. At the northern end stands the **Castelo do Queijo** (Cheese Castle), so-named because it was built upon boulders that apparently looked like cheese. From here, Avenida da Boavista (and bus #502) runs straight back into the city.

Vila Nova de Gaia

The quickest way to Gaia from Porto's upper town is to take the Funicular dos Guindais (see p.275) down from near Praça da Batalha and walk across the bridge; alternatively, buses #900, #901 and #906 run from São Bento station across the bridge and along the Gaia riverfront • For the upper station of the Teleférico de Gaia, take metro Line D from Ⓜ Aliados/São Bento to Ⓜ Jardim do Morro

Cross to the south side of the Rio Douro, over the Ponte Dom Luís I, and you leave the city of Porto for the once-separate town of **Vila Nova de Gaia**, which has now been absorbed as a neighbourhood. The riverfront here – facing Porto's Ribeira – also has a long line of cafés, bars and restaurants; cruise boats dock along the esplanade, while the wooden craft with sails are known as *barcos rabelos*, the traditional boats once used to transport wine casks downriver from the Douro port estates. The views are, if anything, better from Gaia than from the Porto side, looking back across to a largely eighteenth-century cityscape, with few modern buildings intruding in the panoramic sweep from the Palácio de Cristal gardens to the cathedral towers.

The port wine lodges

Gaia, of course, is completely synonymous with the **port wine** trade (see p.275) – you can't miss the dozens of company lodges and warehouses (known as *caves*), some in business for more than three centuries, that splash their brand names across every rooftop, facade and advertising hoarding. They almost all offer **tastings and tours**, conducted in English, with a view to enticing you to buy. Tours of the smaller, lesser-known companies tend to be more personal than those of larger producers, but they are all pretty informative and you'll soon know the difference between a tawny and a ruby, and which vintages are best.

Teleférico de Gaia

Lower station at Cais de Gaia, upper station at Ⓜ Jardim do Morro • Daily: end of April to end of Sept 10am–8pm; end of Sept to end of Oct 10am–7pm; end of Oct to end of April 10am–6pm • €5 one-way, €8 return; children half-price • ☎ 223 723 709, �W gaiacablecar.com

The best way to explore Gaia – and to take some dramatic aerial shots of Porto and the river – is to ride the **Teleférico de Gaia**, or cable car. It connects the upper station, near the

top level of the Ponte Dom Luís I, with the far end of the Gaia riverside, in a five-minute, 600m journey that sweeps right above the rooftops of the historic port wine lodges.

ARRIVAL AND DEPARTURE
PORTO

BY PLANE

Porto airport (☎ 229 432 400, ⓦ ana.pt) is 13km north of the city in Maia. Metro Line E (daily 6am–1am, every 20–30min; one-way travel ticket €1.85 (plus a one-off cost of €0.60 for a rechargeable ticket) takes you directly into the centre in around 30min – to Casa da Música (for Boavista hotels), Trindade, Aliados or Bolhão (for city-centre hotels), or São Bento or Campanhã (for onward train services). Taxis from the airport into the centre cost €20–25 – make sure you get one from the authorized rank outside the terminal.

BY BUS

Buses to Porto arrive at various stops and garages all over the city, though most are fairly central. Eurolines (international services) and several other companies use Campo 24 de Agosto, 1km east of the centre (ⓜ Campo 24 de Agosto); Garagem Atlântico, Rua Alexandre Herculano, near Praça da Batalha, is a hub for several companies including the national operator Rede Expressos (ⓦ www.rede-expressos.pt); Rodonorte (Estremadura, Ribatejo, Minho, Trás-os-Montes; ⓦ rodonorte.pt) and Santos (Beiras, Trás-os-Montes, Lisbon; ⓦ santosviagensturismo.pt) stop on Rua Ateneu Comercial, near Bolhão market; Minho services tend to stop near Praça da República, north of the

centre (near Trindade metro); while Renex (Estremadura, Ribatejo, Lisbon, Algarve and Minho; ⓦ renex.pt) stop at Campo dos Mártires da Pátria 37, next to Palácio da Justiça.
Destinations Amarante (up to 10 daily; 1hr); Barcelos (7 daily; 1hr 45min); Braga (every 1hr 30min; 1hr 15min); Bragança (6 daily; 3hr 30min); Chaves (5–10 daily; 2hr); Coimbra (8–10 daily; 1hr 30min); Guimarães (6–12 daily; 1hr); Lamego/Peso da Régua (3–5 daily; 3hr); Lisbon (hourly; 3hr–3hr 30min); Viana do Castelo (hourly; 1hr 15min); Vila Real (6–9 daily; 1hr 30min–2hr).

BY CAR

Driving into Porto is to be avoided, if possible – the city centre is congested and the one-way system confusing. You don't need a car to see the city, so the best advice is to park where you can and use public transport. Major suburban metro stations have parking – particularly at the football stadium, Estádio do Dragão – or use one of the sign-posted city-centre car parks or garages; following signs for "Centro" or "Aliados" will send you into the maelstrom. Garage parking is expensive – around €1/hr between 8am and 8pm, slightly cheaper overnight – but you'll have little choice if your hotel doesn't have parking, as on-street metered parking is limited to 2hr (though it's free after 8pm and at weekends).

5

Car rental Most international companies have both downtown and airport offices; if you need a vehicle for exploring further afield it's far easier to pick up your car the day you leave Porto. Local companies include Auto-Jardim (ⓦ auto-jardim.com) and Guerin (ⓦ guerin.pt).

BY TRAIN

Estação de Campanhã International, intercity and ALFA Pendular trains arrive at the Estação de Campanhã, 2km east of the city centre. With a ticket to Porto you can simply change here onto any local train for São Bento station (see below), a 5min ride away. Campanhã is also on the metro, or it's a €5 taxi ride into the centre.

Destinations Barcelos (14 daily; 1hr–1hr 20min); Coimbra (hourly; 1hr 15min–1hr 50min); Espinho (every 10–30min; 15–30min); Lisbon (hourly; 3hr 20min–4hr); Pocinho (5 daily; 3hr 30min); Régua (13 daily; 1hr 45min–2hr 20min); Viana do Castelo (every 1–2hr; 1hr 30min–2hr).

Estação de São Bento This is the city-centre station for suburban and regional services. There's a metro station here and taxis outside, though note that São Bento can be a bit chaotic, with hawkers and touts much in evidence. You can buy tickets for any train at São Bento (even for Campanhã departures). There are also weekend summer steam train services between Régua and Tua (see p.291).

Destinations Aveiro (every 10–30min; 40–55min); Barcelos (14 daily; 1hr–1hr 20min); Braga (every 30min–1hr; 1hr); Guimarães (hourly; 1hr 5min); Pocinho (5 daily; 3hr 30min); Régua (13 daily; 1hr 45min–2hr 20min); Viana do Castelo (every 1–2hr; 1hr 30min–2hr).

Train information There are information offices at both stations, or call ☏ 707 210 220 or consult the CP website, ⓦ cp.pt.

GETTING AROUND

You'll be able to walk – more like climb – between all the city-centre attractions, but you'll have to use public transport to get out to the the Serralves art museum, the coast and airport. There's an extensive **bus** network, and a swift **metro** system, while a **funicular** and a couple of old **tram** lines still remain in service. The local transport authority, **STCP** (☏ 808 200 166, ⓦ www.stcp.pt), has a useful website (English version available), and information offices (Mon–Fri 8am–7.30pm, Sat 9am–12.30pm) in Campanhã train station and Casa da Música and Trindade metro stations. At the time of writing, a **rivertaxi** was being set up between Vila Nova de Gaia— by the Sandeman Port Wine Lodge—and the Ribeira.

TICKETS AND PASSES

Andante card To use public transport you need a rechargeable Andante card, which costs €0.60 and is available from ticket machines and from other marked Andante shops and kiosks (*Lojas Andante*). You credit the card with one, two or ten trips – the whole region is divided into concentric colour-coded zones, though everywhere you're going to want to go in Porto all falls within the same central zone 2. A single trip in the central zone costs €1.20 – you can change transport for free within the hour. It sounds complicated, but in practice it isn't, and you can change the instructions on the machines in every station to English.

Andante Tour pass If you're doing a lot of travelling, buy an Andante Tour pass (€7 for 24hr, €15 for 72hr), which is valid on all metros, buses and local trains (and is available on arrival at the airport from the Tourism Office in the Arrivals Hall).

Porto Card The turismos sell the Porto Card (€13 one day; €20 two days; €25 three days), which gives unlimited bus, metro and funicular travel plus discounts or free entry at many museums and monuments, tours, wine cellars, bars, restaurants and shops. There's also a streamlined one-day version (no transport included) for €5.

BY BUS

Major city bus stops include Praça Almeida Garrett opposite São Bento station, Praça da Liberdade at the bottom of Avenida dos Aliados, Jardim da Cordoaria, and the interchange at Casa da Música metro station.

BY METRO

The metro system (ⓦ metrodoporto.pt) runs on six lines, A to F, underground in the city centre and then overground to the airport and to suburban destinations. Hours of operation are daily from 6am to 1am (departures every 10–30min), and you need an Andante card (see above) to use the system. Other than for the ride in from the airport, or for the trip up the coast to Matosinhos or Vila do Conde, the metro isn't particularly useful for sightseeing, though there are handy city-centre stops at Trindade, Aliados, Bolhão and São Bento, and you can also use it to go to the Casa da Música at the Rotunda da Boavista and FC Porto's stadium, Estádio do Dragão. A spectacular ride to experience is Line D (from Trindade, Aliados or São Bento), which crosses the river to Vila Nova de Gaia along the top tier of Ponte Dom Luís I.

BY TRAM

Porto's trams (*eléctricos*) run 5km from the Ribeira along the river to Foz do Douro (25min), with a branch from the Igreja do Carmo at Cordoaria in the city centre (using this, change halfway at Massarelos, by the tram museum). The service operates daily (9.15am–7pm; departures every 30min). Pay a flat €2.50 fare or 24hr ticket for €8.

FIVE GREAT PORT WINE LODGE TOURS

Around thirty port wine lodges in Vila Nova de Gaia are open for tours – our pick of the best is below. Most of the lodges are open daily all year round. Some charge an entrance fee for their tours, such as the Sandeman and Taylor, Fladgate and Yeatman, but most just charge a couple of euros and the amount is deducted from anything you buy.

Cálem ⓦ calem.pt. One of the best visitor centres, especially informative about the wine's history and the port-wine production process. No need to pre-book a visit. Daily: May–Oct 10am–7pm; Nov–April 10am–6pm.

Graham's ⓦ grahams-port.com. Originally founded by a Scottish family, this lodge has a splendid tasting terrace overlooking the river. Book your visit via the website. Daily: April–Oct 9.30am–6pm; Nov–March 9.30am–5.30pm.

Ramos Pinto ⓦ ramospinto.pt. The famous advertising posters of this Portuguese company did much to popularize port in the 1900s – there's a really good museum housed in the 1930s' period offices.

May–Oct daily 10am–6pm; Nov–March Mon–Fri 9am–5pm; April Mon–Fri 10am–6pm.

Sandeman ⓦ sandeman.eu. The black-hat-and-cape cut-out provides the most recognizable of company logos and the lengthy tour includes an explanatory film and a good museum. Tour prices range from €6 to €35. Daily: Nov–Feb 9.30am–12.30pm & 2–5.30pm; March–Oct 10am–12.30pm & 2–6pm.

Taylor, Fladgate & Yeatman ⓦ taylor.pt. Founded in 1692, and still an independent family firm, Taylor's has panoramic views from its salon, terrace and restaurant. Price for tour is €12 and whilst there's no fixed schedule, tours leave roughly every 30–40 minutes. Daily 10am–6pm.

BY FUNICULAR

The quickest way from the city centre down to Ponte Dom Luís I (for Vila Nova de Gaia) and Ribeira is via the Funicular dos Guindais (every 10min: May–June & Sept–Oct Sun–Wed 8am–10pm, Thurs–Sat 8am–midnight; Aug daily 8am–midnight; Nov–April daily 8am–8pm; €2.50 each way, or use Andante card); the upper entrance is below Praça da Batalha, down Rua Augusto Rosa; the lower is right by the bottom tier of the bridge. After a 90m crawl through a tunnel, the carriage drops rather thrillingly down a steep gradient beside the medieval city wall.

BY TAXI

A typical taxi ride across town costs €6–7, and most squares and major stations have taxi ranks (or call Radio Táxis ☎ 225 073 900).

TOURS AND CRUISES

River cruises Porto's stock-in-trade is the river cruise along the Douro. Services are daily and frequent in the summer, much reduced between November and February.

The cheapest is the 50min bridges cruise (€10), though there are also evening and dinner cruises, and full-day or weekend cruises, with prices ranging from €55 to €200. The longer cruises all operate via the port wine town of Peso da Régua, halfway along the Douro, where – depending on your choice – you're shuttled around a port wine lodge or take a trip on a steam train.

Tours There are a number of ways to explore the town: open-top bus tours such as the Hop-On-Hop off tour (ⓦ hop-on-hop-off.com) from €12; free walking tours (ⓦ panchotours.pt); bike tours (from €25) and Segway tours (from €50) with Bluedragon City Tours (ⓦ bluedragon .pt); and even helicopter tours from €165 (ⓦ thefunplan .com). Or try out a Taste Porto Food Tour (☎ 967 258 750, ⓦ tasteporto.com), which takes you around the food markets and focuses on local gastronomy. Porto Tours, Torre Medieval, Calçada Dom Pedro Pitões 15, close to the Sé (daily 10am–7pm; ☎ 222 000 073 or ☎ 222 000 045, ⓦ portotours.com), can book all kinds of tours, including river cruises and trips on the steam train; trips can also be booked at the city turismos and São Bento train station.

INFORMATION AND ACTIVITIES

INFORMATION

As well as the year-round turismos listed below, where you can pick up a useful map and information, there are two summer-season information points, one in Campanhã train station and the other on the Ribeira waterfront.

Turismo Central Rua Clube dos Fenianos 25, top of Avenida dos Aliados (daily: June–Oct 9am–8pm; Nov–May 9am–7pm; ☎ 223 393 472).

Turismo Sé Casa da Câmara, Terreiro da Sé, opposite the

cathedral (daily: June–Oct 9am–8pm; Nov–May 9am–7pm; ☎ 223 393 472).

Turismo Vila Nova de Gaia Avenida Diogo Leite 242, next to Sandeman (Mon–Sat 10am–1pm & 2–6pm; ☎ 223 703 735, ⓦ cm-gaia.pt), is geared almost exclusively to pointing you towards the port wine lodges.

Loja de Turismo Praça Dom João I 43, one block east of Aliados (April–Oct Mon–Fri 9am–7.30pm, Sat, Sun & hols 9.30am–3.30pm; Nov–March Mon–Fri 9am–7pm, Sat,

5

Sun & hols 9.30am–3.30pm; ☎ 927 411 817), is useful for general enquiries about northern Portugal.

Websites The city council's website, ⓦ portoturismo.pt (also in English), provides the same sort of information as the turismos, while there's more information about Porto and the north of Portugal on ⓦ visitportoandnorth.travel. For a different view of the city, check out ⓦ oportocool .wordpress.com, a blog of the city's fashionable hotspots (blog is in Portuguese).

TOURS AND ACTIVITIES

Football FC Porto, European champions in 2004 and winners of the Europa League in 2011, play at the landmark Estádio do Dragão in Antas, off Avenida Fernão Magalhães (ⓦ www .fcporto.pt; ⓜ Estádio do Dragão). Match tickets cost €15–60 depending on the opposition and seat location, or there are year-round stadium tours (July & Aug daily, otherwise Thurs–Sun only; €10; see website for schedules). The city's second team, Boavista FC, play at Estádio do Bessa, Rua 1 de Janeiro, off Avenida da Boavista (ⓦ boavistafc.pt), west of the centre.

Tours Cooltours Oporto (Rua da Armenia 50, Porto; ☎ 222 010 213, ⓦ cooltouroporto.com) offer package trips and group or small personalised trips around Porto (€65), as well as further afield such as to the Minho region.

ACCOMMODATION

Porto has been undergoing a tourism boom and has a wide range of accommodation. Rooms start at €38 for a **hostel** room, though depending on the part of town, many of the older guesthouses can be dog-eared, noisy or dodgy, or all three – budget on €60 for something decent and en suite. Note that hostel accommodation offers dorm or double rooms, and the Portuguese treat hostelling more as a B&B style of accommodation therefore rooms are clean, neat and spacious. Nearly all the cheapest accommodation is in the city centre rather than in the medieval streets nearer the river – there are concentrations along Rua de Cedofeita, Rua do Alamada, around Avenida dos Aliados and near Praça da Batalha. There's more and more **boutique accommodation** in and around the city centre and Ribeira, while the upmarket suburbs of Boavista and Serralves, west of the centre, contain most of the city's **four- and five-star hotels**, though the suburban location is a drawback for sightseers. Only a few hotels have their own parking, but some have negotiated cut-price deals with nearby car parks.

CITY CENTRE

★**Duas Nações** Pr Guilherme Gomes Fernandes 59 ☎ 222 081 616, ⓦ duasnacoes.com.pt; map pp.266–267. Don't be fooled by the slightly run-down exterior This is a real budget gem, whose updated rooms have a satellite TV, fan and central heating, and are double-glazed against the street noise. It's popular with backpackers, who favour the low-cost bunk-style dorms (sleeping four). Double rooms also offered. Best to book ahead if you want a private bathroom. Breakfast is not included, but there's a café just outside. No credit cards. Dorms €15, doubles €38

Grande Hotel de Paris Rua da Fábrica 27–29 ☎ 222 073 140, ⓦ hotelparis.pt; map pp.266–267. Consistently recommended, the *Grande Hotel de Paris* is actually more of a guesthouse in price and feel. The building retains many original fittings, with period furniture and high ceilings, while nice touches proliferate – thick bathroom towels, a small garden, and a good breakfast served in a splendid drawing room. Rear rooms have balconies and old-town views. €82

Grande Hotel do Porto Rua de Santa Catarina 197 ☎ 222 076 690, ⓦ grandehotelporto.com; map pp.266–267. Porto's oldest hotel (three stars) is steeped in nineteenth-century mercantile style, with lots of polished marble and crystal chandeliers, and an echoing gilt-tinged restaurant where breakfast is served. It's also in a very handy location, on the main pedestrianized shopping street. Rooms are a little on the dowdy side, but prices are pretty good, and even better during special promotions. Limited parking available. €85

Infante Sagres Pr Dona Filipa de Lencastre 62 ☎ 223 398 500, ⓦ hotelinfantesagres.pt; map pp.266–267. A boutique makeover has transformed Porto's central five-star into a glamorous, contemporary design hotel. The antique Persian carpets, crystal chandeliers, Chinese porcelain and stained-glass windows are all still there, but now you can also expect funky Portuguese custom-made furniture and chic cosmopolitan style. There's an open-air patio, good restaurant and Asian-style spa, plus parking nearby. €190

Pão de Açúcar Rua do Almada 262 ☎ 222 002 425, ⓦ paodeacucarhotel.pt; map pp.266–267. The building's a rather fab 1930s survivor, and while the rooms could all do with a style injection you do get shiny parquet floors and a fair amount of space. No question, though, that the best rooms (€120) are the half-dozen at the top that open out onto a private terrace overlooking the town hall. €100

★**Porto Gallery Hostel** Rua de Miguel Bombarda 222 ☎ 224 964 313, ⓦ gallery-hostel.com; map pp.266–267. Located in the trendy quarter of Miguel Bombarda, *Gallery Hostel* offers en-suite luxury four- or six-bed dorms or double rooms in a renovated 1906 townhouse. Family-run, it also houses local artists' exhibits which opens to the public on Saturdays. The chill-out area is a key feature with small bar and living room with garden. There's another townhouse just down the street offering five double rooms, all with different artistic themes and a private garden, offering more privacy. Dorms €20, doubles €70

Rivoli Cinema Hostel Rua Dr. Magalhães Lemos 83 ☎ 220 174 634 or ☎ 968 958 637,

5

rivolicinemahostel.com; map pp.266–267. Co-owned by a bunch of art-grad, film-crazy friends, the classy *Rivoli* fills a bright and airy townhouse with film-themed four-bed dorms and double rooms, all sharing toilets and showers. It's by no means backpacker-only, but it is funky and communal – one big breakfast table, an outdoor roof terrace, kitchen and lounge – and they also organize events like poker nights and evening drinks. It's easily missed: go through the red door facing the Rivoli Teatro Municipal. Prices are a couple of euros/person higher at weekends. Dorms €25, doubles €58

★**Rosa et al Townhouse** Rua do Rosário 233 ☎916 000 081, rosaetal.pr; map pp.266–267. Seven boutique-style elegant suites occupy an impressively restored townhouse in an artsy and residential district near Soares dos Reis museum. There's afternoon tea (served 4–6pm) and regular classes such as Portuguese gastronomy can be attended. All rooms come with hardwood floors, warm lighting and classy bathrooms with clawfooted baths. €170

RIBEIRA

★**1872 River House** Rua Do Infante D.Henrique 133 ☎222 039 033, 1872riverhouse.com; map pp.266–267. Opened in 2014, this completely renovated, eight-roomed (four street, four river view) riverhouse offers original features such as thick stoned walls and a stained-glass entrance walkway. There's no time limit on breakfast – you can eat as late as you want. Free pick-up from airport if room booked directly with the hotel. All rooms boast monsoon rainshower bathrooms, chandeliers, and have a quaint style, however it's worth paying the €40 extra for a riverview room (€195). It's surprisingly quiet at night, given its popular location. €155

Carris Porto Ribeira Rua do Infante D. Henrique 1 ☎808 203 615, carris-porto-ribeira.hotel-rn.com; map pp.266–267. Just a few steps up the hill from the Ribeira waterside, this stylish four-star makes a decent base. It's been carved out of five old buildings, creating a dramatic lobby space of soaring stone arches and cutaway floors, with a stylish tapas bar off to one side. Handsome rooms feature hardwood floors, earth-toned fabrics and stylish bathrooms, while breakfast is several levels down in a restaurant that sits under huge granite arches and pillars. €146

Guest House Douro Rua Fonte Taurina 99 ☎222 015 135, guesthousedouro.com; map pp.266–267. Super-cool waterfront B&B with windows right on to the Douro – a chic choice for a weekend getaway. Not all rooms have the river views (others look over the medieval street outside), but there's a sharp sense of style throughout and you couldn't be closer to the action. Note: no guests allowed after 1am. There's parking nearby. €150

★**Pestana Vintage Porto** Pr da Ribeira 1 ☎223 402 300, pestana.com; map pp.266–267. Enjoying the Ribeira's best location, atop the medieval wall next to the river, this cluster of old buildings has been transformed into a boutique-style four-star hotel. Most rooms face the Douro, and corner rooms also overlook the bridge. A contemporary bar and restaurant occupies a raised terrace above the river, where a few outdoor tables are lit by candles on the walls. €190

NORTH OF THE CENTRE

América Rua de Santa Catarina 1018. A 30min walk from the centre or bus #701/#702/#703 from Mercado do Bolhão ☎223 392 930, hotel-america.net; map pp.262–263. Located in the slighly run-down area towards the top of Rua de Santa Catarina, the *América* is a well-regarded mid-range choice with bright and relatively spacious rooms. It also benefits from private underground parking, and a bar. €75

★**Castelo de Santa Catarina** Rua de Santa Catarina 1347. A 35min walk from the centre or bus #701/#702/#703 from Mercado do Bolhão ☎225 095 599, castelosantacatarina.com.pt; map pp.262–263. This turreted folly of the most romantic kind makes a superb in-the-city retreat. The rooms aren't grand or expensive, but are furnished in period style and are perfectly comfortable, while breakfast is eaten in the lush *azulejo*-tiled gardens. There's parking, but no bar. €76

EAST OF THE CENTRE

★**Pestana Palacio do Freixo** N108 ☎210 407 600, pestana.com/en/hotel/freixo-palace; map pp.262–263. Porto finally has its own luxury *pousada*, a couple of kilometres east and upriver of Ribeira. The magnificently restored Baroque *Palácio do Freixa* dates from 1742, and enjoys a majestic riverside location. The main building sticks with period style and houses restaurant, bar and public rooms, while contemporary guest quarters – superbly appointed and many with classic Douro river views – are set in an adjacent former flour factory. Facilities are top-notch, from the outdoor infinity pool with river view to the indoor pool and spa, and the elegant restaurant and bar mean you don't have to make the slightly inconvenient trip into town and back if you don't wish to. €175

WEST OF THE CENTRE

Boa-Vista Esplanada do Castelo 58, Foz do Douro ☎225 320 020, hotelboavista.com; bus #500 from São Bento; map pp.262–263. Ocean and river views are the thing at this traditional villa, set over the road from the fort at Foz do Douro – it's worth paying the extra €10 or so (and booking in advance) to be able to see the water. It's only a three-star, and rooms are comfortable if unexceptional, but there's a fine rooftop pool and sun terrace, plus bar, restaurant and parking. €95

5

Hotel da Música Mercado do Bom Sucesso, Largo Ferreira Lapa 21 ☎ 226 076 000, ⓦ hoteldamusica .com; Ⓜ Casa da Música and taxi; map p.262–263. Located in the Bom Sucesso Market, this non-smoking hotel has 82 rooms, some with limited mobility access, and is conveniently located right by the Casa da Música (see p.271). All rooms are en suite and musically themed and inspired by local and international composers. There's a decent hotel restaurant that's attached to the marketplace too. **€99**

Pousada de Juventude Rua Paulo da Gama 551, Pasteleira, 4km west of the centre ☎ 226 177 257, ⓦ microsites.juventude.gov.pt/portal/en; bus #504 from Ⓜ Casa da Música, or #207 from São Bento; map pp.262–263. It's a bit of a way out, and not ideal for night owls, but Porto's main hostel has wonderful views of the Douro as it drains into the Atlantic. Dorms are four-bed max, and there are 24 en-suite doubles, another ten without bathrooms, and one self-contained apartment that sleeps four people. It's essential to book ahead in summer. Dorms **€15**; doubles **€40**; apartment **€70**

VILA NOVA DE GAIA

★ **The Yeatman** Rua do Choupelo ☎ 220 133 100, ⓦ the-yeatman-hotel.com; map p.273. The most glamorous choice in town, this spectacular hotel with 82 rooms is the business venture of one of Porto's most famous port wine families. It sits amid historic port wine lodges but is thoroughly boutique in character, with dramatic views of Porto from room balconies and the Michelin-starred restaurant alike. You get two infinity pools, one is indoors and connected to the fancy spa, and the other is outdoors – both have amazing panoramic views. It wouldn't be a wine hotel without a wine cellar, and guests get a private tour with the sommelier of what's considered to be one of the best collections of Portuguese wine in the world. Rates are room only and vary considerably throughout the year. Doubles **€300**, suites **€1,300**

EATING

Both sides of the Douro have become the default places to spend the evening. Along Porto's **Cais da Ribeira** a dozen largely touristy fish restaurants are installed under the arches, with more simple places hidden along the backstreets. Over the bridge in **Vila Nova de Gaia** there's a mix of traditional fish places and international restaurants and bars. For cheaper meals look in the **city centre**, either around the university (facing the Jardim da Cordoaria) and near the Clérigos church (on streets such as Rua dos Caldeireiros) or up Rua do Bonjardim, or near Praça da Batalha. In the main market, the Mercado do Bolhão, you can also eat a very cheap lunch at a couple of little cafés amid the flower stalls. For the best local fish restaurants, you need to take the metro out to **Matosinhos**, a 30min ride from the centre.

CITY CENTRE

★ **Antunes** Rua do Bonjardim 525 ☎ 222 052 406; map pp.266–267. Rustic restaurant that famously uses only wood-fired ovens to prepare the daily house specials – notably melt-in-the-mouth roast pork, served with gravy and sticky roast potatoes. Add a dessert and a carafe of house *rosado*, and you'll eat for €15. Mon–Sat noon–3pm & 7–10pm; closed four weeks in Aug/Sept.

Café Majestic Rua de Santa Catarina 112 ☎ 222 003 887, ⓦ cafemajestic.com; map pp.266–267. Best known of the city's *belle époque* cafés, with perfectly preserved decor (celestial cherubs, bevelled mirrors, carved chairs and wood panelling) and braided waiters flitting about to the strains of *The Blue Danube*. Come for coffee or afternoon tea – or maybe have a Caesar salad, club sandwich or *francesinha* for lunch (snacks from €6, mains €13–20). Mon–Sat 9.30am–midnight.

★ **DOP** Palácio das Artes, Largo São Domingos 18 ☎ 222 014 313, ⓦ ruipaula.com; map pp.266–267. Well-known chef Rui Paula has returned to his native Porto to wow punters with more of the creative Portuguese cuisine that made his name. The sleek downtown premises are "a place to taste and be bold" – so expect a twist on tradition, like suckling pig in a cider sauce, or *caldeirada (fish stew)* with *gnocchi*. There are menus at €70 and €80, with wine pairings another €30 – and while you should just be able to rock up for lunch, dinner reservations are advised. Mon 7.30–11pm, Tues–Sat 12.30–3.30pm & 7.30–11pm.

YOU'VE BEEN WARNED – PORTO'S DINNER SPECIALS

Porto's menus go big on grilled fish, seafood and *bacalhau*, but the most authentic **local speciality** is *tripas* (**tripe**) – the story goes that the inhabitants selflessly gave away all their meat for Infante Dom Henrique's expeditions to North Africa, leaving themselves only the tripe, and it's been on the menu ever since, cooked *à moda do Porto* (stewed with *chouriço* and white beans). Courtesy of returning emigrants, meanwhile, is the **francesinha** ("little French thing") – a mighty chunk of steak, sausage and ham between toasted bread, covered with melted cheese and a peppery tomato-and-beer sauce. Don't plan on doing anything much after chowing down on either of these Porto belt-tighteners.

Padorea Ribeiro Praca Guilherme Gomes Fernandes 21–27 ☎222 005 067, ⊛padariaribeiro.com; map pp.266–267. OK, it's a chain bakery but is well located in the centre and has a traditional feel. Popular with tourists and locals alike it serves light snacks such as mozzarella and smoked salmon toast, soups, as well as delicious pasteries (with a good coffee for around €3.50). Mon–Sat 7am–8pm.

Rota do Chá Rua Miguel Bombarda 457 ☎220 136 726, ⊛rotadocha.pt; map pp.266–267. Push on through the rarified tea shop, stocked with tins and caddies of exotic brews, and you'll find a hideway café with a magical Eastern tea-garden with shaded seats and arbours. It's a great place for a lazy afternoon with a book, a big pot of fancy leaves and a cookie or two, or there are daily lunches (€7.50) and Friday- and Saturday-evening dinners (€13.50). Mon–Thurs 11am–8pm, Fri 11am–midnight, Sat noon–midnight, Sun 1–8pm.

★**Tascö** Rua do Almada 151A ☎222 010 763, ⊛soldoutarena.com; map pp.266–267. A traditional Portuguese restaurant serving meat, fish and seafood dishes such as octopus, steak and cod. Well located near to Aliados Square and Metro, you can expect to pay €16 for steak, side of potatoes and glass of wine or sangria with local dessert. Portions are perfectly sized too. Daily noon–1am.

Taxca Rua da Picaria 26 ☎222 807; map pp.266–267. The best place in town for ham or pork sandwiches (their speciality), soups and octopus salad (prices start at around €5). Sit and enjoy with a glass of wine or tankard of beer with your food. The décor includes hams hanging above the bar. *Taxca* is popular with locals and tourists, so it does get busy – be patient, it is worth the wait. Mon–Tues 12–10.30pm, Wed–Sat noon–2am.

RIBEIRA

Casinha Sao Joao Cais da Ribeira 9 ☎220 197 889; map pp.266–267. Quaint *petisco* (like tapas) bar located under stone arches, just as you enter Cais Da Ribeira by the bottom tier of the bridge, therefore offering great views. Dishes include mixed cheese and meat platter (€15) and various meat and fish dishes. Tues–Sun 11am–11pm or whenever the last person leaves.

★**Rib** Pr da Ribeira 1 ☎966 273 822; map pp.266–267. New restaurant in the Ribeira district, specialising soley in meat dishes – if you're not into steak, it's probably not for you (the clue's in the name). Whilst it's not cheap, the food is certainly worth it. Expect to pay up to €40/person for a three-course meal with wine. Starters include dishes such as egg, truffle and asparagus, and the bar serves excellent cocktails. Daily 12.30–3.30pm & 7.30pm–2am.

Terreiro Largo do Terreiro 11–12 ☎222 011 955; map pp.266–267. Restaurant and snack bar right by the river with seating inside and out. Although predominantly a fish restaurant (specialities include shell and fresh fish), they

also serve the famous Portuguese dish *Francesinha* (see box opposite). Menu ranges from €10 (tapas) up to about €40 e.g. lobster dish. Daily noon–3pm & 7–11pm.

The Winebox Rua dos Mercadores 72 ☎222 034 100, ⊛thewineboxporto.com; map pp.266–267. A pretty tasteful environment of granite and wood accompanies this tapas, restaurant and wine bar which offers a choice of over 230 wines. A variety of dishes on offer such as pork pieces marinated in a spicy sauce for €8.50 or grilled shrimps for €10.40. Platters such as Iberian cured meat cost €14.50. Popular, so it's best to reserve ahead. Daily 8.30am–midnight.

WEST OF THE CENTRE

★**Capa Negra** Rua do Campo Alegre 191 ☎226 078 380, ⊛capanegra.com; map pp.262–263. A great diner-style grill house that is packed during weekends, festivals and holidays, and serves food until late. They champion their *francesinhas* but the steaks are just as good, or there's an extensive menu from shellfish to omelettes (most mains are €10–€20). Jump in a cab from the centre; it won't cost much to get here. Mon–Sat noon–2am, Sun noon–midnight.

VILA NOVA DE GAIA

3maisarte Largo Joaquim Magalhães 12 ☎223 758 255; map p.273. At the bottom of the hill from *Yeatman's Lodge*, this delightful tiny warehouse is more of a community organisation that sells local arts and crafts, rescues cats and also offers wine and tapas. Great for a small snack at lunchtime and the perfect spot to combine wine, art and creativity. Pay about €7 for a selection of cheeses, meat cuts and a glass of wine. Daily 11am–11pm.

Barão de Fladgate Taylor's, Rua do Choupelo 250 ☎223 772 951; map p.273. It's a punishing uphill hike to get here (unless you take a taxi), but you're rewarded by the finest river and bridge views from the terrace of Taylor's port wine lodge restaurant – it's lovely for an alfresco lunch. A fleet of smart waiters is on hand, but it's not really formal and not outrageously expensive either (mains around €15). Many dishes have a slug of port in the recipe, while others (like soya burger with wild rice, or pasta and New Zealand mussels) make a change from the prevailing traditional Portuguese cuisine. Mon–Sat 12.30–3pm & 7.30–10.30pm, Sun 12.30–3pm.

★**Casa Adão** Av Ramos Pinto 252 ☎223 750 492; map p.273. Simple family-run riverfront restaurant with low prices (€6–14) for grilled meat and fish, from steak and pork to salmon and sea bass. They also serve bigger platters of mixed grilled fish and the like, for two or more people (€20–30). They are used to tourists, but it's the locals who pack in here at lunch (there might be a wait for a table), and with house wine at €5 a litre there's not much work done in nearby offices in the afternoon. Daily noon–3.30pm & 7–11pm.

5

FESTA DE SÃO JOÃO

Porto lets its hair down during the exuberant celebration that is the **Festa de São João**, St John's Eve (the night of June 23–24), in honour of John the Baptist, patron saint of the city. Be warned – for one night only it is considered fair game to bash total strangers over the head with plastic hammers, while Chinese lanterns drift off into the night sky. There are free concerts throughout the night and a massive firework display at midnight over the river at Praça da Ribeira. The bacchanalian party forms only part of the wider city festival, the **Festas da Cidade**, that runs throughout June and celebrates the start of the summer with concerts, dances, vintage car rallies, regattas, sardine grills and other entertainments – like the competitive *cascata* displays (dolls depicting Santo António, São João and São Pedro, complete with miniature houses, trains and cars).

MATOSINHOS

★**Salta o Muro** Rua Heróis de França 386 ☎229 380 870; ⓜBrito Capelo; map pp.262–263. The "Jump the Wall" is an engaging, if cramped, family-run *tasca* on a dockside Matosinhos street full of fish restaurants. Others might look more enticing, but stick with it – a handwritten menu offers the catch of the day, plus some home-style specials (such as *arroz de polvo* or baked sardines), and you'll get three courses, house wine and coffee for under €20. Or order a bottle from the wall racks and make the waiter use his cunning wine-claw. Tues–Sat noon–3pm & 7–10pm; closed Aug.

DRINKING AND NIGHTLIFE

Porto's ever-changing **bar scene** is spread over three distinct areas: down and around Ribeira, across the river in Gaia, and – unsurprisingly – around the university (near Praça Parada Leitão and on "Bar Street", Rua Galeria de Paris). There are more venues in beachside Foz do Douro, but most of the city's best clubs are fairly central (though the hard house and techno clubs tend to be further out, in Ramalde). Most bars don't open until 10pm and stay open until 2am, later at weekends (often until 4am). **Clubs** open (or really only get going) at midnight, and most don't close until 4 or 5am or later, with a standard €5–15 admission fee, more for special events and guest DJs – the entrance ticket usually gets you a free drink.

CITY CENTRE

★**Maus Hábitos** Rua Passos Manuel 178, fourth floor ☎222 087 268, ⓦmaushabitos.com; map pp.266–267. At the top of an innocuous staircase is "Bad Habits", a late-night, in-crowd venue for alternative music (jazz, funk, indie and world) and contemporary arts. It's not as exclusively hip as you might expect, and out-of-towners are more than welcome – coming for the daily veggie lunch is a good way for a first look around, and then you can check out what's coming up and what's on in the gallery. Restaurant Mon–Fri 12.30–3pm; gallery Wed–Sun 10pm–2am; bar Wed, Thurs & Sun 10pm–2am, Fri & Sat 10pm–4am.

Piolho d'Ouro Pr Parada Leitão 45 ☎222 003 749, ⓦcafepiolho.com; map pp.266–267. The best-known of the student bars facing the university, the "Golden Louse" has a long tradition behind it – graduation plaques line the walls, and it used to be quite the revolutionary hangout. It's open virtually around the clock for cheap-skate students nursing budget beers and basic bites to eat – and the sunny terrace is a good spot for sightseers – while there's a line of inexpensive *tascas* around the corner. Mon–Sat 7am–4am.

Plano B Rua Cândido dos Reis 30 ⓦplanobporto.net; map pp.266–267. Spread over two floors in an impressive townhouse, *Plano B* not only hosts different DJs and live band sets over its three rooms, but also an exhibition space for artists. Expect quirky furniture and chandeliers hanging from the ceiling. On Saturdays it opens in the afternoon and offers cheese and wine events. Tues–Wed 10pm–2am, Thurs 10pm–4am, Fri–Sat 10pm–6am.

Tendinha dos Clérigos Rua Conde Vizela 80 ☎222 011 438, ⓦtendinhadosclerigos.com; map pp.266–267. One for rockers – a cave-like bar and club with pool table and dancefloor, that's also a regular venue for up-and-coming bands. Tues–Sat 1–6am.

RIBEIRA

★**Clube Literário do Porto** Rua Nova da Alfândega 22 ☎222 089 228, ⓦclubeliterariodoportofla.word press.com; map pp.266–267. Above the bookshop and below the art exhibition, the literary club's piano bar is an elegant place to sit and chat with a view of the Douro. On Fridays and Saturdays there are concerts and recitals, often involving their mini-grand. Daily 2.30pm–1am.

Está-se Bem Rua da Fonte Taurina 70–72 ☎222 002 249; map pp.266–267. A nice little *tasca* where a pre-club crowd hangs out, probably because drinks are cheap and there's no cover charge. Mon–Sat 6pm–4am.

O meu Mercedes é maior que o teu Rua da Lada 30 ☎222 082 151, ⓦomeumercedes.com; map pp.266–267. The stalwart of the Ribeira scene not only wins the Porto bar name prize ("My Mercedes is bigger than yours")

but is a wonderfully atmospheric joint to boot, a bit like an old stone-walled wine cellar with regular gigs. Wed–Sat 10pm–4am.

★**Vinologia** Rua de São João 28–30 ☎910 404 435, ⓦvinologia.pt; map pp.266–267. French-owned wine-bar-cum-tasting-shop that's a cosy place to get acquainted with Porto's top tipples. The enthusiastic English-speaking staff really know their stuff, and can recommend all sorts of ports from mainly small producers – from €1.50 a glass or tasting sessions from €6–15. Daily 11am–midnight.

BOAVISTA
Labirintho Rua Nossa Senhora de Fátima 334 ☎919

701 490; ⓜCasa da Música; map pp.262–263. Located a couple of minutes off the Rotunda, the *Labirintho* is a great bar in a converted house, with a shaded back garden, gallery space and occasional live music. Daily 10pm–4am.

FOZ DO DOURO
Indústria Centro Comercial do Foz, Av do Brasil 835–0000 ☎220 962 935; bus #500; map pp.262–263. A sophisticated dance club that gets packed in summer – it's not at the cutting edge of Porto's club scene, but it's still an impressively good night that sees Portugal's best DJs play to a cosmopolitan crowd. Thurs–Sat midnight–6am.

ARTS AND CULTURE

The **Casa da Música** concert hall has a wide musical remit, as well as being home of the **Orquestra Nacional do Porto**, one of the country's leading symphony orchestras. Otherwise, concerts of all kinds are held at a variety of venues, while in summer there's usually a series of **outdoor concerts** in the Jardim do Palácio de Cristal and at Serralves. Local **theatre** is almost always in Portuguese, though there's a strong tradition of contemporary dance and other visual and experimental genres. **Tickets** for most shows (usually in the range €10–40) can be bought in advance from the FNAC books and music store (see p.282), which also promotes gigs, events and talks. Porto's daily newspaper, the *Jornal de Notícias* is also a useful source of information.

Casa da Música Av da Boavista 604 ☎220 120 220, ⓦwww.casadamusica.com; ⓜCasa da Música. Porto's major concert hall is a striking building with an international reputation, not just for classical concerts and recitals but early and contemporary music, fado, world, jazz, folk and experimental. Most tickets are €5–20, though some events are free. Ticket office open Mon–Sat 9.30am–7pm.
Coliseu do Porto Rua de Passos Manuel 137 ☎223 394

940, ⓦcoliseudoporto.pt. Main city-centre venue for international acts, from rock, indie and pop to ballet, classical and big-stage musicals. Ticket office open Mon–Sat 1–8.30pm (Aug Mon–Fri 3–7pm).
Teatro do Campo Alegre Rua das Estrelas 57 ☎226 089 800, ⓦwww.planetario-porto.pt; bus from Casa da Música interchange. An innovative playhouse putting on a vibrant blend of music, theatre, cinema, animation

---

PORTO'S FESTIVAL CALENDAR

You can check exact festival and event dates on Porto's tourism website ⓦportoturismo.pt. The following rundown mixes the annual highlights with some under-the-radar choices.

February–March Fantasporto (ⓦfantasporto.com), the respected international fantasy, sci-fi and thriller film festival, has been a fixture in the city since 1980 and runs over ten days.
March–April Festival Intercéltico do Porto – Celtic sounds from Portugal, Galicia, Brittany, Wales, Ireland and Scotland.
May Fazer a Festa (ⓦteatroartimagem.org) – international theatre held in a "theatre village" in the gardens of the Palácio de Cristal.
June As well as popular saints' days for São João (June 23–24) and São Pedro (June 29), June also marks the start of the respected PortoCartoon World Festival (until Sept), one of the biggest festivals of caricature in the world.
July The annual GLBT Porto Pride march

and celebration takes place on the first or second week of July. The International Folklore Festival is held during the last week. The annual Festa da Cerveja (Beer Fest) begins in Foz do Douro and runs through to August.
August São Bartolomeu (Sun after Aug 24) – a procession in Foz do Douro culminating in a cleansing bathe (*banho santo*) in the sea. On the last weekend of August there's the Noites Ritual, an exclusively Portuguese music festival at the Palácio de Cristal.
September The Porto Jazz Festival is held during the month, and the Concurso Internacional de Música (International Music Competition) begins. The Festival Internacional de Marionetas do Porto (FIMP; ⓦfim.com.pt) is a ten-day festival of dance, circus, puppetry and theatre.

5

MARKETS, JUNK AND VINTAGE STUFF

If the **Mercado do Bolhão** (see p.261) whets your appetite, you might want to scour some of Porto's other markets, starting with the long-established Saturday morning flea market, the **Feira de Vandoma** (Passeio das Fontaínhas). There's a more specialist market for **coins and collectables** (Sun morning, Praça Dom João I), while the **Feira dos Passarinhos** (Sun morning, Campo Mártires da Pátria, in front of the Cadeia da Relação) features birds, cages, and birds in cages. The **secondhand** scene is centred on the top (ie, grungier) end of Rua Santa Caterina, where you can buy anything from dodgy old Portuguese vinyl singles to retro household goods and vintage clothes.

and public lectures; there's also a late-opening bar. Ticket office open Mon 2–10.30pm, Tues–Fri 1–10.30pm, Sat & Sun 3–10.30pm.
Teatro Nacional São João Pr da Batalha ☎ 223 401 900, ⓦ www.tnsj.pt. The city's major theatre and opera

venue, for Portuguese and international productions – it's a gorgeously over-the-top building, inspired by Charles Garnier's Paris Opera. The programme is pretty varied and you can see a show for as little as €7.50. Ticket office open Tues–Sat 2–7pm, Sun 2–5pm.

SHOPPING

One of the city's abiding pleasures is its surviving **traditional shops**, often in beautiful Art Nouveau or Art Deco premises, in which you'll find anything from dusty bottles of vintage port to filigree gold jewellery. Even right in the city centre, people still do much of their day-to-day shopping at small, independent shops – in the line of shops below the Clérigos tower, for example, you could, if you so wished, buy an apple, a pair of shoes, a pig's tongue or a bucket. The main **market**, Mercado do Bolhão, still sees brisk business too, though most of the other neighbourhood markets have been eclipsed by the city's modern **shopping centres** – the biggest is NorteShopping, in the northwest at Senhora da Hora (on the metro). Porto's two main **shopping streets** are Rua de Cedofeita and the more upmarket Rua de Santa Catarina – these are where you'll find high-street fashion chains, designer boutiques, jewellers and shoe shops. Rua de Santa Catarina also has its own mall, Via Caterina, halfway up, as well as a few stalls selling beads, cheap jewellery and accessories, and some secondhand and "vintage" shops towards the top end. Rua de Miguel Bombarda (off Rua de Cedofeita) is at the heart of Porto's **"gallery and arts" district** and is the place for designers, delis, and urban arts and crafts.

ARTS, CRAFTS AND DESIGN

★**Arcos de Miragaia** Rua de Miragaia 39–45 ☎ 918 294 551; map pp.266–267. Jorge Andrade's ceramics workshop under the arches is a great place to look for unique ("from my imagination") painted vases, contemporary *azulejo* tiles, and creatively made platters and paperweights. Mon–Sat 10am–12.30pm & 2–7pm.
Lobo Taste Palácio das Artes, Largo São Domingos 20 ☎ 222 017 102; map pp.266–267. The personal project of interior designer Paulo Lobo, who presents his – and other designers' – reimaginings of traditional Portuguese arts and crafts. This means a rather gorgeous shop full of felt hats and flat caps in funky colours, plus contemporary ceramics, clay figures, designer basketware and fancy olive-oil gift sets, with many of the pieces in limited-edition series, signed by the artists. Mon–Fri 10am–7pm, Sat & Sun 4–8pm.

BOOKS AND MUSIC

Chaminé da Mota Rua das Flores 28 ☎ 222 005 380; map pp.266–267. Perhaps the most characteristic antiquarian bookshop (*alfarrabista*) in town, complete with rare tomes, antique decorations and giant music boxes that play punched metal discs. Mon–Fri 9am–12.30pm & 2.30–7pm, Sat 9am–1pm.

FNAC NorteShopping Rua Sara Afonso 105 ☎ 707 313 435 ⓦ fnac.pt; map pp.266–267. The city's biggest selection of CDs, DVDs, books, games and gizmos. Mon–Sat 10am–10pm, Sun 10am–8pm.
★**Lello & Irmão** Rua das Carmelitas 144 ☎ 222 002 037; map pp.266–267. Porto's famous galleried Art Nouveau bookshop (1906), with its staircase just begging for a grand entrance, is a delight beyond words. There's a small café on the first floor. Mon–Fri 10am–7.30pm, Sat 10am–7pm.

FOOD AND DRINK

A Pérola do Bolhão Rua Formosa 279 ☎ 222 004 009; map pp.266–267. A great little grocery, founded in 1917, loved as much for its Art Nouveau facade as for its cluttered stock of *bacalhau*, port wine, cheese, cured sausages and smoked hams. Mon–Sat 9.30am–1pm & 2–7.30pm.
Loja de Vinhos do Douro e do Porto Rua Ferreira Borges 27 ☎ 222 071 669, ⓦ ivdp.pt; map pp.266–267. At the Porto and Douro Wine Institute's handily located shop and showroom you'll be able to taste a few wines and then buy from the well-stocked shelves. It's also a good place to ask about port wine tours or even arrange visits to the institute's labs and tasting chambers. Mon–Fri 11am–7pm.

DIRECTORY

Hospital Santo Antonio Porto's main hospital is located on Largo Prof Abel Salazar, near the university (☎ 222 077 500, ⓦ www.chporto.pt). In an emergency, call ☎ 112.

Left luggage There are coin-operated lockers at Campanhã and São Bento train stations.

Libraries Visit either the Biblioteca Municipal Almeida Garrett at Palácio de Cristal, Rua de Entre Quintas 328 (Mon 2–6pm, Tues–Sat 10am–6pm; ☎ 226 081 000), or the Biblioteca Municipal do Porto on Rua Dom João VI (Mon & Sat 10am–6pm, Tues–Fri 9am–7.30pm, except July & Aug Mon–Fri 10am–6pm; ☎ 225 193 480).

Pharmacies Late-night and 24hr pharmacies (*farmácias de serviço*) operate on a rota basis; details posted in the windows and given in the daily *Jornal de Notícias*.

Police For English-speaking assistance go to the Esquadra de Turismo (Tourism Police Department), a branch of the PSP, Rua Clube dos Fenianos 11, next to the main turismo (daily 8am–2am; ☎ 222 081 833).

Post office The main post office is on Praça General Humberto Delgado, by the town hall (Mon–Fri 8am–9pm, Sat 9am–6pm); there's also an office at Rua Ferreira Borges 73, near the Bolsa (Mon–Fri 9am–12.30pm & 2–6pm).

Vila do Conde

VILA DO CONDE, 27km north of Porto, has become quite a significant resort over recent years, but despite the increase in visitors still retains much of its charm. In part, it's because the villas and apartments overlooking the beach are set away from the rest of town; the medieval centre, 1km inland on the north bank of the Rio Ave, still has its traditional fishing port and quiet, traffic-free streets, while the modern town is a handsome place of boulevards, gardens and cafés. Anchoring the old town's cobbled alleys is the beautiful Manueline Igreja Matriz, while nearby the Friday **market** takes place, where you'll find everything from farm produce to traditional children's toys. Vila do Conde has a fair reputation for festivals too, from food and drink to film, and if you want more than just a beach then it's the best day out from Porto, especially as you can zip there quickly on the metro. The more developed sands of Póvoa de Varzim are just a few minutes beyond, at the end of the line.

Convento de Santa Clara

Largo Dom Afonso Sanches • No public access

The grand eighteenth-century **Convento de Santa Clara** is Vila do Conde's major landmark. It sits high above the old bridge and, while it's not open to the public, it is worth climbing up to the *miradouro* for sweeping views of town and river. Running directly into the north side of the convent is a well-preserved, early eighteenth-century **aqueduct** which once carried water over a reputed 999 arches from Terroso, 5km north of town – the metro line to Póvoa de Varzim now cuts right through part of the remaining course. The other thing to note about Santa Clara is its long tradition of pastry-making – the so-called *doces conventuais* (convent cakes) are now available in cafés all over town, sickly-sweet affairs generally involving industrial quantities of sugar and eggs.

Museu de Rendas de Bilros

Rua de São Bento 70 • Tues–Sun 10am–noon & 2–6pm • €1.07 • ☎ 252 248 470, ⓦ www.cm-viladoconde.pt

Vila do Conde is still known for its traditional lacework and embroidery (*rendas de*

VILA DO CONDE FESTIVALS

A good time to visit Vila do Conde is for the nine-day food fair **Feira de Gastronomia** (third week in Aug, ⓦ gastronomia.vconde.org), or during the renowned crafts fair, the **Feira Nacional de Artesanato** (last week July to first week Aug; ⓦ fna.vconde.org). People also come from far and wide for **Curtas** (ⓦ curtas.pt), the European short-film festival held here for a week every July.

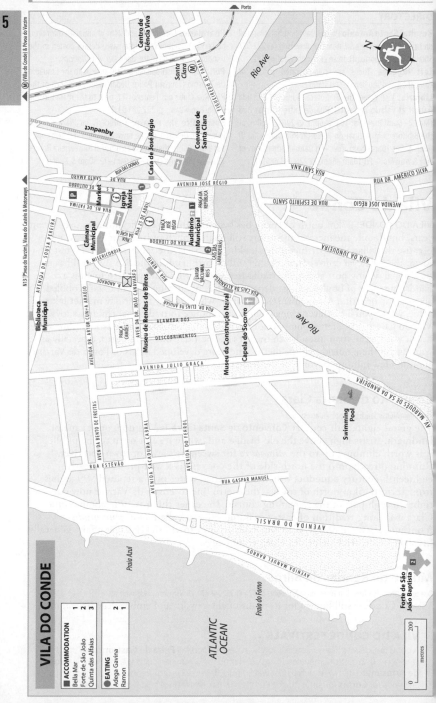

VILA DO CONDE

ACCOMMODATION
Bella Mar	1
Forte de São João	2
Quinta das Alfaias	3

EATING
Adega Gavina	2
Ramon	1

bilros), and there is an active lacework school in the interesting **Museu de Rendas de Bilros**, housed in one of the town's old manor houses. *Rendilheiras* (lace-makers) show off their skills most days, surrounded by lovely examples of lacework and historic lace-making tools and equipment. The museum is also a good place to buy lace, and you'll see more for sale in the market and in shops around town.

Museu da Construção Naval

Rua do Cais da Alfândega • Tues–Sun 10am–6pm • €3.22 • ☎ 252 240 740

Down on the river, walking west takes you through the old **fishing quarter**. Vila do Conde's shipbuilding industry is among the oldest in Europe, and fishing boats reminiscent of fifteenth-century caravels are still constructed here, in the shipyards on the other side of the river. You can trace this heritage (and see replica vessels) in the excellent **Museu da Construção Naval**, housed in the impressive former royal customs house, the Alfândega Régia (1487). Further along the riverside you can't miss the conspicuously Moorish white dome of the **Capela do Socorro**, which bears witness to the conversion of Moorish craftsmen during the Inquisition.

The beach

The **beach** is a good fifteen-minute walk west of the town centre, and boasts long stretches of coarse sand that have been steadily developed right up the coast as far as Póvoa de Varzim. There are rock pools and a few cafés, while to the south the sands come to an end at the mouth of the Rio Ave, marked by the stumpy seventeenth-century **Forte de São João Baptista** (now a hotel), beyond which is a convenient little beach café with an excellent sea view.

ARRIVAL AND INFORMATION

VILA DO CONDE

By metro Metro Line B runs from Porto (Estádio do Dragão) every 20min and takes around 1hr – you need a Z6 Andante card to travel this far (total, with card, €5.80 return). There are two stations: you can get off at Santa Clara, 300m east of the convent, though quicker express services (50min) call at Vila do Conde station, still only 5min walk from the centre.

Information Turismo, Rua 25 de Abril 103 (June to mid-Sept Mon–Fri 9am–7pm, Sat & Sun 9.30am–1pm & 2.30–6pm; mid-Sept to May Mon–Fri 9am–6pm, Sat & Sun 9.30am–1pm & 2.30–6pm; ☎ 252 248 473, ⓦ www .cm-viladoconde.pt).

ACCOMMODATION

Bella Mar Pr da República 84 ☎ 252 631 748. The *azulejo*-lined stone staircase leads to an excellent hostel with cosy, well-kept rooms. Don't expect up-to-the-minute decor and facilities, but the location by the seafront is excellent. **€50**

Forte de São João Av do Brasil ☎ 252 240 600, ⓦ forte .com.pt. The town's seventeenth-century pentagonal fortress now has a contemporary, minimalist style – inside, at least – and the rooms and public areas make the most of the ocean and river views. There's also a wine bar and chic restaurant (reservations advised). **€110**

★ **Quinta das Alfaias** Rua da Trás 220, Fajozes, 10km southeast of town ☎ 252 662 146 or ☎ 919 900 509, ⓦ quintadasalfaias.com. A wonderfully elegant country house set in extensive gardens and orchards, with a large swimming pool and tennis court. It has four en-suite rooms with garden views, plus one suite (€90–110) and a couple of apartments (€110–200) – decor throughout is understated, with plenty of bare granite, and the style is traditional country-house. **€80**

EATING

★ **Adega Gavina** Cais das Lavandeiras 56 ☎ 917 834 517. A small, unpretentious *adega* that overlooks the river and serves freshly caught fish – mackerel, squid and bream – grilled on the barbecue, and washed down with a jug of fruity house wine. A full meal is around €12. Tues–Sat noon–3pm & 7–10.30pm, Sun noon–3pm.

Ramon Rua 5 de Outubro 176 ☎ 252 631 334. The more upmarket place for fish, particularly shellfish – there's outdoor seating in the alley, a good-value set lunch and (providing it's not lobster) mains start at around €13. Mon & Wed–Sun noon–3pm & 7–11pm; closed three weeks in Sept.

5

Penafiel and around

While port wine defines the central and far eastern reaches of the Douro, closer to Porto it's *vinho verde* that holds sway, particularly around **PENAFIEL**, 35km east of Porto. The wine's origins lie with the Benedictine monks, who first grew vines on precipitous valley terraces, while the Benedictine legacy also extends to a handful of glorious **Romanesque churches** secreted amid the hills hereabouts. However, despite the promise, Penafiel itself comes as something of a disappointment. The few old streets of granite mansions behind a handsome Renaissance Igreja da Misericórdia are barely reason enough to stop – certainly not if you're reliant on public transport (the train station is 3km from the centre in any case). Drivers, however, have the option of a pleasant half-day's tour, with wine tasting and church visits breaking up the journey along the Douro.

Quinta da Aveleda

Rua da Aveleda • **Tours** Mon–Fri at 10am, 11.30am, 3pm & 4.30pm • €5.50; reservations required • **Shop** Mon–Sat 9am–noon & 1–6pm • ☎ 255 718 200, ⓦ aveleda.pt • Coming from Porto, leave the A4 at the "Penafiel Sul/Entre-os-Rios" exit

The charming, ivy-festooned **Quinta da Aveleda** is source of the local *vinho verde*. The guided tours include a visit to the bottling hall, and a wine and cheese tasting (and there's more on sale in the rather nice shop), but it's really the gorgeously unkempt, wooded gardens and their follies that make the visit.

Paço de Sousa

10km south of Penafiel, signposted off the N106 • Free

The Romanesque abbey church at **Paço de Sousa** – a pre-eminent Benedictine foundation – is the burial place of Penafiel's local boy made good, **Egas Moniz**, advisor to Dom Afonso Henriques, the first king of Portugal. On a mission to negotiate with the King of León, Moniz displayed the ultimate loyalty by offering himself as a sacrifice – an impressive gesture refused by the king, who rewarded Moniz with his liberty. The panels on Moniz' tomb tell his story, while outside the church is a shaded dell beside the Rio Sousa, just right for a picnic. There are a couple of cafés in the village below.

Boelhe

12km southeast of Paço de Sousa, signposted off the N106 to Entre-os-Rios

Tucked up a minor country road, the church of **São Gens** at **Boelhe** is said to be the smallest Romanesque church in the country, and gains much of its appeal from its impressive position on a hill overlooking the Tâmega valley. From here, the N106 continues south to Entre-os-Rios, where you then have the choice of following the Rio Douro east along either bank (see p.290) towards Lamego and Peso da Régua. You need to call (☎255 810 706) to arrange a visit.

Amarante

A quick drive from Porto takes you to the beautiful riverside town of **AMARANTE**, which hugs both sides of the Rio Tâmega, a handsome tributary of the Douro. Much of the town's history revolves around the thirteenth-century hermit Gonçalo, later made a saint, and most of the attractions bear some link to him. Although Amarante's sights are few, save a photogenic bridge, and a riverside main street of granite houses with wooden balconies, it's popular with weekenders from Porto and

FROM TOP AMARANTE (ABOVE); *QUINTA NOVA DE NOSSA SENHORA DO CARMO*, NEAR PINHÃO (P.299) >

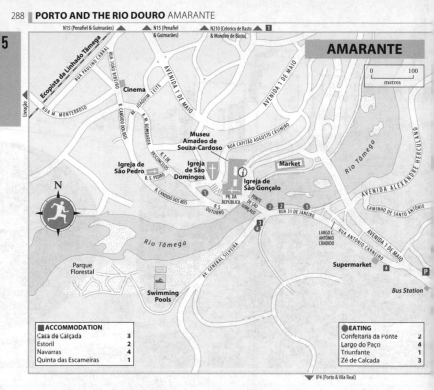

foreign visitors. There's a definite air of prosperity about and it's a fine place to spend the night, with a wide choice of accommodation, much of it still reasonably priced. Wednesdays and Saturdays, the **market days**, are the liveliest, although the action is all over by 3pm. The local hooch, Gatão, a fruity *vinho verde*, can be enjoyed at one of the few late-opening esplanade bars found on the south side of the river near either bridge.

Igreja de São Gonçalo

Praça da República • Daily 8am–7pm • Free

Cross the old stone bridge over the Tâmega and you're confronted by the landmark **Igreja de São Gonçalo**, built on the spot where Gonçalo's hermitage once stood, although the holy site almost certainly dates back to pagan times. The saint's annual festival – now known as the Festas do Junho, celebrated over the first weekend in June – also goes in for a fair amount of pre-Christian jiggery-pokery, not least the traditional exchange of phallic cakes by unmarried couples. Moreover, in the church, a touch of the well-worn saint's tomb allegedly brings forward the happy wedding day for hitherto thwarted lovers.

Museu Amadeo de Souza-Cardoso

Alameda Teixeira de Pascoaes • June–Sept Tues–Sun 10am–12.30pm & 2–5.30pm; Oct–May Tues–Sun 10am–12.30pm & 2–5.30pm • €1 • ☎ 255 420 272

The remodelled Renaissance cloisters around the side of São Gonçalo church contain the **Museu Amadeo de Souza-Cardoso**, largely based around the Cubist and avant-garde works of Amadeo de Souza-Cardoso (1887–1918). Born and brought up in Amarante,

he spent his formative years as an artist in Paris but died young in the influenza pandemic of 1918. He's still relatively little known outside Portugal but the absorbing collection is well worth a look. There are also works by other Portuguese artists, as well as temporary exhibitions and a monthly cinema club.

Igreja de São Domingos

A steep granite stairway climbs from Amarante's main square, past the **Igreja de São Domingos**, whose bell-tower marks the hours. Take a quick look inside the intimate chapel – by the door there is an extraordinary carved wooden tablet showing Christ suspended upside down on the Cross, hoisted by three men operating a rope and pulley.

ARRIVAL AND INFORMATION   AMARANTE

By bus The bus station is on Avenida Primeiro de Maio, a 5min walk south of the river, with regular services to and from Braga (5–7 daily; 1hr 20min), Guimarães (5–8 daily; 50min), Porto (up to 10 daily; 1hr) and Vila Real (every 1hr 30min; 1hr 40min).
By car Driving from Porto (60km) takes less than an hour via the A4 – traffic runs one-way only in town, around the two bridges. Parking is free along the river beside the

market, along the road under the new bridge, and in a car park beyond the hotel *Navarras*; everywhere else you'll need to pay at the parking meters (2hr maximum).
Information Turismo, Alameda Teixeira de Pascoaes (daily: July–Sept 9am–7pm; Oct–June 9am–12.30pm & 2–5.30pm; ☎ 255 420 246, �🖝 amarante.pt/turismo), to the side of the main church next to the museum.

ACCOMMODATION

Casa da Calçada Largo do Paço 6 ☎ 255 410 830, �🖝 casadacalcada.com. A restored palace just above the bridge, stuffed with objets d'art and set in magnificent gardens. The thirty boutique-style rooms and suites vary in size, decor and outlook, while there's also a swimming pool and tennis court in the grounds. The Michelin-starred restaurant, *Largo do Paço* (see p.290), is what brings many here in the first place. **€170**
Estoril Rua 31 de Janeiro 49 ☎ 255 431 291, �🖝 restaurante-estoril.com. A star pick for budget travellers – pleasant, high-ceilinged en-suite rooms and, for a few euros more, a balcony overlooking the river and bridge. Breakfast isn't included, but the cheery attached restaurant is a firm favourite for inexpensive riverside terrace dining – no need to go anywhere else if you're staying. **€40**
Navarras Rua António Carneiro ☎ 255 431 036, �🖝 hotelnavarras.com. This central three-star choice has

seen better days but rooms are shipshape and business-like, there's a proper bath in the bathroom, and you can eat breakfast on the terrace (though the main-road traffic intrudes). Private parking is another bonus. **€75**
★ **Quinta das Escomoeiras** Lourico-Arnoia, Celorico de Basto, 15km north of Amarante ☎ 255 322 785, �🖝 quintadasescomoeiras.com. Set amongst 23 acres of private vineyards and woodland, this wine estate offers nine cosy and individually designed rooms as well as an outdoor pool, sauna and Turkish bath. It's possible to spend at least two or three days enjoying the estate, filling your time with hiking, fishing off the private beach along the river, canoeing or just simply relaxing in the living area. All breakfast jams (also for sale) and juices are made fresh from the estate's fruit, and of course you can sample the wine made on the estate too. Winery tours also available for to non-residents. Small tapas snacks can be prepared in the evening at extra cost. **€110**

CYCLING ALONG THE TÂMEGA

In days gone by, the approach to Amarante was truly scenic, on the old Tâmega branch train line, with rattling wooden carriages snaking along a single-track route up the valley. Although long discontinued, part of the track now has a new lease of life as the **Ecopista da Linha do Tâmega**, a "green route" that's been opened from the old station at Amarante to that of Chapa, a shade over 9km to the northeast. In time, it's planned to extend the **hiking and biking track** as far as Celorico de Basto (22km from Amarante) and Arco de Baúlhe (40km), but even now, the shortish stretch to Chapa makes for a lovely day out, along the river valley, through pine and eucalyptus, over the occasional bridge and past abandoned buildings.

EATING

Many of the places to stay have restaurants attached, though locals tend to eat in the cheaper places found near Largo Conselheiro António Cândido or up in the new town.

Confeitaria da Ponte Rua 31 de Janeiro ☎255 432 034 ⓦconfeitariadaponte.pt. The best place for tea and cakes is right by the bridge, with an ivy-festooned riverside terrace. The nuns of the (now ruined) Santa Clara convent once made the town's famous *doces* (sweets), and you can sample them here, with home-made *bolos de São Gonçalo* (the saint's cakes), *pão de ló* (sponge cake) and others ready to be boxed up and taken away. Daily 8.30am–8pm.

★**Largo do Paço** Largo do Paço 6 ☎255 410 830, ⓦcasadacalcada.com. In one of only two restaurants in the north of Portugal with a Michelin star, chef Vitor Matos does sublime things with local produce in a series of exquisitely presented tasting menus (dinner from €55, lunch from €25). Everything changes with the seasons, but expect a creative twist on traditional dishes, which in autumn and winter might mean things like rabbit stuffed with pistachios and served with a mustard-and-herb crust or roast pigeon with sautéed cherries. Daily 12.30–3pm & 7.30–10.30pm.

Triunfante Rua Teixeira de Vasconcelos ☎255 437 978. A cheery granite-walled *adega*, where there's not much that costs over €5 – rabbit stew, *alheira*, steak, pork and *bacalhau* are generally on the menu. Credit cards are not accepted. Mon–Sat 8am–10pm, Sun 8am–3pm.

Zé da Calcada Rua 31 de Janeiro 83 ☎255 426 814, ⓦzedacalcada.com. The nicest of the riverside choices has a terrace with a water view and serves good regional food (dishes €9–12), from a house *bacalhau* to *posta á Maronesa* (hefty steaks from the nearby Serra do Marão). They have also pioneered a weekday buffet lunch, where €8 gets you a choice of hot and cold dishes. Daily noon–3.30pm & 7–10.30pm.

Along the Douro

The **Douro river route** is one of *the* great European journeys, a careering 200-kilometre ride or stately cruise from Porto to the Spanish border. The full river journey there and back is in a class of its own, and pricey, all-inclusive cruises can take as long as a week, though short tours from Porto (see p.275) or Peso da Régua (see p.292) give you a flavour of the river. In many ways the train is best, though you'll have a lot more scope in a car to visit wineries, stay in rural *quintas* en route and hang around at the majestic dams to watch the boats come through the locks. Be warned that the roads are very winding and often fairly precipitous, though they are all in good condition. It can also take much longer than you think to get from A to B, so give yourself plenty of time.

North bank: along the N108

It's possible to drive all the way along the Douro originating in Porto, following the **N108**, though the first 40km or so is nothing special. Things pick up at **Entre-os-Rios** ("between the rivers"), 12km south of Penafiel, which is the point at which the Douro and Tâmega rivers meet. Stick to the N108 along the north bank and the road is set a fair way inland of the river for much of the route, though you'll get some stunning views at times before finally descending to Peso da Régua, 80km and a good couple of hours later.

South bank: along the N222

Cross the bridge at Entre-os-Rios to the south bank of the Douro, and you're in for a treat of a drive along the increasingly picturesque **N222**. It's undoubtedly one of the best routes in Portugal, with the most compelling section the 40km or so between **Cinfães** and Peso da Régua, where the road winds amongst the terraced hills high above the glinting river. There's the occasional panoramic café, and iron gates at intervals announcing venerable *quintas* tucked into the hillside folds, while at the sleepy spa town of **Caldas de Aregos**, where the Douro has been dammed, there's a quayside marina and an outdoor café. The settlements beyond nearly all boast a Romanesque church, the most significant being **Santa Maria de Carquere**, a twisting 5km above the

THE LINHA DO DOURO – PORTUGAL'S BEST TRAIN RIDE

A engineering marvel when it opened in 1887, the **Linha do Douro** (Douro Line) still thrills passengers today. In its heyday it crossed the border to Spain (for a through service to Salamanca and Madrid) and sprouted some stunning valley branch lines, but even though the branch lines are no more, it's still some ride – 160km of river-hugging track from Porto to Pocinho, via more than 20 tunnels, 30 bridges and 34 stations.

There are regular daily departures **from Porto** (São Bento and Campanhã) and you change on to the smaller Douro Line trains at Peso da Régua (just "Régua" on timetables). **Régua** is where the Douro Line gets most exciting, sticking closely to the river from then on, clinging to the rocks as the river – and track – passes through the Douro gorge. Some of the stations are just a shelter on a platform, used by the local wine *quintas*, though there are useful stops at **Pinhão** (a pretty port-producing town), **Tua** (a cruise halt with a good restaurant) and finally **Pocinho** (for Vila Nova de Foz Côa and its rock art).

Currently five trains a day run from Porto to Pocinho at the end of the line (around 3hr 30min; €13 each way), so you can make the return trip in a day if you take a morning train: there are also summer weekend steam-train services between Régua and Tua. For **timetables**, see ⓦ cp.pt or call ☎ 808 208 208 (local-rate call in Portugal) or ☎ 707 201 280.

small town of Resende. Part of a convent dating back as early as 1099, this is now set amid family vineyards, with extensive views across the rolling hills beyond. The N222 eventually descends to Peso da Régua (though you can also cut south over the hills on the N226 to reach Lamego) and then embarks on its straightest but most river-hugging section, the relatively quick 25km to Pinhão.

Peso da Régua

PESO DA RÉGUA (usually just Régua) was declared the first capital of the demarcated port-producing region in the eighteenth century. While it's Pinhão, further east, that's the more interesting place these days, Régua is still a popular stop – not least because it's the hub of the Douro river-cruise trade, with the boats disgorging hundreds of passengers for lunch, train-trips and wine-lodge visits. Although it's not a particularly pretty place, and is dominated by a motorway bridge, for most of the year there's an agreeable hubbub along the waterside promenade, where ornamental *barcos rabelos* lie anchored on the river. What's more, wine-trade patronage has resulted in some excellent local restaurants and enticing *quinta* accommodation in the vicinity.

Museu do Douro

Rua Marquês de Pombal • Daily 10am–6pm • €6 • ☎ 254 310 190, ⓦ museudodouro.pt

The flagship building on Régua's riverfront avenue is the **Museu do Douro**, which tells you everything you ever wanted to know about the history of the river and its people, as well as the port wine story. It's actually laid across two sites, with a permanent display about the life and culture of the so-called Terra do Vinho on show at the exhibition area on Rua da Ferreirinha (the main inland street), and changing temporary exhibitions at the museum, whether it's photographs of old Douro bridges or shows by regional artists. There's also a restaurant at the museum site and, naturally enough, a wine bar with an esplanade-garden that's open during the summer months.

ARRIVAL AND INFORMATION

PESO DA RÉGUA

By train The train station is on Largo da Estação at the southeastern end of town (towards the bridges), reached along the waterfront avenue.

Destinations Pinhão (5 daily; 26min); Pocinho (5 daily; 1hr 25min); Porto (13 daily; 1hr 45min–2hr 20min); and Tua (5 daily; 42min).

5

By bus Buses stop outside the train station.
Destinations Guarda (daily; 2hr 30min); Lamego (every 2hr; 30min); Vila Real (every 2hr; 40min); and Viseu (2–6 daily; 1hr 10min).
Information The turismo is located at Rua da Ferreirinha (daily 9am–12.30pm & 2–5.30pm, Nov–March closed weekends; ☎254 312 846, ⌨cm -pesoregua.pt) – a 5min walk to the left of the quayside (Porto direction), near the large car park, at the end of Peso da Régua's main street.

TOURS AND CRUISES

Tours Steam train services to Pinhão and Tua (complete with antique wooden carriages, food, wine and music) usually depart on Saturday afternoons between June and October, as well as Sunday mornings in September (€55 return, under-12s €25, reservations at ⌨cp.pt, or at main train stations).
Cruises Between March and November, a huge variety of river cruises with various companies departs from, or passes through, Régua. Kiosks by the quayside sell tickets, or you can consult Porto Tours in Porto (⌨portotours.com) or Régua Turismo for full schedules. Short, hour-long cruises cost around €10, while longer tours run up to Pinhão and back (around €70, including lunch on board), or combine a cruise with a trip on a steam train and a wine lodge visit (around €120).
Vineyard visits The many port wine *quintas* – or vineyard estates – around Peso da Régua offer vineyard tours and tastings. The turismo has plenty of information, as does the Rota do Vinho do Porto information centre, at Régua train station (Mon–Fri 9.30am–12.30pm & 2–6pm; ☎254 324 774), which produces a map of wine-related sites along the Douro (also available online). Douro Verde (⌨douroverde.com) also runs a tourist road-train service from Régua quayside (€7.50) that whisks you up to a viewpoint and throws in a brief lodge visit and tasting.

ACCOMMODATION

Accommodation in Régua itself is distinctly underwhelming, typified by the two high-rise eyesores close to the train station, but there are some fantastic riverside *quintas*, manor houses and wine-hotels within 10km of town. The former Solar da Rede *pousada* at Mesão Frio is under new ownership and at the time of writing was closed for refurbishment but destined to open in the near future.

★**Quinta de Marrocos** Valdigem, 2km east, N222 Pinhão road ☎254 313 012, ⌨quintademarrocos.com. Delightful family-owned *quinta* with four bedrooms on the Douro's south bank where the grapes are still trodden by foot. There's swimming in the river from the estate grounds, B&B in rustic guest accommodation (and meals available for €25), while special weekend stays (€280 for two people) let you experience wine production here at first hand. They also offer cellar visits and tastings (€10). __€75__
Quinta do Vallado Vilharinho dos Freires, 6km northeast, Corgo River road ☎254 318 081, ⌨quintadovallado.com. This historic *quinta* overlooks the Rio Corgo, a tributary, rather than the Douro itself. Owned for a couple of centuries by the famous port wine Ferreira family, the striking house offers winery tours and tastings (well worth doing in any case), plus a selection of beautiful designer guest-rooms – five in the old manor house, and eight more in a sleek, modernist, slate-built extension set on a stunning panoramic terrace (these cost more, around €150). There's also a lovely pool, plus bikes, fishing trips and boat tours available. Doubles __€130__

EATING AND DRINKING

Castas e Pratos Rua José Vasquez Osório ☎254 323 290, ⌨castaspratos.com. Fanciest dining option in town is this impressive designer refurbishment of a warehouse at the old train station now offering restaurant, wine bar, lounge and wine shop, all rolled into one. You can snack in the wine bar on Portuguese and Spanish tapas, while the restaurant (dishes €10–30) goes in for artfully presented contemporary creative Portuguese cuisine. Wine bar daily 10.30am–11pm; restaurant daily 12.30–3pm & 7.30–10.30pm.
DOC Folgosa, 10km east, N222, Pinhão road ☎254 858 123, ⌨ruipaula.com. There's no finer place on the Douro for an alfresco meal than this expensive riverside restaurant with rolling vineyard views from its oh-so-cool dining room and deck – it's only a 10min drive from Régua. Run by chef Rui Paulo of Porto's *DOP* (see p.278), the restaurant serves up sensational contemporary Portuguese food – think tuna carpaccio, *alheira* (sausage) samosa, and sea bass on wild rice. Expect to pay at least €60 per person for a three-course meal with wine. Daily 12.30–3.30pm & 7.30–10.30pm; esplanade bar 11am–late.
Gato Preto Av João Franco ☎254 313 367, ⌨restaurantegatopreto.webnode.pt. Popular with locals, the "Black Cat" is a reliable spot on the Régua quayside for an inexpensive meal. The meze lunch costs around €8, dinner is slightly more. Daily noon–3pm & 7–10.30pm.

Lamego and around

5

Although technically in the Beira Alta region, the charming town of **LAMEGO**, 11km south of Régua, is easily accessible from the Douro, with which it shares a passion for wine – in this case, Raposeira, Portugal's answer to champagne. It's overlooked by the Baroque shrine of Nossa Senhora dos Remédios – another of those decorative Portuguese stone stairways to the skies – which plays host to an annual pilgrimage from late August to early September. There are scores of manorhouses in the handsome town centre, and a series of extraordinary churches, monasteries and fortified buildings in the surrounding verdant valleys, a legacy of the twelfth-century Reconquista, when Lamego was among the first towns to be retaken from the Moors.

Much of Lamego's early wealth derived from its position astride the trade route from the Beiras to the Douro, but the town's real importance is its history: in 1143, Lamego hosted Portugal's first parliament, when a group of clergy and noblemen assembled to recognize Afonso Henriques as the nation's first king. As such, it claims to be the birthplace of country and crown – a fact hotly disputed by Alfonso Henriques' birthplace, Guimarães.

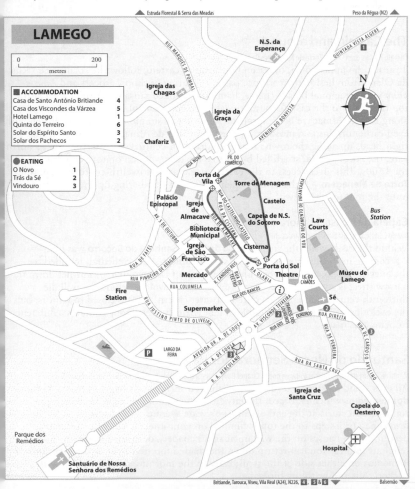

LAMEGO

0 ———— 200
metres

ACCOMMODATION
Casa de Santo António Britiande	4
Casa dos Viscondes da Várzea	5
Hotel Lamego	1
Quinta do Terreiro	6
Solar do Espírito Santo	3
Solar dos Pachecos	2

EATING
O Novo	1
Trás da Sé	2
Vindouro	3

Estrada Florestal & Serra das Meadas

Peso da Régua (N2)

N.S. da Esperança

QUINTADA VISTA ALGERE

RUA MARQUES DE POMBAL

Igreja das Chagas

Igreja da Graça

AVENIDA DO BOAVISTA

Chafariz

RUA NOVA

PR. DO COMERCIO

Porta da Vila

Torre de Menagem

Palácio Episcopal

Igreja de Almacave

RUA DO CASTELINHO/CASTELO

RUA DA CISTERNA

Castelo

Capela de N.S. do Socorro

Law Courts

RUA DO REGIMENTO DE INFANTARIA

Bus Station

Biblioteca Municipal

Igreja de São Francisco

Cisterna

Porta do Sol

RUA DA OLARIA

Theatre

LG. DO CAMÕES

Museu de Lamego

RUA DE FASEL

RUA 5 DE OUTUBRO

Mercado

R. CANDIDO REIS

RUA DO TEATRO

Sé

RUA PINHEIRO DE ARAGÃO

RUA COLUMELA

RUA DOS BANCOS

AV. VISCONDE TEIXEIRA

RUA DOS OUREIROS

TRAVESSA DOS OUREIROS

RUA DIREITA

RUA DE FERREIRA

RUA DE CARDOSO AVELINO

Fire Station

RUA JUSTINO PINTO DE OLIVEIRA

Supermarket

P

LARGO DA FEIRA

AVENIDA DR. A. DE SOUSA

AV. DR. A. DE SOUSA

R. A. HERCULANO

RUA DA SANTA CRUZ

Igreja de Santa Cruz

Capela do Desterro

Parque dos Remédios

Hospital

Santuário de Nossa Senhora dos Remédios

Britiande, Tarouca, Viseu, Vila Real (A24), N226, 4, 5 & 6

Balsemão

5

Sé

Largo da Sé • Daily 8am–1pm & 3–7pm • Free

Lamego's cathedral, the **Sé**, anchors the foot of town, a hybrid structure reflecting several bouts of rebuilding since it was first constructed in the twelfth century. The sculpted Gothic front is still impressive, though the highlight is the rose-planted sixteenth-century cloister, with its pleasing arches and patterned *calçada* floor.

Museu de Lamego

Largo de Camões • Tues–Sun 10am–6pm • €3, free on the first Sun of every month • ☎ 254 600 230, ⓦ museudelamego.pt

Facing the cathedral, and occupying the grand eighteenth-century Episcopal Palace, is the **Museu de Lamego**, whose star exhibit – officially classified as a "national treasure" – is a series of five panels (part of a larger polyptych) attributed to the great Portuguese painter Grão Vasco. They show various scenes, from *Creação dos Animais* (Creation of the Animals) to *Anunciação* (Annunciation) and were completed in Lamego between 1506 and 1511. The museum is also known for its collection of huge sixteenth-century Flemish tapestries.

The Castelo and around

Castelo Always open • Free • **Torre de Menagem** Daily 10am–6pm • Free

To reach the upper town, overseen by Lamego's **castelo**, follow the small, steep Rua da Olaria from beside the turismo, passing an array of shops, grocers and *casas de pasto* selling regional bread, cheese, hams and smoked sausages. A right turn at the top takes you to the castle's southern gate, the **Porta do Sol**, while straight ahead along Rua de Almacave is the **Igreja de Almacave**, a simple Romanesque church with even earlier origins as a mosque. At the top of Rua de Almacave an alley on the right heads up along the town's massive thirteenth-century walls to the castle's north gate, the **Porta da Vila**, straddled by a sorry-looking wooden oratory constructed in the 1700s. This gives access to the **castelo** itself, and its twelfth-century keep, the **Torre de Menagem** – if the tower's open, it's worth clambering up the rickety stairs onto the roof for the views.

Capela da Nossa Senhora do Socorro

Rua do Castelo, just past the Torre de Menagem

Within the castle walls, the small **Capela da Nossa Senhora do Socorro** was built – according to the inscription – on the site of Lamego's first cathedral, founded by the Suevian Idácio, who crowned himself Bishop of Lamego in 435. Further down the narrow street is a small circular *praça*, to the right of which, behind the wall, lies a thirteenth-century subterranean **cisterna** (water cistern). This is closed to visitors, but the enclosing wall itself is remarkable in that virtually every stone contains a different stonemason's mark.

Santuário de Nossa Senhora dos Remédios

Monte de Santo Estevão • Staircase Always open • Chapel Daily: May–Sept 7.30am–8pm; Oct–April 7.30am–6pm • Free

All eyes – and all steps – lead to the celebrated shrine and chapel of **Nossa Senhora dos Remédios** which embraces the city from the summit of a glorious Baroque staircase that starts at the end of Lamego's wide avenue of chestnut trees. It's no fewer than 611 steps to the top – climbed on your knees if you're particularly devout – with pauses on the way up at small chapels, decorated fountains and religious statues. You can return down the shaded forested tracks of the **Parque dos Remédios** on either side of the steps; early in the morning the air is filled with cuckoo calls and warbling birdsong.

> ### THE ENTRUDO DOS COMPADRES AT LAZARIM
>
> The unremarkable village of Lazarim (off the N2 Lamego–Castro Daire road) plays host to one of the oddest rituals to survive in Portugal. The **Entrudo dos Compadres** is a boisterous carnival that has taken place every Shrove Tuesday since the Middle Ages, with cavorting revellers taking to the streets wearing beautifully carved wooden masks, symbolic of the event's licentiousness. From a balcony, two colourful dolls loaded with fireworks are presented to the crowd – the *compadre*, carried by two young women, and *comadre*, toted by two young men. The couples proceed to recite insulting rhymes centring on sexual behaviour, after which the fireworks are lit and the dolls disintegrate in an explosive fury of smoke and flame, marking the end of the old year and the beginning of the new.

The **Festas de Nossa Senhora dos Remédios** (nicknamed the Romaria de Portugal) kicks off on the last Thursday of August, and continues until September 8, with the main pilgrimage and procession on the last day, featuring white-frocked children, and bulls pulling the carriage that transports the image of Our Lady. Of course, it's also an excuse to party and, in addition to the religious ceremonies, there are also floral displays, fairground rides, folk music, dances and concerts all over town.

Capela de São Pedro de Balsemão

Balsemão, 3km northeast of Lamego • Tues–Sun 10am–1pm & 2–6pm • Free

The ancient **Capela de São Pedro de Balsemão** sits in a small square of granite cobbles in the tranquil hamlet of Balsemão. It's a pleasant, signposted, 3km walk from Lamego, that starts at the Capela do Desterro then heads through the old part of town and over the bridge. Believed to have been founded as early as the seventh century, the present chapel's foundations were laid in the tenth century during the Reconquista. Inside the dark, granite interior is the fourteenth-century sarcophagus of the Bishop of Porto, Dom Afonso Pires, who was born in Balsemão. Look out for the unusual statue of Nossa Senhora do Ó – the Ó refers to the shape of her pregnant belly, though others ascribe it to the exclamation uttered when seeing it: *Ó! Nossa Senhora, Mãe de Deus…*

Ucanha

15km southeast of Lamego • Tues–Sun 10am–1pm & 2–6pm • Free • Take N226 (Moimenta da Beira road) for 12km, and look for the signposted left-turn just past Tarouca

For a trip into Lamego's medieval past, take a drive out to the ancient village site of **UCANHA**, where a mighty fortified stone tollgate and ancient bridge (signposted "Torre Fortificada") straddle the lazy river. These sorts of buildings were once a common display of local power and influence – you paid a fee to the manor house to be able to cross the river – and the tollhouse makes for an incongruous sight today in what's a real backwater. Like most other riverside villages, Ucanha also used to maintain a series of open-air washing pools, where the village women gathered to do their laundry and chat. These are no longer in use, but the whole scene is pretty as a picture, with a little bar at either end of the cobbled bridge, and a riverside path that runs up through the woods to a local river beach.

Mosteiro de Salzedas

Salzedas, 18km southeast of Lamego (N226) • Tues–Sun 10am–1pm & 2–6pm • Free • ☎ 254 677 458

At **SALZEDAS**, 3km beyond Ucanha, the mildewed main exterior of **Mosteiro de Salzedas**, an Augustinian – and later Cistercian – monastery overlooks the small village square. It dates from 1168, and was once enormously grand in scale and wealth,

5

though it's been at the mercy of scavengers and the elements since the dissolution of the monasteries in 1834. Inside, a team of volunteers helps to clean and maintain the building, while outside are some abandoned courtyards and cloisters. You're usually free to wander in for a look around, though if you want a guided tour (and the chance of an English-speaker) you need to contact the monastery in advance. There are a couple of cafés in the village square.

São João de Tarouca

17km southeast of Lamego, off the N226 (Moimenta da Beira road) • **Church** Tues–Sun 10am–1pm & 2–6pm • Free • ☎ 254 678 766 • The church is signposted to the right, past Mondim da Beira, 1.5km after the Ucanha junction on the N226, and it's another 3.5km from the turn

Evidence of the central role that Lamego played in the Reconquista, the fight back against the Moors, comes at the village of **SÃO JOÃO DE TAROUCA**, whose monastery of 1124 is thought to be the earliest on the Iberian peninsula to be founded by the Cistercian order – locals claim that Afonso Henrique himself, first king of Portugal, laid the foundation stone. Whatever its erstwhile eminence, the monastery was thoroughly trashed after the 1834 dissolution, leaving a ruined shell of roofless monastic buildings, scattered tombstones and a lone bell-tower. The scale of the ruins is impressive, but only the adjacent Romanesque **church** – consecrated in 1169 – stands in anything like its original form. Inside, there's a fine carved choir and a Baroque organ (1766) whose central figure marks time with his arm during Mass, while *azulejos* in the transepts depict the life of St Bernard, including one of him standing in a wine barrel (a pre-Christian symbol of abundance).

Entry to the church is free, though if a guide accompanies you, you should tip them. There's a café nearby, and five minutes' walk downhill is a lovely Roman bridge over the Rio Varosa – a pleasant spot for a picnic.

ARRIVAL AND DEPARTURE
LAMEGO AND AROUND

By bus Lamego's bus station is located in the town centre, a stone's throw from the main sights.
Destinations Braga (daily; 2hr 50min); Lisbon (2–4 daily; 5hr); Penafiel (3–5 daily; 1hr 40min); Peso da Régua (every 2hr; 30min); Porto (3–5 daily; 3hr); Trancoso (1–2 daily; 2–3hr); and Viseu (3–5 daily; 1hr).
By car The main avenue in town splits into two distinct halves (with separate names) either side of a central roundabout marked by a war-memorial statue

of a soldier. There's metered parking along the bottom half of the avenue (nearest the cathedral) and free parking along the top half (including on the large Largo da Feira market place – though not on market day, Thursday).
By train The nearest train station is at Peso da Régua, 11km to the north: buses to Lamego leave from outside the station every couple of hours (30min), or take a taxi (around €20).

INFORMATION AND TOURS

Information The turismo is at the bottom of Avenida Visconde Guedes Teixeira (April–Sept Mon–Fri 9.30am–7pm, Sat & Sun 10am–1pm & 2.30–6pm; Oct–March daily 9.30am–12.30pm & 2–6pm; ☎ 254 612 005, ⓦ cm-lamego.pt).
Tours The two main local wine producers are the Caves

da Raposeira (ⓦ cavesdaraposeira.com), 1km from town, and the Caves da Murganheira (ⓦ murganheira .com), further out, on the road between Ucanha and Salzedas. For information about visits to local wineries, contact the turismo, since tours and tastings are not always possible.

ACCOMMODATION

LAMEGO
Hotel Lamego Quinta da Vista Alegre ☎ 254 656 174, ⓦ hotellamego.pt. Situated 1km out of town, this 93 bedroomed hotel has an indoor pool and gym, and a cosy dining area with views of the surrounding vineyard countryside. Although the rooms have a slightly 1970s

dated décor and no balcony, it's worth seeing if you can get one overlooking the valley estates below as opposed to the car park at the back. **€76**
Solar do Espírito Santo Rua Alexandre Herculano, entrance also on Av Dr. Alfredo de Sousa ☎ 254 655 060. Comfortable if smallish en-suite rooms in the "Holy

Ghost" guesthouse come with cool parquet floors and a/c. Those at the front with balconies have avenue and shrine views, though you also get some traffic noise. Private parking is a bonus, and there's a *pastelaria* below, from which come your breakfast rolls and croissants and through which you also enter the hotel. **€50**

Solar dos Pachecos Av Visconde Guedes Teixeira ☎ 254 600 300. The smartest town-centre choice is this renovated, granite-walled *solar*. The rooms are light and airy, with baths or showers, and many have avenue views. Prices drop markedly out of summer. **€75**

AROUND LAMEGO

★**Casa de Santo António de Britiande** Britiande, 5km southwest of Lamego, N226 ☎ 254 699 346, ⓦ casasantoantoniobritiande.com. In a handy location for touring the nearby Romanesque churches (bikes are available), this is a delightful, lordly, antique-filled manor house with its own *azulejo*-lined chapel and *pelourinho*, plus lovely orchards, gardens and a pool. There are four charming rooms in the house, and two separate garden apartments, with fireside or alfresco meals available by arrangement, as well as wine tastings and other local activities. There's a minimum two-night stay. Closed Dec–March. Doubles **€110**, apartments **€120**

Casa dos Viscondes da Várzea Várzea de Abrunhais, 10km southeast, signposted off the N226 at Britiande ☎ 254 690 020, ⓦ hotelruralviscondesvarzea.com. A long winding private driveway leads you to a palatial nineteenth-century *quinta* with shady verandas overlooking 180 acres of gardens, orchards and farmland. It's elegantly decorated throughout, with attractive wooden furniture and traditionally tiled bathrooms. Meals, enjoyed in a romantic *azulejo*-lined dining room, are a treat, and there's a pool. **€145**

Quinta do Terreiro Lalim, 7km south of Lamego, off N226 ☎ 254 697 040, ⓦ quintadoterreiro.com. Another of the region's baronial eighteenth-century mansions, where you can stay in one of ten atmospheric granite-walled rooms, some of which have fireplaces. There's also a swimming pool, tennis court and cosy cellar-bar. **€75**

EATING

For simple places serving inexpensive **regional food** in Lamego, head up Rua da Olaria, or at the back of the cathedral along Rua Trás de Sé ("Back-of-the-cathedral street") and Rua Direita. Local specialities include *fumeiros* (smoked meats), particularly *presunto* (ham) and *salpicão* sausages. The town's **food market** (closed Sat afternoon & Sun) is on Avenida 5 de Outubro, and there's a much bigger outdoor **weekly market** on Thursdays (at Largo da Feira), a colourful combination of local farm produce, trailers with grilled chicken, and stalls selling clothes and shoes. The esplanade **bars and cafés** in the middle of the avenue are the hub for summertime evening drinkers and ice-cream addicts.

O Novo Largo da Sé 9, Lamego ☎ 254 613 166. The big draw here is dining at an outdoor table in front of the beautifully sculpted cathedral facade, though luckily the food is pretty good too. Lamego *presunto* is served with fried eggs, or stuffed into grilled trout, while the *bacalhau a casa* is baked with onions. Dishes cost €8–14. Daily 8.30am–10.30pm.

Trás da Sé Rua Trás da Sé 12, Lamego ☎ 254 614 075. The paint-daubed walls are lined with notepaper messages of reviews by previous diners, and the local food and wine is reliably good and fairly cheap (most dishes cost €7–10). There's a short menu, with a handwritten list of daily specials, including the ubiquitous grilled trout stuffed with *presunto*. Daily noon–2.30pm & 7–10pm.

★**Vindouro** Trav da Rua dos Fornos 19, Lamego ☎ 254 401 698, ⓦ restaurantevindouro.com. For a bit of Lamego glam, try this contemporary town-centre restaurant that cooks fancy regional dishes inspired by traditional Douro recipes in its wood-fired ovens. This means things like rack of lamb on ratatouille, *cabrito assado*, or risotto with wild duck and sun-dried tomatoes, with prices around €10–25. It's serious about its wines too, with most of the restaurant's Douro offerings also available to buy. Mon–Fri & Sun noon–10.30pm, Sat noon–11pm.

Pinhão and around

East of Peso da Régua, the minor N222 hugs the south side of the Rio Douro, with the train on the north side, until reaching the small port-wine town of **PINHÃO**, 25km to the east, and the heart of the Douro region. It's a wonderful route and there's a real sense of arrival at Pinhão, where the river broadens and the terraced hills close in. Cruise boats tie up along a broad riverside promenade, where a couple of bars look out over a fjord-like vista and there's a welcome breeze in the evening air. If you've come by car, don't miss the short, winding 7km drive up to the *miradouro* at the small village of **Casal de Loivos** (Favaios–Alijó road) – some say there's no better view along the whole of the Douro.

THE PORT WINE STORY

If ever a drink was synonymous with a country it's **port** – the fortified wine from Portugal's Douro region. For three centuries wine has been shipped down the Douro River to Vila Nova de Gaia, whose famous **wine lodges** (Sandeman, Graham's, Cockburn, Taylor's) reflect the early British influence on its production. A cellar tour here (see p.275) forms an integral part of any Porto visit, while you can also follow the **wine trail** along the Douro by train, car or cruise boat. To find out more, the country's port wine institute, the Instituto dos Vinhos do Douro e do Porto (@ivdp.pt), has a useful English-language website, while the Rota do Vinho do Porto details the region's wine estates, attractions and events.

DEVELOPING A TASTE – THE EARLY DAYS

The clear distinction between port wine (*vinho do porto*) and other Portuguese wines wasn't made until the beginning of the eighteenth century, when Britain prohibited the import of French wines during the War of the Spanish Succession. Portuguese wines quickly filled the void and, following the **Methuen Treaty** (1703), the wine trade became so profitable that adulterated inferior wines were soon being passed off as the genuine article. This led to the creation of a regulatory body in 1756, the **Companhia Geral da Agricultura das Vinhas do Alto Douro**, and, the following year, the declaration of the world's oldest **demarcated wine region** (where port wine could now only legitimately be produced). Yet it wasn't until the mid-nineteenth century that it began to resemble today's fortified wine, when the addition of brandy to stop fermentation became widespread, enabling the wines to be transported over even longer distances.

THE DOURO WINE ROUTE

The port wine grapes are grown in a 600,000-acre demarcated region along both banks of the **Rio Douro**, stretching from Mesão Frio (near Peso da Régua) to the Spanish border. Sheltered by the Marão and Montemuro mountain ranges, around fifteen percent of the region is under vines, which benefit from cold winters and hot, dry summers. The characteristic terraces can be seen along the length of the Douro, and they form a beautiful backdrop to the small town of **Pinhão**, which is now the main centre for quality ports. The grapes are harvested at the *quintas* (vineyard estates) from September to October and crushed. After a few days fermentation is halted by the addition of brandy – exactly when this is done determines the wine's sweetness – with the wine subsequently stored in casks until the following March. The final stage in the wine route is the transportation downstream to the shippers' lodges, where the wine is blended and matures.

WHAT'S IN THE BOTTLE?

Port wine is either **ruby** (ie deep red), **tawny** (made from a blend of differently aged wines) or **white** – the first two are generally drunk at the end of a meal, or with cheese or dessert, the last served chilled as an aperitif. The finest reds are **vintages**, wines from a single year that are bottled two to three years after harvest and left to mature. A vintage is only declared in certain years (just fourteen times between 1901 and 1999, for example), and the wine is only ready to drink at least ten to fifteen years after bottling, when the flavours are at their most complex, the wine deep purple and full-bodied. **Late Bottled Vintage (LBV)** is not of vintage quality, but is still good enough to mature in bottles, to which it's transferred after four to six years in the cask. All other ports are blended and are kept in the cask for between two and seven or more years, with the colour developing into various shades of tawny – they are ready to drink when bottled. Of these, a **colheita** ("Harvest") is a tawny port made from grapes from a specific year and aged at least seven years in the cask; other fine wines are **superior tawnies** dated ten, twenty, thirty or forty years old (the average age of the wines in the blend), while **reserve** ports (both tawny and ruby) are decent blended wines, the best being the tawny reserve ports which have to spend at least seven years in the cask.

ARRIVAL AND DEPARTURE PINHÃO AND AROUND

By train There are five through-trains a day from Porto to Pinhão (2hr 20min), or you can change in Peso da Régua (4 daily; 26min). Onward services are to Tua (5 daily; 15min) – change at Tua for the bus to Mirandela in Trás-os-Montes – and to the end of the line at Pocinho (5 daily; 1hr).

By car Beyond Pinhão, you can only follow the river by

train or boat as the roads (on either side of the Douro) head for the hills, either to the wine- and olive-growing town of

Alijó (15km northeast) or the rock art at Vila Nova de Foz Côa, 60km southeast.

ACCOMMODATION AND EATING

PINHÃO

Douro Rua António Manuel Saraiva 39 ☎254 732 404, ⓦhotel-douro.pt. The best of the two adjacent budget places opposite the station, the *Douro* has a vine-covered terrace and simple en-suite rooms with balconies that overlook the water. It's hard to say what's more disconcerting – the cruise ships or the weekend steam trains, both disgorging their passengers below your window. The downstairs restaurant, which is open to non-guests too, charges more than it should (dishes €9–12), but offers a few fish choices alongside the standard meat menu, and the house wine is excellent. Restaurant daily noon–3pm & 7–10pm. **€60**

Ponte Romanica Rua da Ponte ☎254 732 978. Located across the small bridge over the Pinhão River, at the back of town (Sabrosa road), this is the best of the non-hotel restaurants, with a river view if you get a seat by the window. You'll eat cheaply if you have the dish of the day at lunch, or the à la carte option costs around €20. Daily 11am–3pm & 7–10pm.

AROUND PINHÃO

★**Casa de Casal de Loivos** Casal de Loivos, 7km north of Pinhão, Favaios–Alijó road ☎254 732 149, ⓦcasadecasaldeloivos.com. This old Douro manor house has an intimate house-party feel, and while the small rooms are traditional in decor they all open onto a stunning terrace with a pool, outdoor breakfast area and amazing views. It's the property of a rather exclusive wine producer and if, as a guest, you choose to dine here, be sure to try the wines. You'll find the house in the middle of the hilltop village of the same name, not far from the spectacular *miradouro*. **€114**

Pousada Barão Forrester Alijó, 15km northeast of Pinhão ☎259 959 467, ⓦpousadas.pt. This splendid place is Alijó's main draw, named after the English port pioneer Joseph Forrester, who was made a baron by the Portuguese king and who drowned in the Douro in 1862 (weighed down, it is said, by his money belt). It's a genteel country house, with charming rooms, a formal restaurant, and terraces overlooking palm trees and a pool. **€130**

Quinta de la Rosa 1.5km west of Pinhão, on the north bank of the river ☎254 732 254, ⓦquintadelarosa.com. A working wine estate with nineteen rooms split between the main house and annexe, as well as two gorgeous larger suites (prices up to €140) and a swimming pool. The *quinta*'s own-label wines and olive oil are terrific, which guests can try with a pre-booked lunch or dinner (€25, including wine and port) on their lush vine-covered terrace, which has views to die for. **€90**

★**Quinta Nova de Nossa Senhora do Carmo** Covas do Douro, 10km west of Pinhão, on the north bank of the river ☎254 730 430, ⓦquintanova.com. Truly fabulous, relaxing wine hotel in an eighteenth-century manor house on one of the most beautiful of Douro estates. Views over the vineyards and orchards to the river are stupendous, not least from the infinity pool, while country-chic rooms mix antique carved beds, polished floors and woven rugs with sharply styled, granite bathrooms containing select toiletries. It's a lovely, secluded space, offering its own vineyard tours and cellar tastings, plus bike and hiking trails, while meals are served outside under a century-old vine canopy. It's a 15min drive from Pinhão, or they can pick you up from Ferrão station at the bottom of the hill. **€230**

Vila Nova de Foz Côa

Sitting high above the Côa valley, 60km southeast of Pinhão, the small town of **VILA NOVA DE FOZ CÔA** would attract no interest at all had it not been for the discovery in 1992 of the most extensive array of outdoor **paleolithic art** in Europe. The engravings are of a similar style to those found in caves elsewhere, but their uniqueness lies in the fact that they are carved outside on exposed rock faces in a river valley. With the oldest dated at around 23,000 years, their survival is remarkable, and protected as both National Monument and UNESCO World Heritage Site.

There are three rock-art sites to visit, though the restrictions on numbers and visiting hours mean you can't see more than two in any one day. Depending on how keen you are, this might mean an overnight stop in Foz Côa, though there is not really any reason otherwise to stay. Although the blistering midsummer heat and winter cold makes it hard to believe, the town benefits from a Mediterranean microclimate, proof of which is provided by the locally produced almonds, fruit, cheese, wine and

5

– especially – olive oil, which is among the country's finest. The **monthly market** is on the first Tuesday of the month next to the football field, and the blossoming of **almond trees** draws the crowds in late February and early March.

Parque Arqueológico do Vale do Côa (PAVC)

Museu do Côa Tues–Sun 9am–1pm & 2–6pm • €5 • **Site visits** Tues–Sun 9am–5.30pm • €10 per site, or €12 including museum, nocturnal visit €17 • ☎ 279 768 260, ✉ museu@arte.com.pt, 🖰 arte-coa.pt

The **Parque Arqueológico do Vale do Côa** contains thousands of engravings on several hundred rocks, a good number of which are clustered around the three major sites. The engravings are of horses, deer, goats and other animals, as well as later, Neolithic images of people. Many of the engravings are quite hard to make out, as unlike cave art they are not painted but were scratched or chipped with stones. Depending on the site, visits take place either in the morning or afternoon, though night visits – which benefit from being out of the sun's glare so you can see the engravings more easily – are also sometimes possible. If you only have time to visit one site, Penascosa is considered the most interesting.

Visiting the sites

The **Museu do Côa** (3km east of town, signposted) is the obvious place to start, since it expands in detail upon the discovery and history of the site, and also acts as a booking centre for the park. **Visits to the rock-art sites** have to be booked in advance, which can be done in person or by phone or email – in summer, two or three days in advance is recommended. The fee includes a guide and 4WD transport from the appropriate visitor centre; each trip has a maximum of eight visitors, and children under 3 are not allowed.

Canada do Inferno

From the museum, tours head out to the first site to be identified, that of **Canada do Inferno** (usually morning visits; tour lasts 1hr 30min), which lies near the abandoned Côa dam. It contains a wide variety of engravings, from bison to horses, some of which are very close to the current waterline and many more that have been underwater since the construction of the Pocinho dam upstream raised the level.

Ribeira de Piscos

Trips to **Ribeira de Piscos** (usually mornings; 2hr 30min) head out from Muxagata, 1km off the N102 to Guarda, which has a bar beside the visitor centre. The engravings are spread out along the eponymous *ribeira* down to its confluence with the Côa – a beautiful place, but there's a lot of walking involved. The highlights are a tender engraving of two horses "kissing", some fine engravings of auroch bison (now extinct) and an exceptionally rare, paleolithic engraving of a man.

Penascosa

The least strenuous visit is to **Penascosa** (usually afternoons, 1hr 30min, plus evenings, 3hr), as the jeeps park right next to it. The starting point is the visitor centre in Castelo Melhor, just off the N322 to Figueira de Castelo Rodrigo. Penascosa's highlights include an engraving of a fish (one of very few such depictions worldwide), and a rock containing over a dozen superimposed animals, the meaning of which archeologists are at a loss to understand. The village itself has a gorgeous ruined castle and a couple of café-restaurants.

Quinta da Ervamoira

There's also a private site at **Quinta da Ervamoira** (closed Mon; visits by appointment: ☎ 279 759 229), a secluded vineyard on the west bank of the Côa, accessed from Muxagata. It's owned by the Ramos Pinto port wine company, whose granite estate house is now a museum housing finds from Roman and medieval times.

ARRIVAL AND INFORMATION

By bus In Foz Côa the bus station is on the road in from Pocinho, 200m from the main avenue. Destinations Bragança (2 daily; 2hr); Guarda (Mon–Fri 1 daily; 1hr 30min); Miranda do Douro (4–5 daily; 2hr 10min); Trancoso (2 daily; 40min); and Viseu (2–3 daily; 2hr).

By car Foz Côa is an hour's drive from Pinhão, over the hills along the highly scenic N222.

By train The train from Régua (5 daily; 1hr 25min) or Pinhão (5 daily; 1hr) follows the Douro River as far as its

VILA NOVA DE FOZ CÔA

terminus at Pocinho, which is little more than a railway station, a hydroelectric dam and a couple of restaurants. Vila Nova de Foz Côa is 8km south of Pocinho, and if there's no connecting bus into town, you can take a taxi that will cost around €8.

Information The turismo is in the Centro Cultural, Avenida Cidade Nova (daily 9am–12.30pm & 2–5.30pm; ☎ 279 760 329, ⊛ cm-fozcoa.pt), in the same complex as the library, theatre, cinema and municipal museum.

ACCOMMODATION AND EATING

A Marisqueira Rua de São Miguel 35, down the pedestrianized continuation of the main avenue ☎ 279 762 187. A reliable stop for lunch or dinner *A Marisqueira* serves seafood, as the name suggests, including *arroz de marisco*, but in the end it's just as much a meat-and-potatoes place as anywhere else (meals around €25, lunch for less). Mon–Sat noon–2.30pm & 7–11pm.

Casa Vermelha Av Gago Coutinho 3 ☎ 279 765 252, ⊛ casavermelha.com. The only high-end place in town, with seven rather quaint rooms, plus picture-perfect lawns and a swimming pool. It's on the main avenue and is very easy to find – it's extremely red (*vermelha*). €90

★**Longrovia Hotel** Lugar do Rossio, 15km southeast in the town of Longrovia ☎ 279 849 230, ⊛ naturaempreendimento.com. Set in a peaceful, beautiful location, this hotel and spa offers huge rooms with stone featured walls, heated bathroom flooring and bath tubs. It is worth the drive to base yourself here. They

also have ten private bungalows on the property to rent. Doubles €120, bungalows €160

Pousada de Juventude 1.5km northwest of town off the Pocinho road ☎ 279 764 041, ⊛ microsites .juventude.gov.pt/portal/en. Not a great location if you don't have transport, but it has good facilities and windswept views. It's more like a budget motel, with private rooms as well as dorms (with and without en-suite toilet) with shower room along the hall and also four or six-person apartments with kitchenette. Closed Dec. Dorms €13, doubles €32, apartments €60

Quinta do Chão d'Ordem 5km south, just south of Muxagata, off the N102 ☎ 279 762 427, ⊛ chaodordem .com. Stay in one of the ten bedrooms available on this working farm estate, which boasts a cosy lounge and bar, tennis court and pool, and wine cellar in a converted dovecote. It's an artistically minded place with tasteful decor, and much of the produce, from the wine to the home-cured sausages, comes from the farm. €60

Barca d'Alva

The last Portuguese village along the Douro, **BARCA D'ALVA** is less than 2km from the Spanish border. Surrounded by mountains, and on a placid bend in the Rio Douro, it's a curious spot – on one hand, there's a long-abandoned railway line and a row of elderly cottages; on the other, there's a sparkling quayside with huge pontoons to accommodate the large Douro cruisers which disgorge passengers for a souvenir hunt. A few cafés, restaurants and shops soak up any passing trade, but in the end it's the drive here, from north or south, that really warrants the trip, through beautifully sculpted Douro terraces of olives and vines, with sweeping views across the hills and river gorge. As there's no road along the Douro River in its latter stages after Pocinho, you have to approach via Foz Côa and Figueira de Castelo Rodrigo (in Beira Alta) or Torre de Moncorvo and Freixo de Espada à Cinta (in Trás-os-Montes).

ACCOMMODATION AND EATING

BARCA D'ALVA

Bago d'Ouro Largo das Faias 29 ☎ 271 355 126, ⊛ bagodourohotels.pt. The simple river-facing rooms would suffice for the night, though you'd need a pretty good reason to stay. A daytime visit is more likely, for a browse around the upmarket deli and lunch in the restaurant

(mains from €10), where river fish from the Douro end up in dishes like *migas de peixe* (bread-based fish stew) and *peixinhos fritos* (mixed fried fish). Daily midday–3pm & from 7pm– opening and closing hours are very flexible, but don't expect to turn up at 11.30pm for a meal. €48

The Minho

BOM JESUS DO MONTE

The Minho

It's around 100km from Porto to the mouth of the Rio Minho, a broad river of even broader historical and cultural significance for the Portuguese since it marks the border with neighbouring Spain. The river has lent its name to the entire northwestern province, the Minho – which tourists may see referred to as a rebranded sub-region of Porto and North Portugal – an area which encompasses a range of postcard-worthy landscapes and features that could almost be Portugal in microcosm: dreamy river scenes, high mountains, rolling vineyards, historic towns, dramatic Atlantic beaches, ancient religious foundations and mysterious archaeological sites. Add a modern network of roads – it takes only an hour or so to get from the main towns to remote hiking villages – and a useful regional bus and train network ensures the Minho is an instantly appealing region to visit, as a sort of Portugal-in-a-nutshell experience, easily accessible straight out of Porto airport.

For a start, the region features many Portuguese traditions, whether it's the weekly market at **Barcelos** – a cross between a medieval fair and a vast farmer's market – or the summer *romaria*, or carnival, at **Viano do Castelo**. The Minho's two principal historic towns, both in the south, are also steeped in tradition – handsomely preserved, medieval **Guimarães**, Portugal's first capital, and neighbouring **Braga**, the country's ecclesiastical centre. The Minho coast, meanwhile, as little as half an hour's drive from Braga, is the typical Atlantic swathe of sweeping dunes and wild surf. Known as the **Costa Verde** (Green Coast), it's pretty much one unbroken stretch of sand as far as the Spanish border, punctuated by small-scale resorts and the historic maritime town of **Viana do Castelo**.

Central Minho is characterized by the region's other major river, the **Rio Lima**, which idles through a succession of pretty towns where there's little to do but soak up the scenery – ideally, while staying in one of the manor houses or country homes for which this area is renowned. Further east, the charming Lima valley gives way to the mountains of the **Parque Nacional da Peneda-Gerês**, Portugal's only national park, which stretches north to the Spanish border and east into the province of Trás-os-Montes.

To the north, the Minho region ends – where the country ends – with the **Rio Minho**, across which lies Spain. A string of compact fortified towns flanks the river on the Portuguese side, and the Minho train line from Porto terminates in the best of the lot, the spectacular walled town of **Valença do Minho**, a major crossing point into Spain.

Guimarães

GUIMARÃES never misses an opportunity to remind you of its place in Portuguese history. Indeed, it was here that the country's first monarch, Dom Afonso Henriques, was born in 1110, and the city became the first capital and court of the fledgling

FEIRA DE BARCELOS

Highlights

❶ Pousada de Santa Marinha da Costa, Guimarães Enjoy the views over Guimarães from a delightful hotel fashioned from a medieval monastery. **See p.310**

❷ Citânia de Briteiros Step back to pre-Roman times in the evocative ruins of a magnificent Iron Age hilltown. **See p.311**

❸ Touring the cathedral, Braga Follow the guide as he unlocks the secrets of the country's religious capital. **See p.314**

❹ Feira de Barcelos The spectacular Thursday *feira* is one of Europe's biggest weekly markets. See p.320

❺ Monte de Santa Luzia Ride up the funicular for one of the best views in Portugal from this breezy hilltop sanctuary. **See p.325**

❻ Valença do Minho A walk around the ramparts shows you the best of this historic Rio Minho fortified town. **See p.330**

❼ Ponte de Lima Whether staying in a manor house or boutique hotel – you won't regret a night in dreamy Ponte de Lima. **See p.336**

❽ Soajo, Parque Nacional da Peneda-Gerês The restored village of Soajo offers a glimpse of local life in this remote part of the country. See p.348

HIGHLIGHTS ARE MARKED ON THE MAP ON P.306

kingdom of "Portucale". Although Guimarães subsequently lost its pre-eminent status to Coimbra (elevated to Portuguese capital in 1143), it has never relinquished its sense of self-importance, something that's evident from the omnipresent reminder that *Portugal nasceu aqui* (Portugal was born here), which is the town's motto. With a carefully preserved kernel of medieval monuments, cobbled streets, delightful squares and honey-coloured houses, the old centre retains both a grandeur and a tangible sense of history that's helped earn it UNESCO World Heritage status. But it's far from a museum piece – its contemporary attractions were showcased during its stint as 2012 European Capital of Culture, while the local university lends it a youthful exuberance and lively nightlife, which is at its best during the end of May student-week festivities.

Castelo de Guimarães

Daily 10am–6pm • Castle and chapel of São Miguel do Castelo free; Torre de Menagem €1.50 • ☎ 253 412 273, ⓦ bit.ly/castelodeguimaraes

Occupying a strategically sited hill and partly built into huge granite outcrops, the city's severe **Castelo** was originally built in the tenth century to protect the people of

THE MINHO

HIGHLIGHTS

1. Pousada de Santa Marinha da Costa, Guimarães
2. Citânia de Briteiros
3. Touring the cathedral, Braga
4. Feira de Barcelos
5. Monte de Santa Luzia

6. Valença do Minho
7. Ponte de Lima
8. Soajo, Parque Nacional da Peneda-Gerês

0 — 20 kilometres

OLD CAPITAL, NEW PROJECTS

Guimarães' time as European Capital of Culture, in 2012, prompted a cultural and architectural makeover for the city, though as visitors stick resolutely to the confined streets of the historic old town, the new attractions tend to get short shrift – even though they are mostly located just a few minutes' walk away. The old market building on Avenida Conde Margaride, for example, has been reborn as the **Plataforma das Artes**, an arts and culture space devoted to exhibitions, installations, workshops and other creative projects. Across the way, the converted buildings of a former plastics factory host exhibitions and events at the **Casa da Memória** (Memory House), where the city's history, culture, heritage and industry is explored. Other former industrial buildings have similarly been given a new lease of life as arts and cultural centres, like the **Centro para os Assuntos da Arte e Arquitectura** (CAAA; Ⓦcentroaaa.org) – owned by a local association of artists and architects – or, just out of town, **Fábrica Asa** (Ⓦfabricaasa.eu). The project known as **Campurbis**, meanwhile – a partnership between council and university – aims to reinvigorate the former leather and textile district of Couros, with old factories again being put to new use as a Living Science Centre and Design Institute, among others. Further art and culture can be found at the well-established Centro Cultural de Vila Flôr (see p.311).

6

Guimarães from attack by Moors and Normans. After centuries of use it fell into disrepair – and was used as a debtor's prison in the nineteenth century – but the castle was rebuilt in the 1940s to reflect the era of its greatest prominence under Afonso Henriques, the first monarch to call himself "King of Portugal". It's claimed he was born in the central keep, the **Torre de Menagem**, which is surrounded by seven fortified towers, and if – as is likely – Afonso was baptized here too, then it would have been in the small, squat Romanesque chapel of **São Miguel do Castelo**, nestling among trees just outside the walls. You're free to look inside the chapel and explore within the castle walls, where you can climb up to the ramparts and battlements for fine views of the town. For even better views you can climb the keep itself – reached from inside the walls over a high wooden bridge, followed by 77 steps to the top of a narrow tower.

Paço dos Duques de Bragança

Rua Conde Dom Henriques • Daily 9am–6pm • €5, under-12s free • ☎ 253 412 273, Ⓦ bit.ly/pacodosduques

Dominating the lower part of the castle grounds is the grand **Paço dos Duques de Bragança**, originally built in the fifteenth century and serving as the medieval palace of the all-powerful Bragançan duchy until it fell into decline at the end of the sixteenth century. Successive uses, abandonments and unflattering restorations have rather mucked up its late-medieval majesty, and today part of the interior is used as a museum, housing an extensive collection of paintings (including a room of colourful pieces by modern artist José de Guimarães), applied art and weaponry. The top floor, meanwhile, is reserved as an official residence for the Portuguese president on any visit to the north of Portugal.

Along Rua de Santa Maria

For Guimarães at its most typical – by which we mean prettified and downright picturesque – take a walk along the narrow **Rua de Santa Maria**, which leads down from the castle area into the heart of the old town. You'll pass the impressive Baroque facade of the **Convento de Santa Clara** – now the Câmara Municipal (town hall), with the Biblioteca (library) opposite – before emerging in sloping **Praça de São Tiago**, which is ringed by cafés and restaurants. This forms almost a double square with neighbouring Largo da Oliveira, reached by walking through an ancient stone arcade that runs beneath the old medieval council chambers.

6

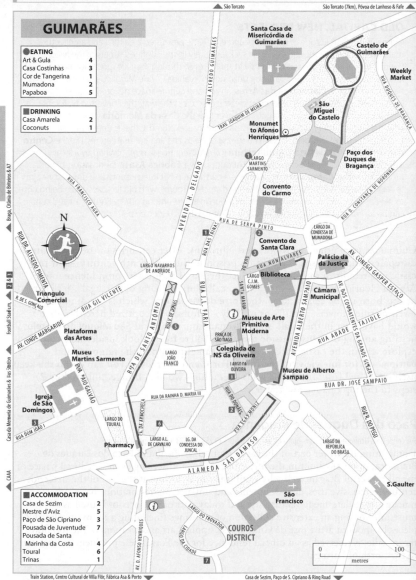

São Torcato

São Torcato (7km), Póvoa de Lanhoso & Fafe

GUIMARÃES

●EATING	
Art & Gula	4
Casa Costinhas	3
Cor de Tangerina	1
Mumadona	2
Papaboa	5

■DRINKING	
Casa Amarela	2
Coconuts	1

■ACCOMMODATION	
Casa de Sezim	2
Mestre d'Aviz	5
Paço de São Cipriano	3
Pousada de Juventude	7
Pousada de Santa Marinha da Costa	4
Toural	6
Trinas	1

Santa Casa de Misericórdia de Guimarães

Castelo de Guimarães

Weekly Market

São Miguel do Castelo

Monumet to Afonso Henriques

LARGO MARTINS SARMENTO

Paço dos Duques de Bragança

Convento do Carmo

RUA ALFREDO GUIMARÃES

TRAV. JOAQUIM DE MEIRA

RUA FRANCISCO AGRA

AVENIDA H. DELGADO

RUA DE SERPA PINTO

RUA DAS TRINAS

LARGO NAVARROS DE ANDRADE

RUA DE S. GONÇALO

RUA DR. ALFREDO PIMENTA

BUA GIL VICENTE

Triangulo Comercial

Plataforma das Artes

Museu Martins Sarmento

AV. CONDE MARGARIDE

RUA PAIO GALVAO

Igreja de São Domingos

RUA DOM JOÃO I

RUA DE SANTO ANTÓNIO

RUA DE PAIOS

LARGO JOÃO FRANCO

RUA J.L. FARIA

PRAÇA DE SÃO TIAGO

RUA DA RAINHA D. MARIA III

LD. DA ARRUCHELA

LARGO DO TOURAL

LARGO A.L. DE CARVALHO

LG. DA CONDESSA DO JUNCAL

Pharmacy

RUA NUN'ALVARES

Convento de Santa Clara

Palácio da da Justiça

LARGO DA CONDESSA DE MUMADONA

Biblioteca

LARGO C.J.M. GOMES

RUA SANTA MARIA

AVENIDA ALBERTO SAMPAIO

Câmara Municipal

RUA ABADE TAJIDLE

AV. DOS COMBATENTES DE GRANDE SALSAR

AV. CONEGO GASPAR ESTANO

RUA D. CONSTANÇA DE NORONHA

RUA DUQUES DE BRAGANÇA

Museu de Arte Primitiva Moderna

Colegiada de NS da Oliveira

LARGO DA OLIVEIRA

RUA DO DONÃES

RUA EGAS MONIZ

Museu de Alberto Sampaio

RUA DR. JOSÉ SAMPAIO

RUA R. DO PEGU

LARGO DA REPÚBLICA DO BRASIL

ALAMEDA SÃO DÂMASO

São Francisco

S.Gaulter

LARGO DO TROVADOR

LARGO DA CIDADE

COUROS DISTRICT

AV. AFONSO HENRIQUES

0   100
metres

Braga, Citânia de Briteiros & A7

Football Stadium

Casa Memória de Guimarães & bus Station

CAAA

Train Station, Centro Cultural de Villa Flôr, Fábrica Asa & Porto

Casa de Sezim, Paço de S. Cipriano & Ring Road

Largo da Oliveira

Legend, history and religion collide in the old town's most attractive square, **Largo da Oliveira**, with its appealingly rustic name (Olive Tree Square), stone arcades and painted houses with wooden balconies. There are no olive trees, though – the name relates to the tale of the Visigothic king Wamba, who is said to have pushed an olive-wood spear into the ground here, and refused to take up his crown unless the spear blossomed. Of course, it did bloom, and the supposed site is marked by a worn stone cross beneath an unusual four-sided **Gothic canopy**. The legend was

enough to inspire Dom João I, who rode out from Guimarães to do battle with Castile at the Battle of Aljubarrota in 1385. Hedging his bets – just in case olive-sprouting miracles weren't the portent he hoped – the Portuguese king also called on the Virgin Mary for help, vowing to endow a monastic church in her honour if the battle went well. The Castilian army was duly scattered to the winds and Dom João I repaid the favour to the Virgin with the construction of the **Colegiada de Nossa Senhora da Oliveira** (Church of Our Lady of the Olive Tree; daily 7.15am–noon & 3.30–7pm), whose magnificent sculpted doorway faces the stone canopy in the square. The monastic buildings associated with the church later passed to the Portuguese state, and it's these that now house the Museu de Alberto Sampaio.

Museu de Alberto Sampaio

Rua Alfredo Guimarães • Tues–Sun 9am–6pm • €3, free on first Sun of every month • ☏ 235 423 910, ⓦ masampaio.culturanorte.pt

Entered around the side of the Nossa Senhora da Oliveira church, the **Museu de Alberto Sampaio** shows off the region's religious treasures, from gold- and silverware to sculptures and frescoes. It's a beautifully restored space, with the collection displayed in the cloister and surrounding rooms, with two items above all taking pride of place. First is the masterpiece of medieval Portuguese silverware known as the *Triptych of the Nativity*, generally claimed to be captured Castilian war booty from the Battle of Aljubarrota, although it was more probably made from melting down the king's silver measuring weights. The other precious relic displayed is João I's battle-worn tunic, handed over by the monarch as a gift to the church that would later embody his victory.

Museu Martins Sarmento

Rua Paio Galvão • Tues–Fri 9.30am–12.30pm & 2.30–5.30pm, Sat & Sun 10.00am–12.30pm & 2.30–5.30pm • €3 • ☏ 253 415 969, ⓦ msarmento.org

The city's archeological collections are held in the **Museu Martins Sarmento**, named after the nineteenth-century archeologist Francisco Martins Sarmento, who was born in Guimarães and first excavated the Iron Age site of Citânia de Briteiros (see p.311). The backdrop to the museum is the former convent of São Domingos, whose Gothic cloister and other rooms display a tantalizing selection of discoveries covering the entire prehistory of northern Portugal. Many of the finds from the Briteiros site and other major excavations in the region are on show in the museum, with highlights ranging from the intricately decorated Vilela votive offering (a 2500-year-old bronze piece depicting a ceremonial procession) to a collection of Iron Age granite warrior statues.

Penha and the Teleférico de Guimarães

Teleférico de Guimarães: Jan–July & Sept–Dec daily 10am–6.30pm; Aug daily 10am–8pm • €5 return, children €2.30 return • ☏ 253 515 085, ⓦ turipenha.pt

The peak of **Penha** (617m) is crowned by a dull grey church but offers spectacular views over Guimarães. The surrounding woods are the locals' favourite spot for a Sunday picnic, reached on paths that skirt round – and sometimes under – enormous moss-covered boulders. To get there, you need to head down Rua Dr. José Sampaio (which starts near the Museu Alberto Sampaio) to the cable car station – the **Teleférico de Guimarães** – which is just a five-minute walk from the edge of the old town. By car or on foot, keep on Rua Dr. José Sampaio and follow the signs, past the *pousada*; the signposted hiking route cuts up the switchbacks and it's about 3km (or a stiff hour) from town.

6

ARRIVAL AND INFORMATION   GUIMARÃES

Guimarães is around 50km northeast of Porto, and around 25km southeast of Braga. It's only a small place, and pretty much everything of interest is located in the old centre, where you'll easily be able to walk from sight to sight.

By bus The bus station is a 15min walk southwest of the centre at the bottom of Avenida Conde Margaride. There are regular daily services to Braga (express buses take 25min, local buses up to 1hr), Porto (1hr), Vila Real (1hr) and Lisbon (up to 5hr).

By car The historic centre is partly pedestrianized, although metered parking is available in the streets around the old town walls. Free parking can be had at the big Largo das Hortas car park (follow signs to the Teleférico); there are also usually spaces on the far side of the Castelo (though not on Fridays, when it hosts a market).

By train The train station is 10min walk south of the city centre – bear left from the station and take the first right down Avenida Dom Afonso Henriques, which takes you to the leafy boulevard of Alameda São Damaso. There are hourly services between Porto Campanha and Guimarães (1hr 10min).

Information The main Turismo da Alameda is at Alameda São Damaso 83 (daily 10am–10pm; ☎ 300 402 012, ⓦ guimaraesturismo.com); there's also a branch office at Praça de São Tiago 37 (Mon–Fri 9.30am–6.30pm, Sat & Sun 10am–6pm; ☎ 253 421 221).

ACCOMMODATION

As well as atmospheric accommodation in the old town, and a just-out-of-town *pousada* with grandstand views, there are also some lovely manor houses in the surrounding countryside offering rather fine lodgings. The former *pousada* in central Guimarães, *Nossa Senhora da Oliveira*, sited right in the heart of the old town was closed at the time of writing, but is expected to reopen as a rebranded hotel in the future.

Casa de Sezim Nespereira, 4km south of Guimarães off the Santo Tirso road – turn right at Covas ☎ 253 523 000, ⓦ sezim.pt. A delightful aristocratic country estate owned by the same *vinho verde*-producing family for over six centuries. Eight of the rooms in the main eighteenth-century *solar* (manor) are furnished with Murano chandeliers and objets d'art, with four-posters in many. There's also a swimming pool and tennis court, and you're welcome to wander the vineyards, while things like walking tours and horseriding trips can be arranged. **€120**

★ **Mestre d'Aviz** Rua D. João I 40 ☎ 253 422 770, ⓦ hotelmestredeavis.pt. The best-value budget place in Guimarães, with pleasant rooms in a lovely converted townhouse, just outside the old centre. The best rooms have balconies, though those in the attic are also atmospheric. It even has its own neat living room and bar. Breakfast is extra. **€52**

★ **Paço de São Cipriano** Tabuadelo, 6km south of Guimarães off the Santo Tirso road – turn left at Covas ☎ 253 565 337, ⓦ pacoscipriano.com. The owners of this stunning fifteenth-century country house have traditionally received pilgrims en route to Santiago de Compostela in Spain, and the property comes complete with a chapel and medieval tower. It's a thoroughly lovely retreat, with its own magical gardens and wooded grounds, plus orchards and vineyards – there are seven elegant rooms and a swimming pool. Afternoon tea and dinner are optional extras, as are guided tours of the estate. It was closed for refurbishment at the time of writing so check for updates in advance of your trip. **€110**

Pousada de Juventude Largo da Cidade 8 ☎ 253 421 380, ⓦ microsites.juventude.gov.pt/portal/en. On a quiet side street, the town hostel partly occupies a renovated mansion, with another part housed in a new wing. It's got dorms, but there are also private rooms and simple four-bed apartments. Other features include its own gardens and courtyard, café, shared kitchen and parking. Dorms **€13**, doubles **€36**, apartments **€65**

★ **Pousada de Santa Marinha da Costa** Lugar de Costa, 2km southeast of Guimarães ☎ 253 511 249, ⓦ pousadas.pt. A 20min walk from town, the finest city choice is the elegant hillside *pousada* fashioned from a twelfth-century Augustinian monastery, which uses its vast granite spaces to impressive effect; for example in the soaring, arched dining room (once the monks' *adega*), the wide, baronial corridors and majestic tiled bar. Water tinkles from fonts, the cloisters are intact, while a romantic terrace offers sweeping city views – and there's a fine swimming pool and lovely hillside gardens as well. Rooms in the main building are in the atmospheric updated monks' cells, though there's more space and better views in the newer wing. **€170**

Toural Largo do Toural, entrance in Largo A.L. de Carvalho ☎ 253 517 184, ⓦ hoteltoural.com. Elegant townhouse renovated into a modern four-star establishment next to the music academy – expect delightful sounds to waft through the window. The rooms are spacious and plush, and there's a pleasant bar overlooking a central courtyard: it also has parking. **€85**

Trinas Rua das Trinas 29 ☎ 253 517 358, ⓦ www .residencialtrinas.com. In a fine townhouse in a great position right in the old town, this good-value guesthouse has eleven modest, en-suite double rooms, which are a bit on the old-fashioned side but are comfortable enough. Rooms overlooking the street have the atmosphere – rear rooms are noisier, although are double-glazed. **€40**

EATING

Old-town Guimarães has plenty of cafés and restaurants, with the best-located being those with outdoor tables in Praça de São Tiago and Largo da Oliveira – though menu-toting waiters go in for the hard sell at times and the food isn't always up to scratch. Local specialities are on the earthy side – like *chispalhada de feijão* (beans, sausage and pig's trotters) and *papas de sarabulho* (a blood and bread stew) – while desserts include the local honey cakes known as *melindres*, and *toucinho do céu* ("heavenly bacon"), a super-sweet concoction of sugar, almonds, eggs and lemon. The city's main festival is the **Festas Gualterianas** (for São Gualter, or St Walter), which has taken place on the first weekend of August every year since 1452.

Art & Gula Largo Cónego José M. Gomes 39 ☎ 253 518 118. The building is an old stone beauty in the historic core, with a first-floor dining room overlooking the square and town hall, and a romantic patio garden at the back. The menu's on the traditional side, *bacalhau* to *porco preto*, but in a restaurant that calls itself "Art & Gluttony" everything is beautifully cooked and presented (dishes €10–13). Tues–Sun noon–3pm & 7–10pm.

Casa Costinhas Rua de Santa Maria 68 ☎ 253 516 248. Sweet little granite house with a tiled bar serving the traditional cakes and pastries known as *doces regionais e conventuais*. Confections like *toucinho do céu* (available here) all once originated in Portugal's convents (*Casa Costinhas* is just around the corner from the old Santa Clara convent), and it's a perfect place to give in to your sweet tooth. Mon–Fri 8am–7pm, Sat 8am–2pm.

★ **Cor de Tangerina** Largo Martins Sarmento 89 ☎ 253 542 009. Hold on to your hats – creative organic veggie food from a good-natured cooperative is unusual enough in northern Portugal, but there's a charming tree-shaded terrace as well in this handsome old townhouse just below the castle. For meals, think things like a vegetable and mushroom *açorda* or tofu and vegetable cannelloni, with mains around €11 and lunch a good deal at €7–9. Otherwise, there are drinks, tastings, foodie workshops and music nights. June–Sept Tues–Sat noon–midnight, Sun noon–7pm; Oct–May Tues–Fri noon–3.30pm & 7.30–10pm, Sat noon–11pm, Sun noon–6pm.

Mumadona Rua Serpa Pinto 260 ☎ 253 416 111, ⊛ restaurantemumadona.com.sapo.pt. The cheapest feed in town at lunch is the set meal that gets you soup, a choice of main dish, drink and coffee, but to be honest it's not much pricier choosing off the menu – generous half-portions start at €5 in this bustling family-run restaurant that sees a largely local clientele (especially for lunch) despite its near-castle location. Mon–Sat noon–3pm & 7–10pm.

Papaboa Rua de Valdonas 4 ☎ 253 412 107, ⊛ papaboa.pt. Very much a restaurant used by the locals in the heart of the medieval city with a pleasant courtyard seating option at the back, main courses range from fish specialities such as sea bass and meat dishes such as pork with sausage mash and chestnut sauce. Prices in the region of €11 for main dishes. Daily noon–3pm & 7–10pm.

DRINKING AND ENTERTAINMENT

BARS

★ **Casa Amarela** Rua do Donães 16–24 ☎ 913 355 111. The "Yellow House" is a funky townhouse just off the historic squares, which mixes a bar, restaurant and live music. Drinks, and weekend gigs and DJs are upstairs in a smallish contemporary bar that opens out on to a roof terrace; good food is served downstairs, from tapas-sized dishes of fried chicken, grilled prawns or daily home-made quiche to *bacalhau*, steak or veggie mains (tapas €4, mains €10–13). Mon, Tues & Sun 10am–midnight, Wed–Sat 10am–2am.

Coconuts Largo da Oliveira 1 ☎ 253 516 664. Of the half-dozen bars on this lovely square, this is the pick of the bunch – with the best views right on to the ancient cross and church, and a studenty interior fashioned from an infilled granite arcade. There are nice cakes and pastries too. Mon–Thurs & Sun 10am–midnight, Fri & Sat 10am–2am.

ART AND CULTURE

Centro Cultural de Vila Flôr Av D. Afonso Henriques 701, on the way to the train station ☎ 253 424 700, ⊛ ccvf.pt. The local cultural centre occupies an eighteenth-century manor house, with a separate theatre wing, plus late-opening café-bar and restaurant. There's an exciting year-round programme, from cinema, live music and theatre to opera, dance and arts workshops – and the terraced gardens are lovely too.

Citânia de Briteiros

Ancient Portuguese archeological sites don't come more mysterious or dramatic than the **Citânia de Briteiros**, an Iron Age hill town that lies roughly halfway between Guimarães and Braga. It's one of dozens in the Minho region, large and small, most of which date back to around 500 BC, although some are considerably older still. Home to a people known as the "Bracari", the extensive site at Briteiros, straddling a

boulder-strewn hill, probably made a last-ditch stand against the invading Romans and was eventually abandoned by around 100 AD. Its significance is enormous – the hillside ruins may appear obscure today, but Briteiros is one of the earliest sites on the Iberian peninsula that could reasonably be described as an urban settlement.

The site

Rua de São Romão, Briteiros • Daily: April–Sept 9am–6pm; Oct–March 9am–5pm • €3, ticket includes admission to Museu de Cultura Castreja • ☎ 253 478 952, ⓦ msarmento.org

The *citânia* was first uncovered by Guimarães archeologist Francisco Martins Sarmento in 1874, who showed evidence of habitation here going back several thousand years, though what's visible today dates mainly from around 200 BC. This era of the so-called Cultura Castreja (Castro Culture) probably saw Briteiros at its peak, home to as many as two thousand people, living in circular huts in family compounds – Sarmento rebuilt two of the dwellings to give an indication of the settlement's feel and look. There's a fair amount of guesswork involved when it comes to interpreting the foundations of more than 150 separate huts, but there are obvious cooking and sleeping areas while the central stones, it's thought, would have provided support for poles holding up thatched roofs. A few of the foundations are more extensive, including a building with stone benches, which may have been a meeting house, as well as two bathhouses – these had their own water supply and separate steam- and cold-water rooms. It displays a surprising level of urban sophistication for the Iron Age – including a clear pattern of streets and defensive walls – and the entire site is a hugely evocative place for a stroll, along rough cobbles and past ancient cork oaks.

Museu da Cultura Castreja

Rua do Solar, Briteiros • Daily: April–Sept 9.30am–12.30pm & 2–6pm; Oct–March 9.30am–12.30pm & 2–5pm • €3, includes admission to Citânia de Briteiros • ☎ 253 478 952, ⓦ msarmento.org

Many of the finds from the site are on show in Guimarães at the Museu Martins Sarmento (see p.309), but once you're out here it's worth also calling in at the **Museu da Cultura Castreja** in nearby Briteiros. It's set inside an old manor house (once the family home of archeologist Francisco Martins Sarmento, and his HQ during the digs conducted at the archeological site), and puts the Citânia de Briteiros into wider context within the world of the Cultura Castreja, which extended throughout northern Portugal and into northwestern Spain. In particular, the museum displays the large, precisely incised stone known as the Pedra Formosa ("beautiful stone"), discovered at Briteiros in the eighteenth century and an object of some fascination for early archeologists. Once assumed to be a sacrificial altar, it's now generally agreed to have formed part of the inner wall in one of Briteiros' ritual bathhouses.

ARRIVAL AND DEPARTURE	CITÂNIA DE BRITEIROS
By car The site is around 15km from both Guimarães and Braga, reached via the small town of Briteiros – here, signs direct you to the *citânia* on the hill above town. There is limited parking, which can be found on	the road before the site and by the entrance. **By bus** A few buses run from Guimarães direct to Briteiros (2–3 daily), from where you can either walk the 2km up to the site, or catch a taxi from the main square.

Braga and around

BRAGA is Portugal's most important religious centre, with churches by the bucket-load. It's also one of the country's oldest and most fought-over towns, probably first founded by the Iron Age Bracari people (hence the name) before falling into Roman hands, after which its history was one of conquest and reconquest. By the time Portugal was

established as an independent country in the eleventh century it was already an important bishopric, and it's remained at the heart of national religious life ever since. Spend some time here and you soon become aware of the weight of ecclesiastical power, embodied by an archbishop's palace built on a truly presidential scale and religious festivities that set the tone for the rest of the country. The city's outlying districts also boast a selection of religious buildings, shrines and sanctuaries, notably

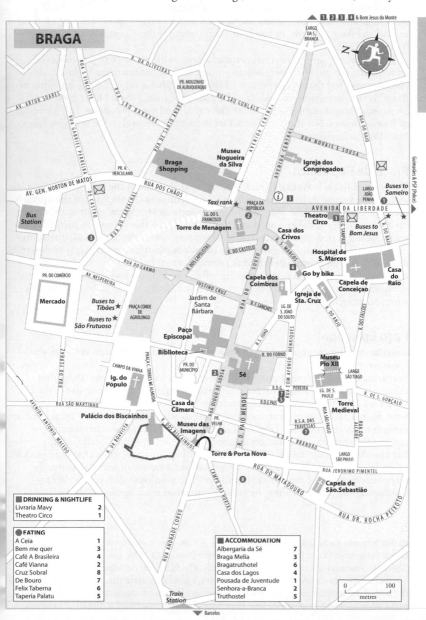

BRAGA

DRINKING & NIGHTLIFE
Livraria Mavy	2
Theatro Circo	1

EATING
A Ceia	1
Bem me quer	3
Café A Brasileira	4
Café Vianna	2
Cruz Sobral	8
De Bouro	7
Felix Taberna	6
Taperia Palatu	5

ACCOMMODATION
Albergaria da Sé	7
Braga Melia	3
Bragatruthotel	6
Casa dos Lagos	4
Pousada de Juventude	1
Senhora-a-Branca	2
Truthostel	5

0 — 100 metres

Portugal's oldest Benedictine monastic foundation at **Tibães**, and **Bom Jesus**, one of the country's most extravagant Baroque creations.

For all that, it would be too easy to fall into the time-honoured cliché that Braga is a traditional, conservative place of stultifying religiosity. True, there might be 35 churches in town, but there's also a fast-growing commercial centre, a renowned university and an underlying cultural vibrancy that led to Braga being named 2012 "European Youth Capital". The refashioned **city centre** is a pleasing place of wide boulevards and traffic-free streets and squares, and it's easy to spend a day or so idling around, drinking coffee in its handsome cafés, some of them century-old survivors from more uptight days.

The smartening-up of Braga has come at a price – the network of fast roads, underpasses and modern tower blocks around the ancient town has angered many residents who feel that the old centre of Braga (the phrase "as old as the cathedral of Braga" is the Portuguese equivalent of "as old as the hills") should have been better preserved. Various tunnelling projects uncovered, and promptly destroyed, a number of Roman houses, but the plus side is that most of the central traffic can now be funnelled underground.

Praça da República

The heart of Braga is **Praça da República**, an arcaded square at the head of the old town, with a wide avenue in front marked by a trio of fountains. At the back of the square is the former town keep, the fourteenth-century **Torre de Menagem**, while in the arcade itself two traditional coffee houses still do the honours – the *Vianna*, in particular, is a gently fading period-piece. Pedestrianized shopping streets shoot off in all directions from Praça da República, like **Avenida da Liberdade**, with its central carpet of flowers, though it's **Rua do Souto** that is Braga's principal street, heading down towards the cathedral. Only in Braga, is the tempting refrain, would you find boutiques and bars alongside a selection of shops where you can buy a silver chalice, a life-sized ceramic saint and a bag of votive candles.

Paço Episcopal

Largo do Paço • No general admission to the palace itself • **Biblioteca** The entrance is on Praça do Municipal • Mon–Fri 9am–noon & 2–8pm • Free

For centuries, the most impressive building in Braga has been the old Archbishop's Palace, the **Paço Episcopal**, a strident statement of intent in the very centre of the city. It's actually "buildings" rather than "building", since it's been extended and reconfigured many times, from medieval castle to aristocratic mansion – most of what survives today (it was much larger still in earlier times) dates from the sixteenth to eighteenth centuries and embraces a variety of architectural styles from Gothic to Baroque. It was under renovation at time of writing. There are some charming gardens around the back too. These days the palace has had a variety of uses and currently accommodates part of the university and both the municipal archives and **library** (Biblioteca), the latter retaining its ornately furnished reading room.

Sé

Rua Dom Paio Mendes, entrance on Rua Diogo de Sousa • Daily: May–Sept 8am–7pm; Oct–April 8am–6.30pm • You can walk into the cathedral for free, but you'll have to buy tickets to see the most interesting parts • ☎ 253 263 317, ⓦ se-braga.pt

The twin-towered **Sé**, or cathedral – properly, the Catedral de Santa Maria de Braga – stands opposite the Archbishop's Palace. It's a rambling structure founded in 1070 on the site of a Moorish mosque after the Christian Reconquest, though only the original main door (at the top of Rua Dom Paio Mendes) survives in its sculpted, Romanesque

form. Everything else is a hotchpotch of often-conflicting styles – Braga's cathedral is no one's real favourite – although Archbishop Dom Diogo de Sousa (1505–1532) did at least have the foresight to commission architect-of-the-day João de Castilho to work on various aspects of the interior and exterior.

Tesouro–Museu da Sé

June–Sept Tues–Sun 9am–12.30pm & 2–6.30pm; Oct–May Tues–Sun 9am–12.30pm & 2–5.30pm • €3

Hardly surprisingly, the most domineering cathedral in Portugal also has the richest **treasury** in the country, containing representative chalices, crosses, goblets, coffers, vestments, paintings and ceramics from across the centuries. It is, dare we say, a bit on the dull side, and the only light relief comes from the displayed shoes of the diminutive Archbishop Dom Rodrigo de Maura Teles (1704–1728), who stood a mighty 1m 20cm tall. He commissioned 22 monuments during his term of office, among them the fabulous shrine at Bom Jesus.

Coro Alto and Capela dos Reis

June–Sept Tues–Sun 9am–12.30pm & 2–6.30pm; Oct–May Tues–Sun 9am–12.30pm & 2–5.30pm • €2

A separate ticket gives you a guided tour of the main chapels and choir, led by an attendant with giant comedy keys, opening and closing vast ancient doors as you go. First up is the Baroque **Coro Alto**, with its majestic carved seats, gilded organ and imposing archbishop's throne – the latter surmounted by a grand eighteenth-century clock stopped at a symbolic three o'clock (the supposed hour of Christ's death). Then it's on to the fourteenth-century **Capela dos Reis** (Kings' Chapel), which is where ecclesiastical and royal power finally collide in Braga. The chapel contains the tombs of Henry of Burgundy and his wife Teresa of León – not only were they the founders of Braga cathedral, but also the parents of Afonso Henriques, first king of Portugal. You'll also be invited to look into the sarcophagus containing the supposedly mummified body of Archbishop Lourenço, though it's tricky to discern much through the clouded glass. Two other chapels are also on the tour – a gilded Baroque monstrosity dedicated to the first archbishop of Braga, now the city's patron saint, and a more sober affair with faded eighteenth-century frescoes and a painted ceiling.

Palácio dos Biscaínhos

Rua dos Biscaínhos • Tues–Sun 9.30am–12.45pm & 2–5.30pm • €2, free on the first Sun of every month • ☎ 253 204 650

To get an idea of how the wealthy lived in the seventeenth and eighteenth centuries, visit the splendid **Palácio dos Biscaínhos**, which was donated to the city in the 1960s on the death of its last aristocratic owner. The Counts of Bertiandos had lived here for over three centuries and the grandiose complex now houses a small museum of decorative arts, paintings and sculpture from the seventeenth to nineteenth centuries, which, together with exquisite tiles and wooden ceilings, demonstrates some of the best Portuguese interior decor of the time. There are pretty landscaped **gardens** behind, complete with a 200-year-old Virginian magnolia tree.

Museu Pio XII

Largo de Santiago 47 • Tues–Sun 9.30am–12.30pm & 2.30–6pm • €2 for each part, or €4 for both plus the Torre Medieval • ☎ 253 200 130, ✆ museupioxii.com

On the southern side of town, in a former seminary, the curious **Museu Pio XII** is divided into two parts: one traces the career of Portuguese portrait-painter Henrique Medina (1901–1988), while the other rounds up a wide-ranging archeological and sacred art collection. In the **Torre Medieval**, opposite, a further section of the museum narrates Braga's history across five floors of a bell-tower – but really, what you come here for is the fine view of town from the top.

Estádio AXA

Monte Castro, 2km north of the city centre • **Tours** Sept–May Mon–Fri 10.30am & 3.30pm; June–Aug 10.30am, 2.30pm & 4pm • 30min tour €3; 90min tour €5 • Reservations essential ☎ 253 206 860, ⓦ scbraga.pt • Bus #5 (every 30–60min) from Avenida Central

Braga's spectacular municipal stadium, known as the **Estádio AXA** – designed by Eduardo Souta Moura for the Euro 2004 football championships, and home of Sporting Braga – has become something of a contemporary icon for the city. It's hard not to be impressed by the architect's vision, which wedged two colossal stands into the Monte Castro hillside, with the bare rock cliff of an old quarry forming one end of the ground. Both long and short tours take in the stadium interior and club museum, though if you're a Portuguese footy fan it's the longer tour you want, which also includes a visit to the changing rooms, press room and VIP areas.

Mosteiro de São Martinho de Tibães

Mire de Tibães, 6km northwest of Braga • Tues–Sun 10am–7pm; guided tours at 11am, 3pm & 4.30pm • €4, under-14s free, free on the first Sun of every month • ☎ 253 622 670, ⓦ www.geira.pt/msmtibaes • Bus #50 (four daily; 30min) runs directly to the monastery from Praça Conde de Agrolongo, though last return is early afternoon; additional services on bus #11 (marked "Padim da Graça") involve a steep 10min walk up to the monastery

The oldest Benedictine foundation in the land – predating even the establishment of the Portuguese nation in the eleventh century – stands a few kilometres from the centre of Braga, close to the village of Mire de Tibães. The **Mosteiro de São Martinho de Tibães** was probably first founded in the tenth century, though its heyday coincided with the

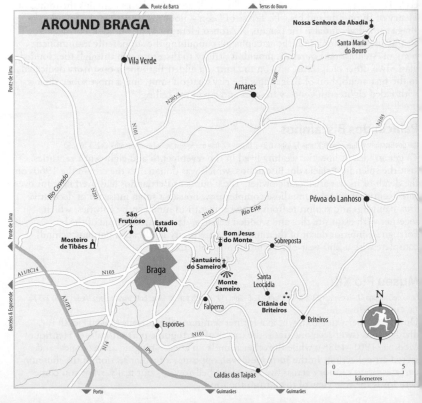

AROUND BRAGA

flourishing of nearby Braga in the seventeenth century, when Tibães was a fabulously wealthy monastery – it was for a time one of the country's main schools for master stonemasons and artists, until its dissolution by the state in 1833.

From the grand cobbled entrance – heavily grooved from the wheels of untold hundreds of carts – the tours (usually in Portuguese) take you round the old stables, and through beautiful **cloisters** lined with eighteenth-century *azulejos* showing the life of St Benedict. It is interesting to compare the ornate grand hall, where bishops were elected, with the spartan monks' cells, though perhaps most impressive of all is the huge church, a mishmash of Baroque, Rococo and Neoclassical styles. You can walk around on your own at other times, when you'll also be able to explore the hundred-acre monastic **gardens**, dotted with chapels, hermits' hideaways and little lakes. There are also two marked trails, a 45-minute one round the cultivated lower slopes, or a 90-minute one that climbs into the surrounding woodlands.

Bom Jesus do Monte

Monte do Bom Jesus, 5km northeast of Braga • Funicular: every 30min, daily 8am–dusk • €1.20 each way, €2 return • Take bus #2, at 10min and 40min past the hour, from Avenida da Liberdade, near the main post office, to the foot of the stairway at Bom Jesus

If the endless churches and religious buildings of Braga leave you cold, the monumental Baroque stairway and pilgrim church of **Bom Jesus do Monte**, sited on a wooded hill 5km to the east, is unlikely to do the same. In the Portuguese way, it's both pilgrimage and picnic site – you might bring lunch and enjoy the wonderful views from the terrace at the top, while other visitors determinedly shuffle up the 116m-long, ornamental zig-zag, granite staircase – doing it on their knees if they are particularly devout. The site was commissioned by Archbishop Dom Rodrigo de Maura Teles in 1723, although the whole complex – staircase, fountains, chapels and church – took sixty years to complete. There's a precise symbolism at work, with fountains representing the Five Senses and the Three Virtues, for example, while the chapels are adorned with sculpted scenes from the Passion of Christ. Linking all, meanwhile, are the bright, white, interleaved staircase walls, climbing to the church at the very top whose altar is dedicated to the inevitable Crucifixion of "Good Jesus of the Mount".

The walk up is certainly an experience, but you can also zip straight to the top using the hydraulic-powered, twin-cabined **funicular**, which was inaugurated in 1882 and is still going strong. The surrounding area is a public park with plenty of family-friendly attractions – woods to walk in, plus formal gardens and hidden grottoes, not to mention the boating lake and pony-cart rides. A handful of day-tripper restaurants cater for the weekend and holiday crowds, and there are even a few hotels and *pensions* too, most taking full advantage of the sweeping views from the Bom Jesus heights.

STAIRWAY TO HEAVEN, PART II

Close to Bom Jesus – 1.5km by road from the bottom of the staircase or a twenty-minute walk uphill beyond the pinewoods at the top – there's a second pilgrimage staircase and shrine with an entirely different feel. The massive, white-domed **Santuário do Sameiro** is impressive in its way, and again affords fantastic views across the city of Braga and beyond. But the nineteenth-century church is swallowed up by masses of surrounding concrete and approached by a grimly monolithic monumental stairway. It's on a similar scale to Fátima – a powerful reminder of the might and authority of the Roman Catholic Church in Portugal – and the main annual festival, on the first Sunday in June, sees the arrival of scores of thousands of pilgrims. There's a second huge event on the last Sunday in August too.

ARRIVAL AND DEPARTURE

Braga is around 60km northeast of Porto, and a quick 45min drive up the motorway. It's a fair-sized city, although the old town – an oval of streets radiating out from the Sé – is easy to see on foot.

By bus The bus station is a 5min walk from the central Praça da República. Local suburban buses operate from a variety of stops, though many use Praça Conde de Agrolongo as a terminus.

Destinations Arcos de Valdevez (10 daily; 1hr 30min–2hr); Barcelos (every 30min–1hr; 50min); Bragança (2–6 daily; 4hr 15min–5hr); Caldas do Gerês (5–11 daily; 1hr 30min); Campo do Gerês (2–7 daily; 1hr 30min); Guimarães (every 30min; 40min–1hr); Lisbon (12 daily; 4hr 30min); Monção (2–4 daily; 1hr 45min); Ponte da Barca (2–4 daily; 1hr 15min); Ponte de Lima (3–10 daily; 30min–1hr); Porto (every 30min; 1hr); Viana do Castelo (4–10 daily; 1hr 40min).

By car A swirl of ring roads and a confusing one-way system does its best to keep you out if you're trying to enter Braga and keep you in when you're trying to leave. If you're using a SatNav, you're going to be hearing a lot of "Recalculating…". There are plenty of central, signposted underground car parks, while the side streets around Praça Mouzinho de Albuquerque are your best hope for finding free parking.

By train The train station lies west of the centre, a 15- to 20-minute walk from the old town, down Rua Andrade Corvo. Direct trains run daily from Braga to Porto São Bento and Campanhã stations (every 30–60min; 55min–1hr 10min); change at Nine (10–20min) for Viana do Castelo and Valença do Minho.

INFORMATION, TOURS AND ACTIVITIES

Turismo Braga Turismo at Avenida da Liberdade 1 (Mon–Fri 9am–1pm & 2–6.30pm, Sat & Sun 10am–1pm & 2–6pm; ☎ 253 262 550, ⓦ www.cm-braga.pt) sells the Braga Card (€5, valid for two days) which gives hefty discounts on most town attractions and bus tours, and a ten-percent discount on some accommodation.

National Park office The HQ of the Parque Nacional da Peneda-Gerês (see p.340) is on Avenida António Macedo in the Quinta das Parretas suburb (Mon–Fri 9am–12.30pm & 2–5.30pm; ☎ 253 203 480, ⓦ adere-pg.pt). It's a 20min walk from the centre, and supplies invaluable maps and walking guides for Peneda-Gerês national park.

Bike rental Rent bikes from Go By Bike (1hr €4, 1 day €12; ☎ 917 741 803, ⓦ gobybike.eu/aluguer) at Rua de São Marcus 76, located by *Bragatruthotel*.

Bus tours The Yellowbus (ⓦ yellowbustours.com) hop-on, hop-off bus tour departs hourly from Avenida Central, passing the Sé and train station, and heading out to Bom Jesus and back (June–Sept 10am–noon & 3–6pm; €10, children €5, includes ride on Bom Jesus funicular; ticket valid 24hr).

ACCOMMODATION

Albergaria da Sé Rua D. Gonçalo Pereira 39–51 ☎ 253 214 502, ⓦ albergaria-da-se.com.pt. If you're on a budget this is a good first place to try, in a great position on a pedestrianized street a stone's throw from the cathedral and close to plenty of places to eat. It's nothing fancy, but the prices are good and there's friendly service. **€45**

Braga Melia Av General Carrilho da Silva Pinto 8 ☎ 253 144 000, ⓦ meliabraga.com. The *Melia* brings a touch of New York style to the suburban ring-road outside the city – from the soaring, urban-chic lobby, restaurant and bar to the fab spa facilities, and indoor and outdoor pool. Glam rooms in sober earth tones look over the roads and city lights below – whisk back the dividing sheen curtain and your room doubles in size, revealing a deep stand-alone bath and sharply styled bathroom. It's a 5min taxi ride to central Braga, and you're just a short drive from Bom Jesus. **€180**

★**Bragatruthotel** Rua de São Marcos 80 ☎ 253 277 187, ⓦ truthotel.com. This once ageing guesthouse has been given a contemporary lift. A good-value choice in a conveniently located, handsome old building where some of the revamped rooms have been designed and decorated by local artists, while the dining area and lobby are designated "art spaces" for changing exhibitions. They've kept right on top of what visitors want; from pillow menu and slippers to bike rental and other services, and there are suites (€75) and family rooms too (€85). They can also sort out nearby parking for you. **€55**

Casa dos Lagos Estrada do Bom Jesus, Bom Jesus 71–73 ☎ 253 676 738, ⓦ casadoslagosbomjesus.com. A charming old manor house up at Bom Jesus (on the road just below the top of the steps), with three spacious, traditionally furnished rooms in the main house (opening out onto a veranda), and some more modern apartments in a separate annexe. There's a kidney-shaped swimming pool and terraced gardens, and the views are sensational from all quarters. **€90**

Pousada de Juventude Rua de Santa Margarida 6 ☎ 253 616 163, ⓦ microsites.juventude.gov.pt/portal /en. Braga's youth hostel has half a dozen eight- and ten-bed dorms, and the bargain prices mean they tend to fill quickly in summer. You'll also need to book ahead if you want one of the three private double rooms. There are lockers for valuables, a kitchen, and a common room with satellite TV and a pool table. Dorms **€12**, doubles **€30**

BRAGA'S FESTIVALS

During **Semana Santa** (Holy Week), Braga is the scene of major celebrations which reach a climax in the three days before Easter Sunday, when local priests bless each house with a crucifix and holy water, while torchlit processions of hooded penitents known as *farricocos* parade by, spinning large rattles. Devout pilgrims meanwhile will be climbing the staircase at Bom Jesus on their knees, and there's a second major pilgrimage here for Pentecost (the seventh Sunday after Easter). Still a religious festival, but rather less buttoned-up, is the shindig associated with the **Festas de São João** (June 23–24), which is preceded by a festival of *gigantones* (giant carnival figures) from June 18–20.

6

Senhora-a-Branca Largo da Senhora-a-Branca 58 📞253 269 938, 🌐albergariasrabranca.pt. A useful place for drivers who want to stay centrally. This hotel is in a quiet location, facing a leafy square, and has garage parking. €55

★**Truthostel** Av da Liberdade 738 📞253 609 020. Under the same ownership as the *Bragatruthotel*, and a similar reboot of an old guesthouse, this is their cheery, more youthful budget haven with rooms to suit most pockets. They've splashed a lot of colour around communal areas, and provided a lounge, continental breakfast and lots of city help and information (there's someone on the desk 24/7). Beds are either in mixed dorms or private singles, as well as simple en-suite doubles and twins, and the best rooms overlook the flower-filled pedestrianized avenue below. Dorms €15, doubles €35

EATING

Braga is known for its old-style cafés, and also has an abundance of **restaurants**, though most of these too are thoroughly traditional in character and cuisine. Local specialities include *caldo de castanhas* (chestnut soup) and *charutos de chila* (cigar-shaped squash pastries), with *rabanadas* (fried slices of milk-soaked bread with a sweet cinnamon sauce) for dessert.

★**A Ceia** Rua do Raio 331 📞253 263 932. A great-value local diner with a rustic feel – you might have to wait for a table, or bag a space at the bar. Spit-roast chickens, *bacalhau* and steaks are served in enormous portions from €5–6 for a *meia dose*. Tues–Sun noon–3pm & 7–10pm.

Bem me quer Rua Andrade Corvo 8 📞253 262 095. Quaint style setting overlooking the town's fountain. The dishes are European, with a focus on vegetarian dishes such as red kidney bean rice or potato gratin, with prices ranging from €5–€10. Mon–Sat noon–midnight & Sun noon–3pm.

★**Café A Brasileira** Largo Barão de São Marinha 📞253 262 104. Originally opened in 1907, serving coffee imported from Brazil, this lovely old café has had a refit or two over the years but still looks the part, with its gilt reliefs, glass-topped tables and monogrammed wooden seats. Smart staff whisk around with snacks, cakes and sandwiches (€2–5), and the outside seats are perfect for watching the world go by. Mon–Thurs 7.30am–midnight, Fri & Sat 7.30am–2am.

Café Vianna Pr da República 📞253 262 336. The Art Nouveau *Vianna* hasn't quite kept its looks – tiles, marble and mirrors are all a bit on the tired side – but there's no arguing with its prime perch by Braga's showpiece fountains. There's a big menu of grills, salads and sandwiches, and it's uniformly good value (dishes €5–10). Mon–Thurs 8am–midnight, Fri & Sat 8am–2am, Sun 10am–7pm.

Cruz Sobral Campo Das Hortas 7/8 📞253 616 648. Traditional setting with a real provincial Portuguese feel, this cosy restaurant serves predominantly meat dishes such as roast goat or lamb with cabbage. Top it off with home-made orange cake (dishes €6–10). Tues–Sun noon–10pm.

De Bouro Rua Santo António das Travs 30–32 📞253 261 609. This former Cistercian monastic lodging house has been buffed up into a *haute cuisine* establishment serving traditional Minho specialities, from *bacalhau a Lagareiro* (salt-cod cooked in olive oil) to *arroz de pato* (rice with shredded duck, served with pine-nuts). Most dishes are around €10, and bigger servings costing €20–25 easily serve two people. Mon–Sat 12.30–3pm & 7.30–10.45pm; closed Dec & Jan.

Felix Taberna Largo do Pr Velha 17 📞253 617 701. A bit more imagination has gone into the traditional dishes served here – it's not straight-down-the-line meat and potatoes – and it's a handsome spot for a bite to eat (mains €9–12). Mon–Thurs 6pm–midnight, Fri & Sat 6pm–1am.

Taperia Palatu Rua D. Afonso Henriques 35–37 📞253 279 772. Cool café-bar that offers up a range of Spanish-influenced dishes (€8–12), from tapas and *revueltos* (fancy scrambled eggs) to steaks and sharing platters. In spring and summer, the small patio garden really comes into its own. Daily noon–2am.

DRINKING, NIGHTLIFE AND ENTERTAINMENT

There is a more contemporary **bar** and **club** scene though it's largely out of town, with most of the action on and around Rua Nova de Santa Cruz, below Bom Jesus, where students from the Universidade do Minho gather. For details of local cultural events, including shows at the Theatro Circo, pick up the monthly what's-on booklet *Braga Cultura* from the turismo.

★**Livraria Mavy** Rua Diogo de Sousa 129–133. The glorious old Cruz bookshop, vintage 1888, with its sculpted wooden ceiling, double-arched glass doors and all, has a new life as a rather hip café-bar. It's a coffee-and-cake place during the day (cheap lunches too) and more of a cocktail and drinks joint at night, with the beautiful interior doubling as a *galeria* for the work of local artists. Daily 9am–2am.

Theatro Circo Av Liberdade 697 ☎253 203 800, ⊛www.theatrocirco.com. The big town-centre theatre is the arts hub for the city, with a full programme, from film to contemporary theatre. There's also a really good theatre café, restaurant and club (entrance around the side at Rua Dr. Gonçalo Sampaio 18), worth checking out in any case.

Barcelos

There's little on first view to suggest that the small town of **BARCELOS** is in any way special – it has a few historical sights, a small medieval centre and an attractive riverside location, and in the normal run of things you might be persuaded to give it half a day. But the truly enormous square in the centre, the Campo da Feira, provides pause for thought, and all becomes clear if you turn up on a Thursday, when you'll coincide with the **Feira de Barcelos**, a gigantic open-air market that has few equals in Europe, let alone Portugal.

Campo da Feira and around

The vast **Campo da Feira** houses Barcelos' market every Thursday from dawn until late afternoon (around 4ish, or whenever the last stallholder closes) – it's been held here since at least the early fifteenth century and, save a few modern refinements, there's still much that a medieval market-trader might recognize. Today the Feira may have its own Facebook page, but the close-set rows of modest smallholders offering up their surplus produce have surely changed little over the centuries. Beyond the fruit and vegetables, eggs, olives, herbs, cheeses, cured meats, breads and pastries there's the supporting framework of an entire rural economy on display here, from agricultural implements and animal yokes to chainsaws and wine-making gear – not to mention piles of cheap clothes, big pants, €10 jeans, counterfeit sportswear, lengths of cloth, brassy Portuguese pop CDs and rustic crafts. The local terracotta, white and yellow pottery – the *louças de Barcelos* – is a big deal, while Barcelos backs up its self-appointed role as "Capital do Artesanato" with a full array of other crafts, from earthenware figurines to traditional basketwork. The market is, in short, as valid a reason to visit Barcelos as you could want; if you can, make a real trip of it by

THE BARCELOS COCK

The legend goes that a Galician pilgrim, en route to Santiago de Compostela in Spain, was wrongly arrested for a crime in Barcelos and sentenced to hang. En route to the gallows, the pilgrim was escorted to the magistrate's house to make one final plea. The judge and his friends were sitting down to a roast dinner, at which the pilgrim proclaimed "As surely as I am innocent, that cock will crow if I am hanged". Up rose the bird from the table and the pilgrim was saved. This tale of the "**Cock of Barcelos**" – its scenes sculpted onto a cross in the town's archeological museum – has endured over the centuries to become a real Portuguese emblem, and you'll see the symbol all over the country, from the ubiquitous rooster-shaped ceramic figures to images reproduced on tea-towels and ornaments.

staying the night before and setting your alarm clock for dawn to mingle with the stallholders as they set up for another timeless day at the *feira*.

Templo do Senhor Bom Jesus da Cruz
Largo da Porto Nova

The gleaming white-painted Baroque **Templo do Senhor Bom Jesus da Cruz**, on the west side of the square, is an obvious landmark. It's fronted by a rather nice formal garden of sculpted hedges and granite walls, while the cafés at the edge of the gardens have the best views in town. Just beware dusk, when birds gather in their hundreds for a chatter in the trees above, with inevitable consequences for anyone sitting or strolling beneath.

6

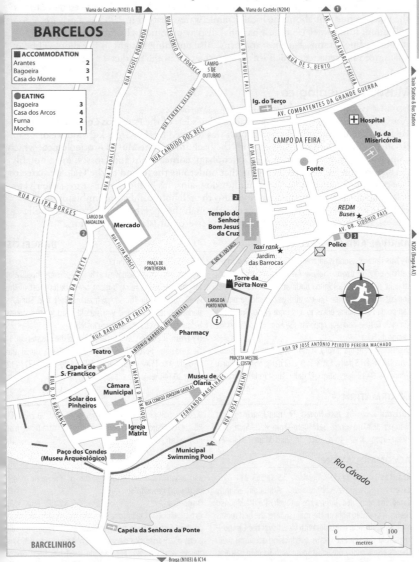

BARCELOS	

ACCOMMODATION
Arantes	2
Bagoeira	3
Casa do Monte	1

EATING
Bagoeira	3
Casa dos Arcos	4
Furna	2
Mocho	1

Torre da Porta Nova

Largo da Porto Nova • Mon–Fri 10am–5pm, Sat–Sun 10am–12.30pm & 2–5pm • Free

Sitting prominently on the southwest side of the Campo da Feira, the solid stone fifteenth-century **Torre de Porta Nova** was once part of the city walls, and was used as a prison until 1932. Now the tower acts as a local handicrafts centre and shop, and is a good place to find out more about Barcelos arts and crafts.

6 Museu de Olaria

Rua Cónego Joaquim Gaiolas • Tues–Fri 10am–5.30pm, Sat & Sun 10am–12.30pm & 2.30–5.30pm • Free • ☎ 253 824 741, ⓦ museuolaria.pt

Housed in the grand eighteenth-century Casa dos Mendanhas, the **Museu de Olaria** is the place to find out about the local ceramic wares. Started in 1963 as a private collection, it has since become a national display of some eight thousand pieces including fine ceramic figurines and urns. Also anything bought in the shop will be of guaranteed provenance, which isn't always the case in the market.

Museu Arqueológico

Paço dos Condes • Daily: April–Sept 9am–7pm; Oct–March 9am–5.30pm • Free

Above the town's medieval bridge stands what's left of the **Paço dos Condes**, once the Palace of the Counts of Barcelos, which was toppled by the Great Earthquake of 1755. Roofless and open to the elements, it's the backdrop to the **Museu Arqueológico**, which comprises a collection of gargoyles, sarcophagi, cornerstones and crosses, most notably the sixteenth-century carved crucifix that underpins the legend of the Galo de Barcelos (see p.320) – labelled "Padrão do Senhor do Galo", it's in the corner nearest the river, just in front of you as you enter. Note also the religious tombstone emblems of the various peoples to have lived in Barcelos through the ages: both Celtic and Catholic crosses, six-point Jewish Stars of David, and five-point Islamic pentagrams.

ARRIVAL AND DEPARTURE

BARCELOS

By bus The bus station is adjacent to the train station on the eastern edge of town – follow Avenida Alcaides de Faria straight ahead for 15min until it becomes Avenida Combatentes da Grande Guerra and you'll emerge on the Campo da Feira. Some buses to and from Porto, Braga and Viana do Castelo also stop opposite the *Hotel Bagoeira* on the Campo da Feira.

Destinations Braga (every 30min–1hr; 50min); Ponte de Lima (Mon–Fri 8 daily, Sat & Sun 1–2 daily; 55min); Porto (Mon–Sat 9–12 daily, Sun 1–2 daily; 1hr 45min); Viana do

Castelo (2–8 daily; 50min).

By car Barcelos is 20km west of Braga – drivers should aim for the Campo da Feira, a giant car park for most of the week, though on Thursdays (market day) and Sundays parking is restricted and you should head for the streets below the Museu Arqueológico instead.

By train The train station is adjacent to the bus station.

Destinations Porto (3–5 daily; 1hr); Valença do Minho (7 daily; 1hr 15min–1hr 50min); Viana do Castelo (11–12 daily; 30–40min).

INFORMATION

Turismo Largo Dr. José Novais 27 (mid-March to Sept Mon–Fri 9.30am–6pm, Sat 10am–1pm & 2–5pm, Sun 10am–1pm & 2–4pm; Oct to mid-March Mon–Fri

9.30am–5.30pm, Sat 10am–1pm & 2–5pm; ☎ 253 811 882, ⓦ cm-barcelos.pt), near the Torre de Porta Nova, just off the Campo.

ACCOMMODATION

Arantes Flat 1, Av da Liberdade 35 ☎ 253 811 326, ⓦ residencialarantes.webnode.pt. Although slightly dated, the blue-tiled *Arantes* has a touch of old-fashioned charm. It's located right on the main square; the best rooms have wrought-iron balconies with views over the Campo – just avoid the cell-like rooms overlooking a central well. There's also a sunny breakfast room with its own balcony,

and a *pastelaria* and *churrasqueira* of the same name occupy the ground floor. **€40**

Bagoeira Av Dr. Sidónio Pais 495 ☎ 253 809 500, ⓦ bagoeira.com. In bygone days, the town's old market inn on the Campo offered really atmospheric lodgings. It's still pretty buzzy on market days, and the restaurant (see p.323) is always worth a visit, but the inn itself has been overly

modernized and sanitized, and there's not much character left – though you do get a top-floor bar and garage parking. **€75**

Casa do Monte Abade de Neiva, 3km west of Barcelos on the N103 (Viana do Castelo road) ☎967 067 779, ⓦsolaresdeportugal.pt. Delightful country manor house set in its own gardens and grounds, with six bedrooms dressed with charmingly rustic furniture. Large gardens and a veranda give wonderful panoramic views and there's a swimming pool and tennis court. Rented as a whole house. **€300**

EATING

★**Bagoeira** Av Dr. Sidónio Pais 495 ☎253 813 088, ⓦbagoeira.com. This showpiece restaurant on the square is the best place in town for regional cuisine, from *rojões* to *cabrito*, with the house specialities like *bacalhau na brasa* and *polvo na brasa*, grilled on huge ranges. Mains are around €6–12, in portions large enough to satisfy hungry market traders who've been up since before dawn. Daily noon–3pm & 7–10pm.

Casa dos Arcos Rua Duques de Bragança 185 ☎253 894 018. Down in the old town, near the river, the traditional old stone house is a local favourite for Sunday lunch. A long menu of regional specialities includes suckling pig and roast pork, while the house-special steak and *bacalhau* are always popular; mains around €10. Mon–Wed & Sun noon–3pm, Thurs–Sat noon–3pm & 7–10pm.

Furna Largo da Madalena 105 ☎253 811 117, ⓦrestaurantefurna.com. At times, the queues for the takeaway charcoal-grilled chicken stretch out of the door, which gives a fairly good idea of what to order. A half-bird, eaten in the restaurant, is yours for under €6, and there's also a big menu of other Portuguese grills and specialities, with most dishes costing €7–10. Tues–Sat 9am–10pm.

Mocho Rua Padra Alfredo Rocha Martins 9 ☎253 054 074. Five-star centrally located restaurant with sleek modern interior and glass patio. Specialising in Spanish tapas, it also offers over a choice of two hundred wines plus local and imported beers. Dishes such as shrimps with garlic and octopus are a speciality for around €7–€12. There's also a wide selection of local cheeses. Daily noon–2am.

Viana do Castelo and around

For a first taste of the Minho coast, the historic maritime town of **VIANA DO CASTELO** is the principal port of call. Sited at the mouth of the Rio Lima, it has a landscaped waterfront, an appealing old town centre overlooked by the heights of Monte de Santa Luzia, and a great beach that lies just across the river. To call Viana a resort is probably a step too far – people certainly do come here in summer to laze on the sands, but the feel in the town at least is of a well-to-do place built on shipbuilding and trade, with elaborate period mansions and good-looking streets and squares to match. Tradition, too, still weighs strongly here, from the age-old Friday market held outside the former bastion walls to the annual *romaria* that ranks as one of the country's most impressive festivals.

Praça da República

Although badly worn, the Renaissance fountain in Viana's harmonious **Praça da República** sets the tone for a town whose earlier patrons spent well and wisely on their

---

THE VIANA ROMARIA

The big event of the year is the pilgrimage-cum-carnival known as the **Romaria de Nossa Senhora d'Agonía** – dedicated to Our Lady of Sorrows. It lasts for several days over the nearest weekend to August 20, and is held in huge esteem by the locals who offer "um abraço dos Vianenses" (a big hug from the Vianense) to anyone who makes the effort to come.

Events kick off with a **religious procession** on the Friday, complete with carpets of flowers, while the Saturday sees a more carnival-like atmosphere with a no-holds-barred **parade** of decorated floats, local villagers in traditional costume and exuberant townsfolk. The blessing of the fishing boats on Monday morning is rather moving, when women in the fishing quarter, east of the centre, decorate their streets and bestow good wishes upon the fleet. And into the mix you can add *gigantones* (carnival giants) at every turn, plus bands, concerts and dances, and spectacular nightly firework displays.

6

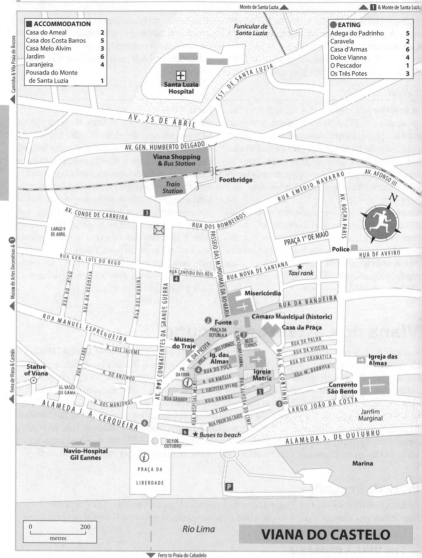

■ ACCOMMODATION

Casa do Ameal	2
Casa dos Costa Barros	5
Casa Melo Alvim	3
Jardim	6
Laranjeira	4
Pousada do Monte de Santa Luzia	1

● EATING

Adega do Padrinho	5
Caravela	2
Casa d'Armas	6
Dolce Vianna	4
O Pescador	1
Os Três Potes	3

VIANA DO CASTELO

public buildings. One side of the square is taken up by the sixteenth-century, triple-galleried **Misericórdia** (almshouse), which forms part of the adjoining **Igreja de Misericórdia**, an impressive eighteenth-century structure lined with superb *azulejos* by master craftsman António de Oliveira Bernardes and his son Policarpo. Behind the fountain, the former **Casa da Câmara** stands foursquare above a medieval arcade – the stone reliefs either side of the coat of arms on the facade of this old city council chamber are of a globe and a caravel, twin symbols of erstwhile Portuguese imperial might. From May to September the square hosts a lively **Saturday-morning market**, while in the quiet streets and small squares to the south of here Viana's old town is at its most charming.

Museu do Traje

Praça da República • Tues–Fri 10am–6pm, Sat–Sun 10am–1pm & 3–6pm • €2 includes entry to Museu de Artes Decorativas • ☏ 258 809 306

On the southwest edge of the square, the imposing yellow wedge – a former bank building – houses the **Museu do Traje**, or Costume Museum. It tells the story of the region's traditional clothes and costumes, from flax-planting to weaving, and displays a colourful array of wedding outfits, work gear and festival clothes, including the extraordinary *croça*, a rain cape made completely from straw.

6

Navio-Hospital Gil Eannes

Doca Comercial • Daily: April–Sept 9.30am–7pm; Oct–May 9.30am–6pm • €3.50 • ☏ 258 809 710, ⓦ fundacaogileannes.pt

Down on the waterfront, moored in the dock off Largo 5 de Outubro, the large white bulk of the **Gil Eannes** was Portugal's first hospital ship, built in Viana in the 1950s to support the cod-fishing boats and crew on the Newfoundland and Greenland seas. Later used as a cargo ship, and then finally scrapped in the 1990s, she returned to her home port after mouldering in Lisbon, and now serves as a floating museum dedicated to the ship's history.

Museu de Artes Decorativas

Largo de São Domingos • Mon–Fri 10am–6pm, Sat–Sun 10am–1pm & 3–6pm • €2, includes entry to Museu do Traje; free Sat & Sun • ☏ 258 809 305

For a sense of the wealth that poured into and out of Viana during its mercantile heyday (from the seventeenth century onwards) it's necessary to walk five minutes east from the main avenue to the **Museu de Artes Decorativas**, which is housed in another of the town's lavish former residences, this time an eighteenth-century palace originally used by the archbishops of Braga. The beautifully maintained interior displays a large collection of ceramics, *azulejos*, furniture and art – often imported from Portugal's former colonies – while a modern extension hosts temporary exhibitions.

Castelo de Santiago da Barra

Guarding the river's mouth, at the western edge of town, is the **Castelo de Santiago da Barra**, commissioned by Philip II of Spain for the defence of the port. Outside the walls here, in the area known as Campo do Castelo, Viana's lively **feira** (market) takes place every Friday, from dawn until early afternoon, or whenever the last vendor leaves.

Monte de Santa Luzia

Santuário de Santa Luzia Daily 8am–7pm • Free • Funicular de Santa Luzia Nov–Feb Tues–Fri 10am–noon & 1–5pm, Sat & Sun 10am–5pm; March–May & Oct Mon–Fri 10am–noon & 1–5pm, Sat & Sun 9am–6pm; June–Sept daily 9am–8pm • €2 one-way, €3 return • A taxi up to the sanctuary costs around €6

For a sensational view of the town, river and Atlantic coast you need to make your way up to the unmistakable landmark basilica on top of **Monte de Santa Luzia**, which looms over Viana do Castelo. The funicular railway is a fun way to get there; otherwise it's a punishing thirty-minute walk up the steps which start just past the hospital – take note of the inscription at the bottom which translates as "My God help me get up". At the summit there's a café and restaurant, picnic tables among the trees, plus plenty of stalls selling "*artigos religiosos*". Other than its monumental presence, there's little interest in the **Santuário de Santa Luzia** itself, though the climb to the top of the dome (marked *Zimbório*) is emphatically worth it. A narrow winding staircase leads right through the building, past traffic lights laid on in summer to keep tourist hordes in check, and emerges on top of the dome itself. It's very steep and – at the top – pretty hair-raising when the wind picks up, but the magnificent views reward every effort.

6

Citânia de Santa Luzia

Monte de Santa Luzia • April–Sept Tues–Sun 9am–noon & 2–6pm; Oct–March Tues–Sun 10am–noon & 2–5pm • €2 • It's located right behind the *pousada*; follow the road up from the sanctuary

It's hardly surprising that such a magnificent – and easy to defend – site as the Santa Luzia hill was settled in very early times; indeed, excavations have revealed that Santa Luzia was continuously occupied from the Iron Age to the end of the Roman period. The remains of a "proto-urban" hilltown or **Citânia** – dating back to at least 500 BC – are located on the highest part of the hill, and the foundations of circular and oval-shaped dwellings, plus walls and paved streets, can be viewed from an extensive raised walkway. You can see very clearly that this was no out-of-the-way rustic backwater, but a town of shepherds, farmers, fishermen, tool-makers, weavers and potters, whose inhabitants went to extraordinary efforts over centuries to build and defend their settlement.

Praia do Cabedelo

Boats May–Sept approximately hourly, 9am–dusk, but check with boatman for the last return; 5min ride • €1.10 each way • **Transcunha buses** Mon–Fri 6 daily, Sat & Sun 1–2 daily; 15min ride • €0.60 each way

Viana's nearest beach, the **Praia do Cabedelo**, is some distance from the historic town centre, south across the Rio Lima. Either take the ferry from the harbourside Praça da Liberdade, or a bus from the bus station, both of which drop you at the north end of the beach, where there's a cluster of café-restaurants and watersports outlets. The long, curving beach itself is terrific, if prone to the usual blustery conditions along this coast, with dunes and sand to spare even on the most popular of sunny days.

Vila Praia de Âncora

15km north of Viana do Castelo • Take the train from Viana station to Âncora-Praia, a 12–17min journey

North of Viana, the whole Minho coast is virtually one long beach. There are small holiday villages all the way up, though the flourishing resort of **Vila Praia de Âncora** is the only one near Viana with any kind of year-round life. It sits in the basin of the Rio Âncora, and has two forts guarding the bay: the Fortim de Cão, south of the estuary, and the better-preserved Forte de Lagarteira, to the north by a bustling fishing harbour. Legend has it that the river and town owe their name to a punishment doled out to the adulterous Queen Urraca of Navarre, drowned in the river by her jealous husband King Ramiro II of Asturias, Galicia and León with an anchor (*âncora*) around her neck. The beach, meanwhile, is a beauty, with an ocean-facing stretch of sand as well as a more sheltered area formed by a kink in the river estuary.

ARRIVAL AND DEPARTURE   VIANA DO CASTELO AND AROUND

By train Bus and train stations are integrated into a transport interchange (Estação Viana), combined with shopping complex and underground car park, located at the north end of Avenida dos Combatentes da Grande Guerra, which runs right through town and down to the river. Trains from Porto run inland via Barcelos, reaching the coast at Viana, then follow the coast north to Caminha.
Destinations Barcelos (12 daily; 25–45min); Caminha (7–8 daily; 20–30min); Porto (3–5 daily; 1hr 45min); Valença do Minho (7–8 daily; 40min–1hr); Vila Praia de Âncora (8–10 daily; 12–17min).

By bus There are bus services all across the Minho from the bus station at the Estação Viana transport interchange (same as train), but if you're heading up the coast to Caminha and

along the Minho to Valença it's usually faster to travel by train.
Destinations Arcos de Valdevez (3–12 daily; 1hr 30min); Barcelos (2–8 daily; 50min); Braga (4–10 daily; 1hr 40min); Caminha (roughly hourly; 30min); Lisbon (2 daily; 5hr); Monção (1–5 daily; 1hr 20min); Ponte da Barca (6–8 daily; 1hr 30min); Ponte de Lima (Mon–Fri hourly, Sat & Sun 7 daily; 50min); Porto (3–14 daily; 1hr 35min); Valença do Minho (1–3 daily; 1hr 15min); Vila Praia de Âncora (2–16 daily; 20–30min).

By car Viana de Castelo is a quick, 1hr drive (80km) up the coast from Porto, with Ponte de Lima a 30min drive (26km) along the north side of the Rio Lima. Parking in town is easy in various places along the waterfront, and while you may have to pay, it won't be much.

MONTE DE SANTA LUZIA, VIANA DO CASTELO (P.325) >

6

INFORMATION AND ACTIVITIES

Information The Viana Welcome Centre is on Praça da Liberdade (Sept–May Tues–Sun 10am–6pm; June–Aug daily 10am–7pm; ☎ 258 098 415, ⓦ vivexperiencia.pt). The main regional turismo is on Rua do Hospital Velho, at Praça da Erva (Mon–Sat 9.30am–12.30pm & 2–6pm; ☎ 258 822 620, ⓦ cm-viana-castelo.pt); it's housed in a lovely building dating from 1468 that was first used as a hospital for pilgrims travelling to Santiago de Compostela in Spain.

Bike rental and tours The Viana Welcome Centre rents out bikes (from €2.50/hour or €11 for a day) and can arrange bike tours (€22.50) and walking tours (€15).

Watersports Several local outfits rent surfing, kite-surfing and windsurfing gear, and can organize lessons and surf schools, including Viana Locals (☎ 258 325 168, ⓦ vianalocals.com) and the Surf Clube de Viana (☎ 258 826 208, ⓦ facebook.com/viandocastelolovers).

ACCOMMODATION

★**Casa do Ameal** Rua do Ameal 119, Meadela, 2km east off N202 (Ponte de Lima road) ☎ 914 206 227, ⓦ casadoameal.com. Handily placed for the town, and a rare retreat, is this granite-walled, whitewashed noble mansion set in its own grounds. There's a pool with manicured lawn and sun-loungers, plus eight charming apartments sleeping two or four people (€140 for a four-bed room) featuring exposed stone walls and vintage furniture. **€90**

Casa dos Costa Barros Rua de São Pedro 28 ☎ 258 823 705, ⓦ casacostabarros.pt. One of the Manueline mansions in the old town, the *Casa dos Costa Barros* offers good-value rooms for visitors, and while it's a pretty traditional setup – with fixtures and furnishings that are defiantly antique – you do get to sleep in one of Viana's characteristic sixteenth-century properties. **€70**

Casa Melo Alvim Av Conde da Carreira 28 ☎ 258 808 200, ⓦ meloalvimhouse.com. The town-centre choice for a gracious stay – a fabulously restored sixteenth-century mansion with elegant but understated rooms inspired by a period or a theme (Baroque to contemporary). Service is faultless, and there's a leafy garden and a good restaurant. Parking is available. **€160**

Jardim Largo 5 de Outubro 68 ☎ 258 822 261, ⓦ hoteljardimviana.pt. An old favourite, overlooking the main road and river at the bottom of town, the *Jardim* has straightforward rooms over five floors, enhanced by views of river, town or Monte de Santa Luzia, depending on which you choose. It's a bit noisy at the front, but pretty good value, especially considering the huge breakfasts. **€65**

Laranjeira Rua Cândido dos Reis 45–47 ☎ 258 822 261, ⓦ hotelaranjeira.com. Renovated townhouse with a bit of a budget boutiquey feel – some rooms are on the small side but the best ones have balconies facing Monte de Santa Luzia. There's garage parking too. **€85**

★**Pousada do Monte de Santa Luzia** Monte de Santa Luzia ☎ 258 800 370, ⓦ pestana.com. The hilltop *pousada* is all about its fabulous views – beg for a room at the front (ideally 108, or the suite, 107, both with private terraces) to enjoy the best panoramas in Viana, right over the basilica and down to the river and coast. It's a handsome refurb of a 1918 hotel building, with rooms given a cheery, country-chic makeover, while public areas make the most of the view, whether from picture-window restaurant, arcaded terrace, grand lounge or stepped gardens. There's also an outside pool, backing on to the archeological remains and boasting more sweeping vistas from the sun-loungers. **€200**

EATING

Viana's old town squares and wide avenues are made for dining alfresco, and there are plenty of places to soak up the atmosphere. For a historic backdrop aim for the cafés in lovely Praça da República, while in summer the riverfront comes into its own – there are restaurants and garden bars overlooking the docks and marina, and a few flash bars set alongside the renovated riverside promenade.

Adega do Padrinho Rua Gago Coutinho 162–164 ☎ 258 826 954. There's a family feel and a down-to-earth folksy interior, though the belting traditional music might force you out on to the street-side tables. It's strictly local on the menu too, with a wide choice of meat and fish grills (€7–12), from pork to squid, all served in gigantic portions. Mon & Wed–Sun noon–3pm & 7–11pm.

Caravela Pr da República 62–68 ☎ 258 822 553. The outdoor tables on the square by the fountain are hard to resist, but have a peek at the interior too. Hollowed out behind the historic facade is a stylish *pastelaria* with mezzanine seating and counters groaning under the weight of delicious cakes and pastries (ranging from €4). Daily 8am–7.30pm.

Casa d'Armas Largo 5 de Outubro 30 ☎ 258 824 999, ⓦ casadarmas.com. Mansion dining on the riverfront road – tapas and snacks on the terrace (€4–9) or a much fancier grill house experience inside, with anything from lobster to *picanha* on offer (mains €16–22). Daily 12.30–3pm & 7.30–10.30pm; bar open until 2am.

Dolce Vianna Rua do Poço 44 ☎ 258 824 860. Tucked into a little hidden square (if you can find the regional turismo, you'll see the restaurant), the *Dolce Vianna* does pretty good wood-fired pizzas and almost-Italian pastas

(€6–9); there's also a full Portuguese menu if this all seems dangerously exotic. Daily noon–3pm & 7.30–10.30pm.

★**O Pescador** Largo São Domingos 35 ☏258 826 039, ⓦopescadorviana.com. The top fish place in town is a 5min walk away from the main avenue – come here for the grilled catch of the day (from €10) or share one of the many two-person specials (€21–30), from a *misto de peixe grelhado* (mixed grilled fish) to a monster *bacalhau* platter. Starters are along the lines of mussels, clams, grilled octopus or *escabeche* (poached or fried marinaded) sardines. Mon–Sat noon–3pm & 7–10pm, Sun noon–3pm.

Os Três Potes Beco dos Fornos 7 ☏258 829 928. Undeniably touristy but also thoroughly charming – a sixteenth-century bakery, under a trailing vine, now the venue for live folk and fado music, bolstered by a pricey menu of Minho specialities, from *lampreia* to *cabrito* (dishes mostly €14–17). There are two entrances, both just off Praça da República – look for the cut-out figures in traditional dress. Mon, Tues & Thurs–Sun noon–3pm & 7–11pm.

Along the Rio Minho

At Caminha, 25km north of Viana do Castelo, road and rail turn decisively northeast and inland to run along the south bank of the **Rio Minho**. With Spain ever-present – just across the wide river – and crossings easily made, it's a fairly well-trodden tourist route, and the succession of historic frontier towns are used to Spanish day-trippers and visiting foreigners. You could just about see the lot in a day – from pretty **Caminha** to the country's northernmost town, **Melgaço**, 70km further east – but that would be to rush a region that's more suited to a leisurely stroll in the countryside, old-town rambles and summer afternoons spent at the nearest *praia fluvial* (river beach). With a night to spare, a stay in the fortress *pousada* of **Valença do Minho** is perhaps the best option, though admittedly this is the most touristy of the Minho towns. The **Linha do Minho** train line from Porto, via Viana do Castelo, runs to Caminha and Valença but no further, though there are plenty of local buses onwards to the old spa town of **Monção** and to Melgaço. The best way, however, to see the Minho region is by guided tour, such as with Cooltours Oporto (see p.276).

Caminha

At the broad sandy estuary of the Rio Minho, and straddling the Rio Coura, **CAMINHA** was a thriving port back in the seventeenth century, sending boats out across the empire. Those days are long gone – sleepy and provincial is closer to the mark now – but the thoroughly charming town is still worth a few hours' exploration, or even an overnight stop if you're in the mood for the beach or a quick ferry jaunt across to Spain. The main square, **Praça Conselheiro Silva Torres**, hints at past glories, with its majestic town hall, Renaissance clock tower and sculpted fountain, though it's the magnificently decorated **Igreja Matriz** (follow the street under the arch beneath the clock tower) that reveals the wealth that once flowed through Caminha.

The nearest beach is just 2km southwest at **Foz de Minho** – an idyllic wooded peninsula where the Minho flows into the Atlantic. A wooden boardwalk hugs the water's edge, leading to a sheltered river beach, or head five minutes through the pines to a great Atlantic beach, with a little fortified islet just offshore and Spain visible opposite. There's another good ocean beach at **Moledo**, a further 2km southwest – both Foz and Moledo are signposted off the N13 (Viana road) as you head into town.

ARRIVAL AND INFORMATION   CAMINHA

By train The easiest way to reach Caminha is by train; the station is on Avenida Saraiva de Carvalho, a short walk from the centre. There are daily services to Viana do Castelo (7–8 daily; 20–30min; for connections to Porto) and to Valença do Minho (8–10 daily; 20–30min; for connections to Vigo in Spain).

By ferry Caminha has a ferry link to La Guardia in Spain, a pleasant ride across the river that leaves from beside the bridge over the Rio Coura – signposted "Ferry-boat", the dockside is a 3min walk from the central square. There are services throughout the year (July & Aug continuous service 8am–8pm; Sept–June Tues–Fri hourly 8am–noon

& 2–6pm, Sat & Sun hourly 10am–noon & 2–6pm; foot passengers €1, cars €3).

Information Caminha Turismo, on Praça Conselheiro Silva Torres, is located in the arcade by the clock tower (daily 9.30am–12.30pm & 2–6pm; ☎258 921 952, ⓦ caminhaturismo.pt).

ACCOMMODATION AND EATING

There are some good local accommodation choices in Caminha and, along with Valença, this is the best overnight choice along the river. Half a dozen cafés and restaurants put out tables around the central square; there's more of a bar scene down Rua Ricardo Joaquim de Sousa, which is the road through the arch from the clock tower, heading down towards the Igreja Matriz.

Casa de Esteiró Vilarelho, 1km south of town, N13 ☎914 933 493, ⓦ casaesteiro.com. Originally an eighteenth-century hunting lodge, this charming house – crammed with family mementoes – is set in lovely gardens. There are two spacious suites in the house, plus three self-catering apartments (sleeping up to four people) in a separate house in the grounds. It's got a pool, and is only a few hundred metres' walk from the beach at Foz. Suites €95, apartments €110

Confeitaria Colmeia Pr Conselheiro Silva Torres 33 ☎258 722 456. The nicest café on the square sells a splendid array of local speciality pastries, including an almond-and-cream confection and a divine strawberry tart for €4. There's also a little bar area where you can sample wines that are also for sale. Daily 9am–10pm.

Design & Wine Pr Conselheiro Silva Torres 8 ☎258 719 040, ⓦ designwinehotel.com. Rio Minho visitors of old will scarcely credit some of the changes in these once somnolent towns, and Caminha's *Design & Wine* is typical of what monied tourism has wrought – a noble town mansion with a designer box full of river-facing rooms in over-the-top contemporary, street-art style. A sleek restaurant updates the Minho classics, offering Portuguese "tapas" from *presunto* to clams, alongside mains (€15–18) like *cataplana*, locally sourced meats and risotto. The restaurant is open to non-residents as well. Daily noon–3.30pm & 7.30–11pm. €90

Hotel Porta do Sol Av Marginal, 1.5km south of town, N13 ☎258 710 360, ⓦ hotelportadosol.com. Caminha's biggest resort-style hotel is at the entrance to town, right on the river – you can cross the road and walk up the boardwalk to the beaches at Foz. It's a four-star place with nice enough rooms – they all have a balcony, though not necessarily a water view – plus restaurant with panoramic views, two pools (one for kids), sauna and spa, gym and tennis court. You can get here by train too – it's just 7min walk from Senhora d'Agonia station, the stop before Caminha. €175

Valença do Minho and around

The must-see historic sight along the Minho is the fortress of **VALENÇA DO MINHO** (or just Valença), whose walls and ramparts dominate the riverside and speak volumes about erstwhile neighbourly disagreements. The fortress has repelled innumerable Spanish and French invasions over the centuries, though the impeccably preserved old town has surrendered entirely to a modern-day army of wallet-waving visitors who file in through the narrow town gates and descend upon the gift shops. Even the regional tourist office describes Valença as a "shopping fortress". But most evenings you'll have old Valença to yourself, and can explore at your leisure – the only disadvantage being that many of the cafés and restaurants are either hauntingly empty for dinner or simply shut up shop once their captive audience has left for the day. There's a new town, south of the ramparts, home to all Valença's non-touristy businesses and services, while each Wednesday a huge weekly market is held on the wooded slopes around the old town to the east.

Around the walls and ramparts

The first defensive walls were built here in the thirteenth century, though the current layout – a dazzling system of double ramparts, with two separate old-town areas separated by a deep moat – is a classic piece of seventeenth-century military engineering. The entrance for traffic is through the **Portas da Coroada**, which leads into an outer town defended by half a dozen bulwarks. Another set of gates, the **Portas do Meio**, then leads across a stone bridge into the even older medieval town, again defended by an elongated star-shape of steep, angled walls, towers and turrets. Alternatively, you can come directly into this older part of town via the pedestrian entrance of **Portas do Sol**.

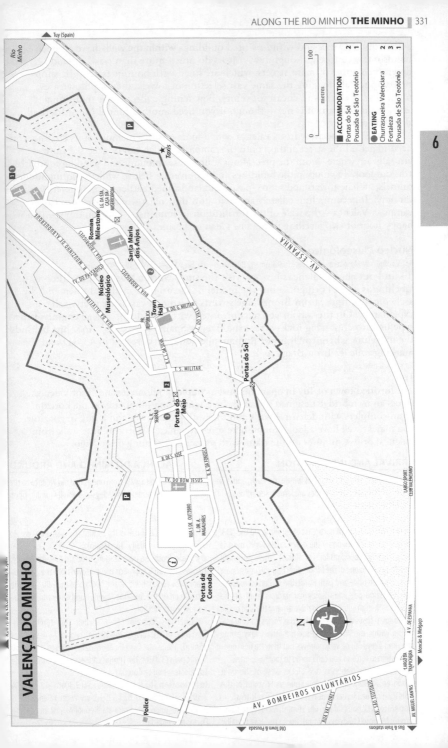

VALENÇA DO MINHO

Tuy (Spain)

Rio Minho

AV. ESPANHA

Roman Milestone

Santa Maria dos Anjos

Núcleo Museológico

Town Hall

LG. DA STA. CASA DA MISERICÓRDIA

RUA J. RODRIGUES
RUA J. RODRIGUES
AV. MOUZINHO DE ALBUQUERQUE
RUA DA OLIVEIRA
RUA DOS PASSADIÇOS DE AL.

PR. REPÚBLICA
R. DO D. G. MILITAR
R. DO VALE
R. CLUB SUAL

T. S. MILITAR

Portas do Sol

Portas do Meio
L. V. SARRÃO

B. DE S. JOSÉ

TV. DO BOM JESUS

RUA 5 DE OUTUBRO
LOR. A. MAGALHÃES
R. A. DA FONSECA

Portas de Coroada

N

Police

AV. BOMBEIROS VOLUNTÁRIOS

RUA VAZ FERREIRA
AV. MIGUEL DANTAS
AV. SÃO TEOTÓNIO
AV. DE ESPANHA

L. ARGOLETA TRAPICHEIRA

Moncão & Melgaço

LARGO SPORT CLUB VALENCIANO

Taxis

P

| 0 | | 100 |
| metres | | |

■ ACCOMMODATION
| Portas do Sol | 2 |
| Pousada de São Teotónio | 1 |

● EATING
Churrasqueira Valenciara	2
Fortaleza	3
Pousada de São Teotónio	1

6

Old Town & Pousada

Bus & Train stations

6

The cobbled lanes and white-painted buildings **within the walls** have all been handsomely restored, though few visitors do much more than trawl up and down the couple of main streets, which are lined with boutiques and gift shops, pretty much all flogging the same vast selection of towels, sheets, pillow cases, nightwear, T-shirts and cheap souvenirs. Bewitching collection of traditional arts and handicrafts it is not – though if you need another Lionel Messi football shirt you're in luck.

If you're to come away from Valença with a more positive memory of its charms, you need to get off the street and up onto **the ramparts**, which can be accessed from virtually anywhere. From the precipitous walls, grassy mounds and winding footpaths, you can look down upon the buildings and the river far below, while exploring hidden tunnels, archaic towers and sentry-posts, and landscaped battlements complete with cannons. It becomes immediately apparent how difficult it would have been to vanquish Valença – the scale of the fortifications is immense – and you can spend a happy hour or two revelling in the fine views to all sides.

Núcleo Museológico

Rua Mouzinho de Albuquerque 67 • Tues–Fri 9.30am–12.30pm & 2–6pm, Sat 10am–noon & 2.30–5.30pm • Free

To find out about Valença's history, visit the small **Núcleo Museológico**. The labelling is all in Portuguese but the model of the original medieval town and the archeological finds, from Bronze Age swords to Roman vases, are pretty self-explanatory. On the way in you're confronted with a model of a siege engine of the type used to chuck big rocks across the river at Spain. Take a look, too, just behind the museum, where you'll find a **Roman milestone**, first erected in 43 AD and marking mile 42 from Braga to Tuy.

Tuy

The fortified town of **Tuy** in Spain lies just a couple of kilometres north of Valença, across an iron bridge designed by Eiffel. It's a tantalizing silhouette on the horizon, again complete with defensive walls and interesting old town, and if you've got time you may as well have a look around here too – it's an easy thirty-minute walk from Valença, or five minutes on the train, with services continuing on to Vigo.

ARRIVAL AND INFORMATION   VALENÇA DO MINHO AND AROUND

Everything of historic interest lies within the walls, and it only takes 15min or so to walk from one end of old Valença to the other. Incidentally, street names are largely superfluous – there are only a few streets and alleys and you'll stumble upon everywhere sooner or later.

By car Valença is 28km northeast of Caminha, up the N13. There's plenty of parking by the outer castle walls, outside Portas do Sol (follow signs for "Fortaleza"), where you might need to pay €1 to one of the blokes directing you into a spare space. You can drive and park inside the walled town too – there's a large pay-and-display car park in front of the turismo – though you'll have to drive around the side of the walled town first and enter through the Portas da Coroada. Driving within the walls might seem a little freaky (some gates and alleys can be very narrow), but there's a rigid one-way system in force so you can't come to too much grief.

By bus The bus station is two blocks west of the train station on Avenida Sá Carneiro, 5min walk south of the walls (go up Rua Miguel Dantas to Largo da Trapichera).

Destinations Lisbon (4 daily; 6hr 30min); Melgaço (8 daily; 40min); Monção (10 daily; 20min); Ponte de Lima (1 daily;

25min); Porto (2–7 daily; 3hr 30min); and Viana do Castelo via Caminha (1–3 daily; 1hr 15min).

By train From the train station, head up Avenida Miguel Dantas and you'll approach the old town from the Largo da Trapichera roundabout, at the bottom of the hill. Continue straight on up the tree-lined avenue and enter through the narrow Portas do Sol.

Destinations Barcelos (7–8 daily; 1hr 15min–2hr); Caminha (8–10 daily; 20–30min); Porto (4 daily, 2hr 15min); Viana do Castelo (7–8 daily; 40min–1hr); and Vigo, Spain (3 daily; 1hr 10min; connections to Santiago de Compostela and La Coruña).

Information The turismo (Mon–Sat 9.30am–12.30pm & 2.30–5.30pm; ☎ 251 823 329, ⌨ www.cm-valenca.pt) is in the old town, on Praça da República just inside the Portas da Coroada.

ACCOMMODATION

Accommodation in town is limited, though if you're heading for the *pousada* you're in for a treat. Otherwise, the choice is between a couple of uninspiring 1970s-style main-road hotels outside the walls (just up from the roundabout, on Avenida dos Bombeiros Voluntários, the Spain road).

Portas do Sol Rua Conselheiro Lopes da Silva 51, just inside Portas do Meio ☎251 837 134, ⓦ residencialportasdosol.com. The only other choice within the walls is an eight-roomed townhouse that's modestly priced for most of the year, though prices rise in summer and other holiday periods. If you're going to stay, try and get one of the four rooms with river views. Breakfast not included. **€35**

★**Pousada de São Teotónio** Baluarte do Socorro, inside the fortress ☎251 800 260, ⓦpousadas.pt. Set right by the northern ramparts, this *pousada* enjoys sweeping views over the Minho from its lounge, sun-room and restaurant, while the outside terraces offer an ideal environment to relax and soak up the scenery. The best rooms also have terraces, as well as white walls and polished wooden floors, offset by vintage carved bedheads, while public areas are big on terracotta tiles and chunky retro furniture. Enter town through Portas do Coroada and drive right through the old town, following the signs – you'll get there eventually. **€185**

EATING

The few old-town cafés and restaurants are much of a pricey muchness – tapas and *bacalhau* to the fore, with a nod to their largely Spanish clientele – and, the *pousada* excepted, it's hard to summon up any real enthusiasm for any of them. Two or three cafés in the cute Praça da República are best for an alfresco evening drink.

Churrasqueira Valenciana Rua Maestro Sousa Morais 8 ☎251 826 547. Pretty much the cheapest place in the old town serves up a grilled half chicken and chips for €5, and other grills for not much more, and you can't say much fairer than that. It's theoretically open daily noon–3pm & 6–10pm, but sometimes closes in the evening.

Fortaleza Rua Apolinário da Fonseca 5 ☎251 823 146. Just outside the Portas do Meio, the house special here is *cabrito* (goat), although the chef also prepares a decent *arroz de marisco*; main courses cost €8–15. Dinner is best enjoyed at the outdoor tables so you can catch the last of the day's sun setting over the ramparts. Daily noon–3pm & 7–10pm.

★**Pousada de São Teotónio** Baluarte do Socorro, inside the fortress ☎251 800 260, ⓦpousadas.pt. The *pousada* restaurant is the best in town, and given that prices in Valença are on the high side in any case, this should be your first choice. Dishes such as pan-fried saltcod with straw potatoes, or chicken with an *alheira* sausage stuffing (main courses €16–21), put a modern twist on the regional cuisine, and there's a good-value, if limited-choice, daily menu for €25. Daily noon–3pm & 7–10pm.

Monção

Like Valença, **MONÇÃO** too, was once fortified to the hilt, though its remaining walls are largely limited to a long stretch above the river, with an elevated promenade offering fine views across the Minho valley into Spain. Below are grassy banks, groves of trees and riverside pathways, with access down to the river through several surviving ancient gateways. It's a pleasant enough place to pause, centred on the spacious, mosaic-cobbled old town square, **Praça Deu-la-Deu**, with ramparts, *miradouro* and promenade at one end, seventeenth-century church at the other, and an attractive grid

PORTUGAL'S WONDER WOMAN

The main square in Monção has an uncommon name, Praça Deu-la-Deu, which celebrates the story of the town's much-heralded medieval saviour, a woman known as **Deu-la-Deu Martins** (the name means "God gave her"). In 1369, with the Spanish at the gates, the town under desperate siege and the mayor on the brink of capitulation, the mayor's wife commandeered Monção's paltry remaining flour stocks, whipped up some cakes and sent them over to the Spanish, offering "more if they needed them". The bold ruse worked, the Spanish forces thought better of attacking such an apparently well-supplied town, and Deu-la-Deu acquired everlasting fame, the honour of a tomb in the Igreja da Matriz, and a questionable modern statue at the head of the square on the *miradouro*.

of narrow streets (reached down Rua 1 Dezembro) that curls around a simple Romanesque Igreja da Matriz. Spanish and Portuguese tourists tend to visit for the town's revived thermal-spa facilities; otherwise the town is liveliest on a Thursday market, or during the local festivals of Corpo de Deus (Corpus Christi, usually second week in June) and Virgem das Dores (Aug).

ARRIVAL AND INFORMATION

MONÇÃO

By bus The local bus station is on the western outskirts of town at Veiga Velha, but most services also stop near Campo da Feira.

Destinations Braga (2–4 daily; 1hr 45min); Melgaço (Mon–Fri 5 daily, Sat & Sun 1 daily; 40min); Porto (2–4 daily; 3hr); Valença (10 daily; 20min) and Viana do Castelo (1–5 daily; 1hr 20min).

By car Monção is 16km east of Valença; the road to Spain crosses the bridge to Salvatierra, just outside town to the

west. There's free parking in Campo da Feira (though not on Thursday, market day), by the bastion walls – for the town centre, walk straight ahead, under the old railway bridge, and at the end of the pedestrianized street turn left for the main square.

Information The turismo (Mon–Sat 9.30am–12.30pm & 2.30–6pm; ☎ 251 652 757, ⓦ www.cm-moncao.pt) is in a small handicrafts and cultural centre, the Casa do Curro, on Praça Deu-la-Deu.

ACCOMMODATION AND EATING

A night in Monção is hardly obligatory – and the nicest places are out of town in any case – but if you fancy it, there are budget rooms advertised in a couple of cafés on the square, and also in the streets around the Igreja da Matriz. Praça Deu-la-Deu is the best place for restaurants and cafés with outdoor tables, a couple of which lie near the *miradouro* with views over to Spain.

Cabral Rua 1 de Dezembro ☎ 251 651 775. Just off the main square (down the road to the side of *Restaurante Central*), this is a rustic place serving unpretentious regional cuisine, from *bacalhau a casa* (fried, with onions, tomatoes and potatoes) to local lamb (dishes €8–12) – there's always fresh fish too. Running along one side of the dining room, an uneven stone wall has become the unexpected receptacle of a collection of escudos, cents, the odd dollar bill and even a Chinese banknote. Mon–Thurs & Fri–Sun noon–2.30pm & 7–10pm.

Hotel Convento dos Capuchos Estrada de Melgaço ☎ 251 640 090, ⓦ conventodoscapuchos.com. The town's top 24-roomed hotel is a stylish conversion of an

eighteenth-century convent just off the road to Melgaço. Contemporary rooms have been fashioned from the old cells, keeping the stone-work and deep-set windows but adding a bit of designer flair; the fancy restaurant, bar service in the cloister, outdoor pool and gardens complete the picture. €173

Solar de Serrade Mazedo, 3km south of Monção, off N101 to Arcos de Valdevez ☎ 251 654 008, ⓦ solardeserrade.pt. This seventeenth-century, twelve-bedroomed manor house belongs to an excellent *vinho verde* wine estate. The rooms have an aristocratic style, some of which boast soaring ceilings, chandeliers and handcarved four-poster beds. €70

Melgaço

MELGAÇO, Portugal's northernmost outpost, has a pretty, restored centre clustered round the towering keep of a medieval fortress. It's another Minho border town, perched high above the river, which merits a short coffee-break and a stroll around its cobbled streets and jasmine-draped cottages. Longer stays probably depend on how much of the local wine you plan to sample – the area around Melgaço produces the finest *vinho verde* in the country.

Castelo

Rua do Castelo • May–Sept Tues–Sun 10am–12.30pm & 2.30–7pm; Oct–April Tues–Sun 10am–12.30pm & 2–5pm • Outer walls free; keep €1

The tenth-century **Castelo** is a shadow of its former self but a walk around the castle walls offers grand views of the old town. Outside the walls, a winding path provides sweeping vistas; inside you can buy a ticket to enter the keep, which contains a few archaeological finds from the area, though it's really the views from the roof that warrant the entry fee.

Solar do Alvarinho

Rua Direita • Daily 10am–12.30pm & 2.30–7pm; bar open later on Fri & Sat nights • ☎ 251 410 195

The local wine headquarters, **Solar do Alvarinho**, is housed in a fine granite mansion (its heraldic emblem dated 1687) on the old town's main street; there's a well-stocked tasting bar and wine shop here, as well as an exhibition area. Melgaço *vinhos verdes* are made from the Alvarinho grape, which produces a full-bodied wine with a much higher alcoholic content (around 12.5 percent) than other *vinhos verdes*, and consequently has the ability to age. The *solar* has details about the local *vinho verde quintas* (estates) which welcome visitors.

6

ARRIVAL AND DEPARTURE

MELGAÇO

By bus There are regular services to and from Monção (2–4 daily; 40min), and weekday buses to Lamas de Mouro in the national park (Mon–Fri 1 daily; 40min) and São Gregório on the Spanish border (Mon–Fri 3 daily; 30min), from where you can pick up connections to Orense.

By car Melgaço is 23km northeast of Monçao, and 11km

southwest of São Gregório on the Spanish border. It also provides easy access to the remote northern part of the Parque Nacional da Peneda-Gerês via the road to Lamas de Mouro. As you drive into town there's plenty of free parking around Largo Hermenegildo Solheiro and the fire station, from where brown signs point you to the castle, a 2min walk away.

ACCOMMODATION AND EATING

Cantinho do Adro Rua Direita 30 ☎ 251 404 904. Sited just below the castle walls, in a pretty square by the church, this place caters to a mostly local crowd. You can get a decent meal here from the simple menu such as *linguiça* (Portuguese sausage) with chips and fried egg – with most dishes costing around €6–8. Daily noon–2.30pm & 7–10pm.

Quinta da Calçada 1km east of town, on the São Gregorio road ☎ 251 402 547, ⓦ quintadacalcada.com. The most charming local accommodation is this seventeenth-century rural manor house with three B&B rooms available; it also has a swimming pool, and gardens and grounds with lovely views. **€80**

The Lima valley

While it's Rio Minho that gives the region its name, it's the area's other river, the **Rio Lima**, which puts heart and soul into the Minho. Its delightful valley – dotted with ancient towns and Romanesque churches, and draped in morning mists – is a byword for beauty in Portugal, and forms an obvious route from Viana do Castelo, where the river meets the sea, eastwards to the Peneda-Gerês mountains. There are minor roads along north and south sides of the river, connecting a cluster of peaceful little settlements on the banks of the Lima and its tributaries, though the fast highway from Viana takes you quickly to the standout town of **Ponte de Lima**, with its famous market held right on the riverbanks. For slower travel around the region, the "Ecovia" bike-and-hike track runs along the riverside between Viana do Castelo, Ponte de Lima and Ponte da Barca.

MEMORY LOSS IN PONTE DE LIMA?

For the **Romans** in Portugal, the rising mists of the **Rio Lima** carried troubling echoes of the River Lethe, or the "River of Forgetfulness", one of the five mythical rivers of the Underworld. The Romans believed that if they crossed the river, or drank any of its water, their memories would be erased and they would never return home – which, according to local legend, is why the otherwise all-conquering Roman legion was brought up short here in the second century BC, its troops refusing to go any further. It took an enterprising general to splash across, and demonstrate that his memory remained intact, before the soldiers would follow. It's a nice tale, embraced by the modern town, which has a phalanx of Roman troop statues lined up on the town side of the river – being encouraged across the Lima by a mounted officer on the other side.

Ponte de Lima

Largely sporting an air of sleepy indifference to the wider world, easy-going **PONTE DE LIMA** takes its name from the stone bridge that spans the wide Rio Lima at this point. It's an attractive town, set back from a handsome, landscaped riverside promenade – the scene is at its best every other Monday when Ponte de Lima's lively open-air market, the **Feira Quinzenal**, sprawls out across the riverside flatlands, where a sea of stalls sells anything from mobile phone accessories to trussed chickens. Ponte de Lima claims the first documented market charter in Portugal, dated 1125, which makes the bi-monthly market the oldest in the country (Feira Quinzenal dates are posted along the riverside and on the town council website). Otherwise, the pedestrianized old centre has no specific attractions beyond its restored stone mansions and tangle of back alleys, but it's one of those places that really repays a lazy day's stroll or a night or two's stopover. Local accommodation, in particular, is in keeping with the well-to-do air in town, with lots of historic manor houses and boutique properties providing a good excuse to stick around for a while.

The bridge and riverfront

There's been a fixed crossing over the river since at least Roman times (see box, p.325). The current **bridge** was rebuilt in 1368 and once had seventeen arches – it's lost three over the centuries to riverbank improvements and raids during the Napoleonic assault in 1809. On occasions, the river encroaches upon the town – on the **Torre de São Paulo**, near the bridge, are marks showing the depth of historic floods, including the particularly severe one of 1987. Further down the riverfront is the old sixteenth-century keep and former prison, the **Torre da Cadeia Velha** (now housing the turismo), with the granite, arcaded

Mercado building (market Mon–Fri 7am–7pm, Sat 7am–2pm), overlooking the riverside, just beyond here. If you keep going along the promenade and under the lime trees you'll see the fifteenth-century convent of **São Francisco e Santo António dos Capuchos**.

Parque do Arnada
Park • Always open • Free • **Museu Rural** • Tues–Sun 2–6pm • Free

Across the bridge from town lies the manicured **Parque do Arnada** (or Parque Temático), whose formal gardens are divided into different styles including Roman and Baroque; there's also a small hothouse. Go through the gardens to the small **Museu Rural**, which houses an interesting collection of archaic tools and farming implements. An annual **Festival de Jardins** (Garden Festival) is held along this side of the river every summer (May–Sept).

ARRIVAL AND DEPARTURE   PONTE DE LIMA

By bus The bus station is outside the old centre, on Rua Conde Bertiandos, 15min walk from the river, though most arriving buses drop passengers closer in.

Destinations Arcos de Valdevez (5–9 daily; 50min); Barcelos (2 daily; 55min); Braga (3–10 daily; 30min–1hr); Ponte da Barca (3–4 daily; 20–30min); Porto (4–7 daily;

2hr 20min); Valença do Minho (1 daily; 25min); and Viana do Castelo (Mon–Fri hourly, Sat & Sun 9 daily; 50min).

By car Ponte de Lima lies 26km east of Viana do Castelo, a half-hour drive on the A27. There's acres of free parking on the riverbank, except on *feira* days, when you'll have to find a space in town where you can.

INFORMATION AND ACTIVITIES

Information Loja de Turismo is in Torre da Cadeia Velha, the tower on the riverfront (Mon–Sat 9am–12.30pm & 2–5pm; ☎ 258 942 335, ⓦ www.cm-pontedelima.pt).
Bike rental Available from around the side of the market

building (daily 9am–8pm; €2/hr, €4 for 4hr, €6 for 8hr) – the Ecovia track (signposted from the old bridge) is ideal for cycling, with rides possible to the Lagoas de Bertiandos nature reserve (14km) and on to Ponte da Barca (18km).

ACCOMMODATION

Accommodation in Ponte de Lima itself is limited, though there is a staid three-star riverfront hotel next to the convent and a cheap guesthouse or two. What the town is famous for is its **rural tourism** properties – bed-and-breakfast and self-catering accommodation in a series of unique and atmospheric properties, from historic manor houses to boutique hideaways.

★**Carmo's Boutique Hotel** Gemieira, 6km east on N203, Ponte da Barca road ☎258 938 743, ⓦ carmosboutiquehotel.com. Providing a real change of

pace from the region's manor houses, the fifteen rooms and three suites (€320) at *Carmo's* occupy a couple of postmodern blocks a few kilometres outside town – you'll drive right past

---

PONTE DE LIMA'S FESTIVALS

As if the huge bi-monthly market wasn't enough, Ponte de Lima offers several other major festivities throughout the year. The market itself goes into overdrive for four days over the second weekend in September with the **Feiras Novas**, or New Fairs, celebrated since 1826 – as much festival as market, with fireworks, fairground rides, folk music and *gigantones* (enormous carnival-like statues). There's a similarly traditional slant to June's **Feira do Cavalo** (Horse Fair), while on the day before Corpus Christi (usually early June) Ponte de Lima comes over positively pagan with its annual ritual of the **Vaca das Cordas** (literally, "Cow of the Ropes"), which involves an enraged and defiant bull being chased through town. This is one of many traditions with its origins in the ancient fertility cults brought to the Iberian peninsula by the Phoenicians – the bull is tied by its horns, led three times around the main church, and then jabbed with goads, after which the unfortunate animal charges through the town's streets before finishing up at the river. It is then led off to the abattoir, as the good people of Ponte de Lima prepare for the more sedate procession of **Corpo do Deus** the following day, which sees the streets covered with ornately patterned flowers. For more cultured pursuits, the annual two-week **Festival Percursos da Música** is held each July, a renowned arts festival presenting recitals, chamber music and opera as well as literature and philosophy events. The town's Teatro Diogo Bernardes is the main venue, hosting a range of shows from dance to fado, with other performances also taking place in local manor houses and on the riverside itself.

6

if you're not careful. Inside, it's a chic, off-white delight of polished concrete surfaces, designer furniture and original art, with uniquely furnished rooms that romantics will love (think canopy beds, floaty fabrics, deep baths, robes and slippers, lotions and potions). There's an indoor plunge-pool and spa (treatments available) and an outdoor summer pool on a grassy slope, with a classy dinner (€35) and drinks served in a book- and wine-filled lair that's less restaurant and more home-from-home lounge-bar (provided, that is, your home was designed by a flash architect). **€250**

Casa de Crasto São João da Ribeira, 1km east of town on N203, Ponte da Barca road ☎ 258 941 156, ⓦ solaresdeportugal.pt. A beautiful seventeenth-century property in verdant grounds, which, legend has it, was partly demolished by the owner in 1896 while looking for hidden treasure – the old kitchen and tower managed to evade his attention. Guest rooms are in the main house, and there's an apartment (sleeps four people) for self-catering. Doubles **€80**, apartment **€140**

Casa de São Gonçalo Arcozelo, 1km west of Ponte de Lima ☎ 258 942 365, ⓦ solaresdeportugal.pt. Views of the town are outstanding from this nineteenth-century house, on the opposite side of the river and about 500m from the old bridge. Although rather elegant and furnished with antiques, it's very much a family home, and the charming garden is a lovely place for breakfast. There's just one double room and a two-person apartment (same price). **€75**

Casa do Outeiro Outeiro, Arcozelo, 2km northwest of Ponte de Lima ☎ 258 941 206, ⓦ solaresdeportugal.pt. Recently renovated stately manor house that dates from the sixteenth century – its vast stone kitchen fireplace is original. The house is surrounded by a garden and woods, next to an old ivy-draped aqueduct, and guests have the run of the grounds and use of the swimming pool. **€80**

Casa do Pinheiro Rua Gen. Norton de Matos 50 ☎ 258 943 971, ⓦ casadopinheiro.pt. A 5min walk from the town centre, this old Minho mansion ("Pine Tree House") springs a pleasant surprise – lovely, high-ceilinged rooms, with the best on the first floor opening onto a lush garden complete with its own small swimming pool. It's a good choice if you want rural-tourism-style accommodation without having to drive. **€65**

★**Moinho de Estorãos** Estorãos, 7km northwest of Ponte de Lima ☎ 258 941 546, ⓦ solaresdeportugal.pt. Rustic charm aplenty in a converted seventeenth-century water mill in an idyllic location, next to a Romanesque bridge, with walking, fishing and swimming all at hand. Accommodation is in a self-catering apartment that sleeps two. Closed November to March. **€85**

Pousada de Juventude Rua Papa João Paulo II ☎ 258 943 797, ⓦ microsites.juventude.gov.pt/portal/en. Handy for the town centre, budget travellers could do worse than the decent modern hostel, which has both shared dorms and private rooms. Dorms **€12**, doubles **€30**

São João Rua do Rosário 6 ☎ 258 941 288. The only real low-cost option in town is near the bridge and riverfront, which means it can be noisy, though you've got a restaurant right below and cafés on the doorstep. Rooms are nice enough for the price – though the cheapest ones have shared facilities. No credit cards. **€40**

EATING

Praça de Camões, by the old bridge, has a ring of outdoor cafés, while the narrow streets behind shelter some old (and not-so-old) *tasquinhas* where you can get stuck into the local *vinho verde*. Regional specialities are earthy to the core – things like *sarrabulho* (rice cooked with blood), *rojões* (roast pork with blood sausage) and *bacalhau com broa* (salt cod baked with corn bread).

Alameda Alameda São João 40 ☎ 258 941 630. By the bridge on the town side of the river, this place has a big outdoor terrace and splendid views, and serves dishes such as beef stew, roast pork or hake in epic portions – a *meia-dose* at €9–10 should suffice. Gets busy on a Sunday so be sure to book ahead. Tues–Sun noon–3pm & 7–10pm.

Casas das Cheias Passeio 25 de Abril 1, next to Torre de São Paulo ☎ 258 741 092. The "House of the Floods" gets it in the neck if the river rises, but in the meantime the affable owners rustle up bargain meals for local diners – big roasts, grills and stews, meat and fish, for €7.50 a *meia dose*, €12 a *dose*, washed down with challenging *vinho verde* from a ceramic jug. It's only a titchy place, and a bit dingy inside, but there are sometimes a couple of tables laid outside, facing the river. Daily 10am–9pm.

★**O Brasão** Rua Formosa 1 ☎ 258 941 890. A classy restaurant in an old stone mansion, just up the hill from the river. The regional cuisine here gets a fancy twist or two, such as steak served with garlic and *vinho verde* sauce, and the weekend special is *rojões a Minhota* or Minho-style roast pork. Dishes cost €9–16. Mon, Tues & Thurs–Sun noon–3pm & 7–10.30pm.

O Mercado Mercado de Ponte de Lima, Rua António Magalhães ☎ 258 753 700. The market building has an upper level with three restaurants including the pick-of-the-bunch *O Mercado* – there's terrace dining in summer and a full menu of regional dishes (€7–12) from *rojões* to *sarrabulho*, *bacalhau* to *polvo*. Daily noon–3pm & 7–10pm.

Os Telhadinhos Rua do Rosário 28 ⓦ tascasdofodinhas .com. For a taste of what Lima used to be like, pop in to this stand-up *tasca* in a back street off the square, where red *vinho verde* is served to you in a little ceramic bowl. Snacks range fom €1 (codfish cakes and beef patties) to €10 (snails) or pig's ear salad at €6. Daily 7am–midnight.

Ponte da Barca and around

Another old bridge over the Rio Lima is the centrepiece of the pretty, historic riverside town – **PONTE DA BARCA**, the "Barca" part of the name referring to the boat that once ferried pilgrims across the river, en route to Santiago de Compostela in northwestern Spain. Nowadays the Lima is spanned by a lovely sixteenth-century bridge, beside which is the shaded Jardim dos Poetas, dedicated to sixteenth-century brothers Diogo Bernardes and Agostinho da Cruz, monastic poets who were born in the town. Like the neighbouring Ponte de Lima, that's pretty much it, save for a fortnightly riverside **market** on Wednesdays (it alternates with the one in Arcos de Valdevez), which draws hundreds of people from outlying hamlets. The only other time the small town becomes animated is for the annual **Feira de São Bartolomeu**, which takes place on August 19–24, with the big day on August 24; don't expect to get any sleep once the party starts.

6

Igreja de São Salvador

Bravães, 4km west of Ponte da Barca, N203

The many Romanesque churches of the Lima valley date from the medieval heyday of the pilgrimage route to Santiago de Compostela. They are often simple in the extreme, though enhanced by animated stone carvings, with the most renowned example being the **Igreja de São Salvador**, in a small hamlet just outside Ponte da Barca. If it's open (it often isn't) you'll be able to see its interior frescoes, but even if it's closed you can check out the vibrant quality of its sculpted doorways, featuring birds, oxen, sheep, people, and even monkeys. The church is right on the road from Ponte de Lima to Ponte da Barca – you can't miss it.

ARRIVAL AND DEPARTURE

PONTE DA BARCA AND AROUND

By bus Buses drop passengers near the bridge.
Destinations Arcos de Valdevez (hourly; 15min); Braga (3–8 daily; 1hr); Lindoso (2 daily; 1hr); Soajo (2 daily; 45min); Ponte de Lima (3–4 daily; 20–30min); and Viana do Castelo (6–8 daily; 1hr 30min).
By car It's an 18km (20min) drive east from Ponte de

Lima to Ponte da Barca (N203); there's free parking in Campo do Curro, the large square to the side of the bridge. The town is handy for the Parque Nacional da Peneda-Gerês – about an hour (50km) on back roads to Caldas do Gerês or a straight 25km run east (N203) to Lindoso in the north of the park.

INFORMATION

Turismo The turismo is on Rua Dom Manuel I (May–Sept Tues–Sat 9.30am–12.30pm & 2–6pm; Oct–April Tues–Sat 9am–12.30pm & 2–5.30pm; ☎258 452 899, ✆www .cmpb.pt) – from the bridge, walk 200m up the main Rua Conselheiro Rocha Peixoto and the office is down a street on the left.
National park office The Adere Peneda-Gerês at Rua

Dom Manuel 1 (Mon–Fri 9am–12.30pm & 2.30–6pm; ☎258 452 450, ✆adere-pg.pt), is a useful source of information about the nearby Parque Nacional da Peneda-Gerês; you can book village accommodation in the park here too. The office is located in a stone house just up the main street, in the sunken square on the left, before the turismo.

ACCOMMODATION AND EATING

★**Casa Nobre do Correio-Mor** Rua Trás do Forno 1 ☎258 452 129, ✆manor-houses-portugal.com. Pick your way around the name and address – "Noble House of the Head Postmaster" on "Back of the Oven Street", no less – and what you end up finding is a tastefully restored seventeenth-century manor house offering genteel accommodation. The ten rooms live up to their noble billing, they are pretty spacious and furnished with antiques, and there's also a pool, sauna, games room and lovely gardens. **€100**
O Moinho Campo de Cûrro ☎258 452 035. Dine on a nice raised terrace in an attractive stone building at the

back of the square by the bridge. Local dishes (€9–15) include things like large, juicy Minho steaks or roast pork served with *papas de sarrabulho*. Mon & Wed–Sun noon–3pm & 7–10.30pm.
Pensão Restaurante Gomes Rua Conselheiro Rocha Peixoto 13 ☎258 452 288. Close to the bridge, on the main road, offering a standard grill menu (dishes €8–11) in a dull dining room. Upstairs, and under separate management, are a few old-fashioned rooms – these are undeniably cheap, and breakfast is served on a balcony overlooking river and bridge. No credit cards. Daily lunch & dinner. **€30**

Arcos de Valdevez

A few kilometres north of Ponte da Barca, the Rio Vez, a tributary of the Lima, is overlooked by the hillside town of **ARCOS DE VALDEVEZ**. It's at its best – no real surprise – along the river, flanked by neat, wooded gardens and with a summer beach (*praia fluvial*) located a few hundred metres downstream from the old four-arched bridge. The old town, such as it is, stretches uphill behind the bridge, culminating in an unusual spiral Manueline pillory in the Praça Municipal. It's very much a traditional shopping town – a bucket, some wellies, a length of hosepipe and a kilo of peaches, no problem; designer clothes not so much. The peak of the town's activity takes place every other Wednesday, when the fortnightly Arcos market springs into action. Its major annual bash, the **Festa do Concelho**, is held over the second week in August, and features the usual giant figures, folkloric entertainments and blazing riverside pyrotechnics.

ARRIVAL AND DEPARTURE   ARCOS DE VALDEVEZ

By car Arcos is 5km north of Ponte da Barca, and makes a useful approach to the Parque Nacional da Peneda-Gerês – it is located just 20km across the hills, on the winding N202 to Soajo.

By bus The bus station, 1km out of the centre near the river, has regular services to Braga (10 daily; 1hr 30min–2hr), Monção (4–6 daily; 45min), Ponte de Lima (5–9 daily; 50min) and Viana do Castelo (5–12 daily; 1hr 30min); arriving buses stop in the town centre on their way to the bus station. You can catch buses to Soajo (Mon–Fri 1–3 daily; 45min) and Lindoso (Mon–Fri 1–3 daily; 1hr) at the stops along the riverside Avenida Marginal.

INFORMATION

Turismo Rua Prof Dr. Mário Júlio Almeida Costa, 200m north of the bridge (April–Sept Mon–Sat 9.30am–12.30pm & 2–6pm, Sun 10am–1pm & 2–5pm; Oct–March Mon–Sat 9am–12.30pm & 2–5.30pm; ☎ 258 520 530, ⌨ www.cmav.pt).

National park office The Parque Nacional da Peneda-Gerês office on Rua Manuel Himalaia (Mon–Fri 9am–12.30pm & 2–5.30pm; ☎ 258 515 338) – turn uphill from the river at the fountain – has walk leaflets and a park map available.

ACCOMMODATION AND EATING

A Floresta Campo do Trasladário ☎ 258 515 163. Overlooking bridge and gardens, this is one of the few options in town for eating alfresco. Regional meats feature, as do fine garlicky beans, all served in generous portions – dishes from around €10. Daily noon–3pm & 7.30–11pm.

Casa dos Confrades Pr Municipal 10 ☎ 258 515 234. Right in the centre, flanking one side of the old square, this stone mansion has the most agreeable accommodation in town. Nice modern rooms face an internal courtyard with its own pool and sweeping views over the hills. €70

★**Quinta da Cortinhas** Paço, 1km south of town, Ponte da Barca road ☎ 258 931 750, ⌨ solaresdeportugal.pt. What was once a summer retreat now offers eight rooms in the lovely main house and another four in handsomely converted stables. Breakfast is served in an ornate tiled dining-room, and guests can also use the basement kitchens. A tennis court and pool in the small leafy grounds add to the appeal. €70

Parque Nacional da Peneda-Gerês

Portugal's first and only national park, the magnificent **PARQUE NACIONAL DA PENEDA-GERÊS**, was established in 1971, and its 700 square kilometres help protect a natural world and a way of life that's all but disappeared from the rest of the country's mountain regions. In the lush valleys oak and laurel line the riverbanks, replaced by holly, birch, pine and juniper at higher elevations; a total of eighteen plant species – including the Serra do Gerês iris – are found nowhere else on earth. Shepherds and farmers inhabit remote granite-built villages, tending primitive domestic animals – *cachena* and *barrosa* cattle, *bravia* goats, *garrano* ponies and the powerful *Castro Laboreiro* sheepdog – that are long extinct elsewhere. In distant forested corners, remnants of the wildlife that once roamed all Europe still survive too, from wild boar to wolves.

If it sounds like a back-in-time backwater – well, parts certainly seem so, and there are high roads across boulder-strewn uplands where you'll rarely see another vehicle (and where goats very definitely have the right of way). But look closely at some of the beautifully kept villages, with their ancient customs and traditions apparently intact, and it's clear that tourism is playing its part in the park's preservation. Restored stone cottages and rustic houses are available for overnight guests in even the most remote of hamlets, while the unmade roads and dirt tracks of twenty years ago have acquired a layer of tarmac and a flurry of brown signs pointing out local attractions.

The park divides into several distinct regions, with the southern area easily seen from the spa town of **Caldas do Gerês**, while mountain-, forest- and water-based activities are centred on nearby settlements like **Rio Caldo** and **Campo do Gerês**. In the centre lie the traditional villages of **Soajo** and **Lindoso** – beautiful places to stay, if you fancy a quiet week hiking or touring – while the wild **Serra da Peneda**, in the north of the park, is one for real mountain aficionados. Here, you'll often have the steep forested valleys, and wind-blown *planaltos* dotted with weird rock formations, entirely to yourself. There's also a far eastern section of the park covered in the Trás-os-Montes chapter (see p.384).

ARRIVAL AND DEPARTURE   PARQUE NACIONAL DA PENEDA-GERÊS

By bus The roads into the park are pretty decent, but bus services are limited during the week and often non-existent at weekends. The main connections are from Melgaço (on the Rio Minho) to Lamas de Mouro in the north; from Arcos de Valdevez and Ponte da Barca (in the Lima valley) to Soajo and Lindoso in the centre; and from Braga to Caldas do Gerês in the south. Note: There are no direct bus services from Porto.

INFORMATION

National park information offices The Parque Nacional da Peneda-Gerês (ⓦadere-pg.pt) has an HQ in Braga (see p.318) and park offices in the outlying towns of Ponte da Barca (see p.339) and Arcos de Valdevez (see p.340). Within the park, the main office is in Caldas do Gerês, with smaller "gateway" offices (marked "Porta do PNPG") in Lindoso, Lamas de Mouro and elsewhere. All can provide maps, hiking guides and information.

Self catering Apart from in Caldas do Gerês, accommodation is limited to a handful of hotels, rural guesthouses and village B&Bs, or camping at a few designated sites. But lots of traditional houses, particularly around Soajo and Lindoso, have been renovated and converted to simple self-catering use and are excellent value, starting at around €50 a night for two people, and up to €150 a night for something sleeping six to eight people (there's usually a minimum two- to three-night stay). There's even a converted monastery, now five-star hotel near the town of Rio Caldo. Bookings are largely through the park organization ADERE (ⓦadere-pg.pt), either online or through any of their park offices. There are also properties available through Aldeias de Portugal (ⓦaldeiasdeportugal.pt) and other agencies.

TOURS AND ACTIVITIES

Tours By far the best way to explore the Park is to take a guided tour, ranging in length and price. Oporto Adventure Tours (ⓦoportoadventuretours.com) can arrange tailor-made trips with knowledgeable guides and with four-wheeled drive vehicles. It's only a 1hr 20min drive from Porto, making a day-trip possible, but staying longer is recommended to get the most out of the region.

Hiking Waymarked trails (*trilhos*) offer plenty of hiking opportunities, from short strolls to day-treks. There's a series of trail leaflets in English (available from park offices and local turismos), mostly for walks of around 10–16km that are fairly well marked with red and yellow pointers (though weather, wear-and-tear and landslides can affect waymarks and routes). The official park map doesn't show footpaths, so you'll need the "Série M888" 1:25,000 topographical maps produced by the Instituto Geográfico do Exército (ⓦwww.igeoe.pt), available online or in Portuguese bookshops.

Caldas do Gerês and around

Easy to reach from Braga, the old spa town of **CALDAS DO GERÊS** (sometimes known as Vila do Gerês) is the park's main resort. Despite a ring of pensions and hotels, it's still just about a village rather than town, spectacularly sited in a densely wooded valley and consisting of little more than a one-way system running either side of a babbling

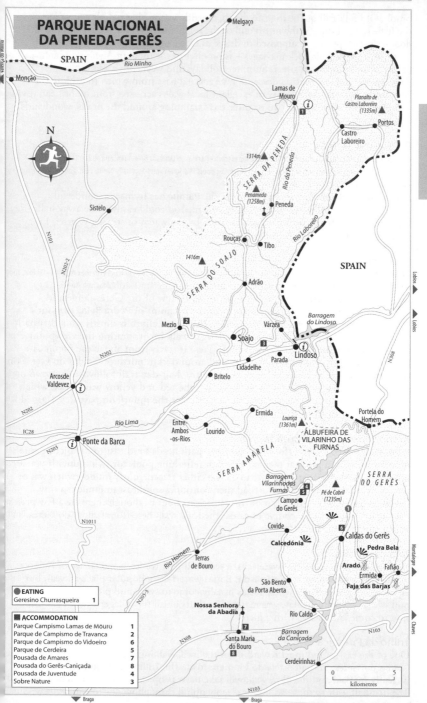

PARQUE NACIONAL DA PENEDA-GERÊS

● EATING
Geresino Churrasqueira 1

■ ACCOMMODATION
Parque Campismo Lamas de Mouro 1
Parque de Campismo de Travanca 2
Parque de Campismo do Vidoeiro 6
Parque de Cerdeira 5
Pousada de Amares 7
Pousada do Gerês-Caniçada 8
Pousada de Juventude 4
Sobre Nature 3

brook. Old folk still queue to taste the therapeutic waters that bubble out of a rock in the little spa building at the north end of the main street – though only those with a doctor's prescription are supposed to drink it. Contemporary pampering, meanwhile – hot tubs to volcanic rock massages – is on offer in the modern Águas do Gerês spa centre, also on the main street. Summer holidays and weekends aside, when day-trippers and spa tourists descend, it's a relaxed base from which to explore the surroundings – there are plenty of excellent local walks accessed from in, or near, town and you could easily spend two or three days tramping around the peaks, woodlands and waterfalls.

Parque das Termas

Entrance over the road from the arcaded gardens at the top of town • **Park** May–Oct daily 8am–6pm, Aug till 7pm; Nov–April Sat & Sun only depending on the weather • **Swimming pools** Mid-June to mid-Sept daily 10am–6pm, Aug till 7pm • ⓦ aguasdogeres.com

Lazy summer afternoons are best spent at the **Parque das Termas**, a wonderful tree-shaded park either side of a gushing stream. You could easily while away half a day here, picnicking while sitting on granite slabs by the water, or stirring yourself for a spot of swimming, tennis or row-boat hire.

Pedra Bela

Drivers can take the road south of Caldas and turn left (signed "Ermida"), or north of Caldas and turn right (by the campsite) • On foot, the most direct approach is to take the cobbled ramp which heads steeply up opposite *Hotel Universal* on Caldas high street

For the best local vistas – a stunning panoramic view of the Gerês range and Caniçada reservoir – make the trip up to the viewpoint of **Pedra Bela**, an hour's walk to the southeast of Caldas do Gerês. The tough climb is mostly on a dirt path which cuts off the road's corners. For a longer walk incorporating the viewpoint follow **trail PR3**, one of the region's best hikes. It starts from above the picnic site opposite the campsite/park-office turning, around 2km north of Caldas do Gerês on the Portela do Homem road. The ten-kilometre, half-day trail follows the *currals* or grazing pastures for cattle ranchers. Look for the red and yellow waymarks, which take you steeply uphill before levelling off to cross the mountain pastures, framed by weird granite outcrops.

Arado waterfalls and Ermida

From Pedra Bela, a delightful four-kilometre path heads southeast to the picturesque **Arado waterfalls**, a popular picnic spot, with refreshing pools for swimming. If you are driving, note the final approach road can be either treacherously muddy when wet or extremely bumpy when dry. The road then continues southeast to **Ermida**, a tiny farming community with an air of true isolation about it, though there are a few places renting out rooms and a couple of cafés. The total walk here from Caldas do Gerês is 11km (about three hours).

Faja das Barjas

Known locally as the Tahiti waterfalls, a scenic 2km drive from the village of **Fafião** brings you to the magnificent **Faja das Barjas waterfalls**, a popular place all year, but especially in the summer where locals usually come to swim and picnic. There's an old mill which, back in the day, was manned in shifts by all the villagers. It's a beautiful spot to come and escape with a picnic.

Trilho da Preguiça

One of the easiest and most rewarding of the local walking trails begins 4km north of Caldas do Gerês on the Portela do Homem road. The **Trilho da Preguiça route** (PR10) is clearly marked and the 4km walk will take most people around two and half hours. The first half, east of the road, heads steeply uphill through woods to a great viewpoint

(1300m). You then descend and continue west of the road on a more gentle, picturesque path through a wooded valley, following a babbling brook with several small waterfalls and rock pools to cool off in.

Portela do Homem
13km north of Caldas do Gerês, N308

North of Caldas do Gerês, the narrow main road twists tortuously uphill into a series of deep wooded valleys through a protected forest, whose trees are indigenous to Portugal. A couple of kilometres before Portela do Homem, a small bridge crosses a stream with a superb natural bathing spot just north of the road, though note that throughout the year, parking and stopping alongside the road is strictly forbidden along this stretch. **Portela do Homem** itself is a mountain pass with a deserted border post, its former customs buildings abandoned and surrounded by grazing cattle; drive right on through to enter Spain and the road to Ourense.

ARRIVAL AND INFORMATION

By car It's 45km to Caldas do Gerês from Braga, around a 40min drive. There's pay-and-display parking along the main street.

By bus Buses stop on the main street, Avenida Manuel Francisco da Costa, with regular services to Braga (5–11 daily; 1hr 30min) and Rio Caldo (6–12 daily; 25min).

Turismo The turismo is located next to the handicrafts centre on the roundabout at the entrance to town (Mon–Wed & Fri–Sat 9.30am–12.30pm & 2.30–6pm;

CALDAS DO GERÊS AND AROUND

253 391 133, geres.pt).

National park office Centro de Educação Ambiente, Lugar do Vidoeiro (July & Aug daily 9am–12.30pm & 2–5.30pm; Sept–June Mon–Fri 9am–12.30pm & 2–5.30pm; 253 390 110), is 1.5km north of town in the Portela do Homem road, in an easily missed building by the entrance to the *Vidoeiro* campsite; it's the best place for walk advice and trail leaflets.

ACCOMMODATION

Gerês has plenty of accommodation, and prices tumble outside July and August (though many of the smaller places are only open from May to October). For budget rooms, try the string of guesthouses overlooking town on Rua do Arnaço, which all have parking for guests; other good-value options are strung out along the road on the 8km down the valley to Rio Caldo.

Águas do Gerês Av Manuel Francisco da Costa 136 253 390 190, aguasdogeres.pt. The town's principal spa hotel is an elegant place, restored several times over and featuring the most stylish rooms in Caldas. There's a fancy pool and spa facilities located over the road, with all sorts of packages available if you want to indulge, while the associated Parque das Termas outdoor park and pools are just a short walk away. **€92**

Hostel Geres Rua do Arnaço 21 253 391 119, hostelgeres.pt. Comfortable, newish hostel at the top end of the road. The living room and terrace have sweeping views of the river and valley below. There are dorms (four people), as well as double rooms – expect to pay more for en-suite doubles. Dorms **€15**, doubles **€25**

Parque de Campismo do Vidoeiro Vidoeiro, 1.5km north of town, Portela do Homem road 253 391 289, vidoeirogerescamping.com; map p.343. Park-run

campsite in shady, wooded grounds, just to the north of town by the river. Advance bookings advised in summer, which you can make in any national park office. Open all year. Per tent **€4.50**, per adult **€4.20**, per vehicle **€4.50**

Quinta Souto-Linho Av Manuel Francisco da Costa 253 392 000. A picture-book house with three bedrooms to rent (not individually), more central than many, uphill just east of the high street. Grand rooms come with polished floors and fine views, and there's also an outdoor pool (open summer only). The price is for the whole house rental. **€165**

★São Miguel do Gerês Rua do Arnaço 43 253 391 360, pensaosaomiguel.pt. A small guesthouse with very friendly owners and pristine rooms, each offering balconies with views over the forested slopes. The bathrooms are showing their age but otherwise this is excellent value, with a generous breakfast to boot. **€40**

EATING AND DRINKING

★Geresiana Rua Augusta Sérgio Almeida Maia 1 253 391 226. Stone walls and crisp white tablecloths set the tone for the best eatery in town, with a decent regional

menu (dishes from €9). *Truta a Minhota* (trout stuffed with *presunto* ham) is always good, or there are grilled meats and a house *bacalhau* served with *grelos* (turnip tops). It's

6

the salmon-pink building above the main street, opposite the spa. Mon, Tues & Thurs–Sun noon–3pm & 7–10.30pm.

Geresino Churrasqueira Lugar do Vidoeiro, 1km north, halfway between town and the campsite ☎ 253 391 574; map p.343. By a cluster of cafés, known as the restaurant of *perri perri* chicken, this has a colossal dining area where you can tuck into well-prepared fish, such as trout and shrimps from €7.50 and pork steak for

€5.50. With an open fireplace, it's a good choice in winter. Daily noon–3pm & 7–11pm.

Lurdes Capela Rua Dr. Manuel Gomes de Almeida 77 ☎ 253 391 208. Popular with the locals, the *Lurdes Capela* serves cheap €7.50 *combinado* dishes of steak and eggs, *alheira* and chips and the like, plus a more varied menu of local dishes (€9–17) from trout to *javali* (wild boar). It's at the bottom of the main street. Daily 11.30am–3pm & 6.30–10pm.

Rio Caldo and around

The village of **RIO CALDO**, 8km south of Caldas do Gerês, sprawls around the two bridges that cross the **Barragem da Caniçada**. Dramatically sited in a bowl surrounded by mountains, the large reservoir is a watersports centre, mainly for windsurfing and waterskiing. The swimming is fine, too, though only in designated areas. For the best views of the water you need to get above Rio Caldo – either by taking the N304 Braga road and staying at the *pousada* (see below), whose austere sanctuary commands a terrace with panoramic views, or heading the other way, 3km northwest to **São Bento da Porta Aberta** along the N304, Campo do Gerês road. Pilgrims gather here at the beginning of July and again a month later (and on most Sundays throughout the year), at which times the traffic up here slows to a crawl.

Nossa Senhora da Abadia

13km west of Rio Caldo, off the N308 to Braga, turning off at Santa Maria do Bouro

One of the most revered places in Portugal, and accessible only by car, is the remote shrine of **Nossa Senhora da Abadia** – although not officially within the Peneda-Gerês national park, it's an easy drive here from Rio Caldo, though it can also be visited as a day-trip from Braga (30km southwest). Pilgrims come to pay homage to the twelfth-century wooden statue of the Virgin and Child and, while the church itself was largely rebuilt in the eighteenth century, outside are two earlier, elegant wings of monks' cells as well as a restaurant. It's pretty quiet for most of the year, though has a far livelier air during the main festival on August 15.

ACTIVITIES	**RIO CALDO AND AROUND**

Watersports Água Montanha in Rio Caldo (☎ 253 391 779, ☻ aguamontanha.com) rents out canoes (from €6/ hr), pedaloes (€12/hr) and motorboats (€35/hr), as well as

offering speedboat rides and family adventure packages, and can also arrange accommodation.

ACCOMMODATION AND EATING

Casa dos Santos ☎ 253 391 212. For cheap rooms up at São Bento, try this homely place (just behind the *Mira Serra* restaurant). It's got simple rooms with fantastic views, a patio garden full of lemon trees, and a rustic bar. The guesthouse also has some self-catering flats (from €60/night), and can organize kayaking and quad-bike activities. **€35**

★**Pousada de Amares** Santa Maria do Bouro, 13km west of Rio Caldo ☎ 253 371 970, ☻ pousadas .pt; map p.343. This gorgeous conversion of a twelfth-century Cistercian monastery, set in the Gerês foothills, has been majestically restored and combines monastic simplicity with daring modern flare – views from the rooms are magnificent, while the cloisters, gardens,

grounds, pool and grand restaurant all add up to a thoroughly spoiled stay. **€229**

Pousada do Gerês-Caniçada 5km south of Rio Caldo, N304, Braga road ☎ 253 649 150, ☻ pousadas.pt; map p.343. This old timber-and-granite hunting lodge has an enviable location, overlooking the reservoir from the southeast with terraces offering sweeping views of the valleys below. It's a very attractive building, with a small-scale feel and lots of nooks and crannies to curl up in. There's also a swimming pool and a fine restaurant with more great views – river trout is a favoured dish here, alongside a decent menu of regional specialities, and you'll eat for around €40 a head. Mon–Thurs & Sun 1–3pm & 7–10pm, Fri & Sat 1–3pm & 7.30–10.30pm. **€190**

Campo do Gerês

CAMPO DO GERÊS is little more than a cluster of houses huddled around a road junction, but it's surrounded by dense woodland and makes a pretty good base for local hikes and adventures. A typical day out on foot is the fine walk from the campsite (see below), following a forestry track east (signposted "Portela do Homem"). This eventually joins the road to Portela do Homem, from where it is a short walk to some superb natural bathing pools (7km/90min each way). Otherwise, there are all kinds of opportunities to rent mountain bikes, go riding or get out on the water at the local reservoir.

6

Museu Etnográfico de Vilarinho da Furna

1km south of Campo do Gerês • Tues–Sun 9am–noon & 1.30–5pm • €2 • ☎ 253 351 888

Sited in quiet woodland not far from Campo do Gerês, the **Museu Etnográfico de Vilarinho da Furna** is an emotive museum dedicated to the former village of Vilarinho da Furna, which was completely submerged by the building of a dam in 1972. There are farm implements, a recreated kitchen, and a series of black-and-white photos recording village life from days gone by. In the nearby dam itself, the **Barragem Vilharinho das Furnas**, a dry summer sometimes reveals the ruins of the old village poking up above the waters.

Just outside the museum, you'll find **Roman column XXVII**, one of a series of carved granite posts lining the road from Santa Cruz, south of Terras de Bouro, to the border at Portela do Homem. This section, known locally as Geira, marks out miles XIV to XXXIV of the Roman Via Nova, a military road built in the first century AD. The route originally linked Braga with Astorga in Spain, a distance of 344km.

ARRIVAL AND ACTIVITIES   CAMPO DO GERÊS

By bus There are direct buses from Braga, via Rio Caldo, to Campo do Gerês (2–6 daily; 1hr 20min).

By car In your own car, it takes under 1hr (45km) from Braga along the N20/307, via Terras de Bouro.

Activities The *Parque de Cerdeira* campsite (see below) has mountain bikes for rent (€25/day), and can also arrange activities like kayaking, horseriding, guided trekking and jeep safaris.

ACCOMMODATION AND EATING

There's a large choice of private rooms and self-catering apartments in and around Campo; just look for the signs. For campsite and hostel, in particular, it's best to book ahead, since this is a popular place to stay for outdoor enthusiasts – August is the really busy month, when prices rise across the board.

Albergaria Stop Rua de São João 915 ☎ 253 350 040, ⓦ albergariastop.com. Rather a nice lodge-style hotel; nothing fancy but the rooms have balconies overlooking an outdoor pool (mid-June to mid-Sept only). It's also got a tennis court and a few other public amenities, plus a decent restaurant open to non-guests (mains €8–12). Restaurant daily noon–2pm & 7.30–10pm. **€52**

★ **Parque de Cerdeira** Rua de Cerdeira 400 ☎ 253 351 005, ⓦ parquecerdeira.com; map p.343. Set in verdant grounds just outside Campo do Gerês, this local campsite is more of an outdoor leisure complex; as well as tent pitches, there's heated wash-rooms, laundry service, bunkhouse accommodation with en-suite four-bed units and some very nice self-catering bungalows (for two or four people).

Whichever accommodation you choose, you'll have use of the open-air swimming pool, games areas, bar and restaurant, and minimarket. Tent plus car **€27**, bunkhouse rooms **€39**; bungalows for two people **€70**

Pousada de Juventude Rua da Pousada 1, Vilarinho das Furnas ☎ 253 351 339, ⓦ pousadasjuventude.pt; map p.343. The place where the dam construction workers once stayed is now the youth hostel, located a 10min walk from Campo do Gerês. It's a brightly presented, efficiently run base for outdoorsy types, with a fairly mixed bag as far as accommodation goes offering not just dorms (four-bed) but also en-suite doubles and four-bed bungalows with kitchenette. Dorms **€13**, doubles **€38**, bungalows **€75**

Lindoso

LINDOSO occupies a spectacular position, surrounded by mountains high above a glittering reservoir. Its prominent castle is a relic of more turbulent times – the village is very close to the Spanish border – though for once the castle isn't the most dramatic

sight in the village. Here, instead, the honour goes to Lindoso's extraordinary collection of around fifty nineteenth-century granite **espigueiros** (grain stores), spread out on the slopes below the castle walls. Protecting the precious grain and the maize for the animal feed was a communal effort in this once-remote settlement, and the *espigueiros* are gathered together accordingly. They are raised off the ground on granite legs and have slots in the side-walls, which keeps the grain and maize away from vermin and allows dry air to circulate – and with each topped by a stone cross, the entire site resembles nothing less than a graveyard of elevated tombs.

Castelo

Museum: April–Sept Tues–Fri 10am–12.30pm & 2–6pm, Sat & Sun 10am–noon & 2.30–5pm; Oct–March, request access at the Porta do PNPG • €1.50

Rising above the village, Lindoso's ruined **Castelo** contains a museum chronicling the castle's military history and displays finds of local excavations. It's free if all you want to do is simply enjoy the guard's-eye view over the valley from the walls and battlements.

ARRIVAL AND INFORMATION   LINDOSO

By car Lindoso is 25km east of Ponte da Barca (N203) and close to the Spanish border. If you're driving from Campo or Caldas do Gerês, the best route is to take the road via Portela do Homem into Spain, up to Lobios, entering Portugal again near Lindoso. There's free parking right beneath the castle walls.

By bus There are a couple of daily buses from Arcos de Valdevez and Ponte da Barca, but the timings usually mean that you would have to spend the night here.

Information Porta do PNPG, Lugar do Castelo (April–Sept daily 10am–7pm; Oct–March Tues–Sun 10am–12.30pm & 2–5pm; ☎ 258 578 141), just below the castle, opposite the church, is a modern information centre for the park.

ACCOMMODATION

Sobre Nature Graçáo ☎ 917 540 404, ⓦ sobrenatura .com; map p.343. Fifteen kilometres from Lindoso, in the tiny village of Graçao, you will find a little piece of heaven. Three old farm buildings, lovingly converted to make plush yet ecologically friendly accommodation, are nestled in a small wooded area, with truly magnificent views over the river and forests beyond. No houses are shared. The owner also has a further two cabins in the village (ⓦ casasdealem.com). One-bedroomed house **€80**, two-bedroomed house **€150**

Soajo

SOAJO is something of a puzzle. Set in a broad, fertile valley, amid a network of ancient cobbled tracks, cultivated fields and watermills, with higher grazing lands beyond, it's both a surviving centre of rustic tradition and designated centre for rural tourism. On the one hand, there are goat-herders, elderly black-clad widows and an ancient *pelourinho* in the time-worn central square; on the other, the stone houses are scrubbed suspiciously clean and linked by pristine paved alleys winding past carefully tended gardens filled with fruit trees and trellised vines. It's an idealized version of rusticity perhaps, but it does mean the village continues to thrive – and that staying in a beautifully renovated traditional house here or in neighbouring Lindoso is a joy (see p.347). It also means that there's a better-than-usual chance of something reasonable to eat with a couple of restaurants on the main road outside the village, and a café or two and a bakery inside the village.

As in Lindoso, the main sight is a grouping of preserved *espigueiros* (grain houses), set apart from the houses on higher ground at the edge of the village. The best local walk is a four-kilometre return route via the neighbouring village of Adrão, along a cobbled lane with ruts worn into the stones over the centuries by ox carts.

ARRIVAL AND DEPARTURE   SOAJO

By car Soajo is situated 20km east of Arcos de Valdevez (N202), a pleasant – and increasingly dramatic – half-hour drive over the hilltops. There's a sign off the main road for the *espigueiros*, where

you can park. From Soajo, it's another 11km over the mountains on to Lindoso (N530), which you reach by crossing a reservoir.

By bus Services from Arcos de Valdevez (Mon–Fri 1–3 daily; 45min) drop you off on the main road at the village entrance.

ACCOMMODATION AND EATING

★**Casa do Adro** Largo da Eiro ☎258 576 327, Ⓦrukatronic.wix.com/casadoadro. By the church in the square (follow the blue signposts), the *Casa do Adro* offers half-a-dozen rustic rooms in a beautiful eighteenth-century house. They make their own wine from the tumbling vines, and you eat breakfast in the old kitchen. There's a minimum two-night stay in July and August. **€50**

Parque de Campismo de Travanca Bouças Donas, Cabana Maior ☎258 526 105; map p.343. A summer only campsite in a clearing in the trees, around 7km

northwest of Soajo (on the Arcos road). Open July and August only. Per tent **€3.60**, per adult **€4**, plus per vehicle **€3.75**

Saber ao Borralho Rua 25 de Abril, just up the main street towards Arcos ☎963 708 986. Specializing in mountain goat, a chicken-and-rice stew and other rustic dishes, this restaurant has very friendly owners and an outdoor terrace with valley views. It's a great place to enjoy a glass of wine and home-made codfish cakes after a day's hiking (€10). Daily noon–2pm & 7–9pm but the times are very flexible.

6

Peneda

Far fewer tourists make the trek to the northern sections of the park, though the small mountain village of **PENEDA** is worth the effort. It's reached by a steep, twisting road and huddles under the towering granite summit of **Penameda** (1258m) – a rather stunning backdrop to the locally renowned **Sanctuário da Nossa Senhora da Peneda**, a miniature version of the pilgrimage church at Bom Jesus near Braga. The village itself is little more than a few religious artefact shops clustered around the main square, and often seems hauntingly empty, but for a couple of days a year at least (Sept 7 and 8) Peneda fills with pilgrims. The original focus of adoration was a curious stone which natural forces had sculpted into the form of a woman, who some said was pregnant. Come Christianity, the stone was adopted as the Virgin Mary and was duly incorporated into the late eighteenth-century church. There she remained until the 1930s, when somebody stole her; a gaudy plastic replacement now stands in her place.

ARRIVAL AND INFORMATION

By car Peneda is around 30km northeast of Arcos de Valdevez, signposted off the Soajo road. It's around the same distance south of Melgaço on the Rio Minho; coming this way, you'll enter the park at Lamas de Mouro, 8km north of Peneda.

Information Porta do PNPG, Lamas de Mouro, Porto Ribeiro (April–Sept daily 10am–12.30pm & 2–7pm; Oct–March daily 10am–12.30pm & 2–5pm; ☎251 465 010, Ⓦadere-pg.pt).

ACCOMMODATION

Hotel da Peneda Lugar da Peneda ☎251 460 040, Ⓦpenedahotel.pt. Former pilgrim lodgings, now rebooted as a twenty-bedroomed three-star hotel, with its own bar and restaurant. **€75**

Parque Campismo Lamas de Mouro ☎251 466 041,

Ⓦcamping-lamas.com; map p.343. The wooded campsite at Lamas has some bungalow shacks in the grounds, ideal for families, a natural pool nearby for swimming and summer activities, and its own restaurant. Camping **€4.20**, bungalows **€55**

Trás-os-Montes

GIMONDE, IN THE PARQUE NATURAL DE MONTESINHO

Trás-os-Montes

The northeastern region of Trás-os-Montes (literally "Behind the Mountains") was once Portugal at its most remote. Cut off from the mainstream over the centuries – beyond the peaks of the Gerês, Marão and Alvão *serras* – this isolated area developed in its own individual ways, characterized by unusual traditions, harsh dialects and hard lives. Many fled to the cities in search of better things, and emigration was high; meanwhile others came to hide, such as the Jews who escaped here from the terrors of the Inquisition. Change came slowly, if at all, and Trás-os-Montes remained a land apart until as late as the 1980s and 90s, when fast new highways started to make inroads into the northern wilds. Investment in agriculture, industry and urban renewal has also done much to change perceptions of the region as backward and conservative, though those views still persist in much of the rest of Portugal.

7

You can get to the main towns more quickly these days, but there are still places where you might feel like the first foreign visitor to arrive, and traditional village life here continues as it has done for decades, if not centuries. This is especially true of the extreme north, hewn from dark granite, which has a challenging climate of long freezing winters and short boiling summers – hence its rather forbidding nickname of the *Terra Fria* (Cold Land). In contrast, the southern region – the *Terra Quente* (Hot Land) – covers the fertile hinterlands of the Douro, Corgo and Tua rivers, and presents a more pastoral landscape of olive groves, vineyards and orchards.

From the Douro and the south, the attractive town of **Vila Real** is the obvious starting point for a tour; it's also handy for access to the dramatic granite scenery of the **Parque Natural do Alvão**. Beyond Vila Real, motorways zip up to the border towns of **Chaves** and **Bragança**, the only other two places in the region of any significant size. Between them they hold the bulk of the historic and cultural interest, while each is also well placed for the great outdoors, with Chaves offering access (via Montalegre) to the eastern section of the **Parque Nacional da Peneda-Gerês** and Bragança acting as the jumping-off point for the magnificent **Parque Natural de Montesinho**. South and east of the Vila Real–Bragança motorway, the landscapes are gentler for the most part but the journeys take longer, on winding routes through far less visited towns and villages. Some places are worthy destinations in their own right, such as dramatically sited **Miranda do Douro**, above a dam on the Spanish border; the Roman bridge over the Rio Tua at **Mirandela**; or the small historic centre of **Torre de Moncorvo**. But often, it's simply the journey that counts, notably the tremendous backcountry route through the fringes of the **Parque Natural do Douro Internacional**, through unheralded towns such as **Mogadouro** and **Freixo de Espada à Cinta**.

BRAGANÇA

Highlights

❶ **Vila Real** Savour spectacular views from this friendly, bustling city, built on a long and dramatically located promontory. **See p.355**

❷ **Boat trip, Miranda do Douro** A Douro cruise with a difference, this exciting boat trip plies the craggy gorge below the historic town of Miranda do Douro. **See p.366**

❸ **São João das Arribas gorge** Enjoy a day's walk from Miranda do Douro to a stupendous viewpoint over the dramatic gorge. **See p.367**

❹ **Bragança** An ancient citadel enclosing

centuries of history dominates this once-remote regional capital. **See p.368**

❺ **Parque Natural de Montesinho** Hike in the hills and valleys before a night at the boutique-style "Lost Lobster" hotel. **See p.372**

❻ **Chaves** The Romans founded this lovely spa town with a picturesque riverside setting, and it's still a joy to visit. **See p.379**

❼ **Piteus das Júnias** Explore this wild and under-visited northwest corner of the Parque Nacional da Peneda-Gerês. **See p.384**

HIGHLIGHTS ARE MARKED ON THE MAP ON P.354

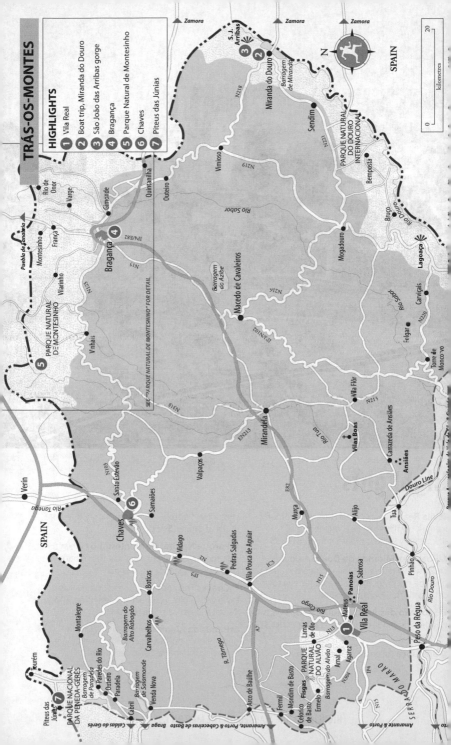

TRÁS-OS-MONTES

HIGHLIGHTS

1. Vila Real
2. Boat trip, Miranda do Douro
3. São João das Arribas gorge
4. Bragança
5. Parque Natural de Montesinho
6. Chaves
7. Pitues das Júnias

N

SPAIN

0   kilometres   20

Vila Real and around

VILA REAL sits on a high spur above the deep valley of the Rio Corgo, a tributary of the Douro. Founded and aptly named by Dom Dinis in 1289, "Royal Town" was once home to the largest concentration of nobility outside Lisbon, although today it has more of an industrial role, as well as being the home of the University of Trás-os-Montes. It's the nearest base for visiting the small but interesting Parque Natural do Alvão (see p.358), while other local attractions include the ancient site at **Panóias** and the **Casa de Mateus** – the country house featured on the Mateus Rosé wine label. Despite its noble heritage, there's little of great architectural interest in Vila Real save the odd surviving mansion, but it's a bustling, likeable place of broad avenues, sunny squares and old-town streets filled with typical old-fashioned Portuguese shops. There's a weekday **market** opposite the Rodonorte bus station: alongside the fruit and veg, look out for for local straw-work and the distinctive gunmetal-grey earthenware crockery (*olaria*) made in the nearby village of Bisalhães.

Museu da Vila Velha

Rua de Trás-os-Muros • Daily 9.30am–12.30pm & 2–6pm • Free • ☎ 259 308 178, ⓦ mvv.cm-vilareal.pt

In a huge granite cube, plonked incongruously amid the old buildings of Vila Real, **Museu da Vila Velha** promises much but delivers just a few bits of crunched archaeology, a stamp collection and lots of empty space. However, there are often interesting temporary shows on the lower level so it's worth popping in to see what's on. Most combine a museum visit with a walk to the end of the promontory on which the town sits, for dramatic views from the crumbling **Capela de São Brás** and its adjoining cemetery. The panorama is wonderful, encompassing an enormous road bridge sweeping the A4 motorway over the deep gorge, with a small reservoir at the bottom.

Igreja de São Pedro

Large dos Bombardeiros Municipais • Daily 8am–7pm

The pleasingly symmetrical Baroque **Church of São Pedro** boasts a beautifully ornate interior, the most impressive element being the barrel-vaulting of the ceiling, which is intricately painted and studded with huge gilt bosses. Look out, too, for the exquisite gilding work throughout and the seventeenth-century tiling.

Casa de Mateus

Largo dos Condes, Mateus, 4km east of Vila Real • Daily: May–Oct 9am–7.30pm; Nov–April 9am–6pm • €11, gardens only €7, wine tastings €4 • ☎ 259 323 121, ⓦ casademateus.com • Buses run from Rua Gonçalo Cristovão, outside Vila Real market (every 30min); a fee is charged for parking at the house

The **Casa de Mateus** (signposted "Palácio de Mateus") is probably the most familiar country house in Portugal, seen on the label of each bottle of Mateus Rosé, one of Portugal's major wine exports. The architect is unknown, though the building is often attributed to the Italian, Nicolau Nasoni (who built the landmark Clérigos church in Porto). It dates to around 1740 – the heyday of Portuguese Baroque – and although there are no real treasures within, the mansion is an enjoyable evocation of its period, full of aristocratic portraits and antique furniture.

The main house ticket price includes a one-hour **guided tour** of the **interior**, including the chapel and special exhibition areas. You don't have to book in advance for these tours, though as numbers are limited you may have to wait an hour for the next one. There are no such restrictions (or tours) for the delightful **gardens**, which are full of ponds, box hedges, statues and shaded avenues. There's also a shop, for local wines and produce, while wine tastings are offered in the *adega* (though not of Mateus Rosé, as you might expect – it's not actually made here).

7

7

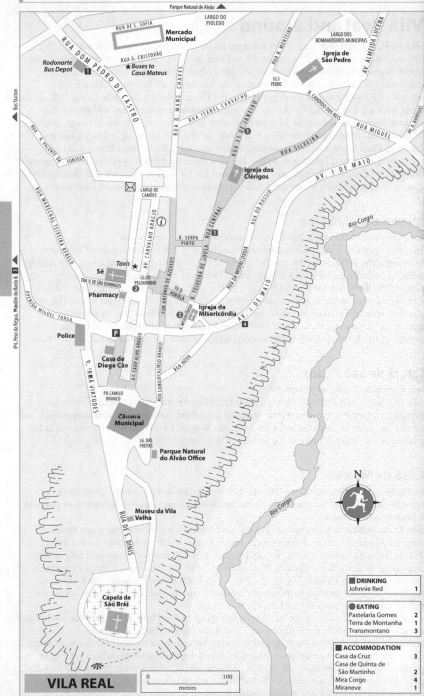

Parque Natural de Alvão

RUA DE S. SOFIA

Mercado Municipal

LARGO DO PIOLEDO

RUA DOM PEDRO DE CASTRO

Rodonorte Bus Depot 1

RUA G. CRISTOVÃO

★ Buses to Casa Mateus

RUA MARG. CHAVES

RUA D. ISABEL CARVALHO

RUA B. MONTEIRO

LARGO DOS BOMBADEIROS MUNICIPAIS

Igreja de São Pedro

AV. ALMEIDA LUCENA

LG.S. PEDRO

R. CANDIDO DOS REIS

RUA 31 DE JANEIRO 1

RUA SILVEIRA

RUA MIGUEL

AV. Z. BARROSAS

Bus Station ◄

RUA A. VALENTE DE FONSECA

RUA MARECHAL TEIXEIRA REBELO

AV. 1 DE MAIO

Igreja dos Clérigos

LARGO DE CAMÕES

✉

ⓘ

AV. CARVALHO ARAUJO

RUA CENTRAL 1

R. SERPA PINTO

RUA TEIXEIRA DE SOUSA

RUA DO ROSSIO

Rio Corgo

7 ◄ IP4, Peso da Régua, Mondim de Basto & 3 ◄

Sé

Taxis ★

TRA V. DE SÃO DOMINGOS

LG. DO PELOURINHO 2

RUA ANTONIO DE AZEVEDO

TV. D. PORTELA

3

RUA MISERICORDIA

AV. 1 DE MAIO

Pharmacy

AVENIDA MIGUEL TORGA

Igreja da Misericórdia

R. MISERICORDIA

4

Police

🅿

AV. CARVALHO ARAÚJO

Casa de Diogo Cão

RUA CAMILO CASTELO BRANCO

RCA NOVA

PR. CAMILO BRANCO

R. IRMÃ VIRTUDES

Câmara Municipal

LG. DAS FREITAS

Parque Natural do Alvão Office

Museu da Vila Velha

RUA DE S. DINIS

Rio Corgo

N

Capela de São Brás

✛

⚓

0   100
metres

VILA REAL

■ DRINKING	
Johnnie Red	1

● EATING	
Pastelaria Gomes	2
Terra de Montanha	1
Transmontano	3

■ ACCOMMODATION	
Casa da Cruz	3
Casa de Quinta de São Martinho	2
Mira Corgo	4
Miraneve	1

Santuário de Panóias

Lugar do Assento, Vale de Nogueiras, 4km east of Mateus, 8km east of Vila Real • Tues 2–5pm, Wed–Sun 9am–12.30pm & 2–5pm • €2 •
The site is hard to reach by public transport, though by car it is well signposted beyond Mateus

The original settlement in the region was out at Panóias, whose fascinating **Santuário de Panóias** is all that remains of a once thriving town. At first sight it seems no more than a field of boulders, but this was the location of the temple of a particularly bloody sacrificial cult, later adopted by the Romans and dedicated to Serapis (a god of Greco-Egyptian origin, lord of life and death). There are three main sacrificial boulders, the uppermost and largest of which displays the remnants of a temple that once stood atop it; the tower above gives a good overview. Much-eroded inscriptions on the boulders are in a strange mixture of Greek and Latin, as the Roman emperor at the time was from a Greek province.

ARRIVAL AND DEPARTURE

By bus The modern new bus station is just northwest the old centre, on the corner of Avenida Cidade de Orense and Rua A. Valente de Fonseca, while Rodonorte (☎ 259 340 710, ⊕ rodonorte.pt) services to Braga, Lisbon and Porto operate from the depot on Rua Dom Pedro de Castro by the *Hotel Miraneve*.

Destinations Braga (5 daily; 1hr 45min); Bragança (10 daily; 1hr 45min); Chaves (6 daily; 1hr 10min); Guimarães

VILA REAL AND AROUND

(5 daily; 1hr 20min); Lisbon (4–6 daily; 5hr); Mirandela (roughly hourly; 1hr); and Porto (15 daily; 1hr 30min).

By car Except for the one-way system around the central avenue, driving into town is fairly straightforward. There's a large underground car park at the southern end of the avenue, or try and find parking spots on Avenida 1º de Maio. For Casa de Mateus and Santuário de Panóias, take the N322 (Sabrosa road) out of town.

INFORMATION

Turismo The super-modern office, with touch-screen info, is on Avenida Carvalho Araújo 94 (daily 9.30am–12.30pm & 2–6pm; ☎ 259 308 170, ⊕ cm-vilareal.pt).

Parque Natural do Alvão HQ Largo das Freitas, behind the Câmara Municipal (Mon–Fri 9am–12.30pm & 2–5.30pm; ☎ 259 302 830, ⊕ icnf.pt).

ACCOMMODATION

Town-centre **accommodation** in Vila Real is pretty underwhelming and it's the *turismo rural* properties in the area that provide the better overnight stay. The town centre has a couple of good deals, however, but don't expect much in the way of luxury.

Casa da Cruz Campeã ☎ 259 372 995 or ☎ 917 523 975, ⊕ casadacruz.com. Three rustic rooms and three apartments, all with lovely carved beds, in an eighteenth-century granite farmhouse, overlooking the Vale de Campeã; it's 12km west of Vila Real, on the N304 (the Mondim de Basto road). There's use of the kitchen, as well as a secluded swimming pool, and breakfast is included. €60
★ **Casa da Quinta de São Martinho** Mateus ☎ 259 323 986, ⊕ quintasaomartinho.com. Some 4km east of Vila Real, 300m from Casa de Mateus, this ivy-swathed country house has two B&B double rooms in the main building and two self-contained apartments (€95) in the garden, complete with spiral staircase and exposed stone walls – the apartments will sleep a family of four. There's a swimming pool, and port-wine tasting in the bar (the friendly proprietor

being president of the Douro wine trail). €80
Mira Corgo Av 1º de Maio 78 ☎ 259 325 001, ⊕ hotelmiracorgo.com. This central four-star hotel is a pretty ugly 1980s edifice, but secure a room overlooking the stepped terraces of the Rio Corgo and you won't be disappointed. There's an indoor swimming pool, and outdoor terraces for the views, as well as secure parking and lots of other guest services. €73
Miraneve Rua D. Pedro de Castro ☎ 259 323 153, ⊕ hotelmiraneve.com.pt. First choice in town for budget travellers, this central, well-run hotel above the Rodonorte bus depot has huge rooms with sweeping views across the surrounding gorges and mountain ridges. Facilities show their age, but breakfast is included and rates on popular booking websites are often very low. €40

EATING

For the cheapest **restaurants** in town, look along Rua da Misericórdia and Rua Teixeira de Sousa; the best **cafés**, meanwhile, are those on the pedestrianized avenue and square, near the Câmara Municipal. Incidentally, Vila Real might be in Trás-os-Montes, but it's also in the demarcated Douro wine region, so decent **wines** are the norm in most restaurants.

★ **Pastelaria Gomes** Largo do Pelourinho 11 ☎ 259 372 076. Around since 1925, this stylish café feels like it

hasn't changed much since it opened. Pull up a green leather chair, order a *galão* and plate of cakes and admire

the vaulted ceiling, Art Deco light fittings and olde-worlde counters. Mon–Sat 8am–7.30pm.

Terra de Montanha Rua 31 de Janeiro 28 ☎ 259 372 075. The tables are set inside huge, antique wine vats in this low-lit, rustic restaurant, and the friendly staff are enthusiastic about the traditional Portuguese menu. There's also a changing selection of hearty *pratos do dia* and a fine red house wine. Mains €10.50–13.50. Mon–Sat 12.30–2.30pm & 7.30–10.30pm, Sun 12.30–2.30pm.

Transmontano Rua da Misericórdia 35–37 ☎ 259 106 457. Meat and fish feature in equal measure at this family-run, unfancy restaurant that packs them in at mealtimes. The speciality here is beef: mountain style and like grandmother used to make. Mains around €9. Mon–Sat 10am–midnight.

DRINKING

Johnnie Red Rua Margarida Chaves 4. Open-all-hours jazz and blues bar, dimly lit with Tiffany lamps and serving any tipple you fancy to some cool background music. Mon–Sat 8am–2am, Sun 2pm–2am.

Parque Natural do Alvão

7

The **Parque Natural do Alvão** is Portugal's smallest natural park, an area of eight thousand mountainous hectares set between Vila Real and Mondim de Basto to the northwest. A mere handful of settlements (with a total population of fewer than seven hundred) hug the boulder-strewn terrain, with every centimetre of arable land between heroically terraced and tended, while other slopes are planted with pine whose scent carries in the air. Life, of course, has been hard and many of the villages are depopulated, but traditional agricultural methods (ox and plough, hand-scythed straw) cling on and some crafts (clog-making, weaving) have been revived. Drive-through visitors in a hurry don't always see the best of Alvão – at first sight, many of the settlements seem moribund or disfigured by ugly recent construction, while there are hardly any facilities within the park, rarely even a place to get a drink. But with just half a day to spare, you can easily do one of the two official **waymarked walks**, while another half-day gives you time to drive around a circuit of the most interesting villages and visit the one standout natural sight, the **Fisgas de Ermelo waterfalls**.

VISITING THE PARQUE NATURAL DO ALVÃO

Access points to the **Parque Natural do Alvão** are Vila Real (5km southeast of the park boundary) or Mondim de Basto (15km from the main village of Ermelo, in the west). The N304 connects the two towns; buses (Mon–Sat only) ply the route, and there are also regular weekday bus services from Vila Real to Agarez and to Lamas de Ôlo, both of which are on the marked walking routes. However, to see the park properly, certainly in a short time, you'll need a **car**. Be aware that signposting in the park leaves something to be desired and some villages are simply not signed at all.

There are **park information offices** in both Vila Real and Mondim de Basto, both hampered by the usual lack of anything you might call information, certainly in English. You could try the generally more helpful Vila Real turismo (see p.357), or consult the comprehensive ⓦicnf.pt.

ACCOMMODATION

There's a distinct lack of **accommodation** (and no camping allowed) within the park, so the only real options are staying in Vila Real or Mondim de Basto. You might also consider the *Pousada de São Gonçalo* in the Serra do Marão, halfway between Vila Real and Amarante and close enough to the park for day-trips.

HIKING

The good news is that, once you've found them, the park's two **walking routes** are well maintained, with proper red-yellow waymarks – you probably won't even need the route leaflets or park map that you might have managed to extract from the information offices.

> **THE TERRAS DE BASTO**
>
> Mondim de Basto is one of three towns with the same suffix: the others are Celorico de Basto, just to the southwest, and the larger Cabeceiras de Basto, 25km north (in the Minho). Together, the three Basto towns and their districts form the **Terras de Basto**, a region whose name comes from a number of life-sized Celtic warrior statues – beautifully incised with Celtic emblems on the torso and a shield on the belly – which were originally laid on warriors' graves. *Eu basto* ("I suffice") was their credo, expressing a willingness to face the enemy (Romans for the most part) single-handed.

Agarez and around

From Vila Real, it's only 5km west to **AGAREZ** village, just above which starts the shorter of the Parque Natural do Alvão's two official walking routes, the **Galegos–Arnal circuit** (7km; 3hr); there's a walk information board on the left-hand side of the Lamas de Ôlo road, just out of Agarez. The route follows a lovely stone path, past an old watermill, before heading steeply up past the dung-spattered Galegos da Serra village to the Escola Ecológica study centre, 1000m high and with majestic views towards Vila Real. From here, the path winds down to the ancient farming hamlet of Arnal (whose chapel has an exterior chain-pull bell), and then you follow the minor road down the pretty Arnal river valley, past grazing cattle, back to Agarez.

Barragem do Alvão and Lamas de Ôlo

Some 9km northwest of Agarez, the **Barragem do Alvão** is the starting point for the second of the Parque Natural do Alvão's two walking trails. The **Barragens–Barreiro–Lamas de Ôlo circuit** (13km; 4hr) is a magnificent high-plateau walk, starting between two dams (*barragens*) and circling around through the villages of Barreiro and Lamas de Ôlo (with the last 2km on the road from Lamas back up to the dams). You're walking at between 1100m and 1200m throughout, with amazing views all the way round, passing through vibrant blankets of purple and yellow heather and gorse, past frog-filled ponds, pine forests and precariously balanced boulders.

Lamas de Ôlo itself is a partly abandoned mountain hamlet of granite houses and traditional *espigueiros* (grain stores). There's a basic café here – no sign, but it's near the bus stop – while the onward road between Lamas and Anta has more magnificent views, with Mondim de Basto and its conical mountain prominent in the distance.

Ermelo and around

There are several possible driving routes through the Parque Natural do Alvão from Vila Real to Mondim de Basto, but the loop through Pioledo and Cavernelhe towards Ermelo is thoroughly recommended, since you can detour to a spectacular rocky ledge overlooking the thundering waterfalls of **Fisgas de Ermelo**, in a craggy valley beyond. The parking and viewing area is some distance from the falls, though a tough hike gets you closer. Entering or leaving the park at the western side, you might as well take in **ERMELO** itself (1km off the N304), a sleepy hamlet that just about stirs itself to claim the title of "largest village in the park". The place has a few cafés, and nothing more in the way of services, but it's interesting to stop and look at the intricately plaited roofs of black slate that are typical of the village.

Mondim de Basto

The small, handsomely sited town of **MONDIM DE BASTO** lies around 10km northwest of the Parque Natural do Alvão, an hour by road from Vila Real (N304) or slightly closer to Amarante, 30km back down the Rio Tâmega in the Minho (see p.286). There's little of

historic interest, but Mondim is ringed by vineyards (they make *vinho verde* around here), and has a pretty floral garden in the centre and a municipal park – not to mention a useful range of accommodation nearby, as well as a couple of adventure-sports outfits that can arrange kayaking or rafting. Lording it over the town is **Monte Farinha** (996m), which from a distance looks like a perfect child's drawing of a mountain; it's an 11km winding drive up to the chapel at the top (follow signs to "N.S Graça" off the N312 Cerva road), and there's also a panoramic café. If you're really keen you can walk, on a well-signposted 14km (5hr) circuit from town, which cuts up through the road switchbacks.

ARRIVAL AND INFORMATION   MONDIM DE BASTO

By bus There are three local buses from Vila Real (Mon–Fri only; first 7.50am) to Mondim. To get to Amarante, you'll need to change at Fermil, 6km to the northwest, which also has connections to Guimarães and Braga. It's a short walk from the bus station to Mondim's public gardens.
Parque Natural do Alvão The park information office is

at Lugar do Barrio, 800m down the Celorico road by the Barrio primary school (Mon–Fri 9am–12.30pm & 2–5.30pm; ☎ 255 381 209).
Turismo The office is on Praça do Município (Mon–Fri 9am–1pm & 2–5pm, Sat & Sun 9am–1pm; ☎ 255 389 370, ⌨ cm-mondimdebasto.pt).

ACCOMMODATION AND EATING

Accommodation in Mondim is none too inspiring, particularly the two very cheapest places on the main avenue near the GALP petrol station. Manor houses out of town are the better choices. Mondim has several chips-with-everything **restaurants**, plus a supermarket, a grocer's shop, chemist and other services.

Casa do Campo Molares ☎ 255 361 231, ⌨ casa docampo.pt. Elegant seventeenth-century manor house, 7km west of Mondim and just south of Fermil (on the Celorico de Basto road), offering gorgeous B&B rooms with a touch of style, plus splendid gardens and a pool with mountain views. A couple of garden apartments have a bit more space (though they aren't self-catering), and there are also two large suites in the main house (€110). Give them some notice and they can usually arrange dinner. **€90**

★ **Quinta do Fundo** Vilar de Viando ☎ 255 381 291, ⌨ quintadofundo.com. This relaxing first choice is set amid acres of *vinho verde* vines, 2km south of Mondim on the Vila Real road. It's packed with family furniture and although the five rooms and two larger suites (€75) are a bit on the ageing side, it's a wonderful spot with a pool, gardens and tennis court. Dinner (€30) is available on request and they also produce their own *vinho verde*. **€50**

Mirandela

Some 65km northeast of Vila Real, **MIRANDELA** is a neat provincial town on the Tua river that's been making an improbable name for itself in recent years as one of the world's jet-ski hotspots, hosting national and European championships. Otherwise, the town's most striking feature is its pedestrianized **Roman bridge**, stretching a good 200m across seventeen arches. There are pleasant riverside gardens and lawns, and – up the hill – a (very) small **old town** with a few surviving Baroque townhouses. There's also a proper, old-fashioned **market building** (walk up pedestrianized Rua da República; best on Thursdays), while grocery stores and delis throughout town sell Mirandela's famed olive oil and olives (much of it *biológico*, or organically produced). The town is also known for its *alheira* sausages, draped across shop windows and served in every restaurant.

ARRIVAL AND INFORMATION   MIRANDELA

By bus Buses all stop on Rua Dom Afonso III, outside the old train station – to reach the town centre, turn right, then right again for the river and the Roman bridge, from where the road veers into the main Rua da República.
Destinations Bragança (13 daily; 1hr); Miranda (1 daily; 2hr); and Vila Real (13 daily; 1hr).

Information The turismo is on Rua Dom Afonso III, next to the old train station (mid-June to mid-Sept Mon–Fri 9am–12.30pm & 2–5.30pm, Sat 10am–1pm; mid-Sept to mid-June Mon–Fri 10am–4pm, Sat 10am–1pm; ☎ 278 203 143, ⌨ cm-mirandela.pt).

PAGAN PIGS

Roughly sculpted **granite pigs** (known as *porcas* or *berrões*) are found all over northeastern Portugal and neighbouring Spain. Most date back a couple of thousand years, and their origins are obscure, though they are thought to have been Celtic fertility idols. The wild boar certainly holds sway in popular culture in these parts, so it's not hard to see where the inspiration lay in the earliest carvings. The most famous example of a *porca* is in the small town of **Murça**, off the IP4, halfway between Vila Real and Mirandela, where it sits on top of a granite plinth above a flowerbed in the town centre. Pig and town, incidentally, give their name to a ubiquitous Douro table wine, Porca de Murça (made by Real Companhia Velha), while the pig is in profile on Murça's *adega cooperativa* (wine co-op), the Caves de Murça. So there's no excuse not to drink the health of Portugal's pagan pigs.

ACCOMMODATION AND EATING

Dom Dinis Av Nossa Senhora do Amparo ☎ 278 097 750, ⓦ hoteldomdinis.pt. A couple of places in town offer cheap rooms, but this large, riverside three-star "*grande*" hotel boasts the only views worth having (a front-facing room with balcony is a must), as well as an outdoor pool. It's on the other side of the river from the old town, across the new bridge (which is adjacent to the old one). **€69**

★ **Flor de Sal** Parque Dr. José Gama ☎ 278 203 063. Across the bridge road from the *Dom Dinis* hotel, this is a sleek, chic, contemporary Portuguese restaurant, with a riverside lounge-bar and deck that's just the place to while

away an afternoon. The food is extremely good – fixed-price lunch from €15, otherwise from €40 a head, and it's quite a surprise to find such a place in an out-of-the-way town like Mirandela. Daily: Restaurant 12.30–3.30pm & 7.30–11pm; bar 10am–2am.

Quinta Entre Rios Chelas ☎ 278 263 160, ⓦ quintaentrerios.com. The most agreeable overnight option where a dozen B&B rooms are located on an organic olive-oil estate, complete with small pool and tennis court. It's 3km northwest of town, on the N213 (follow the signs). **€75**

Vila Flôr and around

VILA FLÔR – the Town of Flowers – is 24km south of Mirandela and worth a quick stop if you're on your way into deep eastern Trás-os-Montes. It was given its name in the thirteenth century by Dom Dinis who, on his way to meet Isabel of Aragon, was clearly in a romantic frame of mind. Flowers are not so evident today, though handsome tree-lined squares and a striking twin-towered tiled church provide focus for a stroll. There's also a rather eccentric municipal museum, the **Museu Municipal de Berta Cabral** (not always open), and a few cafés in the old-town streets. Weekday buses call here on the run between Torre de Moncorvo and Mirandela, but you'd hardly want to stay the night here – and in any case you need a car to see the more enticing surroundings, which primarily means the ruins of Ansiães, a twenty-minute drive southwest.

Castelo de Ansiães

The ruins are 5km south of the town of Carrazeda de Ansiães; you'll see the brown "Castelo" signs as you pass through the centre • Always open • Free • ⓦ castelodeansiaes.com

Twenty-one kilometres southwest of Vila Flôr – follow signs initially for Carrazeda de Ansiães – lie the intriguing ruins of an abandoned, medieval walled town. It's barely recognizable as such until you're almost upon it, winding up the 900m-high hillside to a craggy outcrop signposted simply as **Castelo de Ansiães**. You park by the outer gateway and make your way up a stone track, flanked by bramble-covered ruins, to a twelfth-century chapel with a carved Romanesque doorway. Beyond is the main gate and a complete circuit of partially ruined walls, which provides a breezy walk with beautiful views – otherwise, all that remains are fallen boulders and broken stones. It's hard to believe that five different kings, over a

period of 500 years, made this their strategic base in the north – the last inhabitants of old Ansiães left in the mid-eighteenth century, when the nearby new town of Carrazeda de Ansiães was established.

Torre de Moncorvo

The 26km route southeast from Vila Flôr to **TORRE DE MONCORVO** is a dramatic drive, taking you into the steep mountains round the Douro valley. A network of narrow medieval shopping streets, granite-block walls and handsome mansions makes the small town a pleasant place to stop off for a few hours, with everything helpfully signposted, starting with the imposing sixteenth-century **Igreja Matriz** – the largest church in Trás-os-Montes, which took a century to build. A terrace here looks out over the distant hills, while following signs across the main square into the "*nucléo medieval*" takes you to the surviving town gate, the **Porta da Vila**. Aside from a couple of local museums, that's basically all there is to see here, except for the annual burst of enthusiasm for the region's **almond trees**, the blossoming of which draws crowds of visitors in early spring. The sugared nuts are available in any number of local groceries and "*produtos regionais*" shops, along with Moncorvo's famed cherries and lots of good Douro wines.

ARRIVAL AND DEPARTURE TORRE DE MONCORVO

By bus The bus station is out on the main road, the N220. Destinations Freixo de Espada à Cinta (Mon–Fri 2 daily; 45min); Miranda do Douro (2 daily; 1hr 45min); Mogodouro (2 daily; 1hr); Vila Nova de Foz Côa (1 daily; 30min); Vila

Real (1 daily; 45min).
By car Parking is mostly metered in town, though there's a free car park below the flyover on the way up into the old centre.

INFORMATION AND ACTIVITIES

Turismo The office is at is Rua dos Sapateiros (daily 9am–12.30pm & 2–5.30pm; ☎279 252 289, ⓦwww .torredemoncorvo.pt).

Tours CP, the Portuguese rail operator (☎707 210 220, ⓦcp.pt), runs cherry blossom train-and-coach excursions

here in late March and early April. Trains from Porto or Peso da Régua run to Pocinho, from where a tour bus follows a circuit through the hills, with stopoffs for views, walks and lunch, including a visit to Torre de Moncorvo (adults €8 plus return train ticket, bookings essential).

ACCOMMODATION, EATING AND DRINKING

Casa de Santa Cruz Rua Cimo do Lugar, Felgar ☎279 928 060, ⓦcasadesantacruz.com. Drive 13km east of Torre de Moncorvo (off the N220 and on the Freixo de Espada road) to the quiet village of Felgar for a night in an imaginatively restored eighteenth-century manor house, located in a corner of the village square. It has twelve rooms, its own pool and wood-burning heaters; meals are available (around €20) if you reserve ahead. **€85**

O Artur Carviçais ☎279 098 000. Persevere with the drive for this in-the-know spot, 16km east of Torre de Moncorvo on the N220 (Freixo de Espada road). Expect good-value meals served in a cheery roadhouse of

red-checked tablecloths and stripped pine (mains from around €8). Also offers simple rooms above the restaurant. Tues–Sun noon–10.30pm.

O Lagar Rua do Hospital Velho 16, Torre de Moncorvo ☎279 252 828. The best regional food in town – you'll eat well in an old, granite-walled olive-oil warehouse, down the side of the Igreja Matriz, and pay €20 if you stick to the excellent fruity table-wine. Mon–Sat noon–3pm & 7–10pm, Sun noon–3pm.

★**Quinta das Aveleiras** Rua das Aveleiras ☎279 252 285, ⓦquintadasaveleiras.pt. Relax in the surroundings of a lovely wine and olive estate, just out of Torre de

---

AS FAR AS THE EYE CAN SEE

The Trás-os-Montes **almond trees** are explained in the legend of a Moorish prince who married a northern-European princess. Though happy in summer, she grew sad and wistful in winter, and ached for the snow-clad hills of her homeland. The prince hurried to the Algarve, from where he brought back the almond trees, so that from then on, every February when the trees blossomed, the princess beheld white as far as the eye could see.

Moncorvo on the Pocinho road, where classy self-catering accommodation is offered by the night in four restored buildings, sleeping two to six people (up to €220 a night). Pick of the bunch is the amazing circular *pombal* (pigeon house), which makes a unique and romantic bolthole for two – possibly the region's quirkiest guest room. Breakfast is provided in each property and there's a pool, tennis court and bikes available. **€95**

Freixo de Espada à Cinta

The southernmost town in Trás-os-Montes is **FREIXO DE ESPADA À CINTA**, around 40km southeast of Torre de Moncorvo. The mouthful of a name translates as "ash-tree of the sword of the belt" and supposedly refers to Dom Dinis hacking at a nearby tree as he announced the founding of the town. Hidden in the folds of the undulating Douro mountains, Freixo was once considered so remote that prisoners who had been granted an amnesty were allowed to settle here in obscurity. It doesn't feel quite so isolated any more, with a new town straddling one side of the main through-road (N221), and a small, surviving old centre on the other, dominated by a surprisingly grand **Igreja Matriz** with a *retábulo* of paintings attributed to Viseu artist Grão Vasco. There's also a mighty keep, which affords great views from its bell tower, while beneath lies Freixo's spectacularly sited cemetery. Follow the signs ("*praia fluvial*") 4km east out of town, down a series of hairpin bends on the banks of the Rio Douro, and you'll end up at the local river beach and swimming spot.

ARRIVAL AND INFORMATION

By bus Buses to/from Miranda do Douro, Torre de Moncorvo and Mogadouro are infrequent (usually 1 daily Mon–Fri; see santosviagensturismo.pt for timetables), so you risk spending considerably longer here than Freixo really warrants if relying on public transport.
By car The drive here is marvellous, particularly the approach north from Barca d'Alva on the N221 (20km), part of the Parque Natural do Douro Internacional, which follows a beautiful stretch of the Douro River, with viewpoints at strategic intervals.
Parque Natural do Douro Internacional The park's regional office is on Largo do Outeiro, in the modern town centre (Mon–Fri 9am–12.30pm & 2–5.30pm; 279 658 130, icnf.pt).

ACCOMMODATION AND EATING

Cinta d'Ouro Av Guerra Junqueiro 279 652 550, cintadouro.com. Set on the main through-road, opposite the market and municipal auditorium, this is a rather fine restaurant above a bar and shop selling wines and *produtos regionais*. There's good *bacalhau* among other dishes, all at around the €10 mark, and cheap rooms too if you need them. Restaurant daily noon–2.30pm & 7–10.30pm. **€40**

Quinta do Salgueiro 3km north of Freixo on the Mogadouro road (N221) 279 652 007, quintadosalgueiro.com. This *turismo rural* B&B is on a wine and olive estate and offers eight simple, traditionally furnished rooms and suites, all named after plants and animals found hereabouts. There's a rather nice pool in landscaped gardens, and some widescreen views across the hills and vineyards. **€80**

Parque Natural do Douro Internacional

The **Parque Natural do Douro Internacional** covers a long, thin 120km stretch of the Rio Douro as it flows along the border between Portugal and Spain. On the Portuguese side, the park runs from Miranda do Douro in the north, past Mogadouro and Freixo de Espada à Cinta to Barca d'Alva, the latter the point at which the Rio Douro officially enters Portuguese territory; there's also a southern section that encompasses a stretch of the Rio Águeda, further south in Beira Alta (near Figueira de Castelo Rodrigo). The park is extremely dramatic in parts, known for its sheer canyon walls and Mediterranean microclimate, and this combination of mild winters and its isolation from large human populations has led to the preservation of a rich variety of **animal species**, including a few surviving wolves and wildcats, as well as boar, otters,

bats and amphibians. It is also home to over 170 **bird species**, including rare peregrine falcons, golden eagles, black storks and, in summer, Europe's largest concentration of Egyptian vultures.

The main problem for visitors is getting any sense of the park as a whole, since it's so elongated and necessarily remote from anywhere you're likely to be spending much time; you'll see the periodic brown park signs as you drive between Beira Alta and Bragança, but it's not immediately clear what there is to see or do. To make some sense of it, it's best to visit a **park office** (see below) and buy the official map. Armed with this, you can at least drive to the various spectacular viewing areas, to gaze down from the canyon-like cliffs into the Douro far below – that of **Penedo Dourão** is between Barca d'Alva and Freixo; there's another superb vantage-point at **Lagoaça**, 25km from Mogadouro; while close to Miranda do Douro is the magnificent **São João das Arribas** (see p.367). There's also a brown-signposted "Rota dos Castros" **driving route**, along minor roads linking a series of ancient fortified border posts.

INFORMATION AND ACTIVITIES

Information There are park information offices in the small towns of Mogadouro (see below), Miranda do Douro (see p.367), Freixo de Espada à Cinta (see opposite) and Figueira de Castelo Rodrigo, but don't expect much English to be spoken. For official information (in Portuguese), check ⓦicnf.pt.

Hiking A number of waymarked hiking circuits thread through the park, but the route marks are not always properly maintained, and it can be difficult to get hold of the route leaflets, even in the park offices. Undoubtedly the best walk is the circular one from Miranda do Douro (see p.367), which starts and finishes right in town.

Tours and activities Local adventure-tour operators, such as Torre de Moncorvo-based Sabor, Douro e Aventura (ⓞ 279 258 270, ⓦsabordouro.com), offer activities including kayaking on the Douro (€32) and guided day-walks into the park (€20), though they are more geared to groups than individuals (some activities require a minimum of ten people). Your best bet might be a boat trip on the Douro itself – there are daily departures from Miranda do Douro (see p.367) through some of the most dramatic canyon scenery in the park.

Mogadouro

The old frontier fortress of **MOGADOURO** lies on the fringes of the Parque Natural do Douro Internacional. With the winding journey here from north or south half the attraction, it's hard to escape the impression of a town caught between past and present, ready to embrace tourism but not quite sure what it has to offer. Its main sight is the restored **keep** of a twelfth-century castle, set on a hill with extensive views over a patchwork of tilled fields, traditional pigeon houses and an imposing grain elevator – as well as the municipal swimming pool and stadium, and a spreading line of suburban development.

ARRIVAL AND INFORMATION

MOGADOURO

By bus Buses stop in the main square, and services are usually frequent enough not to strand you in Mogadouro.
Destinations Bragança (1 daily Mon–Fri; 1hr 40min); Miranda do Douro (2 daily Mon–Fri; 45min); Torre de Moncorvo (2 daily Mon–Fri; 1hr 15min); and Vila Real (1 daily Mon–Fri; 3hr 45min).
By car Mogadouro is 47km from Miranda do Douro and 58km from Torre de Moncorvo, both of which are better

overnight stops. In the centre of town is the wide, flower-bedded Largo Trindade Coelho, near which there's plenty of parking; the castle tower is visible from here, signposted straight up at Rua Santa Marinha.
Parque Natural do Douro Internacional The park information office is at Rua Santa Marinha 4 (Mon–Fri 9am–12.30pm & 2–5.30pm; ⓞ 279 340 030).

ACCOMMODATION AND EATING

Casa das Águas Ferreas Lugar das Aguas Ferreas ⓞ 279 341 085, ⓦhostalcasadasaguasferreas .com. Built on a hill around 500m southeast of

Mogadouro, via the Estrada Nacional 221, this eight-room modern guesthouse has perfectly appointed rooms with lots of tiling and reproduction antique

furniture, and is preferable to the accommodation on offer in town. €48

Gabriela Sendim ☎ 273 739 180. Halfway to Miranda, 27km northeast of Mogadouro via the N221, the locally famed *Gabriela* is a traditional restaurant-with-rooms, where a massive slab of meat called a Mirandês steak (*posta*) is the order of the day (meals from around €15). Restaurant daily noon–3pm & 7–10.30pm. €50

Miranda do Douro and around

At **MIRANDA DO DOURO**, you arrive at an eastern Trás-os-Montes town with a certain presence. In part, this is due to its location – across from Spain, and set above a magnificent gorge of the Rio Douro – but there's also history and tradition here in abundance. The border town was always at the forefront of fights with the Spanish, and was fortified to the gills in earlier times – until an apocalyptic explosion in 1762 destroyed its castle, killed hundreds and sent Miranda into a gentle decline. After the explosion, Miranda remained a neglected outpost for two centuries – sufficiently remote for a distinct language, **Mirandês**, to flourish. It is still spoken today and even taught in schools: local street and town signs are usually in both Portuguese and the Mirandês equivalent.

Modern Miranda might be small – with just a couple of thousand inhabitants – but it still retains the status of a city and boasts an outsized sixteenth-century cathedral and a charming old-town area from its glory days. What changed the character of Miranda completely, however, was the building in 1955 of the huge **Barragem de Miranda**, just below town. With the dam wall and border just a couple of kilometres away, there's a constant stream of Spanish tourists, who come to view the staggering gorge scenery, take a river trip and wander briefly around town. Stay the night, and you can also see a bit more of the Douro river gorge by driving out to the magnificent local viewing point – or even hiking there on one of the region's finest one-day walks.

Sé and around

The sixteenth-century cathedral, the **Sé**, overlooks Miranda's whitewashed townhouses and the Douro far below. In the eighteenth century, the bishopric was transferred to Bragança and the adjacent Episcopal Palace allowed to fall into disrepair – today, the landscaped ruins form a handsome garden behind the cathedral, encircled by sections of the medieval walls. The **castle** remains, too, have been shored up and prettified, while the old streets and squares around are laid with clacking cobbles and lined with late-medieval facades. Below the castle on the other side of town, Miranda's other river, the tamer **Rio Fresno**, has also been dammed – it's now a landscaped park of whooshing fountains, winding paths and a waterside café.

Museu da Terra de Miranda

Praça Dom João III • June–Sept Tues 2–6pm, Wed–Sun 9.30am–12.30pm & 2–6pm; Oct–May Tues 2–5.30pm, Wed–Sun 9.30am–12.30pm & 2–5.30pm • €2 • ☎ 273 431 164

In the town-hall square near the cathedral, the **Museu da Terra de Miranda** is the repository of the region's stories and traditions, which sounds dull and worthy until you see the exhibits – from children's balloons made out of sheep's stomachs to fearsome-looking pagan masks worn by young men during local festivities. This is also the place to find out more about the town's stick dancers, known as the *Pauliteiros* (see box, p.367), whose performances enliven many a traditional festival.

Barragem de Miranda

Down the vertiginous hill below town lies the **Barragem de Miranda** hydroelectric dam and border – the road runs over the dam wall into Spain and on towards Zamora. It's

BAGPIPES AND STICK MEN

Trás-os-Montes is the heartland of the Portuguese **gaita-de-foles** (bagpipes), the main melody instrument of Trás-os-Montes traditional music. It's similar to the Scottish Highland war-pipe in shape but closest to the *gaitas* of Spanish Galicia and Asturias, all of which are drawn from the Moorish tradition (*ghaita* being the Moroccan word for a pipe). The old tradition of the pipes survives principally in Miranda do Douro, kept alive by Mirandês *gaiteiros* who play regularly for the **Pauliteiros**, local men in traditional outfits who prance around clattering wooden sticks together rhythmically – rather like an English morris dance. Like many such manifestations in the north (the stone pigs, the bonfire celebrations, the masked revels), it probably dates back to Celtic times. It's a performance which is more often seen at large nationwide festivals than in their home town, though the *Pauliteiros* make a special appearance every year during the Santa Bárbara *festa* (starts the Sunday following August 15). At this time you will also hear the local folk music, a tradition maintained at the town's *Casa da Música Mirandês* (music institute), by the ruined castle on Largo do Castelo.

7

one of the largest hydroelectric dams in the country and marks the point at which the Portuguese Rio Douro transforms itself into the Spanish Rio Duero. Boat trips through the gorge (see p.368) are an obvious attraction and they run year-round.

São João das Arribas gorge

The circular walk (20km; 6hr) from Miranda to the gorge at **São João das Arribas** is the best use of a spare day in Miranda do Douro, though you can also drive there (partly on dirt roads, in good condition) for a picnic, or take a lovely **boat trip** through the gorge (see p.368). The walk is waymarked with red-and-yellow paint stripes, and though many are faded they are still all (mostly) visible, making route-finding fairly straightforward. There is also a leaflet available in the town's park office (see below) showing the route; be prepared for barking dogs at farms all the way round.

The **route** starts by the turismo, where you follow the brown "Castros de Vale de Águia e de Aldeia Nova" sign – the road through the shops and buildings soon turns to a dirt track and the waymarks begin. At Castro de Vale de Águia (2.5km) are the first amazing views over a double bend in the river; at the rustic-in-the-extreme hamlet of Vale de Águia (4.5km) follow the "Aldeia Nova" sign along a tarmac road to Aldeia Nova (6.5km), where there's a bar (probably closed) and a sign for "São João das Arribas" and "Castro". Down this track, at the small chapel of **São João das Arribas** (8km), are simply extraordinary views of the Douro gorge, plus remains of the Iron Age, later Roman, *castro*. It's a great place for a picnic.

The no-risk return is to go back the way you came, though the actual waymarked route runs west through Pena Branca (12km) and then south to the Fresno River where you cross the low bridge (16km) and then head up past farms until you crest a hill and see Miranda (20km) ahead.

ARRIVAL AND DEPARTURE

MIRANDA DO DOURO

By bus Buses stop by the traffic circle, opposite the fire station.

Destinations Bragança (Mon–Fri 2 daily; 1hr 30min); Freixo de Espada à Cinta (Mon–Fri 2 daily; 1hr 15min); Mirandela (2 daily; 2hr–2hr 30min); Mogadouro (3 daily;

45min); Torre de Moncorvo (3 daily; 1hr 45min).

By car The town is split into old and new by a landscaped traffic circle, high above the river. There's lots of free parking all around here, and it's just a couple of hundred metres' walk up the avenue and through the walls into the old town.

INFORMATION AND ACTIVITIES

Turismo The office is on the main traffic circle (Mon–Sat 9am–12.30pm & 2–5.30pm; ☎ 273 430 025).

Parque Natural do Douro Internacional The park

information office, on Rua do Convento (Mon–Fri 9am–12.30pm & 2–5.30pm; ☎ 273 431 457), is in the old town, at the back of the Episcopal Palace

ruins (it's not immediately obvious, but is opposite the church that has been converted into the Biblioteca Municipal).

Boat trips From the quay (*cais*) at the dam, near the municipal swimming pool, Europarques (☏ 273 432 396, �𝕨 europarques.com) runs year-round boat trips on the Douro through the dramatic rock gorge (at least one departure daily; €16).

ACCOMMODATION

Miranda boasts a sizeable range of places to stay, all bar one clustered into two or three streets in the new part of town, just off the traffic circle. They are nothing particularly special, but anything down Rua do Mercado (the street closest to the top of the gorge) enjoys superb views.

★**A Morgadinha** Rua do Mercado 57 ☏ 273 438 050, �𝕨 hotelmorgadinha.pt. Though not much to look at from the outside, this is the best of the guesthouses on this street, with good-value, spick-and-span en-suite rooms – open your curtains in the morning to amazing dam views, and then gawp some more from the balcony over breakfast. **€40**

Parador Santa Catarina Largo da Pousada ☏ 273 431 005, ⟲ hotelparadorsantacatarina.pt. Right on the edge of the modern development outside the old town, with twelve well-appointed rooms offering dizzying views into the gorge – as do the bar and upmarket restaurant. **€110**

Santa Cruz Rua Abade Baçal 61 ☏ 273 431 374. The only place to stay in the old town, with an entrance on the square by the castle ruins. It's been done up over the years – the rooms are modern but unexceptionally basic and occasionally musty, but at these prices they're good value for money. **€35**

EATING AND DRINKING

Locals maintain that Miranda is home to some of Portugal's most tender meat, in the form of *posta à Mirandesa*, basically a huge wedge of steak. You can sample it at just about every **restaurant** in town, although there's a never-ending local debate as to which place serves the best. You can have a **drink** in the places below, or enjoy tables under the trees at the lively café-bar in the Episcopal Palace gardens.

Capa d'Honras Trav do Castelo 1 ☏ 273 432 699. Old-town restaurant (just through the walls, on the right) that takes the flowing medieval capes traditionally worn during important events as its theme. As for the food, it's aimed at tourists – meat grills and *posta* and no fewer than a dozen versions of *bacalhau*, with most dishes costing around €13. Daily noon–3pm & 7–10.30pm.

★**O Mirandês** Rua D. Dinis 7 ☏ 273 431 418. This hotel restaurant gets our vote for prime *posta à Mirandesa*, prepared by cooks beavering away in full view of the dining room, which looks out over the Fresno River. There's a straightforward menu of grills, meat and fish, and €20 gets you the works. Find it just off the traffic circle, below the old town avenue (the road is signposted "Universidade"). June–Sept daily noon–3pm & 7–10.30pm; Oct–May Mon–Sat noon–3pm & 7–10.30pm.

O Moinho Rua do Mercado 47 ☏ 273 431 116. All the restaurants on Rua do Mercado offer cavernous dining rooms with big windows onto the gorge, and menus aimed squarely at Spanish day-trippers. This is no different, but it does also serve pizza and pasta and is remarkably good value, since you can easily eat for €10–12. Daily noon–4pm & 7–10pm.

Bragança

BRAGANÇA is the historic capital of Trás-os-Montes, settled since the very earliest times but acquiring a regional, and later national, importance from the twelfth century onwards. It's this medieval period that gave Bragança its distinctive hillside profile of a well-preserved old town and soaring castle keep, sitting inside a complete circuit of forbidding granite walls. Known as the Cidadela (citadel), it's the embodiment of the town's dynastic history under the sway of the dukes of Bragança – the extended family of Portuguese kings and emperors who ruled from 1640 (following independence from Spain) until the advent of the Republic in 1910.

Despite its historical weight, hit Bragança out of the short summer season and things can seem a bit dreary. Nowhere else in the north will you see just how down on its luck Portugal is, with derelict buildings and long-deserted shops dominating every street. On these days retire to the **citadel**, the main **museum** and **riverside gardens**, the most compelling reasons for a visit. Just to the north broods the Parque Natural de Montesinho (see p.372), though you'll need your own wheels to visit as public transport is threadbare.

7

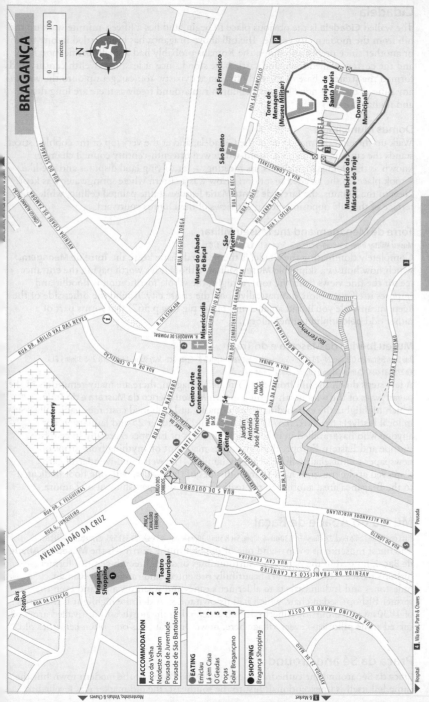

BRAGANÇA

N

0   100
meters

CIDADELA

São Francisco

Torre de
Menagem
(Museu Militar)

Igreja de
Santa Maria

Domus
Municipalis

São Bento

RUA SÃO FRANCISCO

RUA S! CONDESTÁVEL

RUA JOSÉ BECA

RUA S. JOÃO

RUA SERRA PINTA

RUA T. COELHO

Museu Ibérico da
Máscara e do Traje

São
Vicente

Museu do Abade
de Baçal

RUA MIGUEL TORGA

RUA CONSELHEIRO ABILIO BEÇA

R. DA ESTACADA

Misericórdia

R. MARQUES DE POMBAL

RUA DOS COMBATENTES DA GRANDE GUERRA

RUA DAS MORGADINHAS

Rio Fervença

ESTRADA DE TURISMO

RUA DR. ABILIO VAZ DAS NEVES

RUA DR. H. D. CONCEIÇÃO

RUA EMIDIO NAVARRO

Centro Arte
Contemporânea

TRAV. DA MISERICÓRDIA

RUA H. ANIBAL

PRAÇA
CAMÕES

RUA DA PRAÇA

Sé

PRAÇA
DA SÉ

Cemetery

Cultural Centre

RUA ALMIRANTE REIS

RUA DO PAÇO

LARGO DOS
CORREIOS

RUA 5 DE OUTUBRO

RUA ABI. HERCULANO

RUA DR. A. REBUÇA

Jardim
António
José Almeida

RUA DR. A. ALMADA

RUA DR. A. ALMEIDA

RUA ALEXANDRE HERCULANO

RUA DR. F. FELGUEIRAS

RUA G. JUNQUEIRO

AVENIDA JOÃO DA CRUZ

PRAÇA
CAVALEIRO
FERREIRA

Bragança
Shopping

Teatro
Municipal

RUA DA ESTAÇÃO

Bus
Station

AVENIDA DR. FRANCISCO SÁ CARNEIRO

RUA CAV. FERREIRA

RUA DO LORETO

RUA ADELINO AMARO DA COSTA

AVENIDA 22 DE MAIO

AVENIDA CIDADE DE ZAMORA

R. OMÓO RAMIRO RAMÃO

Pousada

Pousada

Vila Real, Porto & Chaves

Hospital

Montesinho, Vinhais & Chaves

Market

ACCOMMODATION

Arco da Velha	2
Nordeste Shalom	4
Pousada de Juventude	1
Pousada de São Bartolomeu	3

EATING

Emiclau	1
Lá em Casa	2
O Geadas	5
Poças	4
Solar Bragançano	3

SHOPPING

| Braganca Shopping | 1 |

Cidadela

The walled **Cidadela** is the obvious place to begin, and lies a fifteen-minute walk up the hill from the modern city centre. The hill above Bragança has been settled in one form or another since prehistoric times; the Romans probably had a small fortification here; and the current walled town and castle have stood since at least the twelfth century and formed the strategic base of the early Bragança dynasty. You can get up onto the **walls** any time of day, but don't let small children run around freely as there are long drops and no handrails.

Domus Municipalis

Walk up through the main gate of the Cidadela, and at the very top of the cobbled street stands the curious, pentagonal, multi-windowed fifteenth-century council chamber known as the **Domus Municipalis**. Its meetings – for solving land disputes and the like – took place on the arcaded first floor; below was a cistern where springwater was kept. Next to the Domus, the **Igreja de Santa Maria** features a fine painted ceiling, while the terrace of the café opposite offers great views of the Domus courtyard.

Torre de Menagem and the Museu Militar

Museu Militar Tues–Sun 9am–noon & 2–5pm • €1 • ☎ 273 322 378

Completely dominating the citadel is the restored castle keep, the **Torre de Menagem**, which now houses a skippable **Museu Militar**, although it's worth paying the entrance fee for the fine views from the top. At night, the whole fortification is floodlit and imposes itself even more dramatically upon the entire city. Round the other side of the keep, meanwhile you'll find an ancient granite pig (see p.362) that forms part of a rather odd **pelourinho** (stone pillory).

Museu Ibérico da Máscara e do Traje

Rua Dom Fernando O Bravo 24–26 • Tues–Sun: June–Sept 9am–1pm & 3–6pm; Oct–May 9am–12.30pm & 2–5.30pm • €1 • ☎ 273 381 008, ⓦ museudamascara.cm-braganca.pt

A few steps down the hill from the Torre de Menagem, there are many reminders of the pagan ways of the wild north in the modern **Museu Ibérico da Máscara e do Traje**, which highlights the extraordinary ritual masks and ribboned costumes habitually seen in local **festivals** (see box, p.371) held between December 25 and January 9. For anyone who has travelled in other mountain areas of Europe, especially in central Europe and Eastern Europe, these costumes made out of anything from strips of newspaper to horsehair will be strangely familiar. The weird-and-wonderful garb displayed at the museum hails from both sides of the border, with one floor dedicated to the Bragança area, another to the region around the Spanish town of Zamora.

Museu do Abade de Baçal

Rua Consilhiere Abilio Beça 27 • Tues–Fri 9.30am–5.30pm, Sat & Sun 9.30am–6pm • €3 • ☎ 273 331 595, ⓦ mabadebacal.com

The finest museum in town – and one of the best in the north – is the **Museu do Abade de Baçal**, housed in the handsome surroundings of an eighteenth-century former bishop's palace. The exhibits are beautifully presented, and range from Roman milestones and Indian caskets to aldermen's canes and weathervanes, and even the former Bishop's sedan chair, which had its own toilet. A definite highlight is the series of 1930s watercolours by Alberto de Sousa depicting the northeast's unrivalled array of carved stone pillories – every village here, however mean, has one, often centuries old.

Praça da Sé and around

Praça da Sé, around the cathedral, is essentially the centre of the modern town but the cathedral itself is unexceptional. Just to the southeast, the old market was levelled to

create the large square of **Praça do Camões** (part of the market facade was left *in situ*), with its shard of modern sculpture; the square is also home to a cultural centre and library (in a former convent), a contemporary art centre (with changing exhibitions) and landscaped town gardens.

The riverside

A walk down along the **Rio Fervença** is perhaps the best surprise – an ingenious network of paths, boardwalks and footbridges hug and crisscross the river as it rushes through a small gorge below town. You can follow this out under the castle walls, past olden-days reminders – chicken sheds, cabbage patches, tumbledown cottages (and one rather splendid gnome garden) – and in under ten minutes you're in open countryside.

ARRIVAL AND INFORMATION

By bus Local and long-distance buses operate out of what was once the train station, at the northern end of Avenida João da Cruz (note the benches, set on wheels on false old tracks). The various companies all post timetables at their office windows, including services across the border into Spain (Zamora and onwards).
Destinations Braga (2–6 daily; 4–5hr); Chaves (1 daily; 2hr 10min); Lisbon (6–8 daily; up to 7hr 30min); Miranda do Douro (Mon–Fri 1 daily; 1hr 20min); Mirandela (13 daily; 1hr); Mogadouro (Mon–Fri 1 daily; 1hr 30min); Porto (at least hourly; 3hr); Vila Real (at least hourly; 1hr 30min); Vinhais (1 daily; 30min).

BRAGANÇA

By car Bragança is 120km northeast of Vila Real, via Mirandela, on the fast IP4/A4, or a very winding but picturesque 100km east of Chaves (N103). In Spain, the nearest big city is attractive Zamora, around 100km southeast. Driving into the city is easy; parking is a different matter, as the centre is almost all metered. For free, all-day parking, your best bet is up at the citadel.
Information The turismo is on Avenida Cidade de Zamora (Oct–May Mon–Fri 9am–1pm & 2–5.30pm, Sat 10am–12.30pm; June–Sept Mon–Sat 9am–1pm & 2–6pm; Oct–May Mon–Fri 9am–1pm & 2–5.30pm, Sat 10am–12.30pm; ☏ 273 381 273, ⊚ cm-bragança.pt).

ACCOMMODATION

There's a fair amount of cheap, if uninspiring, signposted central accommodation, or consider staying outside the city in one of the *turismo rural* options (see p.378) within the Parque Natural de Montesinho, most under half an hour's drive away. The nearest **campsite** to town, the *Parque Campismo do Inatel*, on the França road, isn't actually that good – there's better summer camping in the park at Rio de Onor (see p.376) or Cepo Verde (see p.378).

Arco da Velha Rua D. Fernao ☏ 966 787 208, ⊚ turismobraganca.com. A restored townhouse inside the *cidadela* – on your immediate right as you come through the main (west) gate – offering by-the-night self catering accommodation with a homely, intimate feel. There are only a couple of rooms (sleeping up to five in total) and advance bookings are essential. Parking available. €90
Nordeste Shalom Av Abade Baçal ☏ 273 331 667, ⊚ hotel-shalom.com.pt. An obvious choice for budget travellers, this very professionally run hotel near the hospital, about a 10min walk south of the Teatro Municipal,

has wood-rich rooms, pristine bathrooms with baths, 24-hour reception and heavy discounts in low season. Breakfast is included and there's a café, ATM and supermarket next door. €45
Pousada de Juventude Av 22 de Maio ☏ 273 329 231, ⊚ pousadasjuventude.pt. Roughly 1km west of the centre, this modern hostel has a mix of accommodation, from smallish dorms to neat little private rooms (some suitable for families, €54) and a decent range of facilities, including laundry service and café-bar. Dorms €13, doubles €32
★**Pousada de São Bartolomeu** Estrada do Turismo

BRAGANÇA'S FESTIVALS

Bragança's major festivals include the **Festa de Nossa Senhora das Graças** (Aug 12–22), featuring lots of cultural events and traditional music, and the **Romaria de São Bartolomeu** (Aug 24), an annual religious celebration involving solemn processions and rather wilder concerts and night-time festivities. The **Feira das Cantarinhas** (May 2 & 3) is a crafts fair dedicated to the clay water jug (*cantarinha*) which was once used to store the gifts given to a bride on her wedding day.

📞 273 331 493, 🌐 pousadas.pt. High up on the opposite side of the river to the centre, Bragança's best address is all about its castle and countryside views. Built in the late 1950s, it has a comfortable, country-house feel, rooms with wood-block floors and big balconies, plenty of exposed stone and a bar sporting a huge fireplace. There's a good regional restaurant (meals €40–50), and an inviting circular pool. It's 1km by road from the centre – follow the signs – and you can walk down to river and town (steeply uphill on the way back) in around 15min. **€130**

EATING AND ENTERTAINMENT

Bragança is a traditional town full of traditional **restaurants**; woe betide vegetarians. Although it's a university town, there's not much in the way of **nightlife** save a couple of bars in the Cidadela and some others in an arcade, a 5min walk down Avenida Dr. Francisco Sá Carneiro.

RESTAURANTS

Emiclau Rua Almirante Reis 31–35 📞 273 324 114. Down a flight of steps off Rua Almirante Reis, this basement eatery has a pretty standard, unoffensive dining room where you can enjoy meat and fish (beef dishes and *cataplana*) and the occasional regionally flavoured special. Mains €6–18. Daily noon–3.30pm & 6–10pm.

Lá em Casa Rua Marquês de Pombal 7 📞 273 322 111. A convivial place, decked out in the kind of faux-rustic style so beloved of northern restaurateurs. It's the usual meat and fish menu, though the chef goes light on the local mountain critters. Mains €6–12.50. Daily noon–3pm & 7–11pm.

O Geadas Rua do Loreto 📞 273 324 413, 🌐 geadas.net. Locals consider this the best choice in town for authentic regional food, from river trout to *cabrito* (kid), with dishes ferried to your impeccably-set table by a fleet of uniformed waiters (meals around €30). It's a short way out of the centre, just a 10min walk from the Sé. Mon–Sat noon–4pm & 7pm–midnight.

Poças Rua Combatentes da Grande Guerra 200 📞 273 331 428. A reliable family-run place, usually popular enough to fill a couple of floors, and serving excellent-value mains (€6–16), including mountain fare such as wild boar or partridge with chestnuts – washed down with a great *vinho da casa*. Rare in these parts, they also do a vegetarian menu (€16). Daily noon–10.30pm.

★ **Solar Bragançano** Pr da Sé 34 📞 274 323 875. Enjoyably old-fashioned *casa típica*, where you dine in chandelier-hung, oak-panelled rooms, or in the garden in summer. Mains start around €7.50, though for the regional dishes of which the restaurant is most proud – pheasant with chestnuts, say, or partridge cooked with grapes – it's more like €15 a serving. Tues–Sun noon–3pm & 7–10pm.

ARTS AND MUSIC

Teatro Municipal Pr Prof. Cavaleiro de Ferreira 📞 273 302 744, 🌐 teatromunicipal.cm-braganca.pt. The town's cultural anchor is this impressive wedge of modern architecture that boasts a good year-round music and theatre programme.

SHOPPING

Bragança Shopping Av Sá Carneiro 2 📞 273 323 261, 🌐 brancashopping.com. Near the bus station is the city's sparkling new shopping centre with international and Portuguese chain stores galore – and possibly the cause of so many empty shops elsewhere in town. Daily 10am–10pm.

DIRECTORY

Hospital Avenida Abade Baçal (📞 273 310 800).
Pharmacy Farmácia Confiança, Avenida João da Cruz 76 (📞 273 323 226).
Police PSP, Rua Dr. Manuel Bento 📞 273 303 400; GNR, Avenida General Humberto Delgado 📞 273 331 864.

Post office Largo dos Correios (Mon–Fri 8.30am–5.30pm, Sat 9am–12.30pm).
Taxis There's usually a fleet of taxis parked on Avenida João da Cruz, on the opposite side from the cafés, or call 📞 273 322 138.

Parque Natural de Montesinho

There are still a few places in Portugal that truly feel like the middle of nowhere, and the **Parque Natural de Montesinho** is one of them. Located in the far northeast, hard up against the Spanish border, the heather-clad hills, its verdant grass plains and dense oak forests look much as they have done for centuries. The park itself – lying north and west of Bragança – covers 751 square kilometres, and has a dwindling population of eight thousand distributed between ninety-odd

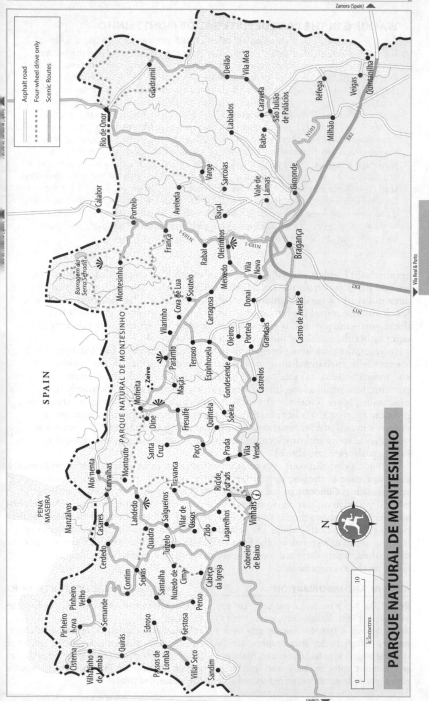

PARQUE NATURAL DE MONTESINHO

WALKING IN THE PARQUE NATURAL DE MONTESINHO

There are currently a dozen waymarked **hiking trails** (*pecursos pedestres*) in the Parque Natural de Montesinho, mostly short (half-day, from around 8km), and well marked and maintained, though you should always expect changes and variations over time. There are free, glossy foldout brochures for each, available from the park information offices (see p.379); they are in Portuguese but the route maps are useful. Boards at the starting points (usually in village centres) also show the routes; the waymarks are the usual red-and-yellow stripes and arrows. The walk at **Molmenta** provides a good introduction to the scenery, though if we had to pick just one route it would be that at **Montesinho**, which is a higher, more dramatic rock-and-reservoir circuit. The **Vilarinho** route is also interesting, winding through the *serra*'s characteristic heather-clad hills and oak woods, though the route-marking is less than perfect on this – you have to be prepared to cross a river or two and not panic when you lose the waymarks at times. The park has also marked out a **two-day trail** (55km) that loops around Vilarinho and Montesinho (where you'd stay the night) – this uses red-and-white paint markers (which sometimes duplicate parts of other trails). Finally, if you were really keen to see more of the park on foot, consider staying at the *Lagosta Perdida* in Montesinho (see p.377), which has prepared a series of self-guided hiking trails for guests that fan out from the village.

granite-built hamlets and villages, many of which have had so little mainstream contact that they retain their old Roman or Visigothic names. In many ways it's the same old story of rural abandonment, echoed by the similar desertion of many of the distinctive round pigeon houses (*pombal*, plural *pombais*), that are a feature of the region – the pigeons, it seems, like the people, prefer an easier existence in the cities rather than pecking out a living in the countryside.

However, the park hasn't been entirely bypassed by modern life. Villages substantially unchanged since medieval times are connected by new roads and show the unmistakable signs of *emigrante*-funded brick-and-concrete construction, while a long line of wind turbines snakes across the northern mountains. More positively, the local councils and park authorities are trying to promote tourism that's beneficial to the region. A flurry of brown signs points visitors towards *aldeias preservadas* (preserved villages), archeological and nature sites, picnic spots and tiny local museums, and there's also a good network of hiking paths (see box above).

With just a day, and your own car, the western loop from **Vinhais** to **Moimenta** would show you some of the best scenery (and has one of the finest short walks). Contrasting villages such as **Gimonde** or fascinating **Rio de Onor** are also easily seen from Bragança, while if you plan on staying overnight in the park the no-contest winner is **Montesinho**, with its boutique guesthouse and excellent walking. Otherwise, **accommodation** in the park is scarce, and cafés, shops and **restaurants** even more so – you may be better off heading 20km or so north up the França–Portelo road to the Spanish town of Puebla de Sanabria, where there are good hotels and restaurants and a better campsite than either on the Portuguese side.

ARRIVAL AND INFORMATION

PARQUE NATURAL DE MONTESINHO

By car The two main access points for the park are Bragança and Vinhais, but public transport within the park is limited – you can only reach a very few villages by bus from Bragança, and the timetable does not allow for easy day-trips. Having your own transport opens up many more possibilities, especially in the far eastern and western sections of the

park, home to countless little villages just waiting to be discovered.

Information You can pick up a free park map and walking brochures at the park information office in Vinhais (see p.379), part of an excellent interpretation centre that's an essential visit in any case. There's official park information (in Portuguese) on ⓦ icnf.pt.

TORRE DE MENAGEM, CHAVES (P.381) >

Eastern park: Gimonde to Rio de Onor

There are local STUB buses from Bragança bus station to **Gimonde** and up to **Rio de Onor** via **Varge**. In neither case are you going to be able to make much of a day-trip, because of inconvenient departure times, but as there's good accommodation, a restaurant and a waymarked walk in Gimonde, and a summer campsite in Rio de Onor, an overnight stay might be the answer.

Gimonde and Varge

GIMONDE, 5km east of Bragança, is a collection of mostly traditional houses where the rivers Onor, Sabor and Igrejas all meet near a Romanesque bridge. Heading back towards Bragança there's a signposted turn for Rio de Onor, which leads you first through **VARGE**, where there are more ancient houses and a decent café-restaurant by the bridge. Beyond Varge is a bleak landscape of moorland, set against wild mountains that are dusted with snow as late as May.

Rio de Onor and around

Postcard-pretty **RIO DE ONOR**, on the Spanish border, is 25km north of Bragança, a half-hour drive though longer on the bus. Curiously, there are twin settlements here – one in Spain (called Riohonor de Castilla) and one in Portugal – but two stones marked with an "E" and "P" respectively, and a change from cobbles on the Portuguese side to tarmac on the Spanish, are all that have delineated the frontier for years. Until recently, the locals even mostly spoke a hybrid dialect known as *Rionorês*. The twin villages are sited in a lush valley on either side of the Rio Onor: schist-built houses with wooden balconies flank skinny alleyways, though some of the houses have been renovated, and there's a new bridge and parking area. Facilities are limited to an old **bar** in the Portuguese "half" of the village – complete with animal heads, antique keys and walking sticks – and a **shop** (signposted "Tienda"), down to the right on the Spanish side.

If you can get someone to point out the track you can walk over the hills on the old route to **Guadramil** (7km) and back, for a look at an even more decrepit village. There's also a road, which provides a diverting circuit for drivers, back to Gimonde (30km), via Guadramil, Deilão and São Julião de Palácios.

ACCOMMODATION AND EATING   EASTERN PARK

GIMONDE

Restaurante Típico Dom Roberto Rua Coronel Álvaro Cepeda 1 ☏ 273 302 510, 🖰 amontesinho.pt. Gimonde village has become something of a personal fiefdom of the family who run the restaurant by the bridge, with its cosy bar and rustic dining room (regional dishes from around €10, cheaper lunch available). Not only do they sell their own smoked sausages and other local produce, but they have self-catering accommodation in half a dozen restored properties around the village, ranging from the old teacher's house to the manorial *Quinta das Covas*. An

information office and shop by the restaurant can show you the options; prices are room only (and €10 cheaper outside peak summer months), though breakfast is available. Restaurant daily noon–11pm. €55

RIO DE ONOR

Parque de Campismo de Rio de Onor ☏ 273 927 061. There's a tree-shaded campsite at the entrance to the village on the Bragança side. Facilities are limited but it does have a café. Closed Oct–March. Pitch €4.50, plus €4.25 per adult

Central park: França, Montesinho and around

The main touristed route in the Parque Natural de Montesinho is the central spine north of Bragança, up to **França**, Portelo and then on to Puebla de Sanabria in Spain, with a side turning for **Montesinho**. The easy drive from Spain, and proximity to Bragança, mean the villages seem to have a little more about them than further east or west, and restored houses and riverside picnic areas are the result. STUB buses ply the route, and will get you to Montesinho if you want to stay the night.

França

Ten kilometres north of Bragança, unassuming **FRANÇA** is locally famous for its chestnuts (widely available in Bragança restaurants) and *chouriço*, while the village still has a number of tumbledown streets which remain rooted in the distant past. You can potter about by the **Rio Sabor** here quite happily, and a good track (left, off the main road, after the bridge) follows the course of the river for some way. There's a small café-bar in the village by the bridge, and horseriding and trekking with the Centro Hípico de França (€12 for a 30min trek; ☎273 919 141, ⍵centrohipicofranca.com).

Montesinho

Flanked by wind-whipped pine plantations and dramatic granite outcrops, the hardy village of **MONTESINHO** packs centuries of history into its manure-mottled streets. Chickens cluck behind wire in carefully tended allotments, while winter wood lies stacked up against solid slate-roofed houses, many of which have been handsomely restored. There's local honey on sale, and an artisan or two at work, but it's still hardly what you'd call touristy. It is the end of the line as far as the road is concerned (roughly 8km northwest of França), but the walking around here is magnificent, with a particularly good marked circular trail (8km; 3hr) running up to the mountain-ringed, turbine-flanked **Barragem da Serra Serrada**.

7

ACCOMMODATION AND EATING   MONTESINHO

There's plenty of rustically restored self-catering accommodation in the village (busy in July & Aug); you can also ask about rooms at the *Café Montesinho*, or at the other café in the *Casa do Povo* ("parish rooms"), by the water fountain, where they'll serve you a beer or a fearsomely murky shot of *licor Giesta*, which is home-made *aguardente* mixed with honey.

★**Lagosta Perdida** Rua do Cimo 4 ☎273 919 031, ⍵lagostaperdida.com. One of the best places to stay in the park, the "Lost Lobster" is a boutique restoration of an old granite house in the middle of the village, run by a convivial Dutch–English couple. Chestnut-wood beams, polished floors and exposed stone set the tone for half-a-dozen agreeable guest rooms and enchanting public areas, including an amazing central space with glass roof. There's eco-friendly solar- and olive-stone-fired power and a heated outdoor pool, while meals are also contemporary in style, using locally sourced ingredients. Dinner is €15 a head; room rates drop to €95 between Oct and April. They also offer horseriding at their riding centre in França (see above). **€125**

Western park

For the western portion of the Parque Natural de Montesinho, access is easiest from the town of Vinhais (see p.378), 31km west of Bragança. There's no useful public transport, so a car is essential, but you'll be able to see the best of the local scenery and the dramatically sited villages of **Moimenta**, **Dine**, **Vilarinho** and **Gondesende** in a single day, combining driving and some walking.

Moimenta

Leaving Vinhais on the Spain (Espanha) road, through Rio de Fornos, it's a quick half an hour on a good road, through increasingly dramatic countryside, before arriving at tranquil **MOIMENTA**, 23km north. There are new villas on the road above, but in the heart of the village Moimenta unfolds its charms slowly – filled with old stone cottages and rows of sagging wooden houses perched precariously atop granite pillars. The **circular walk** from here (8km; 2–3hr) – look for the route-marker on the top road, by the green park information board – winds up to a viewpoint before taking in two bridges on the babbling Rio Tuela, the second a gorgeous medieval span with ancient stone-cobbled path leading all the way back up to the village. There's a very small shop in Moimenta, with an occasionally open tavern next door, and a café on the road above the village – you'll barely be able to get so much as a

bag of crisps in any of them, though you might muster the fixings of a picnic in the shop. (Don't count on it: when asked where the nearest place to eat is, the villagers simply shrug and say "Spain").

Dine
A new road runs from Moimenta over heather-and-gorse moorland towards Mofreita, with sweeping views north to Spain and the wind turbines on the distant snow-capped mountains. When you reach the Mofreita road, turn right (for Vinhais) to find the enchanting village of **DINE**, constructed on descending cobbled streets that afford sweeping views of the valley. A cave excavation here unearthed bones, cooking implements, flints and arrowheads dating back to 4000 BC, and you might find someone in the small **interpretation centre** by the church who can show you around.

Vilarinho
East of Mofreita, on the Bragança road, there are signposted diversions – to the *aldeia preservada* (preserved village) of Zeive, for example – before you drop down into the more pastoral lands around the dung-spattered hamlet of **VILARINHO**. This has another good waymarked walk (8km; 3hr), as well as two basic village cafés, including the magnificently misnamed *Café Tropical*.

Gondesende
From Vilarinho, it's 16km back to Bragança, or you can cut south at Cova de Lua towards the Vinhais road again. You'll run through more pretty hamlets, such as **GONDESENDE**, which has a couple of *turismo rural* places offering rooms in self-catering houses, as well as the single biggest tourism complex in the region, the *Cepo Verde* campsite.

ACCOMMODATION AND EATING   GONDESENDE

Cepo Verde Lugar da Vinha do Santo, Gondesende ☎273 999 371, ⓦmontesinho.com. Rustic campsite and stone-and-wood cabins set amid chestnut and oak trees, just up from the N103 Vinhais road. There's an outdoor pool and restaurant too. Online booking possible. Closed Oct–March. Pitch **€3.95**, plus **€4.25** per adult; cabin **€40**

Vinhais
Some 31km east of Bragança and 65km west of Chaves lies the small, gritty town of **VINHAIS**, the western gateway to the Parque Natural de Montesinho (see p.372). The town is reached via the **N103**, which skirts the park's southern fringes and offers a twisting white-knuckle ride through some of northern Portugal's wildest terrain. The tiny, walled old centre of Vinhais hugs a prominent mound above a wide valley to the south, while a catwalk-style terrace just off from the main through-street offers some amazing views down over manicured municipal lawns and ornamental waterways, and out to the immaculately tended fields of the surrounding countryside. Vinhais is known for its ability to smoke any type of animal product – signs in town advertise it as the "Capital do Fumeiro" (Smoked Meat Capital) – and the various different types of sausage made in the region, including *chouriço*, *salpicão* and *alheira*, are all celebrated in an annual festival, the **Feira do Fumeiro** (second weekend in Feb; ⓦfumeiro.org).

Just across from the Vinhais turismo on the main road, an information board marks the start of a 9km circular **walking trail** on farm tracks and paths. The route runs via the **Parque Biológico de Vinhais** (daily 9am–9pm; free entry, fees for activities; ☎273 771 040, ⓦparquebiologicodevinhais.com), an eco-park just outside town, which offers nature trails and plenty of animals – from deer to donkeys – as well as accommodation (see opposite).

Centro de Interpretação do Parque Natural
Casa da Vila • Tues–Sun 9am–12.30pm & 2–5.30pm • Free • ☎ 273 771 416, ⓦ icnf.pt

If you're heading for the Parque Natural de Montesinho, stop in at the **Centro de Interpretação**, an imaginatively conceived information centre in the Casa da Vila in the old town, with plenty of interesting audiovisual displays and useful pointers towards visiting the park's museums and archeological sites (*núcleos*).

ARRIVAL AND INFORMATION   VINHAIS

By Car Vinhais is on the scenic road between Bragança and Chaves; you'll certainly need a car to get here, as it's served by just one daily bus from both towns.
Information The modern turismo is on Rua Nova da

Calçada, the main road through town, near to where buses stop (Mon–Fri 9am–1pm & 2–5pm, Sat & Sun 10am–1pm & 2–5pm; ☎ 273 770 309, ⓦ cm-vinhais.pt).

ACCOMMODATION AND EATING

Casa de Mencha Rio de Fornos, 3km north of Vinhais ☎ 934 143 171, ⓦ casadamencha.com. A simple country house with a couple of cosy bedrooms, kitchen, a log fire and a balcony with views. To find it, drive out of Vinhais on the Spain/Montesinho park road. No meals available. **€60**
Parque Biológico de Vinhais Alto da Cidadelha, Vinhais ☎ 273 771 040, ⓦ parquebiologicodevinhais.com. On the outskirts of Vinhais, this eco-park has camping

and cabin accommodation on site and an associated inn, the simple *Hospedaria do Parque*, 3km away in the village of Rio de Fornos. The cabins (€65) sleep four to eight people, and have a little kitchen; rooms at the inn (€35) are more for groups. Tent pitch €3, plus €3 per adult
Vasco da Gama Rua da Calç. 24 ☎ 937 314 251. Typically neat and tidy *churrasqueira* on the main road through town offering a menu of inexpensive grilled meat and fish. Daily noon–2.30pm & 7–10pm.

Chaves

Arguably the most attractive town in Trás-os-Montes, riverside **CHAVES** lies 12km from the Spanish border, which tells you all you need to know about its erstwhile strategic importance – as do the connotations of its name, which means "keys". It's also a minor spa town, founded as Aquae Flaviae in 78 AD by the Romans, who built an impressive bridge here across the Rio Tâmega in the first or second century AD. After the Romans came a long line of squabbling forces, from Visigoths and Moors to the Spanish and French, which explains the surviving fortresses, towers and walls that ring the medieval old town. The history is obvious from the monuments, but the welcome surprise is the evident charm of Chaves, from its handsome squares and balconied old-townhouses to its intricately-planted flowerbeds and riverside gardens. The spa is an obvious money-spinner, but many pass over the chance to take the waters, preferring instead to sample Chaves' other significant attractions – namely its smoked hams, sausages and red wine.

> ### PUTTING THE FIZZ BACK INTO THE SPAS
> It was the Romans who first developed the spas of northern Portugal, not only in Chaves (their name for the town was **Aquae Flaviae**) but also at several other nearby thermal stations. Even now, for example, **Carvalhelhos** spring water is a big deal in Portugal – it comes from a small town around 25km west of Chaves in the Barroso hills. But it's the historic spa of **Vidago**, 17km south of Chaves down the Rio Tâmega, that has the highest profile, centred on the opulent Art Nouveau *Vidago Palace Hotel* (ⓦ vidagopalace.com), transformed into a five-star resort by top architect Álvaro Siza Vieira. A similar renovation has taken place 20km south of Vidago at the old spa of **Pedras Salgadas**, source of another famous Portuguese mineral water, where there's new accommodation and revitalized spa facilities as well as more resort and leisure outlets.

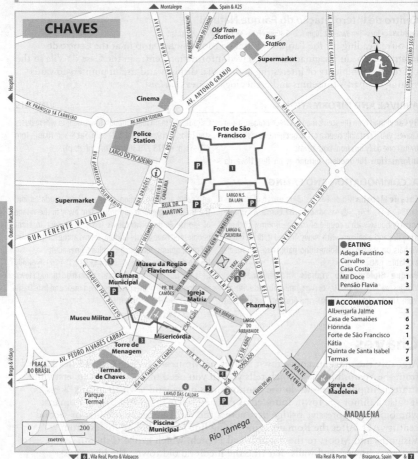

Ponte Trajano and the river

The wide curve of the Rio Tâmega is crossed by the sturdy Roman bridge, the **Ponte Trajano** (after the Emperor Trajan); it's closed to most traffic so you can easily stroll across and examine the Roman milestones erected in the middle. With its modern repaving job, the bridge doesn't feel old at all when you are actually on it – descend to the river banks to admire its ancient chunky arches. Both sides of the river have landscaped promenades, and a couple of newer footbridges allow you a riverside circuit. The characterful Madalena district, just across the Roman bridge, is almost like a separate village with its crumbling houses and handsome public gardens.

Termas de Chaves and Parque Termal

Largo das Caldas • ☎ 276 332 445, ⊛ termasdechaves.com

The main gardens on the town side of the Roman bridge, past the municipal swimming pool, are the site of the **Termas de Chaves** spa buildings and **Parque Termal**, in front of the landmark *Hotel Aquae Flaviae*. The spa complex has a bunkerish feel – Baden-Baden or Marienbad it ain't – and the various treatments offered here aren't

really for casual visitors, though in summer you can visit the *nascente* (spring) in the circular, part-covered building in the square outside to take a drink of the waters. These emerge at a piping 73°C (the hottest spring water in Iberia) and are dispensed free by a white-coated medic.

Torre de Menagem and the Museu Militar

Museu Militar Mon–Fri 9am–12.30pm & 2–5.30pm, Sat & Sun 2–5.30pm • €1, includes entry to Museu da Região Flaviense

Up the hill from the river, the squat fourteenth-century keep, the **Torre de Menagem**, is almost all that's left of Chaves' castle (various bits of surviving wall crop up here and there around town). Inside is the **Museu Militar**, the highlight of which are the views of the town and the surrounding hills from the terrace battlements (though the terrace isn't always open). The little floral **gardens** below the tower are a delight – the ideal picnic spot with a view.

Museu da Região Flaviense

Praça de Camões • Mon–Fri 9am–12.30pm & 2–5.30pm, Sat & Sun 2–5.30pm • €1, includes entry to Museu Militar • ☎ 276 340 500

The main town museum, the **Museu da Região Flaviense**, is set on Praça de Camões, the town hall square, in a palace that once belonged to the Dukes of Bragança. It's a tiny, one-room affair but displays some Roman-era artefacts, from coins and fragmented mosaics to engraved altars and milestones, as well as pre-Roman gold jewellery, spearheads and a Venus statue bearing the same plump features as those found in other far-flung regions of Europe.

Rua Direita and around

The old town streets beyond the Torre de Menagem are highly attractive, such as atmospheric **Rua Direita** with its leaning houses and antique wooden balconies. Traditional **shops** are still much to the fore and it's not hard to find butchers, bakers and probably even candlestick makers if you looked hard enough. Traditional black pottery, straw- and wicker-work are all widely available, as are loops of *alheira* sausage and smoked Chaves hams – the shelves of the town's butcher's shops (*talho* in Portuguese) prove that not a single piece of the pig goes to waste in these parts.

Forte de São Francisco

Chaves's military past presents itself most forcefully in the dramatic, high-walled, seventeenth-century **Forte de São Francisco**, a short walk up from the town centre. It was originally a convent, but was fortified during the Peninsular Wars, and then eventually converted again, this time into a rather grand hotel. No one minds if you walk in through the main gate and have a snoop around, though the vista-rich ramparts are now out of bounds; you can of course have a drink or meal within the walls at the hotel's bar and restaurant (see p.382). It's also possible to take a peek into the **Church of Nossa Senhora do Rosário**, still a working place of worship.

ARRIVAL AND INFORMATION
CHAVES

By bus The bus station (for Auto-Viação do Tâmega services; ☎ 276 332 384, ⓦ avtamega.pt) is a 10min walk north of the centre, behind the fort. There's a handy supermarket above the platforms, next to the old train station.

Destinations Bragança (1 daily; 2hr 10min); Coimbra (2–3 daily; 3–4hr); Lisbon (3 daily; 6hr 30min); Porto (6 daily;

2hr 15min); Vila Real (4–5 daily; 1hr 10min), Vinhais (2 daily; 50min).

By car Chaves is around 65km northeast of Vila Real, and it's a quick drive on a good road. You can be in Spain in 10min and in the city of Ourense (90km) under an hour later. There is ample parking in Chaves, often free (look for the word "gratis"), particularly in

the streets around Forte de São Francisco and down by the riverside gardens.

Information The turismo is at the top of the Terreiro do Cavalaria gardens (Mon–Fri 9am–6pm, Sat & Sun 10am–1pm; ☎ 276 348 180, ⓦ chaves.pt); little English is spoken.

ACCOMMODATION

Accommodation is plentiful, but spa business fills even the cheapest places in summer, so advance reservations are recommended. In winter you can have entire hotels to yourself. Some town-centre budget places are a bit long in the-tooth; the best place to look for cheap rooms is down Rua do Sol, on the way to the river. There are also some nice options out in the sticks, though you'll definitely need a car to reach them.

IN TOWN

Albergaria Jaime Rua Joaquim José Delgado ☎ 276 301 050, ⓦ albergariajaime.com.pt. This handsome, salmon-pink villa has been operating as a guesthouse since the late 1800s, although with rooms in a large rear extension it's now firmly in the hotel category. Rooms are reasonable without being remarkable, but it's a decent choice, with parking nearby. €60

Florinda Rua dos Açougues ☎ 276 333 392. Quirky old family-run place with cool rooms, polished hardwood floors and trim bathrooms. Breakfast is taken in the busy function room and includes some tasty home-made jams. €40

★**Forte de São Francisco** ☎ 276 333 700, ⓦ fortesaofrancisco.com. A chapel with tape-recorded Mass in the reception hall sets the tone for this atmospheric four-star hotel located in the fortress. The conversion is a sensitive blend of old and new, with pool, bar, replica traditional tavern and a restaurant offering a pricey take on updated regional cuisine. €100

★**Kátia** Rua do Sol 28 ☎ 276 324 446. The pick of the bunch on this street of cheaper options has friendly service and fine little rooms (some with balconies) above a good,

inexpensive restaurant. You'd be hard pressed to find anything better in town for this money. €45

Termas Rua do Tabolado ☎ 276 333 280. A concrete hulk close to the river that's a classic case of better inside than out – you get nice big rooms with laminate floors and full bathrooms, heating and a/c and, though it can be noisy out front, it's all pretty good value for money. Parking nearby. €35

OUT OF TOWN

Casa de Samaiões Samaiões ☎ 276 340 450, ⓦ hotel-casasamaioes.com. A cross between an upmarket hotel and a *turismo rural*, this seventeenth-century *quinta* combines traditional four-poster beds with rather more contemporary furnishings. It's 5km south of Chaves, set within lovely landscaped grounds complete with a charming pool that offers great views. €95

Quinta de Santa Isabel Santo Estevão ☎ 276 351 818, ⓦ quintadesantaisabel.com.pt. A traditional Trás-os-Montes country house with gardens and vineyards, 7km east of Chaves and 500m off the N103 to Bragança. Self-catering accommodation is in one of five rustic stone cottages which sleep two to four people. €40

EATING

There are lots of **restaurants**, all pretty reasonable though few stand out from the crowd. Good Chaves *presunto* and local sausages are on every menu; at Christmas particularly it's traditional to eat octopus (*polvo*), brought up dried from the coast, then boiled with potatoes and greens. Two or three **cafés** by the Roman bridge are the best places for a sundowner, and there are mini nightlife enclaves on Largo das Caldas (by the riverside gardens) and at the upper end of Travessa Cândido dos Reis.

★**Adega Faustino** Trav Cândido dos Reis ☎ 276 322 142, ⓦ adegafaustino.pt. Pass through huge red doors to find a cavernous former wine merchant's store, with a cobbled floor and huge barrels lined up behind the bar. The wine is good, and it's great for *petiscos*, including things like bean salad and *presunto*, and grilled main dishes, with almost everything costing between €4 and €9. Mon–Sat noon–midnight.

Carvalho Largo das Caldas ☎ 276 321 727. Rated as the best in town for regional food, and consequently more expensive than most (mains €10–16), but certainly the place to try the definitive *arroz de fumeiro* (rice with smoked meats) or *alheira* (sausage). There's always fish, too, and not just the ubiquitous *bacalhau* or *truta*.

Tues–Sat noon–3pm & 7–11pm, Sun noon–3pm.

Casa Costa Rua do Tabolado ☎ 276 323 568. Primarily a grill place, with a menu of dishes costing from €8.50–17. The speciality is *bacalhau à Costa* (oven-roast, with onions) or a gigantic Mirandês steak – half portions are available. There's also a vine-covered rear garden with bench-style tables, though it's not always open for dining. Daily 11am–3pm & 7pm–midnight.

Mil Doce Rua Dr. Augusto Figueiredo Fernandes 3. Lots of places sell Chaves' signature pastry, the *pastel de Chaves* (minced meat in a puff pastry case), but at this unassuming bakery-café they come straight from the oven. Daily 7.30am–7.30pm.

VIDAGO PALACE HOTEL (P.379) >

★**Pensão Flavia** Trav Cândido dos Reis 12 ☎961 693 890. A very odd concept for rural Portugal, the idea here is that your table is flooded with scrumptious *petiscos* (snacks), after which you order a main course and drinks. At the end you pay what you feel the meal was worth – there are no set prices or menu. The dining room is a large, light, characterful space below street level, full of rural knick-knacks and bottles of wine. The only downside is that staff speak no English. Mon & Wed–Sun 12.30–2.30pm & 7.30–10.30pm.

Montalegre

Some 45km west of Chaves, and a 10km detour off the N103, the historic frontier town of **MONTALEGRE** is the entry point to the eastern stretches of the Parque Nacional da Peneda-Gerês – though you'll really need your own transport to get into the park, as there are no onward buses. Even if you go no further, it's worth making the trip to Montalegre, not least for the sudden looming of its dramatic medieval **castle** as you approach town, lording it over the surrounding plains. You can walk up to the surviving keep and ruined walls (always open; free), and then saunter through the few immaculately restored old-town streets below, and while this takes just twenty minutes, Montalegre is charming enough to stretch your visit to take in lunch. There are half a dozen restaurants in town, most near the diminutive *pelourinho* square, just below the castle. All are big on the local Serra do Barroso produce, namely its huge steaks, smoked meats (*fumeiros*) and ham (*presunto*). There's even a whole festival dedicated to the products, the annual **Feira do Fumeiro e Presunto** (fourth week of January).

Around 8km south of town, a road leads to the huge **Barragem do Alto Rabagão**, around which you can pick up signs to swimming spots, old villages and walking trails.

INFORMATION   **MONTALEGRE**

Information The turismo is at Terreiro do Açougue 11 (daily 9am–1pm & 2–5.30pm; ☎ 276 510 205).

Into the Parque Nacional da Peneda-Gerês

The easternmost parts of the **Parque Nacional da Peneda-Gerês** lie in Trás-os-Montes, cut off from the main section in the Minho region by the Barragem de Paradela and the towering Serra do Gerês mountain range. Drivers already in the main park can approach from the south on the stunning mountain route from **Cabril**, but from Trás-os-Montes it's much easier to drive via Montalegre, from where the park and its villages are well signposted; you should be able to pick up walking leaflets from Montalegre's turismo (see above), but even without them you'll be able to find the trails, as they are adequately signposted. The best walk is at **Pitões das Júnias**, which is itself the single best target in this section of the park.

Pitões das Júnias

It's a terrific drive to **PITÕES DAS JÚNIAS**, 25km northwest of Montalegre, and set in one of the wildest corners of Portugal. The clustered brown-stone, red-tile buildings of

---

DEAD DRUNK

Montalegre is one of the Serra do Barroso settlements where you'll come across the so-called *Vinhos dos Mortos* – **Wines of the Dead**; try asking in local bars and restaurants. This is basically wine that matures in bottles buried underground, a practice that originated in 1809 when villagers, keen to protect their wine stocks from the invading French hordes, hid their bottles. When they dug them up again they were delighted to find that the contents tasted considerably better.

the village are framed by the most extraordinary jagged peaks (*pitões*) of the Gerês mountains, and the surroundings simply beg you to get out of your car and walk. Happily, there's an enjoyable **waymarked trail** (4km; 1hr 30min) that descends a stone path into a hidden valley where a gloriously sited, twelfth-century monastery and plunging waterfall await. Follow the brown signs for "Mosteiro" and "Cascata" and then the paint marks, which take you first to the monastery, then along a stepped boardwalk to the waterfall viewing point before looping back to the village. Pitões may be isolated, but it expects visitors: there's a car park at the top of the village.

ACCOMMODATION AND EATING PITÕES DAS JÚNIAS

Casa do Preto Pitões das Júnias ☎276 566 158, ⓦ casadopreto.com. An agreeable village restaurant and bar – the food is excellent, including produce from their own smokehouse. They also have decent guest rooms in an adjacent building. **€50**

Tourém

From the Pitões das Júnias turnoff on the Montalegre road, it's 10km north to the traditional village of **TOURÉM**, across a wild plateau of heather and roaming cattle. This is a drive that needs no excuse, though Tourém itself is a gem, albeit one very liberally coated with dung. It sits in a neatly cultivated valley by a **reservoir** (where there's swimming), with a bridge connecting it with Spain on the other side. Another easy, marked **trail** (2.5km) heads through the village past a communal stone oven, before climbing to a viewpoint above Tourém.

Paredes do Rio to Outeiro

The road from Montalegre runs southwest, passing **PAREDES DO RIO**, which sits high above the Rio Cávado in the valley below. Paredes itself is an ancient little place, notable for its *espigueiros* (grain stores).

Three kilometres further on, **OUTEIRO** is another charming cluster of old stone houses, this time overlooking the placid waters of the **Barragem de Paradela**, ringed by gnarled peaks. From here, you can head down over the dam and take the wild road towards Cabril for access to the main section of the park, or head south to **Venda Nova** and its own dam, 18km southeast on the main N103 (Chaves road).

ACCOMMODATION AND EATING PAREDES DO RIO

Estalagem Rocha Paredes do Rio ☎276 566 147, ⓦ estalagemrocha.com.pt. This guesthouse has neat little rooms, and a rather more renowned rustic restaurant, cooking meat from its own farm (dishes around €10). Restaurant daily noon–10pm. **€40**

Cabril

The 15km minor road running south from Paradela to **CABRIL** climbs through wild mountain scenery of jutting granite outcrops before descending to the Rio Cabril and an old village surrounded on all sides by mountains. When the nearby Salamonde dam was created, parts of the village were submerged and the old bridge is still half under water. There's a nearby signposted campsite, and rooms available in a couple of simple local places, though it's only 8km on to Ermida in the Minho section of the park, with the main centre of Caldas do Gerês a similar distance beyond that.

ACCOMMODATION AND EATING CABRIL

Ponte Novo Cabril ☎253 659 882. Overlooking the new bridge, this bar-restaurant has a riverside terrace for drinks, while inside you can eat a hearty stew or grilled trout (dishes €7–11). April–Sept daily noon–10pm; winter hours variable.

Alentejo

TEMPLO ROMANO, ÉVORA

Alentejo

The Alentejo covers a huge area, around a third of the country, stretching south from the Rio Tejo (including the old Ribatejo district covered in chapter 2) to the northern mountain ranges of the Algarve – the name derives from the words *além do Tejo*, beyond the Tejo River. This is Portugal's garden, the bulk of the region given over to huge cork plantations, wheat fields and vineyards – and though much of it is flat, the region repays exploration, offering unexpected surprises, from ancient dolmens and superbly sited castles to Roman ruins and sweeping Atlantic beaches. Much of the population make a living from the huge agricultural estates known as *latifúndios*, which are handed down from generation to generation – many have been in existence since Roman times. The vast farms are generally wildlife-friendly – the Alentejo is home to wild boar and hundreds of species of bird, from black stork to great bustard.

For most visitors, the region's major draws are its towns, two of which have UNESCO World Heritage status: the spectacular fortified town of **Elvas**, and **Évora**, whose Roman temple, medieval walls and cathedral have put it firmly on the tourist circuit. Elsewhere in **Alto Alentejo** (Upper Alentejo), you'll find the dazzling hilltop villages of **Monsaraz** and **Marvão**, and the marble towns of **Estremoz** and **Vila Viçosa**, where the local marble quarries have given an opulent look to many of the buildings. South of Évora, in the plains of **Baixo Alentejo** (Lower Alentejo), the attractions lie further apart and can be difficult to see without a car. However, there are some good overnight targets, including the main town of **Beja**, as well as nearby **Moura**, **Serpa** and **Mértola**, all enjoyable historic towns with a wealth of accommodation. The coast, too, is an unexpected joy. Only a few small resorts – prime among them **Vila Nova de Milfontes** – attract summer crowds, but the beaches are superb and you can reach them all by public transport.

Évora

ÉVORA is one of Portugal's most historic and unspoilt cities: indeed its Roman temple, Moorish alleys, circuit of medieval walls, ensemble of sixteenth-century mansions and ochre-trimmed, whitewashed houses have resulted in its being awarded UNESCO World Heritage status. A vibrant university helps support a modern town that spreads beyond the old walls, though its current population of around 56,000 inhabitants is fewer than in medieval times, and its compact centre is easily explored within a day or two. Évora's agricultural roots are recalled on the second Tuesday of each month, with a huge **open-air market** held in the Rossio, south of the city walls, and in the lively **Mercado Municipal** (closed Mon) on Praça 1 de Maio, where you can sample local produce – beneath the fish section is a wine cellar that offers tastings; it also hosts farmers' markets most weekends. The town's big annual event, the **Feira de São João**, takes over the city during the last ten days of June, with handicraft, gastronomic and musical festivals.

VILA NOVA DE MILFONTES

Highlights

❶ **Templo Romano in Évora** Enjoy a sunset drink near Évora's most impressive Roman remains. **See p.391**

❷ **Cromeleque dos Almendres** The Iberian peninsula's largest Neolithic stone circle, near Évora, is a hugely atmospheric site. **See p.397**

❸ **Saturday market at Estremoz** A classic Portuguese market, selling everything from earthenware to cheese, all locally made. See p.399

❹ **Elvas** Admire one of Europe's most perfectly preserved walled towns. **See p.408**

❺ **Monsaraz** Stay the night in one of the

traditional houses in this fortified hilltop village. See p.413

❻ **Serpa** Walk the walls of this sleepy but picturesque town, with its own castle. See p.417

❼ **The Rota Vicentina** Walk a section of this superb long-distance marked trail that wends its way down the west coast of the region. See p.429

❽ **Vila Nova de Milfontes** The Alentejo coast is quite distinct from that of the Algarve, with the estuary town of Vila Nova its finest resort. See p.429

HIGHLIGHTS ARE MARKED ON THE MAP ON P.390

Praça do Giraldo is the city's central hub, with the main historic kernel just to the east. Within the surrounding city walls are several distinct old-town areas, with another concentration of sights in the streets between the main square and the public gardens. Meanwhile, to the north of the centre you can follow the course of the medieval **Aqueduto do Água Prata** (Silver Water Aqueduct), into whose ever-rising arches a row of houses has been incorporated. Wherever you wander, nothing is more than a ten-minute walk from Praça do Giraldo.

HIGHLIGHTS

1. Templo Romano in Évora
2. Cromeleque dos Almendres
3. Saturday market at Estremoz
4. Elvas
5. Monsaraz
6. Serpa
7. The Rota Vicentina
8. Vila Nova de Milfontes

ALENTEJO

0 — 20
kilometres

Brief history

The original settlement was probably founded by the Celts, but it was the Romans who fortified the city in 57 BC. Its position on trade routes allowed Évora to flourish and soon after, the Temple of Diana was erected. In 715, Tariq ibn-Ziyad began a 450-year period of Moorish rule which established the city's maze of narrow alleys. It was recaptured by the Christians in 1165, who began to construct the cathedral in 1186 (though it was not finished until the fourteenth century). The period from 1385–1580 saw the city prosper when the royal House of Avis established their court here, and it was during this period that most of Évora's finest buildings were built. In 1553, the Jesuits founded a highly-rated university, but this was closed down by the King's chief minister, Pombal, in 1759; he distrusted the Jesuits' influence. The Vauban-style defensive town walls were constructed in the seventeenth century under the French engineer Nicolas de Langres and remain little changed today. Once the Portuguese court moved nearer Lisbon, Évora drifted into relative obscurity for much of the nineteenth and twentieth centuries. However, the university was re-established in 1973, and in 1986 the town was awarded UNESCO World Heritage status as "the finest example of a city of the Golden Age of Portugal". It is now thriving again thanks to its lively student population and as a popular tourist destination.

Templo Romano (Temple of Diana)

Largo do Conde de Vila Flor

The graceful ruins of **Templo Romano** stands at the very heart of the old city. It was built in the first or second century, supported by fourteen granite Corinthian columns, making it undoubtedly the most impressive Roman building in the country. Popularly known as the Temple of Diana (the Roman goddess of hunting), it was more probably dedicated to several Roman gods. The little square in front of the temple has an alluring kiosk-bar, while from the terrace you can look north across the rooftops – and see just how small contemporary Évora is, with the fields beginning only a few hundred metres away.

8

Igreja dos Lóios and Palácio dos Duques de Cadaval

Largo do Conde de Vila Flor • Tues–Sun 10am–6pm • €7 • ☎ 967 979 763

Directly opposite the Roman temple is the former conventual church, **Igreja dos Lóios**, dedicated to São João Evangelista, and belonging to the Duques de Cadaval, who still live in part of the adjacent ancestral palace. Inside the church – through the Gothic doorway – are some extraordinary floor-to-ceiling *azulejos*, created by one António Oliveira Bernardes early in the eighteenth century. They show scenes from the life of São Lourenço Justiniano, founder of the Lóios order. Hidden among the pews, two small trapdoors stand open to reveal both a Moorish cistern (the church and convent were built over an old castle) and a grisly ossuary containing the bones of the convent's monks. You can also visit the private art collection of the Cadaval dukes, housed in a few public rooms of the **Palácio dos Duques de Cadaval**, which wrap around an attractive patio garden: its café is open to the public.

The Sé

Largo Marquês de Marialva • Daily 9am–5pm, closes from 12.30–2pm from Oct–May • Church €1.50; church and cloister €2.50; church, cloister and tower €3.50; combined ticket with museum (see p.392) €4.50

The construction of Évora's impressive cathedral, the **Sé**, began just twenty years after the Christians defeated the Moors in 1165 – hence its somewhat military-looking battlements and substantial towers. Its beautiful, if rather sombre, interior is lit up by two huge Gothic rose windows. The more jaunty main chapel was an eighteenth-century Baroque addition attributed to João Frederico Ludovice (1673–1752), a German-born

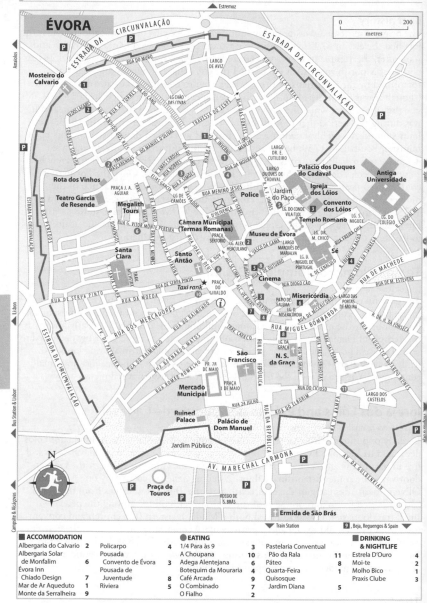

ÉVORA

Estremoz

0   200
metres

Mosteiro do
Calvario

LARGO
DE AVIZ

Rota dos Vinhos

Palácio dos Duques
do Cadaval

Antiga
Universidade

Teatro García
de Resende

Megalith
Tours

LARGO
DUQUES DE
CADAVAL

Igreja
dos Lóios

Jardim
do Paço

Police

Convento
dos Lóios

Santa
Clara

Câmara Municipal
(Termas Romanas)

Templo Romano

Santo
Antão

Museu de Évora

Sé

Taxi rank

Cinema

Misericórdia

São
Francisco

N. S.
da Graça

Mercado
Municipal

Ruined
Palace

Palácio de
Dom Manuel

Jardim Público

AV. MARECHAL CARMONA

N

Praça de
Touros

Ermida de São Brás

Train Station

Beja, Reguengos & Spain

■ ACCOMMODATION				● EATING				■ DRINKING & NIGHTLIFE	
Albergaria do Calvario	2	Policarpo	4	1/4 Para às 9	3	Pastelaria Conventual		Estrela D'Ouro	4
Albergaria Solar de Monfalim	6	Pousada Convento de Évora	3	A Choupana	10	Pão da Rala	11	Moi-te	2
Évora Inn Chiado Design	7	Pousada de Juventude	8	Adega Alentejana	6	Páteo	8	Molho Bico	1
Mar de Ar Aqueduto	1	Riviera	5	Botequim da Mouraria	4	Quarta-Feira	1	Praxis Clube	3
Monte da Serralheira	9			Café Arcada	9	Quiosque Jardim Diana	5		
				O Combinado	7				
				O Fialho	2				

architect best known for his work on the Mosteiro Palácio de Mafra. The Gothic cloister is an attractive, tranquil space, though for most people the highlight is to climb up the tower onto the cathedral's cambered roof, which offers dazzling views over the town.

Museu de Catedral

Largo Marquês de Marialva • Tues–Sun 9am–11.30am & 2–4pm • €4; combined ticket with Sé (see p.391) €4.50

The **Museu de Catedral**, housed in the Cathedral chapter room, shows off the historic

economic clout of the church. Its priceless treasures include a jewel-encrusted reliquary and a thirteenth-century ivory and wood statue of the Virgin, whose midriff opens out to display various Biblical scenes.

Museu de Évora

Largo Conde Vila Flor • Tues–Sun 9.30am–5.30pm • €3, free on the first Sunday of the month • ☎ 266 730 480, ⓦ museudevora.imc-ip.pt

The fascinating and well laid out **Museu de Évora**, housed in a beautiful former bishop's palace, is best known for its collection of fifteenth- and sixteenth-century Flemish paintings which were once displayed in the city's convents and churches. Highlight is a *retábulo* consisting of 19 pieces commissioned by the Bishop of Évora from Flanders in 1495, cementing the strong medieval trade links between the two countries. There are also still life canvases by Portuguese painter Josefa da Óbidos (1630–1684) and archeological remains from Portugal's "Golden Age of Discoveries", including an ornate marble window-frame from a former Queen's palace (1506). In the basement, an archeological display includes finds from local burial mounds and Roman excavations, along with remains from Islamic houses.

Termas Romanas

Câmara Municipal • Mon–Fri 9am–5.30pm • Free • ☎ 266 777 000

One of the city's most significant Roman remains was uncovered in 1987 beneath the town hall, the **Câmara Municipal**, where during office hours you can walk in to view the **Termas Romanas** (Roman Baths), which date to the first century AD. Look down on it and you can see an arched brick doorway marking the entrance to an extraordinary sunken room which houses a circular steam bath 9m in diameter.

Antiga Universidade

Rua Cardeal Rei • Term time only Mon–Fri 9am–8pm, Sat 9am–6pm • €3 • ☎ 266 740 800

In one of the liveliest corners of the city, you'll find the **Antiga Universidade**, whose beautiful courtyard is entered from Rua Cardeal Rei. Founded in 1559 by Cardinal Henrique, the future "Cardinal King", the university was closed down by the Jesuit-hating Marquês de Pombal during the eighteenth century, but reopened in the 1970s. You are free to wander in and view the brazil-wood ceiling, *azulejos* and double cloister of marble columns.

Igreja de São Francisco and Capela dos Ossos

Praça 1 de Maio • Daily 9am–12.30pm & 2.30–5pm • €3 • ☎ 266 704 521

On the eastern side of Praça 1 de Maio is the **Igreja de São Francisco**, best known for its bizarre **Capela dos Ossos**, the "chapel of bones". During the fifteenth and sixteenth centuries, there were 42 monastic cemeteries in town which took up much-needed space. The Franciscans' solution was to move all the remains to one compact, consecrated site. This is the ghoulish result: a room lined with the bones and skulls of around five thousand former monks, inscribed with the reminder of our mortality: "*Nós ossos que aqui estamos pelos vossos esperamos*" ("Our bones that lie here are waiting for your bones"). You can also visit a fairly uninspiring religious museum and walk onto a terrace overlooking the square.

Jardim Público and the Palácio de Dom Manuel

Palace: Mon–Fri 10am–noon & 1–5pm, Sat 1–5pm • Free

Just to the south of Praça 1 de Maio, the **Palácio de Dom Manuel**, with its reconstructed gallery – incorporating inventive horseshoe arches with strange serrated edges – lies

within Évora's **Jardim Público** (Public Gardens). It was from the palace that Vasco da Gama is thought to have received the commission that changed the direction of the Portuguese empire, as the explorer established the sea route to India. From the garden walls, you can look out over the southern edge of the city, and see the **Ermida de São Brás** (Mon–Fri 10am–1pm & 3–7pm, Sat 10am–1pm & 3.30–7pm, Sun 10am–1pm; free; ☎ 266 708 362) just outside the city walls – this small church has been identified as an early work by Diogo de Boitaca, pioneer of the Manueline style.

ARRIVAL AND DEPARTURE   ÉVORA

By bus The bus station (Terminal Rodoviária) is five minutes' walk from the western city walls along the Lisbon road; it's a ten-minute walk in total to Praça do Giraldo, or you can take one of the regular Trevo buses (see below).

Destinations Arraiolos (1 daily; 1hr 10min); Beja (2–4 daily; 1hr 15min–2hr); Elvas (3–4 daily; 1hr 30min); Estremoz (1–4 daily; 40mins–2hr); Faro (3 daily; 4hr); Lisbon (hourly; 1hr 40min); Moura (1 daily; 1hr 25min); Portalegre (1–3 daily; 1hr 25min–2hr 30min); Reguengos de Monsaraz for Monsaraz (2 daily; 35min–1hr); Santarém (2 daily; 2hr); and Vila Viçosa (3 daily; 1hr).

By car Unless you are staying at a hotel with parking, drivers should park in one of the (mostly free) car parks

around the walls, as the city centre has few parking places. There's always space on the massive Rossio (except on open-air market day). The Trevo bus Linha Azul Sul or Norte (Mon–Fri 8am–8pm, Sat 8am–2pm; every 15min; €1 includes parking; ⓦ trevo.com.pt) acts as a park-and-ride service, circling all the car parks around the city walls and running into the historic centre.

By train Évora's train station is 1km southeast of the centre, with regular services from Beja (4 daily; 2hr 20min) and Lisbon (3–4 daily; 2hr 10min). From the station, walk up through the Rossio and follow Rua da República straight ahead to reach Praça do Giraldo, the city's main square: it's a €6 taxi ride or a short ride on the Linha Azul Sul bus (see above).

INFORMATION AND TOURS

Information The turismo is at Praça do Giraldo 73 (daily: April–Oct 9am–7pm; Nov–March 9am–6pm; ☎ 266 777 071, ⓦ www2.cm-evora.pt/guiaturistico/) and posts useful bus and train timetables.

Bike rental ⓦ longaventura.pt rents out bikes for around €18/day, which includes delivery. Ask about the Ecopista, a twenty-kilometre route along an old railway line.

Tours Knowledgeable local professor Libânio Merteira Reis (office in boutique at Rua 31 de Janeiro 15A ☎ 266 739 240, ⓦ evora-mm.pt) runs customized tours round town and

out to nearby megaliths, from €10 for half a day. You can also take guided 2–3hr tours to the local megalithic sites with Ebora Megalithica (☎ 964 808 337, ⓦ ebora megalithica.com) for around €25/person.

Wine tours The helpful Rota dos Vinhos do Alentejo, Praça Joaquim António d'Aguiar 20–21 (☎ 266 746 498, ⓦ vinhosdoalentejo.pt; Mon 2–7pm, Tues–Fri 11am–7pm, Sat 10am–1pm), supplies a wine-route booklet detailing all the region's vineyards and arranges vineyard visits (book in advance).

ACCOMMODATION

Accommodation prices in Évora are higher than in the rest of the Alentejo, but there's a more agreeable choice of places here than virtually anywhere else in the south, from simple rooms in family houses to ducal palaces. Outside the city, a large array of country houses also offer accommodation, most within a short drive. In summer you're advised to book in advance to guarantee a bed, though the turismo may be able to help.

★**Albergaria do Calvario** Trav dos Lagares 3 ☎ 266 745 930, ⓦ adcevora.com. Stylishly converted inn partly set in a former sixteenth-century olive press that supplied olive oil to the adjacent convent. The plush rooms are arranged round an inner courtyard, and there's wi-fi and underground parking. The owners are keen foodies and provide an excellent organic breakfast, as well as tapas served in the bar. Mention *Rough Guides* when you book and you'll get a free room upgrade. **€110**

Albergaria Solar de Monfalim Largo da Misericórdia 1 ☎ 266 703 529, ⓦ monfalimtur.pt. The steps and sumptuous terrace leading to this restored summer ducal palace promise much, though the 25 rooms are a little less

impressive. Pretty Alentejo furniture and furnishings decorate the communal areas, while breakfast is taken on the terrace, which has superb views. Parking (for a daily fee). **€78**

Évora Inn Chiado Design Rua da República 11 ☎ 266 744 500, ⓦ evorainn.com. It's easy to miss the entrance to this good-value guesthouse, which is on four floors of a central townhouse – its name comes from the contemporary furniture and art on the walls, some of which is for sale. The best rooms are at the top, which overlook the old town at the back, but all are individual and filled with funky furniture and fittings. There's also a communal lounge and kitchen. Breakfast extra. **€60**

★**Mar de Ar Aqueduto** Rua Cândido dos Reis 72

266 740 700, ⓦ mardearhotels.com. This ultra-modern five-star spa hotel extends behind an eighteenth-century palace. The best rooms, with glass-walled bathrooms, face onto a lovely garden with its own pool nestled against the city walls (some rooms face over a backstreet). A gym and restaurant complete its attractions. **€146**

Monte da Serralheira 3km south ☏ 266 741 286, ⓦ monteserralheira.com. Dutch-owned farm with good-value apartments (sleeping two or four people) each with terrace, sitting room, small kitchen and TV. It's very peaceful, there's a nice communal pool and table tennis, and you can rent a bike or ride a horse. Breakfast extra. **€70**

Policarpo Rua Freiria de Baixo 16 ☏ 266 702 424, ⓦ pensaopolicarpo.com. A former ducal summer palace with sixteenth-century *azulejos*, a granite staircase and fine views from many of its rooms. The rooms are fading a little (you pay €20 more for en-suite rooms), but they still have charm; breakfast is eaten on the terrace. Parking. No credit cards. **€40**

Pousada Convento de Évora Largo do Conde de Vila Flor ☏ 266 730 070, ⓦ pousadas.pt. One of the country's finest *pousadas*, housed in the former Convento dos Lóios and wrapped round superb inner courtyards, one with a pool. The rooms are lovely – many with traditional furniture, including some dramatic four-poster beds – and some in former monks' cells. You can also eat top-notch Alentejan specialities (mains €18–20; reservations required) in the sumptuous cloisters. **€230**

Pousada de Juventude Rua Miguel Bombarda 40 ☏ 266 706 050, ⓦ pousadasjuventude.pt. In a very grand building is this excellent youth hostel with pristine double rooms and four-bed dorms. There's a pleasant communal lounge and a roof-top terrace with summer bar and great views. Dorms **€14**, doubles **€42**

Riviera Rua 5 de Outubro 49 ☏ 266 737 210, ⓦ riviera -evora.com. A fine central option, with 21 individually styled rooms with stripped wooden floors, Alentejan rugs, pretty bedspreads and little marble bathrooms. Some rooms are more attractive (and bigger) than others, but all are good value. **€75**

EATING

CAFÉS

Café Arcada Pr do Giraldo 7, at Rua João de Deus ☏ 266 741 777. The nicest perch in town, by the fountain at the top of the square, for perusing the comings and goings – better for cakes and pastries than meals. Mon–Thurs & Sun 8am–9.30pm, Fri & Sat 8am–10.30pm.

Pastelaria Conventual Pão da Rala Rua do Cicioso 47 ☏ 266 707 778. This small, traditional café with *azulejos* on the walls has a counter filled with cakes and pastries whose recipes were originally concocted by nuns in local convents. Mostly egg- and almond-based and perfect for those with a sweet tooth, they have risqué names such as *beijinhas de freira* (nun's kisses). Daily 7.30am–8pm.

Páteo Beco do Espinhoso, off Rua 5 de Outubro ☏ 919 549 745. Tucked at the end of a tiny alley, this lovely patio café-bar has tables and chairs under the shade of olive and lemon trees, a tranquil spot for a drink – it also does soups, snacks and decent meals (from around €15) and hosts occasional exhibitions. Daily 11.30–midnight (closes 8pm and Sun afternoon from Oct–April).

Quiosque Jardim Diana Largo do Conde de Vila Flor ☏ 266 707 642. The outdoor kiosk by the temple is the finest place in the city for a beer, as the fading sun dapples the cathedral and temple columns. Given its location, it's amazingly low priced. Daily 8am–9pm (closes 7pm in winter).

RESTAURANTS

¼ Para as 9 Rua Pedro Simões 9a ☏ 266 706 774. Lively local that serves the best fish in town – pricey mains (fantastic boiled hake, garlic shrimps) from €14, but go for the huge *arroz de tamboril* or *marisco* and you can easily share the rice dishes between three people for €30 or so. Also superb starters such as cheese baked with oregano. Mon, Tues, Thurs–Sun 12.30–3pm & 7.30–10pm.

A Choupana Rua dos Mercadores 16–20 ☏ 266 704 427. Close enough to the main square to attract tourists aplenty, but good enough to appeal to locals, too, who tend to eat at the counter rather than in the adjacent tiled dining room. Grilled fish and meats such as *alheira* (chicken sausage) from €9–12. Daily noon–1am.

Adega Alentejana Rua Gabriel Victor do Monte Pereira 21A ☏ 266 744 447. You'll find an authentic slice of the Alentejo at this rustic restaurant and bar, which is lined with agricultural implements, plates and giant barrels. Regional dishes feature the likes of *migas* and *açorda* (a garlic bread sauce cooked with meats), along with huge portions of grilled meats, from €9. The daily specials are chalked on a board. Mon–Sat noon–3pm & 7–10pm.

★ **Botequim da Mouraria** Rua da Mouraria 16A ☏ 266 746 775. This tiny bar with counter seating serves excellent regional food, mainly tapas-style dishes (scrambled eggs and wild asparagus, roast peppers, wild mushrooms in garlic from €5–16) and a few market-fresh mains (say steak, or deep-fried squid with crispy potatoes from around €13). Mon–Fri 12.30–9.45pm.

O Combinado Rua de Machede 95a ☏ 266 700 627. Near the university, this small but popular local does very good value dishes such as *alheira* sausage, salmon and a fish of the day for under €10, and a bargain tourist menu at around €12. Arrive early or book in advance. Mon & Wed–Fri 9.30am–3pm & 7–10pm, Sat & Sun 11am–10pm.

O Fialho Trav das Mascarenhas 16 ☏ 266 703 079, ⓦ restaurantefialho.com. One of the city's top restaurants,

8

ALENTEJAN WINES

The art of wine-making in the Alentejo was already well established when the Romans occupied the country's vineyards, but it is only relatively recently that **Alentejan wines** have become widely recognized as some of the best in Europe. Many of the region's vineyards were torn up in the eighteenth century to protect the newly demarcated port wines from the Douro region, while during the last century the Salazar regime encouraged farmers to replace their vines with wheat. It was only in the 1970s that wine co-operatives were re-established, and heavy investment in modern wine-making techniques saw the quality rise dramatically. What makes the wines stand out from elsewhere is that they are made from **local grape varieties** which thrive in the harsh soils: Touriga Nacional, Aragonez and Alicante Bouschet, Trincadeira and Periquita for the reds; and Antão Vaz, Arinto and Roupeiro for the whites. The region's cool winters, warm summers and perfect conditions for ripening grapes give the wines a full-bodied if youngish flavour. Many of the producers allow **visits** (usually around €6, which includes tastings), where you can find out about the wines, then sample them over dinner – several of the vineyards have restaurants as well as tasting rooms – while the larger ones, such as the *Herdade dos Grous* (see p.421), offer tours of their estate by jeep or even horseback. The best place to start is the headquarters of the Rota dos Vinhos do Alentejo (ⓦvinhosdoalentejo.pt) in Évora (see p.394), which can arrange tours to most of the nearby vineyards. Recommended estates to visit include Esporão (see p.414); Quinta do Carmo near Estremoz (ⓦbacalhoa.com), which is part-owned by the Lafite Rothschild group; and Adega Mayor (ⓦadegamayor.pt) in the Serra de São Mamede, whose landmark headquarters is a stunning white edifice designed by Portugal's most famous architect, Álvaro Siza Viera.

specializing in traditional regional specialities such as partridge, hare and wild boar with apple sauce from around €14–18, and the wine list is excellent. Appetizers are particularly good (spinach with prawns, stuffed crab), as are the desserts. Tues–Sun noon–3pm & 7–10pm.

Quarta-Feira Rua do Inverno 16 ⓣ 266 707 530. This simple but appealing Moorish Quarter tavern has a menu of mostly meaty Alentejan classics – *borrego, bife, lombinhos, rojões* – from €12.50. Mon–Sat 1.30–3pm & 7.30–9.30pm.

NIGHTLIFE AND ENTERTAINMENT

When the students aren't around, Évora goes to bed pretty early, but a few **bars** can provide a bit of late-night drinking – keep an eye out for flyers for club nights. **Concerts and cultural events** are advertised in the *Agenda Cultural* booklet, available from the turismo.

Estrela D'Ouro Largo de São Vicente/Rua Miguel

Bombarda 1–7. With tables outside on a pretty square, this is an arty bar with chandeliers and modern art on the walls. There's also a downstairs café section. Daily 5pm–late, café open from 9.30am.

Moi-te Largo Alexandre Herculano 8 ⓣ 266 702 473. The big attraction about this small bar is its lovely patio garden laden with lemon trees, a lovely spot to while away an evening. Daily noon–3am.

Molho Bico Rua de Aviz 91 ⓣ 266 748 235. A pub-like music bar with tables out the front on an attractive square. There's live music most nights from 11pm, when things can get very lively. Daily 11.30am–3am.

Praxis Clube Rua de Valdevinos 21A ⓣ 266 708 177. The town's only central club is the place to show your moves, especially in term time when the students are in town. There are two dancefloors, an esplanade and various chill-out areas. Tues–Sat 11pm–6am.

DIRECTORY

Hospital Hospital do Espírito Santo, Largo Sr da Pobreza ⓣ 266 740 100.

Police Police station (PSP) on Rua Francisco S Lusitano, near the Roman temple ⓣ 266 702 022.

Post office Rua da Olivença (ⓣ 266 745 480; Mon–Fri 8.30am–6.30pm).

Taxis There's a rank in Praça do Giraldo, or ⓣ 266 734 734.

Around Évora

Leave at least an afternoon or two to explore Évora's environs, which have some significant attractions. Some, like the castle at **Évoramonte**, warrant a quick stop en route elsewhere, though the famed carpet town of **Arraiolos**, just to the north, is a popular day- or overnight trip from the city. The administrative district of Évora also contains over a dozen

megalithic sites – dolmens (funerary chambers), menhirs (standing stones) and stone circles – which have their origins in a culture that flourished here before spreading north as far as Brittany and Denmark. The stones of **Os Almendres**, in particular, provide one of the country's most extraordinary sights. With your own car, you can easily combine a visit to Os Almendres with the dramatic dolmen of **Zambujeiro**. While it's tempting to take the fast road to Beja and the south, there's an attractive detour to be made into deepest rural Alentejo, via the small historic towns of **Viana do Alentejo** and **Alvito**. From Évora the first stop, Viana do Alentejo, is a simple twenty-minute drive down the ruler-straight N254. There's no reliable public transport along this route – you'll need a car.

Anta Grande do Zambujeiro

Brown archeological signposts at Valverde – 7km southwest of Évora, down the N380 (Alcáçovas road) – lead you through the university's agricultural faculty grounds to the **Anta Grande do Zambujeiro**, a huge burial chamber lying sheltered under a corrugated-iron roof. The last 1km of the approach is along a dirt track which is usually fine for cars if it hasn't been raining, but you can always leave your vehicle and walk if you're unsure.

Zambujeiro is the largest dolmen in the country, comprising eight standing stones which lean inwards to form a funeral chamber 8m high, with a six-metre diameter. The capstone is missing and the chamber itself is fenced off for safety reasons, but the twelve-metre-long approach corridor is still largely intact. The moving of such enormous stones must have challenged the ingenuity of the Neolithic builders, and there's still a real sense of mystery here, the only sound that of chirruping crickets in the ancient olive trees.

Os Almendres

The Iberian peninsula's largest and most impressive stone circle lies 13km west of Évora, just south of the small village of Guadalupe. To get here directly from Évora, take the N114 towards Montemor/Lisbon and follow the signs from Guadalupe. If you're approaching from the south, from Escoural and Valverde, you need to turn left in Guadalupe, at the *Café Barreiros*.

You are directed out along a dirt road (largely flat and in good condition, fine for cars), reaching the **Menir dos Almendres** after 2km. This is a single, three-metre-high standing stone set in a quiet olive plantation five minutes' walk from the road. Despite its obvious Neolithic origins, the local legend has it that it is the tomb of an enchanted Moorish princess, who appears once a year on the eve of São João and can be seen combing her hair.

Another 2.5km along the dirt road there's a parking area beside the extraordinary **Cromeleque dos Almendres**, where no fewer than 92 stones are aligned for 70m down a dusty hillside. Placed here in several phases, between six and seven thousand years ago, they are thought to have been erected in a horseshoe shape as some kind of astronomical observatory and site of fertility rituals. Even today, the power of the site is undeniable, the stones resembling frozen figures gazing across the surrounding cork plantation to a distant Évora.

Arraiolos

ARRAIOLOS, 21km north of Évora, is known for its superb **carpets** (*tapetes*), which have been handwoven here since the thirteenth century. Modelled on carpets from Persia, they have been much prized for centuries and adorn the interiors of any Portuguese manor or palace worth its salt. For carpet enthusiasts, Arraiolos is a dream – every second shop sells them, and you can spend €40 on a small square or €1500 or more on a fine example.

8

Carpets aside, it's a very pretty small town, with a ruined hilltop castle and brightly whitewashed houses trimmed in lavender. In the paved central square, Praça Lima e Brito, there's a sixteenth-century pillory and some ancient dye chambers, 500 years old, preserved beneath glass.

ARRIVAL AND INFORMATION
ARRAIOLOS

By bus There is one bus daily between Arraiolos and Évora (1hr 10min).

Information The turismo (Tues–Sun 10am–1pm &

2–6pm; ☎ 266 490 254, ⓦ cm-arraiolos.pt) is at Praça do Município 27, in the town hall.

ACCOMMODATION

Pousada de Arraiolos Nossa Senhora da Assunção ☎ 266 419 340, ⓦ pousadas.pt. The lovely *Pousada Nossa Senhora da Assunção* is a serene hideaway, 1km or so out of

town on the Pavia road. Set in beautiful grounds, it's built into a sixteenth-century former convent, though the rooms and pool are in a very contemporary style. **€175**

Viana do Alentejo

Castle Tues 2–5.30pm, Wed–Sun 10am–1pm & 2–5.30pm, • Free • Buses from Alvito (Mon–Fri 1–2 daily; 20min) and Évora (Mon–Fri 1–2 daily; 35min)

VIANA DO ALENTEJO is a typically dozy southern-Alentejan town, which nonetheless preserves a highly decorative **castle**, full of Mudéjar and Manueline features. The walls were built on a pentagonal plan by Dom Dinis in 1313, and the interior ensemble of buildings was expanded under Dom João II and Dom Manuel I in the late fifteenth century. From this latter period dates a sequence of elaborate battlements, with their witch's-hat towers and pinnacles, and the beautiful Igreja Matriz (parish church), which has a superbly carved door.

Alvito

ALVITO, 10km south of Viana do Alentejo, is a small town with great charm and an abundance of Manueline features. It's dominated by its **castle** built in 1494 and now a *pousada* (see below) – it's a curious Manueline–Mudéjar hybrid, a style seen also in the much smaller sixteenth-century **Ermida de São Sebastião**, on the edge of town, from where there are fine views across the cultivated plains below. In the few streets between the castle, the parish church and the town-hall clock tower, many of the houses have carved sixteenth-century windows and door frames, and if you seek out the town gardens, small market and typical *pelourinho* in the handsome main square, Praça da República, you've easily occupied an hour or two.

ARRIVAL AND INFORMATION
ALVITO

By bus Buses run between Alvito and Évora (Mon–Fri 1–2 daily; 50min) and Viana do Alentejo (Mon–Fri 1–2 daily; 20min).

Information The turismo is at Rua dos Lobos 13 (Mon–Fri

9am–12.30pm & 2–5.30pm, Sat 10am–12.30pm & 2–5.30pm; ☎ 284 480 808), and can point you in the direction of local rural guesthouses.

ACCOMMODATION AND EATING

A Varanda Pr da República 9, Alvito ☎ 284 485 135. Opposite the castle on Praça da República, this baronial-style restaurant serves innovative mains such as *feijoada de gambas* from €15, and if that's not enough, you can also enjoy a cocktail at its *Bar Lady Di*. Daily noon–3pm & 7.30–11pm.

Pousada de Alvito Castelo de Alvito, Alvito

☎ 284 480 700, ⓦ pousadas.pt. You'll certainly feel secure if you stay in the town *pousada*. The fifteenth-century castle was converted into a hotel in 1993, and now boasts very stylish rooms – some with fab views over town – a swimming pool in the garden and a quality if pricey restaurant serving local produce. **€110**

Évoramonte castle

Tues 2–5pm, Wed–Sun 10am–1pm & 2–5pm; closed second weekend of each month • €2 • 29km northeast of Évora along the N18 towards Estremoz • Buses (Mon–Fri 3 daily) between Estremoz (20min) and Évora (50min) can drop you off on the main road, though it's a long uphill hike to the castle – realistically, you'll need a car

The castle at **ÉVORAMONTE** sits impressively atop a steep hillock high above the main road and modern village. While the castle stands on Roman fortifications, what you see today dates from 1306, with a Renaissance-style keep added in the sixteenth century. It was here in 1834 that the regent Miguel was finally defeated and the convention signed that put Pedro IV on the Portuguese throne. Legend has it that the signing took so long that there was only stale bread left to eat, causing the invention of the well-known Portuguese dish *açorda* (a soup of bread, coriander, garlic and olive oil). You can visit the three vaulted chambers inside the castle, though the terrace views are the main highlight.

The upper medieval village rings the castle mound and, with care, you can clamber around the walls and gate towers, and then wander down the cobbled main street to the small church and cemetery; head to the modern settlement on the main road for cafés and restaurants.

Estremoz

The sleepy but highly appealing walled market town of **ESTREMOZ** lies in the centre of a district rich in marble quarries – so much so that the material is used extensively in the most common-place surroundings, as you'll see when you wander its marble-clad streets and squares. It was once an important border settlement where Dom Dinis, an early monarch who set about fortifying Portugal's frontiers, chose to locate his hilltop palace. Meanwhile, down in the lower town, the vast main square known as the Rossio – properly, the Rossio Marquês de Pombal – has long been the site of one of Portugal's finest **markets**, held every Saturday. It starts and finishes early, so it pays to stay over in town on Friday night if you can. The Rossio also hosts Estremoz's annual **festival** (first weekend in Sept), as well as the huge five-day agricultural shindig in April known as the **Feira Internacional de Agricultura e Pecuária**, which mixes cattle shows, concerts and handicrafts.

8

Torre das Três Coroas

Pousada de Santa Rainha Isabel, Largo de Dom Dinis • Access via the *pousada*; ask at reception • Free

The castle in Estremoz is now a *pousada* (see p.401), set within the star-shaped ramparts of the upper town, where Dom Manuel welcomed Vasco da Gama before he set sail for India in 1497. You're free to climb the thirteenth-century **Torre das Três Coroas** (Tower of the Three Crowns), from where there's a splendid panoramic view across the plains to the castle of Évoramonte, 15km away. In front of the tower, there's a modern statue of Isabel, Dom Dinis's queen, who devoted her life to the poor, giving away food and money with unseemly enthusiasm for a monarch. The statue recalls a well-known episode, whereby her husband challenged her to reveal what was beneath her skirt: the bread she had hidden there had been miraculously turned into roses.

Museu Municipal Professor Joaquim Vermelho

Largo de Dom Dinis • Tues–Sun 9am–12.30pm & 2–5.30pm • €1.60 • ☎ 268 339 219

Set in a nineteenth-century hospice opposite the Torre das Três Coroas, the **Museu Municipal** offers a fascinating insight into traditional Alentejan life and Estremoz handicrafts. A maze of rooms, including the building's former kitchen, displays rugged domestic utensils, hand-painted country furniture and intricately carved cork figures and tableaux. Best known of all, however, is the pottery of Estremoz, from dandy figurines and rural scenes to floral pots and jars inlaid with marble

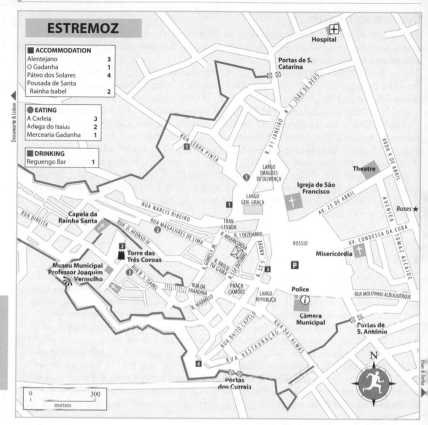

ESTREMOZ

ACCOMMODATION
Alentejano	3
O Gadanha	1
Páteo dos Solares	4
Pousada de Santa Rainha Isabel	2

EATING
A Cadeia	3
Adega do Isaías	2
Mercearia Gadanha	1

DRINKING
Reguengo Bar	1

chips. There's a huge collection in the museum (as well as a ceramics *atelier* in the courtyard), with a story or tradition attached to each item – such as the role the pottery used to play in gypsy weddings. During the wedding procession, the bride would make a sudden dash for freedom across the marketplace, hotly pursued by the groom. With bride eventually captured, a fine Estremoz dish was thrown into the air and the couple pronounced man and wife at the moment that the dish fell to the ground in pieces.

ARRIVAL AND INFORMATION

ESTREMOZ

By bus Buses stop outside the old train station, from where it's a two-minute walk down to the Rossio.
Destinations Elvas (6 daily; 45min); Évora (1–4 daily; 40min–1hr 30min); Lisbon (7–9 daily; 2hr–2hr 30min); and Portalegre (2–8 daily; 45min).
By car Estremoz is 46km northeast of Évora. There's plenty

of free parking in the Rossio (except on Saturday market day) and also outside the *pousada* in the upper town (follow signs for "Castelo").
Information The turismo is on the south side of the main Rossio (daily 9am–12.30pm & 2–5.30pm; ☎ 268 339 227, ⊕ www.cm-estremoz.pt).

ACCOMMODATION

Alentejano Rossio Marquês de Pombal 13–15 ☎ 268 337 300 ⊕ alentejanohotel.com. A traditional place overlooking the Rossio, with a dozen simple but good value rooms that come with flowery painted Alentejan

furniture, brass beds and marble bathrooms. There's wifi, a bar and café downstairs and a proper old country-style restaurant on the first floor, serving good regional food (daily 7am–midnight; mains €9–10). **€35**

★ **O Gadanha** Largo General Graça 56 ☎ 268 339 110, ⓦ residencialogadanha.com. The best bargain in town – an immaculately kept place, the large rooms come with a/c, tiled floors and decent bathrooms. Rooms 303 and 304 have terraces with castle views. It's good for families, too, as most rooms can easily accommodate an extra bed or divan. Breakfast not available. €35

Páteo dos Solares Rua Brito Capelo ☎ 268 338 400, ⓦ pateosolares.com. There's a very genteel ambience in this beautiful town mansion ("sober but rustic" they say, which is just about right). Rooms vary (suites have fireplaces and fancy massage baths, while interconnected rooms are good for families), and there's

a pool and gardens and an upmarket terrace restaurant (mains €15–22) that offers the nicest alfresco dining in town. Parking. €120

★ **Pousada de Santa Rainha Isabel** Largo de D. Dinis ☎ 268 332 075, ⓦ pousadas.pt. The period-piece palace scores heavily on the charm front, with dramatic vaulted public areas, and guest rooms with carved wooden beds, Arraiolos carpets and scintillating views. A pool and lovely gardens are hidden within the battlemented walls, while the restaurant (mains from €17–22; open to non-guests) offers a slick variation on the usual Alentejan cuisine, with specials such as pork with honey and garlic octopus. Parking. €120

EATING

A Cadeia Quinhentista Rua Rainha Santa Isabel ☎ 268 323 400, ⓦ cadeiaquinhentista.com. Near the *pousada*, the old sixteenth-century jail is now a high-end café-bar (with a great terrace) and restaurant, serving Alentejan specialities such as *açorda* and grilled meats (around c15), as well as quality local wines. Café-bar daily 11am–midnight; restaurant daily 12.30–3pm & 7.30–10pm.

★ **Adega do Isaias** Rua do Almeida 21 ☎ 268 322 318. Don't be put off by the local bar at the front, but head into the back dining room, lined with giant wine

jars. It serves most of its food straight from the huge outdoor chargrill – steak, lamb, pork, squid and more, from around €9. Mon–Sat noon–3pm & 7–10.30pm; closed 2 weeks in Aug.

Mercearia Gadanha Largo Dragões de Olivença 849 ☎ 268 333 262. Part deli and part hip restaurant-bar, with a delicious array of *petiscos* (mushroom croquettes, lamb with herbs, sardines) as well as meaty mains from around €12.50–15. You can also pop in for a drink or cake from the counter, with seats outside on an attractive square. Tues–Sun 10am–11pm.

DRINKING

What nightlife there is in sleepy Estremoz can be found along Rua Serpa Pinto.

Reguengo Bar Rua Serpa Pinto 87 ☎ 964 108 247. The main destination on Rua Serpa Pinto is this spacious music bar with occasional live music. There's an appealiing leafy

garden where you can nurse a drink or two until the small hours. Daily 9pm–2am.

Alter do Chão

North of Estremoz, the narrow but fast N245 thunders across the olive- and cork-lined plains to **ALTER DO CHÃO**, 48km away. It's a handsome town, with the rounded towers of its castle facing directly onto a shaded central square, though the chief reason for a visit – well worth the drive – is to see the royal stud farm.

Coudelaria Alter-Real

Tapada do Arneiro, signposted 3km north of town • 1hr 30min guided tours Tues–Sun at 11am & 3pm (English spoken) • €7.50 • ☎ 245 610 064, ⓦ alterreal.pt

The **Coudelaria Alter-Real** stud farm was founded by royalty in 1748 and Alter-Real Lusitano horses have been greatly sought after ever since – the Lisbon Riding School and the Portuguese mounted police both use them. Guided visits show you the cosseted stallions in their vaulted stables, as well as the *picadeiro* (riding ring) and a collection of antique carriages. Some tours start with an impressive falcon-flying demonstration, and there's also a small museum and the possibility of arranging a riding lesson in the *picadeiro* (from €25). The annual stud show and sale is every April 24, a great day for a visit.

8

ACCOMMODATION AND EATING

ALTER DO CHÃO

Casa Arlindo Correia Alter Pedroso, 3km east of Alter do Chão ☎ 245 612 301, ⓦ pateoreal.com. For a real getaway-from-it-all retreat, stay at this rural guesthouse in the little hill village of Alter Pedroso. There are just four cosy rooms (or you can take the whole house for €175 a night) and guests have the use of a kitchenette and living room – or head down to town for a meal in their associated restaurant, *Páteo Real*. No credit cards. **€45**

Páteo Real Av Dr. João Pestana 37 ☎ 245 612 301, ⓦ pateoreal.com. Easily the best place for lunch, just down from castle and square. It has a lovely vine-shaded terrace where you can enjoy a good meal of daily changing specialities, from roast lamb to *migas* with wild asparagus (dishes from around €8), and simple rooms upstairs to stay (from €75). Mon & Wed–Sun noon–11pm.

Crato

CRATO – 13km north of Alter do Chão – is an ancient agricultural town that has clearly seen better days and larger populations and is really only a coffee stop if you're driving – unless of course you fancy a night at the glam *pousada* (see below). A trio of imposing churches and the elegant **Varanda do Grão Prior** (an arcaded granite balcony) in the pretty main Praça do Município attest to the boom years of the sixteenth century. Indeed Crato's largely fifteenth-century castle was once among the mightiest in the Alentejo. In the centre of town, you can't miss the dominant colour scheme – white with mustard-yellow trim – that adorns every single house, mansion to cottage.

From Crato, it's a 7km drive west along the N363 (towards Aldeia da Mata) to the **Anta do Tapadão**, which is reckoned to be the best-preserved dolmen in Portugal. The leaning stones are visible atop a small rise in the middle of grazing land away to the left; access is by foot along a farm track.

ARRIVAL AND DEPARTURE

CRATO

By bus There are 1–2 daily buses to Crato from Portalegre (20min).

ACCOMMODATION AND EATING

Pousada do Crato, Flor da Rosa Mosteiro da Flor da Rosa, 2km north of Crato ☎ 245 997 210, ⓦ pousadas .pt. This impressive Gothic monastery was founded in the fourteenth century but reopened in 1995 as a stylish hotel. The gardens are laid out in the insignia of the Order of Malta, in honour of the warlord Nuno Álvares Pereira, whose father founded the monastery. It's a magnificent building, marrying contemporary style with the convent buildings – there's a games room in the upper cloister, outdoor pool and a lovely restaurant. **€160**

Portalegre

PORTALEGRE is the capital, market centre and transport hub of Alto Alentejo, a busy commercial centre of around twenty thousand people in the foothills of the Serra de São Mamede. Despite its attractive whitewashed old quarter, it's not the most appealing of the Alentejo's towns, but it's Portalegre's industrial history that makes it warrant a visit. Until the end of the seventeenth century, the town was a major textiles centre, though the 1703 Methuen Treaty largely put paid to the trade. However, reminders of a prosperous past still survive and lend the town a certain character. The largest tapestry factory – once housed in a Jesuit college in the lower town – has been beautifully restored as city council offices, while the great brick twin chimneys at the very top of town belong to the **Fábrica Robinson**, a cork factory originally established by an enterprising Yorkshireman.

All roads converge on the **Rossio**, the nineteenth-century square with a fountain that's at the heart of modern Portalegre. Beyond here the **town gardens** flank Avenida da Liberdade, the lower part featuring a renowned plane tree (*plátano*), planted in 1848, whose spreading branches are now so long they have to be supported by pillars.

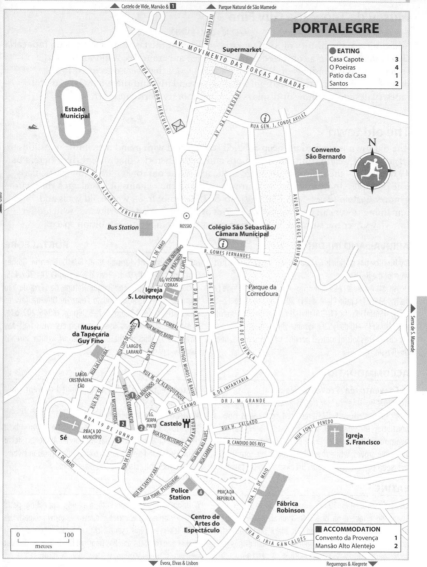

PORTALEGRE

AV. MOVIMENTO DAS FORÇAS ARMADAS

Supermarket

● EATING	
Casa Capote	3
O Poeiras	4
Patio da Casa	1
Santos	2

RUA ALEXANDRE HERCULANO

AVENIDA DA LIBERDADE

Estado
Municipal

RUA GEN. J. CONDE AVILEZ

Convento
São Bernardo

N

RUA NUNO ALVARES PEREIRA

Bus Station   ROSSIO

Colégio São Sebastião/
Câmara Municipal

AVENIDA GEORGE ROBINSON

R. GOMES FERNANDES

RUA 1 DE MAIO

RUA DE OUTUBRO

R. PRACINHA

R. CAPELA

L.G. VISCONDE
CIDRAIS

Igreja
S. Lourenço

R. DA MOURARIA

R. 31 DE JANEIRO

Parque da
Corredoura

RUA M.ª POMBAL

RUA MUROS BAIXO

RUA DE OLIVENÇA

Museu
da Tapeçaria
Guy Fino

RUA LUIS DE CAMÕES

RUA DA SEGURA

LARGO E.
LARANJO

RUA SEIÇA

RUA ANTIGOS MUROS DE BAIXO

LARGO.
CRISTÓVÃO FAL-
CÃO

RUA DA SÉ

RUA MISERICÓRDIA

RUA M. DE ALBUQUERQUE

RUA BENUINO CEIA

B. DE INFANTARIA

DR J. M. GRANDE

RUA DE COMÉRCIO

❶

RUA 19 DE JUNHO

L.G.
SERPA
PINTO

R. DO CARMO

Castelo ⚔

RUA FONTE PENEDO

Igreja
S. Francisco

PRAÇA DO
MUNICÍPIO

Sé

❷

❸

RUA DOS RESTEIROS

RUA H. SALGADO

R. CANDIDO DOS REIS

RUA 1 DE MAIO

RUA DE ELVAS

R. LUIZ BARAHO

RUA GARRETT

RUA 15 DE MAIO

RUA DA SANTA CLARA

RUA TORRE PESSEGUEIRO

❹

PRAÇA DA
REPÚBLICA

Police
Station

Centro de
Artes do
Espectáculo

Fábrica
Robinson

RUA D. IRIA GANÇALVES

■ ACCOMMODATION	
Convento da Provença	1
Mansão Alto Alentejo	2

0   100
metres

▼ Évora, Elvas & Lisbon   Reguengos & Alegrete ▼

8

▶ Serra de S. Mamede

Fábrica Robinson

Rua Dom Iria Gonçalves 2A • Tues–Sat 10am–1pm & 2.30–6pm • Fee for some exhibits • ☎ 245 307 532 ⓦ fundacaorobinson.pt

In 1848, Englishman George Robinson bought up a disused eighteenth-century Franciscan convent and expanded it into a cork factory, which became one of the town's main employers. Today the factory has been turned into a state-of-the-art cultural centre. It hosts various temporary exhibitions, as well as housing a small museum space tracing the history of Portuguese cork production and George Robinson's influence on Portalagre, which included founding schools and the local fire brigade. The building is also the centrepiece of a large urban regeneration project designed by leading architect Eduardo Souto Moura.

Museu da Tapeçaria Guy Fino

Rua da Figueira 9 • Tues–Sun 9.30am–1pm & 2.30–6pm • €2.10 • ☎ 245 307 530

You can trace the history of local tapestry-making in the fascinating **Museu da Tapeçaria Guy Fino**, housed in a converted mansion. There are examples of old looms and a selection of the hundreds of different shades of wool that were once used in the manufacture of tapestries. Exhibitions change regularly, and there may be classical tapestry designs on show or displays of contemporary Portuguese art.

The old town

The old town is reached up steep cobbled streets lined with grand mercantile mansions, a legacy of the wealth from silk workshops and textile factories that once thrived here. **Rua 19 de Junho** – the main thoroughfare at the top of the old town – has some particularly fine examples. In nearby Rua do Carmo, you'll find the remains of Portalegre's thirteenth-century **Castelo** (Tues–Sun 9.30am–1pm & 2.30–6pm; free), whose old walls and remaining tower can be accessed via a series of modern wooden walkways, which offer fine views over the surroundings; there's also a small temporary-exhibition space.

ARRIVAL AND INFORMATION   PORTALEGRE

By bus The bus station is on Rua Nuno Álvares Pereira, just west of the Rossio.

Destinations Beja (1–3 daily; 3hr–4hr); Castelo de Vide (2 daily; 20min); Crato (1–2 daily; 20min); Estremoz (2–8 daily; 45min); Évora (1–3 daily; 1hr 25min–2hr 30min); and Lisbon (5–10 daily; 2hr 45min–3hr 40min).

By car There's lots of metred parking by the gardens, near the Rossio.

Information The turismo is at Rua Guilhermo Gomes Fernandes 22 (daily 9am–1pm & 2–6pm; ☎ 245 307 445, ⓦ cm-portalegre.pt). The Parque Natural da Serra de São Mamede HQ is at Rua Augusto César de Oliveira Tavares (Mon–Fri 9am–12.30pm & 2–5.30pm; ☎ 245 203 631, ⓦ natural.pt), and has useful pamphlets with half-day waymarked walks in the *parque natural*, which spreads north and east of town.

ACCOMMODATION

★ **Convento da Provença** Monte Paleiros, 4km north of Portalegre, on the Marvão road ☎ 245 337 104, ⓦ provenca.pt. This restored convent is now a boutiquey *turismo rural*. Nine cool, tile-floor and oak-beam rooms look out over a pool and surrounding cork and olive groves, while the public areas have comfy sofas overseen by suits of armour. Breakfast can be taken on

the terrace in the shadow of the ruined convent walls and arches. **€85**

Mansâo Alto Alentejo Rua 19 de Junho 59 ☎ 245 202 290, ⓦ mansaoaltoalentejo.com.pt. The town's best choice up in the old town has traditional Alentejan decor (flowery painted headboards, country furniture) in twelve neat and decently sized en-suite, a/c rooms. **€45**

EATING

Casa Capote Rua 19 de Junho 56 ☎ 245 906 185. Swing-door tavern on one side, typical local restaurant on the other, where you can eat black pork and other grilled meats from €9.50 as well as a few fish dishes for a little more. Tues–Sat noon–3pm & 7–10pm, Sun noon–3pm.

O Poeiras Pr da República 9–15 ☎ 245 201 862. This tiled bar stays blissfully cool on a hot day and serves good value grilled chicken, pork and tuna steaks at around €6–8. Tues–Sun noon–3pm & 7–9.30pm.

Patio da Casa Rua Benvindo Ceia 1 ☎ 967 467 645.

A bright little café-bar with a highly appealing patio garden where strawberries and lettuces grow beneath the trees. It serves crêpes, sandwiches and salads (€2–6), fruit shakes and cocktails and has frequent live music sessions at weekends. Tues–Sun noon–3pm & 7–9.30pm.

★ **Santos** Largo Serpa Pinto 4 ☎ 245 203 066. You can eat on the outdoor deck in a pretty square, or in the rustic dining room. It's good for pork and fish (mains €6–10), while the mention of *sobremasas* brings out a mini photo album of amateur shots of puds on tables. Mon, Tues & Thurs–Sun noon–3pm & 7–11pm.

ENTERTAINMENT

Centro de Artes do Espetáculo Pr da República 39 ☎ 245 307 498, ⓦ caeportalegre.blogspot.com. The arts

centre has a great programme of music, dance, theatre and film, from world music gigs to symphony orchestras.

FROM TOP MARVÃO (P.407); COUDELARIA ALTER-REAL, THE NATIONAL STUD FARM (P.401) >

Castelo de Vide

Twenty kilometres north of Portalegre, the small town of **CASTELO DE VIDE** throws up one of the nicest surprises in the Alto Alentejo. A castle rises up above a fairy-tale townscape of bright white houses, while steep cobbled streets and placid squares are lined with well-watered pots of geraniums, tumbling house plants and two-metre-high sunflowers. Mineral springs pepper the local hills and the town is full of public fountains in shaded gardens and gleaming *praças* – at the top of town, Praça Alta provides sweeping views across the plain. It's one of those places that begs an aimless, meandering stroll, and it's very easy to find you've spent a couple of days here doing not very much at all quite happily.

With a car or a bike you can also spend an enjoyable day tracking down dolmens, menhirs and *antas*, which are the remains of an important **megalithic** culture that once flourished between the modern-day settlements of Castelo de Vide, the Barragem de Póvoa and the village of Póvoa e Meadas, 10km to the north. The turismo has useful leaflets and more information.

Judiaria

The lower town stretches from the pretty public gardens to the main Igreja de Santa Maria, behind which are the cobbled lanes of the **Judiaria** – the old Jewish quarter – which was first established by Jews fleeing the Inquisition in Spain. It's a jumble of carefully kept cottages with distinctive granite door-frames, many with brilliant floral displays carpeting the steps. In one small square sits the **Fonte da Vila**, a Renaissance marble fountain dispensing Castelo de Vide's famed mineral water.

Sinagoga

Rua da Judiaria • Daily: May–Sept 9am–1pm & 3–6pm, Oct–April 9am–1pm & 2–5pm • Free • ☎ 245 901 361

Just off the precipitous Rua da Fonte lies the thirteenth-century **Sinagoga**, the oldest surviving synagogue in Portugal. From the outside it doesn't look very different to the houses from which it was originally adapted, but inside the tabernacle survives as part of a small museum detailing the life of Jews in the town.

Castelo

Daily: May to mid-Sept 9.30am–6pm; mid-Sept to April 9.30am–5pm • Free

At the top of the hill you reach the walls and gateway of the **Castelo**, whose four-square keep squats within the wider fortifications of the original *burgo medieval* (medieval village). You can clamber up to the top of the castle from where the views over the green and grey plains beyond are magnificent, while across town you can see the walls of the **Forte de São Roque**, Castelo de Vide's other defensive bulwark (always open; free) – though there's nothing much to see inside.

ARRIVAL AND INFORMATION   **CASTELO DE VIDE**

By bus Buses from Lisbon (2 daily; 4hr 10min) and Portalegre (2 daily; 20min) drop you at the central *pelourinho* by the town-hall clock tower, on Rua Bartolomeu Álvares da Santa.
By car There's ample free parking in clearly marked bays all around the main square and street.

Information The turismo is at Praça Dom Pedro V, just behind the town hall, through the arch (daily: June–Sept 9am–7pm; Oct–May 9am–12.30pm & 2–5.30pm; ☎ 245 908 227, ⓦ castelodevide.pt).

ACCOMMODATION

★**Casa Amarela** Pr D. Pedro V 11 ☎ 245 901 250, ⓦ casaamarelath.pt. The most noble address in town, in keeping with the general ambience, is this lovely yellow mansion, its carved stone windows overlooking the main square. Beautiful rooms with plenty of space, marble bathrooms, antiques and polished wood. Parking. **€100**

Casa Machado Rua Luís de Camões 33 ☎ 245 901 515, ⓦ casamachado.com.pt. You'll find modern, spick-and-span rooms, sharing a patio and kitchen, at the western (bottom) edge of town, 300m from Porta São João. No credit cards. **€30**

Melanie Largo do Paço Novo 3 ☎ 245 901 632. Best value of the budget guesthouses at the western (town centre) end of the public gardens is provided by this friendly, English-speaking place with five nice, spacious rooms. No credit cards. **€35**

EATING

★Dom Pedro V Pr D. Pedro V ☎ 245 901 236 ⓦ dpedrov.com.pt. The place for quality regional dishes, from the usual grills to *arroz de lebre* (rice with hare) and *arroz de tamboril* (rice with monkfish). Mains cost €11–20, and you'll be hard pushed to resist trying one of the *doces conventuais*, the rich convent-recipe desserts that close any blow-out meal in these parts. Daily noon–10.30pm.

Os Amigos Rua Bartolomeu Álvares de Santa 43 ☎ 245 901 781. "The Friends" is just that, a cheery *churrasqueira* run by guys who dish up grilled platters (goat, pork, chicken and *bacalhau*) for €8–12 (most dishes feed two). It's great to eat out on the street, where the several cafés and bars over the road add to the general gaiety. Mon, Tues & Thurs–Sun noon–3pm & 7–10pm.

Marvão

By the time you've negotiated the winding road up to **MARVÃO** you're ready for sensational panoramas, and the remote border outpost doesn't disappoint. From the dramatically sited rocky outcrop high above the undulating *serra* there are unbeatable views, while within a complete circuit of seventeenth-century walls lies a higgledy-piggledy town of fewer than a thousand residents, inhabiting neat houses with granite windows and pitched red roofs. It's a fixture on the tourist trail of course, although many do no more than drive up for a quick look around, so spending the night here is an attractive proposition. There are few actual sights in the village save an impressive ruined **castle**, a couple of historical museums, and some displays in the **Casa da Cultura** (daily 9am–1pm & 2–5.30pm; free), housed in the old town hall at Rua 24 de Janeiro 1. Useful amenities cluster along the central Rua do Espírito Santo, where you'll find the tiny village shop, the post office and an ATM. But in the end, it's just as rewarding to simply climb the switchback cobbled streets or the (unguarded) outer town walls, or sit awhile in the impeccably kept terrace gardens.

Castelo

Entrance on Rua do Castelo • Daily 10pm–7pm • €1.30

The town takes its name from Marvan, a Moorish ruler, and it was the Moors who built the town's first fortifications in around the eighth century. It passed into Christian hands in 1166, and the following century, Dom Dinis built the **Castelo** and walled town that stands today. You can admire a huge *cisterna*, just inside the main entrance, still full of water, designed to supply the entire village, though most impressive of all are the views from the walls.

Cidade Romana de Ammaia

Estrada da Calçadina 4, 7km south of Marvão on the Portalegre road • Daily 9am–12.30pm & 2–5.30pm • €3 • Follow the signs for São Salvador de Aramenha from the Portagem junction • ☎ 245 919 089, ⓦ ammaia.pt

The **Cidade Romana de Ammaia** is located in a beautiful site in a wooded hollow, with Marvão high on its bluff in the distance. Sheep graze across the Roman remains, which include parts of the south gate, a bath complex, forum and temple, while a small museum occupies the kitchen and basement of an old Roman house.

ARRIVAL AND INFORMATION   **MARVÃO**

By bus Buses from Portalegre (Mon–Fri 1–2 daily; 40min–1hr) stop just outside the Portas de Rodão.

By car Marvão is 12km from Castelo de Vide and 17km from Portalegre. It's best to park at the village gate, the Portas de

Rodão. You *can* drive further into the village, following signs for the turismo and castle, but it's narrow and unnerving.
Information The turismo is on Largo da Silverinha, by the main town gates (daily 9am–12.30pm & 2–5.30pm; ☎ 245 909 131, ⓦ cm-marvao.pt), and can give details of local walking routes and companies offering horseriding.

ACCOMMODATION

Casa do Árvore Rua Doutor Matos Magalhães ☎ 245 993 854 ⓦ casadoarvoremarvao.com. A gleaming, traditional townhouse whose five genteel rooms have wooden floors, carved pine beds and great views from the living room and terrace. €60

★**Casa Dom Dinis** Rua Dr. Matos Magalhães 7 ☎ 245 909 028, ⓦ domdinis.pt. On the corner across from the turismo, this house has charming rooms featuring striking murals and paintings, and there's a terrace with views (great for sunset-watching), though you can also pay extra for room 15, which has its own private terrace. €50

El-Rei Dom Manuel Largo de Olivença ☎ 245 909 150, ⓦ turismarvao.pt. You'll find this spruce mid-range option in the first square through the gate, and there's parking right outside. It's worth paying €10 extra for the rooms that face out with expansive views, and some have little balconies or terraces. The in-house restaurant is a moderately priced place, too (mains around €10–18). €65

Pousada de Santa Maria Rua 24 de Janeiro 7 ☎ 245 993 201, ⓦ pousadas.pt. The smartest place in the village is the small-scale *pousada*, converted from former village houses. Rooms are cute and cosy, and while not all have views, those that do are blessed, while the restaurant (which shares the views) is the finest in Marvão (mains from €20). €100

EATING AND DRINKING

★**Casa do Povo** Trav do Chabouco 2 ☎ 245 993 160. The killer attraction is the café terrace with big views to die for, though for a full meal, you'll need to go to the upstairs dining room where the outlook is equally impressive. There's a very good value three-course menu for around €9, or go a la carte for the likes of *porco a Portuguesa* (cubes of pork and potatoes) and *pescada*, from around €8. The local Portalegre wine is a bargain at around €7 a litre.

Mon–Wed & Fri–Sun: café 9am–midnight, restaurant 12.30–2.30pm & 7.30–11pm.

O Castelo Trav da Carredoura 1 ☎ 245 993 411. A bustling lounge café-bar whose big draw is the leafy terrace with swing seats, a resident parrot and fine views. There's a good value set lunch for around €9 together with sandwiches, salads and snacks (€3–6). Mon–Thurs & Sun 9am–11pm, Fri & Sat 9am–midnight.

Elvas

The attractive hilltop town of **ELVAS** was once one of Portugal's mightiest frontier posts, strategically positioned just 15km from Spanish Badajoz, to the east across the Rio Guadiana. Its star-shaped walls and outlying forts of Graça and Santa Luzia are among the best-preserved military fortifications in Europe, a factor that subsequently helped gain the town UNESCO World Heritage status. Its military significance long past, and down to a population of around 25,000, it looks largely to tourism these days – Spanish day-trippers pop over to climb the steep cobbled streets and sit in the restored central square, the **Praça da República**, ringed by cafés and dominated by the mighty but ultimately underwhelming Igreja de Nossa Senhora da Assunção.

The vibrant **Monday market** (held on alternate weeks) is another big attraction, held just outside town behind the aqueduct. Otherwise, the town's main annual bash is its week-long **Festa de São Mateus**, starting on September 20 and including the largest procession in southern Portugal.

Brief history

Today's fortifications date largely from 1643–53, built during the Wars of Restoration with Spain (1641–68). Under the direction of a Dutch Jesuit, Padre Cosmander, an already impressive circuit of walls was supplemented by extensive moats and star-shaped ramparts. The result is considered to be the finest example of the Dutch school of fortifications anywhere in the world. In 1644, the garrison withstood a nine-day siege by Spanish troops, and in 1658, with its numbers reduced by an epidemic to a mere thousand, Elvas saw off a fifteen-thousand-strong Spanish army. During the Peninsular Wars in 1811, the fort provided the base from which Wellington successfully attacked Badajoz.

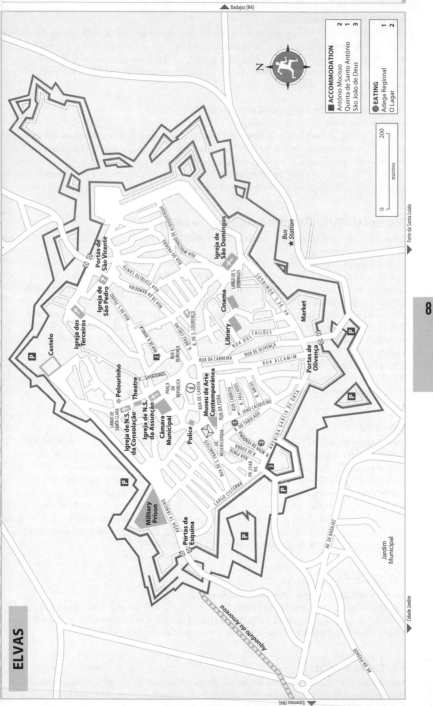

ELVAS

▲ Badajoz (N4)

N

ACCOMMODATION	
António Mocisso	2
Quinta de Santo António	1
São João de Deus	3

EATING	
Adega Regional	1
O Lagar	2

0   200

metres

▶ Forte da Santa Luláà

8

Portas de
São Vicente

Igreja de
São Domingos

Igreja de
São Pedro

Bus
★ Station

Castelo

Igreja dos
Terceiros

Cinema

LARGO DE S.
DOMINGOS

Library

Market

RUA DOS CHILÕES

AV. DE S. DOMINGOS

Pelourinho

Theatre

RUA DA CARREIRA

RUA DE OLIVENÇA

RUA ALCAMIM

Portas de
Olivença

PRAÇA DA
REPÚBLICA

R. SAPATEIROS

Museu de Arte
Contemporânea

RUA DA FEIRA

RUA CABRITO

R. FALCATO

R. ARCOS

Igreja de N.S.
da Consolação

Igreja de N.S.
da Assunção

Câmara
Municipal

LARGO DE
SANTA CLARA

Police

R. JOÃO CASQUEIRO

R. DO TABOLADO

AVENIDA GARCIA DE ORTA

RUA PINTO

R. DE ÉVORA

RUA NOVA DA MISERICÓRDIA

LARGO CISTERNA

PR. 25 AB.

Military
Prison

AVDA 14 JANEIRO

Portas da
Esquina

AV. DE BADAJOZ

Jardim
Municipal

Aqueduto da Amoreira

▶ Cidade Jardim

◀ Estremoz (N4)

Largo de Santa Clara

An intriguing sight lies up the steep street behind Igreja de Nossa Senhora da Assunção in **Largo de Santa Clara**, a tiny, cobbled square built on a slope around a splendid sixteenth-century **pelourinho**. Criminals were chained from the four metal hooks near the top – the strung-up n'er-do-wells were unlikely to have appreciated the pillar's artistically twisted Manueline column.

Igreja de Nossa Senhora da Consolação

Daily 10am–1pm & 3–6pm; Oct–April closes at 5pm • Free

The plain exterior of the small **Igreja de Nossa Senhora da Consolação** gives no clue as to the richness within. Inside you'll find a series of beautifully decorated columns rising up to a patterned cupola, while the walls are lined with ornate *azulejos*. The octagonal shape of the chapel probably pays homage to the Knights Templar: the sixteenth-century church replaced an older Knights Templar chapel that once stood nearby.

Museu de Arte Contemporânea de Elvas

Rua da Cadeia • April–Sept Tues 2–6pm, Wed–Sun 11am–6pm; Oct–March Tues 1–5pm, Wed–Sun 10am–5pm • €2 • Ⓦ cm-elvas.pt/en /museu-de-arte-contemporanea

Housed in an eighteenth-century former hospital and church, with an impressive marble entrance hall, the low-key **Museu de Arte Contemporânea de Elvas** (MACE) displays works from the António Cachola Collection by Portuguese contemporary artists. Only a small proportion of the 600-strong collection is on display at any one time, but you can expect to see impressive works by the likes of designer Fernando Brízio and Dalila Gonçalves' landscape made from used biros. In addition, there's furniture by big-name designers – Ron Arad, Marc Newson, Philippe Starck and Frank Gehry – plus ceramics by Anish Kapoor, as well as fashion from designers including Dries van Noten, Versace, Dolce et Gabbana and Jean Paul Gaultier. An over-the-top, hand-painted cape called *Virgin and Child* by Alexander McQueen is fittingly displayed in the beautiful, tiled former chapel.

Castelo

Sítio do Castelo. • Tues–Sun: April–Sept 9am–1pm & 2–6pm, March–Oct 10am–5pm • €2 • ☎ 268 626 403 Ⓦ cultura-alentejo.pt

A pretty little quarter of whitewashed mansions and cottages surround Elvas' **Castelo**, to the north of the old town. A Roman fort was first built here, which was then developed by the Moors, though what you see today largely dates back to modifications made in the late fifteenth century. You can go into the central courtyard, where there's a small café, but you need to pay to visit a small exhibition space and climb the battlements, where there are magnificent views over the surrounding plains (a view you can also enjoy from terraces outside the castle walls). Only from here do you start to appreciate the extent of the town's dramatic fortifications.

Forte de Santa Luzia

Tues 1–5pm, Wed–Sun 10am–5pm • €2 • ☎ 268 628 357 Ⓦ cm-elvas.pt

The star-shaped **Forte de Santa Luzia**, 1.5km to the south on the Spain road, was built in 1687 and used as a prison in Salazar's time. It's now a military museum, worth visiting for the chance to look across at the impressive ramparts of Elvas.

Forte da Graça

Tues–Sun 10am–5pm • €5, or two-hour guided visits at 10am, 1pm, 3pm & 5pm, €8 • ☎ 268 625 228 Ⓦ fortegraca.aiaradc.org

Resembling Elvas in miniature, this astonishing complex a couple of kilometres north

of town is one of the world's strongest bulwarked forts, built between 1763 and 1792 under the direction of the English-born Count Lippe. It is protected by 144 cannons, which helped the outpost stand firm during several military campaigns. If you want to hear about its detailed history, take one of the tours, or you can take yourself round the substantial barracks, underground cistern, governor's house, chapel and outer walls. There are amazing views back over Elvas and its aqueduct, and across to Badajoz in Spain. There's also a café by the main gates (free to enter).

Aqueduto da Amoreira

The dramatic **Aqueduto da Amoreira**, at the western entrance to town, was constructed between the late sixteenth and early seventeenth centuries. Its series of arches on five levels extend for seven kilometres and the chunky structure was a major factor in Elvas' invincibility – even under siege, the town had enough water to supply its citizens.

ARRIVAL AND INFORMATION   ELVAS

By bus The bus station is outside the walls on the Spain road: it's a longish walk in to the centre, so it's best to take a taxi for a few euros.
Destinations Estremoz (6 daily; 45min); Évora (3–4 daily; 1hr 30min); Lisbon (7 daily; 2hr–3hr 30min); Portalagre (1–3 daily; 1hr 25min–2hr 30min) and Vila Viçosa (2 daily; 35min).
By car Elvas is 40km east of Estremoz. There's parking by

the entrances to the old town, though you can also follow the "Castelo" signs up through town – the narrow streets are a bit hair-raising at times, but there's a pay car park under Praça da República and lots of free parking by the castle.
Information The turismo is on Praça da República (Mon–Fri 9am–7pm, closes 6pm from Oct–March; Sat & Sun 9.30am–6pm; ☎ 268 622 236, ⓦ cm-elvas.pt).

8

ACCOMMODATION

António Mocisso Rua Aires Varela 5/Rua de João d'Olivença 23 ☎ 268 622 126, ⓦ residencial-antonio -mocisso.webnode.pt. Popular budget place in the jumble of streets (signposted) off the main square. The rooms are fairly compact, but you get a private bathroom, fridge, wi-fi and a/c at the lowest rates in town. Your room could be in one of several buildings nearby. No credit cards. Breakfast not included. **€35**
★**Quinta de Santo António** Estrada de Barbacena, off the Portalegre road, 5km northwest of Elvas ☎ 268 636 460, ⓦ qsahotel.com. A very relaxed, informal rural estate with rambling wooded gardens, courtyards, fountains and an excellent large swimming pool. The

handsome rooms have parquet floors, marble window seats and antique beds, and there are some two- and three-bedroom apartments too, plus a moderately priced restaurant. Child-friendly, there's a playground and various activities on offer including donkey rides on request. **€120**
São João de Deus Rua de João de Quintal 1 ☎ 268 639 220, ⓦ hotelsaojoaodeus.com. This beautifully restored four-star hotel right by the walls is the finest place in the town centre. Formerly a convent, it retains its grand sense of space and an interior of *azulejos* and warm colours. The rooms mix contemporary and traditional style, the restaurant occupies the old convent refectory, and there's a small terrace pool with city views. Parking. **€80**

EATING

Elvas has a fairly good selection of **restaurants**, covering all price ranges. The best place to buy picnic supplies is the early-morning food **market** held Monday to Saturday at the bottom of Rua dos Chilões, by the walls. Elvas is not a late-night kind of place, but the **cafés** overlooking Praça da República can be relied upon for daytime drinks (or meals) and stay open until around midnight.

Adega Regional Rua João de Casqueiro 22b ☎ 268 623 009. This popular place has a spacious back dining room and a small terrace with tables on the street. The long menu packs in a good selection of fish, such as *lulas com bacon* and grilled octopus, along with the usual meat dishes (all €9–12). Unusually, there are also some vegetarian options, including a fine potato, mushroom and asparagus gratinado.

Mon & Wed–Sun 11am–4pm & 7pm–midnight.
O Lagar Rua Nova da Vendoria 7 ☎ 268 626 247. Good regional cuisine accompanied by a blessed blast of the air conditioning. Good for fish and seafood, with clams, cuttlefish, *bacalhau*, and *arroz de marisco* sitting alongside the usual grills, and the *porco alentejana* is excellent. Most dishes cost €9–12. Mon–Wed & Fri–Sun 11am–4pm & 7–10pm.

Vila Viçosa

The pretty town of **VILA VIÇOSA** is dominated entirely by its ducal palace – the last residence of the Portuguese monarchy – and by the coachloads of tourists who descend upon it for a quick visit before being whisked off again. Because of that, it's actually quite a pleasant place to spend the night, with an unhurried small-town atmosphere that survives the daily imposition of visitors. As at Estremoz, marble is the dominant building material: the road from Borba, 5km away, is lined on either side with enormous marble quarries, and in town everything, from the pavements to the humblest building, is made of the local stone.

Brief history

The dukes of Bragança established their seat here in the fifteenth century, originally in the castle and then, from the early sixteenth century, in the Paço Ducal. The family were always an influential part of Portugal's ruling elite, but it was only after Spain's Philip II took over the Portuguese throne in 1581 that the Bragança family became truly powerful. After sixty years of Spanish rule, Portuguese soldiers rebelled and occupied the palace at Lisbon. The Duke of Bragança was the obvious choice to take back the throne from the Spanish and he duly became Dom João IV of Portugal. From 1640 until the birth of the Republic in 1910, the dynasty continued to rule as monarchs.

Although the Bragançan dukes and kings had lavish palaces all over the country, they often chose to stay in Vila Viçosa – indeed it was here that Dom Carlos slept the night before he was shot in a republican uprising in the capital in 1908. His son, Manuel II, also used the palace frequently before his eventual exile to Britain two years later. Afterwards, the family was banned from entering Portugal until 1950 so, it is alleged, that when the current duke, Dom Duarte Pio – who still considers himself heir to the throne – was born (1945), it was in the Portuguese embassy in Berne, Switzerland, to ensure any possible future right of succession.

Paço Ducal

Terreiro do Paço • April–June & Sept Tues 2.30–5.30pm, Wed–Fri 10am–1pm & 2.30–5.30pm, Sat, Sun & hols 9.30am–1pm & 2.30–6pm; July & Aug Tues 2.30–6pm, Wed–Fri 10am–1pm & 2.30–6pm, Sat & Sun 9.30am–1pm & 2.30–6pm; Oct–March Tues 2–5pm, Wed–Fri 10am–1pm & 2–5pm, Sat, Sun & hols 9.30am–1pm & 2–5pm • Tours €6; Treasury €2.50; Armoury €3; Chinese porcelain collection €2.50; Coach museum €2 • ☎ 268 980 659 ⓦ fcbraganca.pt

One whole side of the gleaming marble palace square is taken up by the **Paço Ducal**, which can only be seen on an obligatory one-hour guided tour. This is usually in Portuguese and none too revealing – and you might well pass up on the opportunity to visit the armoury, treasury, coach museum and Chinese porcelain collection (separate charges for all) that also form part of the complex. You are led dutifully through formal

---

DON'T PICK THE FLOWERS

Every two years, the pretty little whitewashed town of **Redondo** (18km southwest of Vila Viçosa) bursts into bloom during the extraordinary **Ruas Floridas**, a week-long flower festival with a difference. In a revival of a nineteenth-century tradition, the cobbled old-town streets are covered in flowers, shade canopies, human figures, exotic animals and life-size scenes made entirely from coloured paper. Each street is responsible for choosing a theme, so you might walk up to the castle through a steamy jungle complete with elephants and parrots and back down along a Brazilian beach; caricatures of the local women wash clothes in a paper river, while wild boars root in paper acorns. At lunchtime, every single restaurant in Redondo is crammed with local families and visitors; at night there are marching bands, dances, concerts and bullfights. The event is biennial (odd years) and is usually held from the last day or two in July through the first week in August (exact dates on the local town council website ⓦ cm-redondo.pt).

chambers and halls filled with regal furniture, glowering oil paintings and faded tapestries, and it's only in the more intimate private apartments that you get any real sense of the lives of the penultimate king, Dom Carlos, and his wife Marie-Amélia. There's a *Hello!* magazine fascination in gazing at the old family photographs and everyday objects on display which reveal their taste in fashion and food.

The old Bragança dukes were buried opposite the palace in the chapel of the **Mosteiro dos Agostinhos**, while the duchesses had their own mausoleum in the **Convento das Chagas**, just to the side of the palace – part of this is now the *pousada*. Before you leave Terreiro do Paço square, walk a little way up the road out of town (to Borba), where on the left the **Porta do Nós** is a Manueline stone gateway formed into the knot symbol of the Bragança family.

Castelo and around

Av dos Duques de Bragança • Same hours as Paço Ducal• €3 • ☎ 268 980 128 ☺ cbraganca.pt

Avenida dos Duques de Bragança runs from the palace square past the thirteenth-century hilltop **Castelo**, built by Dom Dinis. It was the original home of the Bragança family before their larger, more lavish palace was built. The interior now houses the Museu de Arqueologia e Muse de Caça (museums of archaeology and hunting) which are less interesting than the building itself. Note that you don't need to pay to climb the outer castle walls for views over town.

The original population of Vila Viçosa was based below the castle inside the walls of the old town. A few cobbled streets, white cottages and a sixteenth-century *pelourinho* are all that remain, along with the **Nossa Senhora da Conceição**, the pick of Vila Viçosa's 22 churches, filled with eighteenth-century *azulejos*.

8

ARRIVAL AND INFORMATION

VILA VIÇOSA

By bus The bus station is opposite the municipal market at the foot of Largo Dom João IV – cross the square and it's a 200-metre walk up any of the streets ahead of you to the elongated main square, Praça da República.
Destinations Elvas (2 daily; 35min); Évora (3 daily; 1hr); Lisbon (3 daily; 2hr 40min–3hr 45min).

By car Vila Viçosa is 35km southwest of Elvas, and 17km southeast of Estremoz. There's plenty of free parking in front of the palace or over in the town centre by the main squares.
Information The turismo is on Praça da República, in the town hall, near the upper (church) end (daily 9.30am–12.30pm & 2–5.30pm; ☎ 268 889 317, ☺ cm-vilavicosa.pt).

ACCOMMODATION AND EATING

Os Cucos Mata Municipal ☎ 268 980 806 ☺ cucus.web .pt. At the top of the market square, in the town gardens, this spacious and popular place is particularly good for fish and there's a changing list of daily specials (*javali, bacalhau* etc) – you'll eat well for around €20. Daily 12.30–3pm & 7.30–11pm; closed 2 weeks in Aug.

★ Pousada de Dom João IV Terreiro do Paço ☎ 268 980 742, ☺ pousadas.pt. Regal accommodation right by the palace in a converted sixteenth-century convent that retains its echoing halls, corridors, nuns' cells and cloister. Rooms are elegant and the pool and gardens at the back

are a hit with families. The restaurant (mains from €20) is the glam dining spot in town, and there's nothing nicer than breakfast overlooking the orange trees. Parking. **€130**

Solar dos Mascarenhas Rua Florbela Espança 125 ☎ 268 886 000, ☺ solardosmascarenhas.com. On the road between the palace and the main square, this converted mansion has stylish three-star accommodation, plus an outdoor terrace and decent pool. You can expect to pay an exta €20 or so per night at weekends. The restaurant, *Do Paço* (mains €15–18, closed Tues), offers a classier take on regional cuisine than most local places. **€105**

Monsaraz and around

MONSARAZ – known locally as Ninho das Águias (Eagles' Nest) – is perched high above the border plains, a tiny village nestled into fortified walls close to the Spanish border. With a permanent population of only a few hundred, Monsaraz has just two main streets that run parallel to each other, Rua Direita and Rua de Santiago.

The **Igreja Matriz** lies at the heart of the village, just off the main square that's home to a curious eighteenth-century **pillory**. The village does its best to attract visitors with a series of little galleries, craft shops and restaurants, but it's really the **castle**, the higgledy-piggledy streets and magnificent views from the walls that keep people coming: to the north and west, you survey a typically flat Alentejan plain of vineyards and olive groves, while to the south and east a watery expanse glitters far below the village, part of Europe's largest artificial reservoir behind the dam at Alqueva (see p.416).

Four thousand years ago, the region around Monsaraz was an important centre of megalithic culture, and various **dolmens** (covered temples or tombs), **menhirs** (standing stones) and stone circles survive today. An hour and a half's driving circuit takes in most of these, and if you throw in lunch and a vineyard visit at nearby Reguengos that's a good day out.

Castelo

The **Torre das Feiticeiras** (Witches' Tower) looms from the **castle** at the southern end of the village, part of a chain of impressive frontier fortresses, once ruled over by the Knights Templar and later the Order of Christ, who ensured the fortified town stayed in Christian hands long after it was taken from the Moors in 1167. You can clamber along the outer walls for more stunning views, around a central space within the castle that was for a time used as a bullring.

Cromeleque do Xerez

1.5km below the village; leave Monsaraz and follow the signs at the first roundabout for the Convento do Orada

The most impressive megalithic monument in the surroundings is the **Cromeleque do Xerez**, a square "circle" of 49 granite stones with a towering four-metre-high central menhir, which is thought to have been built to host fertility rites in Neolithic times. Park by the low walls near the convent and it's a two-hundred-metre walk to where the stones have been re-erected – they were moved here from their original site when the Alqueva dam was flooded.

São Pedro do Corval

It is an easy twenty-minute drive to **São Pedro do Corval**, off the Reguengos road, known for its ceramics workshops, many of which line the road. Some of these might tempt you to stop for a browse around – a few of the workshops and galleries also stock the hand-woven woollen scarves, rugs and blankets in which the region specializes.

Herdade do Esporão

Reguengos de Monsaraz, 15km west of Monsaraz • 1hr 30min tours at 11am, 3pm & 5pm • €6 • reservations on ☎ 266 509 280, ⓦ esporao.com • Wine bar daily 10am–6pm • Restaurant daily 12.30–3.30pm

Just south of the wine town of Reguengos, **Herdade do Esporão** is the oldest wine estate in the region, dating back to 1267 – though viniculture here has been bought bang up to date under Australian wine-maker David Baverstock. As well as seeing the wine presses, cellars (including a 17-metre deep tunnel of barrels), bottling plant and vineyards, you can also visit the restaurant and bar to sample the estate's own olive oil as well as its wine. Visitors can also tour the estate by bike or jeep and visit a medieval tower.

ARRIVAL AND INFORMATION	MONSARAZ AND AROUND
By bus From Évora, you have to catch a bus to Reguengos de Monsaraz (2 daily; 35min–1hr) and change there for	Monsaraz (Mon–Fri 3–5 daily; 35min). Buses stop right outside the town gates.

By car Drivers should use the car parks outside the gates.
Information The turismo is on Rua Direita (daily 9.30am–12.30pm & 2–6pm; ☎ 266 557 136, ⓦ cm-reguengos-monsaraz.pt).

ACCOMMODATION

Several houses along Rua Direita and its continuation advertise **rooms**, sheltered behind thick walls in traditional Alentejan homes – cool in summer, warm in winter – many with stone floors, painted furniture, terraces and balconies. Prices are broadly similar (€70 a room including breakfast), cheaper outside peak summer season.

Casa Dona Antónia Rua Direita 15 ☎ 266 557 142, ⓦ casadantonia-monsaraz.com. A good first point of call, *Casa Dona Antónia* has a homely cottage interior and a lovely patio garden. The six double rooms and one suite are simple but cool and clean, and if you can stretch to an extra €10, you get a view thrown in. **€60**; suite **€90**
Estalagem de Monsaraz Largo de São Bartolomeu 5 ☎ 266 557 112, ⓦ estalagemdemonsaraz.com. Partly built into the walls, just outside the village, this superb inn is in a lovely old building. There are dazzling views from most rooms, as well as a lovely pool in a garden laden with lemon trees. Its restaurant, *Sabores de Monsaraz*, is also good. **€80**
Monte Alerta Apartado 101, Telheiro ☎ 966 768 307, ⓦ montealerta.pt. A couple of kilometres from Monsaraz, *Monte Alerta* is a gorgeous rural retreat which has eight varied but pretty rooms, plus a pool, jacuzzi and fine gardens. **€85**

EATING

Casa do Forno Trav Sabrosa ☎ 266 104 008. This welcoming place has a small terrace and a cosy interior serving Alentejan meat specialities such as *borrego no forno* (roast lamb), lamb chops and *migas* (most mains €9–11). Mon & Wed–Sun noon–9.30pm.
★ **Xarez** Rua de Santiago 33 ☎ 266 557 052. The town's top choice is the stylish *Xarez*, just inside the main gate, which has a terrace with terrific views, an attractive stone interior and serves tasty tapas such as local cheeses, spicy sausages and hare tart. Main courses start at around €11, and usually include *bacalhau* and a fine steak cooked on a hot stone. Mon, Wed & Fri–Sun 11am–midnight.

Moura

The pleasantly provincial town of **MOURA**, 50km south of Monsaraz, is a surprisingly opulent place full of grand mansions, pretty squares and pedestrianized shopping streets. It's also the closest town to the controversial **Alqueva Dam** (see box, p.416). The Moors occupied the town from the eighth century until 1232 – an Arabic well still survives in the old town – and Moura is named after a Moorish maiden, Moura Saluquia, who ostensibly threw herself from the castle tower in despair when Christians murdered her betrothed and overran the town. The discovery of naturally carbonated thermal springs in the late nineteenth century prompted Moura's eventual prosperity; the spa water still dribbles from the Fonte das Três Bicas (Fountain of Three Spouts), but the spa no longer operates. Nevertheless, the adjacent **Jardim Doutor Santiago** gardens (daily 8am–dusk) make a pleasant place to stroll, with lots of shady trees. West of here rises the Manueline Igreja de São João Baptista, with the entrance to the castle beyond, just past the large market building.

Castelo

Calçada do Castelo • Mon–Fri 9am–12.30pm & 2–5.30pm, Sat & Sun 9.30am–12.30pm & 2–6pm • Free • ☎ 285 250 400

Built by Dom Dinis over a Moorish citadel, the **Castelo** was largely destroyed by the Spanish Duke of Osuna in 1701, though one Moorish tower still survives, the **Torre de Menagem** (tours at 10am, noon, 3pm & 5pm). Inside is a motley collection of weapons, though most people head straight up to the top to enjoy the vista. The castle grounds, which have been attractively landscaped, also provide good views – best from the top of the bell-tower – and form the background for various music and dance events that take place throughout the summer (see the turismo website for details).

8

THE BARRAGEM DE ALQUEVA

In 2002 the floodgates opened on the controversial **Barragem de Alqueva** (Alqueva Dam), filled by the waters of the Rio Guadiana and several tributaries. At 250 square kilometres (of which 69 square kilometres are in Spain), it's Europe's largest reservoir. Plans for the project started decades ago under the Salazar regime, with the aim of providing reliable irrigation in this arid region and jobs in the agricultural and tourism industries. There are many who still lament the destruction of over a million oak and cork trees in its construction and the resulting threats to the habitats of golden eagles and the even rarer Iberian lynx, plus the submerging of over two hundred prehistoric sites. Meanwhile, the inhabitants of the former village of **Luz** on the east bank of the Guadiana, now submerged, were relocated to a facsimile village above the waterline which, despite similarities of appearance, has become something of a failed experiment; the younger villagers having left and the older ones are deeply dissatisfied.

The government points to the benefits of the dam, not least the hydroelectric plant, switched on in 2004, which provides enough electricity to supply the Évora and Beja districts combined. Smooth roads also now radiate from the dam, which has become something of a tourist attraction in its own right, the deep waters lapping on one side, a sheer drop on the other. Small marinas have also been built to provide watersports and boat trips (around €10 for an hour) or you can stay on houseboats; see ⓦ amieramarina.com for details.

The Moorish quarter and the Núcleo Árabe

Núcleo Árabe Rua da Mouraria 11 • Tues–Sat 9.30am–12.30pm & 2.30–5.30pm • Free • ☎ 285 208 040 ⓦ mouraturismo.pt

Although Moura's Moorish occupation ended in 1232, a significant Moorish population remained in the part of town just to the south of the castle, off the elongated Praça Sacadura Cabral. Once a teeming hive of alleys, the former **Moorish quarter (Bairro da Mouraria)** is now a quiet residential neighbourhood, whose few narrow cobbled streets only spring to life once the heat of the day diminishes. Here you can still see the fourteenth-century "Poço Arabe" – the old Arab well – which forms the centrepiece of the **Núcleo Árabe**, a small museum that houses a collection of Arab artefacts.

Lagar de Varas do Fojo

Rua São João de Deus 20 • Tues–Sun 9.30am–12.30pm & 2.30–5.30pm • Free • ☎ 285 253 978

Of Moura's few modest museums, the **Lagar de Varas**, just around the corner from the *Hotel de Moura*, is the most interesting. Housed in an old municipal olive-oil plant, which operated before machines took over in 1841, it is a beautifully cool, dark building featuring the restored wooden presses and vats plus a small exhibition about the production of olive oil.

ARRIVAL AND INFORMATION | MOURA

By bus Buses will either drop you centrally, at Praça Sacadura Cabral, by the castle, or at the bus station, outside the old train station, at the top end of Moura: from here, it's a 10–15min walk into the centre.

Destinations Beja (Mon–Fri 6 daily; 1hr 30min); Évora (1 daily; 1hr 25min); Lisbon (1 daily; 3hr 10min); Serpa (Mon–Fri 6 daily; 40min).

Information The turismo (daily 10am–noon & 3–5pm; ☎ 285 208 040, ⓦ cm-moura.pt) is inside the castle grounds.

ACCOMMODATION AND EATING

A few pleasant **cafés** face the gardens and castle on Praça Sacadura Cabral, where you will also find the large fruit and vegetable market. In the narrow streets running back from here, there are plenty of **cafés and restaurants** serving inexpensive snacks and typically generous portions of Alentejan food. Rua Miguel Bombarda is the main pedestrianized shopping street.

Hotel de Moura Pr Gago Coutinho 1 ☎ 285 251 090, ⓦ hoteldemoura.com. Moura's top hotel, signed to the south of town, is set in a former seventeenth-century convent which was turned into a hotel in 1900. Its facade is

completely covered with *azulejos*, and inside there's a grand staircase, lavish rooms, patios, mirrored doors and a rambling garden with a swimming pool. €40

O Trilho Rua 5 de Outubro 5 ☎ 285 254 261. First choice for food is *O Trilho*, which serves bumper portions of regional dishes such as *gaspacho* soup, *roast lamb*, duck rice and *carne de porco à alentejana* (pork with clams and potatoes) from €9–13, as well as various dishes of the day. Tues–Sun noon–3pm & 7–10pm.

Santa Comba Pr Sacadura Cabral 34 ☎ 285 251 255, ⓦ hotelsantacomba.com. The town's back-up option is right by the castle: decent-sized rooms with air conditioning and cable TV, though front-facing rooms can be noisy. Parking. €38

Serpa

Thirty kilometres southwest of Moura, and the same again east of Beja, the small market town of **SERPA** offers the classic Alentejan attractions – a walled centre, a castle, and narrow, whitewashed streets of handsome bougainvillea-clad houses and lush gardens. The town has at various times been occupied by Celts, Romans and Moors, and its highest point is capped by the remnants of its **Castelo**. Beyond these few attractions, the delight of Serpa is in wandering its quiet, little-visited streets that spread for just a few hundred metres within the encircling walls. Centre of the settlement is the **Praça da República**, with its appealing cafés, while arched gates provide access to the more modern town beyond. To the south, the leafy **public gardens** provide shade in the hottest part of the day. The town's annual **feira** takes place on the closest weekend to Aug 24, and there are big celebrations each Easter in honour of Nossa Senhora de Guadalupe.

8

Castelo and Museu Arqueológico

Alcáçova do Castelo • Tues–Sun 9am–noon & 2–5pm • Free • ☎ 284 544 663

Originally built by Dom Dinis in the fourteenth century, Serpa's attractive **Castelo** was partly blown up by the Spanish in the eighteenth-century War of Succession – parts of a toppled tower balance precariously above the entrance. The keep survived and now houses an archeological museum tracing Serpa's history back to Roman times, though labels are in Portuguese. You can also climb the surviving battlements for great views, and to track the course of Serpa's eleventh-century **aqueduct** (closed to the public), which retains an antique chain-pump at one end – this is best seen from just outside the town walls, on Rua dos Arcos. Near the castle entrance, the thirteenth-century **Igreja de Santa Maria** contains an altarpiece of intricate woodcarving, surrounded by seventeenth-century *azulejos*.

Museu Etnográfico

Largo do Corro • Tues–Sun 9am–12.30pm & 2–5.30pm • Free • ☎ 284 540 100 ⓦ cm-serpa.pt

Flanking the eastern town walls, the small **Museu Etnográfico** (Ethnographic Museum) offers an interesting account of the changing economic activity of the town and the area as a whole. Its exhibits include a selection of ancient agricultural implements, olive presses and traditional local costumes.

ARRIVAL AND DEPARTURE · SERPA

By bus The bus station is off Avenida de Paz in the modern southwest of town, ten minutes' walk from the old centre. Destinations Beja (6 daily; 35min); Lisbon (1–3 daily; 3hr 45min); and Moura (Mon–Fri 6 daily; 40min).

By car Cars can enter the walled town for access only, but you wouldn't want to risk the narrow streets in any case. There's plenty of parking all around the walls, with nothing more than five minutes' walk away.

INFORMATION

Turismo Within the walls at Rua dos Cavalos 19 (April–Sept daily 10am–7pm; Oct–March daily 10am–6pm; ☎ 284 544 727, ⓦ cm-serpa.pt).

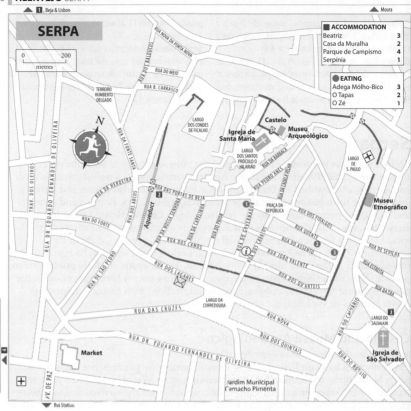

SERPA

ACCOMMODATION
Beatriz	3
Casa da Muralha	2
Parque de Campismo	4
Serpínia	1

EATING
Adega Mólho-Bico	3
O Tapas	2
O Zé	1

ACCOMMODATION

Beatriz Largo do Salvador 10 ☎284 544 423, ⓦresidencialbeatriz.com. This smart guesthouse near the church also has three apartments with kitchenettes (€60) – all rooms have private bath, wi-fi and a/c, and there's parking too. **€45**

★**Casa da Muralha** Rua das Portas de Beja 43 ☎284 543 150, ⓦcasadamuralha.com. The only place to stay within the town walls, it's right by the aqueduct gate, with lovely rooms opening onto a tree-shaded courtyard garden. All rooms face the garden, with painted Alentejan furniture, traditional cane ceilings and cool tile floors. Breakfast is a good spread of local produce. Discounts for longer stays. **€75**

Parque de Campismo Eira de São Pedro ☎284 544 290, ⓦcm-serpa.pt. Serpa's well-equipped municipal campsite is at the southwest corner of town, a bit closer in than the bus station, near the swimming pool complex (to which there's free access). Pitch **€6**

Serpínia Rua Serpa Pinto 34 ☎284 544 055, ⓦresidencialserpinia.com. On the main road into town from Beja, this modern guesthouse has pleasant doubles with small balconies. There's a spacious breakfast room, wifi, parking and a small pool at the back. **€45**

EATING

Adega Mólho-Bico Rua Quente 1 ☎284 549 264 ⓦmolhobicaserpa.com. The weekend family favourite – a rustic grill house with stone floors and wooden benches, serving regional specialities (pork, fish, steaks etc) from around €8–12. Mon, Tues & Thurs–Sun 11am–2am.

O Tapas Rua Quente 17 ☎284 544 063. As the name suggests, tapas is the speciality here – local sausage, cheese etc – though it also does fresh fish and grilled meats (around €10) and good local wines. Friendly staff, but service can be slow when it's busy. Mon–Wed & Fri–Sun 11am–4pm & 6pm–midnight.

O Zé Pr da República 10 ☎968 441 404. This café-restaurant has alluring tables on the main square, with a little inside dining room serving good-value *bacalhau* and a fine mixed grill (mains from €7). Daily 9am–4pm.

Beja and around

BEJA is the main town of the Baixa Alentejo (Lower Alentejo), though its population only numbers around 35,000. Its inland position means that it's frequently the hottest place in Portugal, something to bear in mind if you plan a visit during the summer months. Once past the modern suburbs, you'll find a laidback old quarter with a historic **convent** (now a museum), and an impressive **castle** dating from the thirteenth century. You can take in the sights in the compact historic centre in half a day, though it's not a bad night's stopover in any case, with plenty of good cafés and restaurants.

Commanding a strategic position in the centre of the plains, it has long been an important and prosperous city. Founded by Julius Caesar in 48 BC, it was named Pax Julia, in honour of the peace accord signed here between Rome and the Lusitanians, but later became Pax Augusta and then just Pax – this gradually became corrupted to Paca, Baca, Baju, and finally Beja. You can still experience the Roman influence to the north, at the atmospheric **Ruinas Romanas de São Cucufate**, where the history of three separate Roman villas is laid bare in a series of extensive excavations and reconstructions.

Museu Regional (Convento de Nossa Senhora de Conceiçao)

Largo da Conceição • Tues–Sun 9.30am–12.30pm & 2–5.15pm • €2, free on Sun, also includes entry to Museu Visigótico • ☎ 284 323 351,
Ⓦ museuregionaldebeja.net

The highly impressive **Convento de Nossa Senhora da Conceição** was founded in the fifteenth century, with an array of Manueline arches and latticed embellishments that enliven its low roofline. The convent was dissolved in 1834 and today houses the excellent **Museu Regional**, with displays of rescued church art and Flemish paintings gathered in the galleries around the convent cloister. It's the sumptuous tilework, however, that first catches the eye – the walls of the cloisters and chapterhouse are tiled from top to bottom with sixteenth- and seventeenth-century *azulejos*. There's also a striking Rococo chapel, dripping with gold leaf. A stunning fifteenth-century Mudéjar terracotta grille once linked the convent to the neighbouring palace – it was through this delicate tracery that the convent's most famous resident, Sister Mariana Alcoforado, first glimpsed her lover (see box, p.421).

Upstairs is a small archeological section, where Roman stonework and inscriptions remind you of Beja's erstwhile importance. Much of the collection was found at the extensive site of **Pisões**, 7km southwest of town (signposted from Aljustrel road; by appointment only on ☎ 284 311 800; free), where the walls of a Roman dam and the remains of rural buildings of the first to fourth century AD can still be seen.

Museu Jorge Vieira – Casa das Artes

Rua do Touro 33 • Tues–Sun 9.30am–12.30pm & 2–6pm • Free • ☎ 284 311 920

A short walk up Rua do Touro from the Museu Regional brings you to the **Museu Jorge Vieira**. It's a quirky private showcase for the work of contemporary sculptor Jorge Vieira, whose surreal terracotta sculptures – part feminine, part grotesque – show a clear Cubist lineage from Picasso and Braque.

Igreja da Misericórdia

Praça da República • Mon–Fri 10am–4pm • ☎ 213 614 200

At the top of the Praça da República, you can't miss the sixteenth-century **Igreja da Misericórdia**, whose large arched porch once housed the town's meat market. Now it is home to a small handicrafts shop selling attractive cork products and ceramics produced by a local arts co-operative (until around 1pm).

8

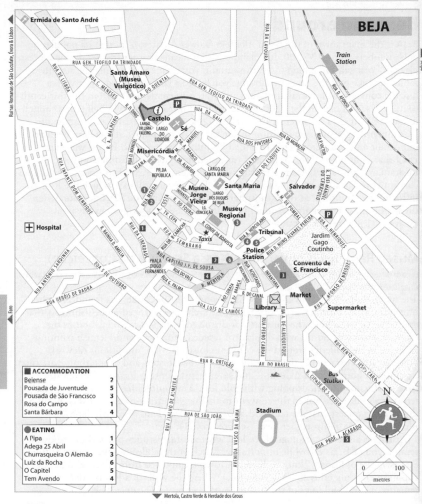

Mertola, Castro Verde & Herdade dos Grous

Castelo

Largo Dr. Lima Faleiro • April–Oct daily 9.30am–noon & 2–5.30pm; Nov–March 9.30am–noon & 2–4.30pm; Torre de Menagem closes 30min before castle • Free

Beja's impressive fourteenth-century **Castelo**, built by Dom Dinis, looms large beyond the town's unassuming cathedral. Its 40-metre-high **Torre de Menagem** boasts decorative battlements and dizzying views, making those from the walls below seem tame. At the time of going to press, the Torre was closed for renovations and visits may involve a small fee. The castle's internal courtyard now houses the town's turismo.

Igreja de Santo Amaro (Museu Visigótico)

Largo de Santo Amaro • Tues–Sun 9.30am–12.30pm & 2–5.15pm • €2, free on Sun, also includes entry to Museu Regional (see p.419) • ☎ 284 321 465

Beyond the castle walls, the small, whitewashed **Igreja de Santo Amaro** is one of the country's few extant buildings to date from pre-Moorish times, with motifs on its

columns being dated back to the seventh century. Inside, the small **Museu Visigótico** displays an important collection of Visigothic archeological remains – look out for the amazing fifth-century iron sword, its handle inlaid with gold and amber.

Herdade dos Grous

Around 19km south of Beja just off the IP2 in the village of Albernoa • Daily 9am–6pm; wine tours from €5–25 depending on group size • ☎ 284 960 000, Ⓦ herdade-dos-grous.com

Set in some of the Alentejo's most beautiful countryside, the **Herdade dos Grous** is one of the region's top wine estates, with 73 hectares of vineyards. They also make their own olive oil, breed cattle and champion show-jumpers, and can arrange fishing in the estate's private lake. Visitors can tour the winery, or explore the 730-hectare estate on foot, by tractor (€9), on horseback (€20), or even by hot-air balloon (€140; min four people). If you fancy a longer stay at this upmarket rural resort, there's a top-notch restaurant (daily 12.30–2.30pm; Fri–Sun 7.30–9.30pm), and smart accommodation (rooms from €125).

8

Ruinas Romanas de São Cucufate

30km to the north of Beja and 1km beyond Vila de Frades in Lugar de São Cucufate • May to mid-Sept Tues 2.30–6.30pm, Wed–Sun 10am–12.30pm & 2.30–6.30pm; mid-Sept to April Tues 2–5.30pm, Wed–Sun 10am–1pm & 2–5.30pm • €3 • ☎ 284 441 113, Ⓦ www.cm-vidigueira.pt

The **Ruinas Romanas de São Cucufate** is a peaceful, rural spot, shrouded in landscaped grounds of rosemary, thyme and lavender. The first Roman villa was built here in the middle of the first century AD, but replaced by two successively grander constructions, with baths, grain stores, oil presses and servants' quarters. The third villa was abandoned in the fifth century and later reoccupied in medieval times as a monastery – the old wine cellar was eventually decorated with frescoes in the seventeenth century, after which the whole complex was abandoned once more. You can go inside a couple of the extremely rickety-looking ruins, used in spring by nesting birds.

ARRIVAL AND INFORMATION | BEJA

By bus The bus station is five minutes' walk southeast of the old centre.

Destinations Évora (2–4 daily; 1hr 15min–2hr); Faro (3 daily; 2hr 50min); Lisbon (7–11 daily; 2hr 15min–3hr); Mértola (Mon–Fri 3 daily; 1hr 15min); Moura (Mon–Fri 6 daily; 1hr 15min); Portalegre (1–3 daily; 2hr 40min–3hr 45min); and Serpa (6 daily; 35min).

By car Beja's old quarter is a circular tangle of streets, enclosed within a ring road that has largely replaced the town walls. Negotiate the one-way system and you can get fairly close to the historic centre by car, and there's signposted parking at various points (some of it metered, free at the weekends) – anywhere around the castle,

gardens or bus station is convenient.

By train Beja is on a branch off the Linha do Alentejo from Lisbon, which usually means changing trains at Casa Branca for trains to Lisbon (3–4 daily; 2hr 15min) or Évora (3–4 daily; 2hr 15min). The train station is five minutes northeast of the town centre.

By bike Bikes are available for free use around town – you'll see the racks – though you have to go through a form-filling procedure (take ID) at the turismo first.

Information The turismo is inside the Castelo (daily 9.30am–12.30pm & 2–6pm; ☎ 284 311 913, Ⓦ cm-beja .pt), and can provide details of the town's various festivities throughout the year.

ACCOMMODATION

★**Bejense** Rua Capitão J. Francisco de Sousa 57 ☎284 311 570, ⊛hotelbejense.com. Beja's oldest hotel, first opened in 1889, is now a lovely space with boutique touches, filled with tiles, flowers and family photos. Contemporary-styled, high-ceilinged, a/c rooms have large bathrooms, satellite TV and free wi-fi. It's a welcoming place, with a bar; breakfast is served in a bright first-floor dining room. **€46**

Pousada de Juventude Rua Prof Janeiro Acabado ☎284 325 239, ⊛pousadajuventude.pt. The youth hostel is close to the bus station, with a good-sized common room, internet facilities and bike rental. The modern dorms are four- or six-bedded, and there are also six en-suite doubles. Dorms **€13**; doubles **€32**

★**Pousada de São Francisco** Largo D. Nuno Álvares Pereira ☎284 313 580, ⊛pousadas.pt. Sumptuous *pousada* set round the cloisters and church of a former thirteenth-century convent – not surprisingly, the atmosphere is serene, with plush rooms modelled from former cells whose small windows keep out the heat. The excellent-quality restaurant and bar have outdoor tables in a palm-dotted garden with its own spacious pool and tennis courts, there's a sauna and Turkish bath, and the only sound at night is the odd nightjar. Parking. **€125**

Rosa do Campo Rua da Liberdade 12 ☎284 323 578, ⊛rosadocampo.pt. Good for groups, with some large rooms of three beds or more, in a well-converted 1950s townhouse. It's a light, bright place, thanks to open planning and unusual roof lighting. No credit cards. **€40**

Santa Bárbara Rua de Mértola 56 ☎284 312 280, ⊛hotelsantabarbara.pt. Good-value, a/c rooms with tiled floors and small en-suite showers/toilets. The best rooms overlook the pedestrianized street and have pocket-sized balconies. There's also a small bar. **€48**

EATING

A Pipa Rua da Moeda 8 ☎284 327 043. A barn-like restaurant with high ceilings hung with old yokes. Big, filling meaty mains from €8, though half portions suffice for most. Good house wine too. Mon–Sat noon–3pm & 7–10pm.

★**Adega 25 Abril** Rua da Moeda 23 ☎284 325 960. There's an Alentejan farmer somewhere missing his tools, because they're all on the walls in this huge rustic *adega*. Try the *arroz de bacalhau* or the giant pork steaks with home-cooked crisps. Mains from €8. Tues–Sat 12.30–3pm & 7–11pm, Sun 7–11pm.

Churrasqueira O Alemão Largo dos Duques de Beja 11 ☎284 311 490. The queues out the door at lunch are for the takeaway side of the operation – slip through into the simple tiled dining-room for unglamorous but inexpensive charcoal-grilled sausages, steaks and chicken from €7.50. Mon–Sat 10am–10pm.

Luíz da Rocha Rua do Capitão J. Francisco de Sousa 63 ☎284 323 179. In business for over a century, the café and tea room downstairs are famed for cakes and pastries. Pop in for a *bica* and snack or an evening brandy, or head upstairs for inexpensive meals. Daily 8am–11pm.

O Capitel Largo Eng. Duarte Pacheco ☎284 327 555. *O Capitel* has a sunny raised terrace facing an attractive square and the Tribunal building, a good spot for a drink or snack. At night, many move inside for the sports TV. Mon–Sat 8am–2am.

Tem Avendo Rua Alexandre Herculano 25 ☎284 328 956. Overlooking an attractive square, this is a good place to sample Alentejan dishes such as *migas* with tomato and mackerel, *carne do porco Alentejana* and *cozido* stews. The half portions at around €6 are usually plenty to fill up on. Mon–Fri & Sun noon–2.45pm & 6–10.15pm.

Mértola and around

MÉRTOLA, 54km southeast of Beja, is as beautifully sited as any town in the south, set high on a spur above the confluence of the Guadiana and Oeiras rivers, guarded by the ruins of a Moorish frontier castle. It makes a fine place to stay the night, or longer, with a compact, somnolent old town full of attractions, and quiet rural surroundings that form part of the **Parque Natural Vale do Guadiana**: the N265 through the park to Serpa is one of the loveliest drives in Portugal. The region is home to the rare black stork and other endangered species, and the local hills, riverbanks and valleys have some excellent walks, especially round the old mining village of **São Domingos**.

Mértola's history goes back as far as Phoenician times, when it was an important river port, and it was later fortified and expanded by both Romans (as Myrtilis) and Moors (Martulah), before being taken by Dom Sancho II in 1238 as part of the Christian Reconquest. With the walled town occupying such a small area, successive conquerors and settlers simply built on what they found, which provides Mértola with its current

MÉRTOLA AND THE GUADIANA RIVER (P.422) >

CORKING STUFF

While travelling through the southern Alentejo, you'll pass mile upon mile of cork oak groves – so it may come as no surprise to learn that the district provides around fifty percent of the world's entire supply of **cork**. It has been an important Portuguese export since the late nineteenth century and a major crop for over seven hundred years.

Cork (*quercus suber*) consists of a layer of spongy cells called phellogen that appear under the bark during the first year of growth. The cells grow radially outwards to form a durable, impermeable material with excellent thermal properties – it's ideal to guard the tree against pests, fire and extremes of temperature, and also ideal as a material for humans to exploit. Importantly, the cork tree is also able to regenerate itself when a layer of cork is removed throughout the tree's life (usually over a hundred years) – and each regenerated layer is thicker than its predecessor. Using a curved axe, cork farmers are therefore able to strip away rectangular layers of cork every nine years, the time it takes for the cork layers to be 4–6cm thick – ideal for wine stoppers. The world's most productive cork tree, the 230-year-old **Whistler Tree**, in the northern Alentejo, has produced enough corks to stop up 100,000 bottles from a single harvest.

Cork trees cannot be harvested until they are at least 25 years old, and as a result, cork groves tend to be superb habitats for **wildlife**. Unfortunately this self-sustaining crop is under threat because of the growth in plastic and screw-top wine stoppers, forcing many farmers to rip up the cork groves for more viable crops, and destroying ancient habitats in the process.

---

fascination – the evidence of thousands of years of habitation visible in almost every building and street.

Museu de Mértola

Tues–Sun: July to Sept 9.45am–1pm & 2–6.15pm; Oct to June 9.15am–1pm & 2–5.45pm • €2 per museum, or €5 combined ticket for all museums plus Castelo & Alcáçova do Castelo • ☎ 286 610 100 ⓦ museus.cm-mertola.pt

Mértola has imaginatively created a series of ten mini-museums, allowing you to trace the town's art and history in a series of small, well-designed **exhibitions**. Most lie within the old walled town, signposted and easily found. The various exhibitions deal with a single facet of the town's history, such as the **Núcleo Romano**, showing the foundations of a Roman house discovered under the Câmara Municipal. In the **Núcleo Arte Islâmico** are gathered the inscribed funerary stones, glazed tableware and decorated urns discovered within the Moorish quarter, housed in a former granary, while the tiny **Núcleo da Arte Sacra** in the Misericórdia church concentrates on religious art, notably the three retables from the parish church depicting Sancho's ousting of the Moors. A co-operative set up to revive the traditional weaving industry showcases its methods in the **Oficina de Tecelagem**, next to the turismo. The most moving exhibit is five minutes' walk away in the modern part of town, where the **Basílica Paleocristã**, in Largo do Rossio do Carmo, preserves thirty funerary stones in a partial reconstruction of an early Christian temple. These inhabitants – "a man of social standing", or simply "son" or "daughter of" – were buried here, outside the city walls, over 1500 years ago.

Castelo and Alcáçova do Castelo

Tues–Sun: July to mid-Sept 9.30am–12.30pm & 2–6pm; mid-Sept to June 9am–12.30pm & 2–5.30pm • €2 each, or €5 combined ticket for Castelo & Alcáçova do Castelo plus all museums • ☎ 286 610 100 ⓦ museus.cm-mertola.pt

From the **Castelo**, the layout of the walled old town and modern settlement beyond becomes clear. The arched main door and winding entrance lead into the central keep, which is Moorish in origin, though the rest of the castle dates from the thirteenth-century Christian Reconquest. The earlier Islamic inhabitants lived within the castle walls and, later, in the Moorish quarter, just outside, which now forms the **Alcáçova do Castelo**, an excavated site with iron walkways over the ruins of the Moorish village as well as earlier Roman cisterns, a Christian baptistery and a later Christian cemetery.

Igreja Matriz

Largo da Igreja • Wed–Sun 10am–1pm & 3–7pm • Free

The small parish church at the foot of the castle, the **Igreja Matriz**, is unusual for Portugal in that you can still clearly see its original incarnation as a Moorish mosque. Built in the twelfth century, it became a church around a hundred years later but retains its Moorish arched doorway and a *mihrab* – a space behind the altar used for Muslim prayer.

Mina de São Domingos

North of town, across the bridge, the very attractive road to Serpa winds for 17km to **Mina de São Domingos**. The former pyrite and copper mines here were the largest in Iberia and until World War II were owned by a British company, whose reputation for harsh treatment of their workforce made them very unpopular hereabouts. The mines closed in 1965 and much of the scarred landscape has been imaginatively landscaped into woodlands around a large lake with an attractive river beach, a fine place for a stroll. You can also look round some of the old mining machinery and visit a miners' cottage, Casa do Mineiro, a titchy space of just sixteen square metres.

ARRIVAL AND INFORMATION   MÉRTOLA

By bus Buses stop by the main Serpa/Beja traffic circle in the new town – follow the signs for "Mértola/Vila Real" for the five-minute walk down the road to Largo Vasco da Gama at the foot of the old town.

Destinations Alcoutim (Mon–Fri 1 daily; 50min); Beja (Mon–Fri 3 daily; 1hr 15min); Lisbon (1 daily; 3hr 45min); and Vila Real (1–2 daily; 1hr–1hr 30min);

By car Don't even think of driving into the walled town

– there's metered parking close to the walls or by the bus stops, though note there is a one-way system round the newer part of town.

Information The turismo (daily 9am–12.30pm & 2–5pm; ☏ 286 610 109, ⓦ visitmertola.pt) at Rua da Igreja 31, just inside the walls (signposted), hands out a useful map and has free internet access.

ACCOMMODATION

★**Beira Rio** Rua Dr. Afonso Costa 108 ☏ 286 611 190, ⓦ beirario.pt. The best rooms at this cheerful place (en-suite, most a/c) have balconies directly overlooking the peaceful river (€10 extra). A good buffet breakfast can be eaten on the terrace, and there's parking and free wi-fi in public areas. **€30**

Convento de São Francisco 1km out of town on the Alcoutim road ☏ 286 612 119, ⓦ conventomertola.com. This 400-year-old former convent (open for public visits on Sunday, €6) is primarily an artist's retreat where you can stay in tasteful, rustic surroundings either in pretty studios with a terrace (two-night minimum stay), or a room in the convent itself with its own veranda and

kitchen). They also let out a bucolic "off grid" cottage (sleeps two; €300 a week) in the grounds, with views over the river and town. Breakfast on request. **€60**

Museu Rua Dr. Afonso Costa 112 ☏ 286 612 003, ⓦ hotelmuseu.com. Tucked down by the river, this is the town's best modern option. The name comes from the fact that parts of a Moorish settlement and Roman store were revealed as it was being built – you can see an excavated Moorish building through a glass floor in reception. The best of the small but comfortable rooms face the river, and there's also a bar, riverside terrace, bike hire and parking. Breakafast extra. **€50**

EATING AND DRINKING

A Esquinha Rua Dr. Afonso Costa 1 ☏ 286 611 081. With a fine view of the river and bridge from inside (and a small terrace at the front), this is one of the more upmarket restaurants. There's a good range of mains including lamprey, wild boar and *bacalhau* dishes, from €9–15. It's on the main street into town from the Beja/Serpa roundabout. Wed–Sun 11am–11pm,

Mon 11am–2pm.

O Rapuxo Av Aureliano Mira Fernandes ☏ 286 612 563. The best of a row of local places at the western end of the avenue, beyond the Beja/Serpa roundabout. This has fine fish, meat (including wild boar) and decent house wine. You can eat well here for around €15. Mon–Sat noon–3pm & 7pm–midnight.

ACTIVITIES

Boat trips/Kayaking/Bike hire Beira Rio Náutica, based at the *Beira Rio* guesthouse (see above), runs 45min

boat trips up the river from €10/person; they also rent out kayaks from €5/hr and bikes from €10/day.

Alcácer do Sal and Comporta

Coming from Lisbon and the west, **ALCÁCER DO SAL** is the first town of the Baixo Alentejo, 52km from Setúbal. It is one of Portugal's oldest ports, founded by the Phoenicians and made a regional capital under the Moors – whence its name (*al-Ksar*, "the town") derives. The other part of its name, *do Sal*, "of salt", reflects the dominance of the salt industry in these parts; the Sado estuary is still fringed with salt marshes.

Few stop longer than to stretch the legs – both Beja and the coast are less than an hour away – but it's an attractive enough place to spend some time, particularly along the waterfront promenade where there are various cafés and restaurants. A couple of roads back from the promenade, at its western end, lies a charming quarter of medieval houses where storks nest on any tall tower. Further uphill, above the town, stands the Moorish **castle**, now a luxury *pousada* (see below), from where you can look out over the Rio Sado and the distinctive green paddy fields which are still cultivated for rice.

Comporta

From Alcácer do Sal, the minor EN253 follows the banks of the Sado estuary to the nearest stretch of coast at **Comporta**, 26km west. It's a lovely drive and worth it, as the **beach** – signed just to the north of the village off the EN253-1 – is simply magnificent, a giant stretch of soft sands served by a couple of seasonal beach café-restaurants, popular hangouts for wealthy Lisboetas. You can continue up the EN253-1 onto the Tróia peninsula for the ferry to Setúbal (see p.122).

INFORMATION AND ACCOMMODATION   ALCÁCER DO SAL

Information The turismo is on Largo Luís de Camões (Mon–Sat 9am–5pm; ☎ 265 247 013, ⓦ cm-alcacerdosal.pt).

★**Pousada Dom Afonso II** Castelo de Alcácer do Sal ☎ 265 613 070, ⓦ pousadas.pt. The former Moorish castle is now home to the fabulous *Pousada Dom Afonso II*, one of the classiest of the chain. The ancient shell of the castle makes a dramatic setting for the surprisingly contemporary rooms, and there's also a swimming pool and top-notch restaurant. **€155**

Santiago do Cacém and around

South of Alcácer, the only place that might tempt you to stop before the Alentejo coast is **SANTIAGO DO CACÉM**, an unassuming provincial town capped by a hilltop castle, with a decent regional museum and the fascinating Roman ruins of **Miróbriga** on its outskirts. It is close, too, to the impressive lagoon and beach at **Lagoa de Santo André**, and also marks the starting point of the 340km-long Rota Vicentina walking trail (see p.429).

Museu Municipal

Praça do Município · Tues–Fri 10am–noon & 2–4.30pm, Sat 2–6pm · Free · ☎ 269 827 375

In the centre of town, the white facade of the **Museu Municipal**, facing the municipal gardens off Avenida Álvares Pereira, was formerly a prison where "enemies" of the Salazar regime were locked up. You can see one of the recreated cells and experience how harsh and spartan life must have been for the prisoners. The building has been a museum since the 1970s, and it also displays coins and architectural finds from the area, as well as recreations of traditional Alentejan bedrooms from the late nineteenth century.

Castelo

The modern town centres on its market, with what's left of the old town spreading up one of the hills to the **Castelo** (free access) which was Moorish in origin but later rebuilt by the Knights Templar. The castle's defensive role became redundant by the

nineteenth century, so the council decided it would make a handy place for the local cemetery for the neighbouring church. You can, however, still climb up to the battlements, a steep fifteen-minute walk up from town, for some fine views over town.

Ruinas Romanas de Miróbriga

Herdade dos Chãos Salgados • Tues–Sat 9am–12.30pm & 2–5.30pm; Sun 9am–noon & 2–5.30pm • €3, free Sun 9am–noon • ☎ 269 818 460, ⓦ cultura-alentejo.pt

The impressive **Ruinas Romanas de Miróbriga** are a short drive from town or around twenty minutes' walk – follow the Lisbon road (N120), and the ruins are signed right by a windmill on the hill. The site, which lies isolated amid Arcadian green hills, was probably inhabited during the Iron Age, but the Roman city here dates from the first century AD. For two hundred years Miróbriga thrived on trade, a planned town set around its forum and temple, with recreational zones and residential areas – a "new town" of its era. By the fourth century AD it was in decline, and was then lost to history until the sixteenth century, and only first excavated in the nineteenth.

The ruins are extensive, scattered over the hills below the small interpretation centre. On top of the highest hill were three temples, one of which has been reconstructed. Below here was the commercial centre, complete with paved streets, houses and shops: one of the houses retains some second-century **wall paintings**, while the **baths complex** displays its underfloor heating. Alongside sits a beautifully preserved Roman **bridge** from the first century AD.

Lagoa de Santo André

Fifteen kilometres northwest of Santiago do Cacém, a sand beach separates the calm waters of the lagoon of **Lagoa de Santo André** from the wild Atlantic. The warm waters of the lagoon, only a couple of metres deep, are fringed by an extensive *reserva natural* of pinewoods and reeds, and development is consequently limited. There's a beach café and a couple of restaurants at the road's end, while beyond lie kilometres of empty beach – though take care when swimming, as the undertow is notorious.

Badoca Safari Park

Herdade da Bodaca apartado 170 • Daily 10am–5pm • €17.50, children €15.50 • ☎ 269 708 850, ⓦ badoca.com • It's 7km out of Santiago do Cacém, just off the IP8

Just inland from the Lagoa de Santo André, at Vila Nova de Santo André, the **Badoca Safari Park** is a great place for families. The main attraction is an hour-long tractor "safari" around a large enclosure where giraffe, zebra and deer roam free. There are also various shows and feeding sessions throughout the day.

ARRIVAL AND INFORMATION

SANTIAGO DO CACÉM AND AROUND

By bus The bus station in Santiago do Cacém is in Rua Moçambique in the centre of town, near the market.
Destinations Lagoa de Santo André (Mon–Fri 3 daily; 30min); Lisbon (approx hourly; 2hr 15min); Porto Côvo (1–2 daily; 1hr); Vila Nova de Milfontes (3–4 daily; 1hr

20min); and Zambujeira do Mar (1–2 daily; 2hr).
Information Santiago do Cacém's turismo is in Parque da Quinta do Chafariz, 100m from the bus station (Mon–Sat 9am–1pm & 2–5pm; ☎ 269 826 696, ⓦ cm -santiagocacem.pt), and hands out a useful town map.

ACCOMMODATION

SANTIAGO DO CACÉM
Dom Nuno Av Álvares Pereira ☎ 269 823 325, ⓦ albdnuno.com. Accommodation is limited in Santiago do Cacém, but if you do want to stay this is a good central choice. The four-storey building is modern and rooms are

decently sized. There's also a bar and small outside pool – a big bonus in the summer. Parking €80

LAGOA DE SANTO ANDRÉ
Al Tarik Condomínio Turístico Dhanani, Lagoa de Santo

8

VASCO DA GAMA

Vasco da Gama (1460–1524) was one of Portugal's greatest explorers – you'll find places named after him all over the country as well as a town in India, a football team in Brazil and even a crater on the Moon. He was born in **Sines**, the son of the town governor. In the 1490s he worked for João II protecting trading stations along the **African coast**. His successes persuaded the next king, Manuel I, to commission him to find a potentially lucrative **sea route to India**. He left Lisbon in July 1497 with a fleet of four ships, reaching southern Africa in December – they named it **Natal** ("Christmas" in Portuguese). By the following May they reached Calicut in southwest **India**, and obtained trading terms before departing in August 1498. The scale of their voyage can be gauged by the fact that Vasco da Gama did not return to Portugal until September 1499, and arrived with just two of his ships – half the crew had died. But Vasco da Gama was richly rewarded by the king, his journey inspiring Camões to write *Os Lusiadas*, Portugal's most famous epic poem. Vasco da Gama returned to India twice more, the final time in 1524 when he contracted **malaria** and died in the town of Cochin. You can visit his **birthplace** in the otherwise missable industrial town of Sines, where the Casa de Vasco da Gama in Sines' castle records his eventful life (Tues–Sun 10am–1pm & 2–5pm, July & Aug open til 6pm; free; ☎ 269 632 237, ⓦ sines.pt).

André ☎ 269 708 600, ⓦ hotelaltarik.com. The apartment-style *Al Tarik* has clean and spacious self-catering rooms in a modern block, close to a minimarket and just inland from the lagoon – it's well signed. **€85**

8 The southern Alentejo coast

Once south of the industrial town of **Sines** – avoidable unless you are on the trail of Vasco da Gama, who was born here, or visiting for the Festival Música do Mundo (see boxes above and p.433) – you'll encounter one of the least developed coasts in Portugal, a wild, scrubby expanse of low hills and wave-pounded cliffs. Low-key resorts cluster round the various cove beaches that you can find right along the coast, including pretty **Porto Côvo**. Further south, **Vila Nova de Milfontes** is the main – and by far the nicest – Alentejan resort, while **Almograve** and **Zambujeira do Mar**, further south still, are both small seaside villages with stupendous beaches, a short drive from the northern Algarve.

Porto Côvo

The former fishing village of **PORTO CÔVO** is a popular weekend retreat for Lisboetas, and its tiny heart is now surrounded by modern holiday villas. The small centre consists of just a few cobbled, whitewashed streets around the attractive central square, Largo Marquês de Pombal. It's very crowded in August – when it turns into a sort of Lisbon-on-Sea – but for most of the year the predominant sound is the whistle of the Atlantic breeze. To reach the coast, head along the main pedestrianized **Rua da Vasco da Gama**, where you'll find most of the village's dozen cafés and restaurants, plus a bank with ATM and various shops selling beach gear and souvenirs. Bear left and steps lead down to a small fishing harbour where you can take a **boat trip** (June–Sept only; ☎ 963 051 176, €10) to the nearby **Ilha do Pessegueiro** (see opposite).

The beaches

Bear a couple of hundred metres north of town for the nearest cove **beach**, a lovely sandy wedge below cliffs – it's generally sheltered even when the sea is rough elsewhere. Continue north along the coast and it's a ten-minute walk to **Praia Grande**, the appropriately named "Big Beach", especially so when the tide is low; it's got its own café-bar, so you could easily spend a day here. Clifftop paths run north and south of town providing access to other coves and beaches. **Praia da Samouqueira** is named after the extraordinary rock formations and is popular at low tide.

Ilha do Pessegueiro

The next beach south of Porto Côvo is at **Ilha do Pessegueiro** (Peach Tree Island), reached by car off the Porto Côvo–Vila Nova de Milfontes road. However, it's much nicer to walk, following the coastal path south from Porto Côvo. It's only a couple of kilometres and en route you'll pass the remains of a Bronze Age burial site.

The name actually applies to the mainland beach, another beautiful duned stretch of sand sitting below a small sixteenth-century fort. The island itself – with the matching ruins of another fort – is a few hundred metres offshore, clearly visible from Porto Côvo and reachable from there on local fishing **boats**, though not all are licensed to actually land on the island.

ARRIVAL AND INFORMATION

PORTO CÔVO

By bus Buses stop near Largo do Mercado, a short walk from the seafront.

Destinations Almograve (summer 5 daily, winter 1–2 daily; 35min); Lisbon (summer 5 daily, winter 1–2 daily; 3hr); Santiago do Cacém (summer 5 daily, winter 1–2 daily; 1hr); Vila Nova de Milfontes (summer 5 daily, winter 1–2 daily; 20min); and Zambujeira (summer 5 daily, winter 1–2 daily; 55min).

Information The turismo (Mon–Fri 9am–noon & 1–5pm; ☎ 269 959 124, ⓦ sines.pt) is on Rua do Mar.

ACCOMMODATION

Ilha do Pessegueiro Camping Estrada da Ilha ☎ 269 905 178, ⓦ ilhadopessegueirocamping.com. The campsite, which also lets out bungalows, is a fair way inland on the road from Ilha do Pessegueiro to Vila Nova de Milfontes, but it is spacious with a minimarket and restaurant. Pitch €12, bungalow €90

Parque de Campismo Porto Côvo Estrada Municipal 554 ☎ 269 905 136, ⓦ campingportocovo.pt. On the Vila Nova road out of town and open all year, this has good facilities, including a children's playground, minimarket and pool (the latter only open in summer). Pitch €13

Porto Côvo Rua Vitalina da Silva 1–2 ☎ 269 959 140, ⓦ hotelportocovo.com. Popular with Portuguese families, this is Porto Côvo's top choice, a few minutes' walk beyond the market building – it's a modern place wrapped around a small pool, with air-conditioned studios and one-bed apartments with a kitchen. €90

Zé Inácio Rua Vasco da Gama 38 ☎ 269 959 136. This is the best of several places offering rooms on the main street, a bright white building with large, comfortable rooms above a restaurant (so can be noisy) – the nicest rooms have sea views. No breakfast. €60

EATING AND DRINKING

A Ilha Praia da Ilha do Pessegueiro ☎ 269 905 113. This is a great little beach restaurant where you can choose fresh fish from the counter – it also serves interesting dishes such as fried eels. Mains around €11. Daily 8am–1am (closes earlier in winter).

Doce Mar Rua Vasco da Gama 35 ☎ 269 905 176. On the main street, *Doce Mar* is a good breakfast or lunch spot: dishes up inexpensive snacks and pastries, with outdoor seating. Mon, Tues & Thurs–Sun 8am–midnight.

★ **Marquês** Largo Marquês de Pombal 10 ☎ 269 905

8

THE ROTA VICENTINA

The Rota Vicentina is a 340km long-distance footpath which runs from Santiago do Cacém in the Alentejo to Cabo de São Vicente in the Algarve. The northern, Alentejan half has two alternative routes: Porto Côvo is the beginning of the 115km-long **Trilho dos Pescadores** (Fisherman's Trail), that follows coastal tracks long used by the local fishermen. Opened in 2012, it's relatively well marked with coloured arrows, and tracks the coast via Milfontes (a taxing first section, 20km), Almograve (15km further), Zambujeira (another 22km) and into the Algarve at Odeceixe (18km on). It's tough going, much of it along towering cliffs, but no section is longer than 25km which means – in theory – you always have accommodation and a place to eat at the end of your day's walk. The inland alternative is the **Caminho Histórico** (Historic Way), which follows ancient pilgrimage routes from Santiago do Cacém, mostly inland, to Cabo de São Vicente. Be aware that, as with all Portuguese trails, way-marking can be sporadic and poorly maintained, so if you tackle the path, take a good map or GPS system – but it is worth the effort, as the routes embrace some of the loveliest scenery in the country. Full details are on ⓦ rotavicentina.com, which also includes five shorter, circular alternatives.

036. The *Marquês* is more like a classy Lisbon *cervejaria* than a local restaurant, with lovely tiles, stand-at-the-bar beers, oysters, fresh-from-the-tank lobsters, *feijoada* and other delights from around €12–15. Mon, Wed–Sun 12.30–11.30pm.

ACTIVITIES

Horseriding You can go horseriding on the beaches around Pessegueiro (one hour from €30) with Herdade do Pessegueiro, Ilha do Pessegueiro (☎269 959 036, ✆herdadepessegueiro.com).

Vila Nova de Milfontes

VILA NOVA DE MILFONTES – 20km south of Porto Côvo – is the main and most attractive resort on the Alentejo coast, but though it gets very busy in high season, it's Portuguese families who predominate, injecting good humour and a relaxed atmosphere. The attractive whitewashed streets of the old town huddle around a striking, ivy-wreathed sixteenth-century castle facing the estuary of the Rio Mira. Built in 1599 to guard the town from North African pirates, the small castle was a hotel for many years, but is now closed to the public.

The beaches

The town's long, sandy river beach lies just a few minutes' walk to the west. Swimmers need to be aware of the strong river currents – the town beach has roped-off swimming areas that you should heed – and even more so at the beaches either side of town, where the breakers can be fierce. Swim close to the locals, however, and you shouldn't have anything to worry about. Even though the town beach is spacious, it gets busy in high season, when you might want to take the **ferry** (July & Aug daily 9am–3.30pm every 30min; €5 return ☎964 200 944) from the jetty at the foot of the castle across the estuary to **Furnas**, a long, sandy beach also accessible off the main coast road.

ARRIVAL AND INFORMATION VILA NOVA DE MILFONTES

By bus Buses stop on Rua Antonio Mantas, near the bank. Destinations Almograve (Mon–Fri 2 daily; 25min); Lisbon (4 daily; 3hr 30min); Portimão (1 daily; 2hr 10min); Porto Côvo (summer 5 daily, winter 1–2 daily; 20min); Santiago do Cacém (3–4 daily; 1hr 20min); and Zambujeira do Mar (summer 5 daily, winter 2 daily; 35min).

Land-train A little land-train runs approximately every 30min from the campsite via the centre of town out to the end of the river beach (May–Sept 9.30am–1.30pm & 3–7.30pm, until midnight in Aug; €3; ☎917 911 309).
Information The turismo is on Rua António Mantas (daily 10am–1pm & 2–6pm; ☎283 996 599, ✆cm-odemira.pt).

ACTIVITIES

Boat trips In summer, various boat trips run from the town quay up the Rio Mira. Expect to pay around €6 for one-hour trips on traditional Moliceiros boats, or around €20 for half-day trips to the town of Odemira.
Canoeing, pony treks and bike hire Half-day canoe hire is available at €30 for two from Ecotrails (✆ecotrails.info), which also offers 1hr 30min pony treks from €35 and bike hire from €16/day.
Surfing and paddle boards Surf Milfontes, Rua Custódio Brás Pacheco 38A (☎914 732 652, ✆surfmilfontes.com), offers surf camps, surfboard rental and lessons (from around €40); it also rents out paddle boards (€35 for two hours).

ACCOMMODATION

★**Apartamentos Dunamar** Rua dos Médos 2, off Av Marginal ☎283 998 208, ✆dunamarmilfontes.com. In a prime location, high above the estuary, these a/c studio and one-bedroom apartments sleeping 4–6 people (with balconies and kitchenette) have great views and are just a few minutes' walk from the beach and town. Parking; breakfast not included. **€85**
Cais Rua dos Carris 9 ☎283 996 268 ✆pensaodocais .pt. This is the best budget choice in town, especially if you have one of the rooms with estuary views, but even if your room doesn't have the best aspect – they are all fairly spacious with traditional furniture and modern bathrooms – there's always the lovely vine-covered patio or first-floor terrace. No credit cards. **€45**
Casa Amarela Rua D. Luís de Castro e Almeida ☎283 996 632 or ☎934 204 610, ✆casaamarelamilfontes .com. The "yellow house" is the project of a gregarious backpacking owner, who has decorated stylish en-suite

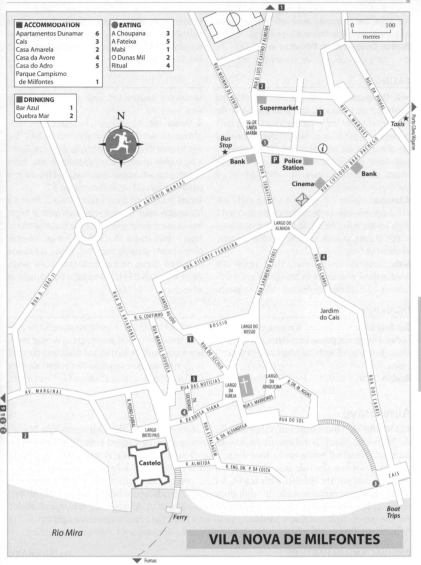

ACCOMMODATION
Apartamentos Dunamar	6
Cais	3
Casa Amarela	2
Casa da Avore	4
Casa do Adro	5
Parque Campismo de Milfontes	1

EATING
A Choupana	3
A Fateixa	5
Mabi	1
O Dunas Mil	2
Ritual	4

DRINKING
Bar Azul	1
Quebra Mar	2

VILA NOVA DE MILFONTES

8

rooms (some with terrace or balcony) with art from his trips. Some rooms sleep up to four people (€20/person) and there's a kitchen, lounge and free internet access. A separate mews-style block a couple of minutes away has more en-suite rooms arranged around a large terraced area and kitchen. Laundry facilities available. Breakfast not included. No credit cards. **€65**

Casa da Arvore Bairro da Alagoinha 31 ☎918 658 755, ⍟alojamentomilfontes.com. This contemporary guesthouse lies in a peaceful side street (apart from the happy sounds from the adjacent primary school) close to the tourist office. The four rooms are of different sizes, the nicest (the Fire Room, €30 extra) opening onto a tree-shaded courtyard. A generous breakfast uses local ingredients, and massages and evening meals are available on request. **€79**

Casa do Adro Rua Diário de Notícias 10 ☎283 997 102, ⍟casadoadro.com.pt. Tucked into the historic centre, this seventeenth-century townhouse is packed with family clutter – but the rooms are stylish and fresh, the best with balconies. There are also two terraces, a communal lounge

and fridge, and a charming owner who indulges guests with free drinks, fruit and home-made cake. **€85**

Parque Campismo de Milfontes 283 996 104, campingmilfontes.com. This big campsite just north of town is set among shady trees and has excellent facilities, including slightly high-density teepees and bungalows. It also has a great swimming pool (for a small fee). Pitches from **€20**

EATING

★**A Choupana** Av Marginal 283 996 643. This wooden bar and restaurant is right on the coast, down the cliff steps at the far end of the beach road: waves crash below you at high tide. An outdoor grill cooks up meat and the catch of the day, with mains from €13. But while the food's fine it's not really the main event – the views and the sunsets are the thing. Daily 8am–midnight, closed Mondays in winter.

A Fateixa Largo do Cais, off Rua dos Carris 283 996 415. A superb location on the riverbank below town, and a shady terrace, makes this a good bet. It's fair value too – platters of squid, sardines, mackerel, swordfish and tuna, all around €9. Daily noon–12.30am.

Mabi Largo de Santa Maria 25A. A simple café which makes a great choice for breakfast, if you're self-catering – it dishes up delicious filled croissants, sandwiches, pastries and fresh orange juice. Daily 8am–midnight.

O Dunas Mil Marginal da Praia 283 996 420, dunasmil.com. The best fish restaurant in town, five minutes along the coast road and high up on the right. There's a big outdoor terrace, and they specialize in *arroz* dishes (including one with lobster). Great mixed fried fish and tiger prawns, too, from €11–12. Daily noon–3pm & 7–10pm.

Ritual Rua Barbosa Viana 4 283 998 648. *Ritual* is a fashionable tapas bar and restaurant, with a bright interior studded with pillars and a small outdoor terrace. Tapas – from around €5 – includes *batatas bravas* or *alheira* (white sausage) croquettes, or you can choose from main courses such as mushroom risotto, pasta, steaks and salads (€9–12). There's also a good choice of wines. Mon–Sat 6–11pm.

DRINKING

Bar Azul Largo do Rossio 20. A relaxed, classy bar in a lovely old townhouse, playing a mix of jazz, rock and blues music, best enjoyed with their refreshing strawberry mojito. Daily 9pm–4am; Fri & Sat only in winter.

Quebra Mar Praia da Franquia Apartado 51 283 969 333. This has a decent restaurant, but the main draw here is the "tropical" terrace right on the river beach, where you can down cocktails and drinks until the small hours. In summer there are regular theme nights and guest DJs. Daily 9am–4am; closed Thurs and earlier in winter.

Almograve

ALMOGRAVE, 10km south of Vila Nova de Milfontes (west of the Odemira–Vila Nova de Milfontes road), is a diminutive, low-key resort sat on a rugged stretch of coastline. Its beach, reached below some low cliffs, is spacious and alluring at low tide, but greatly diminishes when the tide is in. However, there are also many kilometres of high dunes to north and south, riddled with tracks, where you can find quiet spots. For a lovely eight-kilometre circular walk through dunes and a landscape where badgers and otters roam, check the website en.rotavicentina.com. South of Almograve, drivers can make for the promontory of **Cabo Sardão**, a dead-end road that culminates in a clifftop lighthouse, from near where there are magnificent panoramas of the rocky coastline.

ARRIVAL AND DEPARTURE   ALMOGRAVE

By bus Buses stop in the modern village, a block of houses and villas which sits back from the beach – a road and board-walk run over the dunes to a huge car park above the sands. Destinations Lisbon (summer 5–6 daily, winter 1 daily; 3hr 15min–3 hr 45min); Porto Côvo (summer 5 daily, winter 1–2 daily; 35min); Vila Nova de Milfontes (Mon–Fri 2 daily; 25min); and Zambujeira do Mar (summer 6 daily, winter 1 daily; 20 mins).

ACCOMMODATION AND EATING

Natura Maris Dunas Residence Av da Praia 283 647 115, naturamarisresidence.com. On the way to the beach you'll pass the best place to stay, with some rooms facing the dunes, and it also has its own pool and a decent restaurant. Popular with walkers, it also has family rooms for four (€80). No breakfast. **€50**

Pousada de Juventude Rua do Chafariz 283 640 000, pousadasjuventude.pt. This sleek, modern youth hostel is ideally located close to the beach and has dorms for four, five or twelve people. Dorms **€15**, doubles **€45**

THE SOUNDS OF THE ALENTEJO

Every summer, you can enjoy two of Europe's top music fesitvals on the Alentejo coast. The otherwise missable town of Sines hosts Portugal's biggest festivals of world music every July. The **Festival Músicas do Mundo** (ⓦfmm.com.pt) has taken place annually since 1999, with a main stage alongside Sines's castle and other events held at the beach or the Arts Centre; some also spill over to Porto Covo. Folk, traditional sounds and jazz predominate and recent acts have included Billy Bragg, London-based the Comet is Coming, Mali singer Oumou Sangaré and Bilan from Cape Verde. Day-tickets are a modest €15 or so.

Just down the coast at Zambujeira do Mar is the **Festival Sudoeste** (ⓦmeosudoeste.pt), usually held in mid-August. An annual event since 1997, the festival turns this sleepy coastal resort into a mecca for up to thirty thousand music lovers. Three stages are set up for four days of concerts which, in recent years, have included sets by the likes of The Prodigy, Wiz Khalifa, Jessie J and the Ting Tings. One of the stages is dedicated to reggae. Camping is free on the site during the five days (€95), or you can buy a day-ticket which is usually around €50.

Zambujeira do Mar

The southernmost Alentejan resort is the small village of **ZAMBUJEIRA DO MAR**, 29km south of Vila Nova de Milfontes. The main street stops at the top of the cliff, whose rocky outcrops give some daytime shade to the handsome beach below. If the main beach is too crowded – and it gets smaller as the tide rises – there are good alternatives less than three kilometres' walk north or south, reached by clifftop paths. Zambujeira is small and laidback, attracting both locals and a backpacker crowd – it is particularly lively for the **Festival Sudoeste** (see box above). New villas have been tacked on to what was a tiny fishing village, and facilities are adequate: there's a small market, a bank, a few shops and half a dozen restaurants, all within a couple of hundred metres or so.

8

ARRIVAL AND INFORMATION   ZAMBUJEIRA DO MAR

By bus The bus stops at the top of the main approach road (which is closed to traffic from June–Sept); timetables are posted in the newsagent's window.

Destinations Aljezur (June to mid-Sept 1 daily; 1hr); Almograve (summer 6 daily, winter 1 daily; 20 min); Lisbon (July–Aug 5 daily, other months 1 daily; 3hr 40min); Porto Côvo (summer 5 daily, winter 1–2 daily; 55min); Sagres (June–mid-Sept 1 daily; 1hr 30min); Santiago do Cacém (summer 4 daily, winter 1–2 daily; 2hr); and Vila Nova de Milfontes (Mon–Fri 2 daily; 25min).

Information The turismo is on Rua da Escola (Tues–Sat 10am–1pm & 2–6pm; ☎283 961 144, ⓦcm-odemira.pt) and has details of private rooms: it can also check on space at the numerous rural-tourism properties in the surroundings.

ACCOMMODATION

Alojamento Sudoeste Av do Mar 47 ⓦalojamentosudoeste.com. Very close to the clifftop, in an attractive modern building built in traditional style, this has largish, clean rooms with fridges, the best with balconies overlooking the sea. **€50**

Onda Azul Rua da Palmeira 1 ☎283 961 450 ⓦondaazul.pt. You'll find good-sized, modern rooms and quiet surroundings at the *Onda Azul* just east of the main street: it's above a decent restaurant. **€65**

Parque Campismo de Zambujeira ☎283 958 407, ⓦcampingzambujeira.com. The smart, local campsite is about 1km inland on the main approach road, and has a café-bar, swimming pools, games room and minimarket, as well as some apartments (€75) to rent. Pitch **€18**

EATING

Rita Largo de Miramar 1 ☎283 961 317. The address is "Seaview Square" and you'll see why if you bag a window seat at this café-restaurant near the clifftop. Despite the fantastic coastal views, prices are very reasonable for the likes of chicken kebabs, tuna and octopus salad and fresh fish (from €7–11). The tables outside in the square are also appealing for a daytime snack. Daily noon–3pm & 7–10pm.

The Algarve

PRAIA DO AMADO

9

The Algarve

With many of the country's safest and loveliest beaches, and a year-round balmy climate, it is not surprising that the Algarve is Portugal's most popular region for holidaymakers. Inevitably, this also means that stretches of the coast – in particular from Faro west to Albufeira – are heavily developed, though even here the beaches are first-rate, as are the facilities. Elsewhere in the Algarve, especially around Sagres and Tavira, the surroundings are more attractive, with laidback resorts and low-key development.

To the west of **Vilamoura**, you'll find the rocky outcrops and cove beaches for which the Algarve is best known, especially around the main resorts of **Albufeira, Armação de Pêra** and **Lagos**. The coast becomes progressively wilder as you head west, where attractive smaller resorts include the former fishing villages of **Burgau** or **Salema**, and the historic cape of **Sagres** – thought to be the site of Henry the Navigator's naval school. The string of villages along the rougher west coast, as far as **Odeceixe**, are quieter still, with limited facilities but fantastic wild beaches ideal for surfing.

The eastern coast between Faro and the Spanish border is very different. Most of it is protected within the **Reserva Natural da Ria Formosa**, a series of barrier islands fronted by extensive sandy beaches. That means taking a short boat trip to reach the sands, which has helped preserve the towns from large-scale development. The resorts here have a more Portuguese feel than those in the central stretch, and first-choice bases here would be **Faro** itself – capital of the entire region – as well as **Olhão, Fuseta, Cabanas** or **Tavira**, all of which offer easy access to the sandbank islands.

Inland Algarve is still relatively undeveloped, especially around **Alcoutim** on the Spanish border. The Roman ruins of **Milreu** and the market town of **Loulé** are both worth an outing from Faro, while the old Moorish town of **Silves** is easily accessed from Portimão. Towards the west of the region, **Caldas de Monchique** is a quaint spa town in verdant woodland that makes up much of the picturesque **Serra de Monchique** mountain range.

GETTING AROUND AND INFORMATION
THE ALGARVE

By bus Buses link all the Algarve resorts and main inland villages. The principal regional bus companies are EVA (ⓦ eva-bus.com) and Frota Azul (ⓦ frotazul-algarve.pt), who sell three-day (€29.50) and seven-day (€36.50) passes. Several companies operate regular daily express buses between Lisbon and the Algarve (around 3hr 30min) including Rede Expressos (ⓦ rede-expressos.pt), Renex (ⓦ renex.pt) and EVA (ⓦ eva-bus.com). EVA also runs a number of international buses from the Algarve, the most useful being the service from Lagos via the coast to Seville

(5hr 50min; €36 return). A good (unofficial) source for timetables is ⓦ algarvebus.info.

Destinations Lisbon to: Albufeira (6–8 daily; 3hr 10min); Alvor (6–8 daily; 4hr 10min); Armação de Pêra (6–8 daily; 3hr 20min); Faro (6–8 daily; 3hr 45min); Lagos (3–8 daily; 4hr 35min); Olhão (5–6 daily; 4hr); Portimão (3–6 daily; 3hr 40min); Tavira (3–4 daily; 4hr 20min); Vilamoura (4 daily; 5–6hr); and Vila Real (5–6 daily; 4hr 45min).

By car Car hire is relatively inexpensive and will allow you to reach the more out-of-the-way inland villages

Highlights

❶ Olhão With a superb market in its highly atmospheric old town, Olhão is also the departure point for boat trips to some fabulous offshore-island beaches. **See p.445**

❷ Ilha de Tavira Take the ferry to this sizeable island with an enormous stretch of dune-backed beach – the best in the eastern Algarve. **See p.452**

❸ Rio Guadiana The river marking the border with Spain offers some of the region's least spoilt scenery, meandering north to the pretty village of Alcoutim. **See p.459**

❹ Boat trip, Lagos Explore extraordinary rock formations and grottoes on a boat trip from the historic town of Lagos, from where Portugal's navigators once set sail. **See p.479**

❺ Surfing in Sagres The beaches around Europe's most southwesterly town are rated as some of the best in Europe – whatever your surfing skills. **See p.488**

❻ West-coast beaches A stunning variety of wave-battered sandy strands grace the dramatic and largely undeveloped west coast between Sagres and Odeceixe. **See p.491**

HIGHLIGHTS ARE MARKED ON THE MAP ON PP.438–439

9

THE ALGARVE'S BEST BEACH RESTAURANTS

As you'd expect with so much coastline, the Algarve boasts some excellent beachside restaurants serving superb fresh fish as alluring as the sea views.

Beach Bar Burgau Burgau p.485
Boia Bar Salema p.486
Estrela do Mar Armação de Pêra p.470

Mar e Sol Praia da Rocha p.475
Rei das Praias Praia dos Caneiros p.471
Restinga Alvor p.476

and inaccessible cove beaches. The main east–west A22 highway from Lagos to the Spanish border offers fast and easy access to the region, linking with the A2 to Lisbon just northeast of Albufeira. Note, however, that the A22 operates a complex toll-charging system (see p.29).

By train The Algarve rail line (timetables on ☎808 208 208, ⓦ cp.pt) runs from Lagos in the west to Vila Real de Santo António on the Spanish border, calling at most major

towns en route (you may have to change at Tunes, Faro or Tavira, depending on your destination). There are also fast daily connections between Faro and Lisbon. Details are given in the Guide.

Information A comprehensive calendar of cultural events can be found in *Agenda*, available free from tourist offices, cultural centres and larger hotels, and online at ⓦ cultugarve.com. For general information, check the official tourist-board website ⓦ visitalgarve.pt.

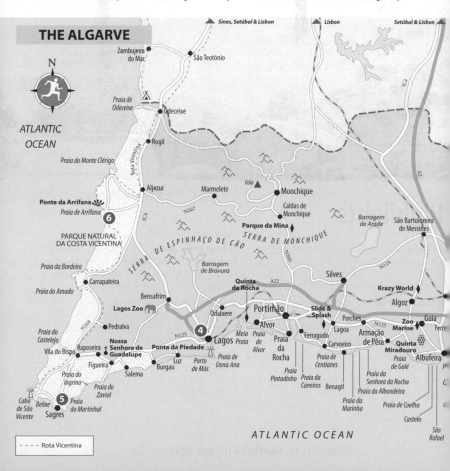

Faro and around

9

With its international airport, impressive shopping centre and ring of high-rise apartments, **FARO** has something of a big-city feel. However, the central area is a manageable size, boasting attractive mosaic-paved pedestrianized streets and marina-side gardens, while its university contributes to a nightlife scene, at its most animated during term-time.

In summer, boats and buses run from the centre of town out to some excellent local **beaches**: the closest to town is the generous swathe of sand at **Praia de Faro**, while a ferry makes the short hop to the village of Farol on the Ilha de Culatra (see p.447).

Originally a Roman settlement, the town was named by the Moors, under whom it was a thriving commercial port that supplied the regional capital at Silves. It then became Christian, under Afonso III in 1249, but was largely destroyed by the Great Earthquake of 1755 – so it comes as no surprise that modern Faro has so few historic buildings left. What interest it does retain is centred within and around the pretty **Cidade Velha** (Old Town), which lies behind a series of defensive walls overlooking the mudflats.

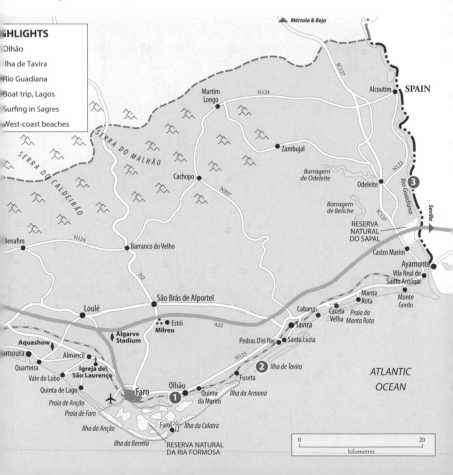

HIGHLIGHTS

Olhão
Ilha de Tavira
Rio Guadiana
Boat trip, Lagos
Surfing in Sagres
West-coast beaches

9

FARO

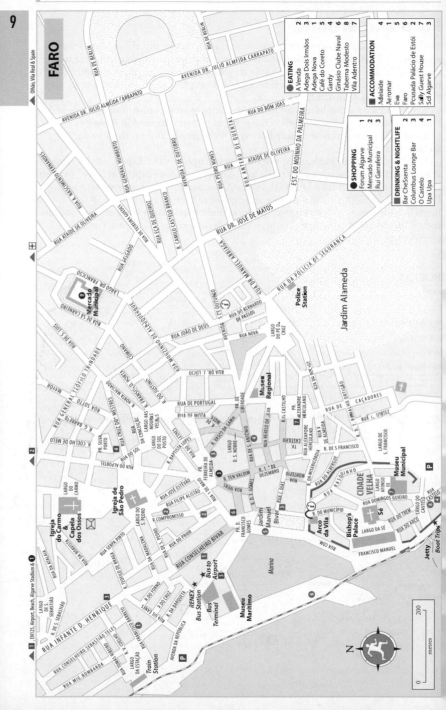

Olhão, Vila Real & Spain

● **EATING**

A Venda	2
Adega Dois Irmãos	3
Adega Nova	1
Café do Coreto	5
Gardy	4
Ginásio Clube Naval	6
Taberna Modesto	8
Vila Adentro	7

■ **ACCOMMODATION**

Adelaide	4
Aeromar	1
Eva	5
Faro	6
Pousada Palácio de Estói	2
Sally Guest House	7
Sol Algarve	3

● **SHOPPING**

Forum Algarve	1
Mercado Municipal	2
Rui Garrafeira	3

■ **DRINKING & NIGHTLIFE**

Bar CheSsenta	2
Columbus Lounge Bar	3
O Castelo	4
Upa Upa	1

Jardim Alameda

Police Station

Museu Regional

Igreja do Carmo & Capela dos Ossos

Igreja de São Pedro

CIDADE VELHA

Museu Municipal

Bishop's Palace

Arco da Vila

Sé

Jardim Manuel Bivar

Marina

RENEX Bus Station

Bus Terminal

Bus to Airport

Museu Marítimo

Train Station

Jetty

Boat Trips

EN125, Airport, Beach, Algarve Stadium &

N

0   200
     metres

Cidade Velha

The only part of Faro to have survived the town's various historic upheavals is the **Cidade Velha**, or Vila-Adentro ("town within"), an oval of cobbled streets set within a run of sturdy walls. Bright-white houses are fronted by decorative balconies and tiling, a few now serving as antique shops, cafés or art galleries. The most central entrance is through the eighteenth-century town gate, the **Arco da Vila**, next to the turismo. From here, Rua do Município leads up to the broad Largo da Sé, which is lined with orange trees and flanked by the cathedral and a group of palaces, including the former eighteenth-century bishop's palace.

Sé

Largo da Sé • Mon–Fri 10am–6.30pm (closes 5pm Oct–May), Sat 10am–1pm • €3

Parts of Faro's squat **Sé** (cathedral) date back to 1251. The impressive structure became the Algarve's principal cathedral in 1577, but was sacked by the English under the Count of Essex in 1596 and then partially destroyed by the 1755 earthquake, so much of what you see today – a mixture of Gothic, Renaissance and Baroque styles – dates from the eighteenth century. Inside there's fine eighteenth-century *azulejo* tiling, though for most people the highlight is to climb the bell tower for superb views over the old town and the mudflats beyond.

Museu Municipal

Largo Dom Afonso III 14 • June–Sept Tues–Fri 10am–7pm, Sat & Sun 11.30am–6pm; Oct–May Tues–Fri 10am–6pm, Sat & Sun 10.30am–5pm • €2, free on Sun until 3.30pm • ☎ 289 897 400, ⓦ cm-faro.pt

One of the oldest museums in Portugal, Faro's impressive **Museu Municipal** was founded as an archeological museum in 1894. Housed in a sixteenth-century convent with a beautiful cloister, its highlight is an almost intact mosaic showing the Roman god of water, Neptune, and the Four Seasons. Dating from the third century, it was originally excavated near the city's train station. Also on display are some fine Roman statues from Milreu (see p.442), exquisite Moorish lamps, vases and bowls, and a variety of Baroque and Renaissance paintings. The collection also includes Futurist works by Carlos Porfírio, one of the country's leading twentieth-century artists. In front of the building stands a forthright, crucifix-carrying statue of the conqueror Afonso himself, king between 1249 and 1279.

Around the marina

At the **marina**, attractive town gardens and outdoor cafés overlook the rows of sleek yachts, and at the end of the day much of Faro gathers to promenade here. At the northern end of the harbour is the small **Museu Marítimo** (Mon–Fri 9am–noon & 2.30–5pm; €1), a modest maritime museum with displays of model boats and local fishing techniques. Heading southwards from the marina along Rua Comandante Francisco Manuel, you can follow the railway line for an attractive walk along the seafront, with the town walls on one side and the mudflats on the other. A small arch through the old town walls offers another approach to the Cidade Velha, while from the jetty opposite here, ferries depart to the local sandspit beaches.

Museu Regional

Praça de Liberdade 2 • Mon–Fri 10am–1.30pm & 2.30–6pm • €1.50, free on first Sun of the month • ☎ 289 878 238

Faro's likeable little **Museu Regional** is a refreshingly low-tech ensemble of items representing traditional Algarve culture – perfect for an hour or so on a rainy day. There are agricultural implements, musical instruments, recreations of house interiors and model fishing boats. Perhaps of most interest are the black-and-white photos that show what the town and local beaches looked like before the advent of tourism.

9

Igreja do Carmo and the Capela dos Ossos

Largo do Carmo • May–Sept Mon–Fri 10am–1pm & 3–6pm, Sat 10am–1pm, Sun only for Mass at 9am; Oct–April Mon–Fri 10am–1pm & 3–5pm, Sun only for Mass at 9am • Church free; Capela dos Ossos €3

For ghoulish delights, it's worth seeking out the Baroque **Igreja do Carmo**, which enlivens an otherwise dull part of town. At the back of the church, you can buy a ticket to view the **Capela dos Ossos** (Chapel of Bones), set in an overgrown garden at the rear. The chapel is completely lined with the bones and skulls of monks disinterred from the cemetery next door and carefully arranged into neat geometric patterns.

Igreja de São Pedro

Largo de São Pedro • Daily 8.30am–12.30pm & 3–6.45pm • Free

The **Igreja de São Pedro** is an attractive church originally built by the local fishermen in the late sixteenth century, though remodelled after the earthquake of 1755. Its finest decorative work is an altar (to the left of the main altar) whose central image is a gilded, wooden *Last Supper* in relief.

Praia de Faro

Buses #14 and #16 run from the marina gardens, or the stop opposite the bus station, calling at the airport en route and stopping just before the narrow bridge to the beach itself (daily every 45min, 7.15am–8pm; 30min); there are also summer ferries to Praia de Faro from the jetty below Faro old town (June–Sept 6 daily; first boat 9.30am, last return 7.30pm; €6 return; ☎ 917 634 813, ⓦ silnido.com); ferries also run from Faro to the Ilha de Culatra (see p.447)

Faro's nearest beach, **Praia de Faro** – the only sandspit beach linked by a bridge – is a long sweep of beautiful sand with both a sea-facing and a more sheltered lagoon-facing side. Its proximity to both the airport and Faro means it's somewhat developed, with bars, restaurants and villas crammed onto a narrow strip – though out of season you'll probably have the sands to yourself. The beach is situated on the Ilha de Faro, southwest of town. In July, the area between the beach and the airport hosts the **Faro Bike Concentration** (ⓦ www.motoclubefaro.pt), Europe's largest meeting of bikers, with plenty of live entertainment. Billy Idol and Portuguese star David Fonseca have appeared in recent years.

Milreu

Estói, 11km north of Faro • Tues–Sun: May–Sept 9.30am–1pm & 2–6.30pm; Oct–April 9am–1pm & 2–5.30pm • €2 • ☎ 289 997 823, ⓦ monumentosdoalgarve.pt • Take the Estói bus from Faro bus station, which passes the site entrance

The Roman site at **Milreu** (pronounced *mil-rio*) is the Algarve's principal Roman excavation, just south of the attractive town of Estói. The lavish villa that once stood here was inhabited from the first century AD and was constructed round a central peristyle – a gallery of columns surrounding a courtyard. You can also see the remains of one of the oldest Christian churches in the country, which was converted from a former Roman temple in around the sixth century. Southwest of the villa is an impressive bathing complex, with an underfloor heating system and striking fish mosaics – there's also an *apodyterium*, or changing room, sporting arched niches for clothes. A small visitor centre shows what the villa would have looked like in its heyday.

ARRIVAL AND DEPARTURE   FARO

FARO AIRPORT

Flights land at Faro's international airport (flight information ☎ 289 800 800, ⓦ ana.pt), 6km west of town, where there's a bank, ATMs, car rental companies and tourist office (daily 8am–11.30pm; ☎ 289 818 582). There are no direct public transport services to other

resorts from the airport, which means heading first into central Faro.

Taxis into Faro A taxi from the airport into the centre of town (15min) should cost €12–14, plus €2.50 for any luggage that goes in the boot; there's also a twenty percent surcharge between 10pm and 6am, and at weekends.

Buses into Faro Local buses #14 and #16 run from the airport to the centre (25min), costing €2.25 (departures roughly every 45min from 7am–8pm; buy tickets on board). Both stop outside the bus terminal in town (see below) and, further on, at the Jardim Manuel Bivar ("Jardim" on the timetables) by the harbour.

FARO TOWN

The compact town is simple to negotiate on foot, and all the hotels, restaurants and bars are extremely central. There is a town bus service, but you'll only need it to get to the beach and back to the airport.

By bus Faro's bus terminal (📞 289 899 760) is on Avenida da República, just back from the marina. There's an English-speaking information office inside, though it's not always staffed. The RENEX bus terminal (for express buses to Lisbon, Porto and the Minho) is opposite.

Destinations Albufeira (approx hourly; 50min–1hr 15min); Castro Marim (5–9 daily; 1hr 35min); Estói (Mon–Fri 10–12 daily, Sat & Sun 9 daily; 20min); Fuseta (4 daily; 45min); Lisbon (6–8 daily; 3hr 45min); Loulé (Mon–Fri every 30–50min; Sat–Sun 2–4 daily; 40min); Monte Gordo (Mon–Fri 7–11 daily, Sat & Sun 4 daily; 1hr 30min); Olhão (Mon–Fri every 20–30min, Sat & Sun approx hourly; 20min); Portimão (7 daily; 1hr 45min); Quarteira (approx every 30min; 40min); Tavira (7–11 daily; 1hr); Vilamoura (approx every 30min; 50min); and Vila Real (7–11 daily; 1hr 40min).

By car There's plenty of metered parking around the harbour; free parking can be found in the streets around the train station or in the large Largo de São Francisco, just east of the old town.

By train The train station is on Largo da Estação, a few minutes' walk north of the marina.

Destinations Conceição (10–13 daily; 45min); Ferreiras, for Albufeira (4 daily; 25min); Fuseta (10–13 daily; 20min); Lagos (7–9 daily; 1hr 40min); Lisbon (5 daily; 3hr 5min–3hr 30 min); Monte Gordo (10–13 daily; 1hr 5min); Olhão (10–13 daily; 11min); Portimão (7–9 daily; 1hr 25min); Porto (2 daily; 5hr 45min); Silves (7–9 daily; 1hr–1hr 15min); Tavira (10–13 daily; 35min); and Vila Real de Santo António (10–13 daily; 1hr 10min).

INFORMATION

Tourist office Faro's turismo, Rua da Misericórdia 8–12 (Mon–Fri 9am–6pm, Sat–Sun 9am–1pm & 2–6pm; 📞 289 803 604, 🌐 cm-faro.pt) provides town maps and posts local and long-distance bus, boat and train timetables.

Regional tourist office Avenida 5 Outubro 18–20 (Mon–Fri 9am–6pm; 📞 289 800 400, 🌐 visitalgarve.pt) is a good source of information on the area as a whole.

TOURS AND ACTIVITIES

Boat trips Various boat trips depart from Faro's jetty, below the old town walls, including the highly recommended trip to the Ilha Deserta (daily at 11.30am & 4pm, weather permitting, last return 7pm; €25; 📞 917 811 856, 🌐 ilha-deserta.com), in the Parque Natural da Ria Formosa. The most southerly point of mainland Portugal, the island's official name is Ilha da Barreta, and there's little there, save one pricey café and a great beach.

Watersports and birdwatching Specializing in eco-tourism, Lands (📞 289 817 466, 🌐 lands.pt) runs kayaking and sailing tours in the Ria Formosa, along with birdwatching, bike rental and walks around the region.

Land train A fun Comboio Turístico (land train; hourly 10am–dusk; €2.75) trundles from the marina to the Sé and through the modern town before skirting back to the marina via the market.

ACCOMMODATION

Adelaide Rua Cruz das Mestras 9 📞 289 802 383. *Adelaide* offers some of the best-value rooms in town, all with attached bathrooms and cable TV, and there's an airy breakfast-room-cum-snack-bar. Some rooms sleep three or four. €55

Aeromar Av Nascente 1, Praia de Faro 📞 289 817 542, 🌐 aeromar.net. By the bridge to Faro's beach, this simple hotel has decent rooms above a restaurant with beach or (distant) airport views – you pay a little more for a terrace. A good option if you have an early flight. €70

Eva Av da República 1 📞 289 001 000, 🌐 hotel-eva -faro.h-rez.com. The town's top hotel, offering bright rooms, the best (€10 extra) with balconies looking across to the old town or the marina. There's a great rooftop pool and restaurant, and a courtesy bus to the local beach. Parking available. €92

Faro Pr Dr. Francisco Gomes 2 📞 289 830 830, 🌐 hotelfaro.pt. Modern four-star above (and accessed via) an office block. Largely geared to business travellers, the rooms are minimalist with minibar, cable TV and a/c; the best are on the top floors with views over town. The main attraction is the sunny roof terrace with its own restaurant and fine marina views. Free shuttle boat to Farol in summer. €150

Pousada Palácio de Estói Rua São José, Estói 📞 289 990 150, 🌐 pousadas.pt. Around 11km north of Faro, this was the former nineteenth-century palace of the Viscount of Estói. Now it's a classic blend of old-style opulence – wood panelling, gilt mirrors and high ceilings – and contemporary flair, with a pool in the top part of the ornate former gardens, modern rooms, a

9

plush bar and quality restaurant serving gourmet regional food. **€200**

Sol Algarve Rua Infante D. Henrique 52 ☎ 289 895 700, ⊛ hotelsolalgarve.com. A popular two-star hotel, with bright rooms on several floors (there's a lift) and its own café. Bathrooms are spotless, the rooms have a/c and cable TV and breakfast (included) is served in the downstairs dining room or on the little internal patio. Parking available. **€85**

Sally Guest House Pr Alexandre Herculano 6 ☎ 289 829 825, ⊛ sallyinfaro.wix.com/sally-en. Welcoming English-run place that has a mixed bag of airy, bright rooms with high ceilings and cable TV – the cheapest ones are on the ground floor with shared bath (€35) and there are also larger family rooms (€90). Some have showers and small balconies, and you can use the communal kitchen and lovely roof terrace. No breakfast. **€55**

EATING

Faro's attractive pedestrianized shopping area is the heart of the town, home to innumerable **restaurants**, **cafés** and **bakeries** – the latter stocked with various almond delicacies, the regional speciality.

CAFÉS

Café do Coreto Jardim Manuel Bivar ☎ 289 243 896. Glass kiosk café-bar with prime seating facing the marina. Serves everything from croissants to ice cream, cakes, beers and full meals (pizzas, crêpes etc from €10). Daily 8am–midnight.

★**Gardy** Rua de Santo António 16 ☎ 289 824 062. Popular local *pastelaria* whose seats are always at a premium – excellent cakes, pastries and coffee, and good-value lunches from around €8. They also have a takeaway branch at Rua de Santo António 33 that sells the delicious local almond pastries. Mon–Sat 8.30am–8.30pm.

Vila Adentro Pr D. Afonso III 17 ☎ 289 052 173. Set in two fifteenth-century townhouses, the interior of this café-restaurant is beautifully tiled in *azulejos* depicting moments from Faro's history. There's an old well in the floor and steps allegedly leading to a secret tunnel, once used to escape sieges. The main courses (fish and grills from around €11) are less dramatic but the cakes are certainly tempting. Daily 10am–midnight.

RESTAURANTS

Adega Dois Irmãos Pr Ferreira de Almeida 15 ☎ 289 823 337, ⊛ restaurantedoisirmaos.com. Opened in 1925 by two brothers (*dois irmãos*) in a former welder's shop, this attractive tiled place is one of the oldest of the city's fish restaurants. The day's catch can be expensive (around €15), though the *pratos do dia* are usually better value. Despite the number of tourists passing through, service remains courteous and efficient, and there's a

pleasant garden. Daily noon–4pm & 5.30–11pm.

Adega Nova Rua Francisco Barreto 24 ☎ 289 813 433, ⊛ restauranteadeganova.com. This old-fashioned *adega* seats diners on long, shared benches in a barn-like building. With sports events shown on TV, it's a buzzy place, serving big portions of good-value Portuguese food and jugs of local wine; you'll eat well for around €15. Order *bife na pedra* and you can cook your own steak on a sizzling stone, brought to your table. Daily noon–11pm.

★**A Venda** Rua do Compromisso 60 ☎ 289 825 500. Small locals' joint with a living-room like interior – comfy sofas and paintings on the wall – this is a great place to sample *petiscos* (snacks; most €3.50–6) such as salt-cod rissoles and blood sausage. There are great veggie options too, from scrambled egg with peppers to bean croquettes. Bench-like seats outside face an attractive cobbled backstreet. Tues–Sat noon–11pm.

Ginásio Clube Naval Doca de Faro ☎ 289 823 869. The main draw here is a great terrace overlooking the tidal mudflats and the coast. The catch of the day includes fresh fish and seafood, often langoustine, clams and oysters, plus good-value rice dishes (around €9). Tues–Sun noon–3pm & 7–11pm.

Taberna Modesto Largo do Castelo 2 ☎ 916 577 044. This basic diner has alluring outdoor tables set out in the old town. There's a long menu of fish (including surprisingly tasty fried eels), meat and seafood at €7–15. Mon–Sat 12.30–3.30pm & 7.30–11pm, Sun 12.30–3.30pm.

DRINKING AND NIGHTLIFE

Faro's bars and clubs are concentrated along the pedestrianized Rua Conselheiro Bivar and the parallel Rua do Prior. Things get going around midnight; soon afterwards, drinkers spill out onto the cobbled alleys to party.

Bar CheSsenta 24 Rua do Prior ☎ 931 194 314. Small and smoky, this is Faro's main live-music bar, featuring everything from rock and pop to reggae and world music most weekends. Daily 9pm–4am.

★**Columbus Lounge Bar** Jardim Manuel Bívar, cnr Rua João Dias ☎ 289 813 051. Fashionable bar with

outdoor seats (press the buzzer for service) beneath the arcades of a former hospital, plus a cosy lounge area inside. It serves up fine *caipirinha* cocktails and hosts occasional live music. Daily 11am–1am.

O Castelo Rua do Castelo 11 ☎ 919 846 405. Superbly sited in the old town facing the Ria Formosa, this is a large,

multi-purpose space with a pricey restaurant, café and bar. The broad terrace is a great spot for a sunset drink and there's also a stage for live music (fado on Mondays). Mon–Sat 10am–4.30am.

Upa Upa Rua Conselheiro Bivar 51 ☎ 965 410 620.

Laidback and relatively early-opening music bar, with a mixed clientele spilling onto outdoor tables on the widest stretch of this pedestrianized street. Daily 9pm–4am; Oct–April closed Sun.

SHOPPING

Forum Algarve EN125 ☎ 289 889 300, ⓦ forum algarve.net. You'll pass this giant shopping centre when heading into Faro from the airport – it's a brisk 15min walk from town up Rua Infante Dom Henrique. The attractive, Moorish-style pedestrianized complex has over 100 local and international shops, cafés, restaurants, a multiplex cinema and a hypermarket. Daily 10am–midnight.

Mercado Municipal Largo Dr. Francisco Sá Carneiro ☎ 289 897 250, ⓦ mercadomunicipaldefaro.pt. Faro's

bustling town market sits in a very grand building on three floors. There's a giant supermarket in the basement, while on the ground floor, stalls sell everything from dried figs and olives to fruit, cheese, honey and fresh fish. There are also restaurants and souvenirs. Most shops Mon–Fri 8.30am–7pm, Sat 9am–1pm.

Rui Garrafeira 28 Pr Ferreira de Almeida ☎ 289 821 586. This deli-cum-off licence sells a fantastic array of traditional sweets, cheeses, preserves and wines from the region. Mon–Sat 8.30am–8pm.

DIRECTORY

Football/live music International games are sometimes played at the 30,000-seat Algarve Stadium (☎ 289 893 200, ⓦ parquecidades-eim.pt), the centrepiece of a cultural centre and sports park called Parque das Cidades, 6km north of Faro on the Loulé road. It also hosts various events including concerts – check the website for details.

Hospital Distrital de Faro, Rua Leão Penedo (☎ 289 891 100,

ⓦ www.hdfaro.min-saude.pt). For emergencies call ☎ 112.

Police Rua da Policia de Segurança Pública 32 (☎ 289 822 022).

Post office Largo do Carmo (Mon–Fri 8.30am–6.30pm, Sat 9am–12.30pm).

Taxis There's a rank in Praça Dr. Francisco Gomes, by the town gardens; otherwise call ☎ 289 895 795.

Olhão and the islands

There are few actual sights in **OLHÃO**, 8km east of Faro, but with a vibrant market, attractive riverfront gardens and atmospheric backstreets, it's an appealing place to spend some time. It also makes a great base from which to visit the surrounding sandbank islands of **Armona** and **Culatra** or the **Quinta da Marim** environmental centre. The largely pedestrianized old town boasts some superb tile-fronted buildings, quirky shops and bars, while the flat roofs and narrow streets are striking and give a North African look to the place – perhaps not surprisingly, as Olhão had traditional trading links with Morocco. The town was granted its charter by exiled king João VI to thank the local fishermen who sailed a small boat, *O Caíque de Bom Sucesso*, across the Atlantic to Brazil in 1808 to give him the good news that Napoleon's troops had left Portugal. The amazing journey was completed with the most basic navigational aids, and a replica of the boat is now moored on the water behind the market: it occasionally runs boat trips along the coast – ask at the turismo for details.

Mercado Municipal

Avenida 5 de Outubro • Mon–Fri 7am–2pm, Sat 6.30am–3pm

The town's most obvious focus is the bustling **Mercado Municipal**, set in two early twentieth-century redbrick buildings on the harbourside. Open from the crack of dawn, it sells meat, fruit and vegetables on one side, fish on the other, the latter full of tuna steaks the size of hubcaps and alarmingly large octopus and squid. Come on a Saturday morning and the market extends along the riverfront, a riot of chickens, flowers, fruit and local characters. In August, the gardens on either side host the

9

Festival do Marisco (Seafood Festival; ⓦfestivaldomarisco.com) with food stalls and nightly entertainment over five days.

Nossa Senhora do Rosário

Praça da Restauração • Tues–Sun 9.30am–noon & 3–6pm • Free

The old town's most prominent building is the seventeenth-century parish church of **Nossa Senhora do Rosário**, right in the middle of town. Outside, at the back of the church, an iron grille protects the chapel of **Nossa Senhora dos Aflitos**, where townswomen traditionally gathered to pray for their sailors when there was a storm at sea – if you look through the grille, you'll see the curious wax *ex voto* models of children and limbs left to bring good fortune.

Museu da Cidade

Praça da Restauração • Tues–Fri 10am–12.30pm & 2–5.30pm, Sat 10am–1pm • Free • ☎ 289 700 184

Behind the church of Nossa Senhora da Soledade, the small but appealing **Museu da Cidade** has a small collection of archeological finds from the region, from Bronze Age

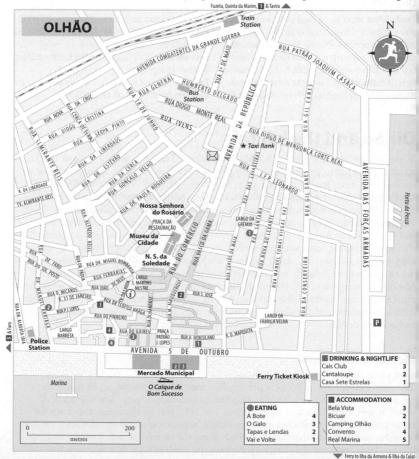

> **FERRIES TO ARMONA AND CULATRA**
>
> Separate **ferries to** Armona and Culatra leave from the jetty at the eastern end of Olhão's municipal gardens, five minutes' walk east of the market. The timetable (also at ⓦ olhao.web.pt, or call ☎ 289 702 121) is posted at the ticket kiosk here; if the kiosk isn't open, you can buy tickets on the ferries. The **Ilha da Armona** (15min; see below) is accessible all year round, as are the villages of Culatra (35min) and Farol (45min) on the **Ilha da Culatra** (see below). Note that in summer you can also get the boat to Farol from Faro (see p.448).

pots to Islamic vases. Upstairs there are relics of Olhão's industrial heritage, with model fishing boats, oil presses and old black-and-white photos.

Ilha da Armona

Ferries make the 15min journey from Olhão (June & Sept 9 daily; July & Aug first departure at 7.30am, then roughly hourly until 8pm; Oct–May 4 daily, first departure 8.30am, check last return with ferry driver; €3.70 return)

Ferries from Olhão drop their passengers at the southern end of **Ilha da Armona**, at the island's only settlement, a charming medley of tightly packed holiday homes with neatly tended gardens of hibiscus, oleander and cacti; Armona's only shop is on the main pathway that heads to the main Atlantic-facing beach. It's a 25-minute walk to the Atlantic, where there's a giant curve of soft sandy beach. The section of **beach** where the path emerges can get busy in high season, but it doesn't take much effort to escape the crowds – just walk east, though pay attention to the signs as the currents can be strong. Continue east up the beach for two hours and you'll end up at **Praia da Fuseta**, opposite Fuseta town on the mainland (see p.449).

There are a few seasonal cafés at the Atlantic-facing beach but the bulk of the island's facilities are near the ferry terminal where you'll find a cluster of decent cafés and restaurants (most closed from October to March). There are no hotels on Armona, and camping on the beach is frowned upon, but there are some basic **bungalows** available to rent (see p.448).

Ilha da Culatra

Ferries run to the Ilha da Culatra from Olhão's jetty (June to mid-Sept 6 daily; July & Aug 7 daily; mid-Sept to May 4 daily; €3.70 return to Culatra (30 min), €4.30 return to Farol (45 min; see box above); there's also a service from Faro to Farol on the Ilha da Culatra (40min), departing from the jetty below Faro old town (June to mid-Sept 5 daily; first boat at 9.30am, last return at 7pm; €5 return; ☎ 917 634 813, ⓦ silnido.com)

Ilha da Culatra is a 6km-long strip of dunes dotted with narrow lagoons and faced by a wonderful sandy beach. The ferry from Olhão makes two stops on the Ilha da Culatra, calling first at **Culatra**, a working fishing village – you dock by a harbour bursting with fishing boats. When not at sea, fishermen gather to mend their nets, or hang out in the bars of the main town, which has a permanent population of about a thousand. There are no cars – the main street is little more than a pavement – but it has its own school, church and assorted local fish restaurants. Walk south through the main street and across the boardwalks to reach the superb stretch of beach.

The second stop on ferries from Olhão (also reachable in summer via ferries from Faro), **Farol** is more geared to tourists, with fishermen's huts, seasonal restaurants and holiday homes gathered below a lighthouse, from where the beach stretches to the west: the further you walk, the quieter it becomes.

Quinta da Marim

3km east of Olhão, just off the N125 Olhão–Tavira road • Mon–Fri 8am–8pm, Sat & Sun 10am–8pm • €2.50 • ☎ 289 704 134, ⓦ icnf.pt • Regular buses from Olhão and Fuseta drop you on the main road, from where it's a 5min walk

Quinta da Marim is a slightly neglected-looking environmental educational centre and

9

headquarters of the **Parque Natural da Ria Formosa**. It's a lovely quiet spot, set amid scrubby dunes and mudflats dotted with pines and gorse, well worth a half-day visit. You can follow a 3km-long **nature trail** that leads from the car park past the visitor centre, along which you'll be able to view storks' nests, and the remains of Roman saltpans. Its highlight is one of the country's last remaining tidal mills; there's also a café at the visitor centre.

ARRIVAL AND INFORMATION

OLHÃO AND THE ISLANDS

By bus Olhão's bus terminal is on Rua General Humberto Delgado, a 5min walk north of the centre.

Destinations Faro (Mon–Fri every 20–30min, Sat & Sun approx hourly; 20min); Lisbon (3–4 daily; 4hr); Tavira (9–10 daily; 40 min); Vila Real de Santo António (10 daily; 1hr 20 min).

By train The train station is at the northern edge of town,

off Avenida dos Combatentes da Grande Guerra.

Destinations Faro (10–13 daily; 11min); Tavira (10–13 daily; 20min); Vila Real de Santo António (10–13 daily; 50 min).

Information The turismo is at Largo Sebastião Martins Mestre 6A (Mon–Fri 9.30am–1pm & 2–5.30pm; ☎ 289 713 936, ⓦ www.cm-olhao.pt).

ACTIVITIES

Football Olhão's football team, Olhanenses, has flown the flag for the region in the top Portuguese league in recent years, though its only league championship was in 1924. They host league matches on alternate weekends from September to May at the small Estádio José Arcanjo (ⓦ scolhanense.com).

Guided walks and boat trips Natura (☎ 918 056 674,

ⓦ natura-algarve.com) offers a range of activities including guided walks and boat trips into the Ria Formosa lagoon, ranging from leisurely 2–3hr birdwatching cruises which include a visit to an oyster farm (all year; €35), to adrenalin-charged 2hr powerboat rides to spot dolphins (June–Oct; €45).

ACCOMMODATION

Olhão does not have a great choice of **accommodation**, so book in advance in high season. For self-catering options, try ⓦ whiteterraces.com, which lets out some great traditional houses in the old town (minimum three-day lets); many have roof terraces with sea views, and some have their own pool. There's also one simple option on the Ilha da Armona.

OLHÃO

Bela Vista Rua Dr. Teófilo Braga 65–67 ☎ 289 702 538. A longstanding favourite, with a range of simple, bright a/c rooms – some are completely tiled, others lack windows – arranged around a flower-filled courtyard; there's also a roof terrace. No breakfast. **€45**

Bicuar Rua Vasco da Gama 5 ☎ 289 714 816, ⓦ pension bicuar.com. Central, sparklingly clean guesthouse on a quiet pedestrianized street, with a variety of rooms, including family rooms (€70) and triple rooms (€58). All are well furnished with cable TV, most have private showers and balconies overlooking the old town, and guests can use a communal kitchen. Great views from the roof terrace. No breakfast. **€50**

Camping Olhão Pinheiros de Marim ☎ 289 700 300. Around 3km east of town, next to Quinta da Marim, this upmarket site is set in substantial grounds and has its own pool (small fee charged), playground, tennis courts, minimarket, restaurant and bars. It's served by regular buses from Olhão. Pitch **€8.50**

★ **Convento** Trav António Bento 10 ☎ 912 463 233, ⓦ conventoolhao.com. This unsigned guesthouse on a small back alley close to the market is a stunning example of an artfully renovated Cubist townhouse. Rooms are

wrapped round a beautiful tiled inner courtyard on two levels, and come with stripped wooden floors and colossal beds; some have walk-in showers. Narrow steps lead to a series of little roof terraces, with sun loungers, a plunge pool and superb views over town. A sumptuous breakfast is served in a cool dining room. Sublime. Two-night minimum stay in high season. **€115**

Real Marina Av 5 de Outubro ☎ 289 091 300, ⓦ real-marina.com. The town's top hotel is an unattrac-tive modern building that offers a range of luxurious facilities – most of the pristine rooms come with large sea-facing balconies and flatscreen TVs. A glass lift shuttles from the ground floor, with its spa and restaurant, past the first-floor deck where there's a heated open-air pool. **€200**

ILHA DA ARMONA

Parque Orbitur Ilha da Armona ☎ 289 714 173, ⓦ orbitur.pt. *Orbitur* operates a series of simple beachside holiday bungalows sleeping up to five on the island of Armona, all a short walk from the ferry terminal off the main path to the beach. Reservations advised; one-week minimum stay in high season. Closed Nov–March. **€93**

EATING

OLHÃO

★ **A Bote** Av 5 de Outubro 122 ☎ 289 721 183. Near the fish market, this lively restaurant serves meat and fish dishes from an outdoor grill, accompanied by mounds of potatoes and salad, from €8. Mon–Sat 11am–4pm & 7–11pm.

O Galo Rua da Gazeta de Olhão 7 ☎ 964 709 746. With a cosy interior and tables lined up on a cobbled alley, this has a short but quality menu (mains €12–15): clams, *carne de porco Alentejana* (cubes of pork with clams) and steaks, plus a good range of veggie dishes such as lentil and aubergine curry. Daily 8am–2am.

Tapas e Lendas Rua Dr. Manuel Ariega 18 ☎ 289 706 429. This attractive tapas bar has seats outside and an upstairs terrace. It serves a good range of drinks and excellent tapas such as goats' cheese with honey in filo pastry, local cheeses and sausage (around €4.50). Mon 6–10pm, Tues–Sat noon–3pm & 6–10pm.

Vai e Volte Largo do Gremio 2 ☎ 968 027 125. Set in an attractive little square, this serves an all-you-can-eat buffet of mixed fish of the day – always sea-fresh – with salad, potatoes, garlicky *açorda* sauce, bread and olives, all for around €12. Tues–Sun noon–3pm.

DRINKING

OLHÃO

Cais Club Mercado Municipal, Loja 49, Av 5 de Outubro ☎ 289 723 044. The liveliest of a row of bars behind the market, with outdoor tables facing the water – though most hit the inside bar and dance area as the night wears on. There's regular live music, usually rock on Fridays. Daily 2pm–4am.

Cantaloupe Mercado de Verdura, Av 5 de Outubro ☎ 289 704 397. Fashionable jazz bar with alluring outdoor

tables facing the water. There are weekly jam sessons on Thursdays, and live music most Saturdays. Mon & Wed–Sat 10am–2am, Sun 10am–8pm.

Casa Sete Estrelas Trav Alexandre Herculano 6. If you fancy engaging with some of the local characters and fishermen, head to this rough-and-ready bar with football-themed decor. There's dirt-cheap wine from the barrel, animated banter and oodles of character. Tues–Sun noon–midnight.

Fuseta

Around 10km east of Olhão, and served by regular bus as well as the main Algarve rail line, the fishing town of **FUSETA** (or Fuzeta) is one of the Algarve's least "discovered" resorts, probably because of its shortage of accommodation. It is not the region's most beautiful town, but it does retain some character as a working fishing port. Its daily routine revolves around its fishermen, whose colourful boats line up alongside the river in town, though in summer Fuseta also attracts a lively community of campers. The two communities usually mingle at the line of lively kiosk-cafés spreading down from the ferry stop towards the river beach.

The town's backstreets straddle a low hill facing the lagoon, sheltered by the eastern extremity of the Ilha da Armona. Many of the local fish find their way to the small covered **market** on Largo 1° de Maio, on the road running parallel to the river. On Saturdays the market expands into a flea market that lines the adjacent pedestrianized Rua Tenente Barrosa. Continue up this road to reach the town's little palm-tree-lined central **square**.

The waterfront of modern shops and apartments faces broad gardens that are largely taken over by the campsite. Beyond this is the **estuary beach**, a fine stretch of white sand that weaves up to a wooden lifeboat house, though more exhilarating and cleaner waters are found over the lagoon on the Ilha da Armona (see p.447).

Praia da Fuseta

Ferries run from Fuesta to Praia da Fuseta (April–Sept daily approx every 15min 9am–6pm, and often later; Oct–March 4 daily from 9am, last return at 5.45pm • €1.60 return; ☎ 289 794 210 ⊛ harmoniafusetatours.pt); you can also reach the sands by Aquataxis (€5 per person one-way; ☎ 962 539 810)

Regular **ferries** shuttle from the fishing quay at the back of the campsite across the lagoon to **Praia da Fuseta** on the eastern end of the Ilha da Armona. The beach immediately opposite the ferry stop gets fairly crowded in high summer, but you only have to walk for ten minutes to have the beautiful, low dune-backed sands all to

9

yourself. In 2010, all the buildings on this stretch were destroyed in a storm, so it's best to take your own supplies.

ARRIVAL AND DEPARTURE   FUSETA

By bus Buses from Faro pull up at the waterfront near the campsite (4 daily, 45min).
By train The train station is to the north of town, a 10min

walk from the waterfront. It has regular services to Faro (10–13 daily; 20min), Olhão (10–13 daily; 12min) and Tavira (10–13 daily; 15min).

ACCOMMODATION

Monte Alegre Apartado 64 ☎ 289 794 222, ⓦ monte -alegre-algarve.de. Around 2km northwest of Fuseta (signposted Bias Sul) and run by welcoming Germans, *Monte Alegre* consists of three well-equipped apartments sleeping up to four (€540 per week), and a superb studio with its own terrace. There's an outdoor swimming pool, stables for horse rides and a pond full of resident frogs; all

rooms have satellite TV and kitchenettes. Minimum one-week lets in high season. Studio (per week) €504
Parque de Campismo da Fuseta ☎ 289 793 459, ⓦ roteiro-campista.pt. Beautifully positioned waterside campsite beneath the trees, with its own minimarket and bar. It gets pretty full in high summer, so it's best to book in advance. Pitch €13

EATING AND DRINKING

Fuseta Tapas Rua Tenente Barroso 59 ☎ 289 791 093. On the main pedestrianized square, this has a good range of *petiscos* (snacks) such as mushrooms with garlic and coriander, *chouriço* snails or *pasteis de bacalhau* (salt-cod cake) from €4, as well as the usual mains from €10. Tues–Sun 11am–3pm & 6pm–midnight.

Skandinavia Rua Tenente Barroso 11 ☎ 289 793 853. Near the market, the food here is not at all Scandinavian – it has friendly service and excellent seafood, grilled meat and fish at €8–10, with outdoor tables spilling onto the pedestrianized street. Mon & Wed–Sun noon–3pm & 6–11pm.

Tavira and around

Despite its inland position, **TAVIRA**, 30km east of Faro, is the most interesting and attractive of the eastern Algarve's towns. It straddles both sides of the broad Rio Gilão, the old town made up of white mansions with hipped roofs and wrought-iron balconies. Many visitors stay longer than planned – particularly after a visit to the superb island beach of the **Ilha de Tavira**, which lies within easy reach of the town by year-round ferry. There are also several quieter spots in the area, such as the holiday village of **Pedras d'el Rei** and nearby beach at **Barril** and, for some excellent seafood, the fishing village of **Santa Luzia**.

Founded as long ago as 400 BC, Tavira was a powerful port trading with North Africa until the river began to silt up in the seventeenth century. It was also an important religious centre, with most of the town's 21 churches built in the fifteenth and sixteenth centuries. Following the Great Earthquake of 1755, Tavira was largely reconstructed, hence the graceful eighteenth-century townhouses and mansions that you see today. The old bridge was mostly built in 1667 on the foundations of a Roman structure; the other central bridge was put up by the army in 1989 as a temporary measure, but has held firm ever since. In the old-town streets on both sides of the river, numerous houses retain fine old doorways with traditional knockers in the shape of hands.

The riverfront

With its tranquil vistas and palm-lined gardens, the **riverfront** is the best part of Tavira for a wander. There are no sights as such north of the river, though the old streets hide many of the town's best restaurants. South of the river, the former town market building, **Mercado da Ribeira**, houses a handful of small boutiques and waterfront cafés, with its central space hosting temporary exhibitions.

Heading east, fishing boats and restaurants line up as far as the flyover. In summer, you can catch direct ferries to the Ilha de Tavira from here. Head under the bridge and

you'll see the large new town **market** (Mon–Sat 8am–1.30pm), whose bustling interior is filled with an array of fruit and vegetables.

Núcleo Islâmico

Travessa da Fonte • Tues–Sat 9am–4.30pm • €2, combined ticket with Palácio da Galeria €3 • ☎ 281 320 540, Ⓦ museumunicipaldetavira.cm-tavira.pt

Tavira is proud of its Islamic heritage and the interesting **Núcleo Islâmico**, spread over three floors, pays it homage. After an introductory video you visit the main exhibition

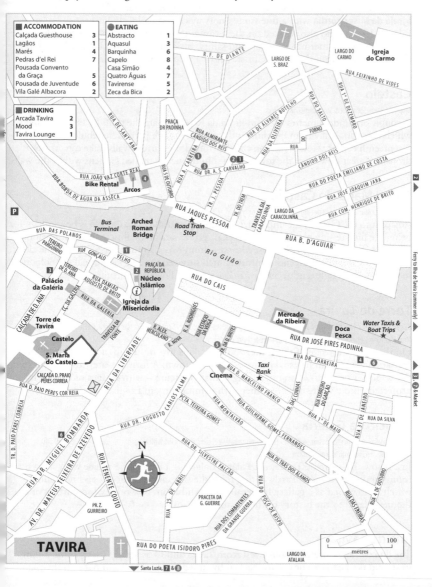

ACCOMMODATION
Calçada Guesthouse	3
Lagãos	1
Marés	4
Pedras d'el Rei	7
Pousada Convento da Graça	5
Pousada de Juventude	6
Vila Galé Albacora	2

EATING
Abstracto	1
Aquasul	3
Barquinha	6
Capelo	8
Casa Simão	4
Quatro Águas	7
Tavirense	5
Zeca da Bica	2

DRINKING
Arcada Tavira	2
Mood	3
Tavira Lounge	1

TAVIRA

0   100
metres

Santa Luzia, 7 & 8

9

area which displays pots, tiles and utensils from the time Tavira was under Moorish rule. Most impressive is a section of an earth-and-stone wall left *in situ*, though the museum's most valuable item is the Tavira Vase, dating from the eleventh century and lined with clay figures, probably made as part of a wedding dowry.

Igreja da Misericórdia

Rua da Galeria • Tues–Sat 9.30am–12.30pm & 2–6pm • Free

From the arcaded **Praça da República**, with its little modern amphitheatre by the river, it's a short climb up into the old town following Rua da Galeria. Ahead stands the **Igreja da Misericórdia** with a fine stone doorway carved by local master mason André Pilarte (1551), who also worked on the Jerónimos monastery in Lisbon (see p.80); it depicts a series of mermaids, angels and saints. Inside there's a striking *azulejo* interior showing scenes from the life of Christ, below a wooden vaulted ceiling.

Castelo

Mon–Fri 8am–5pm, Sat & Sun 10am–7pm • Free

A couple of hundred metres up from Praça da República are the ruins of Tavira's **Castelo**, which dates originally from the thirteenth century, though parts were rebuilt in the seventeenth century. Today you can clamber round the narrow walls (take care of steep drops) for great views over the town, or relax in the neatly tended gardens within the walls.

Santa Maria do Castelo

Alto de Santa Maria • Limited opening times for Mass only

Adjacent to the Castelo, the impressive church of **Santa Maria do Castelo** is best known for being the final resting place of Paio Peres Correia, a warrior knight credited with helping to take back Tavira – and much of the Algarve – from Moorish rule in 1242. Only the clock tower of the original thirteenth-century church survived the 1755 earthquake. Look out for the beautiful eighteenth-century *azulejos* showing flowers and fruits.

Torre de Tavira

Calçada da Galeria 12 • Visits every 30min: Feb–June Mon–Fri 10am–5pm; July–Sept Mon–Fri 10am–5pm, Sat 10am–1pm; Oct–Jan Mon–Fri 10am–4pm • €4 • ☎ 281 322 527, ⊛ torredetavira.com

On the northwest side of the castle, you can take a lift to the top of the 100m-high **Torre de Tavira** for an unusual perspective of the town. A former water tower built in the 1930s, it now acts as an interesting **Câmara Obscura** – with images of the town projected onto a white disk, together with commentary in English.

Palácio da Galeria

Calçada da Galeria • Tues–Sat 9am–4.30pm • Exhibitions usually €2, combined ticket with Núcleo Islâmico €3 • ☎ 281 320 540, ⊛ museumunicipaldetavira.cm-tavira.pt

Just below the Torre de Tavira, the **Palácio Galeria** is a handsome palace with sixteen rooms and sixteen roofs. Partly dating from the sixteenth century, it's a fine building which is now used as a gallery for temporary exhibitions of work by local artists or on themes related to the history of the town.

Ilha de Tavira

The **Ilha de Tavira** stretches southwest from Tavira almost as far as Fuseta, some 14km west, and the beach is enormous, backed by tufted dunes. The main path on the island

BOAT TRIPS TO ILHA DE TAVIRA

In summer you can catch ferries direct to Ilha de Tavira from the riverfront in **Tavira** (daily approx hourly: June & Sept 9am–6.30pm, last return at 7pm; July & Aug 8am–7.30pm, last return at 8pm; Oct 10am–4.30pm, last return 5pm; €2 return; ☎917 634 813, ⊛silnido.com). There's also a year-round ferry that departs from the jetty at **Quatro Águas**, 2km east of Tavira, reachable via a thirty-minute walk or the road train (see below). **Ferries** (daily: Oct–June 9am–6.45pm; July–Sept 8am–11pm; €1.50 return) take just five minutes to cross from Quatro Águas to the island. In high season they run every fifteen minutes or so; at other times they run roughly hourly – always check with the ferryman what time the last boat returns. Alternatively, you can take a **water taxi** – Aquataxis (daily from 8am to dusk; ☎964 515 073) do the ride from Quatro Águas for around €8 per person.

runs from the jetty through a small chalet settlement to the **beach**, where there are umbrellas and pedaloes for rent, and half a dozen bar-restaurants. In high summer this part of the beach is packed, though you only have to walk fifteen minutes or so to be clear of the crowds, and out of season you'll probably have the place entirely to yourself.

Santa Luzia

2km west of Tavira

SANTA LUZIA is an earthy working fishing village which bills itself as the "King of the Octopus", with a number of seafood restaurants catering to day-trippers. Having strolled along the palm-lined waterfront and admired the octopus traps on the jetty, most people settle for a leisurely meal. In summer, local fishermen will ferry you over to the Ilha de Tavira (see p.452) and also run two-hour trips into the lagoon for around €25 a head.

Barril

Weather permitting, the miniature train from Pedras d'el Rei runs daily to Barril (8am–dusk, approx every 15–30min; €1 one-way)

From the bus stop and car park next to *Pedras d'el Rei* holiday complex, 4km from Tavira, you cross a short causeway to the terminal of a rather ancient-looking **miniature train**, which shuttles over to the beach at **Barril** on the Ilha de Tavira. Alternatively, you can walk alongside the tracks, past thousands of fiddler crabs on the mudflats beyond (10–15min). Once there, you'll find attractive former fishermen's houses that have been turned into a cluster of slightly pricey café-restaurants; there's also a small shop, showers and toilets. A long stretch of alluring sands lies beyond the lines of anchors wedged into the dunes. Head around 1km west to **Praia do Homen Nú** ("nude man beach") – one of the country's few official clothing-optional beaches.

ARRIVAL AND INFORMATION

TAVIRA AND AROUND

By bus Tavira's bus terminal is by the river on its south side; it's a 2min walk east to the old bridge and Praça da República.
Destinations Cabanas (Mon–Fri 9–11 daily, Sat–Sun 3 daily; 15min); Faro (7–11 daily; 1hr); Fuseta (9–11 daily; 25min); Lisbon (3–4 daily; 4hr 20min); Olhão (9–11 daily; 45min); Pedras d'el Rei (Mon–Fri 9 daily; Sat–Sun 2 daily; 10min); Santa Luzia (Mon–Fri 10 daily; Sat–Sun 3 daily; 15min).
By car Drivers will encounter a complicated one-way system in Tavira's central area; it's best to head for the free car park by the bus station.
By train Tavira's train station is 1km southwest of the centre of town, straight up the Rua da Liberdade and at the end of Avenida Dr. Mateus Teixeira de Azevedo.

Destinations Conceição (10–13 daily; 8min); Faro (10–13 daily; 35min); Fuseta (15 daily; 5min); Monte Gordo (10–13 daily; 25min); Olhão (10–13 daily; 25min); Vila Real de Santo António (10–13 daily; 30min).
By road train A fun way to get your bearings is by taking the road train, which does a circuit from Rua Jaques Pessoa via Praça da República out to Quatro Águas (daily approx hourly 10.50am–dusk; €4 a circuit, or €6 for a day-pass).
By taxi Taxis line up opposite the cinema, or call ☎281 325 746.
Information The turismo is at Praça da República 5 (Mon–Fri 9am–1pm & 2–6pm; ☎281 322 511, ⊛cm-tavira.pt).

9

ACTIVITIES

Bike rental Tavira's Abilio Bikes, Rua João Vaz Corte Real 23a (Mon–Sat 9am–1pm & 3–7pm, Sat 9.30am–3pm; ☎ 281 323 467, ⓦ abiliobikes.com), rents out bikes from €7 a day.

Boat trips Sequa Tours (☎ 918 763 020, ⓦ sequatours .com) runs 1hr boat trips round Tavira's lagoon for €12 per person, as well as 90min birdwatching tours from €20.

ACCOMMODATION

TAVIRA

★ **Calçada Guesthouse** Calç. de Dona Ana 12 ☎ 926 563 713 ⓦ calcadaguesthouse.com. Set in a low-rise traditional building, the interior of this British-run guesthouse is surprisingly spacious thanks to creative architecture, with a breakfast room overlooking a little garden and a terrific terrace with views over the river (where breakfast is served in good weather). Cosy rooms have walk-in showers and extremely comfy beds, some with small terraces. **€100**

Lagâos Rua Almirante Cândido dos Reis 24 ☎ 281 328 243. On the north side of the river, this place has simple but attractive rooms clustered round a pretty rooftop patio. It's above the top-notch budget restaurant *Zeca da Biça* (see p.456). **€55**

Marés Rua José Pires Padinha 134–140 ☎ 281 325 815, ⓦ residencialmares.com. *Marés* has pleasant rooms – the best have balconies facing the river – with tiled floors and *azulejos* in the bathrooms; there's also a roof terrace and sauna. Family rooms (€100) available too. **€90**

★ **Pousada Convento da Graça** Rua D. Paio Peres Correia ☎ 281 329 040, ⓦ pousadas.pt. Set in an immaculately converted sixteenth-century convent around beautiful cloisters and with its own church, this *pousada* is hard to fault. Most of the plush rooms look down over the old town or a rural hillside, while the swimming pool sits inside Tavira's old town walls. During renovation work, the remains of a Moorish settlement were found and these can be viewed through a glass partition in the bar. There's also a highly rated restaurant that uses local ingredients. **€240**

Pousada de Juventude Rua Miguel Bombarda 36–38 ☎ 281 326 731, ⓦ pousadasjuventude.pt. Behind the facade of a lovely historic cultural centre lies a pristine modern youth hostel with four-bedded dorms and small but very pleasant doubles. There are outdoor terraces, a lounge with pool, a communal kitchen and summer bar. Dorms **€17**, doubles **€47**

ILHA DE TAVIRA

Camping de Tavira Ilha de Tavira ☎ 281 321 709. Great for some island living, this busy campsite is just a minute from the sands, off the path between the ferry terminal and the beach. Pitches are beneath the trees and it has a well-stocked minimarket and café. Closed Oct–Easter. Pitches **€12**

QUATRO ÁGUAS

Vila Galé Albacora Quatro Águas ☎ 281 380 800, ⓦ www.vilagale.pt. Despite its address, this hotel is actually on the opposite side of the estuary from Quatro Águas, 4km east of Tavira. It's a former tuna-fishing village that has been tastefully converted into a four star hotel, with rooms in the old fishermen's houses either facing the river estuary or the enormous central courtyard (though some face the car park). The flower-filled courtyard also contains a large pool, games room, restaurant and bar; inside there's another pool and a health club. Parking available. **€180**

SANTA LUZIA

Pedras d'el Rei Santa Luzia ☎ 281 380 600, ⓦ pedrasdelrei.com. The apartments and villas at this little resort just east of town are perfect for families, set in beautifully landscaped grounds. There's a central lawn area focused around an outdoor pool and overlooked by a café, bar and restaurant. Facilities include a playground, children's club, aviary and well-stocked shop, and residents get free passes for the train to the beach at Barril. **€120**

EATING

TAVIRA

Abstracto Rua António Cabrita 34 ☎ 917 043 274. Small, fashionable restaurant which gives a modern twist to its fish and meat dishes (€9–16), such as scallops, prawns in a curry sauce, or pork with apple and fennel. Mon & Wed–Sun 11am–3pm & 6–10pm.

Aquasul Rua Dr. Augusto Silva Carvalho 11 ☎ 281 325 166. A hip and jazzy place on a quiet street, serving imaginative cuisine with an Italian influence: lamb risotto, pasta and with a veggie dish of the day. Main courses are all €13–15, though pizzas are less (from €9.50). Tues–Sat 6.30–10.30pm.

Barquinha Rua José Pires Padinha 142 ☎ 281 322 843. The best of the somewhat touristy places facing the river. Excellent *bacalhau à brás* (salted cod with egg and potatoes) and good fresh fish from €10. Mon, Tues & Thurs–Sun noon–3pm & 7–10pm.

★ **Casa Simão** Rua João Vaz Corte Real 10 ☎ 281 321 647. This is where the locals go to fill up on Portuguese steaks and grills (€6–9). Portions are huge, service is friendly, and the house white is a refreshing *vinho verde*. It's a bustling place full of Portuguese families, so get there early to guarantee a table. Mon–Sat 11am–11pm.

Tavirense Rua Marcelino Franco 19. For some of the best

TAVIRA (P.450) >

9

cakes and pastries in town, try this old-fashioned *pastelaria* opposite the cinema, where the locals go for breakfast and for daytime refuelling. Daily 7am–2am.
Zeca da Bica Rua Almirante Cândido dos Reis 22–24 ☎281 323 843. Always busy – book or get there early to guarantee a table – this unglamorous but excellent-value restaurant has tasty mains – grilled sardines, pork steaks and the like – for around €8. Mon, Tues & Thurs–Sun noon–3pm & 7–10pm.

ILHA DE TAVIRA

Pavilhão da Ilha Ilha de Tavira ☎961 571 528. Between the ferry and the beach, this is the best place on the island for a full meal, with moderately priced fish and grills (from around €10) and a lively bar area. April–Oct daily noon–10pm.

QUATRO ÁGUAS

Quatro Águas Estrada das Quatro Águas ☎281 325 329. Out by the ferry stop and overlooking the river, this highly rated seafood restaurant specializes in dishes such as *cataplana de marisco* (fish stew), *bacalhau*, and excellent prawn and shrimp kebabs. Mains €12–15. Tues–Sun noon–3pm & 7–10pm.

SANTA LUZIA

Capelo Av Engenheiro Duarte Pacheco 40–42 ☎281 381 670. Santa Luzia's best fish restaurant – slightly pricey but with a spacious *azulejo*-lined interior and a lovely outdoor terrace. Fresh fish, eels and clams from €14 upwards. Mon, Tues & Thurs–Sun noon–2am.

DRINKING

TAVIRA

Arcada Tavira Pr da República 8 ☎915 087 048. A small slice of sophistication in central Tavira, this small, fashionable bar with outdoor seats on the square serves a good range of cocktails from €6 as well as shots and all the usual beers, wine etc. Mon–Thurs & Sun noon–2am, Fri–Sat noon–3am.
Mood Estrada das Quatro Águas ☎927 079 154. Wedged beneath the flyover by the river, this sports bar attracts a young crowd thanks to its two bowling lanes and

lively bar. Theme nights feature regularly, including *kizomba* (Angolan music and dance) nights and DJ sessions most Saturdays from midnight. Thurs–Sat 9pm–6am.
Tavira Lounge Rua Gonçalo Velho 16–18 ☎281 381 034. Spacious lounge-bar with comfy sofas, arty ceramics for sale and a menu featuring cocktails, a range of drinks, inexpensive *petiscos* (snacks) and a terrific terrace with seats overlooking the river. A good chillout spot. Mon–Thurs & Sun noon–2am, Fri–Sat noon–3am.

Cabanas

Six kilometres east of Tavira – past the golf course at Benamor – lies **CABANAS**, named after the fishermen's *cabanas* (huts) that formed the original settlement. Today a kernel of backstreets is still made up of pretty fishermen's houses along with a line of low-rise shops, cafés and bars facing a picturesque river estuary edged by a neat wooden walkway. Moored fishing boats testify to the village's former mainstay, though today the economy is largely driven by tourism thanks to the glorious sands on **Praia de Cabanas** over the estuary. Ferries (April–Oct 9am–dusk, every 15min; €1.50 return) shuttle passengers to the beach from a small jetty opposite *Restaurante O Monteiro* in the east of town. Cross the dunes and you're faced with kilometres of golden sand, plus a couple of seasonal beach cafés.

ARRIVAL AND DEPARTURE

CABANAS

By bus 9–11 buses run daily from Tavira to Cabanas (15min), stopping at the west end of the waterfront.
By train The nearest station to Cabanas is 1km north at Conceição, on the Tavira–Vila Real train line – you'll have to walk into the centre from the station.

Destinations Conceição to: Faro (10–13 daily; 45min); Fuseta (10–13 daily; 20min); Olhão (10–13 daily; 30min); Tavira (10–13 daily; 10min); Vila Real de Santo António (10–13 daily; 20min).

ACCOMMODATION AND EATING

Casa Viana Largo Armação da Abóbora 5 ☎281 325 730, ⍵casa-viana.com. Near the jetty, this friendly guesthouse is the best budget option in town. The large and spruce air-conditioned rooms are in a modern

building with a terrace on the seafront road. Closed late Dec. **€105**
★**Forte de São João da Barra** ☎281 370 495, ⍵fortesaojoaodabarra.com. This stunningly converted

seventeenth-century sea fort is probably the most sublime place to stay in the entire region. Once you're inside the colossal castle gate, you enter a serene space with a big grassy courtyard and a swimming pool in one of the ramparts overlooking olive groves and the sea. The most atmospheric rooms, with cool stone interiors and period furniture, are in the old castle building, though there is an annexe with more modern fittings. €175

★**Noélia & Jerónimo** Rua da Fortaleza 3 ☏ 281 370 649. In a modern building at the eastern end of town, with a terrace facing the water, this is the place to come for inventive home-made cuisine. Try the superb dory with coriander rice, or the octopus fritters. It also does fabulous salads, fresh tuna and a range of rice dishes for two, with mains around €11. Reservations advised in season. Daily 12.30–3pm & 7–10pm.

Pedro Rua Capitão Batista Marçal 51 ☏ 281 370 425. On the way to the jetty, this large, traditional building has an outdoor terrace and a long list of moderately priced fish (€10–12), seafood and rice dishes. Daily 11am–11pm.

Cacela Velha

Perched on a low cliff facing the estuary, 10km east of Cabanas, the whitewashed village of **CACELA VELHA** is a reminder of how the Algarve must have looked half a century ago. Apart from a few café-restaurants, there are no tourist facilities, just a pretty church and the remains of an eighteenth-century fort – and even that houses a maritime police station and is closed to the public. Offering exhilarating views from its clifftop, Cacela is highly picturesque and, despite the Quinta da Ria/Quinta da Cima golf courses just to the west, it's rarely overrun by visitors. The only time the place gets busy is during the **Moorish Nights** in July – a four-day festival of Arabic food and Moorish-inspired events, including a souk.

The beach below the village has been rated as one of the best in the world, and it would be hard not to agree. To get to it, follow signs to "Fábrica", just west of the village, around 1km downhill. From here a ferryman can take you over to the beach for €1.50 single (daily in summer, but only during good weather the rest of the year).

ARRIVAL AND DEPARTURE

CACELHA VELHA

By bus There is no public transport to Cacela Velha, though you can ask to be let off the Tavira–Vila Real bus on the highway, just before Vila Nova de Cacela, 2km inland, from where it's a 15min walk a side-road to the village.

ACCOMMODATION

Cantinho da Ria Formosa Ribeira de Junco ☏ 281 951 837, ⓦ cantinhoriaformosa.com. Around 1.5km from Cacela Velha, near Fábrica and the golf course, the eight rooms in this blue-edged rural hotel have satellite TV and air conditioning, and views over the garden or fields. There are stables attached, and horse rides are on offer for around €20 an hour. €80

Vila Real de Santo António and around

VILA REAL DE SANTO ANTÓNIO (aka Vila Real) is a pleasant border town, the terminus for the trans-Algarve railway line. The ferry across the Guadiana from here to Ayamonte is still the most fun way to cross the border, but the construction of a modern road bridge just north of the town in the 1990s greatly affected the town's former role as the Algarve's main access point to Spain. Nevertheless, it's still an interesting place to spend a few hours, exploring a central grid of streets that radiates out from a handsome main square, **Praça Marquês de Pombal**, ringed by orange trees, low white buildings and pleasant outdoor cafés. The square is named after the king's minister, who helped rebuild the original town after it was destroyed in a tsunami following the 1755 earthquake. Indeed the grid plan, dating from 1774, is very similar to that of Lisbon's Baixa.

On the north side of the square, Rua Teófilo Braga, the pedestrianized main street, leads inland from the riverfront Avenida da República to the **Centro Cultural António Aleixo** (Sept–June Mon–Fri 10am–1pm & 3–7pm; daily in July & Aug;

9

> ## DAY-TRIPS FROM VILA REAL TO AYAMONTE
>
> For a fun day out, hop on a ferry from Vila Real's harbour to the Spanish border town of **Ayamonte**, with its tapas bars and palm-lined squares. It's a lovely twenty-minute ride across the Rio Guadiana, with the forts of Castro Marim visible to the west and the impressive bridge to the north.
>
> **Ferries** run daily to Ayamonte from Vila Real (July to mid-Sept every 30min from 8.30am, last return at 9pm Spanish time; mid-Sept to April hourly from 8.45am, last return at 7pm Spanish time; May–June hourly from 8.45am, last return 8pm Spanish time; €1.80 each way). For more **information** visit ⓦinfoayamonte.com, and remember that Spanish time is one hour ahead of Portuguese.

free; ☎281 542 100, ⓦcm-vrsa.pt), the town's former market building, now used as an innovative space for temporary exhibits and the occasional film and which also dispenses tourist information. The streets surrounding the cultural centre have a certain low-key charm, bristling with linen shops, electrical retailers and grocers, while the riverside **gardens** offer fine views across to the splash of white that is Ayamonte in Spain.

Monte Gordo

Vila Real's nearest beach lies 5km east of town at unglamorous **MONTE GORDO**, the last resort before the Spanish border. It's the most built-up of the eastern holiday towns, with its own **casino** (ⓦcasinomontegordo.solverde.pt), and high-rise hotels overlooking the superb wide, clean sands, on which fishermen still tend to their nets after their stint at sea. In June expect to see a profusion of Harley-Davidson riders who descend for an annual bikers' meet.

Castro Marim

The little village of **CASTRO MARIM**, 5km north of Vila Real, is dominated by an impressive **castle** (daily: April–Sept 9am–7pm; Oct–March 9am–5pm; €1.10), built by Afonso III in the thirteenth century and once the headquarters of the Order of Christ (see p.500). The chapel within the castle was regularly visited by Henry the Navigator, though most of the building was destroyed by the 1755 earthquake. It's a good place for a wander, with fine views of the bridge to Spain from its walls; a small **museum** displays local archeological finds. The castle is also the centrepiece of the village's **Medieval Days Festival** over the last weekend in August, with recreations of medieval life and plenty of entertainment, including access to the sixteenth-century **Fort of São Sebastião** on the opposite hill, which is otherwise usually closed.

Reserva Natural do Sapal

Unrestricted access • Free • ☎ 213 507 900, ⓦ natural.pt

The marshy area around Castro Marim forms the **Reserva Natural do Sapal**, where flamingos stop off to feed. One of the reserve's most unusual and elusive inhabitants is the 10cm-long, swivel-eyed, opposing-toed, Mediterranean **chameleon** – a harmless, slow-moving lizard that's severely threatened elsewhere by habitat destruction. The reserve's website has details of local walks.

ARRIVAL AND DEPARTURE   VILA REAL AND AROUND

By bus Buses to Vila Real either stop by the ferry terminal by the river or at a terminus just north of the train station.
Destinations Alcoutim (Mon–Sat 1–2 daily; 1hr 15min); Castro Marim (Mon–Fri 12 daily, Sat & Sun 2 daily; 15min);

Faro (6–9 daily; 1hr 40min); Lisbon (4 daily; 5–6hr); Manta Rota (Mon–Fri 4–6 daily, Sat 2 daily; 25min); Mértola (Mon–Fri 1 daily; 2hr); Monte Gordo (every 30min; 10min); Odeleite (Mon–Fri 1 daily; 30min); Olhão (10 daily; 1hr 20min); Seville

(2 daily; 2hr 30min); Tavira (9–10 daily; 40min).
By train Vila Real is the eastern terminal of the Algarve railway; the station is a 5min walk north of the riverfront.

Destinations Faro (10–13 daily; 1hr 10min); Monte Gordo (9–10 daily; 5min); Olhão (10–13 daily; 55min); and Tavira (10–13 daily; 30min).

INFORMATION

Castro Marim turismo Rua Dr. José Alves Moreira 2–4, on the main street (daily 9am–1pm & 2–7pm; ☎281 531 232).
Monte Gordo turismo Avenida Infante Dom Henrique, east of the casino (Mon & Fri–Sun 9.30am–1pm & 2–5.30pm, Tues–Thurs 9.30am–7pm; ☎281 544 495,

ⓦ cm-vrsa.pt), with details of private rooms in town.
Boat trips Rio Sul (☎281 510 200, ⓦ riosultravel.com) offers regular day-long boat trips from Vila Real up the Guadiana to the pretty riverside village of Foz de Odeleite; prices start at around €50 per person, which includes food and drinks.

ACCOMMODATION

VILA REAL DE SANTO ANTÓNIO
Baixa Mar Rua Teófilo Braga 3 ☎ 281 543 511. This simple guesthouse has small, functional rooms – the best are at the front, with great views over the river. No breakfast, but plenty of cafés nearby. **€60**

MONTE GORDO
Parque Municipal de Campismo Estrada Municipal 511 ☎281 510 970, ⓦ cm-vrsa.pt. Monte Gordo's campsite

is enormous, attractively set beneath pines near the beach on the Vila Real road. It gets very busy in season, but there's usually plenty of space the rest of the year. Pitch **€14**
Vasco da Gama Av Infante D. Henrique ☎281 510 900, ⓦ vascodagamahotel.com. This may be high-rise but inside it has a certain old-fashioned charm, and its position overlooking the beach can't be faulted. Facilities include tennis courts, pool, restaurant and playground. The best of the large en-suite rooms have sea views. **€155**

EATING AND DRINKING

VILA REAL DE SANTO ANTÓNIO
Caves do Guadiana Av da República 80 ☎281 544 498. A reliable place on the riverfront road for a quality meal at moderate prices, with a pleasant vaulted interior. Mains include *caldeirada* (a type of fish stew) and tuna steaks, at around €9. Mon–Wed & Fri–Sun 11am–3pm & 7–11pm.
Cuca Rua Dr. Sousa Martins 64 ☎963 474 786. Close to the old market building, this is a good budget choice, with just a handful of tables. Recommended are the mixed fish and *bacalhau à brás*, from around €7. Mon–Sat noon–3pm & 7–9pm, Sun noon–3pm.
Sem Espinhas Av da República 51 ☎281 544 605. The

upmarket choice for dining in Vila Real, this has a spacious interior with a semi-covered courtyard. Along with the usual staples – *cataplana* (fish stew), steaks, fresh fish – it also serves some more creative dishes: shrimp with sweet potato, cod gratin and seafood pasta. Mains from €12. Daily 11am–10.30pm.

MONTE GORDO
Jaime Praia de Monte Gordo ☎281 512 361. A little west up the beach from the casino, this simple beach shack draped with soccer scarves serves lunchtime snacks and is a great spot for a beer overlooking the fishing boats. Daily 9am–7pm; Oct–April closes at 6pm.

Alcoutim

Some 40km north of Vila Real – and best approached by car along the road that hugs the Guadiana River – is the extremely attractive border village of **ALCOUTIM**. It has a long history as a river port, dominated in turn by Greeks, Romans and Arabs who all fortified the heights with various structures; the **castle** (daily 9am–7pm, closes 5.30pm Oct–March; €2.50) dates from the fourteenth century and offers fine views over the river. The entrance fee includes access to a small archeological **museum** by the main gates, which traces the history of the castle, its active service in various battles and the remnants of earlier structures on the site. From the castle, cobbled backstreets lead down to the small main square, below which is the appealing riverfront. Currents are too strong for safe swimming, but you can take a boat across the river (around €1.50 single) to the Spanish village of **Sanlúcar**, a mirror image of Alcoutim, with its own ruined castle; or swim at the river beach (*praia fluvial*) in a small tributary off the Mértola road.

By bus There are infrequent buses to Vila Real (Mon–Sat 1–2 daily; 1hr); Castro Marim (Mon–Fri 1 daily; 50min); and Mértola (Mon–Fri 1 daily; 50min).

Information A small turismo (Mon–Fri 9am–1pm & 2–6pm; ☎ 281 546 179, ⓦ cm-alcoutim.pt) is located on

Rua 1 de Maio, just off the main Praça da República.

Boat trips, kayaking and bike hire Fun River, next to the quay on Rua do Município (☎ 926 682 605, ⓦ fun-river .com) runs boat trips (1hr €18; half-day €50), and rents out kayaks (€10/hr) and bikes (€10–15 per day).

ACCOMMODATION, EATING AND DRINKING

Central de Ida Afonso Rua Dr. João Deus 10A ☎ 281 546 411. This friendly family house, just up from the main square, lets out simple but spotless en-suite rooms with TV. No breakfast. **€35**

O Soeiro Rua do Município 4 ☎ 281 546 241. The town's best-positioned place to grab a coffee, with outdoor tables facing the river; it also has an outside grill for great lunches and an upstairs restaurant serving local specialities (from €9) such as lamprey (an eel-like fish). Mon–Fri 10am–11pm.

Pousada de Juventude Alcoutim ☎ 281 546 004, ⓦ pousadasjuventude.pt. The smart fifty-bed youth hostel is around 1.5km north of the village; cross the bridge

beyond Praça da República and follow the signs. As well as dorms and double rooms, it has apartments with a kitchenette (sleeping four; €70), its own canteen and a swimming pool. There's disabled access, bikes for hire, and they can arrange kayaking on the river, too. Dorms **€13**; doubles **€35**

Riverside Tavern Av Duarte Pacheco 3 ☎ 281 546 527. What little nightlife there is in Alcoutim can be found in this restaurant-bar, with a pool table, music, TV, and attractive outdoor terrace. The food is no great shakes, but there's frequent live jazz, fado and quiz nights. Daily 10am–midnight.

The central Algarve resorts

The central Algarve from Faro to Lagos encompasses some of the region's best beaches – but also its most intense tourist development. Despite this, **Quinta do Lago**, **Vale do Lobo** and **Vilamoura** are low density and upmarket: purpose-built resorts with great facilities including marinas, top golf courses and tennis centres. These resorts don't have much traditional culture, though there's a little more of that at neighbouring **Quarteira**, a high-rise resort with a fine town beach and a renowned fish market.

Quinta do Lago

☎ 289 390 700, ⓦ quintadolago.com

Almancil is the turn-off point for the vast, luxury holiday resort of **QUINTA DO LAGO**, with its own golf courses and sports complex. Most day-visitors, however, head straight for the great beach, the **Praia do Ancão**, reached over a wooden bridge from the car park at the end of the main Avenida André Jorge. The bridge heads across the western extremity of the **Parque Natural da Ria Formosa**; it also marks the start of two marked nature trails that lead either side of the inland waterways.

Vale do Lobo

☎ 289 353 000, ⓦ valedolobo.com

Just to the west of Quinta do Lago, facilities are similar at the resort of **VALE DO LOBO**, where a great beach is backed by more serious-money hotels and swanky villas, with golf courses and a riding school nearby. The resort has a 24-hour reception as you enter the complex, which can help with booking accommodation – though nothing is very cheap.

Vale do Lobo Tennis Academy

☎ 289 357 850, ⓦ premier-sports.org

Just south of the main Vale do Lobo resort lies the plush **Vale do Lobo Tennis Academy**, the most famous in the country. You can book lessons and coaching sessions, though as the world's top players come here to practise, courts get reserved well in advance.

Igreja de São Lourenço

Almancil • Mon 3–6pm, Tues–Sat 10am–1pm & 3–6pm; closes 5pm mid-Oct to mid-April• €2.50

Built in the early eighteenth century, the church of **São Lourenço** is famed for its superb tiled interior depicting the life and martyrdom of St Laurence, which is thought to have been painted in 1730 by influential artist Policarpo de Oliveira Bernardes. The church is around 12km northwest of Faro, near the Almancil turn-off from the N125, but is hard to reach without your own transport.

Quarteira

QUARTEIRA, 22km west of Faro, was one of the first fishing villages to be developed in the Algarve, and remains high-rise and downmarket. Stick to the palm-lined seafront promenade with its attractive stretch of beach – **Praia de Quarteira** – and it's a pleasant enough destination, which remains largely Portuguese in character. The main attraction is the bustling fish and vegetable **market** (Mon–Sat 8am–3pm; Sun vegetable market only 8am–2pm) by the working fishing harbour, to the west end of town, though there's also a good flea market each Wednesday (roughly 9am–2.30pm), on the road to Almancil.

Aquashow

Semino, EN396 • Daily: May 10am–5pm; June & Sept 10am–5.30pm; July 10am–6.30pm; Aug 10am–7pm • €29, children €19 • ☎ 289 315 129, ⓦ aquashowpark.com

At Semino, on the road between Quarteira and Loulé, **Aquashow** makes for a fun day out for families. There's a theme-park area with various rides including a rollercoaster through water, plus regular shows (sea lions, parrots and reptiles) throughout the day. But the big attraction is the **water-park zone** which includes a panoply of slides, chutes and pools, including the terrifying vertical White Falls and a descent down a helter-skelter in the dark. Note that in high season the park closes its gates when it hits four thousand people: in June or September it's quieter and there are fewer queues.

ARRIVAL AND INFORMATION
QUARTEIRA

By bus Quarteira's bus terminus is a couple of blocks back from the beach, on Avenida Dr. Sá Carneiro, with regular services to and from Faro (approx every 30min; 40min).

Information The turismo is right by the beach on Praça

do Mar (July–Aug daily 9am–1pm & 2–6pm; Sept–June Mon–Fri 9am–1pm & 2–6pm; ☎ 289 389 209).

Road train A road train trundles along Quarteira's seafront, running around town and back to the market every hour or so (May–Sept daily 10am–dusk; €2).

ACCOMMODATION AND EATING

A Caravela Lardo do Mercado, Loja 17, Quarteira ☎ 289 312 280. Opposite the fish market, this is a good option for quality fish and seafood (lobsters languish in bubbling glass tanks), with well-presented mains at €10–13. It also does *picanha* (garlicky beef) and steaks. Tues–Sun 12.30–3pm & 7–10.30pm.

Aquashow Park Semino, EN396 ☎ 289 317 550, ⓦ aquashowpark.com. Right by the waterpark, this is a stylish modern four-star hotel whose plush rooms (which can interconnect for families) face the park or, better, the local woods and outside pool. The hotel has indoor and outdoor pools, a gym, spa and family

activities, and guests have free access to the adjacent Aquashow park – check on the website for some very good online deals. €178

Beira Mar Av Infante de Sagres 61–63, Quarteira ☎ 289 314 748. Just past the turismo heading east on the seafront, this fab *pastelaria* serves an alluring range of cakes, pastries and inexpensive lunches, with seats facing the sea. Tues–Sun 7am–8pm.

Miramar Rua Gonçalo Velho 8, Quarteira ☎ 289 315 225. Near the market, this long-time favourite has a charming plant-lined internal terrace. The decent double rooms either look out over this, or have sea views. €80

Vilamoura

Now virtually merged with Quarteira, **VILAMOURA** is a constantly expanding resort with a bewildering network of roads signposted to upmarket hotels and exclusive leisure facilities,

9

including five renowned **golf courses**, all within reach of the impressive main beach, Praia da Marina, and Praia da Falésia, just to the morth. Vilamoura is perhaps *the* place in the Algarve to come and practise your swing, while another indication of the kind of clientele Vilamoura attracts is the ritzy **marina**, bristling with yachts and lined with pricey international cafés, and the departure point for numerous boat trips (see below).

Museu Cerro da Vila

Avenida Cerro da Vila • Tues–Sun 9.30am–12.30pm & 2–6pm • €2 • ☎ 289 312 153

The only historical sight in Vilamoura is just to the northwest of the marina, where the **Museu Cerra da Vila** archeological site displays the vestiges of a late Roman, Visigothic and Moorish colony. You can make out the foundations of a Roman mansion, baths and a fish-salting tank, together with well-preserved Roman mosaics laid out in a scrubby field.

ARRIVAL AND INFORMATION   **VILAMOURA**

By bus Regular buses between Vilamoura and Faro (approx every 30min; 50min) drop you next to the casino, one block from the Praia da Marina.
Road train A road train runs from the marina and through the main town to Praia da Falesia (daily; hourly from 10am–dusk; €3.50).
Boat trips Various stalls around the marina offer boat trips along the coast (€25 or so for a 2hr trip) and dolphin-watching (up to €60 for a full-day excursion).

ACCOMMODATION, EATING AND DRINKING

O Tasquinho do Manel Escola de Vela ☎ 289 315 756. Part of Vilamoura's sailing school, this simple place lacks the pretensions of the marina-side restaurants but has very moderately-priced fresh fish (around €10) and great views from the outdoor terrace. Tues–Sun: May–Sept 11am–3pm & 7–11pm; Oct–April 11am–3pm.
Sete Rua Clube Náutico Loja 7, Marina de Vilamoura ☎ 289 313 243. A fashionable chrome-and-steel café-bar part-owned by Portuguese soccer star Luís Figo, and named after his shirt number (*sete* means seven). A good spot for a quiet drink by day, it gets lively after dark. Plasma TVs show the latest soccer action and guest DJs feature. Daily 9am–3am.
Tivoli Marina Apartado 65, Marina de Vilamoura ☎ 289 303 303, ⊛ tivolihotels.com. This enormous modern place is typical of the accommodation here – with every conceivable comfort, and giant rooms overlooking the marina or the beach. **€320**

Loulé

LOULÉ, 18km inland from Faro, has always been an important centre of commerce and is still best known for its markets. It has recently grown to a fair size, though its compact centre doesn't take long to look around. The most interesting streets, a grid of whitewashed cobbled lanes, lie between the remains of its Moorish castle (now a museum) and the thirteenth-century Gothic **Igreja Matriz**, with its palm-lined gardens in front.

Museu Municipal

Rua Dom Paio Peres Correia 17 • Tues–Fri 9am–6pm, Sat 10am–4pm • €1.75 • ☎ 289 400 600

The remains of Loulé's castle enclose a mildly interesting **Museu Municipal**. Its main exhibit is an archeological collection that includes a range of Roman, Moorish and early Portuguese finds from Loulé and the surrounding area, as well as the foundations of a twelfth-century Moorish house, displayed under a glass floor. Head up the steps to the side of the museum to a kitchen, set out in traditional Algarve style. You can also access the remains of the castle walls from here, for good views across town.

Mercado Municipal

Rua José Fernandes Guerreiro • Mon–Sat 7am–3pm • ⊛ loule-mercado-municipal.pt.algarve-portal.com

Loulé's most atmospheric attraction is its covered fruit and vegetable **market**, just

ALGARVE MARKET DAYS

Many of the Algarve's main towns have a vibrant **market day**, with traders selling everything from fresh fruit and vegetables to ceramics, clothes and local crafts. The following is a selection of the best markets in the main towns.

Albufeira First and third Tuesdays of the month
Castro Marim and Vila Real Second Saturday of the month
Ferragudo Second Sunday of the month
Fuzeta First Thursday of the month
Lagos and Alvor First Saturday of the month

Loulé Saturday mornings
Monchique Second Friday of the month
Monte Gordo Fourth Saturday of the month
Olhão Saturday mornings
Quarteira Wednesday mornings
Tavira Third Saturday of the month

southeast of the main Praça da República in a red early-twentieth-century onion-domed building with Moorish-style windows. Try and visit on a Saturday morning, when the market spreads into the surrounding streets – a medley of stalls selling everything from pungent cheese to cages of live chickens.

Mercado Semanal

Sunday 9am–1pm • The market is about 15mins walk northwest of central Loulé; follow the signs to "IP1/Boliquieme"

With stalls selling a motley collection of clothes, ceramics and agricultural produce, Loulé's main **Saturday morning market** is held on a patch of open ground beautifully framed by a pair of dazzling white churches, including the curious, modern, beehive-shaped **Nossa Senhora da Piedade**. At Easter, the church is the starting point of a procession into town for Mãe Soberana, one of the Algarve's most important religious festivals.

ARRIVAL AND DEPARTURE   LOULÉ

By bus Buses from Albufeira (8–10 daily; 45min) and Faro (Mon–Fri every 30–50min, Sat–Sun 2–4 daily; 40min) pull in at the bus station on Rua Nossa Senhora de Fátima, a couple of minutes' walk north of the centre.

ACCOMMODATION AND EATING

Flôr da Praça Rua José Fernandes Guerreiro 44 ☎ 289 462 435. For good-value food, first choice is *Flôr da Praça*, opposite the Mercado Municipal, with fish and grills (from €8) served in a bustling place with old photos and seashells on the walls. Mon–Sat 12.30–2.30pm & 7.30–11.30pm.

Loulé Jardim Pr Manuel de Arriaga 23 ☎ 289 413 094, ⊛ loulejardimhotel.com. A block south of Rua Nossa Senhora da Piedade, this welcoming three-star hotel boasts a bar, a small pool and smallish but comfortable rooms with cable TV. **€100**

Albufeira and around

ALBUFEIRA has long been one of the Algarve's most popular resorts – and it's easy to see why. The old centre is a highly picturesque medley of whitewashed houses atop low sandstone cliffs facing a fantastic town **beach**. But beyond, hundreds of modern buildings lie strung across the hillsides that spread east and west, around the town's **marina**, a collection of brightly coloured, Lego-like modern shops, bars and apartments clustered round in-your-face yachts and speedboats. If you're looking for unspoiled Portugal, this isn't it, but Albufeira is undeniably fun, attracting a varied mix of holidaymakers.

Although the 1755 earthquake destroyed much of the town, there's still a Moorish feel to a few parts of central Albufeira – its original Arabic name, *Al-Buhera*, means "Castle-on-the-Sea". There are some fine beaches either side of the town, too. **Praia da Oura** and those further east towards **Praia da Falésia** are the more developed, while the cove beaches to the

9

west, up to the swathe of sands at **Praia de Galé**, tend to be quieter. Inland, Albufeira is the nearest base to a couple of the Algarve's best family-orientated **theme parks**.

Largo Engenheiro Duarte Pacheco and the beach

The focus of Albufeira is the somewhat tacky **Largo Engenheiro Duarte Pacheco**, a modern pedestrianized square with benches beneath palms and exotic trees. After dark, it's a magnet for families and promenaders, often serenaded by live performers and buskers. From the square, Rua 5 de Outubro leads – through a tunnel – down to the town beach, **Praia dos Penedo**, as good as any in the region, flanked by strange tooth-like rock formations. Sadly all that is left of the *pescadores* (fishermen) who once graced the Praia dos Pescadores, just to the east, is a concrete statue commemorating their trade.

Museu Arqueológico

Praça da República 1 • July & Aug Tues, Sat & Sun 9.30am–12.30pm & 1.30–5.30pm, Wed 9.30am–5.30pm, Thurs & Fri 2–10pm; Sept–June Tues, Sat & Sun 9.30am–12.30pm & 1.30–5.30pm, Wed–Fri 9.30am–5.30pm • €1 • ☎ 289 599 508

Just above the tunnel to the beach, in the old town hall, the **Museu Arqueológico** presents a rather sparse but well laid-out collection of artefacts gathered from the area from Neolithic times to the present. There are fragments of mosaics from a Roman villa, Visigothic rock tombs and jars, and even an Islamic silo excavated *in situ* beneath the museum.

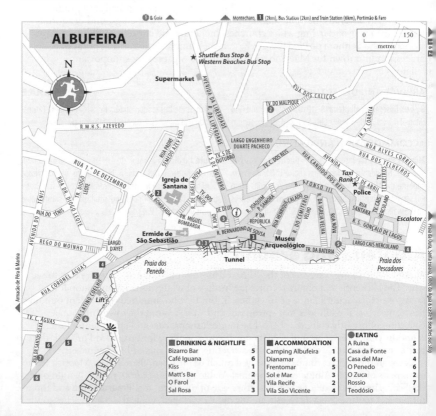

■ DRINKING & NIGHTLIFE		■ ACCOMMODATION		● EATING	
Bizarro Bar	5	Camping Albufeira	1	A Ruina	5
Café Iguana	6	Dianamar	6	Casa da Fonte	3
Kiss	1	Frentomar	5	Casa del Mar	4
Matt's Bar	2	Sol e Mar	3	O Penedo	6
O Farol	4	Vila Recife	2	O Zuca	2
Sal Rosa	3	Vila São Vicente	4	Rossio	7
				Teodósio	1

The eastern beaches

Buses to the beaches (blue or green routes, every 30–60min) run daily from Albufeira bus station or from the stop at the the top of the escalators above Praia dos Pescadores

Immediately east of Albufeira is a string of superb, cliff-backed cove beaches, all of which can be reached by local buses. You can walk to the first, **Praia da Oura**, just 2km away, by heading east from the Praia dos Pescadores and up along a rocky bluff along a coastal path. Praia da Oura has been extensively developed, however, and you might want to push on by bus to **Santa Eulalia**, 4km further east, or neighbouring **Olhos da Água**, another 7km east – both former fishing villages with attractive beaches.

The western beaches

Buses from Albufiera to São Rafael and Galé depart from the top of Avenida da Liberdade (8 daily Mon–Fri)

Most of the development west of Albufeira is set back behind a series of idyllic cove beaches. Busy **São Rafael**, 3km west, and slightly quieter **Castelo**, 1km further on, sit above small beaches that only become crowded in peak season. A delightful clifftop path links the two resorts via the best cove found on this stretch, **Praia da Coelha**; it's reached down a sandy track, with little development apart from a seasonal beach café. Five kilometres west of Albufeira, you reach the extensive sands of **Praia de Galé**, where the beach spreads all the way to Armação de Pêra (see p.469).

Quinta Miradouro

Álamos, Apartado 5008 • Mon–Fri 10am–1pm & 2–5pm • Shop free; tours €7.50, or €25–30 including transport from nearby resorts • ☎ 968 776 971, ⓦ winesvidanova.com

Just south of Algarve Shopping off the main EN125 (go past the car parks east of the shopping centre) lie the open fields of **Quinta Miradouro**, a wine estate owned by British singer Cliff Richard. This is actually one of three farms that form a wine co-operative which produces strong **Vida Nova wines** – named after the "new life" the farms have breathed into exhausted vineyards. The co-operative has become something of a pilgrimage for Richard fans, who can be found posing for photos outside his nearby farm, Quinta do Moinho. Quinta Miradouro visits appeal equally to wine buffs, and include a talk about wine production, a look round the estate and the chance to sample recent blends, which you can purchase from the shop.

Guia

Buses run from Albufeira's bus terminal to Guia (daily, every 30min; 15–40 min)

If Porto is known for its wine, then **GUIA**, 9km northeast of Albufeira, is synonymous with its **chargrilled chicken**, served in a string of specialized restaurants; we recommend one of the best (see p.468), but all of them are pretty good. Shot through by a busy highway, the only other reason to stop in Guia is for couple of fine churches: the seventeenth-century **Igreja Matriz**, and the Baroque **Nossa Senhora da Guia**, the latter sporting a particularly striking interior of sumptuous blue-and-white *azulejos*.

Zoo Marine

EN125, Guia • Daily: Easter–June & Sept 10am–6pm; July & Aug 10am–7.30pm; Oct 10am–5pm • €29, under-10s €19 • ☎ 289 560 300, ⓦ zoomarine.pt • No public transport, but Zoo Marine offers a transit service; check the website for details

Around 7km northwest of Albufeira, off the N125, **Zoo Marine** is squarely aimed at families. Tickets allow entry to a variety of swimming pools, fairground rides, animal enclosures and an aquarium. There are also various shows that take place throughout the day, featuring performing parrots, sea lions and dolphins.

9

Krazy World

Lagoa de Viseu, Algoz • Easter–June & Sept–Oct daily 10am–6pm; July–Aug daily 10am–6.30pm, Nov–Easter Fri–Sun 10am–6pm; some attractions closed in winter, when prices are reduced • €13, under-13s €8 • ☎ 282 574 134, ⓦ krazyworld.com • Buses from Albufeira to São Bartolomeu de Messines stop near the entrance; check the website for details of special buses from local resorts

Krazy World, around 13km north of Albufeira, is a sizeable zoo-cum-theme-park. Low-key and set in attractive farmland, the neatly landscaped park has crazy golf and traditional rides, a mini zoo-cum-petting-farm and a reptile zone complete with enormous pythons, crocodiles and a turtle city; there are some swimming pools to cool off in, too.

ARRIVAL AND DEPARTURE

ALBUFEIRA AND AROUND

By bus Albufeira's bus terminal, Central de Camionagem (☎ 289 580 611), is around 2km north of town on Rua dos Caliços. A red-route shuttle bus runs from the bus station to Avenida da Liberdade every 30min (7am to 10pm; Oct–May until 8pm; €1.40), which is a 5min walk from the central square, Largo Engenheiro Duarte Pacheco.
Destinations Armação de Pêra (Mon–Sat 14 daily, Sun 5 daily; 15–20min); Faro (approx hourly; 50min–1hr 15min); Guia (6–9 daily; 15min); Lagos (5–12 daily; 1hr 25min); Lisbon (6–8 daily; 3hr 10min); Loulé (8–10 daily; 45min); Olhos d'Água (every 30min; 15min); Portimão

(Mon–Fri approx hourly, Sat & Sun 4 daily; 45min); Silves (5 daily; 45min).
By train Albufeira's nearest train station is 6km north of town at Ferreiras; a bus connects it with Albufeira's bus terminal every 45min or so (daily 7am–8pm), or a taxi costs about €12.
Destinations Ferreiras to: Lagos (9 daily; 1hr 10min); Faro (4–9 daily; 25–35min); Portimão (7 daily; 45min); and Silves (7 daily; 30min).
By car Central Albufeira is not an easy place to find a parking spot; it's best to follow signs to the out-of-town car parks.

GETTING AROUND

By bus If you're in Albufeira on a package holiday, you might well be staying in one of the resort-villages on either side of town. The blue bus route is useful, running from the bus station via Areias de São João, Oura and Santa Eulalia to Montechoro. If you plan to use the buses a lot, consider a *bilhete turístico* day-pass for €4, or buy a *cartão recarregável* (rechargeable card; €3) on which you

can load ten journeys for €8. Otherwise it is €1.40 a ride.
By road train A road train runs from the top of the escalator at the eastern end of Praia dos Pescadores out to Montechoro (every 20min; Oct–May 9am–11pm; June–Sept 9am–1am; €2.50 single, or €4 for a day-pass; ⓦ turistrem.com).
By taxi There's a taxi rank on Avenida 25 de Abril. To order a cab call ☎ 289 583 230.

INFORMATION AND ACTIVITIES

Information The turismo (Mon–Fri 9am–1pm & 2–6pm; ☎ 289 585 279, ⓦ cm-albufeira.pt) is on Rua 5 de Outubro, by the tunnel to the beach.
Boat trips Dreamwaves (☎ 962 003 885, ⓦ dreamwave

algarve.com) runs daily boat trips to local caves, plus dolphin watching, speedboat rides and cruises on a mock pirate ship, all €20–50. The trips leave from Albufeira's marina, downhill and 2km west of the town centre.

ACCOMMODATION

Camping Albufeira Estrada de Ferreiras ☎ 289 587 629, ⓦ campingalbufeira.net. Around 2km to the north of town, off the N396, this is expensive but well appointed, complete with swimming pools, restaurants, bars, shops and tennis courts. There are regular red-bus route connections from the bus station. One-week minimum stay in high season. Pitch €20
★**Dianamar** Rua Latino Coelho 36 ☎ 289 587 801, ⓦ dianamar.com. Top choice in town is this well-run Swedish-owned guesthouse in the nicest part of Albufeira, near the cliffs above the beach. En-suite rooms are pristine and breezy, and those at the top have great sea views, as does the communal roof terrace. Larger rooms can accommodate families. Price includes a Swedish-style breakfast, afternoon

cake and a welcome bottle of wine. €70
Frentomar Rua Latino Coelho ☎ 289 512 005, ⓦ frentomar.com. Simple, clean rooms on a quiet side road. Get one with a sea view (€15 extra) and you won't be disappointed, though these are usually snapped up quickly. Closed late Oct to Easter. No breakfast. €90
Sol e Mar Rua José Bernardino de Sousa ☎ 289 580 080, ⓦ grupofbarata.com. Though somewhat characterless and in need of an update, this four-star hotel is in a great position, with its entrance above the tunnel to the beach. It stretches down five floors to exit right on the beach, and the room balconies overlook the sands; there's live entertainment and a small covered swimming pool. Parking available. €156

FROM TOP FISH RESTAURANT, ALVOR (P.475); RIO GUADIANA FROM ALCOUTIM (P.459) >

9

Vila Recife Rua Miguel Bombarda 12 ☎ 289 583 740, ⓦ grupofbarata.com. This rambling hotel has its own garden and small pool. The communal areas are lined with *azulejos*, and while the en-suite rooms are on the small side they are comfortable, and the best have fine views. Closed Nov–April. **€76**

Vila São Vicente Largo Jacinto d'Ayet 4 ☎ 289 583 700, ⓦ hotelsaovicentealbufeira.com. A stylish hotel (adults only) built in traditional style with tiled floors and whitewashed walls. It has its own small pool and a terrace facing the beach. If you can afford the €60 extra, you get splendid sea views. All rooms are en suite with TVs and a/c. **€105**

EATING

ALBUFEIRA

A Ruína Cais Herculano ☎ 289 512 094. Partly built into the old town walls, overlooking the beach, with rooms and terraces at various levels. The lower, beachside area is the best place for those with kids, as they can play in the sand while you eat. Fresh fish is the thing to go for, but check the price carefully when you order and expect to pay over €25 a head. Daily: April–Sept 12.30–3pm & 7–11pm; Oct–March noon–2.30pm & 6.30–10.30pm.

Casa da Fonte Rua João de Deus 7 ☎ 289 514 578. A popular spot set around a beautiful Moorish-style courtyard complete with *azulejos* and lemon trees – get there early if you want a courtyard table. There's a long menu, with mains from €12 – the fish kebabs are recommended. Daily noon–midnight.

Casa del Mar Rua Miguel Bombarda ☎ 289 515 246. A spacious, modern seafood restaurant with a lovely terrace overlooking the beach. It's not cheap – mains from around €15 – but the staff are knowledgeable and will guide you through the menu. Good choices include the fish kebabs or salmon burgers. Daily 10.30am–10pm.

O Penedo Rua Latino Coelho 15 ☎ 289 587 429. With tasteful contemporary decor and a terrific terrace overlooking the beach, this small, arty place serves a varied menu including chicken *piri-piri*, *bacalhau à brás* (salted cod with egg and potatoes) and pasta dishes, at €9–15. Daily 11am–3pm & 6.30–11pm; closed Jan.

O Zuca Trav do Malpique 6 ☎ 289 588 768. Despite its proximity to the main square, this is the locals' choice – a simple, family-run restaurant serving good-value, tasty meat and fish from around €8. The tourist menu is recommended: around €14 for three courses and drinks. Daily noon–3pm & 6pm–midnight.

★ **Rossio** Rua Dr. Santos Silva 58 ☎ 964 063 481. A good value local with friendly service and tables outside on a little square. Fish and meat dishes from around €9; go for the *rodizio de peixe* (mixed grilled fish, around €14) and you'll have half the day's catch on your plate. Tues–Sun noon–3pm & 6–10pm.

GUIA

Teodósio Rua do Emigrante 50, Guia ☎ 289 561 318, ⓦ teodosio-reidosfrangos.com. You'll need a car to reach this giant restaurant, around 1km from central Guia on the Algoz road, but its popularity is clear from the hordes who pack out its ample spaces – this is one of the best places in town for grilled chicken, served with or without *piri-piri*, and both delicious and good value (full meals around €14). The interior is unglamorous, but it's certainly a buzzing spot. Daily noon–3pm & 6.30–10.30pm.

DRINKING AND NIGHTLIFE

At night, the focus of Albufeira's lively bar scene is the pedestrianized **Rua Cândido dos Reis**, where a good-time crowd parades past handicraft stalls and a menu of live soccer, or sit at bars which vie with each other to play the loudest music. Late-night clubs can mostly be found in the suburbs east of the centre, especially around Oura's Avenida Dr. Francisco Sà Carneiro (aka The Strip).

Bizarro Bar Esplanada Dr. Frutuosa Silva 30, Albufeira ☎ 289 512 824. This attractive bar is high above the eastern end of the beach, with superb views over the sands from its front terrace. Mon–Sat 10am–midnight.

★ **Café Iguana** Rua Latino Coelho 59, Albufeira ☎ 289 513 011. An attractive café-bar on the clifftop, whose terrace has fantastic views over the town and the beach. Serves baguettes and snacks as well as a range of cocktails. Daily 8am–midnight.

Kiss Rua Vasco da Gama, Areias de São João ☎ 289 590 280, ⓦ kissclubalbufeira.com. With five bars and two dancefloors, this is Albufeira's best-known club. It often hosts international guest DJs (keep an eye out for flyers) though can get somewhat lairy. It's 2km east of the old town; green and blue bus routes pass nearby. Daily: May–Sept 11am–midnight; Oct–April 11pm–6am.

Matt's Bar Av Dr. Francisco Sà Carneiro (The Strip), Oura ☎ 289 590 280, ⓦ mattsbar.net. Hip and fun bar/club with guest DJs, great music and alluring cocktails. May–Sept daily 8pm–4am; Oct–April Fri & Sat 8pm–4am.

O Farol Praia dos Pescadores, Albufeira ☎ 289 591 618. Once a fisherman's shack, this has been reborn as a modern beach bar/restaurant, with a superbly positioned terrace touching the sands. A great spot for a sundowner, it also does good-value meat and fish dishes from €10.

Daily: May–Sept 9am–midnight; Oct–April 9am–7pm. **Sal Rosa** Pr Miguel Bombarda 2, Albufeira ☎ 289 513 089. A small, arty lounge bar with Moroccan-style cushions and lovely tiles on the walls – the back terrace has fine views over the beach. It serves decent tapas, and drinks include a long list of regionally-influenced cocktails: try the Algarvian Daiquiri, with almond liqueur, lime and honey. Daily noon–midnight.

DIRECTORY

Banks and exchange ATMs are grouped around Largo Eng. Duarte Pacheco and along Avenida da Liberdade.
Health centre Urbanização dos Caliços, 2km north of the centre (Mon–Fri 8am–8pm; ☎ 289 598 400). The nearest hospital is in Faro or Portimão.
Markets On the first and third Tuesday of each month, a lively flea market takes place 2km north of the centre at Urbanização dos Caliços.

Pharmacy Farmácia Alves de Sousa, Avenida da Liberdade 103B (☎ 289 512 258).
Police Contact GNR at Avenida 25 de Abril 22 (☎ 289 583 310).
Post office In the new town on Rua Pedro Álvares Cabral (Mon–Fri 9am–6pm).

Armação de Pêra

ARMAÇÃO DE PÊRA, 15km west of Albufeira, fronts one of the largest beaches in the Algarve, which spreads east all the way to Galé. Beach aside, it is not the greatest looking of resorts; high-rise buildings and apartments straggle along the town's main through-road, tempered only by a pedestrianized promenade overlooking the central part of the sands. The remains of Armação de Pêra's fortified walls are at the eastern end of the resort, where a terrace in front of a little white chapel provides sweeping views. But the town **beach** is fine and if the main section is crowded, just head further east, beyond the cluster of traditional boats on the fishermen's beach towards Galé, where things are quieter. Aside from the beaches, the other local attraction is 4km up the main N125 at **Porches**, where the most famous of the Algarve's chunky and hand-painted pottery comes from – the main road is lined with shops that sell it.

The western beaches

The 10km or so of coast between Armação de Pêra and Centianes is largely flat and scrubby, with a series of delightful cove beaches that have mostly escaped any large-scale development, though you'll need a car to reach them. The closest to Armação de Pêra, 2km west, is **Praia da Senhora da Rocha**, boasting fine caves and strange rock formations below a pretty clifftop chapel. **Praia da Albondeira**, 5km west of Armação, marks the start of a superb coastal footpath that runs for 4km along clifftops all the way to Benagil. A couple of kilometres west of Albondeira, the footpath passes **Praia da Marinha** below a craggy red-sandstone cliff, with the only trace of development being a seasonal beach restaurant and a tasteful villa complex a little up the hill.

After a further couple of kilometres, the path (and road) winds round to the next bay at **Benagil**, a tiny village consisting of a cluster of buildings with a couple of cafés above

---

THE ALGARVE'S TOP FIVE COASTAL SPOTS

The Algarve is known for its wonderful **beaches** and dramatic **coastline** – here are our five favourite places.

Benagil This pint-sized village marks the start of a superb clifftop path past an awesome sea cave. See above
Ilha de Tavira Miles of soft, dune-backed sand without a hotel in sight. See p.452
Praia da Bordeira A wild and wonderful stretch of sand in a remote corner of the Algarve. See p.492
Praia da Figueira You'll have to walk to get here, but it's worth It to find this often-deserted beach. See p.486
Praia de Odeceixe Follow the river valley to a superb bay with sheltered river swimming and a wide sandy beach. See p.494

9

a narrow gully, its fine beach sitting beneath high cliffs. Fishing boats can take you out to an amazing sea cave, as large as a cathedral, with a hole in its roof. You can also walk to the top of it on the path that starts uphill by the restaurant *Algar* just above Benagil; take care of deep drops.

West of Benagil, the scenery changes again with coastal development crowding in around another appealing beach at **Praia de Centianes**, 3km away. From here, the road is lined with villas and apartments all the way to Carvoeiro.

ARRIVAL AND INFORMATION ARMACÃO DE PÊRA

By bus Armacão de Pêra's bus terminal is at the eastern end of town, a 10min walk from the seafront.
Destinations Albufeira (6–14 daily; 20min); Faro (6–8 daily; 1hr 20min); Lagos (6–12 daily; 1hr 15min); Lisbon

(6–8 daily, 3hr 20min); Porches (6–8 daily; 10min); Portimão (6–14 daily; 30min); Silves (5–7 daily; 25min).
Information The turismo is on the seafront Avenida Beira Mar (Mon–Fri 9am–1pm & 2–6pm; ☎ 282 312 145).

ACCOMMODATION, EATING AND DRINKING

★**Estrela do Mar** Largo 25 de Abril ☎ 282 313 775. This simple shack right on the fishermen's beach (you can watch fishermen tending their nets from the terrace) is Albufeira's best place for a budget meal, offering bargain Portuguese staples for €9–11; the grilled sardines are superb, as is the *bacalhau*. Tues–Sun 10am–midnight.
Holiday Inn Algarve Av Beira Mar 1 ☎ 282 320 260, ⓦ crimsonhotels.com/holidayinnalgarve. Right on the seafront, this plush, modern hotel has a pool and terrace overlooking the beach; there's also a restaurant, gym and live entertainment, but it's often block-booked by package holiday companies. €184
Parque de Campismo Armação de Pêra ☎ 282 312 260, ⓦ camping-armacao-pera.com. The shady campsite faces the unspoilt wetlands 1km out of the

centre, back up the N269-1 towards highway N125. It's well equipped, with its own pool, supermarket, restaurant and gardens; three-night minimum stay in high season. Pitch €16
Rosa Mar Rua D. João II, Apt.389 ☎ 282 320 620, ⓦ novorosamar.com. If you don't mind high-rise living, these spacious apartments are good value. In a block back from the tourist office, they have heavy Portuguese decor, and some have sea-facing balconics. €75
Zé Leiteiro Rua Portas do Mar 17 ☎ 282 314 551. Small and usually packed, this is a fabulous place to sample the fishermen's latest catch: there's no menu, just an all-you-can-eat mixed grilled fish with salad and boiled potatoes for around €13. Mon, Tues–Sat noon–3pm & 6.30–9.30pm.

Carvoeiro and around

A whitewashed former fishing village nestled into sea cliffs, the small resort of **CARVOEIRO** must once have been very attractive, but now its small cove beach has to support the prostrate bodies of hundreds of tourists shipped in to what has become an overblown resort. The beach is pleasant enough, though, with fishermen running boat trips from here to nearby caves for around €20.

Algar Seco

Road trains depart from Carvoeiro's seafront (April–Sept Mon, Wed–Thurs & Sat–Sun 10am–10pm; €3 round-trip)

Just 1km east of Carvoeiro lie the impressive rock formations of **Algar Seco**, where steps lead down low cliffs to a series of dramatic overhangs above blow holes and grottoes. They are accessible via the coast road, or by a road train that trundles out from Carvoeiro every hour or so.

Praia da Caneiros and Praia Pintadinho

There are two superb cove beaches a few kilometres to the west of Carvoeiro, though you'll need your own transport to reach them from town. First up is **Praia da Caneiros** (served by regular buses from Portimão and Ferragudo), with a rock stack jutting from the sea off its lovely beach and a superb beachside restaurant, *Rei das Praias* (see p.471).

A couple of kilometres further on, **Praia Pintadinho** is almost as appealing, with a simpler café-restaurant.

Slide & Splash

Vale de Deus • Daily: April, May and mid-Sept to Oct 10am–5pm; June 10am–5.30pm; July & early Sept 10am–6pm; Aug 10am–6.30pm • €27, under-10s €19 • ☎ 282 340 800, Ⓦ slidesplash.com • It's a short drive from town, just outside Lagoa, signposted off the N125, or there's a dedicated bus (check the website for details) that leaves Carvoeiro at 9.30am

For a change from the beach, the water chutes, slides, pools and aquatic fun at the **Slide & Splash** theme park make a great half-day outing, especially for older children, though there are small pools for younger kids. There are also displays of parrots, reptiles and falconry at various times throughout the day, and cafés and a restaurant on site.

ARRIVAL AND INFORMATION

By bus Buses stop near Carvoeiro beach, with regular services from Lagoa (every 40min; 10min) and Portimão (5–8 daily; 35min). Buses from Faro go via Lagoa (7–10 daily; 1hr 35min–2hr), where you'll have to change for

CARVOEIRO AND AROUND

the Carvoeiro bus.

Information Carvoeiro turismo (Mon–Fri 9am–1pm & 2–6pm; ☎ 282 357 728, Ⓦ cm-lagoa.pt) on Largo de Carvoeiro, just behind the beach, can help with private rooms.

ACCOMMODATION, EATING AND DRINKING

A Fonte Escadinhas do Vai-Assar 10, Carvoeiro ☎ 282 356 707. Just west of the main street, *A Fonte* is one of the few restaurants in Carvoeiro with a local flavour, and there's an outdoor terrace, too. It serves good-value rice dishes and fresh fish from €11, as well as excellent *piri-piri* chicken. Daily noon–2.30pm & 6–10.30pm.

Casa Rei das Praias Vale da Azinhaga ☎ 282 491 416, Ⓦ reidaspraias.com. Just inland from the sands at Praia da Caneiros, this modernist villa is extremely stylish and includes indoor and outdoor pools, gym and spa. Plush, airy and spacious rooms come with terraces and minibars. **€180**

O Castelo Rua do Casino 59–61, Carvoeiro ☎ 282 208

518, Ⓦ ocastelo.net. This small guesthouse has modern rooms, the best with a superb view over the beach (€25 extra) – take the road that overlooks the beach uphill above the tourist office and it's a 5min walk. Breakfast extra. Minimum stay of one week in Aug and three days Easter to mid-Oct. **€65**

★ **Rei das Praias** Praia da Caneiros ☎ 282 461 006, Ⓦ restaurantereidaspraias.com. One of the Algarve's loveliest beach restaurants, set on stilts above the sands of this alluring cove. It's not cheap (mains from around €15), but the fresh fish and seafood are second to none – or you can just enjoy a cocktail, or a reasonably priced sandwich in the bar area. Daily noon–11pm.

Ferragudo

Facing the sprawl of Portimão across the Rio Arade estuary, **FERRAGUDO** is an attractive former fishing village centred on a strip of palm-fringed gardens that spread up to the cobbled main square, **Praça Rainha Dona Leonor**. A waterfront promenade lined with fish restaurants skirts the estuary – you can take various boat trips from here, most linking up with those departing from Portimão (see p.472). The old town spreads steeply uphill behind the estuary, its warren of atmospheric cobbled backstreets gathered around Ferragudo's church, with a terrace that offers great views. The town has an estuary **beach**, which gets progressively more appealing as it approaches the impressive **Castelo de São João do Arade**. The castle (closed to the public) faces its partner fort in Praia da Rocha across the river, both of which were built in the sixteenth century to defend Portimão against attack.

The nearest ocean beach lies a couple of kilometres south, where you'll find the broad sands of **Praia Grande** at the mouth of the Rio Arade, with a scattering of restaurant-bars.

ARRIVAL AND INFORMATION

By bus Buses to and from Portimão (roughly hourly 7.55am–7.40pm; 15min) stop on the main road by Praça

FERRAGUDO

Rainha Dona Leonor.

Information The travel agent Beroli, Rua 25 de Abril 40

9

(daily 10am–noon & 5–7pm, closes weekends Oct–May; ☎282 461 100, ⍟beroli.de), is the best source of local information, and can arrange tours, boat trips and accommodation.

ACCOMMODATION AND EATING

A Ria Rua Infante Santo 27 ☎282 451 790. A small, friendly restaurant which lacks the outlook of some on this stretch, but serves good-value fish and grills (from €10–15) and a wide array of rice dishes, including a tasty *arroz de tamboril* (monkfish rice) – it's one of the first places you'll come to along the main harbourfront. Tues–Sat 10am–midnight.

Casa Grande Rua Vasco da Gama 18 ☎914 570 363, ⍟casa-grande.pt. The "big house" is aptly named, a spacious place with a huge front patio facing onto the riverfront road. There's an excellent list of local wines (from €2 a glass), plus regional tapas (local cheeses, sausage and hams from €3) and frequent live music, often fado. Check the website for the lineup. Mon–Sat 6pm–2am.

One2Seven Rua Mouzinho de Albuquerque 12 ☎916 542 351 ⍟one2seven.org. At the top of the hill above town, this is a surprisingly large, ultra-modern boutiquey hotel. Belgian-run, the sleek designer rooms are spacious, the best with terraces overlooking the river (€20 extra); there are also two-room apartments (from €169). There's a lovely pool area and free bike hire; breakfast is extra. Minimum one week stay in high season. **€128**

Portimão

Sited on the broad estuary of the Rio Arade, **Portimão** has made its living from fishing since pre-Roman times, but today it's a sprawling modern port of around forty thousand people. Few of Portimão's buildings made it through the 1755 earthquake – the **Igreja da Nossa Senhora da Conceição** is a rare survivor, retaining a fourteenth-century Manueline door, though most of the church was rebuilt in the late seventeenth century. The surrounding streets are pleasant enough, filled with shops selling lace, shoes, jewellery, ceramics and wicker goods, while the main **shopping streets** are around the pedestrianized Rua Diogo Tomé and Rua da Porta de São José.

The most attractive part of town is the **riverfront**, where a series of squares – Largo do Dique, Praça Manuel Teixeira Gomes and Praça Visconde de Bivar – are filled with outdoor cafés by gushing fountains. Heading up the river and under the road bridge you'll find a series of open-air restaurants serving inexpensive grilled-sardine lunches. The narrow streets just back from the bridge – off **Largo da Barca** – are Portimão's oldest, with more than a hint of their fishing-quarter past.

ARRIVAL AND DEPARTURE

PORTIMÃO

By train The train station is inconveniently located at the northern tip of town, but a bus runs into the centre every 45min (Mon–Fri only); a taxi costs about €6, or it's a 15min walk.

Destinations Faro (7–9 daily; 1hr 25min); Ferreiras, for Albufeira (7 daily; 45min); Lagos (7–10 daily; 20min); Silves (6–9 daily; 15min).

By bus Buses from all destinations pull up in the streets around Largo do Dique, close to the river.

Destinations Albufeira (Mon–Fri approx hourly, Sat & Sun 4 daily; 45min); Armação de Pêra (14 daily; 30min); Alvor (Mon–Fri 5 daily, Sat 3 daily; 20min); Caldas de Monchique (Mon–Fri 9 daily, Sat & Sun 5 daily; 30min); Carvoeiro (5–8 daily; 35min); Faro (7 daily; 1hr 45min); Ferragudo (hourly; 15min); Lagos (hourly; 40min); Lisbon (3–6 daily; 3hr 40min); Monchique (Mon–Fri 9 daily, Sat & Sun 5 daily; 45min); Praia da Rocha (every 15–20min; 5min); Silves (Mon–Fri 9 daily, Sat & Sun 5 daily; 45min).

INFORMATION

Information The turismo (Mon–Fri 9.30am–5.30pm; ☎282 402 487, ⍟cm-portimao.pt) is on Largo 1 de Dezembro, inside the Teatro Municipal.

British consulate Apartado 609, Avenida Guanaré (Mon–Fri 9.30am–2.30pm; ☎213 954 082, ⍟british-consulate.net/Portimao.html).

ACTIVITIES

Boat trips All along Portimão's riverfront, you'll be approached by people offering boat trips along the coast to see the local grottoes (2hr for around €25), while 3hr trips (around €40) also go up the Rio Arade to Silves (departure times depend on the tides). Santa Barnarda (☎282 422 791, ⍟santa-bernarda.com) is a good option, offering

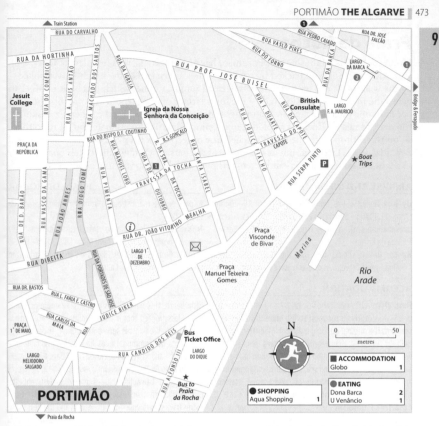

PORTIMÃO

▼ Praia da Rocha

half-day cave tours (€35) and all-day trips (around €70) on a *caravela* sailing ship.

Race track Autódromo Internacional do Algarve, Sitio do Escampadinho (☎ 282 405 600, ⌨ autodromodoalgarve .com) is a modern race track, just north of the A22 motorway, which has held the World Superbike Championship and other top motorbike and car racing events. It also offers go-karting (from €15 for 5min) and the chance to drive various high-performance and classic cars on the track (from €100).

ACCOMMODATION

Globo Rua 5 de Outubro 26 ☎ 282 405 030, ⌨ hoteisalgarvesol.pt. With Praia da Rocha down the road, there's not much cause to stay in Portimão, but if you do, this is the best option: boutiquey touches to the rooms, and with its own gym, bar and great top-floor views. **€95**

EATING

Dona Barca Largo da Barca ☎ 282 484 189. The town's most famous restaurant offers superb fish and regional dishes (around €9), served at outdoor tables in an attractive square. Specialities include *feijoada de buzinas* (shellfish with beans). Mon–Sat noon–11pm.

U Venâncio Zona Ribeirinha Entre-Pontes 4 ☎ 282 423 379. The best of the row of smart but inexpensive fish restaurants north of the old bridge, on the riverfront. Go for the *rodízio* – all the fish you can eat for around €14; other main courses atart at €9. Tues–Sun 10am–10pm.

SHOPPING

Aqua Shopping Rua de São Pedro 72 ☎ 282 413 536, ⌨ aquaportimao.pt. Opened in 2011, this modern shopping centre, 1km northwest of the riverfront, features 117 stores including a hypermarket and a whole host of local and international shops, from Primark, H&M and Mango to Massimo Dutti, as well as a range of appealing restaurants, cafés and bars. Most shops daily 9am–11pm.

9

Praia da Rocha

PRAIA DA ROCHA, 3km south of Portimão, has one of the Algarve's broadest beaches, a fantastic swathe of sand backed by low cliffs. The eastern end of the beach is overlooked by the walls of an old sea fort, the **Fortaleza da Santa Caterina**, which was built in 1691 to guard the mouth of the Rio Arade – the fort's terrace offers splendid views across the ocean in one direction, and over a modern marina and the estuary the other way. Sadly, the rest of Praia da Rocha is a splodge of ungainly high-rise hotels, bars and a casino that sit on the clifftop, with the beach reached down steep steps from the elevated main street, Avenida Tomás Cabreira. But at least most of the bars, restaurants and hotels boast fine views of the sands and sea – and it remains pretty lively whatever time of year you visit.

ARRIVAL AND INFORMATION   PRAIA DA ROCHA

By bus There's a bus from Portimão every 15–20min (7am–11.30pm; 5min; ☎282 470 777, ⓦvaivem .portimaourbis.pt), stopping in front of the *Hotel Jupiter* on Estrada da Rocha.

By car Drivers should note that the main coast road, Avenida Tomás Cabreira, is one-way west to east; it is best

to park on the main street in from Portimão, Estrada da Rocha.

Information The turismo (May to mid-Sept daily 9.30am–6pm; mid-Sept to April Mon–Fri 9.30am–1pm & 2.30–5.30pm; ☎282 419 132) is on the pedestrianized section of Avenida Tomás Cabreira.

ACCOMMODATION

Bela Vista Av Tomás Cabreira ☎282 450 480, ⓦhotel belavista.net. This is the most stylish place to stay on the seafront. The original building is a mock-Moorish mansion built in 1918 by the wealthy Magalhães family as a wedding gift, but the addition of a modern wing has added a swish restaurant, pool and spa. The rooms and communal areas are an exquisite mixture of carved wood, stained glass and yellow, white and blue *azulejos*. Parking. **€280**

Casa Três Palmeiras Apartado 84, Praia do Vau, 2km west of Praia da Rocha ☎282 401 275, ⓦcasatres palmeiras.com. In a sublime position on a clifftop above a

little beach, this sleek villa is a superb example of 1960s chic. Glass-fronted rooms curve around a terrace with a pool, where breakfast is served in summer. There are just five rooms, but communal areas are spacious and tastefully furnished. Parking available. Closed Dec & Jan. **€214**

★ **Vila Lido** Av Tomás Cabreira 2 ☎282 424 127, ⓦhotel vilalido.com. A beautiful, blue shuttered, early twentieth-century villa, in its own small grounds facing the fort. The front rooms have superb views over the beach, and the best come with their own terrace. Very friendly owners, and a superb breakfast is served on the terrace. Closed Nov–Feb. **€120**

EATING

Cervejaria Marisqueira Praia da Rocha Rua Bartolomeu Dias, Edifício Colunas ☎282 416 541.

Just off Avenida Tomás Cabreira, with an outdoor patio and bustling interior, this attracts a largely Portuguese

PRAIA DA ROCHA

■ ACCOMMODATION		● EATING		■ DRINKING & NIGHTLIFE	
Bela Vista	2	Cervejaria Marisqueira		Bar Miradouro	2
Casa Três Palmeiras	1	Praia da Rocha	1	Katedral	1
Vila Lido	3	Mar e Sol	2	Moonlight Bar	3

crowd for good-value daily specials from around €8: try the fried fish with tomato rice. Mon–Sat noon–3pm & 6–11pm.

★**Mar e Sol** Areal da Praia da Rocha ☎ 282 431 122.

Best value of the row of beach restaurants, each under a carapace of steel girders. Good salads, fresh fish and grills (around €10) and a great place to catch the sunset. Mon & Wed–Sun 10am–11pm.

DRINKING AND NIGHTLIFE

Bar Miradouro Av Tomás Cabreira miradouro. Superbly positioned kiosk café-bar, next to a natural rocky viewpoint above the beach – outdoor tables catch the last of the day's sun. Good for snacks, smoothies and cocktails. Daily 10.30am–3am, closes 8pm Oct to Easter.

Katedral Av Tomás Cabreira ☎ 282 417 900, ⓦ katedral-disco.com. Housed in a futuristic cube on the clifftop, this is the largest and highest-profile club in town,

with an early opening bar downstairs. Wed–Thurs 1–6am, Fri & Sat 1–7am; bar open from noon.

Moonlight Bar Av Tomás Cabreira Ed. Guiomar Lj.7 ☎ 282 417 918, ⓦ moonlightbar.com. The best of a row of attractive clifftop bars on this stretch, with bright decor, lively sounds, sports TV and a superb terrace facing the beach to while the night away. Daily 10am–4am.

Alvor

Set slightly inland on the Rio Alvor, the port of **ALVOR**, 6km west of Praia da Rocha, briefly achieved fame as the place where Dom João II died in 1495. Although much of the town was razed in the 1755 earthquake, it still boasts a sixteenth-century **Igreja Matriz** with Manueline doors and pillars carved into fishing ropes and plants. Despite the inevitable development, the old core around the church and the central Praça da República retains some character, while the **harbour** itself is a delight, lined with colourful fishing boats and aromatic fish restaurants. Two-hour **boat trips** to various places along the coast leave from here (around €25 a person).

From the harbour it's a short walk uphill to the ruins of Alvor's **castle**, which dates back to the thirteenth century but now houses a children's playground. From here, Rua Padre David Neto leads onto Rua Dr. Frederico Romas Mendes, the main street lined with bars and restaurants. This stretches down to the riverside **Largo da Ribeira**, marked by a modern statue of a fish, where you'll find half a dozen fish restaurants overlooking the picturesque Rio Alvor. Head right as you face the river and a path leads up the estuary for a tranquil walk; bear left and it's a ten-minute stroll past fishermen's huts and riverside cafés to the **Praia de Alvor**, an enormous beach backed by café-bars.

Quinta da Rocha

On the peninsula between the mouths of the rivers Alvor and Odiáxere, **Quinta da Rocha** is an extensive area of copses, salt marshes, sandy spits and estuarine mudflats, forming a wide range of habitats for different types of animals – including 22 species of wading bird. It has successfully held off development via a series of high-profile court cases. Birdwatching tours of the protected wetlands are run by a voluntary environmental group, A Rocha (ⓦ arochalife.pt). To explore independently, take the turning off the main N125 opposite Mexilheira Grande and follow any of the tracks into the wetlands (there are no marked trails).

ARRIVAL AND INFORMATION   ALVOR

By bus Buses pull in on the eastern edge of the old town, with services from Lagos (6 daily, Sat & Sun 4 daily; 20min); Lisbon (6–8 daily; 4hr 10min); and Portimão (6 daily, Sat & Sun 4 daily; 20min).

Information The town's turismo is in the centre of town at Rua Dr. Alfonso Costa 51 (daily May–Sept 9.30am–7pm; Oct–April Mon–Fri 9.30am–1pm & 2–5.30pm; ☎ 282 457 540).

9

ACCOMMODATION AND EATING

Despite its resort status, Alvor has a surprising lack of central **accommodation**. Most of the hotels are away from the centre, with a cluster of high-rise options a good 2km east of the town facing the beach. **Bars and restaurants**, however, are plentiful, mostly clustered around the waterfront Largo da Ribeira and its approach roads.

Ar de Mar Rua de São João 14 ☎919 724 619, Ⓦalvorardemar.com. Up in the old town, this guesthouse has fresh, brightly coloured rooms, the best on the top floor with balconies and views over the coast (€10 extra). Breakfast is taken in a funky lounge. **€85**

Buganvilia Rua Padre Mendes 6 ☎913 129 573, Ⓦhospedariabuganvilia.com. Just down the hill from the turismo, this modern guesthouse has spotless en-suite rooms. There's also a roof terrace and decent downstairs restaurant. One-week minimum stay in Aug. No breakfast. **€70**

Chefe João Rua Marquês de Pombal 37 ☎282 457 077. This titchy place on Alvor's main road has just half a dozen tables inside and a couple on the street, but it is worth squeezing in for good value *piri-piri* chicken, sardines and tuna steaks for €8–9. No credit cards. Daily 6–11pm.

Churrasqueira Mercado de Alvor Mercado de Alvor ☎282 458 248. Up near the castle, by the market, this local grill house serves bargain chicken, with or without *piri-piri*, for under €8, along with other dishes. Tues–Sun 8.30am–midnight.

★**Restinga** Praia de Alvor ☎282 459 434. Down on the beach, 1km south of the town, this bar-restaurant sits on the cusp of a large dune and offers great views to go with its moderately priced meals (mains around €14). As you'd expect, fish and seafood are the things to go for, but leave room for its famed desserts such as fig or lemon pie or the incredibly sweet egg-based *Dom Rogrigo*. Daily 9am–11pm.

Zé Margadinho Largo da Ribeira 9 ☎282 459 144. Operating since 1890, this bustling place is opposite the old fish market, with outdoor tables on a prime spot facing the river. Excellent freshly grilled fish from around €11. Daily 10am–10pm.

Silves

Eighteen kilometres northeast of Portimão, with a superb castle whose dramatic ring of red walls gradually reveal themselves as you approach, **SILVES** is well worth at least a half-day's visit. While under Moorish occupation, the town was the capital of the Algarve – indeed it was the Moors who named the region *al-Gharb* ("the west"), and built Silves into a well-fortified and sophisticated stronghold. The town's golden age came to an end in 1189 with the arrival of **Sancho I** and his large, unruly army of Crusaders, who laid siege to thirty thousand Moorish inhabitants in the citadel for three months. When the Moors' water and food supplies finally ran low, they agreed to open the citadel gates in return for Sancho's guaranteeing the safety of its inhabitants. The Crusaders, however, ignored Sancho's pledge and killed some six thousand Moors as they gleefully took the fortress. Silves passed back into Moorish hands two years later, but by then the town had been irreparably weakened, and it finally fell to Christian forces for good in 1249.

Fortaleza

Daily: Oct–May 9am–5.30pm; June & Sept 9am–7pm; July & Aug 9.30am–8pm; last entry 30min before closing • €2.80, combined ticket with Museu Arqueológico €3.90

Silves's Moorish **Fortaleza** is slightly less impressive inside than seen from a distance, despite recent renovations of the fairly sparse remains within the walls. There's a Moorish-style garden, café and access to the wonderful vaulted thirteenth-century water cistern, the **Cisterna Grande**, which once served the town. Some 7m in height and supported by six columns, it can hold enough water to supply 1200 people for a year, and was used by the modern town up until the 1980s. The cistern is said to be haunted by a Moorish maiden who can be seen sailing across the underground waters during a full moon. The castle walls offer impressive views over the town and surrounding hills.

Sé

Rua da Sé • Mon–Fri 9am–5pm • €1 • ☎ 282 442 472

Sited below the fortress, Silves's **Sé** (cathedral) was built between 1242 and 1577 on the site of the Grand Mosque. It's an impressive edifice that was the Algarve's most important church until the bishopric moved to Faro shortly after the 1755 earthquake. The tombs lining the cathedral walls are of bishops and Crusaders who died taking Silves back from the Moors.

Museu Arqueológico

Rua das Portas de Loulé 14 • Daily 10am–6pm; last entry 30min before closing • €2.10, combined ticket with Fortaleza €3.90 • ☎ 282 444 832

Below the Sé is Silves's engaging **Museu Arqueológico**, which romps through the history of the town from the year dot to the sixteenth century via displays of local archeological finds. At the centre of the museum is an Arab water cistern, which boasts an 18m-deep well – you can also access some of the old town walls from here.

ARRIVAL AND INFORMATION · SILVES

By train The train station lies 2km out of town (a taxi will cost around €5), with regular services to Faro (7–9 daily; 1hr–1hr 15min) and Lagos (7–9 daily; 35min).

By bus Buses stop near the market on the riverfront at the foot of town, with regular services to Armação de Pêra (4–10 daily; 35min) and Portimão (Mon–Fri 9 daily, Sat & Sun 5 daily; 45min).

Information The main turismo is in Praça do Município (Mon–Fri 9am–1pm & 2–6pm; ☎ 282 440 800, ⓦ cm -silves.pt), which doubles as an exhibition space tracing Silves's Moorish heritage. There is also an information post by the car park near the market building (Mon–Fri 9am–1pm & 2–6pm; ☎ 282 442 255).

ACCOMMODATION

Colina dos Mouros Pocinho Santo ☎ 282 440 420, ⓦ colinahotels.com. Across the river opposite the fortress, this modern hotel is the top choice in town, with an outdoor pool. Slightly tired rooms, but with superb views over the town. __€82__

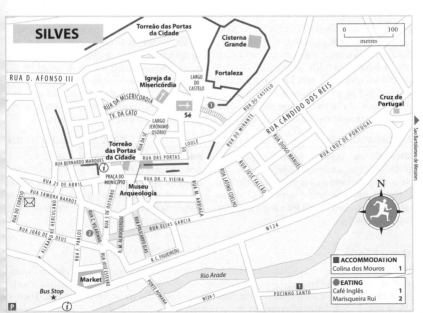

9

EATING

★**Café Inglês** Rua do Castelo 11 ☎282 442 585, ⓦcafeingles.com.pt. The town's social hub, up by the castle, is a fun and funky restored townhouse which sells delicious home-made snacks as well as full meals, including pizzas, curries and pasta, from around €9; it has a roof terrace, outside seats, live music at weekends, poetry nights and the occasional art exhibition. Tues–Fri & Sun 10am–1pm, Sat 1pm–1am.

Marisqueira Rui Rua Comendador Vilarinho 27 ☎282 442 682, ⓦmarisquearui.com. Despite its humble appearance, this is justifiably rated for its seafood, with fantastic fish soup and a very long menu including *massa de peixe* (fish stew with pasta); main courses start at €11. Mon & Wed–Sun noon–11pm.

The Serra de Monchique

The **Serra de Monchique** is a rolling mountain range separating the Algarve from the neighbouring Alentejo district. Its slopes are made up of deciduous oaks and chestnut woods and it's one of the few areas of Portugal that shows off dazzling autumn colours. Its highest peak – at nearly 900m – is **Fóia**, from where, on a clear day, the views stretch over the south coast of the Algarve and west across to Cabo de São Vicente. Sadly this area also bears the brunt of the summer fires that seem to rage annually, though the woodland is generally quick to recover.

Parque da Mina

Sítio do Vale de Boi • Daily: April–Sept 10am–7pm; Oct–March 10am–5pm; closed Mon Nov–Feb • €10, under-12s €6 • ☎962 079 408, ⓦparquedamina.pt

Some 15km north of Portimão, the **Parque da Mina** is a small theme park on the site of a disused mineral mine. There are woodland walks, demonstrations of traditional crafts, a mini-farm and an old distillery, as well as the chance to visit the display gallery of the former copper, quartz and iron mine, which was operational until the 1960s.

Caldas de Monchique

Set in a beautifully wooded ravine, **CALDAS DE MONCHIQUE** was a spa even in Roman times and was once popular with Portuguese royalty. It was sympathetically restored in 2000, transforming a somewhat ramshackle spa resort into a tourist village – and the results have been fairly successful. The cobbled, tree-shaded main square, fronted by the pseudo-Moorish windows of the former casino (now an exhibition hall), is surrounded by lovely nineteenth-century buildings and the wooded setting is a delight. At the foot of the village, the modern **thermal spa** (ⓦmonchiquetermas.com) offers specialist treatments – including water massage, jet-showers and a steam room.

ACCOMMODATION   CALDAS DE MONCHIQUE

Albergaria do Lageado Caldas de Monchique ☎282 912 616, ⓦalbergariadolageado.com. This pleasantly old-fashoned inn has tiled floors, white walls and elderly bathrooms, but the rooms (not all a/c) are spacious and airy; there's a pool and a decent restaurant. Closed Nov–March. **€60**

Villa Termal Caldas de Monchique ☎282 910 910, ⓦmonchiquetermas.com. Five renovated hotel buildings around the village, all with similar, comfortable facilities and shared use of an outdoor pool and kids' club; the *Central* is the best choice, with rooms in the historic former casino building. **€100**

Monchique

MONCHIQUE, 6km from Caldas de Monchique, is a sizeable hilltown best visited for its **market**, held on the second Friday of each month (by the helipad): check out the local smoked hams and distinctive wooden furniture – especially the x-shaped chairs. There's also a weekly Sunday market on the main square, Largo 5 de Outubro, though the

town is liveliest during the **Feira dos Enchidos Tradicionaes** (Traditional Sausage Fair) in March, when restaurants lay on special menus. The old town is dotted with beautifully crafted metal sculptures of local characters made by a contemporary Lisbon artist, which you can spot on the waymarked route to the ruined seventeenth-century monastery of **Nossa Senhora do Desterro**, signed uphill from the bus station. Only a rickety shell of this Franciscan church remains, but it's a lovely fifteen-minute walk up.

Fóia

There's a beautiful, winding 8km drive from Monchique up to the Serra de Monchique's highest peak at **Fóia**, though the summit itself – bristling with radio masts, and capped by an ungainly modern complex sheltering a café-restaurant and shop – can be an anticlimax, especially if clouds obscure the views. On a clear day, however, the vistas are superb.

ARRIVAL AND INFORMATION   MONCHIQUE

By bus Frequent buses run from Portimão to Monchique's bus station (Mon–Fri 9 daily, Sat & Sun 5 daily; 45min) on the main Largo 5 de Outubro. Most of these stop in the centre of Caldas de Monchique (30min) en route, though some stop on the main road a minute's walk above the spa's main square.

Information Monchique's turismo (Mon–Fri 9.30am–1pm & 2–5.30pm; ☎282 911 189, ⓦcm -monchique.pt) is on Largo de São Sebastião, 100m up the steep Fóia road.

ACCOMMODATION AND EATING

Abrigo da Montanha Corte Pereiro, Monchique ☎282 912 131, ⓦabrigodamontanha.com. A couple of kilometres out on the Fóia road, this country inn is great if you want to stay in rural solitude, with a pool, fine views from most of the wood-floored rooms, and its own restaurant. **€75**

A Charrete Rua do Dr. Samora Gil 30–34, Monchique ☎282 912 142. A great, traditional restaurant specializing in award-winning "mountain food" – bean stew with chestnuts, stuffed goat, roast pork and the like from around €14. Mon, Tues & Thurs–Sun 10am–10pm.

Estrela de Monchique Rua do Porto Fundo 46, Monchique ☎282 913 111. The best budget accommodation option in Monchique is this simple but welcoming guesthouse, a stone's throw from the bus terminal, with decent double rooms. No breakfast. **€35**

Lagos

LAGOS is one of the Algarve's most attractive and historic towns, its centre enclosed in largely fourteenth-century walls at the mouth of the Ribeira de Bensafrim. For all its historical significance, Lagos's main attraction is its proximity to some of the region's best beaches. To the east is the long sweep of **Meia Praia**, while to the west – from **Praia de Dona Ana** to **Porto de Mós** – you'll find the series of coves, caves and rock stacks for which the Algarve is best known. Boat trips run along the coast all year round, while a popular side-trip is inland to **Lagos Zoo**.

Brief history

During the early 1400s, **Prince Henry the Navigator** lived for much of his time in Lagos while he was developing his sea school in nearby Sagres. Over the next century it was from Lagos that many of Portugal's great **explorers** set off for the New World, including local boy Gil Eanes, who in 1434 became the first European to round Cape Bojador (today's Western Sahara). In 1577, Lagos became the administrative capital of the Algarve and within a year, Portugal's Crusader king **Dom Sebastião** gathered his troops in the town before their disastrous failed Crusade to Morocco, when the king and most of his court were killed in the battle of Alcácer-Quibrir; in Praça Gil Eanes, an oddly undignified statue commemorates the monarch. Much of Lagos was destroyed in the 1755 earthquake and Faro took over as capital in 1776. As a result the town

9

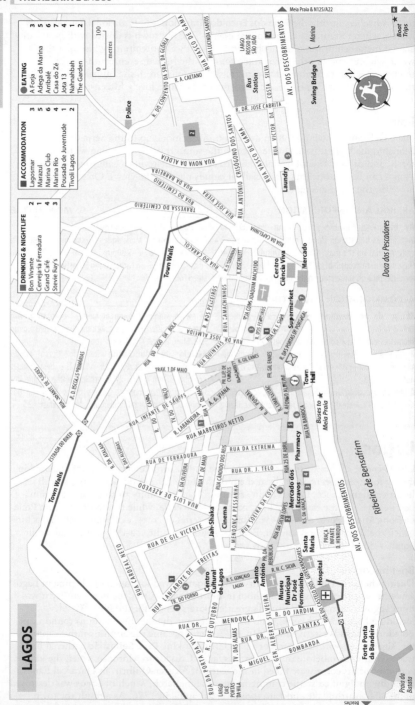

LAGOS

▲ Meia Praia & N125/A22

6

Boat Trips ★

Marina

Swing Bridge

Doca dos Pescadores

Ribeira de Bensafrim

AV. DOS DESCOBRIMENTOS

Praia da Batata

◀ Beaches

■ DRINKING & NIGHTLIFE

Bon Vivante	2
Cerveja'ria Ferradura	1
Grand Café	4
Stevie Ray's	3

■ ACCOMMODATION

Lagosmar	3
Marazul	5
Marina Club	6
Marina Rio	4
Pousada de Juventude	1
Tivoli Lagos	2

● EATING

A Forja	3
Adega da Marina	5
Aribalé	6
Casa do Zé	7
Jota 13	4
Nahnahbah	1
The Garden	2

0   100
metres

Police

Bus Station

Largo Rossio de São João

Centro Ciência Viva

Mercado

Supermarket

Town Walls

Town Walls

Town Hall

Buses to Meia Praia ★

Pharmacy

Cinema

Jah-Shaka

Mercado dos Escravos

Santa Maria

Santo António

Museu Municipal Dr José Formosinho

Hospital

Centro Cultural de Lagos

Forte Ponta da Bandeira

Laundry

RUA VASCO DE GAMA

RUA LUCINDA SANTOS

COSTA SILVA

RUA VICTOR SA

R. DO CONVENTO DA SRA. DA GLORIA

R. A. CAETANO

RUA NOVA DA ALDEIA

RUA DA BARREIRA

RUA DO CEMITERIO

TRAVESSA DO CEMITERIO

RUA ANTONIO CRISÓGONO DOS SANTOS

RUA VASCO DE GAMA

R. DR. JOSÉ CABRITA

RUA JOSÉ VIEIRA

RUA DA CAPITANHA

RUA DO CARACOL

R. TORRINHA

R. JOSÉ PALETI

R. DOS PESCADORES

R. DR. JOSÉ ALMEIDA

R. CAMACHINHOS

P.ÇA COMS JOAQUIM MACHADO

R. DOS FERREIROS

RUA E. SILVA

R. DAS PORTAS DE PORTUGAL

RUA QUINTAIS

RUA DR. JOSÉ ALMEIDA

R. DO DISPO DE BOLA

RUA DOS PESCADORES

TRAV. 1 DE MAIO

PR. LUÍS DE CAMÕES

R. CANDIDO GUERREIRO

R. GIL EANES

FR. GIL EANES

RUA INFANTE DE SAGRES

R. DO CAMINHA

TV. DO SAPATES

RUA 1 A. 6. VIANA

R. LARANJEIRA

RUA MARREIROS NETTO

R. AFONSO ALMEIDA

R. LIMA LEITÃO

R. M. POUSAL

R. AFONSO ALMEIDA

RUA DA BARROCA

RUA DA EXTREMA

RUA DE FERRADURA

RUA 1.º DE MAIO

RUA DA OLIVEIRA

RUA CANDIDO DOS REIS

RUA 25 DE ABRIL

RUA DR. J. TELO

RUA DE GIL VICENTE

R. MENDONÇA PESSANHA

RUA SOEIRA DA COSTA

R.S. DA GRAÇA

RUA DA SILVA LOPES

RUA LUIS DE AZEVEDO

ESTRADA DO BIKER

RUA VISANTE DE SAGRES

RUA DR. ESCOLA 5 PRIMARIAS

RUA DAS ALEGRIAS

R. DA ATALAIA

RUA CARDEAL NETO

RUA LANÇAROTE DE FREITAS

TR. DO FORNO

LAGOS

R. S. GONÇALO

PRAÇA INFANTE D. HENRIQUE

PR.DA REPUBLICA

R.H.C. SILVA

RUA DO CASTELO DOS GOVERNADORES

R. S DE OUTUBRO

LARGO DAS PORTAS DA VILA

RUA DE PORTA DA VILA

RUA DR. MENDONÇA

TV. DAS ALMAS

RUA DR. ALBERTO SILVEIRA

R. DO JARDIM

R. MIGUEL

R. GEN. ALBERTO

JULIO DANTAS

BOMBARDA

N

went into a long decline, until **tourism** revived its fortunes in the 1960s. Since then it has developed into a major resort, though it also remains a working fishing port and local market centre.

Mercado dos Escravos

Praça Infante Dom Henrique • Mon–Sat 10am–12.30pm & 2–5.30pm • €6; combined ticket with Museu Municipal and Forte da Bandeira €6 • ⓦ cm-lagos.pt

The most unsavoury aspect of Portugal's historical forays overseas can be seen at the **Mercado dos Escravos**, site of Europe's first slave market, opened in 1444. The current arcaded building was built as a guards' mess in 1691 and later acted as a customs office: it now holds a museum detailing the awful reality of the slave trade in Portugal and elsewhere. Displays on two floors include the written accounts of the first 230 slaves to be sold in Lagos, along with artefacts brought over by them. You can also see the skeleton of a slave that was found dumped on a rubbish tip at the edge of town.

Igreja de Santo António and the Museu Municipal Dr. José Formosinho

Rua General Alberto Silveira • Tues–Sun 10am–1pm & 2–6pm • €3; combined ticket with Mercado dos Escravos and Forte da Bandeira €6 • ☎ 282 762 301, ⓦ cm-lagos.pt

The **Igreja de Santo António**, largely rebuilt after the 1755 earthquake, has a wonderful, lavishly decorated interior – a riot of ornate carvings, gilding and decorative tiles. The church forms part of a visit to the adjacent **Museu Municipal Dr. José Formosinho** – an eclectic collection, to say the least. Alongside barrowloads of Neolithic axe-heads, statuary and local religious art are jars containing misshapen animal foetuses, a display of models of Algarvian chimneys, plus fossils, the 1504 town charter, and assorted swords and cannonballs.

Forte Ponta da Bandeira

Cais da Solaria, Avenida dos Descobrimentos • Tues–Sun 10am–1pm & 2–6pm • €3; combined ticket with Mercado dos Escravos and Museu Municipal €6 • ☎ 282 761 410, ⓦ cm-lagos.pt

Stroll along the waterfront Avenida dos Descobrimentos to see the remains of Lagos's once impregnable walls and fortifications, which include the squat seventeenth-century **Forte Ponta da Bandeira**, guarding the entrance to the harbour. Despite its modest size, this was considered one of the most advanced forts of its age; inside there's a pretty chapel, exhibition space and fine views over the water.

The town beaches

A road train (Easter–Sept hourly 10am–11pm; €3) runs from Lagos marina along Avenida dos Descobrimentos and out via Praia de Dona Ana to Ponta da Piedade

The small **Praia da Batata**, by the Forte Ponta da Bandeira, is the first of a series of lovely cove beaches to the west of the centre. Head up the hill (towards Sagres) and it's about fifteen minutes' walk to the next beach, tiny **Praia do Pinhão**. Five minutes' walk further, across the cliffs, is **Praia de Dona Ana** – the classic Algarve cove, with a restaurant built into the cliffs. Out of season the beach is superb, though in summer the crowds can get overwhelming.

Beyond here, you can follow a path around the cliffs and coast to **Praia do Camilo** – sometimes a bit less crowded – and right to the **Ponta da Piedade**, a headland whose lighthouse is a popular spot from which to watch the sunset. This marks the final point of call for the road train from Lagos.

9

Porto de Mós

Onda Azul bus #2 runs daily from the riverfront Avenida dos Descobrimentos to Porto de Mós every hour (€1.20 or day-ticket €3.60; Ⓦ aonda.pt)

West of Ponta da Piedade, the coast sweeps west to the beach of **Porto de Mós**, another 45 minutes' walk on the coast path, a lovely, broad beach with its own restaurant. The path then continues on as far as Luz, another hour away (see p.484); it's a splendid stretch, high above the ocean, until the obelisk above Luz comes into sight, from where you scramble down the hillside and into town.

Meia Praia

Onda Azul bus #2 runs daily from the riverfront Avenida dos Descobrimentos to Meia Praia every hour (€1.20 or day-ticket €3.60; Ⓦ aonda.pt)

The coast east of Lagos is very different to the western coves, made up of a 4km-long swathe of beach, **Meia Praia**, backed by low dunes and beach restaurants. You can walk to the beach via the marina and fishing harbour in around twenty minutes, and the bus service travels the length of the beach.

Lagos Zoo

Medronhal-Quinta Figueiras, Barão de São João • Daily: April–Sept 10am–7pm; Oct–March 10am–5pm • €16, under-11s €12 • ☏ 282 680 100, Ⓦ zoolagos.com • Onda Verde bus #6 runs to the zoo from Lagos bus station (6 daily; Ⓦ aonda.pt)

Around 8km north of Lagos, just off the main N120, low-key but engaging **Lagos Zoo** is an extensive area of semitropical parkland which houses flamingos, toucans, owls and parrots, small mammals such as wallabies and porcupines, and farm animals in a special children's enclosure. Highlight is the "monkey lake", where gibbons and smaller animals wander semi-free. There's also a shop, restaurant and playgrounds.

ARRIVAL AND DEPARTURE   LAGOS

By bus The bus station (☏ 282 762 944) is a block back from the main riverfront road, Avenida dos Descobrimentos, just east of the centre.

Destinations Albufeira (5–12 daily; 1hr 25min); Aljezur (Mon–Fri 5 daily; 50min); Alvor (4–7 daily; 20min); Armação de Pêra (6–14 daily; 50min–1 hr 15min); Burgau (5–8 daily, 20min); Faro (2–5 daily; 2hr 10min); Lisbon (3–8 daily; 4hr 35min); Luz (Mon–Sat 5–8 daily, Sun 4 daily; 15min); Odeceixe (Mon–Fri 5 daily; Sat–Sun 1 daily; 50min); Portimão (hourly; 40min); Sagres (approx hourly; 1hr); Salema (5–8 daily; 35min).

By train Lagos is the western terminal of the Algarve railway line and its train station (☏ 282 792 361) is across the river, a 15min walk south of the centre via a swing bridge in the marina; taxis are usually available if you can't face the walk (around €4 to the centre).

Destinations Faro (7–9 daily; 1hr 40min); Ferreiras, for Albufeira (9 daily; 1hr 10min); Portimão (7–10 daily; 20min); Silves (7–9 daily; 35min); Tunes, for connections to Lisbon (5 daily; 50min–1hr).

By car There is plenty of parking on the riverside Avenida dos Descobrimentos (metered on the town side of the marina).

INFORMATION, TOURS AND ACTIVITIES

Information The turismo is in the Antigos Paços do Concelho, Praça Gil Eanes (daily 9am–6pm; ☏ 282 763 031, Ⓦ cm-lagos.pt).

Balloon rides Barlavento Balloons (☏ 914 532 300, Ⓦ barlaventoballoons.com.pt) offers hot-air balloon rides across the region (around €200 per person), usually departing from Aeródromo de Lagos, though exact routes depend on weather conditions.

★**Bike tours** Innovative British-run outfit, The Mountain Bike Adventure (☏ 918 502 663, Ⓦ themountainbikeadventure.com), offers various

half- and full-day bike tours inland and along the coast (€25–60).

Boat trips Avenida dos Descobrimentos is lined with stalls offering boat trips to the amazing grottos and sea caves along the surrounding coast, as well as dolphin "seafaris"; most depart from the marina. It's worth shopping around for the best deal, but most cost €15–20 per person for a 45min trip, up to around €50 for half-day excursions.

Surf and bike rental Jah-Shaka, Rua Cândido dos Reis 112 (daily 9am–8pm; ☏ 282 798 006,

ⓦjahshakasurf.com) sells and hires out surf gear and mountain bikes (surfboards and bikes from €15/day) and can also arrange surf lessons and fishing trips.

Surfing and kitesurfing Extreme Algarve (ⓣ918 674 079, ⓦextremealgarve.com) offers surfing and kitesurfing lessons (from €55/day), as well as surfing/kitesurfing holidays, based at its own central Lagos villa.

Tuk-tuk tours Various companies offer tuk-tuk tours of the town and the surrounding beaches for around €10 per person for 90min.

ACCOMMODATION

Lagosmar Rua Dr. Faria e Silva 13 ⓣ282 763 523, ⓦlagosmar.com. This small family hotel is on a (usually) quiet street with its own bar; the best of the smallish rooms have little balconies. Very good low-seson rates. **€90**

Marazul Rua 25 de Abril 13 ⓣ282 770 230, ⓦhotelmarazul.eu. Beautifully decorated guesthouse in the heart of the old town, with bright rooms and communal areas tiled with *azulejos*. Bedrooms (most en suite) vary in size, but all come with TVs and some have terraces with sea views. Closed Jan. **€60**

★**Marina Club** Edifício da Administração, Marina de Lagos ⓣ282 790 600, ⓦmarinaclub.pt. On the east side of the river, just a 5min walk from the pedestrianized bridge into town, this tasteful modern development of swish apartments is wrapped round a large outdoor pool area. Good for families, with studios, one-bed (€250) and two-bed (€306) apartments, all well-equipped, extremely light and spacious, the best with balconies overlooking the marina or pool. There are very good low-season discounts and facilities include an indoor pool, spa and restaurant. Studio **€195**

Marina Rio Av dos Descobrimentos 388 ⓣ282 780 830, ⓦmarinario.com. A friendly, modern four-star facing the harbour (though the back rooms look over the bus station). The rooms are very comfy with balconies and good facilities, and there's also a games room, small rooftop pool and a sundeck. Limited free parking or paid-for garage parking. **€137**

Pousada de Juventude Rua de Lançarote de Freitas 50 ⓣ282 761 970, ⓦpousadasjuventude.pt. A contemporary, well-designed youth hostel, with several dorms plus a few en-suite doubles (book in advance for these). There's a pleasant courtyard, plus laundry facilities and currency exchange. Dorms **€17**; doubles **€45**

Tivoli Lagos Rua António Crisógono dos Santos ⓣ282 790 079, ⓦtivolilagos.com. The town centre's most upmarket hotel, built round a central garden area with its own pool. Not all the rooms are spacious, and some overlook a busy street, but the best have terraces with good views. There are two restaurants, a bar, indoor and outdoor pools, and a health club, plus a courtesy bus to its own beach club at Meia Praia. Parking. **€150**

EATING

★**A Forja** Rua dos Ferreiros 17 ⓣ282 768 588. This is one of the best places in town for fresh fish, at reasonable prices (from around €9): the giant salmon steaks, for example, are superb. It also serves a few meat dishes, salads and tasty starters. Mon–Fri & Sun 12.30–3pm & 6.30–11pm.

★**Adega da Marina** Av dos Descobrimentos 35 ⓣ282 764 284. A great barn of a place with rows of tables serving very good-value food, including huge portions of charcoal-grilled meat and fish; the house wines are great and there's occasional live music. Most mains under €10. Daily noon–2am.

Arribalé Rua da Barroca 40 ⓣ918 556 618, ⓦarribale.com. This quirky place has tables squirrelled into a former gunpowder store above the old town walls; some are outside with views over the river. There's a meaty menu of steaks, meatballs and ribs (from €10) along with fresh fish, a veg dish of the day and tasty tapas (garlic prawns, pork satay, cheeses etc, from €4.50). Daily 12.30pm–1am.

Casa do Zé Rua Portas de Portugal 65 ⓣ282 760 212. On the corner of the market building, with filling fish dishes served at good-value prices, and the outdoor seating attracting a brisk trade. Daily specials cost around €8 and the tourist menu is around €12.50. Daily 6am–2am.

Jota 13 Rua 25 de Abril 58 ⓣ282 762 319. *Jota 13* is a pleasantly old-fashioned restaurant on the main pedestrianized street, with friendly service and huge portions of fish and meat. Recommended are the *arroz de tamboril* (rice with monkfish and seafood), *pescada* (hake) and mixed fish. Mains from €9. Daily 11am–11pm.

Nahnahbah Trav do Forno 14 ⓣ925 736 570. Fun-time café-restaurant famed for its tasty organic burgers (around €9) – including the El Kilo, a self-explanatory heart-attack in a bun for €35. Also serves salads, pasta and cocktails to a youthful crowd, many from the nearby hostels. Daily 6–11pm, bar open till midnight; closed Tues Nov–May, and usually closed Jan–Feb.

The Garden Rua de Lançarote de Freitas 27 ⓣ913 187 142. As the name suggests, the big draw here is a large patio garden, with tables beneath shady trees. There's a bit of everything on the menu, from good cocktails, pasta and burgers (from €7) to Moroccan-influenced mains such as couscous, tagines and *kefta* meatballs (around €10). Daily 1pm–1am.

9

DRINKING AND NIGHTLIFE

Bon Vivante Rua 25 Abril 105 **☎** 282 761 019. This late-night bar/club at the top of the main pedestrianized street has drinking on three floors and a superb roof terrace – a great spot to watch the sun go down. Daily 2pm–4am.

Cervejaria Ferradura Rua 1 de Maio 26A. An old-time *cervejaria* covered in soccer scarves and posters, where locals hole up on stools around a horseshoe-shaped bar and tuck into inexpensive shellfish and *petiscos* (snacks). Mon–Sat 10am–2am.

Grand Café Rua Senhora da Graça 7 **☎** 918 387 510. In a fine high-ceilinged building decked in gold leaf and velvet, this is one of the town's coolest hangouts, with an outside terrace, guest DJs and a lively crowd. April–Sept daily 9pm–6am; Oct–March Fri & Sat 9pm–6am.

Stevie Ray's Rua Senhora da Graça 9 **☎** 282 760 673, **ⓦ** stevieraysbluesbar.com. Lagos's premier jazz, blues and Latin club, with live music every Fri and Sat, plus music other nights in a relaxed and pleasant venue. Tues–Sat 9pm–6am.

DIRECTORY

Banks and exchange Banks and ATMs are grouped around Praça Gil Eanes.

Hospital Rua do Castelo dos Governadores, adjacent to the Santa Maria church (**☎** 282 770 100, **ⓦ** www .chbalgarvio.min-saude.pt).

Pharmacy Ribeiro Lopes, Rua Garrett 22 (Mon–Fri 8.30am–8pm, Sat 9am–7pm, Sun 10am–6pm; **☎** 282 767 024).

Police Largo Convento Nossa Senhora da Gloria (**☎** 282 780 240).

Post office Rua Portas de Portugal, just off Avenida dos Descobrimentos (Mon–Fri 9am–6pm).

Supermarket Intermarché, Avenida dos Descobrimentos 15 (daily 8am–8pm, until 10pm in July and August).

Taxis There are ranks in front of the post office, or call **☎** 282 460 610.

The western Algarve

The coast west of Lagos, as far as Sagres, remains one of the least spoiled parts of the Algarve, largely thanks to the **Parque Natural da Costa Vicentina**, which prohibits large-scale building on the coastline west of Burgau. As a result, the resorts – certainly west of **Luz** at **Burgau** and **Salema** – remain largely low-rise and low-key. Most of the coast is linked by a craggy coast path and you can easily walk between the villages: Salema to Luz, or Luz to Lagos, in particular, are beautiful routes.

GETTING AROUND   THE WESTERN ALGARVE

Bu public transport There are regular buses (6–12 daily) from Lagos calling at Luz (15min), Burgau (20min), Salema (35min) and Sagres (55min). Other local beaches, near Figueira and Raposeira, can't be reached by public transport, but are much less visited as a consequence.

Luz

Five kilometres west of Lagos, the mass of white chalets and villas that makes up the resort of **LUZ** piles up behind a sweeping beach set below towering cliffs. There's not much of a centre to Luz, but it's well worth taking a stroll along the attractive palm-lined beachside promenade that leads from the sands to a *miradouro* beneath the village's old fort – now a restaurant – and the church. Halfway along the promenade, take a moment to peek into the **Termas Romanas** (daily 9am–7pm; free), the remains of a second- and third-century Roman house, with fish-preserving tanks and a bathhouse.

If you fancy a longer walk, you can take the **path to Lagos** which starts at the eastern end of the beach. When you get to the Algarve Sports Club, follow the private road uphill and make the steep scramble up to the obelisk on the cliffs, from where a gentle path careers along the tops to Porto de Mós, Ponte da Piedade and Lagos: the whole stretch from Luz to Lagos should take around two hours in total, and offers some gorgeous views of the unravelling coastline.

Most **accommodation** in Luz is in modern tourist complexes and villas that are usually block-booked in summer, though the hotel and campsite we list below often have vacancies. For self-catering, ⓦ starvilla.com has a good range of quality, decent-value self-catering options in and around Luz. Book early and you can get very good deals.

Belavista da Luz Praia da Luz ☎282 788 655, ⓦ belavistadaluz.com. Around 1km uphill on the road towards Sagres, this is Luz's only hotel proper, a smart four-star with tennis courts, a health club, restaurant and pool. All the rooms are spacious with balconies. **€155**

Camping Valverde Estrada da Praia da Luz ☎218 789 211, ⓦ orbitur.pt. Close to the EN125 highway and a good 3km from the beach, this is nevertheless well-equipped, with a restaurant, bar, pool, supermarket and kids' playground. Pitch **€30**

EATING AND DRINKING

Dolphin Rua da Dalheta 14A ☎282 789 992. This upmarket restaurant in the attractive west edge of town serves unusual dishes with a South African twist: ostrich steak *piri-piri*, vegetable *bobotie* (with rice, soya and sultanas) and couscous, at €13–20. Mon–Sat 6.30–10pm.

Fortaleza da Luz Av das Pescadores 3 ☎282 789 926. Above the west end of the beach, you can dine in style in a seventeenth-century former sea fort with a lovely sea-facing terrace. Organic vegetables and home-made ice creams complement a choice of Algarvian and international cuisine: burgers, pasta, mussel and pork *cataplana* stew (€9–18). There's live music on Thursdays and jazz on Sunday afternoon. Daily 11am–11pm.

Kiwi Pastelaria Av dos Pescadores 4 ☎282 789 646. The perfect beachside café, right on the promenade, serving inexpensive fresh croissants, juices, salads, sandwiches and ice creams. Daily 9am–midnight, closes 6pm Oct to Easter.

Burgau

Once past the modern suburbs, **BURGAU**, 5km west of Luz, is a pretty little former fishing village of narrow cobbled lanes which tumble down a steep hillside to a fine sandy **beach** set below low cliffs. Fishing boats still line the lower roads, which double up as slipways, while narrow alleys weave around to a *miradouro* viewpoint. In July and August the village is somewhat mobbed, but at other times it retains a distinct character, with locals cooking fish on tiny grills outside their homes.

A Barraca Largo dos Pescadores 2 ☎282 697 748. This clifftop restaurant (aka *The Hut*) is a top spot for mid-priced meat dishes and seafood (around €10–15), including the speciality, *cataplana* (fish stew). It's best in summer since, at other times, plastic sheets over the terrace put paid to the wind but also the views. Mon & Wed–Sun noon–3pm & 7–10pm; closed one month in winter.

★ **Beach Bar Burgau** Praia de Burgau ☎282 697 553. This high-profile restaurant has a splendid terrace on the beach – waves crash around it at high tide. It serves tasty fresh fish, grills and pasta (€10–16), or just pop in for tea and cake or a drink. Daily: bar 10am–midnight; restaurant noon–3pm & 7–10pm; closed Mon Oct to Easter.

Burgau Beach Rua da Fortaleza ☎962 505 429, ⓦ burgaubeachhotel.com. On a hillside at the east end of town, this recently renovated three-star hotel has small but decent rooms. The top-floor ones with balconies have superb views, and there's a garden and small pool. **€140**

Casa Grande ☎282 697 416, ⓦ casagrandeportugal .com. At the top end of town on the road towards Luz, this is a lovely old English-run manor set in its own grounds. The rooms (of varying sizes) have soaring ceilings and there's also a converted barn that sleeps four (€145). **€80**

Salema

At the bottom of an attractive valley, **SALEMA** is no longer the thriving fishing village it once was, but its tight warren of fishermen's houses above the eastern end of a fine, sandy bay now form the hub of an attractive resort. Many of the old houses are now converted into inexpensive holiday lets: look for signs in the windows. A plume of modern development spreads steeply uphill, but at least the white villas are in keeping with the old town, and its **beach** only gets busy in high season.

A Maré Praia de Salema ☎ 282 695 165, ⓦ the-mare .com. On the hill above the main road into town, this good-value and attractively renovated house has a lovely sea-facing terrace and airy breakfast room. Self-catering apartments (from €75) and en-suite rooms are of varied sizes but spotless, the best with terraces overlooking the sea. €80

Quinta dos Carriços Praia de Salema ☎ 282 695 201. An excellent campsite with well-spaced pitches in beautifully landscaped grounds with plenty of trees

for shade. Good facilities include a minimarket, restaurant, bar and launderette – there's also a naturists' zone and bungalows sleeping 2–4 (from €50). Pitch €17

Salema Rua 28 de Janeiro ☎ 282 665 328, ⓦ hotelsalema.com. Plonked ungraciously by the cobbled square just back from the beach, this modern hotel block offers small but pleasant rooms with their own balconies and skewed sea views; there's also a bar. Closed Nov–March. €100

EATING AND DRINKING

★**Boia Bar** Rua dos Pescadores 101 ☎ 282 695 382, ⓦ boiabar.com. Salema's top restaurant is a swish place facing the beach, with snappy service; *caldeirada* (fish stew) is the speciality (though you need to order it in advance), otherwise fresh fish (€10–15) is the thing to go for. Also does inexpensive sandwiches. Daily 10am–midnight.

O Lourenço Rua 28 de Janeiro 13 ☎ 282 698 622. Just back from the main seafront car park (head uphill past the *Hotel Salema*), this is a fine local with an attractive patio garden. The good-value menu features fresh fish, chicken *piri-piri* and rice dishes including an interesting chicken *cataplana* (stew). Mains from €9.50. Mon–Sat 10am–midnight.

Praia da Figueira

The small village of Figueira on the N125, around 3km northwest of Salema, is the starting point for a rough track (signed "Forte da Figueira") to the isolated sands of **Praia da Figueira**, that lie below the ruins of an old fort. This is one of the least-visited beaches along this stretch of coastline, mainly due to the fact that it's not reachable by car. The walk takes twenty to thirty minutes but is well worth the effort, especially as the path passes through some lovely countryside. There are no facilities at Praia da Figueira, so take your own food and drink.

Ermida Nossa Senhora de Guadalupe

Estrada Nacional 125, Raposeira • Tues–Sun 10.30am–1pm & 2–6.30pm, closes 5pm Oct–April • Free; exhibitions €2 • ☎ 282 620 140, ⓦ cultalg.pt

Between Figueira and Raposeira, a sign points off the main N125 to the chapel of **Nossa Senhora de Guadalupe**, reached down the old road which runs parallel to the highway. A boxy whitewashed building with sections of exposed brickwork, the chapel was built in the thirteenth century by the Knights Templar, and is thought to have been frequented by Henry the Navigator. Impressively situated in rural solitude, it makes for a pleasant place to stroll around or lay out a picnic. A small, rather unimpressive exhibition space details the chapel's links with Henry the Navigator.

Praia do Zavial and Praia da Ingrina

There's no public transport to Praia do Zavial or Praia da Ingrina, so you'll need a car

The little-visited **Praia do Zavial** can be reached from the small village of Raposeira, which is on the main EN125. It has a great beach which is popular with surfers and a fine café-restaurant.

Another couple of kilometres around the bay from Praia do Zavial lies **Praia da Ingrina**. This is a more sheltered and sandy spot, offering excellent beachcombing and a host of rockpools to explore – great for kids.

9

Sagres and around

SAGRES is the southwesternmost harbour in Europe. Spread over a flat, scrubby headland above a working fishing port, it is not a handsome town, but its dramatic position attracts a growing number of families, backpackers, divers and surfers, drawn by warm waters, surf schools and the string of magnificent local beaches. Modern Sagres is little more than a main road – Rua Comandante Matoso – connecting the lively **fishing harbour** and **Praia da Baleeira** at one end with the small main square, **Praça da República**, at the other, all backed by a new town of white villas and apartments. Praça da República is the main focus of town, an attractive cobbled space lined with squat palms. Sagres's liveliest day is August 15 when celebrations and fireworks mark the local saint's day.

Brief history

Sagres and its rugged cape, Cabo de São Vicente, were once thought to mark the edge of the known world, which is why **Henry the Navigator** is believed to have set up his **school of navigation** here in the fifteenth century. It was here, too, that the **caravel** was developed – a revolutionary boat that could sail further than any European had been before. During Henry's lifetime, Portuguese navigators colonized the Azores and Madeira and began trading with ports along the west coast of Africa. After Henry's death in 1460, his school continued to train and equip sailors who went on to become the most famous of Portugal's great explorers: **Vasco da Gama** (1460–1524), who opened up the sea route to India; **Pedro Álvares Cabral** (1468–1520), who "discovered" Brazil; and **Ferdinand Magellan** (1480–1521), the first European to cross the Pacific. Once Lisbon became the main departure point for the Portuguese explorers, however, Sagres lost some of its importance and slipped back into obscurity. Its small sixteenth-century Fortaleza de Baleeira was damaged by Francis Drake in 1587 and further ruined in the 1755 earthquake; most of today's town was built after tourism revived its fortunes in the 1960s.

The beaches

Most people spend their days in Sagres on one of the excellent beaches, five of which are within walking distance of the town. Three are on the more sheltered coast east of the fortress, with the best, **Praia da Mareta**, just five minutes' walk southeast of the main square. Further on is the slightly scrubby harbour beach, **Praia da Baleeira**, but you're better off walking another five to ten minutes over the cliffs above the harbour to the longest beach, **Praia do Martinhal**, which is particularly good for families and backed by

---

SAGRES SURFING

The west coast of the Algarve has gained a reputation as one of Europe's best **surfing** destinations, with Sagres as its surfing capital. Its position at the bottom corner of Portugal means that there are nearly always excellent surfing conditions, whatever the weather. The swell "wraps" round Cabo de São Vicente, producing relatively gentle waves in the bays between Sagres and Lagos, ideal for the less experienced. With swell sizes of up to 5m, the beaches north of Cabo de São Vicente face the full brunt of the Atlantic so are best for experienced surfers – legs of the **World Surfing Championships** are held at nearby Praia do Amado. Indeed, it can be decidedly dangerous and inexperienced surfers are best off going with a **surf school** – which can give one-off lessons or courses from around €60 a day – or a **surf camp**, which throws in accommodation and transport to the best beaches. Top surf camps and schools in the Sagres region include ⓦfreeridesurfcamp.com, ⓦalgarvesurfschool.com and ⓦinternationalsurfschool.com. If you use another outfit, check that it's an approved surf school at ⓦalgarvesurfschoolsassociation.com.

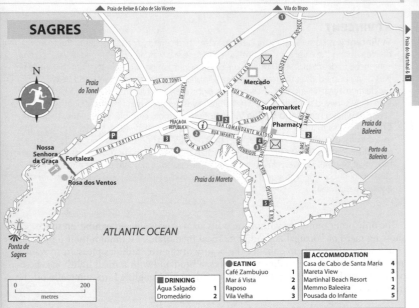

● EATING		■ ACCOMMODATION	
Café Zambujuo	1	Casa de Cabo de Santa Maria	4
Mar á Vista	2	Mareta View	3
■ DRINKING		Martinhal Beach Resort	1
Água Salgado	1	Raposo	4	Memmo Baleeira	2
Dromedário	2	Vila Velha	3	Pousada do Infante	5

a purpose-built resort. West of the fortress, **Praia do Tonel** is a wilder location, popular with surfers. It's a longer walk to the beautiful **Praia de Belixe**, 2km down the road from Sagres to Cabo de São Vicente, which is overlooked by a small fortress (closed to the public). Wherever you swim, take care – there are some very strong undertows, especially on the west side of the fortress.

Porto da Baleeira

Porto da Baleeira is a working fishing harbour, around fifteen minutes' walk from Sagres's main square along Rua Comandante Matoso. It's an earthy kind of place, its waterfront lined with boat-repair yards and fishing fleets – watching the day's catch come in is always an event. Porto da Baleeira is also the departure point for various **diving** excursions (see p.490), and for appealing **boat trips** up and down the coast and out to Cabo de São Vicente.

Fortaleza

Daily: May, June & Sept 9.30am–8pm; July & Aug 9.30am–8.30pm; April & Oct 9.30am–6.30pm; Nov–March 9am–5.30pm • €3, free first Sun of the month • ☎ 282 620 140, ⓦ monumentosalgarve.pt

Henry the Navigator's **Fortaleza** looms over Sagres town, with Rua da Fortaleza running directly up the headland towards its massive bulk; it is better to walk this way than to follow the road signs, which take you on a detour to a giant car park set well back from the fort. You enter the fort via a tunnel through the impressive inland wall – this is all that remains of the defences that once enclosed this dramatic headland jutting into the Atlantic; the rest were brought down by the 1755 earthquake. Opposite the tunnel entrance, you'll see a huge **Rosa dos Ventos** (wind compass) made of pebbles, which was used to measure the direction of the wind. No one is sure whether the compass dates back to Henry's time, though the much-restored chapel of **Nossa Senhora da Graça** alongside is certainly from the fifteenth century.

9

ST VINCENT

St Vincent was born in Zaragoza in Spain in the third century AD and became the town's deacon during the early days of Christianity in Iberia. He was later imprisoned in Valencia and sentenced to death in 304 AD during the days of Christian persecution. It is said that while he was being burned alive, the room filled with light and the voices of angels, and he was proclaimed a martyr and then a saint. In the eighth century, his remains – which had somehow survived the fire – were miraculously washed up in an unmanned boat piloted by ravens at what is now **Cabo de São Vicente**. Perhaps more credible is the theory that Christians took whatever was left of Vincent with them to flee invading Moors, arriving at the safe outpost of the Cape where they later built a chapel to house his remains. In 1173, Afonso Henriques, Portugal's first Christian monarch, had the saint's remains moved to Lisbon. Legend has it that the faithful ravens followed them to the capital, and guarded over him in the cloisters of Lisbon's Sé (cathedral), until the last raven died in 1978. Today São Vicente remains Lisbon's patron saint.

The only other buildings within the walls are a shop, café and **exhibition space** showing maps of Portugal and other nautical memorabilia – though their ugly concrete construction does little to enhance the beauty of the site. Still, it's pleasant to wander around the walls or out to **Ponta de Sagres**, a headland with a small lighthouse beacon offering superb views along the coast, past fishermen dangling lines suicidally off the immense cliffs.

Cabo de São Vicente

The dramatic, cliff-fringed **Cabo de São Vicente** – Cape St Vincent – is the most southwestern point of mainland Europe. The Romans called this Promontorium Sacrum and thought the sun plunged nightly into the sea here – it later became a Christian shrine when the relics of the martyred St Vincent were brought here in the eighth century (see box above). Today, tourist stalls selling trinkets line the approach road to a **lighthouse**, one of the most powerful in Europe: there's a small **museum** (Tues–Sun 10am–6pm, closes 5pm Nov–March; €1.50) tracing the history of the lighthouse, from an original structure in the sixteenth century to the current one which dates from 1908. The other building is a ruined sixteenth-century Capuchin convent, which survived the 1755 earthquake but not the dissolution of the monasteries in 1834: its remaining walls today shelter a small shop and café.

The sea off this wild set of cliffs shelters the highest concentration of marine life in Portugal, including rare birds such as Bonelli's eagle – there's a **birdwatching festival** here in autumn (ⓦbirdwatchingsagres.com). If you can, it's worth visiting the cape at sunset, when the views are breathtaking.

ARRIVAL AND INFORMATION

SAGRES AND AROUND

By bus Buses from Lagos stop just by Praça da República and then continue on to the harbour, Porto da Baleeira. Destinations Cabo de São Vicente (Mon–Fri 2 daily; 10min); Lagos (approx hourly; 1hr); Salema (Mon–Fri hourly, Sat & Sun 6 daily; 30min).

Information The turismo, on the main Avenida Comandante Matoso (daily 9am–1pm & 2–6pm;

ⓣ 282 624 873, ⓦ cm-viladobispo.pt), can give details of local bus timetables and events.

Scuba diving Diverscape, at Porto da Baleeira (ⓣ 965 559 073, ⓦ diverscape.com), offers half-day dive trips from around €90 and various diving courses from around €250, as well as snorkelling trips (€25).

ACCOMMODATION

Casa de Cabo de Santa Maria Rua Patrão António Faústino ⓣ929 346 624, ⓦ casadocabodesantamaria .com. In an attractive modern townhouse on a quiet street,

this has spotless rooms, and two-bed apartments with kitchens and living rooms (€100); the best have their own balconies (€10 extra). Parking available. **€70**

Mareta View Pr da República ☎ 282 620 040, ⓦ maretaview.com. Right on the main square, this bills itself as a "boutique hotel" and it certainly has a clean, modern feel with bright rooms, some facing the sea. There is also a fashionable bar, attractive garden and an Italian-style café downstairs. **€180**

★**Martinhal Beach Resort** Quinta do Martinhal ☎ 282 240 200, ⓦ martinhal.com. This upmarket, family-friendly resort is almost a village in its own right, with a small supermarket, a fantastic spa, various pools, restaurants and playgrounds dotted around the grounds which slope down to Martinhal beach; there's also a gym and access to a whole raft of sports and activities including tennis, padel tennis, kayaking, surfing and cycling. The stylish villas are modern and very well designed for families, while the classy hotel is better for those travelling without kids. Of the three restaurants, *O Terraço* offers excellent fine dining, while the more relaxed beachfront *As Dunas* specializes in fresh fish. **€215**

Memmo Baleeira Rua das Nau ☎ 282 624 212, ⓦ memmohotels.com. This stylish four-star is in a prime location overlooking the fishing harbour, and has a restaurant and bar overlooking landscaped lawns and the pool. Rooms are bright, white and minimalist with flatscreen TV, and there's also a spa, bike hire and in-house surf school. Parking available. **€145**

Pousada do Infante ☎ 282 620 240, ⓦ pousadas.pt. This is an attractive clifftop mansion with Moorish elements and splendid views of the fortress from its bar-terrace. Rooms are large and comfy with luxurious bathrooms. There are also tennis courts, a restaurant and pool in the grounds. Parking. **€130**

EATING

Café Zambujuo Rua do Poço ☎ 282 624 398. On the first turning into town after the road to Martinhal (so best if you have a car), this unassuming locals' place is renowned for its moray eel burgers (around €8), hence its nickname, *Casa da Moreia*. It claims they are unique – and they are surprisingly tasty. A fun place for a beer, too. Mon, Tues & Thurs–Sun 6am–midnight.

Mar á Vista Sítio da Mareta ☎ 282 624 247. On a scrubby patch of ground just off the road to Praia da Mareta, this pleasant restaurant serves a long list of good-value fish, omelettes, pasta and salads (around €11 for mains), with good views from its outdoor tables. Mon–Wed & Fri–Sun 10am–10pm.

Raposo Praia da Mareta ☎ 282 624 168. Lovely wood-and-chrome beach bar-restaurant right on the sands. Food is good value (mains €10–16) if you steer clear of the pricey seafood and wine, or choose the *feijoada de tamboril* (monkfish and bean stew), at €26 for two. By day it's full of surfers enjoying a drink. Daily 10am–10pm.

Vila Velha Rua Patrão António Faustino ☎ 282 624 788 ⓦ vilavelha-sagres.com. The Dutch owners of this traditional restaurant give an international twist to Portuguese ingredients, such as spaghetti with mushrooms and Dutch cheese and pork with mango sauce, served in a pretty white house. Mains from €13. Tues–Sun 6.30–10pm.

DRINKING

Água Salgado Rua Comandante Matoso 8650 ☎ 282 624 297. Bright, lively bar with cool music, a TV and table football. Also does crêpes, pizzas and breakfasts. Daily 10am–3am.

Dromedário Rua Comandante Matoso ☎ 282 624 219. Fashionable little bar-bistro with Egyptian-inspired decor, serving a mean range of cocktails and juices. Occasional live jazz and DJ sessions. Daily 10am–2am; Oct–April closed Tues.

The west coast

The Algarve's **west coast** faces the full brunt of the Atlantic, whose crashing breakers and cooler waters have largely deterred the developers. Nevertheless, the rocky coastline is punctuated by fantastic broad beaches accessible from the small villages of **Carrapateira**, **Odeceixe** or, a little further inland, **Aljezur**. This is popular territory for surfers, campervanners and hardy nudists who appreciate the remote beaches, but be warned: the sea can be dangerous and swimmers should take great care. The designation in 1995 of the stretch of coast from Burgau to Cabo de São Vicente and up through the Alentejo as a nature reserve – the **Parque Natural do Sudoeste Alentejano e Costa Vicentina** – has afforded the rugged scenery a certain amount of protection, though it also means that accommodation is scarce and it certainly helps to have your own transport.

9

Carrapateira and its beaches

Some twenty kilometres to the north of Sagres is the low-key village of **CARRAPATEIRA**. There's not much to the village itself, but most people are drawn by the nearby **Praia da Bordeira**, a spectacular beach backed by giant dunes, a tiny river and crashing surf. A couple of kilometres south of Carrapateira (signed off the main road), there's a further fantastic broad, sandy bay, **Praia do Amado**, with a couple of seasonal cafés. Backed by low hills, it's particularly popular with surfers, and there's a **surf school** here (see p.488).

Museu do Mar e da Terra

Rua do Pescador 7 • Tues–Sat 10am–1pm & 1.30–4.30pm • €2.70 • ☎ 282 970 000

Carrapateira's only real site is the modern **Museu do Mar e da Terra**, at the north end of town up a steep side-road. The museum explores the village's rural past and its relationship with the sea, with a modest assembly of traditional tools and crafts and some evocative photos; there are also great views across the coast from its café.

ARRIVAL AND INFORMATION   CARRAPATEIRA AND ITS BEACHES

By bus Carrapateira has a bus connection with Aljezur (Mon–Fri 1 daily; 25min).

Surf School Carrapateira's Algarve Surf School

(☎962 846 771, ⊛algarvesurfschool.com) offers equipment rental and surf courses from €50.

ACCOMMODATION AND EATING

Casa Fajara Vale de Carrapateira ☎282 973 134, ⊛casafajara.com. You'd be hard pushed to find a better rural retreat than this. It's half a kilometre down a bumpy track (signed right as you leave Carrapateira heading north) in an idyllic valley. Spacious two- and three-bed rooms mostly face out over the grounds, which include a tennis court, pool and various terraces; there's also a simpler room (€128) in a separate building. Activities (yoga, surfing, walks) can be arranged on request. €172

Dunas Rua da Padaria 9, Carrapateira ☎282 973 118, ⊛pensao-das-dunas.pt. The best place to stay in Carrapateira is a very pretty building on the beach side of the village, which has a number of simple rooms (en-suite €10 extra) overlooking a flower-filled courtyard; there are

also six apartments sleeping two (€80), three (€100) or four (€115). €50

★**Micro Bar** Largo do Comércio 7 ☎965 296 492. With tables on the main square, this is the hub of Carrapateira's action, serving a selection of tempting cocktails and fabulous fresh food such as filling bruschetta with aubergine, burgers, salads, and gyros with pork and yoghurt (€7–10). Mon & Wed–Sun noon–10pm, later in summer.

O Sítio do Rio Praia da Bordeira ☎282 973 119. Around 1km back from the beach towards Carrapateira, this is a popular restaurant with an outdoor terrace, offering fresh soup, simple grills and veggie dishes from €10. Mon & Wed–Sun noon–3pm & 7–10pm.

Pedralva

Reached down a bumpy dirt track in a hidden valley – itself miles from anywhere – it is perhaps not surprising that by 2006, the population of **PEDRALVA** had declined to just nine people in a dying village of decaying houses. Roll on a decade and you'll find a thriving tourist village, with neatly tended cobbled alleys weaving through a huddle of pretty whitewashed houses available for **holiday lets**; these get booked up well in advance despite being around 6km from the nearest beach, Praia do Amado. With a couple of restaurants and a bar, the village is great for **walkers**, as it's right on the Via Algarviana long-distance walking route (see p.493), and the letting company also rents bikes for €20 a day.

ACCOMMODATION AND EATING   PEDRALVA

Aldeia da Pedralva Pedralva ☎282 639 342, ⊛aldeiadapedralva.com. Pedralva's cottages have been sympathetically restored, though comforts are simple: no wi-fi or TVs, and most of the rooms are under low wooden eaves. The larger houses (two-beds from

€229) have their own terraces, and there's also a communal barbecue area and an outdoor pool for guests. There's usually plenty of availability out of season, though book ahead at other times. One-bed house from €144

Sitio da Pedralva Pedralva ☎ 282 639 342. Pedralva's main restaurant is a good one, with an attached bar and a lovely outdoor terrace. It serves chicken, veal, burgers and the like (€11–16): recommended is the *bacalhau no pão*, salted cod served in a traditional loaf (€20 for two). Daily 12.30–3pm & 7–10.30pm.

Aljezur and around

ALJEZUR (pronounced *alj-ezoor*), 16km north of Carrapateira, is the liveliest town on this coast, though some way inland from any beaches. The main coast road passes through a prosaic, modern lower town where you find banks, the post office and a range of cafés and restaurants. The more interesting historic centre spreads uphill beyond the bridge over the Aljezur river, a network of narrow cobbled streets reaching up through whitewashed houses to the remains of an eleventh-century Moorish **castle**, a lovely picnic spot and where you can see the remains of the cistern and grain silos. It's a lovely walk up to the castle with sweeping views over the valley, via a cluster of museums – though only the Casa Museu Pintor José Cercas (see below) is really worth a visit.

Casa Museu Pintor José Cercas

Rua do Castelo 2 • June–Sept Tues–Sat 9am–1pm & 2–6pm; Oct–May by appointment only • €2.10, includes entry to all the town museums • Ticket sales and appointments for Oct–May visits via the Museu Municipal on Largo 5 de Outubro (same hours; ☎ 282 991 011)

The **Casa Museu Pintor José Cercas** displays the works and collections of local artist José Cercas, who lived in the house until his death in 1992. His well-observed landscapes and religious scenes are complemented by the attractive house and pretty garden.

Praia da Arrifana and Monte Clérigo

There's no public transport to Monte Clérigo or Praia da Arrifana; drivers may need to park at the top of Arrifana's cliff and walk to the beach as parking spaces are limited

Some 10km southwest of Aljezur, **Praia da Arrifana** is a superb, sandy sweep set below high, crumbling black cliffs which shelter a tiny fishing harbour. The beach is excellent, and surf competitions are sometimes held here. Several simple café-restaurants lie along the road above the beach, all serving grilled fish at moderate prices.

At the top of the cliff – at the headland, **Ponte da Arrifana** – are the ruins of an old seventeenth-century fort, largely destroyed by the 1755 earthquake. From here, you can pick up a coastal walk north, via the remains of an Islamic community at Ponte da Atalaia, all the way to **Monte Clérigo**, a pretty little holiday village of pink- and white-faced beach houses facing a superb, family oriented beach tucked into the foot of a valley. The fine 2hr walk forms part of the signed Trilho dos Pescadores (see p.429) – keep the sea on your left and you can hardly get lost. The views are excellent, down into the deep, green waters and along the fragmented coast. There are some superb deserted strands below – not easily accessible – while the clifftop path, 100m up, runs through the brush- and herb-carpeted dunes, filled with flowers in the spring.

9

ARRIVAL AND DEPARTURE

By bus Buses stop on Aljezur's main street. Destinations Carrapateira (Mon–Fri 1 daily; 25min); Lagos (Mon–Fri 6 daily; Sat & Sun 2 daily; 35–50min); Lisbon (2 daily; 5hr); Odeceixe (Mon–Fri 5 daily; Sat & Sun 1 daily; 30min); Portimão (2 daily; 55min); Santiago de Cacém (2 daily; 2hr 30min).

ALJEZUR AND AROUND

INFORMATION AND ACTIVITIES

Information The turismo (Mon & Fri–Sun 9am–1pm & 2–6pm, Tues Wed 9am–7pm, closes 6pm Oct to Easter); ☎ 282 998 229, ⓦ cm-aljezur.pt), at Rua 25 de Abril 62, the main through-road, does its best to help with private rooms.
Bike rental/tours Algarve Adventure (☎ 913 533 363, ⓦ algarve-adventure.com) rents out bikes for €15 a day (and will deliver to you), and offers guided bike tours from €35 per person.
Donkey treks Burras Artes (☎ 289 998 331, ⓦ donkey -trekking-algarve.blogspot.com) offers one-day donkey treks (€30) along the trails around Aljezur, and on longer tours on request. The donkeys carry your luggage (and children, if required).

ACCOMMODATION

Accommodation options are somewhat limited around Aljezur. The town itself has just one hostel, though there's another on the beach at Arrifana and a campsite nearby. Otherwise, Carpe Vita (☎ 963 256 581, wcarpe-vita.com) lets out a variety of tastefully renovated houses in Aljezur old town, sleeping from two (€95) to four (€105) people.

Amazigh Design Hostel Rua da Ladeira 5, Aljezur ☎ 282 997 502, ⓦ amazighostel.com. Near the market at the bottom of the old town, this funky modern hostel is in a classily renovated old building with lots of bleached wood and exposed brickwork. Geared up for local surfers (surf packages available), there's a pleasant communal lounge and kitchen, decent doubles and dorms sleeping 6–10 people. Breakfast extra. Dorms €17; doubles €99
Parque de Campismo do Serrão Herdade do Serrão ☎ 282 990 220, ⓦ campingserrao.com. The local campsite, 7km northwest of Aljezur, and 4km from the lovely beach of Praia Amoreira, has its own pool, supermarket, restaurant and tennis courts among dense trees. Pitch €17
Pousada de Juventude Urbanização Arrifamar, Lote 43–44, Praia da Arrifana ☎ 282 997 455, ⓦ pousadasjuventude.pt. A smart, modern youth hostel around 1km from the beach as you approach from Aljezur, with doubles and four- to six-bed dorms, its own canteen and fine sea views. Dorms €17; doubles €47

EATING AND DRINKING

III Geração Rua 25 de Abril 14, Aljezur ☎ 282 998 534. A homely restaurant on the main street, with good-value pasta, fish and meat such as chicken *piri-piri* from around €8. The tourist menu is around €13. Daily noon–3.30pm & 6.30–10.30pm, closed Tues in winter.
Mioto Rua 25 de Abril 61, Loja H, Aljezur ☎ 282 998 031. Tucked into a small shopping arcade on the north side of the main avenue, this appealing *pastelaria* does a fine range of cakes and snacks, with an outdoor terrace facing attractive open fields at the back. Mon–Fri 8.30am–5.30pm, Sat–Sun 8.30am–3pm.
Pont'a Pé Largo da Liberdade 12, Aljezur ☎ 282 998 104, ⓦ pontape.pt. Near the market at the foot of the old town, this buzzy restaurant (mains around €10) offers grills, salads and a fine *arroz de tamboril*, served inside a cosy dining room or on an outdoor terrace. DJs and live music most weekends (with later closing) competes with the sound of the resident frogs. Daily 11am–11pm.

Odeceixe

The attractive village of **ODECEIXE** tumbles down a hillside opposite the broad valley of the Ribeira da Seixe, below the winding, tree-lined main coast road. Sleepy out of season, its character changes in summer when it attracts a steady stream of surfers, campervanners and families, lured by a superb beach and a very laidback atmosphere. Everything centres on the single main street and a small square, **Largo 1 de Maio**, where you'll find some lively bars, plenty of cafés, a couple of minimarkets, post office, bank and craft shops.

Praia de Odeceixe

The road train runs from Odeceixe to the beach (approximately hourly 9.30am–7.30pm; (1.50 return)

The beach, **Praia de Odeceixe**, is 4km west of the village, reached down a verdant river valley, the fields either side neatly cultivated with corn. A road train trundles between

village and beach during July and August, but it's a lovely walk along the road as well, following the river to a broad, sandy bay framed by low cliffs. Praia de Odeceixe is one of the most sheltered beaches along this stretch of coast, offering superb surfing and relatively safe swimming, especially when the tide is out. There's lots of parking above the bay, as well as a cluster of houses and cafés, some offering *quartos* (rooms to rent).

ARRIVAL AND INFORMATION   ODECEIXE

By bus Buses (Mon–Fri 5 daily, Sat–Sun 1 daily) run to Odeceixe village from Lagos (1hr 15min) via Aljezur (30min).
Information There's a small information kiosk just above

the beach (July–Sept daily 10am–6pm; ☎ 282 947 255).
Surfing The Odeceixe Surf School (☎ 282 949 152, ⓦ odeceixesurfschool.com) offers 3hr lessons from €55 and rents out equipment from €10/hr.

ACCOMMODATION, EATING AND DRINKING

Casa Celeste Rua Nova 10 ☎ 282 947 150, ⓦ casahospedesceleste.com. Right on Odeceixe's main road, this is a spacious, attractively decorated rooms in a traditional townhouse – avoid the lower rooms which are a bit too close to the street for comfort. **€60**

Chaparro Rua do Correiro, Odeceixe ☎ 282 947 304. Odeceixe's top choice for eating and drinking, opposite *Residência do Parque* – they serve local treats such as *piri-piri* prawns and goose barnacles (mains €7–9), and there's a blackboard menu for the catch-of-the-day as well. If it's warm, you can sit outside at wooden benches to eat. Daily noon–3pm & 6–10pm; closed Wed Oct–May.

Dorita Praia de Odeceixe ☎ 282 947 581. In a superb spot with a terrace just above the beach, this does a good range of fish and seafood – the fish kebabs are

recommended, as are the *petiscos* (snacks) and cocktails. If you fancy staying, there are lovely en-suite rooms (plus a tiny one with shared facilities, €35), the best of which have sea-facing balconies (€50). Daily 10am–10pm.

O Retiro do Adelino Rua Nova 20, Odeceixe ☎ 282 947 352. An excellent-value local restaurant, with tables in a covered courtyard, serving dishes such as *cataplana* (fish stew), grilled octopus and squid at €6–8. Daily noon–11pm.

Residência do Parque Rua do Correio 15 ☎ 282 947 117. On the street by the post office, this friendly backpackers' haunt has a mixed bag of en-suite rooms – the best are on the top floor with small balconies. There's also a hammock lounge downstairs and huge off-season reductions. **€40**

Contexts

History

There is evidence of human life in Portugal going back 30,000 years, to a time when ice covered much of Europe. Around 22,000 years ago, the first Paleolithic hunter-gatherers – concentrated in the sheltered river valleys of the upper Douro and Tejo – began to leave animal engravings on the rocky river flank, most famously around Vila Nova de Foz Côa. The purpose of the etchings remains a mystery, although their unerringly lifelike nature suggests that shamanic ritual may have been involved. Over the following millennia, as the ice receded, early man extended his range further into the part of the Iberian peninsula that later became Portugal.

The first man-made stone structures made their appearance 6000 to 7000 years ago, in the form of communal tombs or **antas** (dolmens), most of which follow a basic design of a circular stone-walled chamber, roofed with flat slabs and originally covered with soil and rubble. Associated with the *antas* is a fertility cult, whose most obvious remains are a series of vertically planted, stone **menhirs** (heavy cylindrical stones, some carved into unarguably phallic forms) – egg-shaped boulders bearing vaginal symbols are believed to be the female equivalents. The largest surviving dolmen in the country is the Anta Grande do Zambujeiro, near Évora, though there are scores of others sited across the Alentejo and Beira regions. There's also a series of Neolithic **stone circles** (most dramatically at Os Almendres, near Évora) whose exact purpose is still unclear, though they may have had religious or even time-keeping significance.

How long this "granite civilization" lasted is unclear, though by 2000 BC it was well integrated into a broader western-European megalithic culture, as testified by the development of symbolic rock art. Particularly fine examples of Neolithic art are the carved shale funerary plaques from Alentejo and the Algarve, mostly in the form of stylized owls or other birds of prey, probably divinities; the plaques may also have been symbols of tribal power or affiliation.

Cultura Castreja

The end of the Neolithic era, around 1000 BC, saw the development of northern Portugal's **Cultura Castreja**, based around fortified hilltop towns – called **citânias** – and villages (*castros*). There were contacts with trading peoples from across the Mediterranean, including the Phoenicians, who settled along Portugal's Atlantic coastline (c.900 BC), and the Mycenaean Greeks. A curious testament to this cultural mingling is found at Panóias, close to Vila Real, where an engraved text next to a sacrificial altar bears a bilingual Latin and Greek inscription dedicated to the Greco-Egyptian deity of Serapis.

c.20,000 BC	5000–2000 BC	700–600 BC
Paleolithic hunters jazz up their caves with animal engravings in the Upper Douro	Neolithic stone circles are erected, most notably near Évora	Celts bring their northern customs to hilltowns such as Citânia de Briteiros near Braga

With the arrival of **Celtic peoples** in Portugal (from 700 BC onwards), life in the *citânias* and *castros* became more sophisticated. The Citânia de Briteiros, near Braga, and Citânia de Sanfins de Ferreira, north of Porto, were both substantial settlements of farmers, artisans and traders who lived in houses on paved streets, defended by formidable walls. Remains and relics from settlements in neighbouring Trás-os-Montes reveal more about this well-established society. The famous granite statues of wild sows and boars – *berrões* or *porcas* – may once have been worshipped as part of a fertility cult (there are notable examples at Bragança and Murça). Meanwhile, from both Minho and Trás-os-Montes come the life-sized statues of Celtic warriors, whose popular name – *figuras de basto* – alludes to their bravery: *eu basto*, "I suffice" (in defending the people), was their motto.

Rise and fall of the Romans

The **Romans** arrived in the Iberian peninsula in 210 BC, spreading out from the Mediterranean coast and quickly colonizing the south. Inland, however, it was a different matter, with the various Celt-Iberian tribes determined to defend their homeland against the invaders. The **Lusitani** of central Portugal in particular are still remembered for their heroic resistance, starting in 193 BC and keeping the Romans busy for years, if not decades. Their leader was one Viriatus, who kept the Lusitani in charge of their own destiny until he was betrayed in 139 BC – the Roman army smashed through and quickly pacified the Portuguese interior as far north as the Minho. Even so, it's easy to believe that in the far north and east, in isolated hilltowns and mountainous areas, the influence of the Romans was never very strong.

By 60 BC the Romans had founded a capital – **Olisipo** (Lisbon) – and established satellite towns throughout the Alentejo, including Évora, Santarém and Beja. Later, the southern Roman provinces became known as Lusitania, with a separate province to the north that covered the Minho, ruled from its main settlement at Braga. There are Roman remains and excavations – major and minor – in all these areas, and while Portuguese Roman archeological sites are generally insignificant compared to those elsewhere in the Mediterranean, the excavations at **Conímbriga** (near Coimbra) do at least give a sense of scale of Roman settlement and occupation.

WHAT DID THE ROMANS EVER DO FOR US?

Well, there are the roads, obviously, and the aqueducts, and the crops, and the language. As elsewhere in Europe and beyond, the influence of **the Romans** in Portugal was far-reaching and long-lasting. They introduced the fundamentally Portuguese staples of olives, vines and cereals, planted on massive agricultural estates (*latifundia*) in the Alentejo that still exist today in their essential forms. Surviving bridges, aqueducts and Roman roads – extremely elegant and amazingly durable – mark out many now-obscure settlements as having once had a more illustrious past. And the very basis of the early Portuguese language derived from the Latin spoken throughout the Empire. Even centuries after the fall of Rome and the end of Empire, when Visigoths and, later, the Moors were the dominant forces in the Iberian peninsula, many people in many towns and villages lived a life that still bore heavy Romanized characteristics, from agricultural methods to legal processes.

First century BC	193–139 BC	711 AD
The Romans occupy southern Portugal, planting vines and citrus fruits	Local warrior Viriatus becomes a scourge of the occupying Romans	The Moors decide Iberia looks a promising place to colonize

By the fourth century AD, as elsewhere in Europe, so-called "barbarian" **Germanic tribes** were nibbling away at the Roman sphere of influence in Portugal, while Christianity was already well established. With the fall of the Roman Empire, the Suevi and then the Visigoths took their opportunities – the latter prevailing after 585, when a unified **Visigothic kingdom** was established across most of the peninsula, ruling from their capital in Toledo, Spain.

The Moors and the Reconquista

The Visigothic kingdom endured until it met its first real political and social challenge – the crossing of the Straits from North Africa in 711 of the **Moors**, largely Berbers from Morocco. Long riven by internal conflict, the Visigothic kingdom collapsed and the Moors advanced, almost without opposition. In Portugal they reached as far as Coimbra and the centre of the country, but preferred the milder south, particularly the established towns and agricultural estates of the Tejo valley and the Alentejo. However, it's the southern coast of Portugal that is most associated with the Moors – the land they knew as **al-Gharb** (Algarve), or "the west", with their capital at the walled town of Silves.

It was a time of civility and no little prosperity. Although the land was held under Muslim law, freedom of worship was granted while the Moors introduced their own **agricultural improvements** – from better irrigation (imported from the harsher climate of North Africa) to the planting of citrus fruits, rice and cotton. Towns as far away from the Algarve as Lisbon, Santarém and Évora acquired a distinct Moorish character that's still evident today.

The unconquered lands between the Douro and the Minho, however, never saw Moorish influence, and it was here that the Christian Reconquest – known in Portugal as the **Reconquista** – first took root. As a region, or county, of the Spanish kingdom of León, by the ninth century this northern land of mountains, forests and rivers was known as "**Portucale**", and by the eleventh century it was big – and occasionally obstreperous – enough to be thought of as a separate country. The nominal "Counts" of Portucale began to flex their muscles and eventually, under Henry of Burgundy, declared their independence. The kingdoms of León and Galicia had other ideas about this fledgling nation, but under Henry's son, **Afonso Henriques**, Portucale moved decisively towards self-determination. Following the battle of São Mamede (1128) – where he defeated his own mother, loyal to the kingdom of León – Afonso declared himself to be prince (and later "king", in 1137) of Portugal and announced that his capital would be at Guimarães.

Reconquest from the Moors followed quickly in the central regions close to Afonso's new power base of **Coimbra**, which became capital in 1143. Santarém and Lisbon both fell in 1147, after mighty sieges, and Afonso's new kingdom spread south as far as the Alentejo. That was the easy part, however, and it took another hundred years or so before the Moorish stronghold of the Algarve was breached – Silves was brutally sacked in 1189 and, though control later ebbed and flowed between Moorish and Christian forces, the writing was on the wall.

When Faro fell in 1249, the borders of the kingdom of Portugal were set – and have remained almost unchanged ever since. The first **Cortes** (Parliament) was called in

1073	1137	1249	1279–1325
Afonso is crowned king of Portucale, a small area to the north of the Moorish Iberia	Afonso Henriques becomes the first king of Portugal proper	Portugal boots out the last Moors from the Algarve	The country's borders are demarcated by a series of forts

> ## THE KNIGHTS TEMPLAR
>
> Founded as a chivalric order in France in the early twelfth century, the **Knights Templar** played an important part in wresting back control of Moorish-controlled land in the nascent state of Portugal. From a castle in Soure in central Portugal – granted in specific exchange for their help against the Moors – the Knights were at the forefront of battles and sieges like that at Santarém, fighting alongside Afonso Henriques as he swept south. They were given authority over lands they had conquered, which made them a power to rival that of the established Church and the other nobles, and in 1160 they moved their headquarters to the strategic site of **Tomar**. Within a century their power and influence in Europe was such that Philip IV of France suppressed the Order (1307), which was later officially dissolved by the Pope in 1312. In Portugal, however, it was too well entrenched in political and religious life simply to disappear – and under Dom Dinis, it was re-established as the **Order of Christ**, which took over the lands and possessions of the Templars, though under royal jurisdiction. The Order continued to play a significant role in the development of Portugal, whose kings and princes became its Grand Masters, thus further enmeshing Church, State and politics to mutual benefit.

Coimbra in 1211, though the country's capital was ultimately transferred to **Lisbon** in 1260 by Afonso III.

Consolidation of the nation

The long reign (1279–1325) of **Dom Dinis** – son of Afonso III – did much to set on a firm footing the Portuguese kingdom that had emerged from the Reconquista. With Castile still nibbling at the borders, new castles were built and towns fortified to safeguard the eastern side of the country – the Treaty of Alcanizes (1297) with Castile eventually granted Dom Dinis the security he craved. Trade and agriculture were prime concerns too, with Dinis' far-reaching reforms earning him the soubriquet *O Lavrador* (the farmer), while an interest in the arts and culture expressed itself in the founding of Portugal's first university at Lisbon in 1290 (later relocated to Coimbra). Dinis also made Portuguese the official language of the country, founded the Portuguese navy, and promoted various other legal and social reforms – in many ways establishing an early national identity for the country that echoed down through the following centuries.

The reigns of Dinis' successors were less tranquil, and the **Burgundian dynasty** – which started with the founding father of the country, Afonso Henriques – ended with the death of the ninth Burgundian monarch, Fernando I, in 1383. Although two years of factional fighting and Castilian intrigue followed, Portugal emerged not only intact but strengthened. With the country's independence under threat yet again from Castile, as rival claimants to the throne squared up to each other, a solution arrived in the shape of João, illegitimate son of Dom Pedro I (the king before Fernando) and Grand Master of the noble House of Aviz.

At the decisive **Battle of Aljubarrota** (1385), fought in the heart of Estremadura, João triumphed against the odds, defeating (indeed, crushing) the powerful Castilian army – with, it's claimed, the help of the Virgin Mary. Divine intervention or not, João built the abbey at Batalha in honour of his victory and was crowned **João I**.

1290	1385	1386	mid-1400s
One of the world's first universities is founded at Coimbra	English archers help Portugal to repel Spanish invaders	The Treaty of Windsor cements Portugal's friendship with England	Henry the Navigator encourages expeditions to the New World

A newly confident Portugal had no further fear of Castilian meddling, and began to look elsewhere for support, trade and alliances. English soldiers had played a part at Aljubarrota, and an Anglo-Portuguese alliance was cemented with the 1386 **Treaty of Windsor** – one of the oldest surviving international alliances in the world – and the subsequent marriage of João to Philippa of Lancaster, daughter of John of Gaunt, in 1387.

Emergence of the maritime empire

Given its geographic location, it was hardly surprising that Portugal looked west and south – across the oceans – from the earliest settled period of its nationhood. There had always been the Crusades to keep knights and nobles occupied, and Morocco and North Africa were also tantalizingly close – João I took **Ceuta** in 1415, which was the first real step towards anything approaching an imperial policy.

However, it was to be João's third son, Henry, who transformed Portugal's maritime fortunes – he's known, aptly, as **Prince Henry "The Navigator"** (1394–1460). Henry became fascinated by the prospects of African trade and exploration and, after being made governor of the Algarve (1419) and then Grand Master of the Order of Christ (1420), was eventually in a position to fund his pursuits. At Sagres, on the Algarve, Henry developed an ocean-going ship, the caravel, which would drive Portugal's later explorations, while cartographers and navigators were quizzed for their expertise.

By 1430 both **Madeira** and the **Azores** had been colonized, and by the 1440s the **west coast of Africa** had been reached – importantly, avoiding the Muslim-dominated land routes across the Sahara and thus opening up a new line of trade for Portugal. The **Cape Verde** islands were explored in 1456 and, two years after Henry's death, in 1462, Sierra Leone was reached. It took another quarter of a century to round the Cape of Good Hope – named Cabo da Boa Esperança by Portuguese mariner **Bartolomeu Dias** – which was the true catalyst for expansion.

In 1498, when **Vasco da Gama** used decades of Portuguese maritime know-how to sail on around Africa and reach India, the economic floodgates opened. Under Dom Manuel I, the Portuguese Crown was to reap the extraordinary rewards of its sailors' endeavours, becoming one of the world's richest countries in the process. With imperial Spain similarly active in the New World, the **Treaty of Tordesillas** (1494) effectively divided the globe between the two countries.

Manuel I and the Golden Age

Four hundred years after it had first carved itself out a niche in the Iberian peninsula, Portugal was a world power. By the beginning of the sixteenth century, the country's **"discoveries"** in Africa and the Orient – and their exploitation for trade – had made Portugal a super-power. There was a Portuguese presence in Brazil (after 1500), India (1505), the Persian Gulf (1515) and Macau (1557), with untold riches – from gold, silver, precious metals, spices and slaves – filling the royal coffers.

The main beneficiary of this trade-built windfall was **Manuel I** (1495–1521), the king known as *O Venturoso* – "The Fortunate" indeed. His reign is often referred to as a "Golden Age" and it's difficult to argue with that assessment when confronted with the

late 1400s	1494	1498	1495–1521
An elephant is paraded around Lisbon as an example of exotic wealth	Spain and Portugal agree to divide the New World's trade routes	Vasco da Gama opens up the Spice Route to India	Manuel donates his name to a flamboyant architectural style

JEWS AND THE INQUISITION IN PORTUGAL

Jews had long settled in Portugal, and in many ways the country seemed more tolerant of the faith than others in Europe. Even when Spain turned decisively against **the Jews** in 1492 – forcibly expelling them en masse – Portugal at first refused to join the clamour. When Manuel I became king in 1495, there was still much sympathy in royal circles for the plight of the Spanish Jews, many of whom relocated across the border. But realpolitik soon intervened and Manuel felt sufficient pressure to order his own expulsion of the Jews in 1496. Many left altogether – to the Netherlands, or to hide away in remote parts of the Portuguese kingdom where the royal writ scarcely reached. There are enclaves in Trás-os-Montes and the Mountain Beiras where Jewish communities survived under the radar for centuries. Others took the official way out by becoming forced converts, known as "New Christians", a process that took on a more public face after 1531 with the activities of the **Portuguese Inquisition** – never as fierce as in neighbouring Spain, but still with the capacity to harm and to change lives forever. Stone crosses carved on lintels over ancient doors in small towns across Portugal tell the story of families forced to deny their old faith and proclaim their new one. Interestingly, in 2015, the government approved a rule which said that descendants of all Jews expelled from the country could claim Portuguese citizenship.

greatest manifestations of this huge wealth – the magnificent buildings erected in his reign that bear the architectural description **Manueline** (a term first used, incidentally, in the nineteenth century). The swirling maritime motifs, the twisted ropes and columns, the elaborate vegetation and heraldic devices – whether at Batalha, Tomar, Belém or Setúbal, these symphonies in stone speak of a desire to make a confident statement about a newly endowed empire.

After Manuel came his eldest son **João III** (1521–57), and the Portuguese empire continued to thrive and expand, as well as making significant new trading contacts in China and Japan. It can barely have seemed possible that it would end, such was its extent, wealth and glory, and yet within twenty years of João's death, Spain was back in charge.

Under the Spanish yoke

The seeds of disaster had already been sown under Manuel I and continued with the reign of his son João III. Such a huge **empire** was hard to administer and local governors difficult to control. The Ottoman Empire had its own ideas about where spheres of influence should be established, Indian and North African ports became difficult to defend, and pirates continued a running battle against Portuguese ships. In addition, although the wealth was pouring in, it was also pouring out again – personally commissioned abbeys and palaces, designed and decorated by the day's leading architects and artists, didn't come cheap.

João's heir was his three-year-old grandson **Sebastião**, most of whose reign was spent under a regency. The boy was devout, came of age in 1568 and promptly set about pursuing new religious and imperial endeavours, unaware that the old ones were already crumbling. Morocco was his eventual target, ostensibly to safeguard Portuguese trading outposts on the India route, but Sebastião was also happy to dress up the

1531	1581	1640	Late 1600s
The Inquisition ruthlessly expels or converts Jewish citizens	Political manoeuvrings see Philip II start a period of Spanish rule	Portuguese troops place a Portuguese Duke on the throne	The country fills its coffers with gold and diamonds from Brazil

invasion as a Crusade. He took an army of seventeen thousand from Lisbon to Cadiz and then to Morocco, where it was annihilated at the battle of **Alcácer-Quibir** (1578) – thousands were killed, including Sebastião himself, riding into battle.

Spain saw its chance and renewed its long dormant claim to Portugal. Sebastião's uncle, Philip II of Spain, scion of the House of Habsburg, saw off a multitude of pretenders in battle and marched into Lisbon to proclaim himself **Filipe I** of Portugal – he was recognized as such by a meeting of the Cortes in Tomar in 1581. Sixty years of direct Spanish rule followed, largely under viceroys appointed by Filipe and his sons, Filipe II and III. Their intention was to rule Portugal as a separate kingdom, though part of a dynastic union, and the country kept its currency, laws and government.

It made no difference to the Portuguese, who were never going to take to Spanish rule. Filipe himself was judged to be an unrightful ruler, and faced loud whispers that the last young Portuguese king, Sebastião, had never died at all, while various pretenders and mysterious Arthurian-style "sleeping kings" emerged from the woodwork over the years. Heavy taxes further upset both the nobility and the population at large, while Spain's own political pretensions – sending an Armada against England, Portugal's long-time ally, for example – simply made Portugal's position worse.

The House of Bragança takes power

With Spain embroiled in the Thirty Years' War, and waging constant battles with France, matters came to a head in 1640 when Filipe III ordered Portuguese nobles to Spain to help put down an uprising in Catalunya. That was enough for many, who kicked Filipe's governor out of his palace in Lisbon and bestowed the throne upon the Duke of Bragança, from one of the most powerful families in the country. He became **João IV** (1640–56), first king from the Portuguese **House of Bragança**, the dynastic family that was to reign until the Republic was declared in 1910.

The newly independent Portuguese Crown made it very clear, very quickly, that Spanish concerns were now of secondary importance. João's oldest surviving daughter, **Catherine of Bragança**, was used as a blatant lure for reviving relations with England and – in the face of continuing Spanish opposition – she was married to Charles II of England in 1661. Continuing skirmishes with Spain – some political, others military – were finally ended by the 1668 **Treaty of Lisbon**, mediated by England, in which Spain recognized Portuguese sovereignty.

The House of Bragança was to preside over something of a second Golden Age for Portugal, kick-started by the fortuitous **discovery of gold and diamonds in Brazil**. The colony had been a source of revenue since the arrival of the Portuguese in 1500, with hardwoods, tobacco, cotton and sugar exported and traded, but the discovery of gold at the end of the seventeenth century – in the inland area that became known as Minas Gerais (General Mines) – changed the game.

The Portuguese Crown, impoverished by the long struggle with Spain, couldn't believe its good luck. It no longer needed to rely on the troublesome Cortes (Parliament) for funding and so simply stopped calling it, and the new-found riches meant that Portugal could buy textiles, manufactured and luxury goods, guns and pretty much anything else it needed from England and other European countries.

Early 1700s	1755	Late 1700s	Early 1800s
Poor decisions and lavish building programmes bankrupt the state	A huge earthquake flattens Lisbon	The Marquês de Pombal rebuilds the capital, modernizes the country and ejects the Jesuits	British forces help to repel Napoleon's invading army

The **Methuen Treaty** of 1703 formalized the trading relationship with England, expanding the market for Portuguese wine while allowing in English cloth tax-free.

The newly absolutist Crown enjoyed its greatest period of prosperity under the long-serving **João V** (1706–50), who did what all monarchs-with-money do – spent it, lavishly. Unequalled in Europe as a patron of the arts, João also built magnificent monuments to his own importance, chief of which was the extraordinary – some say obscene – palace-convent at Mafra, which has almost become a byword for lavish excess.

Pombal and the 1755 earthquake

João was succeeded by his dilettante son, **José I** (1750–77), who had better things to do (mainly hunting, fishing and shooting) than rule a country. From the outset of his reign, power in the land instead was vested almost entirely in the hands of the monarch's Secretary of State, one Sebastião José de Carvalho e Melo, better known as the **Marquês de Pombal** (1699–1782).

Pombal's influence on Portuguese life was incalculable. Although not of royal birth he gave the country a single-minded, regal, autocratic direction, best seen in his reaction to the defining event of the age, the **Great Earthquake of 1755**, when the capital Lisbon was razed to the ground. His response ("Bury the dead, heal the living") was typically pragmatic, and Lisbon itself emerged from the rubble with a new, planned, ordered look that reflected the man himself.

Pombal's reforms chimed with the prevailing Age of Enlightenment, and Portugal's systems of trade, commerce, manufacturing, law and education were all overhauled. Pombal abolished slavery in Portugal, ended discrimination against "New Christian" converts and also took on the established Church – believing in particular that the Jesuits were acting as a brake on further reform. Where there was opposition, it was dealt with ruthlessly, and when an assassination attempt on Dom José I in 1758 implicated the high-ranking Távora family, Pombal had them swiftly executed.

Such a personal hold on power relied on particular circumstances, and with the death of his royal "protector" José I, and the accession of the king's unsympathetic daughter, **Maria I** (1777–1816), Pombal's time was over. His reforms largely endured, however, while in "Pombaline" Lisbon – with its gridded plan, open squares and low-built earthquake-proof buildings – Europe was bequeathed one of its most gracious capital cities.

Napoleon – and the independence of Brazil

While the Portuguese monarchy had largely managed to keep the country out of foreign squabbles for over a century, it was **Napoleon** who dragged Portugal squarely into European affairs. In an attempt to wage economic war against the British he ordered the Portuguese to close their ports to their oldest allies and, when they proved understandably reluctant, Napoleon ordered in his generals, who in 1807 marched across Spain for Lisbon.

The royal family had already fled into exile in Brazil, and it was to be the British who led the fight for Portugal in the ensuing **Peninsular Wars**. British forces landed in Portugal in 1808, under their commander Arthur Wellesley, later Duke of Wellington,

1821	mid-1800s	late 1800s	1910
Safe from Napoleon, the Portuguese royal family return from Brazil	Instability in the court leads to virtual civil war	Lisbon's trams set forth as part of a public works programme	Portugal's last monarch flees to England at the birth of the Republic

and – after victories and setbacks – finally wore the French down. Wellington's fortified "Lines of Torres Vedras" and the significant **Battle of Buçaco** (1810) gave the French army pause for thought, and when Napoleon turned his attention towards Russia he withdrew his army from Portugal in 1812, pursued by Wellington.

Even after the final defeat of Napoleon in 1815, Dom João VI and the Portuguese royal family remained in **Brazil**, with Portugal effectively a British military protectorate. Portugal was destitute – ravaged by war and the comings and goings of invading and protecting armies – and rumblings of domestic discontent grew louder, inspired by the advent of a liberal constitution in Spain, drawn up after the defeat of Napoleon. Brazil meanwhile had been elevated from colony to kingdom in 1815 and was now an equal partner in a "United Kingdom of Portugal, Brazil and the Algarves" – subservient no longer.

In 1820, a liberal Cortes in Portugal formed a government, drew up a new constitution and, a year later, demanded the king's return from Brazil. João acceded but his attempts to maintain his United Kingdom split his family and came to naught. His queen, Dona Carlota, refused to accept the proposed limits on royal authority and was dispossessed of her title and position – becoming a figurehead of reactionary, absolutist opposition. João's son Pedro, meanwhile, was left in Brazil to rule as regent, but instead proclaimed **Brazilian independence** in 1822 (with that independence finally recognized by Portugal in 1825).

The death of the monarchy

The struggle between Liberals and Absolutists in Portugal, and between reform and repression, was set to define the rest of the century. After João VI's death in 1826, Pedro I of Brazil took the same route as his father before him and returned to Portugal as **Pedro IV**, but his reign – as those of his daughter and grandsons – was mired in constitutional conflict that occasionally bordered on civil war. The monarchy – deprived of its cash-cow of Brazil, following that country's independence – was almost bankrupt, and the dynasty became fundamentally split between a Portuguese and a Brazilian line. The enduring influence of the Church stifled social progress, and old imperial interests in Africa were lost as Britain, Germany and Belgium carved up the continent between them; there were industrial disturbances and political unrest as **Republicanism** gained a foothold.

The endgame approached for the ruling family. **Dom Carlos I** (1889–1908) was assassinated as he travelled across Lisbon in 1908, killed by a shot from a Republican crowd. His oldest son also died in the attack, and the younger son, **Manuel II**, took up the throne. He was the last of the Braganças – and indeed the last of all – to be king of Portugal, forced into exile on October 5, 1910, by a **Republican revolution**. The royal yacht sailed from Ericeira to Gibraltar and on to Britain – all attempts to restore his throne failed and Manuel lived on in exile in London until his death in 1932.

The rule of Salazar

The first **Portuguese Republic**, although widely welcomed by parts of society (and rejected by others, notably the Church), never achieved its goals. Divisions among

early 1900s	1916–18	1928	1932–68
Political instability witnesses 45 changes in government in 16 years	Initially neutral, Portugal finally joins ally Britain in the war against Germany	Economics professor Dr. António Salazar makes his mark as an impressive Finance Minister	Salazar rules Portugal as a virtual dictator

A FASCIST REGIME?

It's still a matter of hot debate as to whether **Salazar's regime** was fascist or simply deeply authoritarian and right-wing. The things it was opposed to certainly put it in the prevailing fascist camp – against communism, socialism or liberalism of any kind, with a repressive streak that was mirrored in both Germany and Italy. Political organizations were highly controlled, with his own party, the **National Union**, dogmatically supportive of the regime. Elections were rarely contested, rigid Catholicism became an integral part of the state education system, and censorship of the press was widespread. Salazar established a **secret police force** (the PVDE, later the PIDE) in 1933, modelled on the Gestapo, which kept tabs on left-wing political opponents and jailed many of them in detention camps on the Azores and the Cape Verde islands. During the Spanish Civil War, Salazar offered assistance to the Nationalists and turned over Republican refugees and sympathizers to Franco, knowing that they were certain to "disappear". Salazar's Portugal may not have been outwardly as brutal as Nazi Germany, or post-Civil War Spain under Franco, but there's little doubting the desensitizing effect his policies had on the country for decades.

the Republicans, the cyclical attempts at violent overthrow of the new regime by monarchists, and the weakening of the country's economy kept the Republic in permanent turmoil. There were 45 changes of government in sixteen years, and several brief dictatorships and military uprisings.

Into such a volatile situation stepped **Dr. António de Oliveira Salazar** (1889–1970), a pro-Church professor of economics at Coimbra University, who joined the regime in 1928 as Finance Minister. So effective was he that Salazar was quickly established as the leading light in the regime and appointed **Prime Minister** in 1932, while retaining close control over government spending and economic planning. A new constitution in 1933 gave him overarching, authoritarian powers under Portugal's **Second Republic** – powers that Salazar personally exercised until 1968.

Salazar's so-called **Estado Novo** or "New State" stabilized the economy but sowed the seeds of its prolonged downfall with its narrow, nationalistic outlook. There was no trickle-down effect as far as wealth was concerned, and Portugal remained woefully underdeveloped. The vast agricultural estates of the Alentejo saw no real improvement – scenes of rural work and life in the 1950s could have come straight out of a medieval engraving – and **emigration** was widespread. Large Portuguese populations in France, the US and elsewhere are a direct result of these impoverished years.

Portugal still had an empire, which ardent **colonialist** Salazar was determined to defend as part of "Greater Portugal", but the tide was turning in Africa and India. Goa was lost in 1961, while guerrilla activity increasingly spelled trouble for Portugal in Angola, Mozambique and Guinea-Bissau. The country began to find itself internationally isolated, economically stagnant and out of touch with the rising anticolonial sentiment in the world.

The end came in 1968 when Salazar suffered a brain haemorrhage and was replaced by his long-time colleague **Marcelo Caetano**. Salazar lived on until 1970 (apparently under the illusion that he was still Prime Minister), but the one-man state he had constructed was dismantled surprisingly quickly.

1939–45	1950–65	1960s–1973	1974
"Neutral" Lisbon becomes a hotbed of wartime spies, including Ian Fleming	Salazar funds the construction of the Lisbon metro and a bridge over the Tagus	Portuguese troops increasingly sent abroad to contain uprisings in its colonies	The Carnation Revolution overthrows the old regime

Revolution and democracy

Initially, after Salazar, there were limited government attempts to appease opposition at home, but it was unrest in the colonies that increasingly became the focus of dissent. The wars against the independence movements in Africa took a huge financial and personal toll, and an increasing number of younger soldiers and officers began to question Portugal's colonial isolationism. Many joined the revolutionary **Movimento das Forças Armadas** (Armed Forces Movement; **MFA**), while senior officers – up to the level of General António Ribeiro de Spínola – began openly to support democratic reform and military withdrawal from Africa. Thousands of other young men fled Portugal to avoid conscription.

On **April 25, 1974**, the Caetano government fell to a coup known as the *Revolução dos Cravos*, or **Carnation Revolution**. The signal was the playing of a song on the radio called *Grândola, Vila Morena*', by a banned Portuguese political singer-songwriter; the carnations were the flowers handed to the revolutionary soldiers by the people who came out to celebrate a peaceful coup in which no shots were fired.

It was an exciting and liberating time for Portugal. Although there had been no general clamour for freedom at home before the coup, the days and weeks after April 25 saw a surge in popular political participation, with mass demonstrations and demands for change. A military junta sponsored by the MFA took charge, under the leadership of **General Spínola**, and prepared for eventual civilian government. It was not all plain sailing and the country saw increasing friction between communists and democrats, conservative peasants and liberal urban elite, north and south. The Church was still strong in the conservative north of the country, where ecclesiastical Braga saw itself as a bulwark against godless communism; in the Alentejo in the south, peasants enthusiastically grabbed the land and set up collective farms.

Portugal's first **free election** for half a century was held on the first anniversary of the Revolution, in April 1975, paving the way for a new constitution to replace that of Salazar's Estado Novo. After a so-called "hot summer" of political intrigue, there was one last twist as a communist-led counter-coup by elements of the MFA tried to seize

END OF EMPIRE

The 1974 Revolution had a profound impact on **Portugal's former colonies**, which were not only granted **independence** virtually overnight – with no planning in place – but also lost large parts of their administration and labour force. The Portuguese troops went home, leaving a power vacuum, while hundreds of thousands of Portuguese citizens also relocated back to Portugal – the so-called *retornados*. Guinea-Bissau and Mozambique initially found independence beneficial (though damaging civil wars later followed), but Angola dissolved into full-scale civil war from the outset, which took decades to resolve. In East Timor, thousands were slain as Indonesia invaded in 1975 – they remained in brutal occupation until 1999. Only Cape Verde and Macau avoided bloodshed, though political maturity took time to evolve. In Portugal itself the colonial **retornados** posed yet more problems, as the mother country struggled to house and employ them. Their peaceful integration has been one of modern Portugal's greatest successes – though in the ongoing economic crisis the situation has been reversed, with many thousands of Portuguese people seeking better lives in the thriving economies of Angola and Mozambique.

Late 1970s	1986	Early 1990s	1998
Thousands of refugees flood into Portugal from its former colonies	Political stability is ensured with entry into the European Community	European funds transform the country's infrastructure	Lisbon hosts the successful Expo 98, which spawns a new district and bridge over the Tagus; Portuguese author José Saramago wins the Nobel Prize for Literature

power on November 25, 1975. The Carnation Revolution was safeguarded by the actions of General António dos Santos Ramalho Eanes, who put down the uprising, and new elections in April 1976 finally cemented **democratic government** in Portugal.

The Socialist Party won most seats and former exile **Mário Soares** became Portugal's first democratically elected Prime Minister, with the respected figure of General Eanes elected as President. Ultimately, right and left contested power for the next decade as Portugal came to terms with its new status, but Eanes and Soares provided a crucial consistency. Soares lost office between 1978 and 1983, but Eanes remained as President until 1986 – when he was replaced by none other than Soares, who had the distinction of becoming the first civilian President for sixty years.

Portugal in Europe: the 1980s and 1990s

Portugal's entry into the **European Community** in 1986 brought with it the most important changes since the Revolution. With the help of a massive injection of funds, Portugal enjoyed unprecedented economic growth as roads, industry and communications received heavy investment. In 1992 Portugal assumed the presidency of the European Community, the year when all remaining trade and employment barriers were removed and the EC became the **European Union** (**EU**).

The late 1990s saw a huge boost in Portuguese self-esteem. Lisbon's **Expo 98** was an enormous success, and the following year, **Portugal's last colony** – Macau – was handed back to Chinese rule, largely without the problems encountered by the UK with Hong Kong. Portugal also played a major role in the fate of former colony **East Timor**, which had endured a bloody 24-year rule by Indonesia following the 1974 Revolution. A UN-organized referendum in August 1999 saw an overwhelming vote in favour of independence. The Portuguese had been pushing for this for two decades – the feeling was of a long-standing obligation to a former colony that had finally been fulfilled.

Twenty-first-century Portugal

With EU funds flooding in, the first decade of the new millennium saw the country's infrastructure develop beyond recognition. Ambitious new roads and bridges were built; there was a new transport system in Porto and Lisbon's metro system was greatly expanded; and a series of fancy stadiums were built for the successful **2004 European Football Championships**.

Not surprisingly, Portugal was a flag-waver for the EU, and in December 2007 the draft constitution for the European Union – the so-called **Lisbon Treaty** – was signed in front of the Mosteiro dos Jerónimos in Belém. Portugal will forever be associated with the fundamental workings of the Union as a whole.

However, attitudes towards the EU have changed markedly since the global crash of 2008 and subsequent **European economic crisis**. Portugal plunged towards an inevitable request for an EU bailout, which ended Portugal's second Golden Age of lavish building as abruptly as the earthquake of 1755 had ended the first one. The new buzzword is austerity, managed by right-of-centre Prime Minister Pedro Passos Coelho, a previously little-known former businessman and fado fan who was voted into power in June 2011. He quickly sold off state assets, including some of Portugal's power

1999	2004	2007
Portugal gives up its last colony, Macau	The Euro football championships are hosted in a series of state-of-the-art stadiums	The Treaty of Lisbon is signed in Belém, forming the constitution for the EU

companies to China, and dramatically hiked tax rates. His policies had little effect: by late 2015, unemployment stood at twelve percent, and around twenty percent of the population lived below the poverty line. No wonder nearly half a million people – mostly highly-qualified – had emigrated in the previous three years. When an election was called in September, Coelho's government – despite receiving the most votes – was toppled by a coalition of the Communist Party, the Greens, the radical Left Bloc and new PM António Costa's Socialist Party. Former Mayor of Lisbon Costa vowed to ease austerity while pledging to abide by the EU's budget deficit rules.

Despite massive **social change and economic restructuring**, the economy remains ill-equipped to compete successfully in the international arena. The bulk of Portugal's **industries** remain small or medium in scale, and have now to compete with Eastern European enterprises which have the advantage of lower labour costs and new EU funding. The country is also vulnerable to drought, especially in the south, affecting both **agriculture** – still a significant employer – and tourism. Unforeseen developments have even damaged traditional industries such as cork production: Portugal produces around half the world's cork, but the shift by wine-makers to plastic stoppers and screw caps has threatened livelihoods.

The future?

It's not all bad news. Successive governments have heavily promoted technology in work and education and there's been considerable investment in **communications technology**. Not only does Portugal have one of the world's highest densities of mobile phone use, it's also one of the few European countries with virtually universal high-speed internet coverage.

The country's dependence on imported energy has also been addressed by an ambitious **alternative energy programme**. An enormous solar farm near Moura in the Alentejo supplies the electricity needs of thirty thousand homes, while northern Portugal boasts the world's biggest wind farm. By 2015, 48 percent of Portugal's electricity came from renewable energy and in May 2016, the country spent four consecutive days relying only on renewable energy sources. **Tourism**, too, remains a reliable earner. Porto has joined Lisbon as a major city-break destination, and there is no sign that the popularity of the Algarve's beach resorts is dwindling. Indeed, with uncertainty about the political and social situation in the eastern Med, Portugal is seen as a safe alternative for holiday goers, especially with its relatively low prices. In 2015, Faro airport had its busiest ever year, with the arrival of 6.4 million passengers. In the same year, a record 314 beaches were awarded blue flags and fifty new hotels were opened. Tourism in Portugal is booming.

2009	2010	2015	2016
National superstar Cristiano Ronaldo becomes the world most expensive footballer when he is sold by Manchester United to Real Madrid for £80 million	Portuguese artist Paula Rego is made a British Dame	More than ten million tourists visit the country, breaking all records	Portugal win the UEFA European Championship

Fado – the people's soul

Portugal's most famous musical form, **fado** (or "fate"), opens a window onto the Portuguese soul. It's an urban music, a thing of night-time and bars, the origins of which are debatable but certainly involve influences from Portugal's overseas explorations. The essence of fado is *saudade* – an impossible-to-translate word that is nonetheless usually summed up as a "yearning" or "beautiful melancholy", and it's this that is expressed by the lyrical and sentimental expression of a solo singer, usually accompanied by the *guitarra* and *viola de fado*. The Portuguese are often mystified as to what a non-Portuguese-speaker could get from fado, since so much of its meaning lies buried in the poetic lyrics, but the beauty of soaring vocals over a silvery *guitarra* is certainly seductive.

Two working-class districts of Lisbon – **Mouraria** and **Alfama** – are considered the birthplace of fado, while the university city of Coimbra also has its own separate tradition. In both places – not to mention in towns and resorts across the country – you'll find clubs devoted to fado where you can experience something of the mystery that attaches itself to the art form. Many clubs are expensive, some are tourist-traps, some are both, and you may find the most memorable fado of all is performed by an unadvertised performer – when you're present at a special, real moment of fado you'll know it. **Fado clubs** are social places, with eating, drinking and informality, but during a song set in a good club the waiters don't serve, and the music is treated with due reverence.

Lisbon fado

The greatest name in fado – still – is **Amália Rodrigues**, who had an immeasurable impact upon the direction of fado through her recordings. Born in 1920 in the Alfama district of Lisbon, her death in October 1999 saw three days of official mourning announced in Portugal. Though over the course of her long singing career she ventured into other musical forms, her style and most celebrated recordings have become a central reference point for what people mean by fado.

It's not unusual for well-known Lisboan *fadistas* to run their own clubs. **Maria da Fé** owns the fado house *O Senhor Vinho*, where she and other notables perform. Seated at the long tables in the *Clube de Fado* in Alfama, you might well hear the owner **Mário Pacheco** himself, a fine guitarist and the last to play with Amália, accompanying another celebrated *fadista*, **Ana Sofia Varela**.

Coimbra fado

Coimbra fado has a very different style to that of Lisbon, reflecting that city's ancient university traditions. It's typically performed by students and Coimbra graduates, and is an exclusively male domain. As well as more formal songs that are less personally expressive than the Lisbon fado, there is also a strong aspect of *guitarra*-led instrumentals.

The most famous Coimbra *guitarra fadista* of the latter half of the twentieth century was **Carlos Paredes**, who combined enviable technical mastery with genuine feeling and expression, placing the fado guitar centre-stage alongside the singers it traditionally accompanied. Coimbra's instrumental fado continues to evolve in both traditional and new combinations: most of **Pedro Caldeira Cabral**'s compositions aren't fado as such, but they and his immense virtuosity on the *guitarra* can be seen as part of the legacy of Coimbra fado.

Nova canção and música popular

Coimbra fado also embarked on a new journey towards the modern Portuguese ballad, whose progenitor was the great **José Afonso**. He had a classic, soaring fado-style voice and his first recording, with Luís Góes in 1956, comprised fados from Coimbra together with his own more personal, contemporary songs. It's these, and his drawing upon regional traditional music and fado, that first formed the genre known during the last years of the Salazar dictatorship as **nova canção** ("new song"). Although censorship and the restriction of performing opportunities caused some songwriters to move and record abroad, Afonso remained in Portugal, masking his social and political messages with allegory, when necessary.

After the 1974 Revolution, an ever-growing number of singer-songwriters turned to contemporary matters in their music – social, cultural, political – and *nova canção* became known simply as **música popular**, both drawing on popular tradition while taking on board new influences from Latin America, Europe and North Africa. Afonso died in 1987, but his music is still very much a touchstone, while other singers and songwriters, such as **Amélia Muge**, continue to mix rural and fado traditions. You'll frequently hear songs by Afonso, Sergio Godinho and other *nova canção* leaders in the repertoire of fado singers.

Contemporary fado

Contemporary *fadistas* start with **Mariza**, now a veritable world-music superstar who frequently tours the globe. Also listen out for **Ana Moura**, **Mísia**, **Cristina Branco**, **Carminho**, **Kátia Guerreiro**, **Mafalda Arnauth** and male singers **Helder Moutinho** and **Camané**. At the same time, **Dona Rosa**, a blind former busker, is now receiving international acclaim after years of performing her very personal fado on the streets of Lisbon.

Many performers move in and out of fado, or mix aspects of it with other genres. For example, **Dulce Pontes** began in the world of rock-pop ballads, then for her second CD, *Lágrimas*, she performed fado and while she explores other genres it has remained a strong thread in her music. The music of long-standing Lisbon band **Madredeus** – a manicured blend of classical guitars and keyboards surrounding the songbird vocals of **Teresa Salgueiro** in songs largely by band leader Pedro Ayres Magalhães – while not fado as such is, nevertheless, replete with the reflective melancholy of *saudade*.

Playing fado – guitar and viola

The dominant instrument of fado is the **guitarra**, although its body isn't "guitar-shaped", but that of an Arabic lute, introduced over a thousand years ago by the Moors. Two designs evolved – the Lisbon *guitarra*, usually used for accompanying singers, and the larger and richer version more suited to Coimbra fado, with its strong *guitarra*-virtuoso strand. Both have six pairs of steel strings.

The *guitarra* is usually accompanied by a six-string guitar of the Spanish form, known in Portugal as a **viola**. Though the *viola de fado* is usually a normal Spanish guitar, there is a remarkable range of other specifically Portuguese violas. The version encountered most often, particularly in the north, is the *viola braguesa*, which has five pairs of strings and is usually played *rasgado* (a fast, intricate, rolling strum with an opening hand). A slightly smaller close relative, from the region of Amarante, is the *viola amarantina*, while other varieties include the ten- or twelve-stringed *viola campaniça alentejana* and the *viola beiroa*.

Books

There are plenty of books available in English covering Portuguese history and society, and also lots of fiction in translation. It's always worth checking the latest output from UK publisher Carcanet Press (⑩ carcanet.co.uk). Publishers are given below for books published only in Portugal.

ART, CULTURE AND BIOGRAPHY

Helder Carita and Homem Cardoso *Portuguese Gardens*. A huge, beautiful tome, lavishly illustrated with photographs and plans, with a scholarly text.

Miles Danby *The Fires of Excellence*. Magnificent and detailed study of the Oriental architecture of Spain and Portugal, illustrated with specially commissioned photographs.

Matthew Hancock *Xenophobe's Guide to the Portuguese*. An irreverent and affectionate look by our *Rough Guide* author, at what makes the Portuguese Portuguese. It contains cultural insights ranging from why the nation is so child-friendly to Portuguese driving habits, business etiquette and why coffee and salted cod are so revered.

Patrick Barclay *Further Anatomy of a Winner*. The latest biography of Portugal's most successful football manager José Mourinho, tracing his career from translator with Bobby Robson at Sporting Lisbon to manager of European Champions Porto, and onwards to his second stint with Chelsea via Milan and Madrid.

Anne de Stoop *Living in Portugal*. A glossy coffee-table tome filled with beautifully evocative photographs of Portugal's sights and architectural gems, from palaces and rural houses to *pastelarias* and restaurants.

FICTION

Monica Ali *Alentejo Blue*. Best known for *Brick Lane*, which looked at the difficulties Asian immigrants face in London, Monica Ali here turns her gaze to expat immigrants and would-be emigrants in a small, rural Alentejan village. Ali, who has a holiday home in the region, creates an atmospheric but ultimately inconsequential world where nothing much happens – evoking perfectly the Alentejo.

António Lobo Antunes *An Explanation of the Birds; The Natural Order of Things; Act of the Damned; The Return of the Caravels; The Fat Man and Infinity* and *South of Nowhere*. Psychologically astute and with a helter-skelter prose style, Antunes is considered by many to be Portugal's finest contemporary writer. *The Return of the Caravels*, a modern "take" on the Discoveries, is a good place to start.

Bernard Cornwell *Sharpe's Havoc*. This historical novel follows the exploits of Richard Sharpe, here battling Napoleon's forces in Porto during Wellesley's Portugal campaign of 1809. Filled with spies and intrigue, it's a rip-roaring tale.

Mario de Carvalho *A God Strolling in the Cool of the Evening*. Set in the third century AD, this fascinating novel traces the life of a Roman magistrate whose Lusitanian town is threatened by subversive Christians and the prospect of attack from the Moors. Summing up the circumstances that ultimately destroyed the Roman Empire, the book won the Pegasus Prize for Fiction in 1996.

★**Lídia Jorge** *The Migrant Painter of Birds*. Born near Albufeira in 1946, Lídia Jorge is one of Portugal's most respected contemporary writers. This beautifully written novel describes a girl's memories as she grows up in a small village close to the Atlantic, and in doing so poignantly captures a changing rural community.

Ray Keenoy, David Treece and Paul Hyland *The Babel Guide to the Fiction of Portugal, Brazil and Africa*. A tantalizing introduction to Portuguese literature, with a collection of reviews of the major works of Lusophone fiction since 1945.

Eugénio Lisboa (ed) *The Anarchist Banker and Other Portuguese Stories; Professor Pfiglzz and His Strange Companion and Other Portuguese Stories; The Dedalus Book of Portuguese Fantasy*. These collections of twentieth-century short stories give more than a taste of the exuberance and talent currently proliferating in Portuguese literature. Stories by old favourites – Eça de Queirós, Pessoa, José Régio and Miguel Torga – are included, too.

Yann Martel *The High Mountains of Portugal*. The *Life of Pi* author returns to the themes of religion, man's relationship with animals and sheer weirdness in these three entertaining stories. Taking place over different time periods, the stories (about one of the first car journeys in Portugal, a post-mortem and a Canadian's return to his Portuguese roots accompanied by a chimpanzee) all end up in the high mountains of Portugal – presumably Trás-os-Montes, which is beautifully evoked.

Pascal Mercier *Night Train to Lisbon*. This slow-burner by a Swiss philosophy professor (now also a film starring Jeremy Irons) explores the adventures of an elderly teacher in Bern. Spontaneously giving up his job, he sets off on a train to learn more about an inspirational Portuguese writer. Piecing together the writer's life in 1920s' pre- and

post-revolutionary Lisbon, the teacher begins an insightful journey of self-discovery.

José Rodrigues Miguéis *Happy Easter*. A powerful and disturbing account of the distorted reality experienced by a schizophrenic, whose deprived childhood leads him to a self-destructive and tragic life in Lisbon; evocatively written and a gripping read.

★ **José Luís Peixoto** *The Piano Cemetery*. Loosely based on a real Portuguese marathon runner who died in the 1912 Stockholm Olympics, Peixoto's novel is a dazzling fragmented mosaic of episodes from the lives of carpenters who run a piano workshop in Lisbon. The workshop introduces romance, intrigue and betrayal into three generations of a family fated to repeat each other's mistakes, but who are ultimately bonded by a deep loyalty and love. Beautifully written, it's the sort of book that you want to reread the minute you've finished it.

★ **Fernando Pessoa** *Book of Disquiet*; *A Centenary Pessoa*; *The Education of the Stoic: The Only Manuscript of the Baron of Teive*. The country's best-known poet wrote *The Book of Disquiet* in prose; it's an unclassifiable text compiled from unordered fragments, part autobiography, part philosophical rambling. Regarded as a Modernist classic, the Penguin edition is the most complete English version. *A Centenary Pessoa* includes a selection of his prose and poetry, including his works under the pseudonym of Ricardo Reis. *The Education of the Stoic* was compiled in 1999 from the Pessoa archives in Lisbon. Written under the heteronym the "Baron of Teive", it is a bleak work exploring the impossibility of producing perfect art by an artist who bins all his output before destroying himself.

★ **Eça de Queirós** *The Sin of Father Amaro; The City and the Mountains; Cousin Bazilio; The Maias; The Illustrious House of Ramires; To the Capital; The Yellow Sofa*; and *Three Portraits*. One of Portugal's greatest writers, Eça de Queirós (or Queiroz; 1845–1900) introduced realism into Portuguese fiction with *The Sin of Father Amaro*, published in 1876. It was recently given contemporary treatment in a successful Mexican film, *The Crime of Father Amaro*. Over half a dozen of his novels have been translated into English; always highly readable, they present a cynical but affectionate picture of Portuguese society in the second half of the nineteenth century. His *English Letters*, written during his long stint as consul in England, is also recommended.

José Régio *Flame Coloured Dress*. Like Eça de Queirós, Régio examines how society imposes restrictions on everyday life. *Flame Coloured Dress* is a series of vivid short stories, each one about the struggles of a woman but in very different circumstances, from a society woman to one suffering abject poverty.

Erich Maria Remarque *The Night in Lisbon*. Better known as author of *All Quiet on the Western Front*, German author Remarque writes with a similar detachment in this tale of a World War II refugee seeking an escape route from Europe. One night in Lisbon, he meets a stranger who has two tickets, and within hours their lives are inextricably linked in a harrowing and moving tale.

Mário de Sá-Carneiro *The Great Shadow* and *Lucio's Confessions*. *The Great Shadow* is a collection of short stories set against the backdrop of Lisbon in the early 1900s as the author describes his obsession with great art. Sá-Carneiro, who committed suicide at 26, writes with stunning intensity and originality about art, science, death,

EÇA DE QUEIRÓS

In a series of outstanding novels, the writer **Eça de Queirós** (1845–1900) turned his unflinching gaze on the shortcomings of his native land. While his earlier novels, such as *The Sin of Father Amaro* (1875) and *Cousin Bazilio* (1878), reveal a clear debt to French naturalism in their satirical intent, his mature writings offer a more measured critique of contemporary Portuguese society. Novels like *The Illustrious House of Ramires* (1900) work by gradually building up a picture of decadence and inertia, through an assemblage of acutely observed vignettes tinged with a sardonic but always affectionate humour.

Eça's cosmopolitan outlook was a result of both his background and of the fact that he was extremely well-travelled. Born out of wedlock, he was brought up by his paternal grandparents in the north of Portugal in an atmosphere of liberal political ideas. He studied law at Coimbra University, where he joined a group of young intellectuals (known as the "Generation of 1870") dedicated to the idea of reforming and modernizing the country. His adult years were spent as a career diplomat and for much of the 1870s and 1880s he was a consul in England, first in Newcastle upon Tyne, then in Bristol.

Oddly enough, it was at Newcastle that Eça wrote much of his masterpiece *The Maias* (1888), a complex portrayal of an aristocratic, land-owning family unable, or unwilling, to adapt to changing times. Focusing on three generations of male family members, Eça brilliantly conveys what he sees as a peculiarly Portuguese indolence and hedonism that invariably acts as a curb to good intentions – a condition that becomes a metaphor for the country's inwardness and lack of ambition.

homosexual sex and insanity. Similar themes appear in *Lucio's Confessions*, in which a *ménage à trois* between artists ends in a death.

★**José Saramago** *All the Names; Baltasar and Blimunda; Blindness; The History of the Siege of Lisbon; The Year of the Death of Ricardo Reis; The Gospel According to Jesus Christ; The Stone Raft; The Tale of the Unknown Island; Manual of Painting and Calligraphy; The Cave; The Double; Seeing; Death with Interruptions; Small Memories; The Trip of the Elephant; Cain; Skylight.* Saramago (1922–2010) won the Nobel Prize for Literature in 1998. He wrote prolifically and his work are mostly experimental, often dispensing with punctuation altogether; *Blindness* even avoided naming a single character and was recently made into a successful film, directed by Fernando Meirelles. Start with *Ricardo Reis*, whose theme is the return of Dr. Reis, after sixteen years in Brazil, to a Lisbon where the Salazar dictatorship is imminent and where Reis wanders the streets to be confronted by the ghost of the writer Fernando Pessoa. In *Baltasar and Blimunda*, Saramago mixes fact with myth in an entertaining novel set around the building of the Convent of Mafra and the construction of the world's first flying machine.

Antonio Tabucchi *Declares Pereira; Requiem: A Hallucination; The Missing Head of Damasceno Monteiro;* and *Fernando Pessoa* (with Maria José de Lancastre). Tabucchi (1943–2012) is a highly regarded Italian author who lived in Portugal for many years and is a biographer of Pessoa. In *Declares Pereira* he has recreated the repressive atmosphere of Salazar's Lisbon, tracing the experiences of a newspaper editor who questions his own lifestyle under a regime he can no longer ignore. The book has recently been made into a film by Roberto Faenza. *Requiem: A Hallucination* is an imaginative and dream-like journey

around Lisbon, while *The Missing Head* is a gripping crime novel set in Porto.

Miguel Torga *The Creation of the World* and *Tales from the Mountain*. Twice nominated for the Nobel Prize before his death in 1995, Torga lived and set his stories in the wild Trás-os-Montes region. His pseudonym "Torga" is a tough species of heather that thrives in this rural, unforgiving landscape, where the fiercely independent characters of his books battle to survive in a repressed society. Torga's harsh views of rural life in *Tales from the Mountain* led to the book being banned under the Salazar regime.

Gil Vicente *Three Discovery Plays: Auto da Barca do Inferno, Exortação da Guerra, Auto da Índia*. Three plays from the sixteenth-century scribe who some consider the Portuguese equivalent of Shakespeare, with the original archaic Portuguese versions alongside English translations, and copious notes.

Robert Wilson *A Small Death in Lisbon; The Company of Strangers*. In *A Small Death In Lisbon*, a policeman attempts to find the murderer of a girl found dumped near a beach on the train line to Cascais, opening up a can of worms stretching back to the last World War. *The Company of Strangers* is a thriller based in wartime Lisbon and Estoril. Both are gripping page-turners from a British author who lives in Portugal.

Richard Zimler *The Last Kabbalist of Lisbon*. Kabbalah is a mystical art based on an esoteric interpretation of the Old Testament. American author Zimler, now a resident of Porto, writes an intense and compelling story of a Jewish kabbalist attempting to discover the mystery behind his uncle's murder during the massacre of New Christians in Lisbon in 1506. Based on historical fact, the story has been a bestseller in Portugal, Italy and Brazil.

FOOD AND WINE

Jean Anderson *Food of Portugal*. The best of the cookbooks by non-Portuguese writers; a wonderful tour of the gastronomic horizon with easy-to-follow recipes.

Miguel de Castro e Silva *Recipes from My Portuguese Kitchen; Classic Recipes of Portugal*. An array of tempting menus from a well-known Portuguese chef. In *Classic Recipes of Portugal*, he explains how to prepare 25 of the country's most typical dishes.

★**Tessa Kiros** *Piri Piri Starfish*. A range of great Portuguese recipes, but the big pull here is the photos that are so good you could eat them.

Richard Mayson *The Wines and Vineyards of Portugal*. A wide-ranging, award-winning account of all you need to

know about Portuguese wines by a passionate expert in the field.

George Mendes *My Portugal*. 125 recipes spiced up with anecdotes of a Portuguese childhood from one of New York's top chefs.

Charles Metcalfe and Kathryn McWhirter *The Wine and Food Lover's Guide to Portugal*. A true labour of love, and an encyclopedic guide to the country's finest wine, regional cuisines, gastro destinations, food shops, markets and more.

Ana Patuleia Ortins *Portuguese Homestyle Cooking*. All the classics: easy-to-follow regional recipes collected by a first-generation Portuguese-American, peppered with fun anecdotes, stories and photos.

GUIDES

Brian and Eileen Anderson/Paul and Denise Burton *Algarve Car Tours and Walks; Northern Portugal: Car Tours and Walks*. Good maps and walking instructions make these great little books both for keen walkers or

those simply in search of a rural picnic spot.

Colm Moore, Gonçalo Elias and Helder Costa *A Birdwatcher's Guide to Portugal*. A comprehensive guide to 44 birding sites on the mainland, as well as the best spots

on the Azores and Madeira, together with maps and practical information.

Bruce Sutherland and Stuart Butler *The Stormrider Surf Guide – Portugal*. Part of the Stormrider series, this has great photos and top tips on where to find the perfect

waves. An invaluable guide for serious surfers.

Chris Thorogood and Simon Hiscock *Field Guide to the Wild Flowers of the Algarve*. The best available guide to the region's diverse flora, let down slightly by so-so illustrations and photos.

HISTORY AND POLITICS

Nigel Cliff *The Last Crusade*. A kind of Hilary Mantel treatment of the Age of Discoveries, focussing in particular on Vasco da Gama's mammoth voyage to India. Placing it firmly in the context of earlier crusades, Cliff neatly captures the historical misunderstandings between the great cultures of the East and West.

Peter Daughtrey *Atlantis and the Silver City*. British researcher Daughtrey argues the case that Silves, in the Algarve, was the fabled city of Atlantis, claiming it matches 60 of Plato's clues. A fascinating premise.

Barry Hatton *The Portuguese: A Modern History 2011*. A thorough look at Portugal's history along with an insight into what defines the Portuguese today.

★**Edward Paice** *Wrath of God*. Vivid, readable and evocative account of Lisbon before, during and after the Great Earthquake of 1755.

★**José Hermano Saraiva** *Companion History of Portugal*. An accessible, generously illustrated and concise history of the country written especially for non-specialist foreigners by the author of the bestselling Portuguese original. Includes easy-reference glossaries of historical figures and places.

Ronald Watkins *Unknown Seas: How Vasco da Gama Opened the East*. The fascinating story of Vasco da Gama's voyage and triumphant return, which paved the way for the runaway expansion of the Portuguese empire. It's a well-told tale that rattles along.

Patrick Wilcken *Empire Adrift*. The Portuguese royal family fled from the French invasion to Brazil in 1807 and established a court in exile there for 13 years. It was a move that was to change both Brazil and the path of the monarchy in Portugal, as this lively account of the fluctuating fortunes of João VI and his family shows.

POETRY

★**Luís de Camões** *The Lusiads; Epic and Lyric; Selected Sonnets*. Portugal's great national epic, *The Lusiads* (*Os Lusíadas*) was written in 1572, taking Virgil's *Aeneid* as its inspiration. The Oxford Classics is a good verse translation by Landeg White. *Epic and Lyric* includes extracts from *The Lusiads* together with other shorter poems, while *Selected Sonnets* shows the development of his remarkable lyrical poetry both before and after his experiences in Africa and India.

Sofia de Mello Breyner *The Perfect Hour: Selected Poems*. Evocative selection of translated poems from one of the country's foremost writers, winner of the 1999 Prémio Camões.

Fernando Pessoa *Pessoa: Selected Poems*. Pessoa wrote his poetry under several different identities, which he

called heteronyms. Those wanting a brief introduction to the range of his different "voices" are well served by Jonathan Griffin's elegant translations of four of them. *A Centenary Pessoa* is a superlative anthology of poems, prose, letters and photographs, and the most comprehensive selection of Pessoa's output yet published in English. *Fernando Pessoa*, available only in Portugal (Hazan, Portugal), is a revealing collection of documents and photographs of the author at work, with an introduction by Antonio Tabucchi.

Pedro Tamen *Honey and Poison: Selected Poems*. Lisbon law graduate Tamen is regarded as one of Portugal's leading contemporary poets; his poems of passion capture the distinctive sights and emotions of a country which has moved from dictatorship to democracy during his lifetime.

TRAVEL WRITING

William Beckford *Recollections of an Excursion to the Monasteries of Alcobaça and Batalha; Travels in Spain and Portugal (1778–88)*. There's rarely been a more entertaining traveller in Portugal than the wildly wealthy Beckford – eccentric seems a woefully inadequate description – and his journals and tales still delight.

Paul Hyland *Backwards Out of the Big World*. A fascinating and sympathetic account of a 1990s journey through Portugal by a man who knows the country's people, history and literature as few foreigners do.

★**Marion Kaplan** *The Portuguese: the Land and its People*. A readable, all-embracing volume, covering

everything from wine to the family, poetry and the land. A little dated perhaps, but still the best general introduction to the country.

Rose Macaulay *They Went to Portugal*. Old-school travel writing that takes a Brit's-eye view of visits to Portugal through the ages, from medieval times onwards. There was a follow-up volume, *They Went to Portugal, Too*.

Fernando Pessoa *Lisbon: What the Tourist Should See* (*O que o turista deve ver*) (Livros Horizonte, Portugal). Written in English and Portuguese (but only available in Portugal), Pessoa's 1925 guidebook describes a Lisbon that is largely recognizable today.

Portuguese

If you have some knowledge of Spanish you won't have much problem reading Portuguese. Understanding it when it's spoken, though, is another matter: pronunciation is entirely different and at first even the easiest words are hard to distinguish. But it's well worth the effort to master at least the rudiments – certainly the locals will be pleased you've made an effort and you'll be congratulated on even your most excruciating manglings of the language.

The **pronunciation and phrasebook guide** below will equip you with the basics, and there's also a full **menu reader**, so you shouldn't ever be stuck for choice in a restaurant. For more detail, purchase the *Rough Guide Portuguese Phrasebook*, set out dictionary-style for easy access.

Pronunciation

The chief difficulty with pronunciation is its lack of clarity – consonants tend to be slurred, while vowels are nasal and often contracted to the point of being ignored.

CONSONANTS

C is soft before E and I, hard otherwise unless it has a cedilla – açúcar (sugar) is pronounced "assookar".
CH is somewhat softer than in English; chá (tea) sounds like "shah".
J is pronounced like the "s" in pleasure.
G as in English, except before E and I, when it's also like the "s" in pleasure.
LH sounds like "lyuh" (Batalha is pronounced "Batalyuh").

M as in English, except at the end of a word when it's more like a nasal "-ng" – com (with) is pronounced "kong" (without sounding the G).
Q is always pronounced as a "K".
S before a consonant or at the end of a word becomes "sh", otherwise it's as in English – Cascais is pronounced "Kashkaish", adeus (goodbye) is "a-day-ush".
X is also pronounced "sh" – caixa (cash desk) is pronounced "kaisha".

VOWELS

E at the end of a word is virtually silent unless it has an accent, so that verde (green) is pronounced "verd", while café is pronounced "ca-**feh**".
Ã and Õ The tilde renders the pronunciation much like the French -an and -on endings, only more nasal.
ÃO Sounds something like a strangled yelp of "Ow!"

cut off in midstream (as in pão, bread – são, saint – limão, lemon).
EI and OU Sound like the "ay" in day and the "oh" in dough respectively (though when other two vowels come together they continue to be enunciated separately).

Portuguese words and phrases

GREETINGS AND QUESTIONS

hello; good morning	olá; bom dia	what's this called in Portuguese?	como se diz isto em Português?
good afternoon/night	boa tarde/noite	can you write it down?	pode escrever isso?
goodbye, see you later	adeus, até logo	do you know…?	sabe…?
everything all right?	tudo bem?	could you…?	pode…?
it's all right/OK	está bem	it doesn't matter	não faz mal
I don't know	não sei	you're welcome	de nada
I don't understand	não compreendo		

do you speak English?	fala Inglês?	what's your name?	como se chama?
where are you from?	de onde é?	my name is…	chamo-me…
I am from…	sou de…	what time is it?	que horas são?

USEFUL WORDS AND SIGNS

yes; no	sim; não	youth hostel/	pousada da juventude/
please	por favor/se faz favor	campsite	um parque de campismo
thank you	obrigado/a*	Is there a…near	Há um/a…aqui
sorry; excuse me	desculpe; com licença	here?	perto?
today; tomorrow;	hoje; amanhã; ontem	Do you have a room?	Tem um quarto?
midday, noon/midnight	meio-dia; meia-noite	I'd like a room for…	Queria um quarto para…
where; what	onde; que	one person/	uma pessoa/
when; why	quando; porquê	two people	duas pessoas
how; how much	como; quanto	with two beds/	com duas camas/
with; without	com; sem	a double bed	um casal
here; there	aqui; ali	with a private	com casa de
near; far	perto; longe	bathroom	banho privado
this; that	este/a; aquele/a	It's for one night/	É para uma noite/
now; later	agora; mais tarde	one week	uma semana
more; less	mais; menos	May I see it?	Posso ver?
big; little	grande; pequeno	How much is it?	Quanto custa?
open; closed	aberto; fechado	OK, I'll take it	Está bem, fico com ele
push; pull	empurre; puxe	I'd like to make a	Queria fazer uma
entrance; exit	entrada; saída	reservation	reserva
danger; dangerous	perigo; perigoso	I have a reservation	Tenho uma reserva
toilet/men/women	casa de banho/senhores/senhoras		

*Obrigado agrees with the sex of the person speaking – a woman says obrigada, a man obrigado.

DRIVING AND DIRECTIONS

Which is the road to…?	Qual é a estrada para…?
left, right	esquerda, direita
straight ahead	sempre em frente
air; tyre	ar; pneu
oil	óleo
petrol; diesel (unleaded)	gasolina; gasóleo (sem chumbo)
Fill it up please	Encha, se faz favor
diversion	desvio
roadworks	obras
no entry	passagem proibida
no parking	proibido estacionar/estacionamento proibido
Can I park here?	Posso estacionar aqui?
motorway	autoestrada
tollbooth	portagem
petrol station	bomba de gasolina
driving licence; documents	carta de conduçao; documentos

TRANSPORT

Where is…	Onde é…
the bus station?	a estação de camionetas/terminal rodoviária?
the bus stop for…?	a paragem de autocarro para…?
Is there a bus to…?	Há uma camioneta/autocarro para…?
Where does the bus to…leave from?	Donde parte o autocarro para…?
Stop here please	Pare aqui por favor
Where is the railway station?	Onde é a estação de comboios?
Is this the train for…?	É este o comboio para…?
What time does it leave? (arrive at…?)	A que horas parte? (chega a…?)
I'd like a ticket to…	Queria um bilhete para…
one-way/return	ida/ida e volta

SHOPPING

what's that?	O que é isso?
I want to buy…	Quero comprar…
how much is it?	Quanto é?
I'd like a bag	Queria um saco
slices/sliced	fatias/fatiado

ACCOMMODATION

I'm looking for a…	Procuro…
pension/	uma pensão/
hotel/	um hotel/uma

fresh; can (tinned)	fresco; lata (em lata)	November	Novembro
litre	litro	December	Dezembro
market	mercado		
minimarket/grocery	minimercado/mercearia	**NUMBERS**	
supermarket	supermercado	one	um/uma
organic/organic	biológico/produtos	two	dois/duas
produce	biológicos	three	três
weight/to weigh	peso/pesar	four	quatro
kilo	quilo	five	cinco
unit	unidade	six	seis
bakery; butchers	padaria; talho	seven	sete
bank; exchange	banco; câmbio	eight	oito
bookshop; laundry	livraria; lavandaria	nine	nove
post office; stamps	correios; selos	ten	dez
(two) stamps	(dois) selos	eleven	onze
pharmacy/chemist	farmácia	twelve	doze
includes VAT	incluído IVA	thirteen	treze
		fourteen	catorze
DAYS OF THE WEEK		fifteen	quinze
Sunday	Domingo	sixteen	dezasseis
Monday	Segunda-feira	seventeen	dezassete
Tuesday	Terça-feira	eighteen	dezoito
Wednesday	Quarta-feira	nineteen	dezanove
Thursday	Quinta-feira	twenty	vinte
Friday	Sexta-feira	twenty-one	vinte e um
Saturday	Sábado	thirty	trinta
		forty	quarenta
MONTHS		fifty	cinquenta
January	Janeiro	sixty	sessenta
February	Fevereiro	seventy	setenta
March	Março	eighty	oitenta
April	Abril	ninety	noventa
May	Maio	100	cem
June	Junho	101	cento e um
July	Julho	200	duzentos
August	Agosto	500	quinhentos
September	Setembro	1000	mil
October	Outubro	2000	dois mil

MENU READER

BASICS

Açúcar	Sugar	mexidos/quentes/	scrambled/soft-boiled/
Arroz	Rice	estrelados)	fried)
Azeite	Olive oil	Pão (trigo/centeio/	Bread (wheat/rye/
Azeitonas	Olives	caseiro/intégral)	rustic/wholemeal)
Broa	Cornbread	Pimenta (preta/branca)	Pepper (black/white)
Farinha	Flour	Queijo	Cheese
Manteiga	Butter	Sal	Salt
Massa	Pasta	Salada	Salad
Molho de tomate	Tomato/chilli sauce/	Vinagre	Vinegar
	piri-piri		
		IN A RESTAURANT	
Omeleta	Omelette	Ementa (turística/do dia)	Menu (set menu)
Ovos (cozidos/	Eggs (hard-boiled/	Prato do dia	Dish of the day
escalfados/	poached/	Carta dos vinhos	Wine list

Dose (uma dose/ meia dose)	Portion (full/half)
Pequeno almoço	Breakfast
Almoço	Lunch
Jantar	Dinner
Petiscos	Snacks, tapas
Entrada	Starter
Sobremesa	Dessert
Prato	Plate
Chávena	Cup
Copo	Glass
Garrafa	Bottle
Faca	Knife
Garfo	Fork
Colher	Spoon
Conta	Bill

COOKING TERMS

A vapor	Steamed
Assado/no espeto	Roasted/spit-roasted
Bem passado/mal passado	Well done/rare
Caril	Curry
Caseiro	Home-made
Cozido	Boiled/stewed
Empada	Pie
Ensopado	Soup or stew
Estrelado	Fried
Frio	Cold
Frito	Fried
Fumado	Smoked
Gratinado	Gratin
Grelhado/na grelha	Grilled
Guisado	Stewed
Mexido	Scrambled
Molho	Sauce
Na brasa	Chargrilled, braised
No churrasco	Chargrilled
No forno	Baked
Panado	Breadcrumbed and fried
Picante	Spicy/hot
Piri-piri	With chilli sauce
Quente	Hot
Recheado	Stuffed
Salgado	Salted
Salteado	Sautéed

FISH (*PEIXE*) AND SHELLFISH (*MARISCOS*)

Ameijoas	Clams
Anchovas	Anchovies
Atum	Tuna
Besugo	Bream
Camarões	Shrimp
Caranguejo	Crab
Carapau	Mackerel
Cherne	Sea bream
Chocos	Cuttlefish
Congro	Conger eel
Dourada	Bream
Enguia	Eel
(Peixe) Espada	Scabbard fish
Espadarte	Swordfish
Gambas	Prawns
Garoupa	Grouper
Lagosta	Lobster
Lampreia	Lamprey (similar to eel)
Linguado	Sole
Lulas	Squid
Mexilhões	Mussels
Ostras	Oysters
Pargo	Snapper
Pescada	Hake
Polvo	Octopus
Robalo	Sea bass
Salmão	Salmon
Salmonete	Red mullet
Santolas	Spider crabs
Sapateiras	Common crabs
Sarda	Mackerel
Sardinhas	Sardines
Tamboril	Monkfish
Truta	Trout
Vieiras	Scallops

MEAT (*CARNE*), POULTRY (*AVES*) AND GAME (*CAÇA*)

Almôndegas	Meatballs
Bife	Steak
Borrego	Lamb
Bucho	Haggis
Cabrito	Kid goat
Carne picada	Mincemeat
Coelho	Rabbit
Cordeiro	Lamb
Cordoniz	Quail
Costeleta	Chop/cutlet
Dobrada	Tripe
Entrecosto	Spare rib
Escalope	Escalope
Febras	Thin pork steaks
Fiambre	Boiled/cured ham
Fígado	Liver
Frango/galinha	Chicken
Fumeiros	Smoked meats
Javali	Wild boar
Leitão	Suckling pig
Lombo	Loin, fillet or tenderloin
Medalhão	Medallion
Moela	Gizzard

Paio	Cured sausage
Pata/Pé	Hoof/foot
Pato	Duck
Perdiz	Partridge
Perna	Leg
Peru	Turkey
Picanha	Brazilian sliced rump steak
Pomba	Pigeon
Porco	Pork
Presunto	Smoked ham
Rim	Kidney
Salpicão/salsicha	Smoked sausage/sausage
Tripas	Tripe
Vitela	Veal

VEGETABLES (*LEGUMES* OR *HORTALIÇAS*) AND SALAD (*SALADA*)

Abacate	Avocado
Abóbora	Pumpkin
Agriões	Watercress
Alcachofra	Artichoke
Alface	Lettuce
Alho	Garlic
Alho Francês	Leek
Batatas (fritas/ cozidas/a murro)	Potatoes (French fries/ boiled/Jacket)
Beringela	Aubergine
Cebola	Onion
Cenoura	Carrot
Coentro	Coriander
Cogumelo	Mushroom
Couve	Cabbage
Couve-flor	Cauliflower
Ervilha	Pea
Espargos	Asparagus
Espinafre	Spinach
Fava	Broad bean
Feijão	Bean
Feijão-frade	Black-eyed bean
Feijão-verde/-vermelho	Green bean/kidney bean
Grão(-de-bico)	Chickpea
Nabo	Turnip
Pepino	Cucumber
Pimento	Sweet pepper
Salsa	Parsley
Tomate	Tomato

FRUIT (*FRUTA*)

Ameixas	Plums
Ananás/Abacaxi	Pineapple
Cerejas	Cherries
Damascos	Apricots
Figo	Fig
Framboesas	Raspberries
Frutas silvestres	Berries, forest fruits
Goiaba	Guava
Laranja	Orange
Limão	Lemon
Maçã	Apple
Manga	Mango
Maracujá	Passion fruit
Melancia	Water melon
Melão	Melon
Meloa	Cantaloupe or Carmargue melon
Morangos	Strawberries
Pêra	Pear
Pêssego	Peach
Romã	Pomegranate
Tangerina	Tangerine
Toranja	Grapefruit
Uvas	Grapes

DESSERTS (*SOBREMESAS*), SWEETS (*DOCES*) AND PASTRIES (*PASTÉIS*)

Arroz doce	Rice pudding
Bolo	Cake
Broa de mel	Soft cornflour and honey cake
Doces conventuais	Sweet egg-based "Convent desserts"
Gelado	Ice cream
Maçapão	Marzipan
Mel	Honey
Mil-folhas	Puff pastry (mille feuille)
Pastel de nata/ pastéis de nata	Custard tart/tarts
Pudim, Pudim flan	Crème caramel
Queijadas	Cheese cakes
Suspiro	Meringue
Tarte	Tart
Torta de arroz/feijão/ cenoura/chila de amêndoa/ amendoim/noz/ nata/mel	Roll…with rice/beans/ carrot/pumpkin …with almonds/ peanuts/walnuts or nuts/pumpkin/cream or custard/honey

PORTUGUESE SPECIALITIES

Açorda (de marisco)	Bread-based stew (with shellfish, garlic and coriander)
Alheira	A fried pork-free "sausage" from Trás-os-Montes, traditionally of minced chicken and bread – more like a rissole than a sausage

Ameijoas à Bulhão Pato	Clams sautéed with garlic and coriander (named after a 19th-century Portuguese poet)
Arroz de…	Rice…
…cabidela/pato/ polvo	enriched with chicken blood/with shredded duck/with octopus
Arroz de mariscos	A thick, soupy seafood rice
Bacalhau…	Dried salt cod, soaked and then cooked…
com batatas e grão	with boiled potatoes and chickpeas
à brás	fried, with egg, onions and potatoes
na brasa	roasted with sliced potatoes
à Gomes de Sá	sliced, baked with potatoes, served with boiled eggs and olives; speciality of Porto, named after a 19th-century cod merchant turned chef
à lagar (lagareiro)	roasted in lots of olive oil (a *lagar* is an olive-oil press), served with roast potatoes
com natas	baked with cream
com todos	"with everything", ie boiled potatoes, cabbage and eggs (a Christmas dish)
Bife de atum de cebolada	Tuna steak with stewed onions, cooked in an earthenware dish
Bife à Portuguesa	Beef steak, topped with mustard sauce and a fried egg
Cabrito assado no forno	Oven-baked kid goat
Caldeirada de peixe	Fish stew, with a base of onions, tomatoes and potatoes
Caldo de castanhas	Chestnut soup
Caldo verde	Cabbage/potato broth (with or without *chouriço*)
Canja de galinha	Chicken broth with rice and boiled egg yolks
Cataplana	The name of the copper cooking vessel – most commonly used to cook shellfish, particularly clams (*ameijoas*), with smoked ham, pepper and onion
Chanfana	Goat/kid stew, braised in red wine, a Beiras dish
Coelho à caçadora	"Hunter's rabbit", a stew with tomatoes and garlic
Cozido à portuguesa	Boiled casserole of pork, beef, blood sausage, offal, beans, cabbage and carrots, served with rice
Empada de frango/atum	Chicken/tuna pie
Ensopado de borrego	Lamb stew
Espetada mista	Mixed meat kebab; *espetadas* of squid/ shrimp are also common
Feijoada	White bean stew: *à moda de Trás-os-Montes* (with root vegetables, cabbage, beef and *chouriço*); *à moda do Porto* (with *chouriço* and tripe)
Filetes (de pescada)	"Fillets", nearly always battered or breadcrumbed fish fillets, served with tomato rice
Francesinha	The "little French thing", a Porto speciality – a grilled steak, ham and sausage sandwich, smothered in melted cheese, doused in spicy beer-and-tomato sauce
Frango no churrasco	Barbecued chicken; sometimes with *piri-piri* (chilli) sauce
Frango na púcara	Chicken casserole made with wine, port and brandy (a *púcara* is the earthenware pot it's cooked in)
Isca de bacalhau	Battered cod fishcake
Lanches	Sweet bread/brioche stuffed with ham
Leitão assado	Roast suckling pig
Lulas recheadas	Stuffed squid (with meat and herbs)
Massa(da) de…	Soupy pasta dish, usually with *peixe* (fish)

Migas (à alentejana)	Fried maize-bread-based dish (with pork, garlic and spices)
Papas de sarrabulho	Thick blood-and-bread-based stew with herbs and spices
Pescada com todos	Poached hake, with potatoes, boiled eggs and greens
Porco à alentejana	Pork cooked with clams, served with fried potatoes and pickled vegetables (originally from the Alentejo)
Prego no pão/prato	Steak sandwich; with a fried egg on top
Rodizio	Brazilian buffet of sliced, barbecued meats, served with black beans, rice and salad
Rojões (à Minho)	Cubed pork (marinaded in wine, cumin and garlic), roasted with chunks of blood sausage and potato
Sopa à alentejana	Garlic/bread soup with poached egg on top
Sopa de tomate	Tomato soup, in the Alentejo often made with quails' eggs or beaten egg
Tripas à moda do Porto	Tripe stewed with beans and vegetables
Truta com/recheado com presunto	Trout stuffed with smoked ham

SNACKS AND PETISCOS (TAPAS)

Amendoins	Peanuts
Bifana	A grilled/fried pork steak sandwich
Caracóis	Snails
Chouriço/Linguiça/Paio	Cured sausage
Croquetes de carne/peixe	Meat/Fish croquetes
Empadas de Bacalhau	Dried cod mini-pies
Enchidoe	Smoked sausage
Farinheira	Floury sausage
Morcela	Blood sausage
Pastéis de carne/camarão	Puff pastries stuffed with sausage meat/shrimp paste
Pastéis/Bolinhos de bacalhau	Dried codfish and potato cakes
Pataniscas de bacalhau	Large flat dried codfish cakes
Perceves	Goose barnacles
Prego no pão/prato	A steak sandwich/with a fried egg on top
Queijo fresco	A soft white cottage cheese
Queijo seco/de ovelho/cabra	Cured/Sheep's/Goat's cheese
Tremoços	Pickled lupin seeds

Glossary

Adega Wine cellar, winery (also wine bar or restaurant)
Alameda Promenade
Albufeira Reservoir or lagoon
Aldeia Small village or hamlet
Alto/a Upper (area of a town)
Anta Prehistoric megalith tomb (also dolmen)
Armazém Warehouse
Artesanato Handicraft shop
Avenida Avenue
Azulejo Glazed, painted tile
Bairro Quarter, area (of a town); *alto* is upper, *baixo* lower
Baixo/a Lower (area of a town)
Barragem Dam
Biblioteca Library
Cais fluvial Quayside terminal
Caldas Mineral springs or spa complex

Câmara municipal Town hall
Campo Square, field or sports arena
Capela Chapel
Capela dos ossos Ossuary
Casa de povo Village/community hall
Castelo Castle
Castro Fortified hilltown
Centro comercial Shopping centre
Centro de saúde Health centre
Centro histórico Historic centre
Chafariz Public fountain
Cidade City
Citânia Prehistoric/Celtic hill settlement
Claustro Cloister
Convento Convent (or old church)
Coro Choir stalls (in church)
Correios Post office (abbreviated CTT)
Cruz, cruzeiro Cross

Dom, dona Sir, Madam (courtesy titles, usually applied to kings and queens)

Eléctrico Tramcar

Elevador Elevator or funicular railway

Ermida Chapel, not necessarily a hermitage

Espigueiro Grain shed on stilts

Esplanada Seafront promenade, terrace

Estação Station

Estrada Road

Farmácia Pharmacy

Feira Fair or market

Festa Festival or carnival

Fonte Fountain or spring

Forte, Fortaleza Fort

Freguesia Parish (*junta da freguesia* is the local council)

Grutas Caves

Igreja Church; *igreja matriz* is a parish church

Ilha Island

Infante/a Prince/princess

Jardim Garden

Lago Lake

Largo Square

Livraria Bookshop

Manueline Flamboyant style of Late Gothic architecture developed in the reign of Manuel I (1495–1521)

Menhir Prehistoric standing stone

Miradouro Belvedere or viewpoint

Moçárabe Moorish-Arabic (usually of architecture or a design)

Mosteiro Monastery (or old church)

Mudéjar Moorish-style architecture and decoration

Nossa senhora (N.S.) Our Lady – the Virgin Mary

Paço Palace or country house

Palácio Palace or country house; *palácio real*, royal palace

Parque Park

Parque nacional/natural National/Natural park

Pelourinho Pillory

Poço Well

Pombal Pigeon house

Ponte Bridge

Portagem Tollbooth on motorway

Praça Square

Praça de touros Bullring

Praia (fluvial) Beach (river beach)

Quinta Country estate, farm or villa

Retábulo Altarpiece

Ria Lagoon

Ribeiro Stream

Rio River

Romaria Pilgrimage or festival

Sala do capítulo Chapterhouse

Sé Cathedral

Serra Mountain or mountain range

Solar Manor house or mansion

Termas Thermal springs or spa complex

Torre de menagem Keep or tower (of a castle)

Tourada Bullfight

Vila Town

Small print and index

Rough Guide credits

Editors: Rachel Mills, Olivia Rawes, Polly Thomas
Layout: Anita Singh
Cartography: Deshpal Dabas
Picture editor: Phoebe Lowndes
Proofreader: Stewart Wild
Managing editor: Keith Drew
Assistant editor: Payal Sharotri

Production: Jimmy Lao
Cover photo research: Marta Bescos
Editorial assistant: Freya Godfrey
Senior DTP coordinator: Dan May
Programme manager: Gareth Lowe
Publishing director: Georgina Dee

Publishing information

This fifteenth edition published January 2017 by
Rough Guides Ltd,
80 Strand, London WC2R 0RL
11, Community Centre, Panchsheel Park,
New Delhi 110017, India
Distributed by Penguin Random House
Penguin Books Ltd, 80 Strand, London WC2R 0RL
Penguin Group (USA), 345 Hudson Street, NY 10014, USA
Penguin Group (Australia), 250 Camberwell Road,
Camberwell, Victoria 3124, Australia
Penguin Group (NZ), 67 Apollo Drive, Mairangi Bay,
Auckland 1310, New Zealand
Penguin Group (South Africa), Block D, Rosebank Office
Park, 181 Jan Smuts Avenue, Parktown North, Gauteng,
South Africa 2193
Rough Guides is represented in Canada by DK Canada, 320
Front Street West, Suite 1400, Toronto, Ontario M5V 3B6
Printed in Singapore
© Rough Guides 2017
Maps © Rough Guides

Help us update

We've gone to a lot of effort to ensure that the fifteenth
edition of **The Rough Guide to Portugal** is accurate
and up-to-date. However, things change – places get
"discovered", opening hours are notoriously fickle,
restaurants and rooms raise prices or lower standards. If
you feel we've got it wrong or left something out, we'd like
to know, and if you can remember the address, the price,
the hours, the phone number, so much the better.

Please send your comments with the subject line
"**Rough Guide Portugal Update**" to mail@uk.roughguides
.com. We'll credit all contributions and send a copy of the
next edition (or any other Rough Guide if you prefer) for
the very best emails.

Find travel information, read inspiring features and book
your trip at roughguides.com.

A ROUGH GUIDE TO ROUGH GUIDES

Published in 1982, the first Rough Guide – to Greece – was a student scheme that became a
publishing phenomenon. Mark Ellingham, a recent graduate in English from Bristol University,
had been travelling in Greece the previous summer and couldn't find the right guidebook.
With a small group of friends he wrote his own guide, combining a contemporary, journalistic
style with a thoroughly practical approach to travellers' needs.

The immediate success of the book spawned a series that rapidly covered dozens of
destinations. And, in addition to impecunious backpackers, Rough Guides soon acquired a
much broader readership that relished the guides' wit and inquisitiveness as much as their
enthusiastic, critical approach and value-for-money ethos. These days, Rough Guides include
recommendations from budget to luxury and cover more than 120 destinations around the
globe, from Amsterdam to Zanzibar, all regularly updated by our team of roaming writers.

Visit **roughguides.com** to find all our latest books, read articles and get inspired.

ABOUT THE AUTHORS

Marc Di Duca has been crisscrossing Europe for over 25 years, the last ten as a travel guide author for most major guide publishers. He has penned guides to places as diverse as Siberia and Madeira and also works as a translator specialising in travel and tourism. When not travelling, Marc lives with his Ukrainian wife and two sons in Sandwich, Kent.

Rebecca Hall After extensive global travels, Rebecca now divides her time between her native UK and Greece. She teaches English part time, is a travel writer and proud contributor to *The Rough Guide to Portugal* and *The Rough Guide to Greece* and wryly observes that the chaotic nature of her adopted country suits her personality very well. Follow her adventures at ⊚lifebeyondbordersblog.com. Her debut novel *Girl Gone Greek* can be found on Amazon.

Matthew Hancock fell in love with Portugal when he taught in Lisbon, then walked the 775-mile Portuguese/Spanish border. For this edition he researched and wrote the sections on Lisbon, Coimbra and the Beira Litoral, the southern Alentejo and the Algarve. Now a journalist and editor living in Dorset, he is also author of the *Pocket Rough Guide to Lisbon* and co-author of *The Rough Guide to Dorset, Hampshire and the Isle of Wight*.

Acknowledgements

Rebecca Hall would like to thank many people who helped her on her journey through Portugal. André Apolinário of Taste Porto Food Tours helped with all the initial contacts and continued to be a source of support throughout. Carla and Sérgio of Oporto Adventure Tours for their organization and, of course, Rui Coelho – her guide through the Gerês National Park. Ricardo Lopes of CoolTours Oporto and especially Pepe Rodrigues, her guide through the Douro Valley. Thanks to Gabriella Reynes Opaz of Catavino for her suggestions of places to try and to the many hoteliers, restaurant owners throughout Porto, the Douro and Minho region who gave their time and enthusiasm. And, thanks also to her editor and team at Rough Guides for supporting her through the process.

Matthew Hancock Thanks to Vitor Carrico, António Lacerdo, António Padeira, Ruben Obadia, Raquel Jorge, Marli Monteiro, Cristina Silva, Idália Costa José, Luís Marcão, Eva and Mats at *Dianamar*, Miguel Mateus, Tamsin and Andy at *Calçada Guesthouse*, Patrica David, Rosa Santos, Luke and Paula Pimenta Tilley and especially Mandy Tomlin, Alex and Olivia Hancock-Tomlin for their support and help. Thanks too to the in-house team especially Olivia Rawes, Rachel Mills and Polly Thomas.

Readers' updates

Thanks to all the readers who have taken the time to write in with comments and suggestions (and apologies if we've inadvertently omitted or misspelt anyone's name):

Jose Baeta, Sue Barnard, Luis Sousa Bibi, Solange Bury, Paul Cane, Filipa Cordeiro, Manuela Costa, Antonio Calado da Costa, John Field, George Graf, Will Graham, Evert Hekkema, Egbertien Hermans, Marta Inocentes, Jackie Kennard, Ana Lourenco, Christoph Maier, Marty McGlame, Taly Minkov-Louzeiro, Marian Smith, Sofia Soares, Michiel van Dam, Hanneke Verwimp, Mary Jane Vogel-Friend.

Photo credits

All other images © Rough Guides
(Key: a-above; b-below/bottom; c-centre; f-far; l-left; r-right; t-top)

Index

Maps are marked in grey

Map symbols

The symbols below are used on maps throughout the book

▬▬ ▪▪	International boundary	★	Bus/taxi	⚲	Swimming pool	⚲	Skiing
▬ ▬ ▬	Chapter division boundary	Ⓜ	Metro station	⚤	Boat	⛳	Golf course
▬▬▬	Road	🅿	Parking	⊤	Gardens	⚘	Vineyard
▬▬▬	Pedestrianized road	ⓘ	Tourist office	⌂	Cave	⛰	Mountain range
▭▭▭	Steps	ⓒ	Telephone	⌂	Abbey	〰	Rocks
▪ ▪ ▪	Path	✉	Post office	⛪	Fortress	〰	Cliff
▬▬▬	Railway	✚	Hospital	▇	Tower	⚓	Church
▬ ▬	Ferry route	◆	Place of interest	⛰	Viewpoint	▮	Building
▬▬▬	Wall	⊙	Statue/monument	∩	Arch	▭	Market
●▪▪▪●	Cable car	🗼	Lighthouse	⛺	Mountain refuge/lodge	⬭	Stadium
▬▬▬	Funicular line	∴	Ruins	🏛	Stately home	▭	Park
⊠—⊠	Gate	🌊	Waterfall	⛩	Monastery	▭	Beach
≈	Bridge	〰	Spring	✡	Synagogue	⊞	Cemetery
✈	Airport	⚱	Spa				

Listings key

■	Accommodation
●	Eating
■	Drinking/nightlife
●	Shopping